Writing
Moves

COMPOSING IN A DIGITAL WORLD

Eleanor Kutz · Denise Paster · Christian J. Pulver

FOUNTAINHEAD
PRESS

Our green initiatives include:

Electronic Products

We deliver products in nonpaper form whenever possible. This includes PDF downloadables, flash drives, and CDs.

Electronic Samples

We use Xample, a new electronic sampling system. Instructor samples are sent via a personalized web page that links to PDF downloads.

FSC-Certified Printers

All of our printers are certified by the Forest Service Council, which promotes environmentally and socially responsible management of the world's forests. This program allows consumer groups, individual consumers, and businesses to work together hand in hand to promote responsible use of the world's forests as a renewable and sustainable resource.

Recycled Paper

Most of our products are printed on a minimum of 30% post-consumer waste recycled paper.

Support of Green Causes

When we do print, we donate a portion of our revenue to green causes. Listed below are a few of the organizations that have received donations from Fountainhead Press. We welcome your feedback and suggestions for contributions, as we are always searching for worthy initiatives.

Rainforest2Reef

Environmental Working Group

Designer: Carol Hill

Developmental Editor: Katie Dickman

Books may be purchased for educational purposes. For information, please call or write:

1-800-586-0330

Fountainhead Press

Southlake, TX 76092

Website: www.fountainheadpress.com

Email: customerservice@fountainheadpress.com

ISBN: 978-1-68036-392-0

Printed in the United States of America

Table of Contents

Access the Digital Toolbox at www.fountainheadpress.com/writingmoves.

Part IV of *Writing Moves* is a Digital Toolbox that provides rich digital resources for reading, writing, and collaborating online that can be used by both instructors and students.

Acknowledgments

In our work for this book, we have drawn from insights and understandings we have gained from our many colleagues at UMass Boston, UMass Amherst, Coastal Carolina University, Roger Williams University, and the Benjamin Franklin Institute of Technology, as well as in the larger fields of composition, rhetoric, and literacy and we wish to express our appreciation to them all. Student writers, through their thoughtful inquiries into the digital worlds they inhabit, have deeply enriched our understandings of the literacy practices of those worlds, and we wish to thank, in particular, those whose work and worlds are represented in this book: Ashley Canter, Richard Corrente, Erin Gaglias, Razz Green, Mehdi Hasan, Ben Huff, Laurie Jackson, Alex Slotkin, Nate Jolley, Zacharie Loveless, Hannah Morgan, Christian Nunes, Mary Rufo, Brian Santoro, and Danielle Small. Denise would also like to thank Megan Fahey, Brooke Parker, and Jordan Serviss who used early versions of this text when working as graduate teaching assistants and shared valuable insights. Exchanges with independent bloggers whose posts appear here, Mark Mulligan on genre in music, Mark Schannon on reviews, and Wayne Rhodes whose blog posts about plagiarism laid the foundation for the essay that appears in Part III, brought further insights about practices we explore. We also wish to thank the team at Fountainhead Press, Scott Timian, Felix Frazier, and Amy Salisbury-Werhane for their interest in and support of this project, Carol Hill for her design work, and particularly Katie Dickman for her rich understanding of what we hoped to achieve, for thinking with us through revisions that moved us in that direction, and for guiding our manuscript through the production process. We are deeply indebted to those who pioneered early versions of this textbook, in particular Christian Smith, Alan Reid, and Ata Moharreri who were willing to adopt this text and share their insights with us as we refined the project. We would also like to thank Donna LeCourt for her rich contributions to Denise's and Christian's scholarly and pedagogical work and for guiding their thinking about the complexities of digital contexts. Finally, we wish to thank family and friends for their patient support and encouragement of our work, particularly Ron Thornton and Holly Boyle.

Preface to Instructors

The *Writing Moves* chapters, together, are intended to support a larger and coherent inquiry into the possibilities, concerns, and challenges of composing in a digital world, whether in local, public, or academic settings. They draw on explorations we have undertaken with our own quite diverse students at several different institutions.

Each chapter is designed to support a classroom of active engagement and inquiry in key ways. The first of these ways is *sequencing*. Each chapter moves through a series of smaller inquiries that build to a larger writing project by the end of the chapter. What is especially helpful about this approach is that you can utilize these inquiries in a number of ways: for example, as generative writing prompts for students to complete in or out of class or as discussion starters that can be used for class group work or for online discussions. These inquiries provide instructors with flexibility as they support students' generative thinking and writing.

The second of these ways has to do with how the chapters are organized. Most chapters are built around three main sections: Exploring, Making Connections, and Composing. The Exploring section frames the work of the chapter using real examples of literacy practices in action, and it introduces key concepts that students will be asked to apply. From "Exploring" a particular literacy practice, students move to "Making Connections" where they build on and extend their thinking through a careful and critical reading of a text that has been chosen to highlight the topics being explored in the chapter and the ways in which others have inquired into these topics. By the time students get to the "Composing" section, they are well positioned to develop more substantive ideas as they move through the writing process to compose a text that reflects the goals of the chapter. Many of the projects that ground the composing sections reflect common public and academic genres (such as the literacy narrative, a position argument, and a visual analysis), but all chapters focus on the kinds of inquiry-based writing and discussion posts central to the work of this book and composing projects reflect the book's larger focus on our changing literacies in a digital world.

The "Composing" sections included in each chapter are broken up into smaller sections, what we call moves. By framing the composing process as a series of moves, these sections are designed to help students navigate the writing process more deliberately with detailed discussions of typical moves writers make in composing within a particular genre.

The following moves are included in most chapters:

➤ **Inquiring and Inventing.** In the Inquiring and Inventing section, activities invite students to generate ideas and explore their thinking before they begin the formal composing of a text. In this generative stage, students engage in writing strategies central to academic work, strategies to help them ask questions and prepare them to begin drafting a more formal composition. One of primary reasons we begin the Composing sections with Inquiring and Inventing is to demystify the meaning making process with students, and the activities called for in this section are meant to help students come up with some messy material so they have lots of ideas to choose from as they extend their thinking.

➤ **Drafting and Shaping.** It is in this section that students do the bulk of their composing. We want to name for our students many of the strategies, activities, and considerations that are central to the work of writing. Even in classes where the writing process is central, we could probably be doing more to explain and unmask the real work that is writing, and this section is a step in that direction. As we encourage students to consider a variety of concepts (their purpose, audience, how to draw on multimodality), we also aim in this section to call attention to the sheer options we have as writers and help students develop meta-level understandings.

➤ **Revising and Publishing.** Peer review and revision are central to this aspect of the composing process. The prompts included in these sections are meant to support students' development as writers who also read and respond to others' texts—a skill in and of itself. Our goal is to help students come to see revision as an activity that moves beyond "tidying up" and draws on the rich social context of the classroom. In many of these sections, we also encourage students to consider publishing their writing in broader contexts. For example, in Chapter 15 on "Claiming Positions" we encourage students to enter the public conversation in a variety of ways (on a public class blog, a website). We also encourage them to share selections from their work as tweets or on existing discussion threads. While you might decide not to invite your students to take their work public, this section contains viable options for helping your students make that move.

> **Reinventing and Extending Your Work.** This section provides students with opportunities to re-envision and extend the work they have done in a chapter. By asking students to add more research or transmediate a project as they draw on different modalities, we encourage students to think dynamically about the texts they create and how they might reposition the original piece they composed. As we emphasize to students throughout these sections, reinventing your work is an active process of meaning-making.

As you teach with these various moves, you will decide what seems most productive for you and your students. You can pick and choose from these activities, and we have had success assigning them both in and out of class. Pedagogically, the idea here is not only to support students as writers researching contemporary literacy practices, but also to support teachers in creating classes that center on writing as a social activity: the activities included in the Composing sections are meant to do just that.

In addition to the sequencing of inquiries and the basic structure of each chapter, the chapters in this book have been designed to be modular. That is, not only do they build on one another, they are also designed to be used in a variety of ways and in a number of sequences. For example, odd numbered chapters tend to be more theoretical in nature while even numbered chapters tend to be more project-driven. This means instructors can choose to have students do a more involved writing project at the end of each chapter or combine chapters (1, 2) (3, 4), (5, 6, etc.) to create a longer sequence of activities that lead to more involved formal projects.

Writing Moves offers a comprehensive writing curriculum. Each main part of the book includes a series of chapters (8 chapters in Parts I and II, 4 chapters in Part III), along with additional readings, student examples, and additional resources. Part IV, which is available online at fountainheadpress.com/writingmoves, is a practical, hands-on resource that supports the work of the other parts, suggesting key digital resources and practical strategies for using them in carrying out the sorts of composing projects presented in the main chapters. We anticipate that teachers will use these resources in different ways, as we have done, perhaps focusing on either Part I or Part II, or combining one of these parts with Part III, or selecting chapters across these different parts for a one semester course, or using the book for a full-year sequence that moves from Part I into Parts II and III.

As instructors become more familiar with individual chapters they will be able to choose their own sequence of chapters (or create a custom edition) that meets their specific teaching needs, and we offer several example chapter sequences in the Instructor's Manual that address common approaches and goals of typical first year writing courses, as well as sequences that focus on a specific aspect of composing (multimodality, creating public arguments, doing research into media and literacy practices, etc.). Individual chapters are rich in content and composing activities, and while an instructor could certainly work straight through each chapter as it is laid out in the Table of Contents, the chapters have been designed to be flexible and to work in any number of different combinations. We believe this coherence and flexibility really make this book special.

Chapter Summaries

Part I: Local Contexts and Conversations

Part I focuses on the local contexts in which students communicate with familiar audiences at least partly through digital means. The chapters in Part I guide students in exploring their own digital literacy practices in these contexts and offer examples of other students' explorations. They also draw on the work of other researchers of changing literacy and new media practices, positioning students as inquirers/ researchers alongside others who have undertaken such inquiry.

Chapter 1: Navigating Changing Literacy Contexts

In this chapter we enter the composing world of a representative college writer, Barry, as he contributes to both social and academic online sites, using his example to consider the context of composition, rhetoric, and literacy studies in a digital age and to introduce some key concepts and an overview of what to expect in the chapters that follow. We draw on composition researcher Deborah Brandt's study, "Accumulating Literacy," to consider changes in literacy practices in the twentieth century and the implications for seeing and responding to such change in the twenty-first century. We point to larger themes and concerns that students will explore both through readings and their own inquiry. And we introduce the moves of writing for inquiry and discovery that will underlie the work of each subsequent chapter.

Chapter 2: Narrating Digital Literacy Experiences

Here we follow the work of a student writer, Ashley, as she explores an aspect of her own digital literacy experience and creates and revises a narrative that reflects the new understandings she gains about her uses of a particular digital practice—texting. We consider her complex and recursive process in the context of composition research that focuses on the writing process, and we see how she shapes and reshapes her composition within a classroom community, reseeing her work from the perspective of how it contributes to her class's larger inquiry into changing literacies in a digital age. We also watch as Ashley begins to trans-mediate her written composition into an increasingly multimodal one as she creates a storyboard to guide her in composing a digital story.

Chapter 3: Reading Rhetorical Situations

Here we focus on how rhetorical relationships—connections between writers/composers and their audience—are created and maintained through texts and image. Starting with a student's post on social media, we consider how writers seek to build rhetorical relationships through the texts they share and exchange. We then turn to a research blog post on the topic of Facebook and privacy by researcher danah boyd. Students are first introduced to the reading strategy of annotation, and then asked to engage in two types of reading, participatory and critical, as they work through boyd's piece to consider the kinds of meanings that emerge from particular ways of reading. The chapter also considers how reading practices change as we move from print texts to the screen and offers practical reading strategies for reading effectively online. The chapter concludes with moves for composing extended discussion posts for online course sites.

Chapter 4: Capturing Identity in a Profile

In this chapter we apply our understandings of rhetorical relationships to a common act of composition in the digital world—the composing of personal profiles and profiles of others—and the privacy concerns to consider when composing such online profiles. We consider the profile as a public genre as we read a *New York Times* profile of new media researcher danah boyd and point to a student's profile of a rap musician friend that appears in Part I Additional Readings, and we explore strategies for creating such public profiles, including audio profiles.

Chapter 5: Building Knowledge Collaboratively in Online Communities

Here we focus first on the quick, informal exchanges that take place among friends and family through conversations, texts, and tweets—how they typically build on and extend prior shared knowledge. We then turn to the ways in which ideas are shared and knowledge is created in the digital spaces of classrooms, with the example of a discussion of digital writing. As we continue our consideration of knowledge sharing and knowledge building in learning communities, we draw on a technology newsletter blog post that presents the work of researcher John Seely Brown (whose full article, "Growing up Digital," is included in Part I Additional Readings). The blog post reframes and restates Brown's observations about how literacy and learning have changed in a digital world and the important role of collaborative learning, as well as how shared knowledge (such as Brown's ideas) can be resituated in new compositions to serve new rhetorical purposes. We guide students through the process of working to represent another's work while shaping their own meanings, resituating their new understandings in a particular local context, and circulating what they compose within that context. We consider implications for becoming an effective digital learner in an academic environment and strategies for sharing and building collaborative knowledge.

Chapter 6: Connecting Local Practices to the Wider Culture

In this chapter, we explore questions of identity and culture as we reflect on how the digital exchanges like those of Barry's Facebook friends from his hockey team (Chapter 1) draw from the larger culture of hockey players and fans, guiding an initial inquiry into social identities and how they can be shaped locally, even as they draw on aspects of the wider culture, including the cultures of fandom. We then go on to consider the concept of cultural literacy (a concept further explored in an essay by Eric Liu in Part I Additional Readings) and to explore how the shared knowledge of cultural meanings and references that it suggests applies not only to verbal exchanges and print literacy but increasingly to other "technologies of sharing," including photos and music. A selection from Jose van Dijck's *Mediated Memories in the Digital Age* provides an opportunity for students to make connections between their uses of photography and changes that have occurred in the larger culture of picture taking. Students then explore the process of creating a digital shoebox of artifacts and examples that are relevant to the culture of a local community; they work to identify patterns in that collection, and draw on key concepts to explore larger meanings as they consider how their local communities incorporate the wider culture in their everyday literacy practices.

Chapter 7: Questioning Community Conventions

Here we focus on the role of context in shaping language, style, and genre, exploring how styles of discourse shift in different contexts and how a social identity that draws from a larger culture is reflected in language and style. Drawing from blog posts about language in music lyrics and from student Nate Jolley's study of speech acts and genres in a hip-hop community (included in Part I Additional Readings), we ask students to explore the intersection of speech acts, genres, and culture in settings they observe. A blog post (with an infographic) about genre in music by a music industry expert lets students make connections that contribute to a richer understanding of how genres take shape and function in larger cultural settings and how new media give rise to emerging genres—to new shapes and forms that respond to new contexts and address new rhetorical purposes, while reflecting on the effect of the visual representation of information on their own understanding. We consider how the student's report on the hip-hop community works with features of an academic genre. Finally, we guide students in analyzing how speech acts and genres, along with visual indicators of style, contribute to the cultural identity of a group and in considering how to move between community voices and academic voices as they present this work.

Chapter 8: Analyzing Discourse Communities

Drawing on another student's inquiry, we explore what can be learned from observing interactions in a wholly virtual community, this one formed as a small offshoot of a Star Trek fan discussion group. As they gather more data and extend their analyses, students have the opportunity to apply the concepts of Chapter

7 to a more extended study of a community. We draw on a research study of an online fandom community by communication studies researcher Nancy Baym and consider how she portrays and analyzes an online discourse community, with further examples from a student portrait of an online Goodreads book group that is included in Part I Additional Readings. As students give shape to their own community studies, they begin to draw on other sources, including readings they've encountered in this book, and begin to place their own observations in conversation with what other researchers have discovered—work further built upon in Part III.

Part II: Publicly Circulating Compositions

In Part II we shift our focus to the public contexts in which students are likely to participate as writers/composers and to the tools of analysis and argument that can help us to understand, critique, take positions about, and contribute to those contexts. These chapters guide students in exploring how texts circulate online and how they are reshaped and re-mediated, gaining new meanings and new audiences in the process. Here we further our exploration of rhetorical practices, as reflected in visual and multimodal representations of meanings as well as alphabetic ones. We consider how some common genres on online platforms—the blog post, the review—are being shaped to reach and interact with wider audiences, some forms that critique of digital culture is taking, some of the claims being made about the digital world and how they are supported, and how big and small data work to make arguments and supporting positions. Again we draw on the work of researchers and other writers who focus on these public literacy practices and concerns of a digital age.

Chapter 9: Joining Public Conversations in Digital Contexts

In this first chapter of Part II, we move from a focus on local digital contexts and communities to the larger public world in which digital texts often circulate. The chapter begins by looking at a tweet written by a student, Brittany, that goes viral. Using her experience and analysis of composing this tweet, the chapter proceeds to consider questions about virality, social media norms, and the circulation of posts. This chapter reviews key concepts from Part I and introduces some key concepts of inquiry for Part II, such as how various cultural productions of our digital age, including multimodal texts, can be analyzed and understood and how they are altered as they circulate more widely, moving from local to global cultural contexts. It then turns to questions of ownership as students read Lawrence Lessig's essay, "In Defense of Piracy," which argues for new approaches to copyright law to support both ownership and creative use of copyrighted work, and we consider how he addresses his concerns with a form of social action as he established the Creative Commons site that allows creators to set their own terms for the further use of their work. Finally, we guide students in analyzing a small cultural production, such as a meme, that both speaks to their own interests and has larger cultural significance, as they follow its circulation—mapping out its textual ecology and seeing how writing (and visual and multimodal texts) moves into different spaces and reaches different audiences.

Chapter 10: Practicing Rhetoric in Digital Spaces

Here we extend the focus on rhetorical analysis introduced in earlier chapters and apply it to evolving digital contexts and genres, exploring some of the rhetorical means used to attract an audience in the digital world and considering how traditional rhetorical terms can help extend our understanding of today's rhetorical practices. What makes stories go viral and how do rhetorical concepts help us to understand how public writers are working in the present digital moment? We make connections to an article about why all pop music sounds the same and a New Yorker essay that explores how stories go viral, as well as a student's rhetorical analysis of a widely circulated ad that, once altered, took on new meaning about NFL players and domestic violence. We then guide students through some common moves of composing a rhetorical analysis, as they consider the circulating text they choose to analyze, its cultural context, and the ecology of other texts that contextualize this piece.

Chapter 11: Building Public Knowledge through Online Articles

In this chapter, we build on earlier considerations of knowledge-building in Chapter 5, moving from the sharing of ideas and information in local spaces to the public sphere of online articles and blog posts. How do the digital production practices associated with writing for the web shape both new contexts and audiences for writing and new or altered genres? We begin with an exploration of the ways in which information is being shared online through short, catchy "content articles" with headlines designed to garner clicks and shares, making content go viral and supporting constant, but often superficial, knowledge consumption. We then consider Andrew Sullivan's moves of knowledge-sharing in an article about his blogging practice published both in print and online in *The Atlantic*, before turning to the example of his own blogs and how the design context of a blog interacts with the knowledge being shared through it. Finally, we guide students in creating their own extended blog posts about some aspect of their own digital composing practice and then deciding how they will circulate their work to place it in conversation with the ideas of other bloggers who address similar topics.

Chapter 12: Evaluating Cultural Productions in a Digital Age

Here we continue our exploration of the public spaces in which students might participate as composers of alphabetic and multimodal texts, exploring the many forms of reviewing they might engage in (and considering what makes a good review for various contexts and purposes) before turning to the more extended reviews of cultural production that appear on music review sites and on multi-faceted review sites such as BlogCritics. Building on the work of earlier chapters, we explore how reviews function in a social/cultural context, consider web reviews as an evolving internet genre, and see the ways in which they draw on the sorts of cultural, rhetorical, and textual analysis we've been considering in establishing a basis for evaluation. We connect with two readings, a review of a music production that appeared on *Pitchfork* and an article about how to write effective reviews by Mark Schannon, a reviewer for BlogCritics. We consider the moves of analysis, assessment, and evaluation in composing a review of a cultural production that's meaningful to a particular community as students work with these moves in crafting their own reviews and circulating them in appropriate spaces.

Chapter 13: Analyzing Literature as Cultural Critique

Cultural productions and cultural critique can take many forms, and in this chapter we consider some critical stances on the social effects of our digital world, encouraging students to think about both what this world offers and what concerns it is raising. Here we begin by exploring the ways in which circulating memes often work as cultural critique; we then consider other forms such critique might take, including the work of researchers like Sherry Turkle, before turning to an example of dystopian literature, an excerpt from *The Circle* by Dave Eggers with its concerns about the potential of large technology and social media companies to invade our privacy and change our cultural environment in negative ways. While this chapter draws on tools of literary analysis, working with Eggers's novel locates that work in a particular cultural moment and informs the larger inquiry of *Writing Moves*. Reading such a text necessarily elicits evaluative as well as analytical responses, focusing not only on how Eggers has shaped his work but also on how well he has succeeded in crafting a compelling piece of literature that achieves his rhetorical purposes.

Chapter 14: Reading Visual Culture

While Chapter 13 focuses on a word-based form of cultural production, Chapter 14 explores the ways in which visual representations can be given new meanings in new cultural/historical contexts. We consider images as memes, using the example of Rosie the Riveter and asking students to consider some of the many variations of the classic Rosie image. We introduce some common concepts for the analysis of visual compositions, inviting students to apply them to both a Rosie image they select and to the Rosie the Riveter Trust website. Reading an article on "The Many Faces of Rosie the Riveter" from *The Atlantic* places the Rosie images in a historical context and helps students explore more of its cultural meanings. As students work with still other Rosie images, and place them in the context of other message-focused images such as propaganda posters, they further their understanding of how to analyze visual texts and their contexts in ways that are parallel to the analysis of verbal texts and contexts in Chapter 13. Finally, we guide students through the activities of gathering and curating a set of images and drafting an essay that analyzes the images from multiple perspectives. For the final formal assignment of the chapter, students write an extended analysis of a specific aspect of visual culture that has emerged from their research on a set of images.

Chapter 15: Claiming Positions in Digital Contexts

In this chapter, we try to formalize students' working understanding of argument, giving further consideration to the ways positions might be argued, focusing in particular on positions about social media, and beginning with some informal arguments that have been made for and against joining Facebook. We introduce some common forms of position arguments and the sorts of rhetorical appeals they make. We then make connections to an argument made by Malcolm Gladwell in his essay, "Why the Revolution will not be Tweeted," and consider counterarguments made by others in response, including one drawing on big data from a recent revolutionary context in the Ukraine that's included in Part II Additional Readings. Echoing the work of other chapters on how any text and the arguments it makes can be resituated in new contexts, we look at some student examples from an online discussion of Gladwell's work. And we guide students to consider both Gladwell's own intertextual context, the work of others that he brings into his own, and the context of circulation—where his work has further been used and argued with. Finally we guide students through the moves of framing an argument, setting forth counterclaims, their own claims, and presenting their evidence, considering what's involved in composing an effective argument, including the use of relevant media.

Chapter 16: Putting Data to Work

The topic of data—how it's gathered, how it's presented, and how it serves arguments—is both a growing social concern and a matter to be considered by all thoughtful readers and writers. In this chapter we consider data, big and small, and how such data can be used in building an argument, not top-down from a set position, but bottom up, from gathered data. We begin with a discussion of big data, not just in its potential for violation of privacy, but its important role in helping us understand both the natural and social worlds we inhabit. This chapter asks students to begin by generating questions that might be answered with the collection of big data. We invite them to consider how data visualization—infographics and other visual representations—is rhetorical and can make such data comprehensible and then consider the rhetorical effectiveness of a website that collects data about people's consumption practices and links it to the modern-day slavery involved in the global production of goods. We then make connections to an article by marketing professional Martin Lindstrom on the uses of small data (with a Lego example) and examine his methods and claims. Finally, we guide students in crafting a data-driven argument, supplementing the small data they've been gathering with the relevant big data they can find.

Part III: Researching in Context

In Part III we shift our focus from the local and the public worlds of writing and textual production to the academic, inviting students to build on their work in earlier chapters to more fully enter an academic conversation by placing their findings alongside those of other scholars and shaping a more extended research project. We focus on three common research genres—the ethnographic study, the archival study, and the literature review (each as both a component of the others and as a stand-alone genre). Chapters 17–19 are intended to be used in sequence, moving through key elements of planning research, finding and evaluating sources, and synthesizing research into a final project. Chapter 20 focuses on digital presentation and guides students in planning and constructing an online portfolio of their work.

Chapter 17: Planning Research in Context

While students are somewhat familiar with contemporary research tools and practices, they often lack coherent and consistent approaches to the research they are asked to do. In this chapter, we again ask students to begin by observing and reflecting on their casual, everyday online research practices and then stepping into a more focused process—reflecting on search terms, considering site credibility, and using a research platform as both a repository for information found and a space for reflection: a digital research journal. Using the example of Hannah, whose earlier "Bookworm Buddies" study appears in Part I Additional Readings, we introduce the ethnographic, archival, and literature review research genres, considering how Hannah might proceed with each of these choices to fit her questions and interests and asking students to do the same. At this point, we also address ethical concerns of primary research, with a simple model permission form included on page 415. Our reading for this chapter, from a study of how freshmen conduct course research (from Project Information Literacy), points to common difficulties with formulating effective online searches, identifying and selecting sources, and comprehending and summarizing materials, giving students a starting point for considering their own prior experiences and present understandings. We also use this chapter to consider disciplinary perspectives and to locate topics and questions in webs of conversation, working with Google Scholar to consider communities of readers and audiences. We end this chapter by guiding students through the process of writing a research proposal for the genre of study they choose.

Chapter 18: Finding and Evaluating Sources in Media-Rich Settings

In this chapter we move from the public web to the scholarly web, placing academic databases within a larger online world of information (with the help of an infographic on the deep web), building on the example of Hannah's search activities as she moves to her library's search site and its scholarly databases, and considering again through her example what's involved in collecting and evaluating sources. We consider as well how to manage sources using bookmarking tools, bibliographic tools, writing and organizing tools, and document storage and retrieval tools, as well as how to avoid plagiarism through such planning and organization. We show how Hannah can use effective reading strategies to make connections and work with an article she has chosen, making familiar moves such as quoting, summarizing, and paraphrasing, and we point to Wayne Rhodes's essay "Love and Theft" (in Part III Additional Readings) to consider how building on others' work for "creative remix," whether in composing music or composing new texts, involves both trying on what others have done and carefully documenting that journey. Finally, we guide students through the process of composing an annotated bibliography in which they both summarize their sources and engage in analysis and critique. A student's sample annotated bibliography is included in Part III readings.

Chapter 19: Shaping and Synthesizing Research

While Chapters 17 and 18 focus on more general research strategies and tools, here we more fully address the differences in three research genres, what they look like in a digital world, and how they reflect and support inquiry-based research of the sort students have been reading about and beginning through their own earlier inquiries and projects. We first consider the opportunities and concerns of ethnography focused on the digital environment and the practices and purposes of participants in online settings. Again using Hannah's study of an online book group as an example, we guide students through the process of preparing an ethnographic study, from the more systematic collection and use of primary data to the use of secondary resources for interpretation and analysis, to shaping and structuring an ethnographic report. Likewise, we consider the possible opportunities, purposes, and resources for archival study that the digital environment affords, guiding students through the process of preparing and crafting such a study. Finally, we address the literature review as a stand-alone genre—how it might address questions about the digital world that are beyond the scope of what a student researcher might answer with primary data, the features and uses of the literature review genre, and how to enter the scholarly conversation and shape a literature-based study. We conclude the chapter with a consideration of multimodal possibilities for any of these studies and ideas for their circulation. A student sample literature review and selections from researchers' reviews are included in Part III Additional Readings.

Chapter 20: Constructing a Portfolio

Here we take up questions of curation and design as we take students through a process of collecting and presenting their own work, in digital formats, through an online portfolio. We consider what can be learned from examining the web portfolios of both professional and student writers, considering what we, as readers, discover from such examples, and how that can help those who are creating their own writer's portfolios to reflect on their own purposes and the ways to approach them rhetorically. The moves of choosing a digital platform, selecting artifacts, and considering visual design build on work students have done in earlier chapters, while further discussions of layout, navigation, and potential connections to social media and search engines, guide them through new rhetorical considerations as they move toward peer review and going live with this final display of their work as writers. More guidance about platforms and design can be found in Part IV.

A Brief Guide to Citations

While we encourage students to use the Purdue Online Writing Lab (OWL) to answer many of their questions about writing style, including citation style, we do include a brief guide to the sorts of citations they're most likely to require for the explorations they undertake in *Writing Moves*—including podcasts, images, songs, video clips, and wikis, as well as more traditional scholarly articles.

Part IV: Digital Toolbox (Online at fountainheadpress.com/writingmoves)

The digital toolbox is designed to supplement the work of Parts I, II, and III, offering guidance in the use of online platforms and digital tools that are relevant to the work of earlier chapters. A digital toolbox icon appears at points throughout the book where students might turn to the digital toolbox to further the work they are doing, and we anticipate that Part IV will be used in conjunction with other chapters. This part is divided into six sections, each representing some aspect of what students and their teachers might want to know as they proceed through various sections of the book. The material in this section offers guidance in how to think about using a number of tools and platforms for composing and learning in digital contexts, focusing on how they are designed and what affordances they offer. It does not offer detailed "how-to" for particular tools, but points to online sources for such explicit instruction.

Section 1: Using Digital Tools to Support Reading, Writing, and Collaboration

There are many apps that support the work of readers and writers who are working in digital spaces. In this section, we introduce common apps for reading, generating ideas, and drafting and collaborating on documents. We always encourage students to be observers of their own practices, and they can do this as they try out various apps and see what works in their own contexts.

Section 2: Building a Local Writing/Learning Community Online

We anticipate that some kind of online classroom site will either supplement the work of most face-to-face classes using this book or will offer a platform for a fully online course. We also believe that composition courses have an important role to play in preparing students for the writing and discussions that will take place in their other courses. Here we discuss three common platforms that are commonly used, sometimes together, in college courses: the learning management system, the wiki, and the blog, focusing on the design of each and how each can contribute to the sorts of writing and learning within a classroom community that we explore in this book. We invite our own students to reflect critically on the affordances and limitations of the platforms they work with.

Section 3: Circulating and Publishing to Engage with a Wider Audience

Throughout the book, but especially in Part II, we suggest that students periodically move beyond an audience of their classroom peers to engage with a larger public. In this section we describe the design of public discussion boards, such as Reddit, and microblogging platforms, such as Twitter, where writers might begin to enter a public conversation. We point also to sites for Twitter poetry and fiction; discussion sites for books, movies, and music; and fan sites, as well as to spaces like Hubpages for writing on general topics, spaces for writing in creative genres, and fan fiction groups. We also build on the discussion of blogs in Section 2 to offer suggestions for entering the public blogosphere and using effective blogging strategies.

Section 4: Composing Multimodally

Many of the activities in this book invite multimodal composition, and in this section we offer some preliminary suggestions and strategies for approaching the multimodal online world as a writer, beginning with storyboards for planning and design, thinking about using digital images, whether working through image banks or editing one's own images, designing an audio script and working with audio editing tools (to create a podcast or a digital story with sound and narration), and working with video-editing tools. Elsewhere on the website accompanying *Writing Moves*, we have included some examples of students' digital stories, and we plan to invite submissions of multimodal compositions and other work from other student writers who work with this book.

Section 5: Curating and Archiving Your Research

In this section we suggest some practical strategies and tools for researchers, focusing first on gathering primary data—working with screen capture tools to gather data from online sites and using survey apps to gather responses from participants in a setting. We then consider tools for secondary research—bookmarking tools and citation/bibliography generators. Finally we address the topic of plagiarism detection tools like SafeAssign and TurnItIn, so that students can understand how to use them strategically and make use of the information they offer, while recognizing their limitations.

Section 6: Presenting Your Work

Here we discuss presentation tools like PowerPoint and Prezi—how to think about their design and how to use that design effectively. Because the visual presentation of information has become increasingly important, we also look at infographic builders and word cloud generators, and we encourage students to generate or find appropriate visual displays of information they plan to present. Finally, we offer a brief introduction to website building applications that support writers' presentation of their work to an immediate and larger audience, with some guidance and resources for considering the design of a writer's portfolio.

Preface to Students

Do you use Facebook, Twitter, Instagram, or Snapchat? Do you follow bands and artists you like through their websites, blogs, or on social media? Do you text your friends and family and include pictures more often than you talk on the phone? When you write online, do you consider the platform you're using, the people you're sharing with, and the purpose of your communication? If so, then you already inhabit the world we'll explore in this book. *Writing Moves* is a book about how digital environments are changing how we write; changing how we read and compose texts—texts that may include images, sound, and video as well as words; and changing how we practice the new forms of literacy that are central to today's communication. As we write in these new environments, we learn new writing moves while building on those we've learned earlier, always adapting and reinventing what we know in ways that fit the new contexts we're writing for. The writing we do also moves—circulating quickly and often widely in the digital world through Facebook and other social media posts, through online course sites or public blogs, and reaching ever-wider audiences. Our title, *Writing Moves,* is intended to capture both the new moves writers are making and the movement of that writing to new audiences.

This book offers you a guide for both studying contemporary literacy practices and developing your own repertoire of moves as a writer working in many different contexts. It begins with the question: What does it mean to be literate in the twenty-first century? And it will ask you to explore your experience of literacy as a social activity, one in which we write to build and maintain relationships and share ideas across different settings and contexts, seeing how you use literacy to read and make sense of specific contexts and writing situations, and then make appropriate moves to create texts that will meet the needs of that situation.

The Book's Structure

The book includes four major parts. In Part I, we'll focus on local contexts—on the ways in which the digital world is reshaping communication among friends and family, in dedicated online communities of sports fans or book groups, and in classrooms—settings where you share both common interests and ways of interacting. The chapters in Part I will help you connect what you already know about literacy from the many contexts in which you've been communicating all your life to your current experience of reading and writing in a digital world. We'll then explore the ways changing media contexts are influencing the work of composing, what this means for building rhetorical relationships between writers and audiences, and how this impacts the ways writers produce and distribute their texts. We'll also guide you through several projects involving reflection and observation: a narrative that explores your own digital literacy experiences, a profile of someone engaged in digital literacies, and a study of how a community uses digital literacies to build relationships.

In Part II, we'll turn our attention to some of the rhetorical practices emerging in the larger public and often global contexts where memes circulate, new content is created to capture public attention, and serious arguments about the possibilities and potential dangers of our digital world are offered on new blog and news platforms to a wide group of readers, who respond in turn by commenting, sharing, and contributing to an ongoing conversation. The chapters in Part II will explore the sorts of cultural, compositional, and rhetorical productions that are characteristic of the digital age and how texts get reshaped by our use of digital writing tools. Singers, for example, not only must perform on stage, they must also perform on social media. In digital spaces, composers need to understand how to produce *and* circulate texts if they are to reach an audience and enter a larger, public conversation. Part II looks closer at certain writerly moves for connecting with audiences and entering public conversations through techniques of analysis, evaluation, and argument as vital literacy practices in today's complex digital environments.

Each chapter in Parts I and II is designed to guide you through a series of *inquiries* exploring how your own literacy practices and those of others are being shaped by the new digital practices of the different local, public, and academic contexts you participate in. An inquiry is an ongoing investigation, an exploration that shapes how we look at and think about a set of issues and problems—in this case, how to develop as participants in conversations that take place online and off, and how to understand the larger cultural context that shapes our participation. By organizing the book around a set of inquiries, we want to suggest to you that becoming an effective writer in new settings isn't so much about learning a set of fixed rules you can apply across settings, but more about being a good observer of how members of different communities use all of the composing tools available to them to shape and share their ideas and meanings, drawing on familiar moves for the context and inventing new ones as needed.

Each chapter of Parts I and II includes:

➤ an Exploring section where you'll make an initial inquiry into the topic, with a background discussion of concepts and ideas that are useful in exploring these questions, the issues they raise, and ways of approaching these inquiries;

➤ a Making Connections section where you'll read the work of other writers and researchers who are contributing to our understanding of new literacies and discover something about how to approach questions of literacy and learning in digital culture; and

➤ a Composing section, where you'll develop what you've been learning into a more formal composition that reflects your new understandings, using whatever literacy resources are most appropriate to your purpose and audience.

This Composing section in particular will guide you in generating ideas and giving more coherent shape to your writing, in thinking about the genres of academic and public writing, and in addressing the expectations of readers in such settings to present your ideas in new, hybrid compositions.

In Part III, we focus on the academic world, looking beyond immediate classroom communities to the larger communities of the academic disciplines those classrooms provide entry to, seeing the ways in which the research practices of academic communities are being reshaped with digital resources. The chapters of Part III suggest ways to extend your earlier work through several types of research: reviewing the literature—the reports of others' research—that is available on a topic you're exploring; gathering additional information through archival research—examining materials that have been collected in some form whether in a shoebox of old photos or a collection on Instagram; or ethnographic research—gathering more information about a setting and its participants' digital literacy practices through observations and interviews. Research too has been changed by the development of new digital resources, and we'll show how such resources can help you as you carry out your own extended inquiry and present its results.

For each of Parts I, II, and III, we also include additional readings, examples of student projects, and related references and resources.

In Part IV, we provide a digital toolbox to support your use of digital resources in your composing activities for the three earlier parts of the book. Access Part IV: Digital Toolbox at fountainheadpress.com/writingmoves.

Our goal, in the end, is to guide you in practicing and expanding your own literacies—your ways of reading, writing, and composing—as you enter the new settings of your college life and beyond. And we'll help you shape a semester-long inquiry into what it means to become a writer who is rhetorically aware and can use a variety of resources to compose effectively in the print and digital contexts of the twenty-first century.

Local Contexts and Conversations

Welcome to Part I of *Writing Moves*. Here we begin a larger inquiry into how writing, rhetoric, and research are changing in the digital age in local, public, and academic contexts. We begin by focusing first on the local—on the communities we connect with, at least partly through digital resources, in our social worlds and in our classrooms. We'll consider the ways in which literacy practices have changed and are continuing to change, the ways in which we use digital literacies to build rhetorical relationships with each other, and how we can build more consciously on our prior experience as writers—and as digital composers who are as likely to use images and music as well as words to express our meanings—as we move into new writing contexts.

We've given this book about writing in digital contexts the name *Writing Moves* for several reasons. The first is that we want to emphasize that writing, no matter what context it takes place in, is an active process, one in which we draw on all that we know about how people communicate in a particular context, whether digital or not. In that process, we draw on familiar ways of writing, speaking, and other forms of composing that have developed in that context, but we also reinvent and adapt those ways to our own purposes. As with dance, we learn the moves that people make and then we make them our own. That sense of writing as movement—as changing and adapting to new purposes and context—is central to the kind of writing we'll do in this book.

A second meaning for the book's title is that the writing we do also moves—it doesn't stay in one place, on a piece of paper handed to a professor or tucked away in a notebook or drawer. Digital media foster communication and networks, connecting users both to local communities, like friendship groups or classrooms, and to a global public as well. A post that we make on Twitter or Facebook is likely to be shared, liked, and commented on or reposted as it moves from reader to reader. In classroom communities, digital learning spaces encourage sharing and commenting and the collaborative building and further sharing of new texts. This process of circulation—the movement of texts—accelerates in digital, networked environments, changing the ways in which texts move between their creators and their readers, speeding up both our production and consumption of texts.

In Part I, where our focus is on the local, we will consider how such movement, in both senses, works at a local level, among people who know each other in some way—as participants who share some common interests and purposes and ways of communicating, whether their digital world is an extension of a face-to-face one of family or friends or a sports team, or whether instead they have met only online, through games, fan sites, book clubs, or online courses.

Digital environments, then, are changing our practices as writers and readers—our literacy practices. The ways in which those practices have changed and continue to change will be one of our themes throughout Part I. Such changes affect not only our writing processes, but also the moves and literacy resources available to us. Changes in our literacy tools change our experience as readers and writers, how we form learning communities both outside and inside academic settings, the ways in which we draw our meanings from the widely circulating larger culture, and our styles of language and ways of interacting. As we connect online using digital composing tools, we create and recreate the communities we become part of. Additionally, as writers in those communities, we share and invent new ways of composing.

As writers in digital environments, we are in a good position to become researchers as well. We research both informally, as we figure out what we need to know to participate in any of these communities in any digital context, and also more formally, in the rhetorical relationships we build through our writing. One community that grounds the work of this book is the academic one of your college writing courses, and that in turn is connected to a larger research community of people who are studying our changing literacy practices: how we communicate and shape identities through social media; how the digital photos we take on our cell phones are affecting that process of shaping social identities; how the changing digital music scene can inform our understandings of how we work with language, styles, and genres; and how our learning communities themselves are being reshaped. With a focus on inquiry, we invite you in Part I to become researchers of your own worlds from these various perspectives, reading some of the public and academic writing of those who have studied these topics and contributing what you learn about your local communities to those larger conversations. The chapter inquiries will build to smaller projects of sharing what you've learned, while the larger sequence will contribute to a more multifaceted yet detailed study of one community of your choice as it interacts—at least partly—through digital means. As a writer/composer working in this inquiry context, you'll be using and adapting some of the most common moves of academic writing and many of the typical forms (genres) that have taken shape in that context. This work will provide some of the underpinnings for more extended and formal research studies in Part III.

At the same time, as a writer in a digital world, you've most likely been using a variety of resources in your daily communication—posting images to Snapchat, sharing links through Twitter, and bringing music and videos into your online conversations. As we suggest some of the writing moves that are often made in sharing the results of your inquiries for each chapter, we'll also suggest ways in which digital resources can support your academic writing as well—resources that can help you engage an audience of readers not only with words but with other modes of communication.

Throughout these chapters we have shared some of the work of our own students so that you can see where their inquiries have led and how they are contributing to the larger conversations taking place about our literacies, identities, and communities in the digital world. We now invite you to enter this conversation.

Navigating Changing Literacy Contexts

CHAPTER ONE

CENTRAL QUESTIONS

 1 What are the typical literacy practices of a college writer?

2 How did literacy practices change throughout the twentieth century, and how do they continue to evolve into the twenty-first century?

3 How can we use the typical moves of inquiry-focused writing to engage with this text?

Chapter Preview

In our digital world, we write all the time. We use cell phones to text instead of calling; we share observations, photos, and comments on social media in the evening, rather than waiting until we see friends the next day or the next week; and we read and share and send links to a vast amount of content we find interesting, funny, or troubling. We know how to use a range of digital tools and platforms and how to do so creatively, to engage the interest of our readers, to build on the conversations that are already taking place around us, extending and reshaping them with our own input. As insiders to many digital contexts, we don't have to think much about these actions and interactions—we just carry them out, making quick choices about which emoji to use, which image to post, which link to share, as well as what words to write. We are not simply writers in the traditional pencil and paper sense, but composers who use the full array of possibilities our digital environments offer to shape our communication in multifaceted ways.

As we shift contexts, perhaps from Facebook to Snapchat, or from a face-to-face classroom discussion to an online discussion site, we draw on what we already know from writing, communicating, and composing in those earlier spaces, even as we try to figure out what to say and how to say it in the new setting. We can think of that prior knowledge as part of our literacy, not just our ability to read and write, but to do so in many different ways, for many different contexts. All of those ways—our *literacies*—are the communicative practices we engage in as we build and maintain relationships and share ideas across a range of settings. Our old literacies—our various ways of reading and writing in the different contexts of school or private life—continue, but they are integrated into new literacies for new contexts.

As writers, as readers, as composers who are developing new literacy practices in such ever-changing digital environments, we need to gain a richer understanding of the common practices most of us engage in through what other writers and researchers have learned about those contexts. In turn, we can contribute our own discoveries to everyone's evolving knowledge about the ways in which the digital world is impacting our literacies and our lives. We can then use our new understandings to consider what's involved in composing for the changing literacy environment of a digital, networked world, and to apply that knowledge in our own composing activities.

In this chapter, we'll begin our process of discovery with a focus on how literacies change in different contexts and across different time periods. We'll explore the varied literacy practices of a typical college student who is negotiating digital environments in both his social and his school worlds, read a brief excerpt from a study by a composition scholar about the ways in which literacy practices changed over the twentieth century, and work with the moves of exploratory, inquiry-focused writing.

Exploring
The Composing Worlds of a College Writer

The following vignette offers a brief look at the composing worlds of a freshman college student—those related to his courses and those we can get a hint of through his Facebook page.

Barry is a college student. He's taking four courses: Freshman Composition, Introductory Psychology, Calculus, and an introductory science seminar. He has a work-study job managing equipment for a science lab. He plays hockey. He has a network composed of family, friends, and three roommates. He is thinking of pledging a fraternity and often goes to their parties. He has started dating someone who goes to a different college.

As you read the following account of Barry's literacy experiences, consider the following questions.

- What are the contexts for which Barry reads and writes?
- What are his current literacy practices?
- How are these practices linked to the social worlds he's part of and the identities he takes on in each of those worlds?

Composing for College Courses

Most of Barry's reading and writing is done in the context of the courses he is taking. As a student, he keeps a required reading journal, which he can choose to do in a notebook or in an online blog, and he writes both short, informal papers and longer essays for his English class where, although he feels somewhat shy, he manages to contribute a little to classroom discussions. He reads textbooks and takes notes for his calculus course, and he uses those notes to do homework assignments and prepare for quizzes and exams. He's not a confident calculus student, and he rarely speaks up in the large calculus lecture. However, his professor uses an app that lets students enter responses into their smartphones and displays the results to the class, so Barry can see how his answers compare to those of his classmates.

Barry is taking his psychology course in a fully online version because the meeting times for the face-to-face section of the course conflict with his hockey practices. For that course, he watches and listens to lectures that the professor has recorded, and he participates in online discussions with other students in response to questions the professor posts about weekly topics. The discussion posts give him more of a sense that he is writing for his fellow students, as well as for the professor. The course textbook is an ebook, which he accesses online, and he reads, highlights, and makes notes on his computer (though he sometimes prints out a few pages of difficult material to reread and mark up with a pencil). The ebook includes links to animations, videos, and interactive exercises that help him to understand difficult concepts.

Barry, who is thinking about majoring in biology, feels most confident in his freshman science seminar, which explores current science topics such as HeLa cells, food production, and DNA. This course requires the widest range of reading and composing activities. In addition to doing required reading, he has to go online to find news reports related to these topics and post links to them, saying why they're relevant, on the course website. He also listens, after class, to the MP3 files of the lectures that his science professor posts to the course site, where he can also review the professor's PowerPoint slides from each lecture. For some weeks, he has to undertake various activities with a lab partner and write lab reports. He also works with other students on a team research project. They compose collaborative web pages to report on their work, using a wiki where all members of the team can write, edit, and upload pictures and videos that illustrate the ideas they want to present. Figure 1.1 is an image from his Blue Team's home page, with links to the team's project reports for the semester on topics such as the human genome, food production, and vegetarian diets, along with a humorous picture the group has added.

Figure 1.1: Blue Team's home page

Teams will then show the web pages as they present the results of their research to the class. Their professor will record those presentations, post them to the class wiki, and then ask students to write a review of their team's performance.

In his work as a twenty-first century college student, Barry participates in both spoken and written conversations, both face-to-face and online, as a speaker, listener, writer, and reader, drawing on written text, images, and audio for his own learning and using these different modes of conveying ideas and understandings in his own reports and presentations. Both his spoken and written exchanges are, in essence, conversations in which speakers and listeners, writers and readers, have to figure out how to be understood and how to make the conversation work. Those conversations are tied to particular course contexts, with particular expectations for what's appropriate to bring into the conversation and how to present those ideas. And the communication associated with courses is increasingly **multimodal**, going beyond written words to include other means of representation such as images and sound.

At the same time, although Barry is a freshman learner in each course, his own position feels different in each one. He likes to read and he felt like a pretty good writer in high school, so he feels OK about keeping a reading journal and submitting the essays required for his English class, but he feels awkward about rarely participating in discussions. He feels completely over his head in calculus (although he did OK in his high school course). He likes his introductory science seminar, enjoys working with his team, and feels at home in this small world of future science students who share some common interests. And he is surprised to find that he feels connected to other students in his online psychology course, even though he's never met most of them in person. In their discussion posts, they often share ways in which the topics have come up in their own lives. And as a shy student, he finds it easier to participate in those discussions by writing his comments

Sidenote

Seeing how different contexts shape our written conversations will be a major focus of this book.

multimodal
drawing on more than one mode of expression: words, images, audio, video

online, maybe because he can see what others are posting and how to make the style and content of his own posts fit in.

We can see that Barry, as a college learner, has to adapt his reading and writing to multiple course contexts. At the same time, because digital technologies are continually changing education and learning, as well as much of the larger society, he must continue to adapt and expand his literacies using a variety of technologies and moving adeptly between both online and offline worlds.

In each of his courses, **what** Barry talks about—the subject, the ideas—is different. **Why**—his purpose for each activity—varies as well: to share ideas, to satisfy an assignment, to get a good grade. But part of his purpose is always to create a relationship with his professors or his classmates. There are also differences in **how** he talks, reads, and writes about those subjects—reading carefully for an exam, scanning quickly to find a relevant article on the internet, or taking in visual information from diagrams in his textbook or images on the screen, as well as from printed words or aural information from sound files of lectures on a course site. And he writes in as many different ways—from notes to discussion posts, to essays and projects, using different media—using less formal to more formal language and structure. Some of that writing is collaborative. And **where** his writing goes—whether he is writing an essay for a professor or crafting a discussion post all of his classmates can read online—also shapes the approaches Barry takes in his work. The shifting contexts for his reading and writing, where his work will travel, continually reshape the what, why, and how of his literacy practices.

what, why, how, and where
key concepts for analyzing spoken and written conversations: what—the content of an exchange, why—its purpose, how—the way it's carried out, and where—the contexts in which writing is shared

---

INQUIRY

#1: Composing in college settings

From this narrative account, what sorts of literacy practices do Barry's college courses seem to demand? Look back at the image from the Science Gateway Seminar wiki. What do you see there about the focus of the Blue Team's work, the sorts of writing they post, and their use of an image and of hyperlinks? Why might Blue Team members have chosen this image for a home page that links to their report on the relationship of vegan/vegetarian diet and food production? What might Barry's classmates need to know to be effective composers on this particular site for an audience of other students in this classroom context?

Reflect, in writing, on your current experience as a student and what you need to know and be able to do as a literate participant in your various courses.

Communicating in Social Contexts

Barry's literacy practices outside of his courses also draw on his ability to read and write in appropriate ways for different contexts, but they differ quite a bit from his course-related practices.

Beyond the work for his courses, Barry doesn't tend to read or write anything very long. Mostly he sends and receives text messages, and he sometimes "googles" for information he scans quickly to get what he needs. He has to keep a record of when lab equipment is borrowed and returned for his work-study job. He often visits the website for his hockey team, checking the schedule, reading game reports, and looking up the stats for each player. He stays updated with teammates, but also a wider circle of friends and family by reading and writing quick posts on Facebook.

Figure 1.2: Barry's Facebook page

Although Barry might occasionally post that he's heading to class or studying for an exam, his Facebook page shows us more about his worlds beyond the classroom (Figure 1.2). Barry has several different **social identities** at this moment in his life: college student, future science major, hockey player, boyfriend, and more. All of them are reflected to some degree on his page, but some more strongly than others.

As a social media site, Facebook is set up to show and facilitate social connections among its users. Using the template and options that Facebook makes available, Barry has shared information about his life in several ways: by connecting to a list of friends, by entering information about his high school and college, by updating his relationship status, by adding profile images that show important elements of his life, and by posting to his own wall and to those of his friends. The posts he and his friends make often include interesting images or videos, like the YouTube clip of a professional hockey game that his teammate John has posted to Barry's wall (Figure 1.3). Posts tend to be very short, with informal, colloquial language or slang, and many posts elicit further responses.

social identities
a person's self-concept based on membership in different social groups

Figure 1.3: Pro hockey fight

We can also see that Barry doesn't compose his page alone. Some big compositional elements, such as the placement of information, have already been determined by Facebook's designers (with periodic redesigns), but it's the shared content created by Barry's posts and responses and those of his friends that keep his newsfeed alive.

We'll look more closely at some of the posts and responses on Barry's Facebook page and at what they can tell us about composing for the Facebook context in another chapter. For now, the same framework we use to understand Barry's school literacies can also be used to understand the literacies he engages in outside of the classroom. In exploring our social media practices, we'll again consider not only **what** we post, but **why** we post, and the purposes we're trying to achieve. We'll also consider **how**—the language and style, the form and relative length of the posts and responses, the use of images and links—as well as the ways in which the design of sites like Facebook, Twitter, or Instagram both support and complicate our use of these digital communication tools.

These elements—**what**, **why**, **how** and **where**—represent four key functions that are essential to any act of communication, in any context.

- **What:** representing ideas
- **Why:** building relationships and achieving purposes
- **How:** using words, forms, and modes that are appropriate for those purposes in that setting
- **Where:** the contexts that shape how texts move

It's the context that influences what will be shared, why, and how, like the context of Barry's friendship group from his hockey team vs. the working group of his Blue Team classmates. Increasingly, **where** includes not just the community of participants, but the digital platforms they are using. Facebook gives a particular shape to exchanges, and it would be difficult for the Blue Team to use it as a way to share their research.

INQUIRY

#2: Reading and writing in social contexts

Make a quick list of some of the social contexts in which you read and write at this moment in your life and add some notes about what you read and write about, why, and how for each context. Note the composing tools and strategies you (and your friends, family, coworkers, or teammates) use in one of those contexts. Then think about how you want to introduce yourself in the social context of your current composition class. What would you choose to share about the reading and writing you do in relationship to a particular social context?

Making Connections
Changing Literacy Contexts

By the time you enter a college classroom, you've learned a lot about the kind of writing that happens in school contexts—about reading for information, interpretation, and meaning; about writing a clear thesis, providing supporting evidence, and concluding an essay. You've also learned about language and style, with an awareness of what's considered an appropriate use of language for both in-school and out-of-school settings. But you've also acquired other ways of reading, writing, and composing that are appropriate to other contexts. If you're a baseball fan, you know how to record and interpret baseball statistics; if you've been working part time in a medical office, you've most likely learned what information is recorded on patients' charts, with what terminology, in what form of entry; and if, like Barry, you have been exchanging posts with your friends on Facebook, you've learned a form of social media literacy that involves knowing how to write posts and share other information on that platform.

Some researchers in the field of composition have been studying the different ways people use literacy as they move through different parts of their lives, looking at how both their immediate and larger social contexts shape their reading and writing. They are discovering how particular literacy practices develop and enable people to participate in those social contexts, including Facebook communities and science classrooms, and how composing, as a core literacy practice, has been changing in digital environments. Throughout the following chapters, we'll be exploring similar concerns and their implications for you, as a reader/writer/composer, in a variety of contexts—social, public, and academic—where literacy practices are being significantly transformed in a digital age. But we'll begin here with a look back, to see how literacy practices changed over the twentieth century and to consider what implications those shifts might have for how we approach the rapid changes we encounter in the twenty-first century.

Changing Literacies

We've traditionally thought of literacy as the ability to read and write. In the modern world we don't interact through reading and writing in just one setting, but in many, each with different expectations for the style of language we'll use, for the sorts of things we'll talk about, and for the forms that our exchanges will take. As researchers have focused on the different forms that reading and writing take in different settings, they've begun to talk about literacies, using the plural form to reflect the different ways people have to know how to read and write in their churches or workplaces, and in their literature or physics courses. As a reader and writer today, your literacies are complex and varied, and they go beyond knowing how to work with written text alone. Reading and writing are changing in a digital age. But the fact that what's involved in literacy is constantly changing isn't new, as researchers of literacy practices have discovered.

Deborah Brandt, a professor of English at the University of Wisconsin-Madison, has focused much of her composition research on the literacy experiences of people from different eras and different backgrounds. In this report on some of that research, she begins with an account of the literacy lives of two individuals, an older woman, Genna May, and her great-grandson, Michael May.

BEFORE READING:

Remembering your early literacy experiences

Before you read Brandt's account of her research, think about what you remember of key moments in your own early literacy experiences. How have your own your reading and writing practices changed over time and in new settings?

📖 Deborah Brandt
Author of 4 books:

- *Literacy in American Lives*
- *The Rise of Writing: Redefining Mass Literacy*
- *Literacy and Learning: Reflections on Writing, Reading, and Society*
- *Literacy as Involvement: The Acts of Writers, Readers, and Texts*

AWARDS

- The Modern Language Association's Mina P. Shaughnessy Prize (2002)

- The Grawemeyer Award (2003)

- The Conference on College Composition and Communication's Outstanding Book Award (2003)

FACTS

- She is professor emerita of English at the University of Wisconsin-Madison.

- For nearly 30 years at UW-Madison she taught undergraduate writing at all levels, as well as graduate courses in literacy studies, contemporary writing theory, and research methodology.

- Her research has been supported by the American Council of Learned Societies, the Guggenheim Foundation, National Endowment for the Humanities, the Spencer Foundation, and the U.S. Department of Education, among other sources.

RESEARCH FOCUS

Brandt's research focuses on the social contexts of mass literacy and literacy learning, and on large-scale, structural forces that shape individuals' access to literacy.

READING

Selection from

"Accumulating Literacy: Writing and Learning to Write in the Twentieth Century"[1:1]

by Deborah Brandt

College English, 1995

Genna May was born in 1898 on a small dairy farm in south central Wisconsin, the eighth of nine children of Norwegian immigrants. She spoke no English when she enrolled at the age of seven in a one-room schoolhouse built on land donated to the school district by her parents. Although Genna May would eventually go on to complete high school (as one of a graduating class of thirteen) by boarding in a town ten miles from her farm, she started school at a time when Wisconsin required only that young people ages seven to fifteen attend a local grammar school for twelve weeks a year. (. . .) As a student in "the grades," as she calls them, Genna May wrote spelling lessons on slates, erasing with a wet cloth to go on to arithmetic lessons. She remembers a home with few books and little paper, and she said she would have had no reason to write as a girl except to compose an occasional story assigned by her teacher. After high school graduation in 1917, she enrolled for several months in a private business college in the state capital, just long enough to learn typing and shorthand and win a certificate in penmanship before being placed by the college in the office of a local business that was manufacturing disinfectants for dairy farms. In 1994, Genna May was using writing to record recipes, balance her checkbook, and send holiday

READING

and birthday greetings to family members.

Genna May's great-grandson Michael May was born in 1981 in a sprawling suburb east of Wisconsin's state capital. In the early 1990s he was attending a middle school equipped with computers. The first of four children in his family, Michael remembered that his earliest composing occurred at two years old, when his parents helped him form simple words with magnetic letters on a metal easel and chalkboard in the family's TV room. As a participant in a grade-school enrichment program called Future Problem Solvers, he wrote a letter to his principal arranging to correct erosion on the school playground. In the bedroom of his eight-year-old sister Rhonda was a manual typewriter that their father had bought and used while attending a local technical school, a typewriter that Rhonda was now using recreationally. One weekend Michael's mother brought home a personal computer from her job as a data processor at a national insurance company so that she could learn a new program, and, Michael remembered, she allowed him and his sister to type messages back and forth to each other on it. Asked what made writing important to him, Michael responded that it "has a lot to do with speaking," with "seeing correct words."

These accounts by two members of the same family capture many of the economic and social transformations of twentieth-century America: population movements from farms to urban centers to suburbs; shifts in the economic base from agriculture to manufacturing to information processing; the rise of big business; a rapid escalation in educational expectations; revolutions in communication technology; and the growth of a print culture so saturating that it has become a principal means by which some children learn to talk. Against that backdrop we see the dramatically different social contexts in which Genna May and her great-grandson learned about literacy and its relationship to the world. In the sparse setting of Genna May's prairie farmhouse, paper, hard to come by, was reserved for her father's church work. In Michael May's print-cluttered suburban ranch home, his parents introduced him to writing and reading amid the background chatter of network television. For members of the community in which Mrs. May grew up, the ability to write the words of everyday life often marked the end of formal schooling, while for Michael May these same experiences served as a preparation for kindergarten. In the social dynamic of the rural school district of the 1890s, it would not have been unusual for a teacher to board with her students' families while school was in session. Three generations later, in a twenty-five room middle school, students learned to address their principal by formal letter as a lesson in bureaucratic action.

These accounts complicate the argument that the demand now is simply for more people to achieve a kind of literacy that used to be achieved only by a few—or, as Lauren Resnick has put it, that everyone now has to develop reading and writing skills that used to belong only to an elite. However, to say merely that social changes dictate that Michael May achieve a higher level of literacy and education than his great-grandmother is to miss how the same social changes that demand higher eventual skills are already tangibly present at the scene of his literacy learning, part of the way a two-year-old in the 1980s learned what literacy is. Not even elites of the past have encountered the current contexts in which literacy in its many forms is being practiced and learned.

In fact, these accounts suggest that what is unprecedented about literacy learning (and teaching) in the current climate is not so much a demand for literacy that seems chronically to outstrip supply, but rather the challenges faced by all literacy learners in a society whose rapid changes are themselves tied up so centrally with literacy and its enterprises. If Genna May carved out an early life amid a scarcity of print, her great-grandson must carve one out amid a material and ideological surplus. The setting in which Michael May first encountered the ABCs is layered with discarded and emergent forms of literacy and their histories. With his magnetic slate, he recapitulates in eerie ways a rudimentary ritual of the nineteenth-century schoolhouse at the same time that he must absorb from his parents the meanings that literacy and education have for middle-class families of the late twentieth century. (. . .)

The piling up and extending out of literacy and its technologies give a complex flavor even to elementary acts of reading and writing today. Contemporary literacy learners—across positions of age, gender, race, class, and language heritage—find themselves having to piece together reading and writing experiences from more and more spheres, creating new and hybrid forms of literacy where once there might have been fewer and more circumscribed forms. What we calculate as a rising standard of basic literacy may be more usefully regarded as the effects of a rapid proliferation and diversification of literacy. And literate ability at the end of the twentieth century may be best measured as a person's capacity to amalgamate new reading and writing practices in response to rapid social change.

AFTER READING:

Write about a specific memory you have from your early experiences with literacy, and share your memory with your classmates in a class discussion or on an online course site or blog you create for this course. As you hear or read others' memories, do you find any evidence to support Brandt's claim that an individual's literacy experiences are linked to larger social contexts? More precisely, do you find that differences in literary experiences are linked to economic and social transformations in the larger society?

Defining literate ability

Look again at the last few paragraphs of this reading. We can see that Brandt argues, in a sense, with other researchers who have focused only on the rising expectations that everyone will achieve an "elite" level of literacy that was once achieved by only a few. From her research, she has come to see literacy at the end of the twentieth century as involving a kind of "piling up" of different literacies and technologies (and there has been even greater change in the twenty-first century). What does she see as the situation of contemporary literacy learners, and would you agree that it still holds true? Does her definition of literate ability as "the capacity to amalgamate new reading and writing practices in response to rapid social change" fit with the literacy memories and the current communicative exchanges you and your classmates have begun to explore?

From the last few paragraphs of the reading, we can also see that Brandt is critiquing what is sometimes referred to as the "literacy myth"—the notion that greater levels of literacy mean greater prosperity for both individual and society. What does Brandt see as the situation of contemporary literacy learners and do you think this still holds true in a progressively digital world? What resonances do you see between your current literacy practices and Brandt's description of accumulative literacy? And would you agree or disagree with the idea that greater literacy means greater prosperity at the present moment?

Contemporary Digital Literacies

As digital technologies have developed even more rapidly in the twenty-first century, they have continued to impact our literacy practices. For example, Genna May's literacy practices focused more on reading than on writing. Michael May, who must now be in his thirties, grew up writing and using computers. But the growth of the internet, of online gaming communities, of social media sites like Facebook, and the general emergence of life online has been a much more recent phenomenon and has shaped much-altered literacy practices. These new practices are often referred to as *digital literacies*. They include not only the ability to use digital technologies for reading and writing, but also to use them both critically and creatively for specific contexts and purposes, in ways we'll be exploring.

We've seen that new media compositions are often *multimodal*, involving sound and images as well as printed words. They also bring new designs and arrangements of material, and new ways of expressing our identities, as we can see on Barry's Facebook page. But as researchers have studied what is happening online, they've also discovered other significant elements of digital literacies.

Digital literacies are interactive.

Earlier literacies were also interactive in the sense that writers were interacting with their readers through the texts they produced, while readers were actively taking in what was written. But contemporary digital literacies are more so. While people often read what's posted on an online site without contributing their own ideas, most sites are set up to allow readers to interact with writers. The blog sites being used by most newspapers but also by tech geeks, young mothers, coupon clippers, or almost any other interest group are designed to support the posting of comments by readers and to foster more extended interaction. MySpace offers a platform where bands can create pages for their music and fans can follow them and share what they like. The online sites associated with courses typically have discussion boards, chat rooms, and other features that encourage interaction among students. Online games are inherently interactive—you're either a player or you're not. And even shopping sites ask for our reviews of the products we've purchased and use our past purchases to suggest what we might like in the future.

To say that our contemporary literacies are more interactive is another way of saying that a lot more of our communication is taking place in writing today than at any point in history. It's easy to overlook how radical these changes are because our digital literacy practices seem so normal to us now and so much imbedded in the culture at large.

Digital literacies are often collaborative.

The internet enhances the collaborative potential of our literacy practices. Multimedia sites typically require more collaboration to create, but users too are often expected to take on a more collaborative role in creating the content that's presented on them. Wikipedia offers one striking example. It has forever displaced compendiums of knowledge like encyclopedias and has helped immensely in democratizing the process of knowledge-making, shifting the notion of an encyclopedia from one where a few experts gather and present the knowledge that others read to one where everyone is invited to contribute and to edit what has been contributed. We'll talk about contemporary knowledge-building in Chapter 5. But the creation and wide use of platforms such as wikis that support such collaboration show an ongoing shift in literacy practices, beyond those needed for early uses of computers and the internet.

Digital literacies are also both public and global.

While the internet supports our daily local connections with friends and family, it also supports more public sharing and connection. And because the internet can connect people in distant parts of the globe and because new tools and platforms support interaction among those people, writers and readers and online game-players are interacting with people they've never met in person, around the world. Facebook is available in most countries, and it's likely that some of Barry's classmates are exchanging posts with their friends back home in other countries and that Barry himself has, among his Facebook friends, some who are not currently in the United States.

New applications and platforms permit people from across the globe to connect, to coalesce around a common interest or topic. Facebook surpassed 1.65 billion accounts in 2016. But other platforms—Twitter, Tumblr, Instagram, and Snapchat—continue to emerge and support global connections. With each new wave of applications, our literacies adapt in response.

Digital literacies have brought greater exchange and variation of language from around the world.

Even where English is the primary language used for communication online, as is often the case, that English may reflect local varieties of English as it is spoken in India or Nigeria. The exchanges of blogs and games, but also online courses, may reflect the presence of multilingual participants and alter our expectations of what public English looks like.

INQUIRY

???

#3: Your experience of twenty-first century literacies

Do you or any of your classmates spend time in an online setting or activity that involves interaction with others whom you haven't met face to face? With others who are outside of the United States? With others from different language backgrounds? In collaborative endeavors? What does your own experience with new digital literacies suggest about how they might differ from twentieth century reading and writing practices?

Key Concepts for Studying Contemporary Literacies

Academic communities bring together people who share an interest in knowing and learning more about a particular field of knowledge and who begin to name the key concepts of their field in particular ways. For example, motivation and self-esteem are two important terms out of many that Barry will encounter in his Introduction to Psychology course. Genes and DNA and mitosis are concepts he'll work with as a biology major. We've started introducing concepts in this chapter that are central to the understandings shared by people who study composition and literacy and that will be important to the work of this book as we extend that study to digital environments. Such concepts grow from ongoing work in the field, the research that's done there, and the theories that are developed. Those that prove useful become widely shared, while others drop away.

Key concepts, like the ones we are noting and defining in our chapters, are really tools for thinking—ways of naming important understandings that are shared within a discipline, generalizations that come from looking at many related examples and that help us make sense of what we're seeing. The related concepts of *literacy, literacies,* and *digital literacies,* for example, emerged from: 1) identifying fundamental reading and writing skills and practices, 2) recognizing that those needed skills and practices change in different contexts and individuals develop multiple sets of skills and practices that they can use as they move from one context to another, and 3) seeing that many of our literacy skills and practices are being radically reshaped in new, digital contexts. Sometimes researchers use the term **new literacies** to capture both new understandings that our literacies are embedded or "situated" in our social contexts and the fact that these contexts are, increasingly, digital ones, drawing on digital tools. These evolving literacy concepts create a network of ideas that let us understand much more about what is happening than the concept of *literacy* alone could represent. Some related concepts that we'll draw on for understanding how our literacies are situated are *discourse community, conversation,* and *context.*

new literacies
literacies that are shaped by new contexts and draw on new technologies

Discourse Community

The term **discourse community** combines two ideas: one of community, where people are connected by some shared interests, purposes, beliefs and values, whether through a church, workplace, or fantasy football club; and another that such groups also share ways of using language—ways of communicating. In the formal study of language, literacy, and composition, the term **discourse** is used to refer to language as it is actually used by people to communicate their meanings in real situations (as opposed to clauses and sentences in grammar books that are taken out of normal communicative contexts). When, like Barry's hockey teammates, you share some of the same knowledge, beliefs, and values in a certain area of interest, but also similar ways of talking or writing about these things, and you participate in ongoing exchanges with each other, you belong not only to the same community but to the same discourse community. Discourse community is an academic term—a concept that focuses our attention on the communicative and literacy practices of its members.

When you're a member of a discourse community, communication with other members is easy because you know what others are likely to know, what they're likely to understand, and how they'll expect something to

discourse community
a community of people who share interests and ways of talking about them

discourse
language used by speakers and writers in actual communicative contexts

be said. But all of this shared understanding is implicit—the rules for what to talk about (or what to post on Facebook) and how to talk about it, are almost never explicitly stated. Members of the group know when someone is a newcomer but they don't always know how to say why they know that. When all of the participants in a conversation belong to a common discourse community, they share an understanding of **what** is interesting and worth talking about, **why** they should participate in exchanges, and **how** to contribute appropriately and to build on what has been said by others at any moment, in the **where** of any context.

We have seen that our literacy practices are closely tied to the communities we are part of. Brandt's account shows us how, even in the same family, literacy practices changed significantly as the larger society changed. We can also see, however, that those practices were strongly shaped by the beliefs and values of a small community. We learn, for example, that "in the sparse setting of Genna May's prairie farmhouse, paper, hard to come by, was reserved for her father's church work," and we can imagine that, if we could look closely at how literacy was used in that community, much of it would involve a church—reading the Bible, learning prayers, and listening to sermons the preacher composed. Genna May would have read and done a little writing in two other communities—school and eventually the business office of a manufacturer—but these communities would have been quite distinct from each other, with little overlap.

Our account of Barry's reading and writing practices shows him using literacy in a number of small but sometimes overlapping communities—those associated with his courses, with his team, and with his friends. His Facebook page shows one exchange about the hockey video his teammate posted.

> Barry: haha I like how the announcer wanted buffalo to try to hit thomas to get back at boston
>
> John: haha you shoulda heard the Bruins announcers later in the period, something like: "the Sabres didn't really go after the Bruins too hard after the hit. If Buffalo had hit Thomas, the Bruins would have killed every one of them"
>
> Barry: more like the whole city of boston would have gone to war.

Facebook literacy, as practiced by Barry's hockey friends, involves knowing what topics will be of interest to teammates (and thus worth posting), and that a post of a video link on your timeline requires a short, appreciative "haha" comment about it, which may lead to a sequence of short comments. But it also involves knowing how to create a Facebook page, how to post images and links to videos as well as text, and how to share and comment. Unlike for written literacies practiced in more formal settings such as workplaces and classrooms, text doesn't require capitalization, and the informal tone of the responses is maintained by sometimes representing spoken words ("shoulda").

The different ways in which we use various forms of literacy—how we use them to build or maintain relationships and express ideas—are shaped very much by the communities in which our exchanges take place. Barry's teammates and his larger circle of Facebook friends value maintaining an ongoing social connection, yet they have limited time and may not be at the same colleges. Writing and reading frequent, short posts to their own and one another's timelines about their current activities or interests reinforces what they have in common and helps them to maintain a sense of community, whether the community represented is hockey team friends or the small community being built in a boyfriend/girlfriend relationship. When we get together regularly with any group of people—when we have a sense of belonging to a group of friends, a family, a church, a workplace, or even a classroom, where people share some connections and also share certain ways of thinking and talking about them—we are part of a discourse community.

Conversation

In studying the ways in which members of a discourse community communicate with one another, we use the term *conversation* to represent all types of interactions, whether spoken or written, face-to-face or online, in short comments or in lengthy speeches or articles where one person takes a very long turn while others are silent (but actively listening or reading), among people who know each other personally or only indirectly (as fellow scholars of new literacies, for example). Sometimes the meanings being exchanged are implied rather than stated directly, as in Figure 1.4, where those who have gathered at the Thanksgiving dinner table for "good conversation" seem to be involved in many very different conversations on their cellphones while ignoring the one that could be taking place face to face. Yet the participants are acting on a new shared understanding of what Thanksgiving dinner-table conversation can look like, and perhaps a shared meaning that family members can find value in being in a common space while carrying on the multiple simultaneous exchanges that our networked world allows. But they might also be contributing an implicit statement to the common dinner-table "conversation" that the usual conversation is likely to be boring or filled with tension.

All conversations, whether small and local or extended and public, involve shared knowledge (what), shared purposes (why), and shared ways (how). That shared knowledge might be that a family's Thanksgiving conversations have been contentious, the shared purpose might be to make it through a meal together, and the shared ways might be using cellphones as a way of disengaging, but nevertheless the participants are involved in a common act of communication, as well as the ones they are carrying out individually. In many conversations, particularly the larger public and academic conversations that we'll explore in Parts II and III of this book, we'll generally find the knowledge that participants already shared or that's being shared is more explicit and substantive, and we'll consider what might be involved in "joining the conversation" that's already taking place in the larger world. But we'll find that these shared elements are always present.

Figure 1.4: Conversation in a discourse community

Context

context
the surroundings of a particular text or event

immediate situation
the setting and circumstances that help to shape spoken and written texts in the moment

A discourse community provides part of the **context** (the *where*) for any act of communication or conversation. When people are part of such a community, they understand the larger context of their exchanges—belonging to a team that may play better if its members feel a stronger connection, for example. But they also understand the **immediate situation** of any exchange, like what can be said in person, what's OK to post on Facebook, and what's OK to say when the team has just won or the goalie has made a number of great saves, but might not be OK to say when the team has lost or the goalie has let too many shots get by him. **What, why,** and **how** in any exchange are in turn determined by **where** the exchange is taking place, and among what group of participants at what moment. It's the immediate situation that helps participants determine what's significant—what's meaningful and important enough for the exchange to build on, and what's not so significant. It's the situation of two teammates whose coach has just come down hard on the team for a minor altercation in their last game that makes John's posting of a hockey fight video meaningful in a way that it might not have been otherwise.

Finally, the context for any exchange includes the immediate situation, but also a larger **social and cultural context**, where similar exchanges have gone on over and over again, and patterns have developed that provide the background for what is happening in any particular moment. In Barry's case, that larger cultural context includes the large role professional sports play in American society, the somewhat smaller world of hockey fans, and the still smaller world of players. It also includes a digital culture in which fans form groups and exchange images and videos and information about teams and their strategies, successes, or fights online. In the case of his writing course, it's the cultural context of an American system of higher education, where students are expected to take courses in their first two years that will contribute to their general knowledge and their ability to think and write in a variety of academic courses.

INQUIRY

#4: Observing a written exchange

Look back at the list you made of your current social contexts for reading and writing. Choose one of them and think about, or observe and write down, an actual exchange that was carried out through texting, posting, or any other written mode. Do you think it's typical? Do you think it represents shared and repeated ways of talking or writing? Does it reflect any common understandings or shared values? Does it draw from both an immediate situation and a larger social/cultural context?

Even with widely shared and established concepts, individuals need to develop their own working understandings of what the concept means and how to apply it to their own observations. In the context of this book, all of the concepts we introduce should be seen as working concepts, ideas to be tried on and tested out and refined through your own observations, not definitions to be memorized. It will be helpful to create a glossary of working concepts—your own examples that seem to illustrate each concept, and your own developing definitions. It's important for your evolving understandings that you capture your thoughts at this moment of your own work, not a dictionary definition. You can revisit your glossary and refine and add to your working understandings as you go along.

Below are some working definitions of the concept of a discourse community and some examples that other students have generated. Note that each response is slightly different, but each contributes to a general understanding and represents that understanding in the writer's own words, while the examples help to test that understanding (so that some may be rejected and others added as the inquiry goes on).

STUDENT VOICES

From the reading, my take on discourse community is a social structure that you interact in and live with. I am part of school discourses, work discourses, and also a social group of friends that works as a discourse, and my church community is a discourse community. (Matt V.)

An example of a discourse community is a certain group who is really passionate about football and likes to follow the game in depth, which may include statistics, players, coaches, etc. (Brian)

Any setting of conversation that has distinct and recognizable characteristics. What makes that particular conversation recognizable is that all participants know how the conversation will proceed. Each person has a place in adding their own knowledge into the equation and they know how and when to add it. (Matt S.)

INQUIRY

#5: Starting a working concepts glossary

???

This is a good moment to begin to create an individual or a class glossary of working concepts. Begin by listing new concepts from this chapter that seem significant to you. For this chapter, include *composing, multimodal composition, literacy/literacies, digital literacies,* and *discourse community* as a starting point, adding others as you read more. (We'll be using the key concepts of this chapter in later ones, and you'll have a chance to add and expand on them in your glossary.) From your informal writing and discussions, you should have some ideas about these concepts that you can draw on.

For each concept, put down your current understanding of the concept in your own words (leaving room to expand on this), and one or two examples that make it clear to you. If you're doing this collaboratively, you can capture several wordings and examples from your group. If you've divided up responsibility for particular terms, it would be useful to report back on your group's work and get input from others.

Whether you maintain a glossary of working concepts individually or as a collaborative class effort, we recommend you share and draw on one another's ideas and observations to enrich your own understandings. In our classes, we ask students to post their working concepts to a wiki to create their own working concepts "Wikipedia" they can add to collaboratively throughout the semester, and we've included in Part IV some suggestions for setting up such a wiki glossary that all can access (Figure 1.5).

Digital Toolbox
See Part IV, Section II

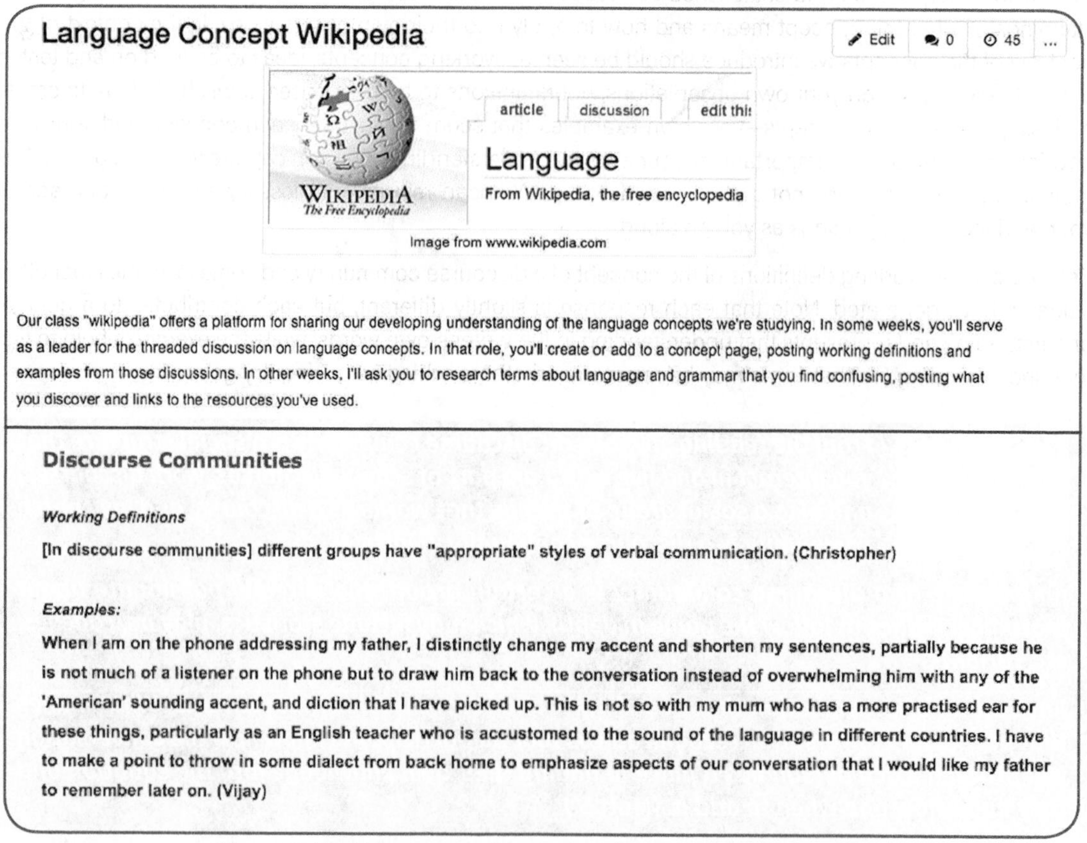

Language Concept Wikipedia   ✏ Edit   💬 0   ⊙ 45   …

article   discussion   edit this

Language

From Wikipedia, the free encyclopedia

WIKIPEDIA
The Free Encyclopedia

Image from www.wikipedia.com

Our class "wikipedia" offers a platform for sharing our developing understanding of the language concepts we're studying. In some weeks, you'll serve as a leader for the threaded discussion on language concepts. In that role, you'll create or add to a concept page, posting working definitions and examples from those discussions. In other weeks, I'll ask you to research terms about language and grammar that you find confusing, posting what you discover and links to the resources you've used.

Discourse Communities

Working Definitions

[In discourse communities] different groups have "appropriate" styles of verbal communication. (Christopher)

Examples:

When I am on the phone addressing my father, I distinctly change my accent and shorten my sentences, partially because he is not much of a listener on the phone but to draw him back to the conversation instead of overwhelming him with any of the 'American' sounding accent, and diction that I have picked up. This is not so with my mum who has a more practised ear for these things, particularly as an English teacher who is accustomed to the sound of the language in different countries. I have to make a point to throw in some dialect from back home to emphasize aspects of our conversation that I would like my father to remember later on. (Vijay)

Figure 1.5: Working concept wiki page and discourse communities page

The Context of Composition Research

At this point, you are probably beginning to see that composition is a field of study, an area of scholarly inquiry, like psychology or biology. Researchers in this field—including perhaps your own instructors—have discovered a great deal about how writers work, how different technologies affect how we write, and why particular forms of writing emerge for different purposes. The study of changing literacies and new literacies represents one strand of this research, but we'll be drawing on other strands and other concepts as well.

The idea that there is a **writing process**, for example, comes out of research from the 1970s. Researchers at the time surmised that, if we can understand how skilled writers write, then we will be able to design a successful curriculum to teach more advanced writing techniques and habits. They found that writers did follow a typical writing process when they composed longer texts, with elements of generating ideas, drafting, and revising through which they moved back and forth, though the process varied as they wrote for different purposes and different contexts. The writing process we will talk more about in Chapter 2 is directly tied to this history.

writing process
the idea that writing involves many different activities, from generating ideas to editing final texts

Recent research within the field of composition has focused on other areas. One of these is **rhetoric**, an ancient and complex field of study that takes as its focus the ways we use language to achieve our purposes to persuade, chide, cajole, or encourage. Contemporary studies of rhetoric focus on how writers respond to different audiences as they try to achieve different purposes with their writing, and we'll explore these understandings further in Chapters 3 and 12. Members of Barry's science seminar team, for example, know they need to draw the interest of their fellow students as they create the home page for the Blue Team's wiki pages if they want their classmates to pay attention to the work they've done. So they decide to post an image of a lion on stilts stalking a giraffe, along with a link to its source, a site about vegetarian/vegan diets (one of their research topics), as well as a link to "other funny stuff." By making this rhetorical move in composing their home page, they show that they can anticipate the concerns of this particular audience, drawing them in and entertaining them while connecting the humorous image to one of the serious topics they are covering in the research they want their classmates to read.

rhetoric
the study of how to achieve purposes in speaking and writing

Still other research within composition considers the ways in which certain textual forms—a news article, a position argument, or a Facebook post—have taken shape over time in particular contexts. In the news, school, or social media context, shared understandings about how to write or speak for particular purposes become established over time, and recognizable **genres** or forms of writing or speaking (much like genres of music) develop.

genres
texts with characteristic forms and styles that take shape in social contexts

Genres arise within discourse communities. When members of a discourse community engage in repeated exchanges with one another, they develop some expectations about the form those exchanges will take. When similar exchanges go on frequently, the repetition gives rise to patterns that may become formalized—the college application essay, the job interview, the joke or the put-down in friends' conversations, or particular forms of social media posts. If we looked at all of the Facebook posts about hockey from Barry and his team-mates, we'd find that the examples we've been looking at are typical. The posts most often include an image from a game or a link to a video. There's often some commentary from the poster about what makes that game moment notable. There's an appreciative response from the reader/viewer that adds to the commentary, to which the original poster responds back. And the exchange goes on, with short back and forth comments, for three or four turns. Barry might call this genre "the hockey team Facebook post," and his team friends all know what's required to make a good one, even if they've never named those elements.

Genre research has shown that within any genre, there are typical moves that people tend to make, but that they might use different strategies to accomplish those moves (Swales[1,2]). A common and repeated move in the Facebook exchanges of Barry's hockey team friends seems to be making a connection to the activity of the pros. These friends accomplish the move by posting links or images at some times, or by briefly mentioning something they read or viewed at others. It's the move of connecting to the larger culture of hockey that's important to this posting genre as it is taking shape in their immediate discourse community, and they use different strategies at different times to make that move. Likewise, one typical move for newcomers in classroom settings, whether online or off, is the act of introducing oneself. You might accomplish the move of introducing yourself with different strategies—by telling a story, by describing your interests, or by naming your goals for taking the class or for your future study. Over time, most participants in your evolving classroom discourse community will share most of these things, drawing on these several different strategies and coming to a fuller picture of who is in this community and why. But your initial choices of strategy for this same move of introducing yourselves may be quite different.

We will be using this framework of moves and strategies as we suggest ways to undertake different composing and research activities in each chapter of this book, so these concepts will become quite familiar to you as we move along.

INQUIRY

???

#6: Identifying informal genres

Observe some of your exchanges like texts or social media posts. Can you identify repeated patterns that might represent an informal genre like the "hockey team Facebook post"? Can you identify key features of that genre? What do participants need to know in order to "do it right"? What larger moves do they make, and what different strategies do they use as they make those moves?

Use the examples you find to add to your own working concept of genre in your glossary.

Composing
Writing for Discovery

What is writing? What does it mean to write or compose well? These questions seem obvious enough, but when we try to answer them we learn quickly that both questions resist easy explanations. In its simplest terms, we might be tempted to define writing as "recorded speech" or even a "technology for communication." Both ways are useful as general definitions, but they tell us very little about our actual experience of writing and the shape it takes on the ground, in our local and online communities, our classrooms, and our day-to-day experiences of the world.

Composition research has shown us that writing is much more than a skill we learn in the classroom. Rather, we can consider writing, and literacy more broadly, as the communicative activities we engage in as we build and maintain relationships and share ideas across a range of settings. *But* writing is also a practice we draw on to construct knowledge, to engage with others' ideas, and to generate the new understandings we'll share in turn. Writing informally about what you're learning is an important way to clarify ideas, discover questions, and make connections to other things you've learned and experienced. Perhaps you've already kept a math journal about your thinking process and questions as you've solved particular problems, or a reading journal for a literature class, and if so, you probably remember more of what you learned and can apply it more effectively than if you hadn't done that writing.

Much of the writing suggested in each chapter will consist of informal inquiry responses—the sort you wrote and discussed after reading Brandt's account of Genna May's and Michael May's literacy practices—which allow you to make connections to your own experience, to follow out your thinking in an exploratory way, and to discuss and share what you discover. These inquiry responses will sometimes focus on readings. Sometimes they'll ask you to observe something in the world around you. Sometimes they'll ask you to step back and reflect on the patterns you're finding across a number of readings, observations, or experiences, or to begin to analyze a cultural scene, visual image, or multimodal text. The inquiries provided in each chapter are meant to provide moments for you to pause and consider and see what you can discover about the topics we'll explore.

In most chapters, the final Composing section will offer you an opportunity to build on these informal inquiries to present your understandings in more developed and complete projects. We will guide you in working with the common composing moves that writers make in completing and sharing the sorts of inquiry the chapter focuses on and suggest different strategies you might use in making these moves.

In each case, we'll focus on four larger types of moves.

Moves of Inquiring and Inventing

These moves tend to be exploratory with a focus on asking questions, generating ideas, and determining **how** you might approach a particular composing activity—on deciding **what** you want to write about and **why**, for your audience and purpose.

Moves of Drafting and Shaping

These moves will focus on the steps writers typically take when composing in a genre that has arisen from similar inquiries, focusing on the **how**—the likely choices you'll be making as you give shape to a text that engages an audience and shares what you've discovered. In Chapter 2, for example, you'll have the opportunity to craft a literacy narrative that reflects on your own digital literacy experiences. Through the process of drafting and shaping, you'll learn to recognize and use common moves made by other researchers like Brandt and to use those moves to invent a shape or form to your writing that suits your purposes and likely audience. You will also learn to recognize when and how you might use multimodal resources or create a fully digital composition.

Moves of Revising and Publishing

These moves will focus on the relationship between the **what**, **why**, **how** and **where** of composition—on what you can learn from sharing your work within your classroom community and how you might further revise it to reflect your own richer understandings as you consider where and how you might publish it in a finished form for local audiences.

Reinventing and Circulating Your Work

In most cases, the exploration of a topic we undertake in any chapter is just a beginning. While in some instances you might end by sharing and publishing your work within your local community, in others you might use the responses of that community to help you expand or reinvent a composition, sometimes by using different modes (images, sound, video) or addressing a new audience, and we'll suggest some of those options in each chapter. Reinvention might also include building on an earlier piece of work for further research, in the ways suggested in Part III of this book.

Your local community might also help you to consider whether and where a composition might be more widely shared and circulated. **Circulation** has become an important consideration for composers in our networked and wired world, where their work can be shared and distributed easily. As texts circulate, they build new audiences, and often reach audiences far beyond those their composers might have initially anticipated. We'll address such wider circulation extensively in Part II, where we focus our inquiry on public contexts, but the understanding that all texts, even local hockey team Facebook posts, can circulate to wider audiences of friends and families, has become an important aspect of digital literacy.

circulation
the movement of texts
through and across
audiences and contexts

In this chapter, we want to use this Composing section to say more about how to work with informal inquiries, rather than more developed compositions. The suggestions for these types of informal writing, thinking, and sharing inquiries will typically ask you to engage directly with the texts you read or the details you observe or remember. They'll suggest bringing some of the words of the text or the details of the observation or memory or a visual image into the response you write and into the conversation you'll be having with your readers, so those readers can see both what you're thinking about and how you're thinking about it. But they won't focus on a particular structure or format, as the book's suggestions for formal project essays and reports may do. Rather, your informal, inquiry-focused responses will be a place to follow out your ideas freely, in an extended way, to work through an analysis, or to report in a preliminary way on what you're finding, without having to worry about the final organization and presentation of those ideas for a particular audience. We expect that you'll share these inquiries with others, to compare what you're discovering and to generate new ideas, or that you'll undertake some inquiries collaboratively, but that your focus will be on the thinking rather than on any final form.

Although it hasn't been studied as much as other genres, such inquiry-focused, informal writing is important to all of our learning and discovery, and it can offer you a chance to explore your thinking and reactions in systematic ways. **Inquiry-focused writing** is a genre of writing that is important for learning and research contexts.

inquiry-focused writing
informal writing that is focused on discovery and ideas rather than final presentation

As we identify the moves that are typical of such writing, we suggest you apply them to one further inquiry in this chapter: a reflection on the understandings you've gained from this chapter and how they connect to the immediate composing context of your course.

INQUIRY

#7: Reflecting on a learning and composing context

Chapter 1 has introduced you to key concepts and a framework of inquiry you will draw on and build on throughout your course and your work with this book. You've stepped into a new conversation about the changing literacies of the digital world and how they affect our work as writers. This is a good moment to reflect on what you've discovered thus far and the questions and speculations this immediate experience leads you to as you look forward to the work of this book and your course.

As you begin this inquiry, quickly scan this book, looking at the table of contents, the set-up of chapters, and additional features (a strategies list, an index) to get a sense of both where we're headed and how.

Then look at the syllabus or course overview from your writing course and any online site that has been set up for your course. What do they tell you about the goals of the course, the work you'll be doing, how the course will be structured, and how your work will be assessed?

Finally, work through the following moves.

WRITING MOVES

Inquiring and Inventing

There are several moves that will contribute to your learning as you engage in exploratory, inquiry-focused writing and that you can apply to Inquiry #7. As we walk through these moves, we'll ask you to try them out as you consider your new writing context and the evolving classroom discourse community you find yourself in at the moment. Remember there's not just one "correct" way of making these moves, but rather a number of different strategies you might use or invent.

1 Connecting

Finding connections among readings, experiences, and observations (your own and your classmates') and making connections between those readings and experiences and the concepts that the book presents are key ways for you to locate yourself in the kind of work this book invites. You've already been making connections to the content in this chapter—to Barry's literacy activity as a college freshman and on social media, and to Genna May's and Michael May's experiences in vastly different social and historical contexts. As you look at your course syllabus and/or course site, what connections can you name between what you've read in this chapter and the course context that has been created for your work? Between what you've found in this first chapter and what you see as you survey the larger context of the book this chapter introduces? Make some notes about what you find.

2 Elaborating

When you elaborate, you follow out details and examples to see what they tell you about the ideas you're exploring. Where have you made connections or noticed elements you think might be important to the larger inquiry you'll be undertaking into the composing and literacy practices of a digital world? What details or examples in the materials have caught your attention and led to your preliminary ideas about the work you'll be doing? Highlight or mark these details in some way.

3 Questioning

Asking questions about what you observe, read, and experience, and finding questions that can guide new stages of your own inquiry into traditional and new literacies and how they are being used in various settings is another useful strategy of inquiry you will use as you move through this book. After reading this first chapter, scanning the book, and examining the materials that give initial shape to your classroom context, what questions are you left considering? What new questions might the points, examples, and concepts highlighted in this chapter suggest to you as a student taking seriously the reading, writing, and communicating accomplished in digital spaces? What questions do you have at this moment about the larger context of your work?

4 Speculating

Speculation is key to academic work as it helps you move beyond your current understandings as you imagine possible answers to some of your questions, asking "what if," and exploring potential connections and relationships. What speculations can you articulate as you come to the end of this chapter? What do you think you might come to see about reading, writing, new literacies, discourse communities, and/or genres as you move through this book and your course? How might looking to the what, how, why, and where allow you to rethink your own approach to writing, the kinds of writing called for in college, or the communicative practices central to networked spaces?

┌─ WRITING MOVES ◄─

Drafting and Shaping

Depending on how your course is structured, you might use different tools and technologies as you draft and shape your inquiries: pencil and paper for quick responses that you'll share in the classroom, contributions to discussions on online course sites, or regular posts to a blog you maintain for this purpose. What matters most is that you do a lot of such writing, collect it, and come back to it—sometimes to draw on and reshape for more formal compositions, and sometimes to see the progress of your own thinking.

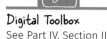

Digital Toolbox
See Part IV, Section II

1 Considering the where

Consider the *where* of this immediate inquiry and of the larger context for your ongoing work. What do you know at this moment about your classroom context and how such informal, exploratory work will be shared? (Will it be shared with your classmates? Just with your instructor? On a printed sheet of paper? On a learning management site, like Moodle or Canvas? On a blog you might later choose to make pubic on the web?) What do you know about the place of inquiry-focused writing in your course and how it will be built on as you move into larger composing activities? Use those understandings as you give shape to some of the ideas you came to as you moved through the last section, as you now focus on the *what, how,* and *why.*

2 Considering the what

What ideas or understandings, what speculations or questions about the work you've begun and anticipate doing do you want to share with others? What will you take as the focus of this inquiry that will start your work in this class? Will you focus on one question? On a series of ideas and questions and speculations? What connections to your experience of this chapter and/or to what you've found in related materials will you focus on? What details and examples will you bring in to help others see what you've found to be important or what you're questioning?

3 Considering the how (but not too much)

We've said that for this sort of inquiry-focused writing, you should not be focusing on form and final presentation in the ways you would for a more formal composition. Nevertheless,

we anticipate that much of such writing will be shared within your classroom community, with that discourse community gradually developing common expectations for this genre of writing, for what it might include, even as it remains informal. At this moment, think about what you hope your classmates might learn from your contribution to a classroom conversation about the work you'll be doing together (a conversation that might take place online or face to face, as a whole class or in small groups, by sharing portions of an inquiry aloud or by reading what others have passed around or posted). How will that sense of a shared purpose and your sense of the classroom community you are entering inform the ways in which you share your thinking? If this writing won't be shared, but kept in a personal journal, that too will influence your sense of *how.*

4 Considering the why

Considering the purpose of each inquiry is helpful. Certainly they are all meant to help support your engagement with the ideas presented throughout this book, but each inquiry might also serve other purposes. In this case, your response, if it will be shared with your classmates, will help you begin to define a common purpose and shared understandings—to begin building a classroom community around the work you'll be doing. It might also act as an introductory move for sharing your thinking, even if you have already done other sorts of class introductions (by going around a room and introducing yourself or by saying a bit about what you hope to gain from your class in an online forum, for example). How do you want to present your early thoughts and questions about your work to your instructor or classmates, to begin shaping the identity you'll be building as a contributor to the conversations of this community?

Revising and Publishing

Your own inquiries will be supported by the work of those in your classroom community. As you engage in the ongoing work of the classroom—asking and answering questions, reading and writing, and sharing your perspectives and discoveries with the other student writers in your classroom—you'll create a common and shared—and continually developing and changing—backdrop of understandings from which each new phase of inquiry will begin.

Your informal inquiries, when shared in the classroom or on an online site, will also help you to contribute to class discussions. Discussions—in groups or as a whole class, online or face to face—can help to support the understandings that can guide your work as a reader, writer/composer, and researcher because they allow you to compare responses and to discover what they have in common. They allow you to see what everyone's assumptions are as you undertake a particular task, to see how different writers have approached particular activities of reading and writing, or to see what common elements appear across the varied experiences all of you have had as you read and compose in many contexts. Looking at the conversations that go on in your classroom can help you see what shared knowledge is being developed there and how. It can also help you understand more about how conversations— whether spoken, written, or multimodal—might be shaped by particular settings. Your informal writing will allow you to generate ideas to bring back to your classroom community.

1 Reading as a reader

In many cases, when students are asked to read other student texts, they are invited to focus on evaluative comments, on pointing out places where students need to tighten up their work or where there is work left to be done. In this case, we want you to read your classmates' inquiries as a reader, as someone who is interested and invested in what they have to say, and as someone who is willing to think with them. As you read a handful of inquiries, note the new understandings, connections, and ideas they bring you to as you consider the work of your classmates in attentive ways.

2 Discussing and connecting to others' work

After reading a few inquiries as a reader, and not as a potential editor or critic, collect your ideas. How can you relate to what others had to say? What new ideas or questions are you now considering? What patterns seemed to emerge from the pieces you read? Share these in a class discussion as a way of thinking through examples, concepts, and points with your classmates as you build a collective sense of community.

While this book will provide a useful guide to the work you'll do in your writing course, that work will be supported by everything that is present in your college writing course: your teacher, the other students, the syllabus, and any other materials that are brought into the course, including whatever you and your classmates contribute and produce. Although the inquiry process—the reading, writing/ composing, and research you'll engage in—will take place within some structured guidelines and directions, the context in which you will be carrying it out will continually be reshaped by what you're learning from those very activities.

Key Concepts

Narrating Digital Literacy Experiences

CHAPTER TWO

CENTRAL QUESTIONS

1 How might stepping back from the flow of events to create narrative accounts and reflect on them offer new understandings and meanings?

2 What can we learn from following the composing process of a student writer creating her literacy narrative?

3 How can you work through your own composing process to develop a digital literacy narrative, and also possibly a multimodal one, involving images and sound as well as text?

Chapter Preview

In Chapter 1 we saw how literacy practices changed over the course of the twentieth century. Chapter 2 focuses on literacy practices in the present moment, particularly those involving digital resources. In it is the first focused inquiry of this book: considering what we can learn by exploring our own literacy experiences in a digital world and what these accounts might contribute to our larger inquiry into the new literacies and changing literacies of the digital age. As we invite you further into an ongoing conversation about writing and composing, we'll also consider what composition researchers have learned about the composing process. Then we'll turn to the work of one writer, following her process as she works to shape a literacy narrative that will be both personally meaningful and meaningful to other readers who are exploring the larger theme of contemporary literacies. We will see what her experiences can tell us about the ways such literacies are altering and/or supporting important aspects of our social interactions and communication. Finally, this chapter will guide you in composing your own literacy narrative, considering both print and digital possibilities.

Exploring Literacy Narratives

One form of inquiry that is particularly useful for understanding how something changes over time—in this case the typical literacy practices of particular communities in different eras—is the reflection on and recounting of a sequence of experiences. Brandt's account of Genna May's and her great-grandson Michael's literacy practices in Chapter 1 drew on her interviews with them and their personal recounting of their experience in response to her questions. She, as the researcher, was drawing on their experiences to gain larger understandings about changing literacies.

This chapter asks you to become the researcher of your own experience, not only recounting some moments that are relevant to your understanding of changing and digital literacies, but also reflecting on that experience and discovering its meanings for yourself.

Narrative Inquiry in Familiar Contexts

It's not unusual for us to use narrative to make sense of our experiences, and in a digital age, those narratives are often shared online, where they become available for others to draw on and to add to their own experience. As the internet makes more stories available, we more often bring outside stories into the conversations of our communities, building shared understandings around the story links we tweet or the video links we post on social media. We can see this happening, for example, on Barry's Facebook page in Chapter 1.

Barry's page contains comments on and links to hockey fights in professional games. We can guess that this must be a common area of shared interest in the larger culture of hockey players and fans because there's a **website**[L2:1] that captures them. At that site, we can find a blog with narrative accounts of the "fight of the week," as well as fight videos that show the actual sequence of events. And we can see that the internet has not only made it possible for a particular subset of sports fans to share stories widely, but also in doing so, to use a wider collection of narrative accounts to give further meaning to their own experiences. In these social exchanges, those meanings remain implicit—perhaps for Barry's team placing a recent hockey fight of their own in context, or alternatively showing how relatively controlled their own team's behavior is within the larger context of hockey as a sport. But a researcher drawing on such examples might find particular patterns that point to larger meanings about the culture of hockey teams or hockey fandom.

Likewise, "mommy blogs" have allowed mothers of young children, who might otherwise feel isolated if they aren't working outside the home, to share their "trials of motherhood" stories, build an online community with others who have similar experiences, begin to see reassuring patterns in others' accounts (like the common experience of the two year old's temper tantrums), and find new meanings ("Two year olds frequently act like this"; "It's a stage of their development"; "I'm not a bad mother because my child acts this way"). Or parents who worry about the impact of technology on their children's lives can share their concerns and strategies[L2:2] and the effects of their screen time rules.

#1: Narrative accounts and community meanings online

People often make connections to others' experiences to help make sense of their own by placing them in a larger context. Look at the posts and links on an online site you participate in and that represents one of your communities. What sorts of events are narrated or linked to and when, and what patterns and possible meanings do you find in such connections?

Or find an online site that includes narrative accounts of events—perhaps a blog for fans of a particular band or singer, for comics or anime fans or artists, for sports fans, etc. (See Part I Additional Readings, References, and Resources for some possibilities.) What information is included in these accounts, how are the events retold, and why do you think this material is being shared with a wider audience? What might be some of the concerns of this community and how might such shared narratives contribute to shared understandings?

Inquiry and the Genre of the Literacy Narrative

While blogs and other online sites expand the narrative resources we can draw on to make sense of our own experiences, allowing us to connect those experiences to those shared in a wider community, we can also gain new understandings through a focused reflection on our individual experiences. Narratives emerge from people's ongoing interest in making sense of the events in their lives and sharing their understandings of those events with others. While all narratives involve a recounting of some sequence of events, there are many narrative genres that take on different shapes as they evolve for different purposes in different contexts, with moves that go beyond the simple narrative accounts of "this happened and then that happened." From the opening "Once upon a time..." of fairy tales to the TV procedurals that begin by placing you immediately in the middle of a crime scene, each narrative genre has common conventions and expectations about how events should be recounted, in what sequence, and how and where background knowledge will be shared.

In composition research, where there is a shared interest in literacy and learning, the genre of the **literacy narrative** has evolved from many accounts collected by literacy researchers like Brandt,[1.1] from the reflections of other composition scholars on their own literacy practices, and from the narrative inquiries into their own literacy experiences that students have shared in their composition classrooms. We know that genres are shaped within particular social contexts, and we will see that the literacy narrative—rather than recounting a wide range of events—focuses only on those that might be meaningful in relation to an inquiry about literacy and its effects on our lives.

The literacy narrative, as a genre that has evolved within educational and research contexts, has come to have some common purposes and ways of achieving those purposes as well as some common composing moves, as we'll see later in this chapter. We'll begin thinking about this genre using the concepts of **where**, **why**, **what**, and **how** that we introduced in Chapter 1. Because literacy narratives are typically written to further an individual inquiry within a larger research context, their content and shape typically arise from a combination of a writer's search for what's personally meaningful and what will be meaningful within that larger context, within communities of others making similar inquiries, and eventually a larger research community (the **where**). Their purposes (the **why**) are typically both personal ("Why did I have such a negative image of my potential as a reader when I was in second grade?") and academic ("What can we learn together from sharing and examining school literacy experiences?").

The **what** then follows from these purposes as the writer selects events that might be meaningful to others in a classroom or research community, as well as to the self. That selection happens through a particular lens: the lens of what we've already come to understand about literacies and how they develop both in school

literacy narrative
a narrative genre that focuses on the literacy experiences of individuals or groups

Sidenote

Min Zhan Lu[2.1], for example, looks to her reading, writing, and communicative practices both in and out of school to question how two dramatically different sets of cultural expectations—Chinese and American—shaped her as a writer, student, and daughter.

and out, and what might contribute to further knowledge about this topic as we consider how our literacy practices are being reshaped in digital contexts.

Finally, the **how** typically includes recounting such key moments and reflecting on their meanings in a way that will interest others and contribute to a larger conversation, in a language and style that suits the composing/research context. A rap artist like Kanye West may capture what might be considered a literacy event ("The problem is I be textin"[2:2]), but in a language and style quite different from the typical literacy narrative, although a college writer might bring some of the language that captures that moment into more formal prose.

Before turning to the literacy narrative of a student, Ashley Canter, begin thinking about a moment in your own experience that might be included in such a narrative. Although you'll be considering the meanings of your larger literacy experience through the lens of digital literacies, you needn't begin there (Ashley didn't), but you might focus on any personally meaningful literacy memory.

INQUIRY

???

#2: Vignette of an experience

Brainstorm some moments of your own learning, literacy, or digital literacy experience and choose one to recount in detail. What details will make this event come alive for your readers? What details help to show its significance for you? Share your vignette with others by reading it to classmates or posting it on your class website or blog and asking for their response. What aspects of your experience do others connect with? What do they think it might mean?

Making Connections
Reflection and Narration

Ashley Canter, the writer of "The Gift of Sisterhood in a Text Message," first used the assignment—to write a personal narrative about an aspect of her literacy/digital literacy experience—as an opportunity to explore moments that were important for her. Writers might work with different processes on their way to a final piece of writing, and knowing more about Ashley's writing process as she worked toward creating the final piece might help you find flexible ways to tell the story of your own literacy/digital literacy experience.

Writing is often a means of coming to new understandings, and as Ashley worked through several drafts of her literacy narrative, she came to discover more about her own purposes beyond completing an assignment and the meanings she was finding. She was able to consider the most effective ways of telling her story to an audience of other college writers, connecting with the sorts of experiences and meanings they might share. We'll follow her process of thinking about **what** she might write about, as well as **why**, and **how**, and how the **where** of her class's larger inquiry ultimately influenced each of these.

invention
generating ideas

The Writer's Process

writing process
the ways in which writers move through different activities as they discover, give shape to, and share their meanings

The writing process has often been presented as a series of fixed stages—beginning with **invention**, then drafting, then revising, and finally editing—and sometimes your writing will move along neatly through these stages. But more often your process will be less linear and messier, and even more multimodal. A long tradition of composition research, beginning in the 1970s, into the thinking and **writing process** of writers with different levels of experience (Flower and Hayes[2:3]), in school and in out-of-school settings (Emig[2:4]), across disciplines (Herrington[2:5]) as well as in workplaces (Odell and Goswami[2:6]) showed that writers engaged in all of these activities of invention, drafting, etc., but that most often they moved through them fluidly, coming up with new ideas at one moment in the drafting process and tweaking a sentence in the next moment. Rereading and rewriting were shown to be an important part of the composing process, and they often led to the generation of even more new ideas during the final revising and editing parts of the process (Sommers[2:7]). Even Facebook writers have been shown to go through similar flexible processes, drafting, reading, and rereading their writing as it progresses, and often revising or editing midsentence (Tayoshi[2:8]).

Composing processes can be messy, and you, too, might realize while working on what you expect to be a final revision that you need to generate new ideas, draft new material, cut out entire sections of what you've written, or rearrange other parts in order to achieve purposes and meanings you can really only discover through the act of writing and through sharing with your readers. This was definitely true for Ashley, whose process evolved through several phases, each of which involved some amount of invention, structuring and drafting, and revision.

Phase 1: Generating ideas and creating a draft

Ashley began with a common invention strategy—**brainstorming**—to generate a list of possible topics. Composition scholar Sondra Perl has suggested a process that emphasizes the connection between mind and body and involves getting comfortable, letting your thoughts flow freely, creating a list of ideas that come to mind, and asking, "What here draws my attention right now? What could I begin to write about, even if I'm not certain where it will lead?" This is a process that calls attention to "what is just on the edge of our thinking but not yet articulated in words" and that she names as offering a "felt sense" of where your writing might go.[2:9]

brainstorming
quickly generating a list of ideas

Ashley thought about possible moments that she might focus on in her literacy narrative, making a quick list of all the possibilities she could come up with and identifying the most promising ones. She wanted to write about literacy experiences that felt meaningful to her, but also that she might make interesting to her readers, and she thought carefully about a number of possibilities before focusing on three: her wheelchair-bound grandmother writing a poem supporting her dreams of being a ballerina, her mother reading a favorite book, and her own storytelling as she invented stories about her stuffed animals. In an early draft that she worked through to a final form, the story of her grandmother was the most fully developed, full of rich detail and offering a clear sense of the significance of this moment and this relationship for her own literacy and learning. For example, she writes,

> I had such confidence that my Grannie would be the first one to throw a rose, with tears of joy and pride gliding down her soft, wrinkled skin. It seemed as though, even though she was never a dancer, my grandmother understood my passion for the art better than anyone.

And

> I remember one line of the poem specifically, it read, "She had danced all day, a very tired girl. She had fallen asleep, still wearing her tutu, dreaming of dancing in Carnegie Hall." As a child I had a simple appreciation for the poem, mature for my age, but not enough to know the sort of impact this work would have on me later in life. Though at the time I didn't know what Carnegie Hall was, I feel that this was my earliest form of being inspired by a written work of another. This is also the earliest time I can remember feeling emotionally connected with a piece of writing and like I could hear the writer's voice in the piece. For my writing today, I try to remember this poem as a way to include voice in my own writing. More than that, I use this poem to remember who my Grannie was and interpret what I think she wanted for me in life.

Ashley was satisfied with this piece of writing; her peer readers gave her very positive responses, and she was happy to submit it as her final version. But writing is always shaped not only by the writer's interests, but also by the social/cultural context in which it occurs, and the context for this literacy narrative was a course focusing on an inquiry into new literacies in a digital age. And although these lovely, descriptive passages met one of Ashley's purposes—exploring moments that were personally meaningful—"I was able to learn the importance of literacy not only inside the classroom, but also on a more personal level"—they didn't speak directly to that larger inquiry into digital literacies.

Phase 2: *Refocusing for a new draft*

freewriting
writing freely without stopping or editing

Ashley began again to generate new ideas, using another invention technique: **freewriting**. Freewriting, popularized by composition expert Peter Elbow, involves writing freely, anything that comes to mind, over a defined period—perhaps 10 minutes—and then pausing, looking for a center of gravity, an interesting idea, and then writing freely about that for another 10 minutes or so. You repeat the process until you've generated some material you want to go on writing about.

> The idea is simply to write for ten minutes (later on, perhaps fifteen or twenty). Don't stop for anything. Go quickly without rushing. Never stop to look back, to cross something out, to wonder how to spell something, to wonder what word or thought to use, or to think about what you are doing. . . Editing, in itself, is not the problem. Editing is usually necessary if we want to end up with something satisfactory. The problem is that editing goes on at the same time as producing. . . .The main thing about freewriting is that it is nonediting. It is an exercise in bringing together the process of producing words and putting them down on the page. Practiced regularly, it undoes the ingrained habit of editing at the same time you are trying to produce. It will make writing less blocked because words will come more easily. . . .
>
> Next time you write, notice how often you stop yourself from writing down something you were going to write down. Or else cross it out after it's been written. . .
>
> The habit of compulsive, premature editing doesn't just make writing hard. It also makes writing dead. [2:10]

focused freewriting
freewriting that begins from a particular starting point, focusing on an idea, image, or theme

From writing the first version of her essay, Ashley realized she really wanted to focus on a family relationship that was important to her, but the ones she'd selected earlier didn't have a direct connection to the contemporary literacies of digital environments. When she thought about where she'd find a connection between the personal and the digital, she realized it was in her daily texting with her older sister. She decided to do some **focused freewriting** around some moments in their relationship, and she listed a number and then explored three: twirling in a field of "puffy wishing flowers" (dandelions that have turned into seeds) when she was young; being encouraged by her sister to live in a college dorm instead of at home; and receiving a text from her sister in the middle of a boring sociology class. When she shared her freewrite with her readers, some could identify with having a supportive sibling, some had made similar decisions about whether to live at home or away at college, and while all were used to texting, some wanted to know more about the texts she and her sister exchanged.

Increasingly, the field of composition focuses on writing in digital environments where multimodal texts are more common, there has been greater interest in the place of the nonverbal—of image and sounds—in generating ideas. In a recent study[2:11], compositionist Jason Palmeri revisits the earlier writing process research and finds that the understandings of the process that emerged earlier were very multimodal, even though they were pre-digital. He finds that Emig saw the thinking underlying verbal composing as drawing from several modalities—visual, aural, spatial—and that Flower and Hayes saw writing as a process of translating other modes of understanding into words—moving from "the multimodal mind to the alphabetic page"—that Perl's felt sense generated images as well as words, that Elbow has focused on capturing the aural qualities of speech, and that Ann Berthoff[2:12], whose work on meaning-making we'll consider in Chapter 5, saw the visual as important to the imaginative act of composing. He argues, then, that "Composition has always been multimodal."

What does this multimodality, not only in digital compositions, but also in any act of composing, mean to a writer like Ashley? We can see that Ashley's earliest list of brainstormed topics includes strong visual and aural images, as she pictures and hears her grandmother reading a poem, visualizes the stuffed animals she told stories to, and remembers the sound of her mother reading a book to her ("In her southern, low, loving voice she would read, 'I'll like you forever, I'll love you for always. As long as I'm living, my baby you'll be.'"). She remembers feeling emotionally connected to these moments, capturing their "felt sense." Her title for her new draft, "Puffy Wishing Flowers," captures the visual image in her mind of twirling with her sister in a field.

As Ashley further explored her relationship with her sister, she continued to generate ideas and to think with images. At this point she turned to an explicitly multimodal tool, the digital bulletin board Pinterest, where she could pin images and words that seemed to capture some of her meanings (Figure 2.1).

Figure 2.1: "The Gift of Sisterhood in a Text Message" Pinterest board

Phase 3: *Considering the context of circulation—connecting personal and social meanings*

Up to this point, in both of her drafts, Ashley had focused on personal meanings, on the significance of the events she was telling about to herself and to her family members, but now she focused more explicitly on the context in which her writing would be shared—within a community of literacy researchers in her classroom and possibly beyond. Although the literacy narratives of any individual will necessarily focus on personal events and personal meanings, what might make them interesting to other readers outside of one's close friends and family is a connection to some larger events or the concerns of the larger society. What made the literacy experiences of Genna May that we read about in Chapter 1 significant was that they represented a major social shift at the beginning of the twentieth century—when a young woman could leave the farm to hold a job that required new and rapidly changing literacy practices. Genna May's experiences certainly meant a lot to her personally, since she remembered them and shared them with researcher Brandt. But it was the fact that her experiences connected with the experiences of so many others that make them valuable to us as readers, as representing, in Brandt's words, "the challenges faced by all literacy learners in a society whose rapid changes are themselves tied up so centrally with literacy and its enterprises."

The events Ashley retells can also point to larger meanings that will engage readers beyond her close friends and family. One point of connection for her readers, for example, was the decision to live at college, and her narrative could have been shaped to speak to the larger freshman college experience and the importance of having a strong support system for making the transition to college.

But Ashley was also writing in a specific course context, one that was focusing on the new literacies of the digital age, and where students were exploring how their own digital literacy experiences could contribute to larger understandings of that subject. Her readers' questions about her texting point there—questions about whether she and her sister use other modes of communication (phone, email, chat, Facebook) when they're not together and about whether they share images with their texts. But there was also a question about why she was beginning a literacy narrative with the memory of being twirled in a field by her sister. These questions, in this context, guided her to think further about both the personal and the social meanings of what she was writing, and we'll read about those meanings in her finished text.

INQUIRY

#3: Using a flexible set of idea-generating strategies

Through brainstorming, freewriting, creating a timeline of related events, searching through photos or other artifacts, or pinning generative images to a Pinterest board, determine the focus of your project. What stories do you have to tell about your literacy experience or the experience of others around you? How are these memories captured? In other writing? In photos? In objects related to the experience? What will you want your readers to know about these experiences and what understandings will you want them to take away from your account of them? How might the literacy experiences you choose work not only to convey the significance they have for you personally, but also to contribute to our larger understandings about literacy, including the new literacies of a digital age? If you are considering presenting a digital version of your narrative project, what visual and sound elements might you use to support your narrative?

Digital Toolbox
See Part IV, Section 1

As Ashley moved through the drafts of her essay, she made a number of decisions with her readers in mind: recreating a key moment in her early experience that related to her use of digital literacies in the present, deciding on the scope of what she'd tell (ending in college, but eliminating many details in between), moving back and forth between details of her experience and some reflections on that experience, and including actual examples of her text exchanges with her sister, along with the visual element of screenshots and other images.

At the same time, the challenge for Ashley was to find a way to expand the frame of her meaningful personal experiences in a way that would engage a larger circle of readers and show how they speak to the concerns of a digital age. As you read Ashley's final draft, you can consider whether and how she has accomplished this.

BEFORE READING:
Participating as you read

As you read, participate in Ashley's experiences as she has presented them. Annotate (mark) the text as you read it, noting places where you are drawn into her experience, where you make connections between her experience and your own or have questions, or find reflections and understandings that seem significant to our larger inquiry about digital literacies.

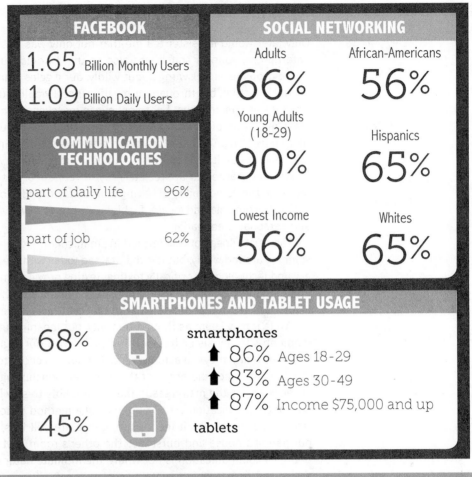

FACEBOOK

1.65 Billion Monthly Users
1.09 Billion Daily Users

COMMUNICATION TECHNOLOGIES

part of daily life   96%

part of job   62%

SOCIAL NETWORKING

Adults
66%

African-Americans
56%

Young Adults (18-29)
90%

Hispanics
65%

Lowest Income
56%

Whites
65%

SMARTPHONES AND TABLET USAGE

68%   smartphones
▲ 86% Ages 18-29
▲ 83% Ages 30-49
▲ 87% Income $75,000 and up

45%   tablets

READING

"The Gift of Sisterhood in a Text Message"
by Ashley Canter

Place annotations here

"Whoooosshhh!"

This was the noise that filled my ears in perhaps one of the most important moments of my childhood.

This was the sound of my older sister, Britney, swinging me around wildly, gripping me at my ankles, my slim, pale arms held out in front of me in glee. She would hold me tightly, making sure I would not fall, and move her body in big, enthusiastic circles, as I spun around with her, upside down, seeing the world pass by in an ornate, colorful blur. The morphed sight of dandelions, or as we called them "puffy wishing flowers" danced in my view. I could faintly hear the sound of a bee making its home in a flower hidden in the distant, fragrant summer grass of our parents' backyard. The most prominent noises, however, were that of my childlike laugh of freedom, of ignorant and completely carefree bliss, as well as my sister's more mature, but equally joyful chuckle. My soft, golden locks hung before me as I spun, and every time I would giggle they would invade my mouth and nose. Here we were, my older sister and I, swinging about foolishly and happily, our only care being that our mom didn't see us playing so haphazardly, as we knew she would worry that I would get hurt, like all good mothers would.

In this moment, the only meaning I found in my sister and I's goofy pastime was to have fun.

Place annotations here

Only later would my sister tell me that not only was this one of the many things she would do to entertain my younger self, it was also so that I would trust her. I would, in that moment, trust her not to drop me as we swung about wildly, our giggles filling the warm, summer air that surrounded us. Not only that, but throughout my life since, I would trust her. Trust her to tell me the truth, even when it was difficult. Trust her to believe in me, even when no one, including myself, did. Trust her to make me aware of my own potential when I felt weak. Trust her to rejoice with me in the moments that I felt strong. Trust her to support and love me even in the difficult moments of our sisterhood. And as crazy as it sounds, this seemingly meaningless youthful act that we participated in, that I have only learned to appreciate fully in retrospect; it taught me to trust my sister and to open myself to the vulnerability of having a big sister, friend, mother-figure, guidance counselor, advocate, fashion advisor, fellow lover of travel, and personal cheerleader.

The trust I speak of was formed in small childhood memories like spinning around wildly, but it is maintained today with the aid of literacy and technology, specifically texting. Texting provides an immediate and intimate way for my sister and I to communicate when we both lead busy lives and aren't able to hold face-to-face conversations.

While it may seem as though this silly, but meaningful childhood moment with my sister has nothing to do with our digital literacy practices today, they are actually directly related. I chose to open with this scene to trace the origin of the close relationship with my older sister. However, the main reason that we are able to stay just as close today is due to our constant flow of communication via texting. Having a method of communicating that allows me to instantly reach my sister makes it feel as though we are still kids, able to run down the narrow hallway of our parent's house and burst into the other's room anytime we need anything. Texting as a form of digital communication is not where the intimate nature of our bond began; however, this digital literacy practice is what maintains such a sense of closeness and immediacy.

My sister and I have had many important conversations via text. However, one that stands out in my mind is the following.

The words "I believe in you" seemed to be so much larger, more alive, perhaps, than any other words I had ever read on a screen. These four simple words leapt off my glowing phone screen and entered my full consciousness and seemed to slither down my body until they hit my stomach, causing a warm, anxious feeling of self-confidence.

She believed in me. And now, through her sisterly love and guidance, I believed in myself. I finally believed that I was making the right decision by staying on campus for my first year of college.

Knowing that my sister believed in me and trusted that I would make the most out of my first-year college experience made all the difference. Entering college, a time of discovery, vulnerability, and change, is a transitional time in both my own, and I believe, other's lives. The comfort of having a support system, a strong sisterly bond, meant that in the late nights of cramming for exams, times of confusion over which minor to choose, or the utter victory of making an A in that unreasonably difficult politics class; I would always have someone that I knew I could pick up my phone and talk to. Every college student,

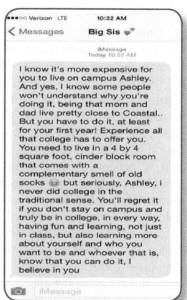

READING

Place annotations here

in my opinion, knows what an exciting, yet challenging time of adjustment the first year of college can be. Due to the age of technology that we live in, not only can I survive the struggles, big or small, associated with one's first year of college with the help of my older sister; but all college students, especially those who go to college far away from their hometowns, can maintain meaningful relationships with their family members.

I trusted my sister as she swung me about wildly at the age of eight and I trusted my sister now at the age of eighteen as she has advised me, in a text message, to live on campus and be the first in my family to achieve my college degree in the traditional way. Not only does texting allow for my sister to advise me in life-altering decisions, like the manner in which I will attend college, but this digital literacy practice also means that I can reach my sister in a matter of seconds about smaller, short-term decisions, like what I should wear for the first day of classes. . .

Here I stand in my dorm room that as she said it would, came with a complementary smell of old socks and sterile cinderblock walls that I have tried hopelessly to enhance with decorations. As I stood in front of the mirror deciphering whether the brown sandals or flats would be better, I knew that only one person could help in this time of "dire fashion emergency," my big sister. I grabbed my iPhone and scrolled through my contacts to find "big sis" written in a neat black font with a pink heart emoji next to it and I began to type (top, right).

Even when I least expect it, the welcoming and high-pitched "ding" of my phone's text alarm reverberates through the walls of my classroom. I look down to find a text that I had a feeling would be from my big sister (right).

I see her words pop up on my phone screen that is placed in my lap, lighting up in a vivid, white font. I'm in Sociology, the monotone voice of my professor drudging in my subconscious. I should be paying attention, yet all I can do is smile and think of how much this casual text from my sister means to me. Not only did she guide me toward one of my better decisions [to go to college in the traditional sense] and help me pick out the best outfit for the first day of class, but she also regularly checks in to see how things are going. Every week I know I will see a text quickly appear on my phone screen, jumping to life in a vivid white font. They read something like (bottom, right).

The previous examples showcase how my sister and I use texting as a way to maintain contact and have meaningful conversations complete with images to further convey meaning and establish a level of conversations as similar to being in person as possible. However, my sister and I's use of texting as a means of digital communication also speaks to a broader issue in today's ever-evolving age of technology. Many speculate that

Place annotations here

the use of digital communication, such as texting, has a negative effect on literacy and weakens the quality of technology users' conversations. I, however, argue that my sister and I's use of texting to maintain contact has exactly the opposite effect. Being that texting allows immediate contact and the ability to attach images or web links, my sister and I are able to make each other feel as though we are actually together even when we aren't. Due to texting, I have been able to communicate with my sister about something as small as my outfit choice for the first day of class to the decision to stay on campus for my first year of college. Not only that, but because of my maintained relationship with my sister via texting, I have used her support and guidance as tools for success in my first year as a college student. Something as simple as a text message has maintained something as important as a sisterhood and ultimately resulted in my academic, personal, and social success as a first-year college student. If texting as a means of digital communication has played such a positive role in my life, there is then proof that society's use of technology today may not be so trivial, and in fact, may actually be having positive effects on our population's literacy practices as a whole.

While some may view today's growing use of technology as a means of communication as a curse, I view my ability to maintain my relationship with my sister via texting as a blessing. Every time I see one of her texts I can't help but wonder where I would be today without the guidance, support, and love from my big sister. A chill runs through my spine at the thought, but this feeling is instantly stolen by a feeling of gratitude. I am and will forever remain grateful for the relationship I have with my beautiful, humorous, inspirational and brave big sister. And I am equally grateful for my ability to live in an age of technology that makes it possible for me to maintain such a bond with someone so monumental in my life. ∎

Sidenote

We can see that Ashley has included both narrative moments and some reflections on those moments as she works through a richer understanding of what she has learned about the role that seemingly simple texting plays in maintaining an important relationship in her life, and in turn, what evidence her own example offers that speaks to larger social concerns about young people's reliance on texting as a primary means of communication.

AFTER READING:
Sharing participatory readings

Share several of your markings or notes from your initial reading of this literacy narrative. As a reader participating in the events Ashley is recreating, where have you connected with or been interested in Ashley's experience? What understandings does she come to herself and share with her readers through what she has told of these events?

Rereading Ashley's narrative from the perspective of a writer

As a writer, what strategies in Ashley's choices of **what**—what to write about, what to include—and **how**—her ordering of the events she's presented, her structuring of a beginning and ending, and her movement between close details and a larger picture—do you find most effective? Are there any that you might adapt for your own literacy narrative or suggest to another writer of such a narrative? Are there some you find less successful? What do you discover about her writer's craft and her relationship to her assumed audience within the context of a college writing class focused on exploring new literacies? Do you think she has met her dual purposes—her **why**—of exploring both personal meanings and contributing her experiences and understanding to a larger conversation about new literacies?

From Written Narrative to Digital Story

Ashley has focused on presenting a written literacy narrative with the inclusion of some visual elements—a handful of pictures and screenshots of texts. But her narrative also provides an opportunity to engage in a more multimodal form of composition—to use even more images and sound as well as text to tell a digital story without relying so heavily on alphabetic writing.

Digital storytelling can be seen as a new form of an old art—the oral storytelling that drew communities together long before the advent of written literacy and that has continued in many forms through the present. The effective oral storyteller makes events come alive and take on meaning for her listeners by recreating those events in the telling. The development of new digital tools has allowed ordinary people, not only film producers, to use images, music, and other sounds, and text as well as their voices to support the telling of their stories and make them come alive. There are a number of tools that support digital, multimodal storytelling and guides to support the process, and you'll find more about these resources in Part IV. But if you're thinking about composing your literacy narrative as a digital story, here are some elements you'll want to consider early on.

Digital Toolbox
See Part IV, Section 4

- The visual/aural quality of the story you want to tell. Stories that offer rich images to their readers can more easily lend themselves to a multimodal digital presentation.

- The actual artifacts you have available. If you've seen a Ken Burns documentary, like *The Civil War*, you've seen how a long, multi-episode story can be made using photos and images of texts such as letters from soldiers, music, and narration. If you have actual photos and documents that are relevant to your story, you have a set of resources to work with.

- The meanings you want to convey. Good writers can set a scene, bring readers into it, and offer a sense of why the events that unfold there are significant, all with their words. But some meanings, like the terrible loss of so many young men in battle and the terrible cost our nation had to pay to end slavery, can be supported powerfully by a few well-chosen images.

- The resources of technology and time available to you. Learning to craft an effective digital story is a large project, and it requires significant planning as well as appropriate resources. It's important not to get bogged down in an ambitious project you can't complete, although you can learn powerful compositional skills with even a small project.

Ashley knew that the moments she was drawn to sharing often involved strong visual images, such as the field of "puffy wishing flowers." She included images to enhance these moments as well as screenshots of the texts she exchanged with her sister. She also included a picture of the outfit she was considering wearing on her first day of college, which she'd asked her sister's advice about, and another of her dorm room. While these images allowed Ashley to compose a multimodal essay, she could have done even more to make the visual central to her story, and she also could have added aural content such as sounds and music she might associate with these experiences or that could elicit certain feelings from her audience.

As you consider creating your own digital composition, you can see some examples of multimodal digital stories by other college students by following the links in this article from the UMass Boston Edtech Newsletter.[L2:3] Or search for "digital literacy narratives" online to find other examples including this one we like that includes students' spoken narratives[L2:4] of digital literacy experiences.

links

INQUIRY

#4: Reflecting on multimodal, digital compositions

Looking at the digital compositions of others can give you a sense of what the possibilities might be for such a composition and whether it's something you might want to think about as you begin to compose your own fuller narrative. Look at some digital stories at the sites we pointed to or others that you find online, whether or not they focus specifically on digital literacies. What seems to make a narrative work as a multimodal or audio composition? What engages you as a listener/viewer and helps you to understand both the experiences the composer is presenting and why those experiences might be significant? Are there elements that don't work as well for you? Think about the vignette you wrote for Inquiry #2. Can you imagine images to go with it? A storyboard for it? Telling it as a spoken story? Write down some ideas of what might be possible.

Sidenote

Online sites change frequently, and the suggestions we give you might not always be available when you go to connect to them, but you're likely to find others.

storyboard
multi-episode story
made using photos and
images of texts such
as letters, music, or
narration

Ashley intended to create a version of this piece using a richer variety of modalities, and she did some planning and sketching in the form of a **storyboard**, a visual layout of all the elements she considered including. Below, you will find a storyboard Ashley created for her current literacy narrative (Figure 2.2). You can imagine her creating a more image- and sound-driven version if she were to recast this as a digital story. By starting with the images, photographs, and screenshots she uses in her current version, she might think of other elements to include and take notes on them—detailing how she might create a recording to tell this story in her own voice or how she might use music to underscore her experiences.

The Gift of Sisterhood in a Text Message

A mutual trust is formed between me and my sister through the silly childhood act of swinging about in a field of "puffy wishing flowers."

This trust is maintained today through digital literacy, such as texting about important decisions.

This trust is also maintained in smaller, yet still significant ways, such as choosing an outfit for the first day of class.

Argue that texting, a form of digital communication, actually strengthens the quality of discourse taking place in our sisterhood.

Technology is having a positive effect on the literacy practices of other college students.

Sidenote

You can find resources to help you with creating your own storyboard in Part IV.

Figure 2.2: Ashley's digital composition storyboard

Composing
Digital Literacy Narrative

As you've read about Ashley's process for composing her literacy narrative, you have most likely done a lot of thinking about composing your own, about what you might focus on, and why, and how. In this chapter, we've focused on the elements of the writing process and how Ashley moves among them flexibly. At the same time she is making some of the common moves that writers make when composing a literacy narrative. While one strand of composition research has focused on the writer's process, another has looked at how genres arise in particular contexts and the typical moves that writers make when composing in those genres for those contexts (Swales[1,2]). These are complementary ways of thinking about the active work of composing, but naming moves situates that work more firmly in a context where other writers have been writing for similar purposes, and we can draw on the shared understandings that have developed about how they typically proceed. It's important to see these moves as suggestions for how to think your way through a piece of writing based on what we know about how many writers proceed with creating a successful composition of this type, but that can be adapted to your own purposes. Such flexibility is increasingly important in digital contexts. For instance, Tayoshi discovered this about Facebook composers:

Writers composing in internetworked, interactive environments (and writing of all kinds is increasingly being mediated through such environments) are negotiating multiplicity in writing task, purpose, audience, and technology. They not only juggle the multiple rhetorical tasks required by one act of composing, they are juggling multiple acts of composing, moving from one to another, making decisions about where to focus their attention and shifting gears between vastly different audiences, tasks, purposes, and genre constraints.[2:9]

You should see these writing moves, then, as another way of naming a process to use flexibly, in response to changing contexts and purposes, not as a set of rules to follow precisely.

> Writing moves are another way of naming a process to use flexibly, in response to changing contexts and purposes, not as a set of rules to follow precisely.

WRITING MOVES

Inquiring and Inventing

We know that writers who are engaged in similar explorations typically move through similar processes. For those who are exploring their literacy experiences, two initial moves of inquiry seem central.

1 Identifying key moments and their significance

You've already begun this process with Inquiry #2 as you've brainstormed moments to focus on in a vignette. That first vignette might or might not be included in a more extended literacy narrative. (Ashley's wasn't.) But it got you started, and by now you've probably identified a number of possible moments that seem significant to your own literacy history and/or current practices, choosing some to keep working with and rejecting others you imagine will speak to others and contribute to their larger understandings. As you begin to build more vignettes, more small narratives around these key moments, you'll want to bring your readers into them, capturing details and recreating these moments.

2 Reflecting on changing literacies in a digital age

You'll want to think more about **why** you're composing this literacy narrative. As with almost any writing project beyond a personal diary, you'll want to connect your own purpose with the likely purposes of your readers, to think about what you want to understand better through this composing exploration and what might interest your readers and offer some new understandings to those readers within a particular context.

Part of your purpose with a literacy narrative is to share the meanings these events have for understanding how our literacies develop and are used in particular social contexts, and you'll want not only to step into moments of your experience, but also to step back from them as well, to reflect on what they might mean in this context. Ashley, for example, focused first on her own favorite memories and had to work toward connecting them to the larger purposes of a collaborative inquiry into literacy/digital literacies, setting aside some moments that didn't speak to these larger purposes. At this moment, you're still not concerned about giving a definite shape to your narrative, but generating further ideas that you might want to share.

WRITING MOVES

Drafting and Shaping

At this point you already have a good idea about **what** you want to share with your readers/viewers/listeners—the key moments you want to focus on that will become the **shared what** of your composer/audience exchange. And you've reflected on **why** these particular moments are significant to you and might be meaningful to them, the **shared why**. As you begin to give shape to a fuller composition, you'll want to think also about **how** you'll do so, keeping in mind a sense of a **shared how**: what your audience's expectations might be, based on how others have approached this type of composition.

There are some key moves that are usually involved in giving shape to a literacy narrative, whether you are composing for an audience that will read a print text or for an audience that will experience a multimodal composition with images and/or sound.

1 Orienting readers/ viewers/listeners

When you lead a friend into a new scene—a party or a sporting event or a family dinner—where you know what's going on but your friend doesn't, you can let that friend stumble around, uncertainly, making awkward mistakes and misinterpreting what's going on. Or you can offer some background before you enter the scene and/or as the event goes along, explaining who is present and what others know that the friend doesn't to guide her or his interactions. As a writer, you always need to orient your readers and provide the shared background knowledge they'll need, but there's always a question about where to do this.

We can see that Ashley chose to begin in the middle of an event, with the "Whooosshhh!" of her sister twirling her around. Then she goes on to introduce her sister and the surrounding scene. It's not until the second full paragraph that she makes it clear that she's going to focus on her relationship with her sister. She could have begun quite differently, introducing her sister and their relationship first, for example, but she decided that she could capture her readers' interest better if she brought them right into the scene. You can decide whether this worked for you or not, as you consider where and how you'll provide the orientation and shared background knowledge that your readers/viewers/listeners will need.

2 Structuring your narrative

You'll want to think more about **why** you're composing this literacy narrative. As with almost any writing project beyond a personal diary, you'll want to connect your own purpose with the likely purposes of your readers, to think about what you want to understand better through this composing exploration and what might interest your readers and offer some new understandings to those readers within a particular context.

Part of your purpose with a literacy narrative is to share the meanings these events have for understanding how our literacies develop and are used in particular social contexts, and you'll want not only to step into moments of your experience, but also to step back from them as well, to reflect on what they might mean in this context. Ashley, for example, focused first on her own favorite memories and had to work toward connecting them to the larger purposes of a collaborative inquiry into literacy/digital literacies, setting aside some moments that didn't speak to these larger purposes. At this moment, you're still not concerned about giving a definite shape to your narrative, but generating further ideas that you might want to share.

3 Using specific and general narrative details

The how, for any narrative, includes bringing in narrative details. Whatever your audience, you'll want to include rich details that will bring them into the moment(s) you've decided to focus on. But you'll also want to move from those details to larger generalizations—larger understandings that they point to. In Ashley's narrative, details of twirling in a field or texts about clothing choices point to larger generalizations about an ongoing close relationship of two sisters, one that texting helps to maintain.

At the same time, in a narrative exploring ways in which her own life has been affected by digital communication, Ashley places her private experience into a broader public context to contest a larger generalization that's often made about digital practices like texting—that it might reduce meaningful communication: "If texting as a means of digital communication has played such a positive role in my life, there is then proof that society's use of technology today may not be so trivial, and in fact, may actually be having positive effects on our population's literacy practices as a whole."

As you recreate moments and make larger statements about their significance, you'll also want to capture the language of those moments if it helps to set the scene. Bringing in the texting language of "whats up" and "lol" makes the exchanges Ashley points to more vivid and enlivens the more formal language in which she represents her larger understandings.

4 Adding transitions

If you've focused on several key moments, crafting vignettes about each, you'll want to be sure you've moved effectively between one and another. Such transitions can also be places for stepping outside of your story for a moment, to reflect on its meaning and point to its significance. Ashley follows her vignette about twirling in the field of puffy wishing flowers with an explanation of why she's chosen to begin her literacy narrative with that moment, pointing toward her larger meanings while moving her readers out of one moment and into another. In digital compositions, transitions are often highlighted with the fading in and out of images or changes in background music.

5 Incorporating images and sounds

If you explore the possibilities of composing your literacy narrative as a digital story, or of recasting a literacy narrative that you've written into a digital form, you'll want to consider the visual and aural qualities of your narrative and how images and sound could contribute to it, the artifacts you have available to you, the ways in which images and sound might enhance your meanings, and the technological and other resources and supports you have available. You might decide to proceed with a digital composition or you might, like Ashley, decide that you could potentially prepare such a composition in the future. If you're trying to decide, you might prepare a quick sketch to explore the feasibility of your project or even a full storyboard for your present composition or a future project.

Because many narratives lend themselves to one form or another of digital storytelling, you're likely to want to consider these options now or in the future.

- You can narrate what you've written using your voice for an audio story. The Moth radio hour[L2:5] on National Public Radio presents podcasts of personal narratives by different storytellers each week and invites listeners to submit their own, offering good examples for working in this medium

- You can compose a multimodal digital story using images, sound, and text

- You can create a hybrid composition with images placed within a print narrative to highlight certain moments and meanings

You'll find resources for these approaches to multimodal composing in Part IV, Section 4.

 link

Digital Toolbox
See Part IV, Section 4

6 Considering other elements of good storytelling

An effective literacy narrative shares some qualities with other good stories, and whether you are composing for a print or digital audience there are common elements to good storytelling. Six such elements (some of which we've already discussed) are described on the <u>digitales website</u>[L2:6] for digital storytelling.[2:13]

> **LIVING INSIDE THE STORY.** Telling it in the first person in your own narrative voice

> **SHARING LESSONS LEARNED.** Highlighting the meaning and significance of what you're telling

> **DEVELOPING CREATIVE TENSION.** Having a problem or question to be solved or answered

> **MAKING A POINT ECONOMICALLY.** So that all details are relevant

> **SHOWING NOT TELLING.**

> **DEVELOPING CRAFTSMANSHIP.** So that all elements are artfully presented

As you draft or do storyboard planning for your print or digital composition, you'll want to consider such elements.

As you work with your materials, you'll most likely circle back through these moves as you keep trying out other possibilities, drafting and composing through several different versions before you come to what feels more final. Writers usually discover new meanings and therefore new threads that they might explore as they write. Staying flexible and being open to new possibilities—but also being realistic about how much time you have to play with your ideas before you settle on a more final draft—is an important part of composing. As you do settle on a more final version of your composition, you'll want to make one more move: editing.

7 Editing

The need for careful editing is part of the shared knowledge of any community of writers, so there's little more we need to say about it here, except to remind you to do it. You might do a rough edit of your composition at this point, waiting for more careful formal editing until you've circulated it to other readers in the ways discussed below, but you'll want to do it at some point.

Information that can guide formal editing—the specifics of how to use words appropriately (usage), how to capitalize and punctuate, as well as key points of formal grammar, etc.—are typically presented in a *style manual*. Your class might be using a print manual or handbook, or a digital version such as the Purdue University's Online Writing Lab (OWL). The <u>OWL sitemap</u>[L2:7] lists all of the topics and the site addresses, and you'll find a variety of resources for writers, along with explanations of almost any editing topic you could think to ask about, as well as a search function to let you search for your own topics.

WRITING MOVES ◄

Revising and Publishing

We often think of composing as a somewhat isolated activity, where we put our words on paper and share them with only a teacher or a limited set of readers. But in the digital age, the things that people compose might be shared widely, often with distant friends or strangers. In Part II of this book, we'll consider how texts are now being circulated and distributed and the impact this is having on our literacy practices. But it is always useful to think of any composition in terms of how and where it might be shared, in wider and wider circles. At the same time, it's also useful to have a real and immediate audience to offer helpful feedback. The process of circulating a composition, getting audience feedback, and revising in response to that feedback, is a key part of any creative endeavor, and something you'll want to implement in any such work, in or out of a classroom context.

A classroom community, whether in a physical space or online, offers you an immediate audience that's knowledgeable about the enterprise you're involved in and your general purposes, providing a rich opportunity to learn to gather and work with feedback, and we'll encourage peer response activities—getting feedback from other writers in the same situation as yourself—throughout the work of this book. You can share your work with others at any moment in the composing process. (Ashley even shared her freewriting with readers.) But you'll certainly want to do so when you've reached what feels like a final version, eliciting feedback that can tell you what you might want to add or alter. Reading aloud to a peer response group can be particularly useful for narratives. More moves for gathering responses from peer readers include the following.

1 Creating and using a generative rubric

You've probably had experience with using rubrics to guide your school writing—a naming of key elements that you should include. Such rubrics are often tied to a grading scheme and can be helpful letting writers know how their work will be evaluated and graded. We use **generative rubrics**, not as a defined list of "must-dos" but as a list of typical elements that writers of a particular genre of composition would be likely to include. These are generative in the sense that they are meant to generate ideas for what might be included and how from the experience that you and your peers have in reading and drafting a particular type of composition—in this case a literacy narrative. A generative rubric is intended to guide a composition in process rather than to give a final evaluation. Such rubrics usually draw on our sense of the typical elements of a genre as writers have used it, and a good way to develop them is to read a number of examples of that genre of writing.

You can create your own generative rubric by brainstorming with other writers to create a list of elements that seem to be part of the literacy narratives you've written or read. Here's a list that emerged from our own classes.

- At least one particular experience or event

- Details that allow the reader to share/understand the experience

- A focus on a larger theme, issue, or concern (in this case related to literacies/digital literacies), with a clear sense of the significance of the event(s) in relationship to that larger framing

- A sense of what new understanding has been gained (or what new questions have emerged) by re-seeing this experience or event in light of the larger focus

- Sometimes a quotation or two connecting the writer's understanding to those of others through the words of another text (another literacy narrative or other research about literacy, the lyrics of a song)

For a digital composition, a generative rubric might include the following additional elements.

- Voiced narration with effective tone and pacing

- Visual images that contribute to and enhance the story's meanings

- A soundtrack that supports the emotional tone

- Use of effective titles, transitions, and special effects

generative rubrics
list of typical elements writers would likely include

2 Using guiding questions for peer response

Writers often begin to share their work with a smaller audience before putting it into wider circulation. Many published writers belong to writers' groups in which they share their work regularly, and most researchers and academic writers get more formal responses to their work as well, as the editors of the journals or publishers they submit it to send it to other readers in their field for peer review. You might use elements you list in a generative rubric as a quick checklist and to guide your discussion with a peer reviewer. Here are some useful first questions for a literacy narrative, and you might want to add your own.

- What interested you? What confused you, where you would like to know more? What caught your attention, or struck you most vividly in what you heard or read? What else do you want to learn?

- What events and details are included and why is the writer telling you about these events? What larger themes do they relate to? What personal and social meanings are brought out? What significance do they have in relationship to a larger exploration of new and changing literacies in a digital age?

- How has the composer structured this telling? And if this is a multimodal composition, what are its elements and where are they used?

- How well does the composition work in terms of what, why and how—in the events and details included (enough to give a picture but not too many), in giving you an understanding of the meaning and significance of these events for the composer personally and in relationship to a larger concern of a digital society, and in how well the overall structuring and style work to bring you into the events and to the understandings the writer is sharing? In a digital composition, are all images and sounds relevant to the meanings and not simply decorative?

- What helpful advice can you give the composer, based on your experience of the composition thus far? What places did you find that were particularly effective for you, and where might you want more details or a clearer sense of the meanings the writer wants to convey? In a digital

composition, do all of the elements of image, music, narration, and text work together effectively for you or are there suggestions you might make to add to or alter these?

3 Revising and reshaping

The responses you receive from those who read/see/hear your composition can tell you how well you've accomplished your purposes and give you advice for composing. Sometimes your readers' responses will lead you to significantly rethink your whole composition, as happened in Ashley's case. More often those responses will lead you to add to or reshape particular parts of the composition you've created. Sometimes seeing your own work in the context of others' compositions during the peer review process will suggest new strategies and moves you might want to try. In any case, revising is an important part of the composing process and should allow you to create a final composition you're proud of.

4 Publishing your work

Once you've finished revising your work into a final form, publish it in some way, making it available to those in your class and perhaps to others. Your class most likely has an online site for posting student work that can be set up for sharing your final products. If you have a class wiki or blog, you can decide together how widely you want particular pages on the wiki or material posted on the blog to be shared.

You might also want to circulate your work by publishing it on a fully public site. We've mentioned places where you can submit podcast stories in this chapter, and you can discover others. Very short digital stories appear on Cowbird.[L2:8]

The Digital Archive of Literacy Narratives (DALN) at Ohio State University[L2:9] accepts literacy narrative submissions.

For writers/composers, one project typically generates ideas for others that can grow out of the first. The next section offers some typical ways in which you might go further with the work you've done in composing a digital literacy narrative.

Reinventing and Circulating Your Work

➤ **Option 1: Recasting your literacy narrative in a different mode.** From a print narrative you might create an audio story or a multimodal digital story, but if you've started with a multimodal composition, you might try recreating it for print, seeing how you can translate images into words.

➤ **Option 2: Resituating your study in relation to what other researchers have discovered about literacy experiences like your own.** Your exploration of your own experience might lead you to new questions and form the kernel of a new research project. The extended research endeavors we suggest in Part III of this book will build on your work in earlier chapters and the understandings you've come to here could contribute to that work.

➤ **Option 3: Reshaping your work for a different audience.** We've been focusing on a community of readers/viewers/listeners who are working toward a richer understanding of literacy practices and the ways in which they are changing in (and changing) our increasingly digital society. But what you've discovered here might be relevant to the research interests of another disciplinary perspective—perhaps sociology, psychology, education—or another setting such as a community program for teens. How might you adapt the work you've done for another audience community that you're part of or might become part of?

➤ **Option 4: Creating a class collection of digital literacy narratives.** Researchers have developed larger understandings about new literacies by collecting narratives from many people and finding patterns of commonality and difference. Brandt's book *Literacy in American Lives*[2:14] draws on many literacy narratives like Genna May's from Chapter 1 to explore patterns of change in the twentieth century. Selfe and Hawisher's collection, *Literate Lives in the Information Age*[2:15] a collection of twenty first-person literacy narratives (out of more than 350 people initially studied), explores the impact of race, ethnicity, class, gender, family, and access to technology in people's experience of new literacies. Selfe curates the Digital Archive of Literacy Narratives (daln.osu.edu/), and the collections that it contains are organized around topics such as "Community Literacy." A multimodal site drawing on black women's literacy narratives[L2:10] from that collection explores themes that emerged in a set of collaborative narratives, offering an audio introduction as well as a written overview essay by Beverly Moss and Elaine Richardson.[2:16]

As a class you can organize your collection of narratives into groups around themes you identify and write a collaborative introduction to the whole collection and to each group within it. Such collections can be a valuable mid-semester or end-of-semester project, allowing you to revisit earlier work and reframe it through the larger understandings you gain from your ongoing inquiry.

Key Concepts

Reading
Rhetorical Situations

CHAPTER THREE

CENTRAL QUESTIONS

1 What is a rhetorical relationship and how can we draw on familiar digital contexts to explore such relationships?

2 How can a research post about a teen's efforts to maintain Facebook privacy from parents help us to understand more about rhetorical relationships in online social contexts?

3 What role can one academic genre, the extended discussion post, play in building shared understandings and fostering a rhetorical relationship within your class?

4 How can we develop different reading strategies to think about how to enter into new rhetorical relationships through our reading?

Chapter Preview

We saw in Chapter 1 that Barry, as a college student, is embedded in a network of relationships, both inside and outside of the classroom. With each act of speaking or writing, Barry has to consider **what** he writes (the content and message), **why** he writes it (his purpose), **how** to do it in a way that will engage others in the conversation, and **where** the interaction takes place (the context). Otherwise, his readers may click over to another Facebook page without posting a response, or skip through the posts he makes on the science wiki without drawing his ideas into the team's final collaborative report. Even when he writes an essay for a course assignment, his readers are actively participating in a conversation with him by reading and thinking about his words.

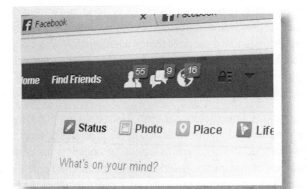

In making these decisions about communication, Barry is taking part in the social and shared process of conversation that is necessary for building and maintaining a relationship with readers. This is what researchers in the field of composition refer to as a **rhetorical relationship**. In this chapter, we'll explore more fully this kind of relationship between readers and writers in specific communicative situations, focusing especially on our roles as readers.

. . . .
rhetorical relationship
the connection built
between writers and
readers through a text

Exploring
Rhetorical Relationships

Whenever a person engages with others in any context, through any mode of communication, a connection develops and some sort of relationship is formed. In Chapter 1, we talked about composition as a field of academic research. In the field of composition, that relationship is seen as part of a **rhetorical situation**—that particular moment or context when two or more people come together to talk about a shared interest or concern. While such situations certainly arise when we talk with others, they also take shape around the texts we write and compose for others who don't have to be present in the same room and who are likely never to have met in person, but who do have some area of shared interest and a way of communicating, in print or online. What brings speaker and listener, writer and reader, and composer and viewer together is some sort of **shared purpose**. That purpose might be to keep a friendship going or to inform others or learn about a topic like the best new bicycles, what a hockey team's season has looked like, or the latest results of a scientific experiment. It might even be to persuade others, perhaps toward a particular political viewpoint or a legal or medical course of action. But each exchange is always motivated by the shared purposes both parties bring to it, by the **why** of the exchange.

rhetorical situation
the full context for a
rhetorical interaction

Rhetoric as an Evolving Practice and Field of Study

What makes these relationships and situations "rhetorical"? In popular usage, *rhetoric* is often used unfavorably to describe manipulative language used by politicians to sway public opinion. Rhetoric, in this definition, is artificial eloquence intended to *persuade* an audience by misleading them. But this type of persuasion is just a small part of actual rhetorical situations and how we participate in rhetorical relationships. The term **rhetoric** derives from the ancient Greek word *rhetor*, a word meaning "to speak." The ancient Greeks defined rhetoric as the art of public speaking and oratory, communication practices that stood at the center of social life and governance in ancient Athens (circa 600 BCE), much as writing and digital media are at the center of social and public life today. The Greek philosopher Aristotle (300 BCE) famously defined rhetoric as "the faculty of observing in any given [communicative situation] the available means of persuasion."[3:1] Rhetoric, in this definition, is the human ability to observe and understand the range of things we might say when engaged in communication with others. Generations of subsequent scholars have drawn on and expanded Aristotle's definition of rhetoric to study the different types of rhetorical situations and relationships that arise in our use of other media, including written and visual texts.

rhetoric
the art of speaking and
writing effectively

In our digital age, rhetoric, as both a language practice and a field of study, continues to evolve. While traditional research on rhetoric tended to focus on political contexts and public speech-making, modern research has extended this civic lens to look at the social nature of rhetorical activity as it unfolds in everyday contexts and local communities, including those maintained online and with digital means. Such research has shifted from an emphasis on how public individuals use rhetoric to an emphasis on the *context* of communication— on the rhetorical situation as the social space that takes shape when people *feel the need* to discuss an issue of shared interest and concern (Bitzer[3:2]). When Barry and his hockey friends make their Facebook posts, it's in response to a felt need to build their friendship by focusing on their shared interests and maintain their small community. *Rhetorical situation* as a concept includes everything in their context, including a need to be addressed, their shared purposes in addressing it, the topics and events they are concerned about, available media, and their use of those digital media to make it happen.

Another useful concept is **rhetorical stance**, the active relationship of a speaker/writer/composer to an audience. Stance has to do with the **how** of an exchange and includes the writer's attitude toward all of the elements of a rhetorical situation as well as the persona or social identity the writer draws on in a particular exchange (Booth[3:3]). Barry and his friends might present themselves as amused or puzzled or annoyed in their hockey fight exchanges. That stance will depend on the persona they want to project and how they think their attitude will be received by the other participants who read a particular example of hockey fight information[L3:1] in a given moment of an ongoing Facebook exchange.

The digital environment in which the hockey friends' exchanges are taking place offers new rhetorical possibilities, but also some limitations and constraints within the rhetorical situation that wouldn't apply to a face-to-face conversation, or one that takes place on a written page. They can easily share photos, videos, and links that contribute to a shared understanding, for example, and they can share their posts at any moment with a wider circle of friends, but the Facebook platform doesn't easily support longer turns and responses. In addition, people often build digital identities in ways that are different from the ones they bring to face-to-face conversations. So, in understanding the shape of a rhetorical situation, we also want to consider the different modes and media used to communicate (voice, written, visual, print, digital) and the benefits and limitations of each for rhetorical action (Zappen[3:4]).

rhetorical stance
the active relationship
between writer and
audience

INQUIRY

#1: Seeing rhetorical situations

???

Look at any brief online or texting exchange and try to map out all of the elements that seem to contribute to the rhetorical situation—all of the persons, events, objects, relationships, needs, identities, and stances that flow within and around it. Does this expanded picture of context contribute to your own understanding of what's involved, in that moment, in building a rhetorical relationship and achieving shared purposes?

Seeing How a Rhetorical Relationship is Built Through Writing

Barry's Facebook is a good example of how a rhetorical relationship is built through writing. His friend John posts these words with a link to another YouTube hockey video:

> John: "(: barry lava did you see this wicked nice goal? Also are you going to be in Boston for New Years again?"

In understanding this particular rhetorical situation, we might begin with the purposes of such a post. One is most likely more interpersonal, to maintain a friendship. Facebook and other social media platforms have become a common way in which friends do that, letting others know, "I'm thinking about you," "I know what you'll find interesting," or "I'm interested in your plans." A second purpose here is most likely to share some specific information in an area of shared interest, in this case about a winning hockey goal by a well-known player (Benoit Pouliot) on a professional team (and if you're interested in hockey, you may be able to **view the video**[L3:1] that John shared with Barry). A third purpose is clearly to get some information about Barry's New Year's plans, but also to show how well he knows Barry—knowing that Barry is a Boston Bruins fan and that he spent last New Year's Eve in Boston. These shared purposes fulfill a shared need by Barry and John to communicate and to communicate in this way via an online post rather than, say, a phone call, which would inevitably give rise to a similar but different rhetorical situation.

link

Within this particular rhetorical situation that includes these participants, their shared connections and interests, and their ongoing conversations both on and off Facebook, as well as the need they're addressing through their exchange at the moment, they are maintaining their relationship by using writing to construct a rhetorical one, drawing on particular personas—John's stance here seems to be that of an "interested friend" who is writing from the social identity that he and Barry share as teammates—and achieving these overlapping purposes. Barry doesn't answer with a Facebook post (although he may have done so by texting or in person), so we don't know exactly how he responded. But any response, even one that is silent, will contribute to the shape of this rhetorical situation and how their rhetorical relationship evolves over time.

As the recipient of a post, Barry was most likely pleased that his friend John was posting for these purposes. But understanding a rhetorical relationship sometimes requires more than understanding the literal meaning of an exchange. If they'd had a disagreement, John could have been making this post to gloss over it, and Barry's response could have been annoyance: "Why does he keep bugging me?" "Maybe I should unfriend him!" While people who know each other well often communicate with shared purposes that are understood by all parties, they can also be at cross purposes some of the time, as anyone who has had a fight with a parent, sibling, or friend knows. To understand this exchange as a rhetorical situation, we need to ask more specific questions about the purpose of each response and how the participants go about the communication.

link 🔗 ▶

While there's a lot we can guess about the purposes of one individual exchange, there is more to be learned from looking at a larger conversational context that informs this rhetorical situation and the relationship it supports. In Chapter 1, John made an earlier post with a YouTube link[L3:2] to a Boston Bruins game. John didn't comment in that post, letting the video with its caption "Milan Lucic hits Ryan Miller" speak for itself. But the exchange that followed that post involved four more turns:

> Barry: haha. I like how the announcer wanted buffalo to try to hit thomas to get back at boston.
>
> John: haha you shoulda heard the Bruins announcers later in the period, something like "the Sabres didn't really go after the Bruins too hard after the hit. If Buffalo had hit Thomas, the Bruins would have killed every one of them."
>
> Barry: more like the whole city of boston would have gone to war.
>
> John: . . . hilarious.

The earlier exchange offers evidence that John's purpose with such posts really is to share information that will interest and/or amuse his friend, maintaining the friendship and trying to elicit a response. We can see that Barry responds to that purpose, adding a comment about the announcer that shows he actually followed the link and watched the video. He then adds a comment that extends John's conjecture about what the Bruins' response would have been if the Sabres had hit Boston's goalie—that not only would the Bruins have killed them, but "the whole city of boston would have gone to war." What we witness in this exchange is how a relationship is built and maintained through an exchange of texts, each text serving multiple purposes and, quite often, seeking to extend the conversation. The exchange ends with John's confirming one-word response, "hilarious," suggesting that, in this particular rhetorical situation, the two friends achieved a sense of shared purpose by developing a shared stance toward the events being discussed, and doing so effectively within the possibilities and constraints of the Facebook digital platform.

We can learn still more about Barry's purposes in communicating by looking at the various kinds of rhetorical situations that arise across many different posts. Barry's own posts often focus on his own team's games, as in this post that seems intended to rally team spirit for his own team before a game:

> Barry: "Big win tonight over UofM, make it happen tribe."

While this post seems intended mainly for his teammates, it also speaks to an audience beyond his team, creating a new rhetorical situation in the process with more participants involved. Eight people—friends and family—showed that they "liked" that particular post by selecting the Facebook "like" icon, conveying the message that they are actively following these Facebook conversations and that they too were rooting for the team.

But Barry does more than play hockey, and each post he makes gives rise to new rhetorical situations. Other posts by him, his friends, and his girlfriend comment on other activities he's part of. When his girlfriend makes an early morning post, "You better be waking your ass up to come get me :)," he doesn't answer directly but makes a new post: "Cara is the coolest." Again, there's a suggestion of shared purposes—that he understands she's prodding him to get going on the long drive to her college. These shared purposes are realized through Barry's awareness of the rhetorical situation when he responds positively, though indirectly, with a hint of sarcasm. Social media platforms like Facebook have introduced new ways for individuals and communities to build and maintain their rhetorical relationships through writing and exchanging texts online. They expand the social and cultural context in which the writer is composing (Figure 3.1).

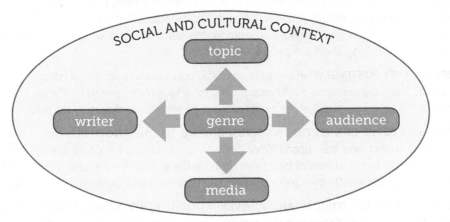

Figure 3.1: Expanded rhetorical situation within a social and cultural context

What understandings can we take away from these ordinary Facebook exchanges that will help us to understand more about how we form and maintain rhetorical relationships?

➤ These Facebook posters—friends, teammates, boyfriend/girlfriend, are actively involved in building their relationships through their posts and likes. They are involved in an ongoing conversation—that is, they are actively using writing in rhetorical ways to maintain and extend conversations and their relations with others. And they know how to do so within the genre of the Facebook post as it has been shaped by their community of friends.

➤ Understanding the purpose of a particular post often depends on knowing something about the rhetorical situation, which includes the larger conversational context like the posts that have gone before; the different relationships between the posters; the worlds they share, whether those worlds are on sports teams, in college classrooms, or in a dating relationship; and the technology and platform used.

➤ Rhetorical relationships in writing aren't exactly the same as full relationships, even among friends. They're created through texts that are written and read. In a full relationship, there are many other channels of communication through looks, touch, and voice. But in thinking about the rhetorical aspects of a relationship, the people posting have only the evidence of the text itself (and whatever they know about the other person's likely purposes from other exchanges) to draw on. In these examples, we can see that both Barry's friend John and his girlfriend Cara add the smile emoticon :) to provide some textual evidence of their stance: that what they've said is intended in a good-humored way.

INQUIRY

#2: Observing Facebook posts as rhetorical relationships

Individuals, organizations, and businesses use Facebook for different purposes. Look at your own Facebook page, the page of a friend, of an organization on your campus, or of a public entity or business. Here are some questions to ask in trying to understand the shape of a rhetorical relationship and the different situations that take shape there.

➤ **WHO IS POSTING?** In friendship circles, it's likely that the posts are being made by the owner of the page and by friends or family who write on one another's walls or timelines. For a business page, it might not be possible to identify an individual poster, but you might be able to guess something about the way someone speaks for the company, and where there are response comments, something about the people who respond.

➤ **WHY ARE THEY POSTING?** What seems to be the purposes of some individual posts or a sequence of posts? From the response comments posted (or a lack of comments) or "likes," can you tell whether the typical purposes of the owner of the page seem to be shared by the readers/visitors?

➤ **HOW ARE PEOPLE CONNECTING AND RESPONDING TO ONE ANOTHER?** How is information presented, shared, and built upon? What kinds of conversations are constructed on the page? What seems to be the stance of the contributors, or the attitude they're taking toward whatever they're posting about? Do they seem to be writing from particular personas or social identities?

➤ **WHAT SORT OF RHETORICAL AND CONVERSATIONAL CONTEXT IS CREATED OR EVOKED THROUGH THESE PAGES?** Could the participants in these exchanges be said to belong to a particular community of like-minded people who come together for a common purpose? Or do you notice cross purposes? What do you seem to have to know or care about to be part of the community?

➤ **IS THERE ANYTHING ELSE YOU NOTICE ABOUT THIS RHETORICAL SITUATION?** How is the rhetorical relationship between the page owner and the "friends" who appear created and maintained within this particular digital environment?

Making Connections
Reading as a Writer

Different media are an essential component of all rhetorical situations and they affect not only what we write and post, but also how and what we read. Facebook, and social media in general, doesn't represent reading and writing as we traditionally think of them. Facebook, for example, uses a variety of visual elements (a topic we'll return to in Chapter 14) with limited posting space, making it less than suitable for a writer to create an extended entry or to develop any ideas at length. That in turn changes our experience of reading and the shape of the rhetorical situation we're taking part in. Nevertheless, the rhetorical relationships created through Facebook can tell us something about how we build relationships through writing, reading, and the ongoing rhetorical situations we create together. We've made some observations about Barry's and John's likely shared purposes from John's posts to Barry's wall, but from Barry's brief responses, we have less sense of how he reads these posts and how the rhetorical relationship is being maintained in the reader's mind and perspective.

But we always read with specific purposes in mind, adapting how we read in response to a rhetorical situation that includes the text, different media, and our changing purposes for reading. When we begin to read, we enter a conversation that the writer has initiated, imagining either a known reader like Barry or an imagined reader like yourself, who will read what's been written and become involved with the writer's ideas and purposes. When we read a longer text, we again enter into a rhetorical situation and must draw on prior experience, as well as prior knowledge about whatever is being shared to help us make sense of what we are reading.

In a moment you'll enter a conversation initiated by an expert on social media, danah boyd (who chooses not to capitalize her name), about how teenagers are finding clever ways to hide personal information, particularly from their parents, as they post on Facebook. boyd posted the article on her public research blog, taking one turn in a larger conversation about Facebook and privacy that many others are contributing to.

Writing for a public audience, boyd is contributing to the rhetorical situation that has emerged in response to the topic of teenagers and social media. To make a valued contribution to this growing social concern, boyd has to create a conversation with readers she doesn't know but can only imagine—a conversation in which she uses specific writing moves to achieve particular purposes, and in the process, build a relationship with potential readers. To build this relationship, she has to connect with these unknown readers and hook their interest. She has to do so in a way that brings all of those unknown readers along and keeps them interested, justifying her demanding their time and attention. As she imagines her readers, she has to think about the rhetorical situation: what readers may already know about the topic, their purposes for reading, and how to keep them involved in the conversation. boyd can assume, for example, that most of her readers are familiar with Facebook, so she doesn't need to explain what it is.

At the same time, her readers are also participating in this rhetorical situation, working with the writer to understand what she's saying and to engage with her ideas. The first moves of engaging with boyd through reading are typically the same ones we introduced in Chapter 1, from the writer's perspective, for inquiry-focused writing: connecting, elaborating, questioning, and speculating. These are all things you'd do if you were participating in a face-to-face conversation, and we'll refer to such reading-to-enter-a-conversation as *participatory reading*. At other times, as with a face-to-face conversation, you might step back to look at it from a more analytical and evaluative perspective, to think about how the exchange itself is working, and how well, and why, in a form of *critical reading*. Both ways of reading are involved in **reading rhetorically**— reading to achieve a larger common purpose with a writer/composer through a written or multimodal text. As one of boyd's readers, we'll ask you to observe your own experience, considering first the ways you read as a participant in this written conversation, but also what you find as you step back from it, reading more analytically and evaluatively.

> **reading rhetorically**
> reading to achieve a larger common purpose with a writer

Participatory Reading

The way in which you read this blog post will be shaped in part by other elements of the rhetorical situation, including the context in which you're reading and the conversations in your classroom that have preceded this reading. You might, as you read, find yourself thinking about your own experiences with Facebook or other online media. You might be reminded of something in your own interaction with a parent. Or you might find yourself focusing on what boyd says about hidden messages. Any of these ways of engaging with the ideas and experiences this writer presents contribute to a **participatory reading**—one that brings you into a rhetorical situation with the text and its writer and allows you to make as many connections as possible with the understandings represented there. You can think of a participatory reading as reading for meaning— reading to find shared purpose with the writer and gain the knowledge and understandings the writer offers.

> **participatory reading**
> reading to connect and engage generously with a text

When reading something for the first time, a participatory reading initially asks us to give the writer the benefit of the doubt and read with the primary intention of really understanding the goals of the writer and the text. In a participatory reading, we ask exploratory questions as we read, such as the following:

- What does the writer say to me through this text?

- How does it contribute to what I know and have thought about? Does it connect with other things I've read or heard or to aspects of my own experience? If not, what can I learn from encountering a very different experience?

- How might I extend and elaborate on the points being made? Are there points where it clashes with what I know, or where I want to add to the text by arguing with it?

- What questions do I have for the writer or for other readers? What further speculation and new thoughts does it lead me to? What might I want to take away from it to think about later?

To enter a rhetorical situation through participatory reading, make notations in the margins of books and articles to trace and record your responses and reactions. This is often a new practice for many students, as writing in books is typically prohibited in high school; but in college, you are often encouraged to make a text your own through your marginal notes. In taking marginal notes, in which you pose questions, talk back to the writer, underline key passages, or refer to other texts you have read, you create a record of your reactions that you can build upon in the future—maybe to come to a richer understanding of a piece and the rhetorical situation it is a part of.

annotation
marking and commenting on a text

Such note taking is called **annotation**. Annotating a text, and doing it well, is a necessary literacy skill for building rhetorical relationships and growing as a reader and writer. As you read boyd's essay for the first time, you'll want to keep track of the conversation you have with her by marking the text and making comments as you read. Actively noting your responses to the reading is a way of capturing your experience and clarifying your own ideas about the writer's points. Such active annotating—going beyond highlighting to comment on what you are finding—helps you to be a more attentive reader and gives you notes to draw on in response to the writer. Annotating is, generally, more successful *without a highlighter*. It is easily done with pencil and paper, as well as with note-taking apps for digital texts, which let readers use comment functions and add annotations.

Although your conversations with writers will go on in your head any time you read, it's important for your own work as a writer that you leave traces of those conversations. When you annotate as you read, you can see what you made of the things the writer had to say, examining the writer's ideas and integrating them into your own thoughts, ideas, and responses. For all of your reading in this book, both of our chapters and the readings we include, we encourage you to annotate the text while you read, making notes in the margin or comment space; commenting on the things that interest, puzzle, or annoy you; and keeping track of the ways in which your own thinking moves in relationship to what you're reading. It will help you clarify the rhetorical situation you are taking part in and you'll soon find that you have a wealth of material to draw on for your own writing.

BEFORE READING:
Annotation

Read and annotate "Social Steganography: Learning to Hide in Plain Sight," leaving tracings of your own conversation with this writer through this text. See sample in Figure 3.2.

Note:

- Where you are struck by something boyd says, where you think she offers new and interesting information or a perspective you hadn't thought of before;

- where you find connections to your own experience, to other things you've read, or perhaps to your ongoing classroom conversation about these topics; and

- where you'd ask her a question or disagree with her if she were present in the room.

AUTHOR'S NAME

born as:	**Danah Michele Mattas**
after mother married:	**Danah Michele Mattas Beard**
in high school after parents' divorce:	**Danah Boyd** (maternal grandfather's name)

no capitalization

1 more balanced look:
danah   ~~Danah~~

2 feels it's self-righteous to capitalize "I" pronoun

AUTHOR TAGS

- author
- researcher
- professor
- scholar
- activist
- blogger
- tweeter
- mom

BUZZWORDS

privacy	culture
context	social media
youth	big data

DISSERTATION

Taken Out of Context
American Teen Sociality in Networked Publics

UC Berkley | Doctorate of Philosophy | 2008

PROFESSIONAL LIFE

Principal Researcher at Microsoft Research | Founder/President: Data and Society

---

SAMPLE

Carmen and her mother are close. As far as Carmen's concerned, she has nothing to hide from her mother so she's happy to have her mom as her 'friend' on Facebook. Of course, Carmen's mom doesn't always understand the social protocols on Facebook and Carmen sometimes gets frustrated. She hates that her mom comments on nearly every post, because it "scares everyone away...Everyone kind of disappears after the mom post...It's just uncool having your mom all over your wall. That's just lame." Still, she knows that her mom means well and she sometimes uses this pattern to her advantage. While Carmen welcomes her mother's presence, she also knows her mother overreacts. In order to avoid a freak out, Carmen will avoid posting things that have a high likelihood of mother misinterpretation. This can make communication tricky at times and Carmen must work to write in ways that are interpreted differently by different people.

When Carmen broke up with her boyfriend, she "wasn't in the happiest state." The breakup happened while she was on a school trip and her mother was already nervous. Initially, Carmen was going to mark the breakup with lyrics from a song that she had been listening to, but then she realized that the lyrics were quite depressing and worried that if her mom read them, she'd "have a heart attack and think that something is wrong." She decided not to post the lyrics. Instead, she posted lyrics from Monty Python's "Always Look on the Bright Side of Life." This strategy was effective. Her mother wrote her a note saying that she seemed happy which made her laugh. But her closest friends knew that this song appears in the movie when the characters are about to be killed. They reached out to her immediately to see how she was really feeling.

Interesting that she opens with this mother-daughter relationship. This makes me think of my mom.

My aunt doesn't recognize these conventions either. She often comments on my friends' post if they tag me. Awkward. It does seem like boyd assumes some shared understandings about how to use social media.

Figure 3.2: Sample annotated text

Place annotations here

"Social Steganography: Learning to Hide in Plain Sight"[3:5]

by danah boyd

Apophenia, August 23, 2010

Carmen and her mother are close. As far as Carmen's concerned, she has nothing to hide from her mother so she's happy to have her mom as her 'friend' on Facebook. Of course, Carmen's mom doesn't always understand the social protocols on Facebook and Carmen sometimes gets frustrated. She hates that her mom comments on nearly every post, because it "scares everyone away…Everyone kind of disappears after the mom post…It's just uncool having your mom all over your wall. That's just lame." Still, she knows that her mom means well and she sometimes uses this pattern to her advantage. While Carmen welcomes her mother's presence, she also knows her mother overreacts. In order to avoid a freak out, Carmen will avoid posting things that have a high likelihood of mother misinterpretation. This can make communication tricky at times and Carmen must work to write in ways that are interpreted differently by different people.

When Carmen broke up with her boyfriend, she "wasn't in the happiest state." The breakup happened while she was on a school trip and her mother was already nervous. Initially, Carmen was going to mark the breakup with lyrics from a song that she had been listening to, but then she realized that the lyrics were quite depressing and worried that if her mom read them, she'd "have a heart attack and think that something is wrong." She decided not to post the lyrics. Instead, she posted lyrics from Monty Python's "Always Look on the Bright Side of Life." This strategy was effective. Her mother wrote her a note saying that she seemed happy which made her laugh. But her closest friends knew that this song appears in the movie when the characters are about to be killed. They reached out to her immediately to see how she was really feeling.

Privacy in a public age

Carmen is engaging in social steganography. She's hiding information in plain sight, creating a message that can be read in one way by those who aren't in the know and read differently by those who are. She's communicating to different audiences simultaneously, relying on specific cultural awareness to provide the right interpretive lens. While she's focused primarily on separating her mother from her friends, her message is also meaningless to broader audiences who have no idea that she had just broken up with her boyfriend. As far as they're concerned, Carmen just posted an interesting lyric.

Social steganography is one privacy tactic teens take when engaging in semi-public forums like Facebook. While adults have worked diligently to exclude people through privacy settings, many teenagers have been unable to exclude certain classes of adults—namely their parents—for quite some time. For this reason, they've had to develop new techniques to speak to their friends fully aware that their parents are overhearing. Social steganography is one of the most common techniques that teens employ. They do this because they care about privacy, they care about misinterpretation, they care about segmented communications strategies. And they know that technical tools for restricting access don't trump parental demands to gain access. So they find new ways of getting around limitations. And, in doing so, reconstruct age-old practices.

Ancient methods

Steganography is an ancient technique where people hide messages in plain sight. Invisible ink, tattoos under hair on messengers, and messages embedded in pictures are just a few ways in which steganography is employed. Cryptographers are obsessed with steganography, in part because it's hardest to decode a message when you don't know where to look. This is precisely why spy movies

READING

LOVE steganography. Of course, average people have also employed techniques of hiding in plain sight for a long time, hiding information in everyday communication, knowing that it'll only be interpreted by some. Children love employing codes and adults generally pretend as though they can't understand pig Latin or uncover the messages that children hide using invisible ink pens purchased from toy stores. Yet, as children grow up, they get more mature about their messaging, realizing that language has multiple layers and, with it, multiple meanings. They often learn this by being misinterpreted.

What fascinates me is that teens are taking these strategies into the digital spaces, recognizing multiple audiences and the challenges of persistence, and working to speak in layers. They are not always successful. And things that are meant to mean one thing are often misinterpreted in all sorts of the wrong ways. But that doesn't mean teens aren't experimenting and learning. In fact, I'd expect that they're learning more nuanced ways of managing privacy than any of us adults. Why? Because they have to. The more they live in public, the more I expect them to hide in plain sight. ∎

Place annotations here

AFTER READING:
Responding analytically as a reader

Once you've read "Social Steganography" and shared your responses with other readers, you'll discover that no two responses from participatory readings are alike. Even the same reader, rereading the essay a second time, will be struck by different things and have different responses, engaging in a new conversation with the text (and thus its writer) each time.

➤ **A FAVORITE ANNOTATION.** Choose your favorite annotation and elaborate on why it's significant to you.

➤ **SHARING FAVORITE ANNOTATIONS.** Contribute to a classroom or online discussion by sharing your favorite annotations and why you chose them to bring your individual responses into a common conversation about boyd's research and what can be learned from the example of Carmen's Facebook writing. What do you see as boyd's purpose(s) in writing about Carmen? How have you and your classmates responded to those possible purposes?

➤ **MAKING CONNECTIONS.** Look back at your annotations of "Social Steganography" to see where you've drawn on your own experiences, and/or where you've gotten a new perspective on social media. Write a journal response in which you describe your experience of reading this essay as a participatory reader. Draw on some of boyd's points by quoting them and respond to them to explore your own thinking and to create the sense of a two-way conversation. See what new understandings you can come to about your own experience or the experience of the young woman, Carmen, described by boyd.

Digital Toolbox
See Part IV, Section 2

Critical Reading

So far we've focused on how you can enter a rhetorical situation by reading boyd's essay in a participatory way, as if you were having a conversation with her. But there are other times, especially in academic settings, when you'll need to step out of this participatory role to think about a piece of writing more analytically, much as we've done in looking at the posts of Barry's Facebook friends, seeing how the piece works to connect with readers, considering its likely purposes, and also evaluating how well it is working for what we imagine the writer's purpose to be. As a writer who will be making your own choices and trying to capture the interest of your own readers, you can learn a lot by working critically with a piece of writing, seeing how it works to build shared knowledge and purposes with readers, and evaluating how well it does this.

As you step back from the written conversation you are having with boyd, you can begin to see more clearly the rhetorical relationship that is forming between her text and your reading of the text. We can begin to see more clearly how the piece is organized, what rhetorical moves boyd makes, what her stance seems to be, and what details she includes. In asking these questions, we look specifically at how the writer has built her text—not only what she has included, but also how much she has included, in what order, and how the picture she portrays moves from step to step. This type of **analytical reading** is the sort of reading we're more likely to do when we return to the text a second or third time, deepening our understanding of the text in the process and seeing how it works rhetorically (a process we'll look at closer in Chapter 12).

analytical reading
reading to understand the writer's purpose and rhetorical moves

What the writer includes depends on what she thinks we (the imagined readers) already know. boyd assumes an audience of contemporary readers who will be familiar with social media and who will have reflected on concerns about privacy. But she also assumes an audience of readers who will accept her introduction of rather obscure and difficult terminology—the term *steganography*—for the act of creating hidden messages that are really in plain sight. She is writing a blog post for an audience of readers who are interested in social media (or they wouldn't be reading her blog), and she can make choices with that audience and a sense of shared purpose in mind.

For an analytical reading of boyd's essay, you'll want to extend your understanding of the rhetorical situation it is a part of. You might look at both what ideas and examples she has put forth and how she has done that. In such a reading, you'll want to consider **how** the writer has proceeded, stepping out of the conversation to identify not only **why**—the writer's purpose and **what**—her choices about what ideas and details to include were drawing on your understanding of the rhetorical situation, but also her choices about how to orient readers, how much background to provide, her choices about language, and more. From your own discussion of her essay, you might have determined that part of boyd's purpose seems to be to enter into the public discussion about privacy on social media sites such as Facebook, in response to a perceived need for others to have some of the information she has gathered through her own research. But she involves her audience and builds a rhetorical relationship by the specific choices she makes in how she structures her essay and the details she includes.

In analyzing this text, we also want to ask questions about the rhetorical situation this text is a part of and the social needs that give it shape. In this case, it is the recent concerns over social media and privacy. The question of online privacy has become a larger social issue that individuals and communities alike are grappling to understand as digital media disrupts some of our basic shared understandings of privacy. On the individual level, people have various ways of dealing with it, from not using platforms like Facebook or Twitter or Instagram at all, to trusting in the site's privacy controls and posting anything they think or do. You can see that Barry and his friends are pretty careful about what they post, keeping their comments focused on general topics like sports, or at most a nudge that any girlfriend might make (and we've respected that privacy as we bring their words to an audience of people who aren't their Facebook friends by changing names and altering pictures and some specific background information, although we've asked permission to use the words themselves for the purposes of this book). And we can also assume that they, like Carmen's friends, know how to read any hidden meanings that might underlie these posts. Such practices are reflected in boyd's essay and the larger rhetorical situation that helps shape how Barry and his friends use language online.

Another form of critical reading is *evaluative,* looking at *how well* the essay works to accomplish what seems to be boyd's purpose within this rhetorical situation. Maybe the example she has chosen doesn't seem representative enough to support her larger point. Maybe Carmen's story leads you to a different conclusion. An evaluative response can focus on what works in the essay, as well as what's not completely involving or convincing. You might ask, "What do I find to be the most effective moments in this essay?" and "Why are they effective?" While our primary focus will be on participatory and then analytical readings in the next few chapters, trying on an evaluative stance with the work of other writers can help you become a better evaluative reader as you work on drafts and revisions of your own writing.

This is a good moment to reread "Learning to Hide in Plain Sight" from an analytical and/or evaluative perspective. For a second reading, particularly when you're reading as a writer who will also be writing articles and posts about new literacies and social media, you'll want to step away from the conversation invited by a written text to reflect more consciously on what it includes, what its purpose is, how it works, and how well it works.

INQUIRY

#3: Responding critically

For an analytical reading, you'll want to take a close look at your annotations from a first reading, and add to them as you reread analytically. A paragraph-by-paragraph annotating to note the main point or main focus of each paragraph in the margin will be particularly useful for an analytical reading.

Look closely at the **what** of boyd's essay—tracing her ideas, her main points, her examples—through your annotations. Then step back to look at the **how** and the **why** of her essay, considering these questions.

➤ **HOW DOES BOYD STRUCTURE THIS ESSAY?** What examples does she bring in? How does she help you connect to her topic? Where does she move in close to give you details of a real teenager's exchange with her mother? Where does she step back from this story and make larger comments about what she sees as its meaning?

➤ **WHY DO YOU THINK SHE STRUCTURES THIS ESSAY IN THIS WAY?** Why does she move as she does from one very specific example to describing a more general human activity that has gone on from ancient times to the present? How does that broad framing about social steganography help her to make her own larger point, and what do you think that point is? What is the social need that boyd is addressing?

➤ **FOLLOW THE LINK TO BOYD'S ORIGINAL BLOG POST.** Does the original context add anything to your observations of the choices she has made to achieve her purposes as a writer in conversation with her likely audience? What does a digital format contribute to the writing?

➤ **WHAT SEEMS TO BE HER STANCE TOWARD HER TOPIC AND HER READERS' UNDERSTANDING OF IT?** What persona or social identity does she seem to be writing from and what sort of relationship might that create (or has that created) with her readers?

➤ **HOW WELL HAVE HER WRITING MOVES WORKED IN ACHIEVING SHARED PURPOSES WITH YOU AS A READER?**

Write an informal journal response in which you imagine yourself in conversation with boyd about how she has written this piece and how well it has worked for you as a reader. Tell her how her moves in writing this essay have supported what seems to be her larger purpose, including and quoting specific examples from the text that illustrate the points you make. Describe the interaction between what she has written and your own response as a reader and why you find what she's written to be effective or confusing in addressing her apparent purposes as a writer.

Imagining such conversations will also give you practice for responding to the writing of other student writers in your class.

See Chapter 18 for a discussion of quoting on page 441.

Extending Rhetorical Relationships to the Digital Page

In further exploring the rhetorical situation that boyd's article is participating in, we cannot ignore the great deal of discussion by both popular writers and literacy researchers about how the reading most of us do online differs from how we've traditionally read in print and about whether those differences are cause for concern. One leading researcher, Maryanne Wolf (who tells the story of how the "reading brain" has developed over time in society and develops in individuals in her book *Proust and the Squid*, 2009),[3:6] argues that reading the printed page has allowed us time to think and to read "inferentially, analytically and critically." Wolf worries that as we scan quickly through digital pages for "sound bites" and "text bites," we'll become "too distracted by and too drawn to the next piece of new information to allow [ourselves] time to think." What's worse, she fears, is that this will alter the reading brain and that many contemporary readers won't develop the "rich networks which are required in order to read at a high level of sophistication."

So what are some of the ways in which digital contexts might change rhetorical situations and how might our typical reading of the digital page alter the sort of rhetorical relationships we develop in reading the printed page? If you observe your own informal online reading behavior, you'll probably find you spend much of your time browsing and scanning, trying to find the bits of information that speak to your immediate concerns, and that you may be distracted from what you started reading by links and sidebars that send you to other pages. Such reading serves a different purpose, and it's important to be aware of *how* you are reading. When scanning a text, you don't get much sense of the context of what you read, and you're unlikely to be reading deeply and reflectively. You are engaged in cognitively complex behavior, but it involves making quick associations and connections and is more like multitasking, rather than maintaining a clear cognitive focus. With scanning, you are unlikely to be significantly involved in developing shared purposes with a writer and building a more extended rhetorical relationship.

While reading in these ways is an important literacy skill, understanding the rhetorical aspects of the texts you are reading often requires more focus and concentration when you read. It is important to develop your abilities to engage deeply with written texts, both print and digital, in the participatory ways we've described above, as well as to step out of a text to read it critically. Such deep reading is something we can learn to do on a screen as well as from a printed page. The fluid nature of digital texts and the new media tools for composing and sharing texts present new possibilities for building rhetorical relationships between writers and readers.

Here are several features of digital texts that may alter your path as a reader in either productive or unproductive ways, depending on your different purposes for reading, and the ways your purposes connect to those of the writer/composer.

➤ **Links.** The ability to make links on the same page, either within a text—perhaps to definitions like that for steganography, or alongside a text—typically to related content, can make it easy to access related information. Such links may alter your reading path, distract you from following the main argument, and take you in new directions. But they can also help you focus on the main content by moving information that might otherwise be in parentheses or a footnote on the page into a different location. And the related information they guide you to can enrich your understanding of the topic. Many sites include breadcrumbs (a trail of terms: news > technology > Facebook) to help you find your way back to your starting point.

➤ **Multimodality.** Adding images and sound to text can enhance the reader's meaning-making and understanding, but like linked text, they can sometimes be distracting.

➤ **Context.** We use what surrounds any text to help us to understand it, and we've seen that the rhetorical situation involves multiple elements of context. For example, the original context for a stretch of text might be a larger book, a print newspaper, or a blog. If we read a segment of text in the context of a book, we'll draw on our sense of the rest of the book as we determine its meaning. The story of Carmen's steganography originally appeared as a post on boyd's own blog, in the context of boyd's other posts on a variety of internet issues (where her prior post is on regulating the use of social media data—another privacy concern). But it also appeared on a multi-authored blog on digital media, *DMLCentral,* along with a post by another writer on how two Brazilian teens broadcast their sexually intimate activity on Twitcam, doing the opposite of the careful hiding that Carmen does to protect her privacy. It now appears in a full book by boyd, *It's Complicated: The Social Lives of Networked Teens,* within a larger chapter on privacy that comes between a chapter on identity and one on addiction to social media.[3:7] In each setting, her essay is situated in a larger conversation, but each of those conversations is somewhat different. (For the same reason, reading a newspaper article on the front page of a paper where it is positioned and given a certain amount of space in relation to other news of the day is different from reading it on the newspaper's online site, where the reader no longer sees it surrounded by the headlines for eight or ten other stories about that day's events, but rather with sidebar links that might connect it to earlier posts on related topics, and followed by a set of readers' comments.)

➤ **Interactivity.** Digital, online texts are interactive. They ask for our attention and engagement in the shape of links, menus, and comments. One of the primary rhetorical purposes of content producers online is to attract and interact with readers. Sites are designed to not only draw in readers, but to persuade them to come back, stay longer, sign up, or post a comment. Surely, writers of print texts are trying to attract readers too, but interactive digital texts draw on different modes and media (from paper to digital) that radically alter our experience of reading.

INQUIRY

#4: Observing print and digital contexts

Choose a newspaper that has both a print and a digital version and read an article that interests you, first in the print context and then in the digital. How do the two contexts affect your reading and your understanding of this article?

Reading on the Screen

As a college student who will do a lot of online reading for class assignments, discussions, and research, you will want to devise strategies that position you as an active reader, as someone making connections, coming to conclusions, and challenging your previously held ideas as you read on the screen as well as in print. Effective reading strategies will not only help you remember the content of texts, but they will also help you draw on those pieces through writing as you participate in discussions in class and online, and as you create compositions where you draw on what you've read.

One larger strategy suggested by people who think about the roles emerging technologies play in learning is *customization*. Scholars like Troy Hicks[3:8] argue that how we customize our devices matters (as we select particular programs for taking notes, others for composing essays, and still others for reading PDFs). As a college student, you will want to figure out the most effective tools for customizing your own devices—the apps or programs that support your reading as you work with digital materials. Of course, you can always print these pieces, within reason, but it is probably

Digital Toolbox
See Part IV, Section 1

worth your time to figure out some tools for reading, engaging with, and archiving your reactions to texts you read on the screen.

Some possible strategies you might want to experiment with include those listed below.

Digital Toolbox
See Part IV, Section 1

➤ Downloading a reading app that allows you to highlight, annotate, and write notes on the texts you read. New note-taking tools are always being created, but popular programs include Evernote and OneNote, and we discuss the use of such tools in Part IV.

➤ Creating a separate document in which you type out sections of a text that seem most striking to you (be sure to get down the page number) and then comment on them. This is similar to a double-entry notebook we'll discuss in Chapter 5, where you create two columns (perhaps by folding a piece of paper down the middle) and write out quotations from a text in the left column and respond to them in the right. Doing this digitally, though, will allow you to search this document for key words later.

Digital Toolbox
See Part IV, Section 2

➤ Keeping an online reading journal, in which you respond informally to all of the texts you read for a class, perhaps using a class website, blog, wiki, or a class learning management system (like Blackboard, Moodle, or Canvas).

In addition to considering how you can annotate digital texts, you might also want to consider possibilities for sharing your annotations with others. Some programs (like Evernote) allow you to share notebooks, allowing you to collaborate on reading notes. Others (like Dropbox) allow you to share folders, where you might upload notes or annotated texts. Still others (like the iPad app Documents, or Adobe) allow you to email PDFs you have highlighted, annotated, and documented. These are just a few options, but many more exist. The best thing to do is to try your hand at a few of these and see what works best for you. As we considered in Chapter 1, one distinguishing aspect of being digitally literate is learning to manage and adapt to constantly changing writing and communication tools.

Digital Toolbox
See Part IV, Section 1

You might also want to consider how you save texts you read on the screen or online. Bookmarking apps (like Delicious or Zotero) allow you to easily return to pieces you have read. Even the simple act of creating a folder on your hard drive for class readings might be helpful. The idea is not to take a particular approach, but to identify and reflect on strategies that help you interact with the digital texts you read.

Digital Toolbox
See Part IV, Section 5

INQUIRY

link

#5: Comparing reading in print and online

Select another post from **boyd's blog**.L3:3 If you initially read and annotated "Social Steganography: Learning to Hide in Plain Sight" as a print text, read online and use a digital tool reading app to comment on this blog post. If you read it in a digital form, be sure you've annotated it with a digital tool. Then read and annotate it in a print version. Compare your own two reading and annotation processes and what you've gained from each.

Composing
Extended Discussion Board Post

discussion post
an inquiry-driven response to texts, ideas, or concepts typically shared with others

The **discussion post** is a recent genre of writing that has emerged as course environments have gone wholly or partially online. Course sites, whether learning management systems like Blackboard or Canvas, class wikis like the one Barry's Blue Team uses, blogs, or other websites, have changed the rhetorical situation of the class discussion, offering new possibilities and also new constraints, as members of the classroom community build rhetorical relationships online as well as, or instead of, face to face. The most common use of the discussion post is to carry on the sort of discussion that has traditionally been a spoken genre, with the purpose of developing a richer shared understanding of a course reading, for instance, laying the ground for working with further readings/further discussions and building a common framework of shared knowledge in the classroom community. And that purpose continues into the written online context. But how the rhetorical relationship is developed and maintained and this shared purpose is achieved in the new online rhetorical situation is a matter for further inquiry. In this Composing section, we will focus on both the typical moves that are made within the discussion post genre and on how these can work to support the rhetorical relationship you are building as a writer of such posts with your readers—the members of your class community.

Once you've annotated boyd's essay, working from a participatory but also a critical reading, you can craft a discussion post to join the conversation that she has initiated as you invite others to engage your thinking. While an in-class discussion offers the opportunity for such conversation, sharing your response in writing can give you more time to work out your ideas in extensive ways and can provide others more time to reflect on and respond to the points you make. And reading and responding to what others have written allows you to engage with their ideas, as well as with boyd's and your own, building a rhetorical relationship with others in your classroom context who will be reading and responding to your thinking throughout the semester. Posting your ideas to an online discussion site—either within a learning management system (LMS) or on a blog or wiki for your course—allows you to access and respond easily to one another's thinking.

Digital Toolbox
See Part IV, Section 2

WRITING MOVES

Inquiring and Inventing

In this chapter, we have focused on the idea of a *rhetorical relationship*, where the writer's purposes and the reader's purposes come together in the text that is created so that, for a successful writing/reading event, a shared purpose or shared **why** is realized. We saw that rhetoricians refer to everything surrounding that relationship as the *rhetorical situation,* and the writer's attitude and the social identity or persona the writer is taking on at the moment as a *rhetorical* stance. We also considered two ways a reader might be involved with a piece of writing—as a *participatory reader* who enters the reading as if it's a conversation, or as a *critical reader* who steps back and thinks analytically about how the conversation is working and why, and evaluatively considering whether it worked as well as possible, what made it successful, and/or what might make it work better to meet the purposes of the writer and/or reader.

This notion of rhetorical relationships helps us think through the moves, strategies, approaches, and processes associated with reading and writing as contextualized activities. These generative moves of inquiry are meant to invite you to think not only about how you will want to respond to boyd's work in your discussion post, but also how you will use that piece as an opportunity to create and support the rhetorical relationships that exist within your classroom. This approach, which emphasizes what you want to say as it pushes you to consider the importance of how you position yourself in such a post, will also help you extend your thinking about boyd's piece and your classroom community. Establishing rhetorical relationships is a move to create and extend shared knowledge, but it is also an undertaking that invites you to consider the social nature of communication as you consider the contexts you write for and how to claim a productive stance in particular rhetorical situations.

1 Considering your classroom context

When you respond to a text in ways that allow you to support rhetorical relationships, you need to think carefully about the context you are writing from and for. In this case, you'll want to consider the shared expectations, values, and ways that are central to your class. What can you say about this particular classroom context based on previous conversations, the structure and focus of the class itself, and the feedback your instructor has provided (on inquiries, more formal writing tasks, and during class conversations)? What does this data lead you to see about this class and the ways of reading, writing, and interacting that are encouraged in this setting? What moves can you make in your discussion post to respond to the expectations that frame this class?

2 Drawing on working concepts

Concepts help us better understand the activities we study. Generating and grappling with the meanings of working concepts is a way to push your thinking as you speak to and from a specific rhetorical situation, one provided by the focus of your classroom community. In this case, working concepts can help you better understand the points boyd makes by drawing on the conceptual

framework provided by your class and this book. By drawing on working concepts central to your class in your discussion post, you can make sure to contextualize your reading of boyd by grounding it in the work your class is engaged in.

To generate your own working concepts, add to your group's wiki page, choosing two or more concepts, giving your working sense of them at this point in your own words. These concepts can be ones introduced by this book or other course materials or additional terms that help you as you enter the classroom discourse community constructed by your class. They should also be concepts that speak to boyd's work in useful ways. Try to be as specific as you can and question how these terms support your developing understandings.

3 Returning to your annotations

As you decide what aspect of boyd's piece you will want to focus on in your discussion post, you should return to the annotations you made in the margins of this text as you completed both participatory and critical readings of it. What were you most drawn to as a reader? What patterns seem to emerge from the notes you took? What questions you noted in the margins might you return to now? How were these annotations working in conversation with other aspects of your class?

WRITING MOVES ◄

Drafting and Shaping

Once you have an idea of what you want to say and how your discussion post will work for the classroom context you are writing for, you'll want to keep the rhetorical relationships you are trying to establish and extend through your post in mind as you shape it. So, you are not just responding to boyd here. Instead, you are using this situation, this writing task, as an opportunity to claim a stance that supports a particular kind of rhetorical relationship. Use these moves to approach this discussion post as a highly contextualized turn in the larger conversation your class is structured around.

1 Stepping into a conversation

Drawing on your various readings of boyd's essay, what points would you finally like to make

about the rhetorical relationship she is creating with her text? Who seems to make up her intended audience, and what purposes does she assume her readers share? What shared background knowledge does she expect that they bring, and what new knowledge does she offer? How does she present what she wants her readers to understand? What evidence does she offer? And what evidence (including quotations from her text) can you use to support the points you want to make about the **why**, **what**, and **how** of her text to contribute to the larger online conversation of your class?

2 Applying working concepts

Return to your generative work defining concepts and use it to provide you with a frame for thinking about boyd and the points she makes about how teenagers use social networking sites. How do they help you talk about her article? What new perspectives do they seem to suggest? How does applying them to boyd's piece strengthen and enrich your understandings of these concepts?

3 Nodding to what has come before

As you shape and reshape your discussion post, think about the conversations that have already taken place in your class. This might mean remembering past class discussions, or rereading old discussion threads, or looking at early posts some of your classmates might have already shared with the class. Nod to some of the points made during these discussions in explicit ways (saying things like, "As Phoebe points out," or "Last week we discussed X, but boyd makes me wonder Y"). These explicit connections will help you contextualize the points you are making and connect with your immediate audience.

4 Crafting a rhetorical stance

As you shape your discussion response and prepare to post it, keep your audience in mind and how you want to address this group. This is not a general audience of readers who may or may not be interested in your ideas; your readers will be made up of your classmates, who have read the same materials as you and are exploring similar lines of inquiry. How can you use that shared enterprise as you compose your extended discussion post to invite them to engage with your thoughts and ideas? How can you position yourself through your writing as a (thoughtful/critical/overwhelmed/underwhelmed/diligent) participant working through your ideas? What impact will the position you craft have on your audience?

WRITING MOVES

Revising and Publishing

The discussion post is a genre built around the act of sharing; these kinds of responses are written for others to read and consider in thoughtful and careful ways. While they can be revised and circulated more broadly, we frame them as communicative acts meant for classroom settings to stress the immediate rhetorical relationships they can foster and support.

1 Reading others' posts

When you read your classmates' discussion posts, see them as turns in a conversation going on in writing. These are not mini-essays meant to deliver a particular and polished reading of boyd. Instead, they are generative, tentative, and, ideally, thought-provoking responses.

2 Responding to others' posts

To extend the rhetorical relationship invited by your classmates' discussion posts, respond to a handful of them by stating the new questions they suggest for you as a reader. You can do this in a brief paragraph.

Key Concepts

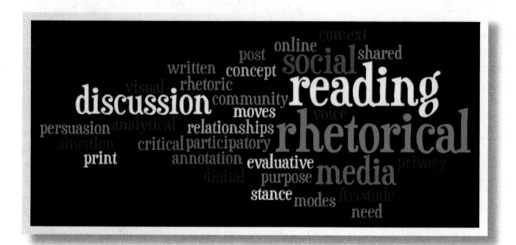

Capturing Identity
in a Profile

1 How does the profile function in digital contexts and how do self-posted profiles present a particular social identity?

2 Why are individuals selected for media profiles? What do these profiles suggest about the importance of context in influencing both how a profile is written and how it is read?

3 What might be included in the profile of a member of a community? As you compose your own, how might you decide what to include?

Chapter Preview

Chapter 2 discussed how reflecting on our literacy experiences can help situate us as we explore writing in a changing world and develop new literacy practices for digital contexts. Chapter 3 explored the concept of a rhetorical relationship and what's involved in building these relationships. Chapter 4 builds on this work as it explores how we can gain insight into what it means to participate in a digital environment by reading and writing profiles of others.

The profile of an individual is a written genre that appears across a wide range of publications and websites, from celebrity magazines to scholarly journals. It has traditionally been used as a way to introduce notable individuals to the public in light of a particular activity, context, or community. Today, the profile has become a common literacy practice for everyday people to introduce themselves and for creating a more public, online identity. As users of social media, we routinely create and share profiles while checking out profiles of friends, potential friends, businesses, and organizations we'd like to know more about.

While the information we find in personal profiles was traditionally shared only in immediate face-to-face communities, in a networked world that information has become more public, shared with a much wider circle of "friends" and potentially read by anyone online. Composing an online profile requires that we think at various levels about our potential audiences, the kind of social identity we wish to express, and how best to build the rhetorical relationships we hope to create. Moreover, while digital media have allowed for easy creation and sharing of profiles, they are also raising real concerns about personal privacy, issues we'll also consider in this chapter.

• • • • • • • • • • • • • • • • • •
social identities
sense of self based on
membership in differ-
ent social groups

This chapter explores the public presentation of self and others, considering profiles you've created for social media and profiles written about others. It builds on the concept of **social identities**—the different ways we choose to present ourselves and how others see us in different social contexts—and it asks you to consider how digital environments are altering the ways in which we create and sustain those identities. Reading a profile of social media researcher danah boyd will help us further explore these issues and prepare you to compose your own profile of another person.

Exploring
Personal Profiles in Digital Contexts

Chances are, you have composed a number of profiles. Maybe you sent an email to your future college roommate to introduce yourself. When composing such an email, you most likely thought carefully about what kinds of information to include. You probably told your roommate-to-be where you are from, a bit about your interests, and about your hopes for the coming semester. You probably didn't explain that you have trouble keeping your laundry off the floor. You selected information in ways that crafted you as a "potential roommate" who will be easy to live with. This is something we do when we compose any profile; by incorporating particular descriptions, details, images, and stories, we actively compose a picture of ourselves, or of someone else, that invites readers to understand a person in a certain way. A profile is based on rhetorical choices, choices that stress some aspects of our (or our subject's) identity, while making other qualities, experiences, and values less visible.

Personal profiles are common in many digital contexts including dating sites, professional sites, and social media. You might also have an online profile for a site associated with one of your courses. On such a page, you might provide a picture of yourself (or an image that represents you in some way), a brief description, and a list of interests you think work to define you. With such a profile, you construct your own public identity in a way you think fits the context, and you are likely to highlight different aspects of who you are as you move from a course site to Twitter to an online dating site. Each specific platform also shapes the profile. Facebook, for example, suggests questions like schools attended and relationship status, guiding you to choose some information to share, and ignoring other elements of your life you might consider equally important. Each site prioritizes different information. The profile you construct for a professional networking site like LinkedIn will look different from one you use on a discussion board about online gaming.

In constructing a personal profile, you are actively building a rhetorical relationship with your imagined audience for anything further you'll write or post. That rhetorical relationship, with its sense of shared purpose and interests, will connect you and your readers and establish the potential for future discourse. If further posts alter this sense of shared purpose, both writers and readers may choose to disconnect, unfriend, or unfollow. With a roommate, however, you're likely to want to keep renegotiating a shared purpose through exchanges beyond that initial email.

Your Digital Profile

Most social media sites like Twitter, Instagram, Facebook, and LinkedIn ask you to create a profile, and those sites are linked to others. For example, you might sign in to a music site with Facebook or share a restaurant review with Twitter followers. Such profiles involve a careful act of composition and self-presentation even when the composition only involves answering a few seemingly simple questions. They allow us to shape a particular rhetorical relationship with those who might read the profile, one that positions ourselves and our readers in particular ways.

We all have different social identities—often as members of particular families, groups, sports teams, churches, and circles of friends—and we emphasize different interests and ways of talking, dressing, and acting as we move from one setting to another. This practice of identity building continues online. We know how to select particular photos, stories, and personal qualities in ways that situate us as members of a community or as strong potential members. This process of selection is central to the profile, and it typically involves choices on our part that consider the contexts where the profile will circulate and what we want to highlight about ourselves.

INQUIRY

#1: Reading and writing digital profiles

Make a quick list of some digital profiles you have composed. Select one of these profiles to reflect on. What was your purpose in composing this profile? What was it you wanted to communicate? What sorts of details, stories, and/or images did you draw on, and what guided your choice of those details? What media did you use? How would you describe the social identity you were presenting? What can you now say about how your process of selection has shaped the identity you are presenting to others in this context?

If you have not created a digital profile, you might look at the profile suggestions on a particular site and consider how they respond to your sense of the identities you share with your friends. Privacy concerns lead many people not to participate in social media, and if that's true for you, you might reflect on why and how the specific details a site calls for could affect your decision.

Profiles and Privacy

For a digital profile, you've certainly made choices about what information to share, and perhaps choices about who will get to see what pieces of that information. There are growing concerns, however, that we may be sharing too much personal information and we're unaware of how widely that information might be shared or what the consequences might be at a future time. According to a recent *New York Times* article, "We Want Privacy, but Can't Stop Sharing,"[4:1] although social media encourages us to stay connected with others by sharing more details about our lives, studies have shown that the more we share, the more likely we are to feel anxiety and depression if we think others are always watching us. Along similar lines, a *Huffington Post* article, "Didn't Read Facebook's Fine Print? Here's Exactly What It Says,"[L4:1] reports on the details of what we agree to when we sign up for Facebook, allowing extensive collection and use of our personal information through data-mining. The article quotes directly from the user terms: "You give us permission to use your name, profile picture, content and information in connection with commercial, sponsored, or related content (such as a brand you like) served or enhanced by us." One concern about Facebook's terms of use is that all of the information you share in your profile, your likes, and your general web browsing when you're logged in are collected and sold to third parties. Much of this information is used for targeted advertising, but other companies and organizations purchase this data for different reasons, such as to assess your potential as an employee or as borrower of a loan. Such data collection and selling is the standard business model for all social media sites today.

In response to wide-scale data collection by social media sites (and governments around the world), there is a growing movement of people who are trying to raise awareness about the tracking of online activity. The nonprofit group Mozilla, for example, creators of the popular web browser Firefox, have developed browser add-ons like Ghostery and Lightbeam to allow users to see what companies are tracking them and to block unwanted access by these companies. The website donottrack.com,[L4:2] funded by dozens of concerned groups around the world, offers a series of short films about the problem of tracking and the data collected through it. Episode 3 focuses specifically on Facebook activity.[L4:3] As writers and participants in a digital world, an important facet of our emerging digital literacies is understanding the data that is collected about us and the policies of the social media sites we use, and to use privacy tools and settings as effectively as possible while always remembering that some tracking of our online data is inevitable.

INQUIRY

#2: Your privacy settings and choices

Read the article about Facebook's fine print[L:4:4] mentioned above. Have you read other articles about privacy concerns? What kinds of issues and concerns do they raise for you?

Using your computer or cell phone, take some time to read through the terms and conditions of a social media site you use. How long is the document? What are the language and terminology like? Is it clear about what data is being collected and shared? Review the privacy options on the site and consider your own settings and choices. You'll find several resources online that guide users through this process, one example being "How to Check Social Media Privacy Settings,"[4:4] from socialmediaexaminer.com.[L:4:5]

links

Making Connections
Personal Profiles as Public Genres

While social media sites allow us to craft our own profiles and shape the identities we want to display to a larger world, we continue to be interested in reading about public figures and discovering what is significant about their lives. Like other more traditional public genres like the newspaper cover story or letters-to-the-editor, the profile continues to be a popular form of writing online. Reading profiles of people involved in a particular cultural context can offer unique insight into that context, and one way to gain a richer understanding of how our literacy practices are changing in a digital age is to learn more about the people who are both studying and engaging in these new practices. Because the profile of an individual typically introduces readers to a person of interest by placing that individual in relationship to a particular activity, context, or community, in reading such profiles we can learn more about not only individuals, but also about the worlds in which they participate.

Understanding Genre

In your earlier English courses you have probably been assigned to write a particular type of essay—a process essay, an argument essay, maybe even a profile, the genre we'll explore here. If so, you've probably been given guidelines about the process to follow: "Choose someone interesting to write about; find information about your subject; describe the person; identify a theme and give information that supports that theme; revise and edit." Or maybe you've received instructions about the form: "Your profile should include an introduction to highlight some aspect of the subject's personality or experience, body paragraphs with examples that show the aspect you're highlighting, including descriptive details and/or the subject's words, and a conclusion that recaptures what you've shown about your subject." These suggestions aren't wrong, but they ignore the social and rhetorical context of the audience you're writing for and why, what conversation you're entering, and how your composition will contribute to it.

We've already discussed that in an actual composing context, the writer's process is more fluid and complex than this typical naming of composing steps suggests, and that when researchers studied the processes of writers at various levels of experience, writing in different contexts, they found both common elements such as drafting or revising, and different patterns of movement through those activities. And we need to think about form in more complex ways and as being more influenced by context as well. To capture that complexity of form, to see how it is shaped and reshaped for different purposes in different contexts, composition research has focused on the concept of **genre**—on how our genres of writing and composing reflect our social practices, and how the idea of making common moves using different strategies can help us see those genres, not as fixed forms with set rules for writers to follow, but as flexible forms that writers can move within and adapt for different contexts and purposes.

Sidenote

Composing guidelines are helpful, but do not ignore the social and rhetorical context of the audience you're writing for and why.

genre
a way of naming the idea that texts involve common moves and shapes that reflect particular social practices

Rhetorical genre studies, a strand of research in composition studies, takes a rhetorical perspective on genre, and has generated some key concepts and shared understandings useful for our further inquiry into composing in a digital world. One important understanding is that genres don't represent fixed forms, but a kind of *social action* (Miller[4.4])—a way of responding to and acting on the world that's repeated for similar purposes in similar contexts. Online dating, for example, presents a "recurrent rhetorical situation" (Miller 151) for people who use dating sites, and successful digital profiles for those sites will include similar content and present it in similar ways (selecting the right screen name, including interests and sounding enthusiastic, etc.). But online dating profiles, like other genres, don't stay fixed; they've evolved and developed and might someday disappear. They didn't exist before the internet, before sites like match.com were created and people discovered this new way to meet potential partners (although print "personal" ads served a similar purpose in a predigital era).

So genres have a recognizable form that can be given a name at a particular moment, but they can also be modified to fit new rhetorical circumstances (Berkenkotter and Huckin[4.5]), and we can see them as "stabilized-for-now" or "stabilized-enough" (Schryer[4.6]) as they take on recognizable characteristics, but these are always in the process of being shaped and reshaped. As newcomers spend time in a discourse community, they start to see what genres have developed there and how to use the typical moves of a genre as it appears at that moment in order to engage with the community and accomplish their own purposes—to get the responses they hope for ("matches" for an online dater). Another key understanding is that genres don't exist in isolation but within systems of related activities (Bazerman[4.7]), so that creating a dating profile is just one composing task, accompanied by choosing the right photo to share, and followed by composing email responses to those who read the profile and make contact, and having an appropriate "first date conversation" with an interesting candidate. Online dating becomes a larger framework of activity within our larger digital culture, with many composing actions and genres.

Our consideration of genre continues in Chapter 7, but for the moment, keep in mind these four points.

① Genres represent repeated **rhetorical actions** (moves) within social contexts/discourse communities.

② Genres evolve and change and can be adapted to new purposes.

③ Any example of a genre will be part of a larger system of related genres/related activities.

④ Composers in new contexts most often learn to use genres by observing others working with them and trying them out.

Reading a Public Profile

Like a personal digital profile, a profile written about public figures and people of public interest is a genre that has arisen in a social context and has taken on a repeated form with typical but flexible moves that reflect the shared interests of a larger community of readers in a particular cultural moment. While the interest in the lives and ideas of public figures is not new, the range of people whose worlds are potentially interesting to many readers has expanded as people become instant celebrities and pop icons in our digital culture. It's not surprising, then, that even a researcher of that culture would be captured in a profile.

Social media researcher danah boyd, whose research into teenagers' Facebook postings we discussed in Chapter 3, is deeply involved in the digital world and its new literacies. The following *New York Times* profile by Pamela Paul presents boyd in light of her work as a researcher of teenagers' digital activity. While it is certain boyd steps into many roles and participates in a variety of contexts, it is her work as a savvy researcher of social media that has drawn attention and is highlighted here. Thus, her profile invites us to consider the relationship between individual and context—how learning more about one representative of that context can give us a clearer picture of what is valued there.

Sidenote

Genres are not fixed forms with set rules, but flexible forms writers can move within and adapt for different contexts and purposes.

rhetorical actions
the repeated moves made within genres to achieve rhetorical purposes

BEFORE READING:
Evoking your prior knowledge

You always come to a reading with some prior knowledge that places that reading in context and provides the basis for some initial shared understanding about what the writer might address. Based on what you already know about danah boyd (from Chapter 3), what aspects of her life and work do you think will be highlighted here? What is it that you, as a reader, want to know about her? Considering the title "Cracking Teenagers' Online Code," what aspects of boyd's life will most likely be central to this piece? Take a look at the images that accompany this text. What do they suggest about the article and its focus? As you read the article for the first time, read as a participant—annotate the places that interest you, that resonate for you, and that make you want to ask questions, make comments, or respond to boyd in some way.

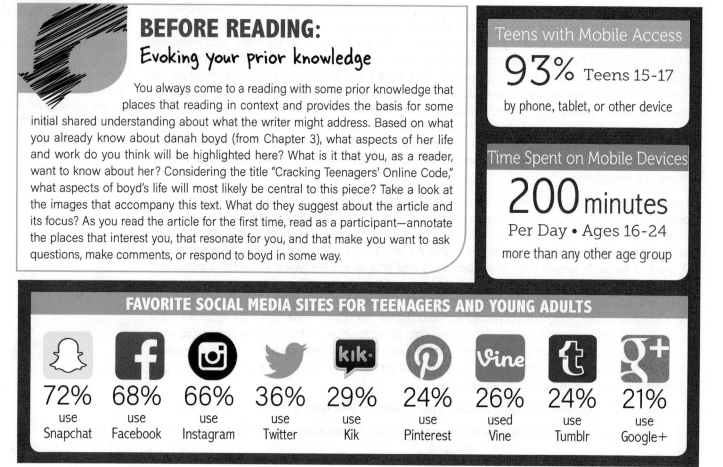

Teens with Mobile Access

93% Teens 15-17

by phone, tablet, or other device

Time Spent on Mobile Devices

200 minutes

Per Day • Ages 16-24

more than any other age group

FAVORITE SOCIAL MEDIA SITES FOR TEENAGERS AND YOUNG ADULTS

72% use Snapchat	**68%** use Facebook	**66%** use Instagram	**36%** use Twitter	**29%** use Kik	**24%** use Pinterest	**26%** used Vine	**24%** use Tumblr	**21%** use Google+

Source: http://www.statista.com/statistics/199242/social-media-and-networking-sites-used-by-us-teenagers/ In U.S. February 2016

READING

"Cracking Teenagers' Online Code"[4:8]
by Pamela Paul
The New York Times, January 20, 2012

Credit Erik Jacobs for The New York Times

Danah Boyd, 34, studies children's use of social media.

With her coordinated zebra-striped scarf, tights and arm warmers (arm warmers?), spiky out-to-there hat and pierced tongue, 34-year-old Danah Boyd provides an electric Gen Y contrast to the staid gray lobby of Microsoft Research in Cambridge, Mass., which she enters in a flurry of animated conversation, Elmo-decorated iPhone in hand. In a juxtaposition that causes her no end of mischievous delight, her laptop bears a sticker of Snow White, whose outstretched arm gently cradled the Apple logo.

But Dr. Boyd – a senior researcher at Microsoft, an assistant professor at New York University and a fellow at the Berkman Center for Internet and Society at Harvard—is a widely respected figure in social media research. With a num-

READING

ber of influential scholarly papers under her name, she travels relentlessly, tweets under the handle Zephoria and has fans trailing her at TED conferences, at South by Southwest and elsewhere on the high-tech speaking circuit.

She is also a kind of rock star emissary from the online and offline world of teenagers. The young subjects of her research become her friends on Facebook and subscribe to her Twitter feed.

"The single most important thing about Danah is that she's the first anthropologist we've got who comes from the tribe she's studying," said Clay Shirky, a professor in the interactive telecommunications program at N.Y.U. and a fellow at the Berkman Center.

There's no shortage of grown-up distress over the dangers young people face online. Parents, teachers and schools worry about teenagers posting their lives (romantic indiscretions, depressing poetry and all), leaking passwords and generally flouting social conventions as predators, bullies and unsavory marketers lurk. Endless back-and-forthing over how to respond effectively—shutting Web sites, regulating online access and otherwise tempering the world of social media for children—dominates the P.T.A. and the halls of policy makers.

But as Dr. Boyd sees it, adults are worrying about the wrong things.

Children today, she said, are reacting online largely to social changes that have taken place off line.

"Children's ability to roam has basically been destroyed," Dr. Boyd said in her office at Microsoft, where a view of the Boston skyline is echoed in the towers of books on her shelves, desk and floor. "Letting your child out to bike around the neighborhood is seen as terrifying now, even though by all measures, life is safer for kids today."

Children naturally congregate on social media sites for the relatively unsupervised conversations, flirtations, immature humor and social exchanges that are the normal stuff of teenage hanging-out, she said.

"We need to give kids the freedom to explore and experience things online that might actually help them," she added. "What scares me is that we don't want to look at the things that make us uncomfortable. So rather than see what teenagers are showing us online about bullying and suicide and the problems they're dealing with and using that information to help them, we're making ourselves blind to it."

These are issues that Dr. Boyd has lived with and knows well.

"At the age of 16, I thought I'd be dead by 21," she said. "I lost 13 classmates to drug overdoses, suicides, accidents and a murder."

Danah Boyd often dresses like her youthful subjects.

Her parents divorced when she was 5 and her father largely disappeared. She was raised by her mother, sometimes in straitened circumstances, in Lancaster, Pa. Bored at school, she rebelled—challenging teachers, lashing out at her mother, hanging out with hackers and languishing in school.

"The Internet was my saving grace," Dr. Boyd said. "I would spend my teenage nights talking to strangers online, realizing there were other smart kids out there."

She also often reached out to adults online, many of whom acted as de facto counselors and mentors. Dr. Boyd's own positive experience on platforms like Usenet and Internet Relay Chat fuels her dismay over attempts to restrict children's use of the Internet today.

She asks, for example, how teenagers can be encouraged to become politically active when so much of that activity takes place online. And she wonders whether gay children grappling with their sexuality might benefit enormously from chatting online with adults who have been through similar situations.

"There are lots of places where it's extraordinarily helpful for kids to talk to adults," she said.

Moreover, grown-ups' panic about teenage online behavior distracts from the potential benefits. Bullying, Dr. Boyd said, occurs more frequently in schools than on the Internet, and in neither case, according to data she cites, is it on the rise.

"The most deadly misconception about American youth has been the sexual predator panic," she said. "The model we have of the online sexual predator is this lurking man who reaches out on the Internet and grabs a kid. And there is no data that support that. The vast majority of sex crimes against kids involve someone that kid trusts, and it's overwhelmingly family members."

A teenage girl who has been sexually molested by an uncle

and who has nobody she can talk to in her hometown might benefit greatly from communicating with a counselor online.

Despite her own teenage rebellion or perhaps because of it, Dr. Boyd ended up at Brown, where she studied computer science, and at the Media Lab at M.I.T., where she got her master's. She earned her Ph.D. from the School of Information at the University of California, Berkeley, working at Google, Yahoo and Tribe at the same time.

She now calls herself an activist and a scholar. Her Twitter handle is "social media scholar, youth researcher and advocate." She is also working on a long overdue book for Yale University Press, "The Social Lives of Networked Teens." (The title, she said jokingly, should really be "It's Complicated.")

In November she was tapped, along with John Palfrey, a director of the Berkman Center, to run the research arm of Lady Gaga's Born This Way Foundation, an organization devoted to empowering youth.

Dr. Boyd's standard mode of research combines traditional quantitative work with deep ethnographic research—embedding herself in youth communities, whether it's middle-class Muslim gangs in Nashville or Ivy League aspirants who navigate social media with startling sophistication.

One of her most influential and contentious papers showed that when teenagers transitioned from MySpace to Facebook, a kind of "white flight" occurred, in which Facebook became more associated with children who aspire to college.

By focusing on a range of issues—sexual predation, teenage suicide, bullying, sexting, drug and alcohol abuse, sexual trafficking—Dr. Boyd has shown, often to the dismay of those in the tech community who believe that the Internet is the ultimate equalizer, that issues of race, class and gender persist in the virtual world just as in the real world. The children in families characterized by alcohol and drug abuse, financial stress, divorce and sexual abuse reveal their struggles online just as they do off.

"She was the first to say that the teenagers at risk off line are the same ones who are at risk online," said Alice Marwick, a postdoctoral researcher at Microsoft who works closely with Dr. Boyd. "It's not that the Internet is doing something bad to these kids, it's that these bad things are in kids' lives and the Internet is just a component of that."

Most broadly, with troubled teenagers and model youth alike, adolescent online behavior is a reflection of what teenagers' social lives have always been: friendship, gossip, flirting, transgressing and keeping it all—good and bad—from parents.

One girl Dr. Boyd knows made her Facebook page sound as if she were depressed so that she could use her mental state as a pretext for breaking up with a boyfriend. When a teenager posts the lyrics to a suicidal love song on her Facebook page, her mother may panic while her friends know it's just a reference to an annoying ex-friend.

"Teenagers try to hide what's really going on in their communication online," said Ethan Zuckerman, director of the M.I.T. Center for Civic Media. "Danah is very good at figuring out how to crack those codes. And she's made a strong case that teenagers are using the Internet in ways that are far more productive and creative and less harmful than people assume."

Most shocking to adults may be how similar teenagers are to them when it comes to online behavior.

"Teenagers absolutely care about privacy," Dr. Boyd said, adding that like adults, they share things to feel loved, connected and supported.

"Teenagers are not some alien population," she said. "When we see new technologies, we think they make everything different for young people. But they really don't. Teenagers are the same as they always were." ■

In demand on the high-tech speaking circuit, Dr. boyd opposes restrictions on teenagers' use of the internet, maintaining that it has many benefits.

AFTER READING:
Responding analytically as a reader

Why was boyd profiled? What might Paul's purposes have been? What more have you learned about boyd's life and her work from this profile? What community(ies) is she seen as representing?

What words of hers are quoted, and what do they contribute to the portrait of her that's developed here? How do her own words, those of others, her visual self-presentation, and even her choice not to capitalize her name contribute to a particular sense of her social identity? (Notice the difference in self-presentation in the three pictures that accompany this post. Why do you think the writer or editor has chosen these visual images?) How does Paul, as the writer, build on the elements of boyd's public social identity, her public persona? Why do you think this profile of an anthropologist and media researcher appeared in *The New York Times* section on Fashion and Style? What does that suggest about its audience? What larger questions emerge about the online social worlds of young people and how to study those worlds?

As discussed in Chapter 3, we enter into a rhetorical relationship with a writer when we read a text. How we read can take many forms, sometimes staying in the flow of the text by reading in a participatory way; sometimes stepping further out from the text to read it more analytically from a writer's perspective, noticing how the writer has constructed the information and meanings being shared; and sometimes looking evaluatively at how well the text seems to work for its intended audience and purposes. Of course, these different ways of reading usually overlap and work together, but it's helpful to be aware of these differences so we can deepen our understanding of a text and adjust how we read based on our purposes for reading.

INQUIRY

#3: Reading analytically as a writer

In her profile, Pamela Paul is writing in the genre of a newspaper profile, published in the Fashion and Style section and posted online. How does she go about establishing a rhetorical relationship with her audience, connecting with them, evoking the background knowledge they might share, and introducing new information?

What information does Paul make central to her profile of boyd? How does she present this information? What do you notice about how this piece is organized? What details about boyd's life are introduced, and in what order? What does Paul assume about readers' background knowledge and what shared knowledge does she create explicitly here? What larger points does Paul make about boyd? What social identity(ies) does she bring out? What does Paul want readers to take away from this profile?

What does this piece suggest about the genre of the profile as it has taken shape in the context of our contemporary digital culture? About some of the shared ways, purposes, and understandings writers might create in this genre and use it to learn about and represent someone other than themselves?

Particular aspects of boyd's social identity are represented in this profile, supported in part by her own public self-presentation. But boyd has also created profiles of her own, so we can see this one example within a system or network of other acts of representation and self-representation. We can go directly to them to see more about both boyd's self-presentation and the social identities she emphasizes for different audiences and different rhetorical purposes.

links

INQUIRY

#4: Further exploration: boyd's online social identities

One of boyd's own profiles appears on <u>a website</u>L4:6 she has set up to showcase her work. A briefer statement appears on her blog, <u>Apophenia</u>.L4:7 Compare the social identities she presents on these sites with those presented in Paul's profile of her. You might also look at the <u>Wikipedia entry</u>L4:8 for her to see what this collective knowledge site has gathered and emphasized.

Our knowledge about danah boyd and her several social identities is enhanced by reading and comparing such profiles of her. We also gain insight into how the profile works as a genre and how it changes, depending on where it is published and the purpose of its composition.

INQUIRY

#5: Reading other profiles

The *New York Times* profile of boyd and those she has composed appear online. Find another example of an online profile of a public person, preferably someone whose life or work can tell us more about an aspect of the digital world. What aspects of the subject's life are showcased in this profile? Why do you suppose these aspects were made visible in this text? How is this profile constructed? What kinds of media does the composer draw on (images, video, sound)? Why do you think this particular profile was composed? What does it tell us about this individual? What does it tell us about the communities, organizations, and/or field this individual is a part of and invested in? What can you learn about profiles in general by looking at this additional example?

Composing
Online Profile

We've discussed that danah boyd, although she probably wasn't known to most *New York Times* readers before her own article and then her profile appeared, was a good choice for a section of the paper (Fashion and Style) that often includes profiles. She represents a community of experts on social media and also users of social media—a topic of general interest to most readers. She also has a colorful style. She's presented primarily in her social identity of "social media guru," and although the profile presents some details about her personal life, she has other identities that aren't explored here. Her profile is suited to a particular audience and context: an audience of educated readers with a general interest in social media and its impact on individuals and communities.

Such profiles don't have to focus on already well-known people. In fact, profiles often focus on ordinary people whose experiences tell us something more about a community or social demographic we want to learn more about. *The New York Times* could have followed danah boyd's original article on teenagers' "hiding in plain sight" with a profile of a teen who uses this strategy, telling us much more, from an insider's perspective, about the teen experience of social media.

Student writer Nate Jolley chose to write about a friend of his who is trying to make it in the world of music—in this case, rap. While his friend has begun to build a local reputation as the rapper Fame, a wider group of readers might not be as interested in reading a profile of him as they might be of more widely known artists like Kanye West or Drake. But such profiles can serve as a powerful way to introduce a new artist to a larger audience, as well as to provide insight into how aspiring musicians use social media to reach this audience. And any reader who is interested in the larger question of how technology and social media are transforming our larger cultural world is likely to be interested in how they are impacting the experiences of young musicians.

Nate Jolley's profile of his rapper friend Fame, "Rise to Fame," appears in Part I Additional Readings. Turn to it, read it, and trace some of the moves he makes as a writer and how he attempts to build a rhetorical relationship with readers. Note that Nate has captured the young rapper's world, in part, by including Fame's own words about this social context. While some terms within that world might seem offensive to those outside it, neither Nate's nor Fame's purpose is to give offense but simply to use the everyday discourse of the rapper community. We'll refer to the moves Nate has made as we consider some of the typical moves of composing in this genre.

Composing a profile offers another opportunity for inquiry into an aspect of our digital literacies. We've seen that boyd represents a community of social media researchers, and the profile written by Pamela Paul highlights this aspect of boyd's professional identity by showing how she mixes personal style with academic research to study teens' use of social media. The profile of Fame shows how a young musician, one of many within a larger music community, is using digital composing tools and social media to create a presence in the music world to truly become the Fame of his self-representation.

As we name some of the typical moves of this genre in contemporary contexts, remember that they are not just typical, but also adaptable, and that you are likely to find your own strategies for accomplishing them as you work within your own rhetorical purposes in a shared inquiry context. Remind yourself also that we learn to work with and use genres for those purposes by trying them out, drawing on what we've observed in other profiles, but making our own versions to see whether they work within their intended community conversation.

WRITING MOVES
Inquiring and Inventing

While there are many possible subjects for profiles, the context in which you're composing will shape your choices as you consider what your work in this genre might contribute to the conversation of your classroom community and beyond. Because that context includes this book and our larger exploration of literacy in a digital world, as you consider possibilities for the profile you will compose you'll want to think about how the person you are profiling uses digital literacies to accomplish his or her day-to-day communication with others. That person doesn't have to be famous or have a public persona, and he or she may have a small presence online. For example, Ashley (Chapter 2) might have profiled her sister, and in doing so, learned more about how her sister uses digital media in other contexts beyond their texting, with other family members and work. Understanding an individual's digital literacy practices will lead to a deeper understanding of that individual, her or his place in a community, the shape of some aspect of the person's current social identity, but also about our larger digital culture.

1 Generating ideas and selecting a subject

Make a quick list of some of individuals you might profile. It doesn't have to be someone actively trying to create a public persona, as Fame is. Select an individual who is a member of a community that you see as significant and whose experience has some relevance to our larger inquiry. Consider your classmates, your fellow students, a faculty member in a field you're interested in, but also a friend or family member or coworker. Think about communities and settings being impacted by digital technology and social media—a classroom using an online learning management system, for example—and what might be learned from an individual's experience of that context.

As you proceed, consider what can you learn about this individual and about the community he or she is a part of. Which of this individual's experiences, values, allegiances, and qualities seem most representative of a particular community? How might understanding more about this individual and this community contribute to the larger exploration of new literacy practices in digital environments?

At this point, you should also ask for this individual's permission to move forward with collecting data as discussed in moves 2 and 3. Chapter 17 highlights the importance of obtaining informed consent in a section titled "Addressing Ethical Concerns" (on page 421), and you will want to keep the issues raised there in mind whenever you collect information tied to individuals (as you will also do if you move through Chapter 8 and compose a community analysis). For this project, telling your potential subject about your research and how you intend to share your profile (who will have access to your final profile) and getting a signed form that allows you to use your subject's words and experiences would be entirely appropriate.

2 Observing your subject and collecting data

Consider the primary data you might draw on in your profile. Some of the research strategies commonly used in composing a profile are observation and interviews. If your subject is involved with a hybrid, digitally enhanced space, you might make observations about how physical spaces merge with digital spaces, as Nate has done. If your subject uses platforms like Instagram or World of Warcraft, you might make observations about that space and how the person you're profiling interacts with it.

If you are able to observe your profile subject, you might want to shadow this individual while she is engaged in an activity that is central to both her life and the focus of your profile. Take notes to try to capture a sense of this individual's lived experience. You'll also want to capture some images, if possible, that represent the person you're profiling or the world that person represents.

3 Interviewing your subject

You'll also want to interview your subject. As you observe this person's digital environment, you're likely to start identifying themes that emerge from your inquiry, ideas about how this person uses digital media to participate in local or larger communities, perhaps. Interviews can be very generative in that they help you develop themes based on your participant's perspective and help you support any larger ideas you see taking shape as you learn more about this person in context.

To conduct an interview, generate a list of questions that point to themes and ideas you hope to highlight in your profile. As an interviewer, you will want to ask more open-ended questions that encourage your profile subject to elaborate and say as much as possible. Ideally you'll record this session using audio or video, but you should plan on taking notes, too, as that might encourage your subject to say more. You might even conduct your interview by phone or email. From what Nate tells us of Fame's life, you can guess some of the questions he asked him: When did you get involved with music? When did you begin to record in a studio? How did you build a fan base? How do you go about recording? How do you use social media? And finally, how would the music industry fare without technology?

Part of your goal as a profile writer is to capture some of your subject's voice in your writing, and collecting and paying careful attention to the person's speech will help with this. Pamela Paul, in her profile of danah boyd, and Nate, in his profile of Fame, both use their subject's own words to capture a more personal perspective of their experience. Paul quotes boyd on her own teenage experience: "The internet was my saving grace," as well as what she has learned from her research, for example, that "issues of race, class and gender persist in the virtual world just as in the real world." Nate uses Fame's words throughout his profile and in his conclusion about the importance of the internet to him: "Without the internet, we wouldn't be able to broadcast our sound at all. There would be no real way for our music to get out there, and I ain't sellin' CD's and shit out of my house. That's dead."

4 Working with the information you've gathered

Once you've gathered your primary data from observation notes and interviews, you'll want to begin to identify patterns in what you've found. What key points emerge from what you've been told or in what you've observed? What seems significant and relevant to what you're trying to learn about this person in this context? Are there other points you'd like to make but can't really support from what you've gathered so far? Can you make further observations or ask further questions to gain more evidence? You won't be able to address everything you notice, so you'll want to focus on those aspects that seem most relevant and of interest to your potential audience of readers.

WRITING MOVES

Drafting and Shaping

Once you've worked out the significance of the things you've observed and heard, the points you might make, and the evidence you can use to support them, you're ready to begin shaping your profile, to consider **how** you'll write it, or what rhetorical moves you'll make. As you do so, you'll want to think about the rhetorical situation you're writing for: your purposes in writing this profile, your audience, and the elements of your composition that will most effectively address your purposes with this audience. You might also think about including other media like images, video, and sound if they seem to lend to the quality and richness of your profile.

Digital Toolbox
See Part IV, Section 4

1 Considering purpose

Your purpose in composing this profile—your own interest in this person and what you want your audience to know and understand—will lead to a sequence of decisions: How will you introduce your subject to your readers? What elements of this subject's life will you share? Which of your observations and of the subject's words will best highlight the points you want to bring out about this individual? The community he/she represents? His/her interaction with the world of digital literacies? Nate's purpose is certainly to give his readers a picture of what's involved in building a reputation as a musician these days, but he may also want to learn more about his friend's life and work. Clarifying your different purposes for writing about this person will

serve as a guide as you, like Nate, begin to shape a more formal profile, using your own developing understanding to guide your choices of what to include.

2 Considering audience and orienting readers

Unlike many news articles, where the writer might be reporting on events for which readers have little prior knowledge, the profile, as a genre, traditionally highlights an individual who is either already known to many or who represents a community that is familiar to readers. While you might not profile an individual who has established such a public persona, you will most likely point to a larger community or context your readers will recognize (as Paul does by highlighting new media scholars and as Nate does by pointing to the community of rappers). So one important task for you, as the writer of a profile, is to imagine what your readers are likely to know about the person and about the community. What shared knowledge do you need to evoke from your readers? What new background information do you need to provide, and where will you add it? Note that readers learn about boyd's status as a researcher in the second paragraph of Paul's profile and in the third paragraph readers learn that she's a "rock star emissary of the online and offline world of teenagers," background information that Paul includes for readers that may not be familiar with this side of boyd. Nate can assume readers know about music tracks, but he explains the insider term "bars" and he doesn't expect all of his readers to know about sound editing tools, so he adds this information later in the profile, after readers have already been introduced to the musician who uses such tools.

You might also consider what preconceived notions—about an individual or about a particular community—you want to build on or push against.

At this point you can ask yourself: How do I want to introduce my subject to my readers? How might I use my introduction to situate this individual in a particular context or in light of a certain social identity?

3 Shaping your composition

As you begin to draft your profile, you'll want to consider the order in which you present your information to your readers. You can see quite different choices in the profiles of danah boyd and of Fame (and you might have made still other choices if you'd been the writer of these profiles).

What details, including descriptive details and the subject's own words, do you plan to weave into this text? What will the inclusion of particular details help you highlight? What might you want to omit or handle carefully? (You might want to omit

language that's intentionally derogatory or insulting, for example, unless part of your own purpose is to understand your subject's purpose in using it and giving an example is necessary to sharing that understanding.)

How do you want to structure this profile? How might you balance specific details and more generalized statements or claims in this piece?

What new understandings do you want your readers to gain from this profile and where will you share these?

4 Incorporating images and/or audio

If you're writing for a platform that supports images and/or sound, you can include these elements to support the points you're making in your profile,

Digital Toolbox
See Part IV, Section 4

or you can plan a composition that builds itself around them. The images in danah boyd's profile highlight aspects of her personality the writer wants to convey. A more complete digital portrait could be created with sound bites from boyd's public talks. And Nate, who has given us a detailed description of his friend's studio, might include photos he has taken of this space as well as social media images from Facebook and other sites for Fame and his rap group, DMP. He could also consider including audio selections from his interview with Fame and examples of his music.

5 Editing

Remember you'll generally want to prepare the cleanest copy of your composition you can before you begin to circulate it.

Digital Toolbox
See Part IV, Section 3 and 6

Sidenote
As you shape your composition, you might also consider drafting a rough outline or working visual map to get a larger sense of the overall shape of your profile with a pencil and paper, or using digital tools for these purposes.

Digital Toolbox
See Part IV, Section 1

WRITING MOVES

Revising and Publishing

When you're working in a community of writers, you might choose to share your work at any point. But certainly once you have a solid draft of your composition you'll want to begin to share it with readers/viewers/listeners to get a richer sense of the audience response to the work you have completed so far. In Chapter 2 we discussed two possible moves: creating and using a generative rubric, and using guiding peer response questions. Another peer response strategy is to have a classmate read your work and then write you a letter (or compose an email) telling you everything he or she now knows about your profile subject. A letter highlights the rhetorical relationship you are building with the person who reads or hears or views your story and invites that person to continue that relationship through an active response.

1 Requesting a letter from a peer reader/listener/viewer

Here are some questions you might ask a peer to address.

- What did you learn about my subject, x, from reading, viewing, or listening to this profile?

- What larger points do you think I was making about x and his/her experience?

- What details were most striking and helped you to gain a sense of x, of x's relationship to the world of new literacies, and of the community x represents?

- Were any details distracting from my larger points, or not needed?

- Was there any additional information that would have been helpful?

- Did the details appear at appropriate moments for building an understanding about x and x's world?

- Are there other things you'd like to tell me at this point about how this piece worked for you and how I might revise or reshape it?

You might want to extend the turns in this exchange, writing back with your own comments in response to what you've learned and further questions about points your reader has made. But at some point, you'll be ready to go on to your next move.

2 Revising your profile

From your exchange with your peer reader, you can decide what additional information you want to bring into this piece, what details might not be relevant, what else you might change as you work on a final revision.

3 Publishing your work

As you think about finalizing this piece, consider how you might share it with others, such as on a course site or class blog or wiki, as described in Chapter 2, or in a more public space. Your college or university might have an online site for publishing student work, for example, and a profile of a student who is using new literacies in a course, to build new relationships with team members, or to stay in touch with family at home, might speak to a larger student audience. Your school newspaper might also offer an outlet for your work. Consider how you can reach an audience for this text and if this wider audience and delivery method call for some further changes to the final version of your composition.

Digital Toolbox
See Part IV, Section 4

Reinventing and Circulating Your Work

Once you've completed your profile you might extend your work in one of several ways.

➤ **Option 1: Creating a composite profile.** If the person you profiled is part of a larger group—a team, a class, a music group—you can extend your individual profile to create a composite profile of that group. Nate, for example, moved from his profile of an individual rapper to create a composite profile of the "mad lyrical" rap group he works with and promotes.

➤ **Option 2: Contextualizing your profile.** To further contextualize the work you do in your profile, select one element that seems central to your profile that extends beyond this one individual—maybe this is a sense of place (what it meant or means growing up in small rural community with no internet vs. a profiled cousin's connected rural world), a sense of shared experience (what it meant to be a stay-at-home mom in the 1960s vs. a profiled mom's connection to other moms through mommy blogs), or a shift in technology (what it meant to go to college before the internet was widely available vs. a profiled classmate's learning with digital technologies), or what it meant to be a young musician making your way in the preinternet age vs. Fame's experience—and find at least one outside source that references this theme. Reframe what you've learned through your profile in light of this larger context.

➤ **Option 3: Finding patterns across profiles.** As with literacy narratives, it can be useful to create a collection of profiles of people who are engaged in different ways in the use of contemporary digital literacies, creating groupings and seeing what patterns emerge across individuals, within groups, or across groups. As you create a collection of profiles, you might want to use the themes you see emerging to suggest an organizational approach as you decide which profiles should be gathering in particular sections (maybe you will organize a section around a focus on social media activity, perhaps you will include another on multimodality). You can then explore the themes that become central to this collection in an introduction that explains to potential readers what this collection suggests about digital literacy practices and what repeated shared ways, expectations, and values it most underscores.

➤ **Option 4: Creating an audio profile.** You might also have the option to create an audio profile, a genre that has become increasingly popular with the use of podcasts. Start by listening to some podcasts that interest you, whether or not they focus on digital literacies. For example, consider looking up the following.

links

· A BBC (British Broadcasting Corporation) series[L4:9] that aims to offer "insight into the character of an influential figure making news headlines," often politicians, journalists, or celebrities

· Popcorntalk Network's[L4:10] profiles of Hollywood figures—actors, directors, etc.

· This American Life, the weekly NPR radio show, which often profiles people who aren't famous but whose stories are often interesting (example: one episode[L4:11] focuses on the stories of several young people who went through an experimental phase of their lives that moved them away from their parents' worlds)

Digital Toolbox
See Part IV, Section 4

Key Concepts

Building Knowledge Collaboratively
in Online Communities

CHAPTER FIVE

CENTRAL QUESTIONS

1 What can we learn by considering the ways in which we share and exchange information in familiar contexts? In digital and networked spaces?

2 How does such sharing change when moving from more informal communities to more formal, academic ones? What can that tell us about how learning is being redefined in digital (and academic) spaces?

3 What are some common moves of "reporting back" and resituating outside knowledge in your local learning community conversations?

Chapter Preview

Up to this point we've been exploring some of the different ways our literacy practices are changing in a digital world and how these changes affect the kinds of rhetorical relationships we build. In developing these understandings, we've looked closely at how different uses of language and literacy help build, shape, and maintain smaller, local discourse communities, while also working to define the social identities of their members and help them achieve shared purposes in their interactions. In this chapter, we will extend this notion of community to the learning communities that are constructed and reconstructed, shaped and reshaped, through our interactions on the web and in academic settings. By analyzing how information is shared and built on online, we can gain a deeper awareness of how communities and individuals actively construct both private and public knowledge using various media.

As we've emphasized throughout these early chapters, regardless of the media used, writers typically have two purposes with any act of communication. One is interpersonal—to establish or maintain some sort of relationship; the other is to convey information through ideas and propositions. As with Barry's Facebook page, in exchanges between friends, the information conveyed literally often isn't very important; rather, it's *the act of communicating* it and maintaining a connection that matters most. Now turning to the learning context of colleges and universities, the focus of communication is more likely to be on presenting information or ideas. There is still an interpersonal aspect to communication in these learning communities: members might try to draw from one another's interests and provide a little entertainment with images and some humor on an online course site like the Blue Team's wiki page (Chapter 1).

While our learning communities, whether face-to-face or online, are still local in the sense that they involve a defined group of people who are involved in a common enterprise of discovering and building shared knowledge, they connect to and draw from a much wider world of knowledge that is easily available online. Knowledge-building in these communities involves not only building on one another's ideas through discussion posts, as we discussed in Chapter 3, but going out into that wider, global world, finding new information and ideas and bringing it back to share locally, much as Barry's research team did with their science-wiki posts.

In this chapter, we look more closely at this fundamental process of knowledge-building and how writers and composers work together in digital spaces to build knowledge-focused rhetorical relationships.

Exploring
Collaborative Learning

When we write in informal contexts, when we're texting or tweeting or posting online with friends and family, we often decide very quickly what we want to say and why. So quickly, in fact, we don't really dwell on our purposes for writing or consider what background information they might need to understand us. However, taking a closer look at some of these informal exchanges, we can see that, just as in more formal, public conversations, we always make rhetorical decisions about what information to share, how to share it, and why.

Sharing Quick Bits of Information

An informal, everyday texting exchange between friends is a good place to observe the process of informal **knowledge-building** in action. Here's an example focusing on the **what**—on the knowledge and information that is being shared within this moment, and in the **where** of a two-person friendship being sustained in this mode—within a particular rhetorical situation:

knowledge-building
the construction of
shared understandings

> >Out Xmas shopping and just drove by a bunch of Xmas trees flocked in purple, pink, and blue snow! Is that tree abuse?
>
> >definitely
>
> >thought so

In this exchange, the literal **what** of the conversation is about Christmas trees "flocked" with colored snow and the possibility of "tree abuse." Understanding the **what** of a conversation is necessary to make sense of it, but it is often just an entry point in understanding how shared knowledge is continually maintained through informal exchanges like this one. In addressing the **what** and making sense of what's being talked about literally, other questions open up about the shape and purpose of this seemingly insignificant exchange, **why** it's happening, and **how** it's unfolding. Without actually knowing the participants we can only guess, but quick exchanges like this, sharing a random moment, are typically used to support a friendship, to express intimacy and suggest "I know you well enough to guess at what might amuse you" or just "I'm thinking about you."

In such informal exchanges, the purpose is likely to be an interpersonal one more than an idea-sharing one. This exchange seems intended to maintain a friendship by affirming a shared perspective on the world, a shared sense of humor, and a shared sensibility. And the **how** is related to this purpose: using an ever-present cell phone to share something quickly in the moment.

Informal exchanges between friends and family make sense to those involved because they are backed by underlying, usually tacit, shared knowledge and a larger shared context. In the above texting exchange, the friends can assume a **shared why**, a mutual purpose behind their interaction. They can also assume a shared understanding of **how**—both general texting conventions (like abbreviating words and phrases) and their friendship-specific use of humor, which in turn shapes the actual information being shared in the words of this exchange.

Group chat technologies and social media sites like Twitter and Snapchat have helped turn texting into one of our most basic literacies. tweets, like texts, have to be brief (less than 140 characters) and they have a similar **how** of abbreviating words and compressing sentences. Tweets, however, are usually intended for a larger public audience of followers (and embarrassing moments arise when people accidently post private information). Snapchat, on the other hand, isn't public and messages are deleted shortly after they are received, leaving no record of the exchange. The content literally disappears, but the relationships remain.

No matter the media or platform, whether a texting exchange, a note passed in class, or a tweet, these informal, daily conversations we have with one another are a central aspect of our experience of literacy and the social process of knowledge-building. And sometimes they have that as their primary purpose. To the right are a couple of examples of tweets from danah boyd (@zephoria), sent over two days.

Speaking to a public audience of followers who are likely to know her work, boyd focuses on sharing just the essential information about her new paper within a rhetorical situation that includes the constraints of Twitter: it addresses research ethics and focuses on a study of "emotional contagion" on Facebook, with an abbreviated link to the actual study (Figure 5.1). She doesn't describe the paper at greater length, assuming that her followers will most likely share the knowledge that her work focuses on teens and can make some meaning from the words "emotional contagion." Boyd also writes as if the existence of the study is already shared knowledge, referring to "the" Facebook study rather than "a" Facebook study, indicating there is a specific study that her audience and followers are potentially aware of. **How** she communicates reinforces the purposes boyd and her followers share. Using a platform like Twitter to send and receive updates on her latest work shows she's immersed in the social media she studies, and reinforces the importance of social media to contemporary communication, scholarly as well as personal.

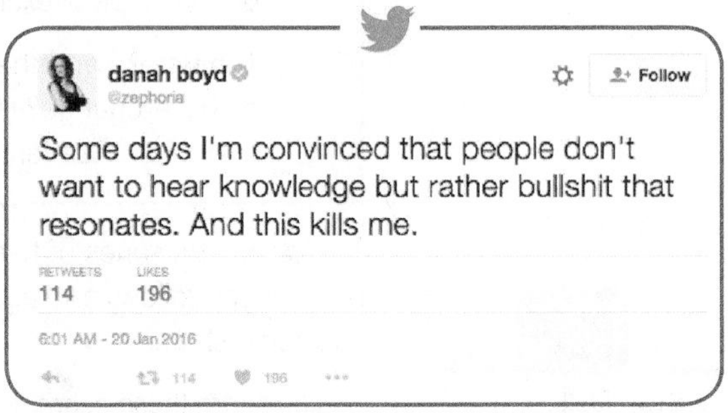

Figure 5.1: danah boyd's January 18, 2016, tweet

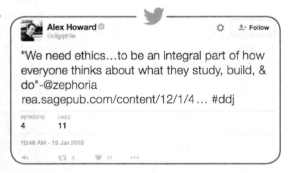

Figure 5.2: danah boyd's January 20, 2016, tweet

The second tweet (Figure 5.2), although addressed to the same followers, seems to have a different purpose: perhaps to let off steam about something happening in the larger cultural context (the fact that it was posted on January 20, 2016, in the middle of a contentious presidential campaign, offers one possible explanation). While her stance was impersonal on the first tweet, here the information boyd is sharing is about her personal response to what's happening at this cultural moment, and her use of informal language, "bullshit" as opposed to "knowledge," and "this kills me" foregrounds that emotional content. Interestingly, more of her followers have retweeted or starred (liked) this second tweet, reminding us of how both the informational and interpersonal functions of knowledge-sharing work together to shape our rhetorical relationships with one another.

Figure 5.3: Extension of danah boyd's tweet

Twitter also enables users to post tweets that relate to other Twitter users, building a common thread of shared knowledge, and there are many such tweets for @zephoria (boyd's Twitter handle). For example, boyd's first tweet above, was extended in Figure 5.3, with a quotation from the paper boyd mentioned.

Such exchanges, as facilitated by different types of social media, help to further our publicly shared knowledge about particular areas of interest. They also raise the question of **where** a text goes (in this case, a tweet), who picks up on it, and for what purposes.

See Part II
where the topic of circulation through media is explored.

Digital Toolbox
See Part IV, Section 3

See Chapter 9
for more about joining
conversations in digital
contexts.

INQUIRY

#1: Seeing how knowledge is evoked and shared in brief digital exchanges

Drawing on one or more examples from your own texting exchanges, group chats, or tweets, identify the following.

➤ The **what** and the **shared what**: both the specific new information and ideas of this exchange and the underlying knowledge both participants can assume to be shared.

➤ The **why** and the **shared why**: both the immediate purposes of these participants in this moment and the larger background of purposes they share. How do these shared purposes affect what information and ideas appear in the participants' words?

➤ The **how** and the **shared how**: both the immediate choices being made in this exchange (like including particular details or using humor) and the larger shared background of ways to interact with others through brief digital exchanges. Again, how do these understandings of how to carry out this type of exchange with this person shape the actual information and ideas being shared?

➤ The **where** and the **shared where**: What is the context that is shaping the what, why, and how of this exchange? How does the community, the platform, the particular moment, and immediate rhetorical situation (the context) affect the information being shared and how?

Then look at a series of tweets from a public figure from one of your areas of interest (perhaps a musician or actor you follow) and again look at what knowledge is shared and assumed, and at why, how, and where it is being shared.

As you share these examples in a group or as a class, what larger shared understandings about such informal written exchanges in a digital environment do you find? How might such exchanges complement spoken exchanges, and why might you typically choose this means of communication (versus a phone call or a Facebook post)? What do you discover about more public tweets (it's also possible to create a private Twitter account) and the expectations and understandings shared by the particular Twitter users and their followers? Do you find that information is shared differently in private vs. public exchanges?

Sharing Ideas in the Digital Spaces of Classrooms

Classes, whether they meet in an online or a physical space, offer a different rhetorical situation from more interpersonally focused rhetorical relationships. They are built around a course subject with a focus on knowledge-building. In typical classroom discussions, whether they are online or face to face, most participants don't know one another well. Because their purpose is focused on learning, the typical **what** of classroom discussions tends to focus more on specific information or ideas related to course content rather than on maintaining more interpersonal bonds.

Here's an example from an online discussion from a first-year writing course about students' experiences of digital writing, with part of one writer's initial post and two responses from different classmates. In the first post (Figure 5.4), writer Rachel McFall describes how she uses digital writing in her life and why, explaining that she uses texts, posts, and email "to instantly shoot off [her] thoughts," emphasizing the immediacy of social media, but also that writing (rather than speaking) allows her to take her time and "rewrite something that it is difficult to put in words."

The Freedom of Digital Writing
by Rachel McFall - Wednesday, January 15, 2014, 11:16 AM

Digital writing is a large part of my life. Like many others, my phone is glued to my hand and I am on my laptop at least once a day. I communicate through text, Facebook messaging, Twitter posts, and email which means I am always using some form of digital writing. I am not a big talker in person or on the phone so being able to communicate through writing is important because it allows me a comfortable way to keep in touch with my relatives in other states and gives me an opportunity to hold long conversations with my friends. I love the idea of being able to instantly shoot off my thoughts and the other person is able to see what I want to say almost immediately. There is no waiting to see the other person or waiting for them to answer a phone and then trying to remember my thoughts and trying to find the right words to say out loud. I can also take my time with digital writing to rewrite something that is difficult to put in words or come up with a response instead of being forced to say whatever comes to mind like in a face-to-face conversation. Digital writing connects me with others easily and allows me the freedom of expression I would not have been able to have in person.

Figure 5.4: Rachel's description of digital writing in her life

In this classroom context where students are exploring the common topic of digital literacy and writing, there is already a larger context of **shared knowledge**—a shared **what** that frames all of the contributions to this conversation. Students are also beginning to build rhetorical relationships that are both informative and interpersonal with a sense of **shared purpose**, a shared **why** that will go on through the course and beyond. And we can see, in the responses that follow, that each person responds directly to Rachel's post by building on details that resonate for her or him, and in a way that helps foster more interpersonal connections appropriate to a course context, beginning with addressing Rachel directly by her name.

Virginia, who doesn't know Rachel personally, also ends with a move that can help to build their online relationship for possible future exchanges, saying she is "looking forward" to reading more of Rachel's posts (Figure 5.5).

Virginia picks up on two ideas from Rachel's initial post: being able to take your time when writing, and being or not being a "talker." You can see how she echoes Rachel's phrases and adds her own points from her own experience to them, making the qualification about not communicating digitally about sensitive issues, for example, but adding the imagery of someone making faces as a possible counterargument.

Re: The Freedom of Digital Writing
by Virginia Jeffords - Tuesday, January 21, 2014, 7:34 PM

Rachel,

You definitely hit on one of my favorite aspects of digital writing, that is, being able to take your time. This is particularly useful when it comes to writing important documents like meaning letters, essays, and creative pieces. I've found myself in the same predicament, not being able to read what I'd written because I'd crossed it out and rewritten it so many times that it just becomes either a large massive scribble or just a page of smudge. I don't often like to communicate digitally about sensitive issues--extreme examples being like breakups, fights, or professing my undying love--because I worry that my words may be more easily misconstrued; however, if I simply cannot do it face to face, for whatever reason, I do appreciate the luxury of having the time to organize my thoughts and rearrange them until I am certain they are perfect.

Touching on your point about not being a talker, I love talking, but I find that I can open up even more, like you, through digital text. It is so much easier to say something to a computer (Ipad, Iphone, etc), just type it in and hit send, than say it in person, whether it's good, bad, exciting, depressing. It is just so much easier to open up to something that doesn't make faces and whose only response is to critique your sentence structure, not the content. I think this can be both good and bad, but I certainly understand exactly where your coming from.

Thank you for sharing. Looking forward to reading more from you!

-Virginia

Figure 5.5: Virginia's response to Rachel's post

In this second response, Nicole, who does know Rachel outside of this course, reaffirms that fact and builds off of it to add new observations about Rachel's feelings about digital writing, adding the phrase "new sense of comfort," and adding her own related experience as well. She, too, looks forward to their ongoing relationship in the context of the course: "I can't wait to see your first paper" (Figure 5.6).

Re: The Freedom of Digital Writing
by Nicole Birkbeck - Thursday, January 30, 2014, 6:31 PM

Rachel, I loved this piece. Maybe the fact that I know you, makes me like it a little more. I know how you interact socially, so I am completely able to see what you mean when you say you feel a sense of comfort in writing digitally. I know I say what I like no matter who is around me, I guess I just never really get nervous, but I agree with you, that writing is a new sense of comfort. It's something that I can't explain. And you are 100% right about having a conversation digitally and it being easier to find the right words. When I write, things come out a lot easier then if I were to say. I guess messages get distorted between my brain and my mouth, and things never come out as I'd like. Even though I may make typos when writing, it still comes out better. I can't wait to see your first paper.

Figure 5.6: Nicole's response to Rachel's post

In exchanges like this, the participants apply what they know from face-to-face conversations—about picking up on what someone else has said, taking turns, and making your own points relevant so others don't just say "Huh?" or "So what?" and about making moves that establish an interpersonal connection in this online rhetorical space. In doing so, they show how they're working out a shared way of communicating (the **how** of this space), as well as a shared **what** and **why** for this particular context **(where)**. Like Facebook or Twitter, online discussion spaces for courses give shape to the communication that takes place there, and these spaces have given rise to the discussion post genre we discussed in Chapter 3.

As you can see from the online discussion example, many of the ways in which we communicate in digital contexts build off of the strategies we already use in face-to-face or print contexts. When we think more specifically about sharing knowledge and building ideas in digital contexts, we find the same thing—that many of the strategies we use in face-to-face or print contexts form the basis for our digital exchanges as well.

INQUIRY

#2: Knowledge-building on a course site

???

Post your own reflections on your experience with knowledge-building on an online discussion site (or add to written classroom round-robin idea-building with each person, adding to a previous person's reflections on paper).

Then, drawing on examples from your own posts and responses, see what you can identify about how you and your classmates build on one another's ideas and information to create shared knowledge, and how you build shared purposes and begin to shape and identify shared ways within the rhetorical space of your course.

Digital Toolbox
See Part IV, Section 2

Making Connections
Learning and Knowing in a Digital World

Writers and thinkers have long noted the potential of the internet for sharing and collaboration. As a networked communications technology, the web enables us to engage in knowledge-sharing on a new, global scale, helping us draw on the "wisdom of crowds" (Surowiecki[5:1]). Through the global reach of the web, many individuals and local communities can exchange ideas and contribute to our general knowledge, offering more diverse perspectives than most local communities could offer.

crowdsourcing
the process of constructing shared understandings by a wider community on digital platforms

Wikipedia offers one example of such crowd-based "wisdom" and collaborative knowledge-building, also referred to as **crowdsourcing**. There the collective knowledge of the world community is gathered and continually refined by ordinary people, both professionals and amateurs, who feel they have something to add to a particular topic, replacing the knowledge of the few experts who are hired to write entries for traditional encyclopedias. Volunteer editors check for accuracy and note where references are needed to support the points being made, bringing still more knowledge into the discussion of a topic, as the expertise of many adds to, builds on, and corrects the knowledge of others.

We tap into this network of collective knowledge all the time. Think of those times when you're sitting around with friends and a question comes up about a world event, a song lyric, or the birthdate of a celebrity. Someone does a quick search on a smartphone to find the already shared information on the internet, and that information is used to support and build on the conversation underway. Or you read a review on Yelp about a restaurant you might go to, on Amazon for a book you might buy, or Rotten Tomatoes for a movie you might see. And you are likely to have made your own contributions to this pool of shared knowledge, contributions that are then available to anyone in the world with an internet connection.

INQUIRY

#3: Knowledge-sharing on public online sites

???

Find a site online where knowledge-building is occurring. This could be a discussion board, a review site, a Wikipedia entry, or a blog with comments—any site where individuals come together to share and exchange ideas. What is considered knowledge here, and how is it constructed in this space?

Knowledge-Building in Learning Communities

In a moment, you will look at two related blog posts on digital learning written by one of the authors of the book you are currently reading, Ellie Kutz. The posts originally appeared on the *Educational Technology Newsletter* hosted by the University of Massachusetts Boston (Figure 5.7). Although written for an audience of teachers interested in how digital media is changing how we learn, the posts are relevant to our conversation here for the way they illustrate knowledge-building in action.

Figure 5.7: Masthead of UMass Boston's Educational Technology Newsletter

Sidenote

Apps like Pages or Dropbox have their origins in our real-world experiences.

. . . .
knowledge-sharing
the process of sharing
information with a
wider community

In writing these posts, Ellie was doing a form of **knowledge-sharing** common in academic settings: reporting back to her university community on something she'd read elsewhere. In this case, she was reporting on an article by John Seely Brown, a researcher and thinker who was the chief scientist at Xerox Corporation, to an audience of readers who might be interested in his ideas about how learning is changing in the digital world. In "Growing Up Digital,"[5:2] which was originally published in *Change*, a higher education journal, Brown was presenting what he had learned about learning at Xerox to an audience of college and university professionals. Ellie's purpose was to share Brown's ideas with other faculty at her university (who might follow up, as you might, by reading Brown's original article, which is included in Part I Additional Readings). Our purpose in including her post here is to give you some ways of thinking about your own learning and also to show you how this academic genre of reporting on an article can work to bring new ideas into a local conversation, just as googling something can bring new information and ideas into a conversation you are having with your friends.

. . . .
double-entry notebook
a two column method
of keeping reading
notes and reflections

Related to the academic literacy practice of reporting back on something you read is the knowledge-building strategy of using a **double-entry notebook** for taking notes on that text and capturing some key ideas to discuss or write about later. Here are its elements.

- Divide a page into two columns.

- Use one column to copy words, passages, and ideas from the text—ones that are most interesting or inspiring for your purposes and most likely to contribute to the common inquiry of your classroom community (and noting page numbers or location). Copying bits of text in this way also serves as an aid to active memory.

- Use the second column as your own active comment space, where you can note why these words interested you and how they might make a contribution to the conversation you're having in your mind with the writer or will have in a classroom discussion, and make some of the moves of connecting, elaborating, questioning, and speculating.

The double-entry notebook goes beyond annotating insofar as it resituates words and ideas in your own framework of thought. It provides a way to be attentive both to the original argument of the piece you are reading and its logic, and to your own purposes as well. The double-entry format, which is also used for observation notes—for capturing the words of an exchange, or a description of an image, or the movements in a video or in a classroom—allows a "continuing audit of meaning" (Berthoff[5:3])—a kind of ongoing dialogue between what you read, observe, or hear, and what you think as you read or observe.

Figure 5.8 shows a few of Ellie's double entry notes from her first reading of Brown's article, with his phrases on one side and her reflections and comments on the other.

Double-Entry Notes: "Growing Up Digital," John Seely Brown

Excerpts ⟶

1. Brown's subtitle: "How the Web Changes Work, Education, and the Ways People Learn"

2. "a transformative medium, as important as electricity." (Brown 2)

3. "A new learning ecology." (2)

4. "Two-way." (2)

5. "This past century's concept of 'literacy' grew out of our intense belief in text, a focus enhanced by the power of one particular technology—the typewriter" (12).

6. "With the web, we suddenly have a medium that honors multiple forms of intelligence—abstract, textual, visual, musical, social, and kinesthetic. As educators, we now have a chance to construct a medium that enables all young people to become engaged in their ideal way of learning" (19).

Reflections/comments ⟶

1. B makes his argument clear from his subtitle, that he thinks the web fundamentally changes all of this.

2. This is a big claim!

3. A whole system of texts and writing, with everything interrelated

4. But the web wasn't really two-way at first; it just pushed more information at us (Web 1.0). Web 2.0 captures the idea of the social, interactive web, the 2nd generation web.

5. Yes. Literacy was all about words and dominant discourses; now literacies/multiliteracies reflect different ways of using and representing language and other means of representation like video, sounds, images.

6. This article was written almost 15 years ago. How much have we used the web in education to support different intelligences/different ways of learning?

Figure 5.8: Ellie's "Growing Up Digital" double-entry notes

You can see that Ellie sometimes agrees with Brown's points, sometimes elaborates on them, sometimes questions them, and sometimes reflects on the implications for her own inquiry about how we're now educating college learners for a digital world.

Reading about Learning and Knowing in a Digital Age

After reading Brown's article, Ellie posted her two-part discussion of it as the opening section of a newsletter issue with a series of posts[L5:1] on the topic of digital learners and online learning communities. Her immediate context was that series of posts within a larger context of a community conversation at her university about teaching and learning in digital environments (and in that context, where she is known personally by many of her colleagues, she writes as "Ellie.") And her purpose was to bring useful knowledge from a world outside of her university community into that local community's conversations about learning.

BEFORE READING:
Using double-entry posts

As you read the following posts to the *UMass Boston Educational Technology Newsletter,* keep your own set of double-entry notes. (You can use the Table function in Word to create a two-column table, or simply draw a line down the middle of a notebook page.) Note key points you want to comment on in one column, and make your own comments and reflections in the other. As you read about what John Seely Brown found about learners who were "growing up digital" and about how he expected new literacy and learning environments to look, reflect on your own experience. Are there points that connect to your own experience as a digital learner, or places where you find a disconnect? How much have the learning environments you've been part of reflected Brown's understanding of what was likely to be happening in a digital age?

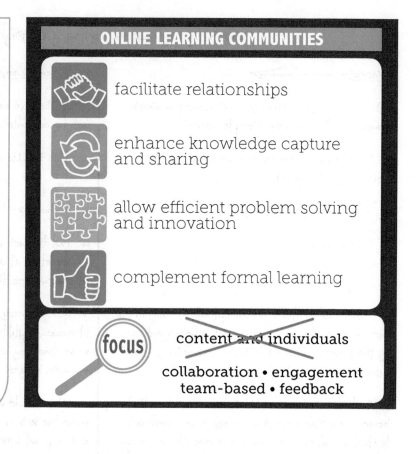

ONLINE LEARNING COMMUNITIES

facilitate relationships

enhance knowledge capture and sharing

allow efficient problem solving and innovation

complement formal learning

focus ~~content and individuals~~

collaboration • engagement team-based • feedback

READING

"Part I. Overview: Digital Learners and Online Learning Communities"[5:4]
by Ellie Kutz
UMass Boston Educational Technology Newsletter, March 26, 2012

© 2016 John S. Dykes c/o theispot

Over ten years ago the innovation guru, John Seely Brown, called our attention to the ways in which learners who were growing up in a digital age were likely to be different from earlier learners with his much-cited and now classic essay: "Growing Up Digital. How the Web Changes Work, Education, and the Ways People Learn" (*Change* March/April 2000). In many of my conversations with faculty about how they are using technology to support their students' learning, a recurrent question is "How do we keep our students involved and engaged online?" To think more about that question, I decided, for this issue, to return to Brown's essay, to revisit his useful and still-relevant insights, and to explore the relationship between digital learners, community, and our classroom practices.

Brown makes several larger points:

· That the web offers a significantly different medium of communication,

READING

- That learners who have grown up in web environments have developed new literacy and learning practices that can be used to support their learning, and
- That the creation and sharing of knowledge goes on most effectively when learners are actively constructing their understandings within communities formed with others who have shared interests and purposes.

I'll briefly review what he had to say about the first two points, but most of this issue will focus on the third, considering

- How the Web has changed literacy, learning, and knowledge-sharing
- What keeps students connected to online communities and what can we learn from the non-academic ones they participate in
- What our faculty have discovered about effective practices for teaching online
- What we need to consider in constructing and managing effective online discussions
- Other digital resources that will be available to faculty through Blackboard.

"Part II. How the Web Has Changed Literacy and Learning"5:5

John Seely Brown was one of the first to see the web as a "transformative medium for social practices" and to explore how the characteristics of the web as a medium of communication would affect learning and learners. What's different about the web as a medium, according to Brown?

- It easily supports two-way communication vs. more typically one-way communication of print or even of older audio-visual media such as movies or television.
- It typically draws on multiple intelligences, "abstract, visual, musical, social, and kinesthetic."
- It can link the efforts of many people (who needn't be in the same physical space) in a common project.

Brown and his colleagues invited 15-year-old digital learners to participate as researchers at Xerox's research center, and identified, through observations of their work, some dimensional shifts in their literacy practices. For these digital learners, they found:

- Literacy involves image and screen literacy: "The ability to 'read' multimedia texts and to feel comfortable with new, multiple-media genres."

- "The new literacy, beyond text and image, is one of information navigation. The real literacy of tomorrow entails the ability to be your own personal reference librarian—to know how to navigate through confusing, complex information spaces and feel comfortable doing so. 'Navigation' may well be the main form of literacy of the 21st century."
- Learning involves a shift from learning in an authority-based, lecture-oriented environment to learning that is "discovery-based"– e.g. web surfing for both entertainment and information.
- Learning is active, involving mucking about vs. being told, and requires making good judgments as you find what you need and build on it.
- Learning has a social as well as a cognitive dimension.

In his essay, Brown reminds us that knowledge is created in communities where participants share both explicit knowledge (knowing what—key concepts, facts, and theories) and tacit knowledge (knowing how—how to shape an interesting question, offer convincing proof) and that people learn the latter from being immersed in a community of practice (a community whose participants are involved in a shared knowledge-creating enterprise) and coming to understand its ways of seeing, interpreting, and acting. The role of members in such a community is both collaborative and participatory and outsiders can become insiders over time by gradually taking on a larger role (moving from lurking to participating in online forums, for example).

One example that Brown offers of such a knowledge-creating community is one formed by repair reps at Xerox, who, in discussing repair problems, kept adding fragments to an evolving process. This "multi-person storytelling process" was augmented with a web-based platform for peer review, so that the stories could be refined and connected to other stories to create a repository of relevant knowledge. Many such knowledge-creating communities now exist in both professional and educational contexts. But Brown also saw the virtual communities that were starting to emerge on the web around areas of shared interest as offering a model for what learning communities might look like in the future—communities where participants would be both consumers and producers of knowledge, interact with many others, and not be bounded by physical proximity. Brown anticipated a shift from using technology to support the individual to using technology to support relationships between individuals and thus to support social learning and even a general culture of learning.

READING

Since Brown wrote his essay, the Web has continued to evolve in the ways he identified and has become an increasingly social environment, while we've come to recognize some of the new literacy practices that learners draw on and need, both outside and inside the classroom. But while Brown envisioned a world of virtual communities rich in knowledge-sharing, the developers of Blackboard and similar systems for higher education were focused on "learning management." We might ask, then, "How are our faculty creating effective online learning communities within that platform, involving the participants, our students, in a knowledge-sharing enterprise?" ■

AFTER READING:
Sharing double-entry notes and elaborating on an entry

Share a few of your double-entry notes with some classmates. What kinds of different issues did you each look at? Did you connect to any of Brown's ideas about knowledge-sharing communities (as captured by Ellie)? Is there any overlap in your observations, your choice of passages? How are your responses similar/different?

After you've had a chance to discuss your double-entry notes with one another, choose one entry and elaborate on it in light of your conversation with your classmates and any new thinking you have done about it. What has changed in your understanding since first noting the passage? What other observations, experiences, arguments, or insights emerge as you think deeper about this passage?

Drawing on Content for New Purposes

Ellie makes certain writing moves as she draws on Brown's essay to motivate the faculty at her university to create effective digital learning environments for their students. Her moves include the following.

summarizing
putting another's idea, point, or argument in your own words

➤ **SUMMARIZING.** Ellie first identifies key points that Brown has made. She can't assume her readers share any knowledge of Brown's work or Brown's article, so she has to create that shared knowledge if she wants to build on it to create her own conversation about digital learning and learners. One way she captures his many points is by making bulleted lists, like the one in her first post:

- that the web offers a significantly different medium of communication;

- that learners who have grown up in web environments have developed new literacy and learning practices that can be used to support their learning; and

- that the creation and sharing of knowledge goes on most effectively when learners are actively constructing their understandings within communities formed with others who have shared interests and purposes.

And she summarizes as well his key points about the literacy and learning practices that his researchers discovered as they worked with the 15-year-old co-researchers at Xerox.

quoting and paraphrasing
including someone's exact words or restating the idea in your own words

➤ **QUOTING AND PARAPHRASING.** Beyond summarizing Brown's key points, Ellie sometimes restates his ideas in her own words, and sometimes quotes his words directly to more exactly capture his thinking. She quotes his definition of literacy as "The ability to 'read' multimedia texts and to feel comfortable with new, multiple-media genres." But she defines his term "community of practice" in her own words: "a community whose participants are involved in a shared knowledge-creating enterprise" to give her community of readers a clearer sense of its meaning.

➤ RESITUATING **IDEAS IN A NEW CONVERSATION.** Ellie resituates Brown's points in her own ongoing conversation with other faculty about teaching in a digital age, asking questions related to their own practices, such as "What keeps students connected to online communities and what can we learn from the non-academic ones they participate in?"

resituating
using someone's ideas for new rhetorical purposes

INQUIRY

#4: Triple-entry notes

At this point, you'll want to think about entering this process of summarizing, resituating and commenting. To examine your thoughts on Brown's work and Ellie's take on it, create a triple-entry notebook (Figure 5.9), with a column for Brown's ideas, a second for Ellie's comments about Brown, and a third column for your own. Ellie is writing in a particular rhetorical situation, as a campus leader in helping other faculty think about how to use digital technologies effectively in their teaching. What do you see about her rhetorical purposes and how they have guided what she's selected to share from Brown's article?

As you fill in this chart, you should pay careful attention to who is saying what as you think about who you'll want to echo and extend. As you share information in academic contexts, crediting people for their ideas is a central move, and this process will help you tease out who said and stressed what as you think about how you want to react.

Triple-Entry Notes on "Growing Up Digital"

➝ Excerpts

Brown's subtitle: "How the Web Changes Work, Education, and the Ways People Learn"

➝ Ellie's take

B makes his argument clear from his subtitle, that he thinks the web fundamentally changes all of this.

➝ Reflections/comments

This seems to come up against boyd's idea that teens are acting in ways they always have. How fundamental are the changes the web and networked communications have introduced?

Figure 5.9: Triple-entry notes on "Growing Up Digital"

INQUIRY

#5: Reflecting on your own digital learning practices

Which of these points about learning apply to you? Reflect on your own learning in digital environments, whether you are learning something for an academic purpose (a class assignment or activity) or a personal or social purpose. Make notes on your process, your thinking and choices, and on what guides you from one moment to the next. What can you say about your own digital learning practices and the process of building knowledge with others?

links

INQUIRY

#6: Looking at the **how**—articles in context

While a restatement of the content of Brown's article could as easily have appeared in print, it was composed for an online, blog-based newsletter. Look at these posts in their original context. Consider the list of articles that appeared in this issue of the newsletter, and then look again at Ellie's posts about Brown.[5:2, 5:3] Do you see ways that the digital context might have influenced the **how** of these posts? Are there writing moves that suggest Ellie had an online vs. print audience in mind? (Ellie adapted this blog platform to a newsletter format by setting it up so all posts for one issue appeared at once.) Then take a quick look at Brown's original article (in Part I Additional Readings), which was originally written for a print journal, although it is available online. How do you think these differences of media have affected each writer's choices? Are there ways in which Brown's article might have been prepared differently for an online audience, or do you think his own composition practice was shaped by his attention to web environments?

Collaborative Knowing

One of Brown's key points that Ellie picks up on in her blog post is that learning and knowing are collaborative activities. As Brown notes,

> It's common for us to think that all knowledge resides in individual heads, but when we factor in the tacit dimension—especially as it relates to practices—we quickly realize how much more we can know than is bounded by our own knowledge. Much of knowing is brought forth in action, through participation—in the world, with other people, around real problems. A lot of our know-how or knowing comes into being through participating in our community(ies) of practice. (15)[5:6]

Web environments have made such collaborative sharing and knowing much easier, across boundaries of time and space. Online course platforms can support collaborative knowing in academic settings. But Brown believes we can learn a lot about learning by looking at the communities that get established in other environments as well. The copy machine repair reps at Xerox showed the value of such shared knowledge-building in that context. At Xerox they found that these tech reps went through several stages in building shared knowledge.

- The tech reps around the world had insights about effective repairs.
- They entered their insights into a common database to create shared documents.
- They reviewed the content of the documents in a peer review process, validating the insights.
- Their insights became part of the shared knowledge of the field, while the authors of individual stories and insights gained **social capital** by being recognized as more central members of this community.

According to Brown, this process was going to save Xerox as much as $100 million per year in improved service (which we hope was shared with the reps who created this "intellectual capital"). But the steps of this process are ones that can work in many situations, and they are much like the ones that have proven useful in the composition classroom.

Sidenote

In a community of practice, people learn by working together, collaboratively.

social capital
symbolic value established when something is important to a given community

> **INQUIRY**
>
> ???
>
> ## #7: Observing collaborative learning
>
> Where have you experienced collaborative learning outside of the classroom? How was important knowledge identified, shared, brought into the conversation from outside of the group, built on, and extended? What identifiable elements shaped how participants did this? What discussion or literacy practices supported the group's learning? What lessons can you bring from that experience to collaboration in a classroom community? To working together online?

Composing

Reporting Back

With collaborative knowing, just pooling the knowledge everyone brings, as Brown's tech reps did, can lead to rich new understandings. But to grow beyond that pool of knowledge, members of the community need to seek out and bring back new information and ideas. That's how Barry's Gateway Science Seminar worked, with teams of students who found articles that helped them make sense of topics like genetic modification or HeLa cells, and who shared what they'd learned with the larger class on the course wiki. And that's how Ellie used the EdTech newsletter, reporting, or having others report, on technology and learning across campus, but also from the larger world, and hosting face-to-face and wiki discussions of what faculty were learning, trying, and discovering. Collaborating in such activities—the information-seeking, the reading, the writing, the sharing of developing understandings—reinforces individual learning while expanding the knowledge of the group.

Here we'll focus on what you might contribute to the shared knowledge of your classroom community as you work with the moves of the "reporting back" genre. But such reporting back is just one step in a collaborative enterprise where you're guided by your sense of your own learning community and what will be of interest there—of what its members might want to know about learning, composing, and practicing the new literacies of a world that's become much more digital since Brown wrote his article, and even since Ellie wrote hers.

⟵ WRITING MOVES

Inquiring and Inventing

We've repeatedly pointed to the influence of the **where**—of the context—on any exchange, and that becomes particularly visible in any situation of collaborative learning and knowing. As you undertake the work of bringing new information and ideas back to your classroom community, you will be guided as much by that context as by your own interests, balancing the two in your own reporting back. Within the common frame of our shared inquiry into how so many aspects of our lives—our writing, reading, and composing; our social practices involving literacy; our learning (and teaching); and even our social identities—are being reshaped in a digital world, there is much you can learn and share from a variety of sources.

1 Generating a list of possible topics and sources

Before you try to locate a source (a text, a lecture, a YouTube video) to report back on to your class, you'll want to generate a list of possible topics to explore within our common frame—topics that have caught your attention and perhaps the attention of your classmates. And even this initial list could be a collaborative one. You might pick up on the ideas and sources represented in this chapter, turning to the Part I Additional Readings to read Brown's original article (which goes into all of the points that Ellie summarized in much more depth). You might turn to the *UMass Boston EdTech Newsletter* to see what other posts appeared there, with tags like digital storytelling, writing, and multimedia. You might Google topics on your list, or search within news sources like *The Huffington Post, Salon,* or *The New York Times* (and news articles often point to other research and researchers). Or you could search YouTube, where you'll find a number of videos on digital learning and literacy and social media, including a talk by danah boyd on **social media and teens**,[L5:4] for example, or TED talks (at **ted.com**) with many talks on a range of topics on technology, education, and design by high-level speakers like **John Seely Brown**.[L5:5] Maybe a talk on a relevant topic is being given on your campus. You might even look up a topic in Wikipedia. Your source doesn't have to be a scholarly article, but you'll want to find something that adds to the knowledge that

links 🔗 ▶

has already been shared in your classroom community. You are likely to go back and forth a bit between topics and sources to find a match.

2 Considering shared interests as you locate a piece to report back on

Once you have a sense of what you would like your source to address, you'll want to read through it or listen to it carefully, keeping a double-entry notebook to capture key points (and if you're listening to a talk you'll find yourself replaying it to capture the words, and hitting pause to take time to connect and question and reflect). You'll want to note sections that speak to you and that seem especially interesting. But you'll also want to keep your classmates' interests in mind. Are there issues or questions you seem to circle around as a class? These are things you might want to report back on.

WRITING MOVES ◀

Drafting and Shaping

Once you have done some work deciding what you will report back on, you will consider how to share new information in ways that will extend the work of your classroom community. Again there are some common moves within this reporting back genre.

1 Representing another's work

When you report back what has been said before, you will need to represent another's ideas in clear ways, as Ellie does when she explains the work John Seely Brown has done looking at digital learners. In order to do this, you initially need to work toward your own understandings, and then share those understandings with others, and your double-entry notebook should help with this process.

- **Summarizing.** If you want to bring back the content of a longer work like Brown's article, you'll need to summarize it, representing its key points in an abbreviated form, as Ellie did by listing Brown's points in her first post. In this case you'll find it useful to create an informal outline of the writer's or speaker's key points and

arguments. For summarizing a shorter work or a useful section of a longer one, you might find that you've captured the key points in your double-entry notebook.

- **Paraphrasing and quoting.** Sometimes putting the writer's or speaker's ideas in your own words works best for sharing them in your own setting, and Ellie mostly **paraphrased** Brown as she represented his points. But you might sometimes want to emphasize a point or share the sense of the writer's words by **quoting** them, as Ellie did with Brown's words about navigation as a new literacy.

> *"The new literacy, beyond text and image, is one of information navigation. The real literacy of tomorrow entails the ability to be your own personal reference librarian—to know how to navigate through confusing, complex*

paraphrasing
putting a specific point made by someone else in your own words and citing it

quoting
drawing on another's exact words in your writing, using quotation marks and a citation

information spaces and feel comfortable doing so. 'Navigation' may well be the main form of literacy of the 21st century."

2 Contributing your meanings and questions

Providing a clear summary or paraphrase, along with a few quotations, isn't enough. You also need to do something with the information you share to make it useful in your classroom context. To do this, turn to the commenting side of your double-entry notebook, where you've been making the generative moves of connecting, elaborating, questioning, and speculating. How do the points you've summarized, the ideas you've paraphrased or quoted, connect to what you've been thinking or what your class has read or discussed? What else can you say to invite your classmates to rethink currently held understandings of digital literacy practices? What new questions does your source suggest that you would like to bring back to your classmates? What new ideas or conclusions does this source point you to? Ellie brings Brown's ideas into the conversations she's been having with other faculty about the question "How do we keep our students involved and engaged online?" and she uses that local question to guide what follows.

When you report back on what has been said, you bring others' views back to your classroom community and share them as a way of considering other perspectives to enrich your shared understandings.

3 Resituating your new understandings in your local context

Your context is likely to provide the questions that frame your inquiry, but also some questions that derive from what you've learned and shared. What will you and your classmates think about together with the new knowledge you've brought back? Ellie asks how her faculty colleagues can use a course management system like Blackboard to create "effective online learning communities within that platform, involving the participants, our students, in a knowledge-sharing enterprise?"—a topic that is picked up in the next article in that issue of the newsletter.

> ❝ The new literacy, beyond text and image, is one of information navigation. ❞

WRITING MOVES ◄

Revising and Publishing

The central purpose of reporting back is to share ideas and understandings with a particular community of thinkers. So, as you share your report, you'll be doing so with others within the same rhetorical situation and extending your existing rhetorical relationships by sharing new information. Your "reporting back" is intended to be exploratory and generative, to push the thinking of your group, rather than to present a fixed set of conclusions. As you share it, you'll be asking for input toward that purpose.

1 Asking for input

As you begin to shape your report, ask a classmate to read it with an eye to how you are extending shared understandings in your classroom community. The following questions will help.

- How am I building upon your current understandings as a member of this class?

- What additional information do you need about what has been said by the person or people whose work I'm drawing on?

- How does this information seem to build upon, challenge, or extend the conversations central to our class?

- What else do you need to understand this report, and where else do you think I should take it to be useful to our community?

2 Revising based on input

After you have a sense of how a classmate sees your report speaking to the current conversations important to your class, you'll want to reshape your piece, making sure you do two things: provide your classroom community with new information (based on what others have said or what others do), and embed that information in the shared understandings of your class. Ask yourself how you can report back in ways that support the rhetorical relationships being established and extended in your class.

3 Circulating your report within your local community

When you've gotten as much as you can at this moment from the work you're drawing on, you're ready to share it more widely within your community. If you have a class wiki, blog, or course site, post it there for discussion or comment. Read through a set of related explorations to see what they collectively add to your class's shared knowledge, and draw on them for further class discussion.

Key Concepts

crowd sourcing 92
double-entry notebook 94
knowledge-building 88
knowledge-sharing 94
paraphrasing 102

quoting 102
quoting and paraphrasing 98
resituating 99
social capital 100
summarizing 98

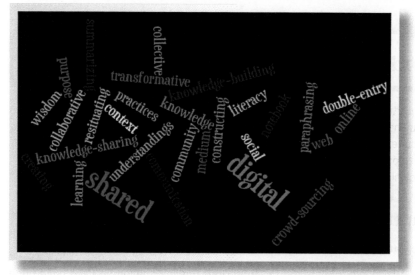

Connecting Local Practices
to the Wider Culture

<table>
<tr><td></td><td>CHAPTER SIX</td><td></td></tr>
</table>

CENTRAL QUESTIONS

1 Where do the shared interests of an immediate community connect to the larger culture? How do members of the community use media to support and shape their group identity?

2 How are photos being used differently in a digital age to circulate cultural knowledge?

3 How can a particular group's use of media present a rich account of the ways in which a local community draws on a larger culture to shape its own identity and meanings?

Chapter Preview

In Chapter 5, we considered how knowledge is built on and shared in both informal and academic contexts, with each participant in an exchange building on and adding to ideas that have previously circulated among friends, in a classroom, or in a larger community of people with shared interests. The **what** of the knowledge already shared or being newly shared was related to the specific local interests of a group—what might be texted by friends or tweeted to followers, discussed on a classroom site, or shared in a university newsletter. In that case, we drew on information published in a higher education journal for those interested in technology and education. But we are all participants as well in building these rhetorical relationships through the writing, reading, and speaking we do, not only in local communities and interest groups, however large, but in a broader, increasingly global culture, drawing on elements of that larger culture to help build local interests and shape local identities.

A **culture** can be defined as all the shared ways and meanings of a group of people, from a small community to a whole nation or beyond, whether joined in a shared physical space or geographically dispersed and connected through shared texts or online media. We can see *what* knowledge is shared within a cultural group by looking to the texts produced by its members, the images they share, the physical objects that are central to their interaction, the music they create or listen to, and any common practices. Anything that is a recurrent focus and interest of their world contributes to their culture. Media also play an important role in the shaping of culture. While our identities and the rhetorical relationships we form still take shape in face-to-face communities, in digital culture these practices now flow across media as we actively participate in a wider culture using the internet and mobile devices to build relationships around the world, regardless of where we are located.

culture
the shared beliefs, values, and practices of a group

Exploring
Media and Shared Meanings

cultural lens
a shared perspective that helps members of a particular culture understand their experiences

cultural representation
references to shared understandings recognizable to members of a culture

We represent our meanings through language, images, music, and objects we see as significant. As we do so, we are applying a **cultural lens**, framing our understandings from the perspectives of our culture(s). When hockey players share images and pieces of information that are easily available to them, they are sharing ideas about the world of hockey that are already present in U.S. (and Canadian) culture. There is a common cultural representation of that world and its meanings that individual players, teams, and fans may connect to or challenge, just as there is a common **cultural representation** of the worlds of punk, hip-hop, or classical music that individual musicians or music lovers might share or challenge. The internet, digital technology, and social media have contributed greatly to the spread of common cultural representations by making it easier for us to compose texts, take pictures, capture video, and share these cultural representations with others.

Sharing Cultural Representations in Online Communities

As shown in the Facebook interactions of Barry and his friends in Chapter 1, within the cultural practices of their online community, references to hockey play a central role in their sharing of meaning. As a participant in these exchanges, Barry typically goes with the flow, viewing what others have posted, commenting (or not), liking, and posting his own examples. But stepping outside of those interactions to see how they work, we might be struck by the extent to which the small texts of their Facebook exchanges link to a larger community of hockey fans and the meanings they derive, perhaps ironically, from such acts as posting links to fight videos. These are members of a relatively peaceful hockey team at a small liberal arts college, playing a game that is often associated with extreme fights and an edge of violence. Do they embrace such fights? Or do they present them as an implied commentary on a contrast between the values of their local hockey culture and those of the larger culture of hockey players and fans?

"Hockey," in this small group culture, involves not just the game they play as team members, but also the game as it is represented in the larger society and captured through YouTube videos or other online postings. Their immediate, physical hockey team community is maintained through the online medium of Facebook. The texts of their individual posts give evidence about and connect two cultural contexts, that of their small community, and that of a portion of the larger society that defines itself as "hockey fans," also maintained significantly through online resources such as blogs, YouTube videos, and other fan sites (and many of these fans do attend actual games as well).

Digital Toolbox
See Part IV, Section 5

INQUIRY

#1: Connections to a larger culture

Select a post on social media that speaks to two contexts, a local community (a group of friends, a family, a collection of teammates, students in a class) and a larger, more global context that informs the local group. Briefly capture the **where** of those two contexts and how the two are connected. Then focus on **what**, describing the post itself and, if possible, capturing an image of it. Does it include words, a video, an image, a link, a repost? What do you notice about **how** the post has been crafted, and **why**? How does it draw on and extend the group's shared knowledge of something in the larger culture? What meanings does this reference to the larger culture allow members of a local community to share? And do those local meanings sometimes play against those that are dominant in the larger culture? (Might Barry's local hockey team draw on hockey fight videos ironically, appearing on the surface to embrace fights that would never be part of their own team culture, as a way of affirming their own contrasting team values?)

Meaning-Making in Cultural Contexts

How do we make sense of our lives, of relationships, the events that we read about online, or the texts we might read in the classroom? We do so not just through the gathering and sharing of information—of facts and details and images and ideas—but also through a process of **meaning-making** in which we review the details of what we observe, read, and hear and then actively seek larger understandings and patterns in the information we've taken in, connecting the **what** of that information to **why** it matters. The knowledge sharing we explored in Chapter 5 involves meaning-making in this way, going beyond gathering new information to consider how that information speaks to the questions and concerns shared within a local learning community. All composing involves acts of meaning-making, of selecting what will be designed or written about, what media to use, and thinking about what might be interesting to a reader/viewer/listener, a potential audience within a particular context. Addressing the **why**—the reader's or listener's implicit or stated questions such as "So what?" "Why are you telling me this?" "Why should I pay attention?"—when communicating with an audience is an essential part of the meaning-making process. If your listener walks away shrugging his shoulders or a friend replies to your Snapchat with a "huh?" you probably haven't communicated in a way that answers that "so what?" or achieved your rhetorical purpose. You haven't successfully shared the meanings you found in that bit of information or found common meanings with the recipient.

Although making meaning for ourselves and in our interactions is a fundamental aspect of human activity, it is also complex. As compositionist Ann Berthoff put it in her book, *The Making of Meaning:*

> Meanings are not things, and finding them is not like going on an Easter egg hunt. Meanings are relationships: they are unstable, shifting. . . We might keep in mind the nature of meaning as a means [of knowing and interpreting], a way to remember that meaning is dynamic and dialectical, that it depends on context and perspective, the setting in which it is seen and the angle from which it is seen. (42–43)[6:1]

One focus of our meaning-making activity is on who we are, what we share with others who are like ourselves, and how to locate ourselves in the world. It is building our sense of self based on the social groups we belong to or identify with, commonly referred to as a **social identity**. Our early sense of who we are is based on family, gender, ethnic or racial identity, or perhaps religious affiliation. As you become an insider to new contexts you acquire new social identities (college student, hockey player, music fan, player of World of Warcraft, geek, etc.), gaining new perspectives, seeing things from different angles, and making new meanings. Education can be seen, in part, as a process of gaining new perspectives from which to understand the world and others to come to an ever-richer understanding of those we might at first see as strange or different to come to a greater sense of their ideas and actions and how these might be shaped in ways similar to our own.

The identities you take on within your immediate social groups, your various social identities, are almost always connected to elements in the larger culture. And the internet, along with social media, has accelerated this process of building connections between local social identities and that larger (and rapidly changing) culture. The culture of fandom, for example (something we'll talk about more in Chapter 8), where fans become dedicated followers of a sports team, a music group, or Harry Potter, has become one significant way in which individuals and small groups define an aspect of their social identities, just as we saw with Barry and his friends and their connection to professional hockey. When people identify actively with fandom of any sort, they both participate in and begin to shape that culture. They might do so through the videos they post or blogs they keep, and there are many hockey fandom blogs, such as one called Transformative Hockey Fandom, where fans post images and commentary and other artifacts.

meaning-making
the process of constructing new understandings based on evidence (what we observe, read, and hear)

Sidenote

Ann Berthoff is the "inventor" of the double-entry notebook suggested in earlier chapters and revisited here.

social identity
a person's self-concept based on membership in different social groups

Cultural Literacy

As we consider how knowledge and meanings are shared from the wider culture to the local group, we need to consider what elements the group draws on from the larger culture, what meanings are commonly shared about those elements, and how the group makes the elements their own to create their own meanings. We can consider many elements of what is repeated and shared: what categories of interest (such as favorite teams or players, violence and fights for hockey fans; favorite singers, lyrics, and genres for music fans) what other elements (such as style of dress or other objects or rituals) contribute to and take on meaning in relation to the larger culture, as well as what images are shared and how; and what texts are created.

The ability to draw on a wide range of cultural meanings and cultural references is often referred to as **cultural literacy**. The term recognizes that we always need a framework of shared knowledge with shared cultural meanings and references for understanding what we read, what we learn, and what goes on in the larger world around us. The concept was first named, in 1987, by composition scholar E.D. Hirsch, who saw its absence as one cause of "a failing system" of American education, and he tried to identify the shared background knowledge needed in order to understand the references in what educated Americans might read—a common core of knowledge needed to participate, as a reader, in the larger conversations of American culture. Hirsch was right in naming such shared knowledge as essential to our practice of literacy to enable the larger conversations of American society: "literacy is far more than a skill and that it requires large amounts of specific information . . .(a) network of information that all competent readers possess" and that it is needed "to foster effective nationwide communications" (Hirsch,[6:2] 2). But his list of "what every American needs to know" was narrowly defined and focused only on a traditional sense of what's culturally important, ignoring how multicultural American history and culture actually had become, even as he was writing (Kutz and Roskelly[6:3]).

Cultural literacy continues to be a useful concept, however, for considering the shared knowledge within our wider culture that allows us both to engage in a national conversation and to bring elements of the wider culture into our local conversations in meaningful ways. In a recent essay in *The Atlantic* (included in the Part I Additional Readings), Eric Liu, a writer who focuses on issues of American citizenship and American identity, revisits this concept and explores what is needed as commonly shared knowledge in the twenty-first century to maintain a shared democratic enterprise, an increasingly diverse and multicultural America, and to allow for the ever-changing new cultural knowledge being created and shared on the internet.

> Literacy in this mediated age is not only verbal. It needs images. . . iconic sounds. . . and pop culture referents. . .The internet has transformed who makes culture and how. . . And as the pool of potential culture-makers has widened, the modes of culture creation have similarly shifted away from hierarchies and institutions to webs and networks. (Liu)[6:4]

And such shared cultural knowledge is, and needs to be, increasingly global in our complexly interconnected world (Banks[6:5]).

While Liu's essay focuses on a broader American identity and participation in our wider democratic society, local identities and local meaning-making often draw on particular areas of knowledge from the wider culture, as we've seen with Barry's hockey friends. Music, in particular, serves as a cultural identifier for many of us, as we build shared interests in particular artists and genres.

Jake, a student at UMass Boston, was studying the ways of a local discourse community made up of the housemates in his Cambridgeport apartment, capturing their exchanges and seeing how the shared what, why, and how of those exchanges both reflected and contributed to their community identity. He found many instances where they referenced things in the wider culture to reinforce their local identity, as in the following example from his final report:

cultural literacy
the cultural knowledge needed to understand shared references and meanings within a given culture

See Chapter 7
for a discussion of music as a cultural identifier and example of genre.

See Chapter 8
for more examples of discourse community analyses.

Cambridgeport speakers also demonstrate cultural literacy with their speech. Names from television police dramas, heavy metal music groups, and local politics are dropped into conversation with frequency. Rarely are they the subject of discussion; more often they are used as analogies, as in this case, where a defective car is compared to a rock band renowned for their elaborate pyrotechnic stage shows:

> SONNY: "[My car] is blowing like blue smoke. . . I feel really trashy blowing blue smoke"

> JAKE: "You feel like you're at a Kiss Concert."

Naming specific icons, whether Kiss or Spider Man, reinforces the bond between the speaker, who recognizes them as common to all present, and the listeners, who can personalize their significance individually. . . Fringe culture in general and its music in particular are among the factors unifying the Cambridgeport subjects and serve as pools of knowledge from which they draw shared references.[6:6]

Jake and his housemates are actively drawing on an aspect of a larger global culture, "fringe culture . . . and its music in particular," to support the local culture and shared social identity they've been creating in their immediate community and to represent their shared local meanings. At the same time, those larger cultural scenes are being both enhanced and altered in a changing digital environment where music groups have websites, online fan groups, Twitter feeds, Instagram accounts, and more to further frame the cultural associations that a group of friends and roommates might draw on.

In her book, *Mediated Memories in the Digital Age,* José van Dijck explores the ways in which our "shoeboxes"—our collections of images, music, videos, etc.—both draw from and connect us to a larger culture. She considers how "individuals make selections from a culture surrounding them yet they concurrently shape that collectivity we call culture" (25), and she explores how they do this through the things they create, collect, and share.[6:7] Our collections, according to van Dijck, help us to shape a personal cultural identity that links to the cultural identities of friends and family as well as to a wider culture, and she explores how new "technologies of sharing" enable us to "form bonds across private boundaries, tapping into a communal or collective culture that in turn reshapes personal memory and identity" ([6:7], 41).

Before she turns to the cultural uses of photographic images—the focus of our reading for this chapter—van Dijck addresses the role of popular music in the chapter titled "Record and Hold." There she writes the following:

> Individual memories almost invariably arise in the context of social practices, such as music exchange and communal listening, and of cultural forms, such as popular radio programs, hit lists, music programs, and so on. These social practices and cultural forms appear almost inseparable from the memory of actual songs; as a sign of their time, popular songs create a context for reminiscence. [And] through these practices and forms, individual memories become collective vehicles for identity construction. Listening to recorded music has always been a social activity: listening with peers or sharing musical evaluations with friends helps individuals to shape their taste while concurrently constructing a group identity. (Dijck 91)[6:7]

We can see how shared musical tastes drawn from the larger culture contribute to constructing a group social identity among Jake's roommates, not only at the times they are actively listening to music, or perhaps going to a KISS concert with blue smoke, but at other moments where they can exchange references to their shared knowledge about fringe music and fringe culture to make and play with shared meanings. And we can see Jake making his own meaning about this activity as he finds patterns in how his housemates draw on "specific icons." By interpreting their activity as demonstrating a form of "cultural literacy," he shares that meaning with his readers in terms that they will understand, applying a concept that has become part of the shared knowledge of their classroom.

INQUIRY

??? #2: Identifying and tracing one element of shared cultural knowledge in a local community

For a group that you interact with at least partly through digital means, identify one element that recurs in your texts, discussions, or posts—recurrent references to or images related to music, TV programs, movies, politics, or any other aspect of the wider culture. A Facebook home page, for example, might serve as a momentary digital shoebox, collecting seemingly random posts/reposts from a variety of friends that nevertheless refer to something in the wider culture. When and how do such references occur, and how do they seem to contribute to group culture, the group's shared meanings, or the cultural/social identities of individual members? Do members also contribute back to an aspect of wider, more global culture by posting to online sites that relate to their shared area of cultural interest, such as fan sites or review blogs?

Making Connections
New Practices and Changing Meanings in a Digital World

As we build on and share our cultural knowledge through digital means in digital environments, we also contribute to changing literacy and rhetorical practices. It's not just the technology that changes, but also the ways we use it and the meanings we assign to it. Creating playlists to listen to on your smartphone is significantly different from finding favorite tracks on a vinyl record, both in the moment of selection and in how and why these favorites might be used and shared, for example. Passing on memes that are circulating on the internet is different from sharing one's own funny photo of a dressed-up pet (and the popular dressing up of pets, as well as circulating their photos and videos, has been another change in the larger culture). And we are increasingly using visual means in rhetorical ways to represent our shared meanings and achieve our communicative purposes. Such **visual representation**, whether it involves capturing images created by others that reflect our feelings or ideas, using photos we take and share, or creating infographics like the ones that appear throughout this book, lets us express those meanings in nonverbal as well as verbal or multimodal ways.

> **visual representation** using visual means to present ideas and information

> **See Chapter 2** for how Ashley uses images in her literacy narrative that reflect her feelings.

Shifts in Technology and Culture

In our reading selection from her chapter, "Pictures of Life, Living Pictures," van Dijck draws on the work of other researchers as she considers how the collecting and sharing of images has changed with the advent of digital photography and then the cell phone camera. She sees that new technology as both contributing to and responding to "a social and cultural climate that increasingly values modifiability and flexibility" ([6:7], 107), as taking photos has taken on new cultural meanings. Before we turn to it, you might take a moment to reflect on your own practices.

INQUIRY

#3: Shifting photographic practices

What sorts of photos has your family collected and how are they archived and used? What sorts of photos do you and your friends take, and how do you share them? And has the composition and use of any of these photos been altered with the advent of selfie sticks? Look at or remember one or two typical examples of each. What is included in each photo and how is it composed? What sort of visual representation does it offer of the meanings shared in each group?

BEFORE READING:

Reflecting on the changing role of photography

Our reading selection includes two parts of José van Dijck's chapter on photography and its changing role in our personal and cultural experience in the digital age. As you read and annotate, what connections do you find to your own experience, either to the ways that photos are being shared and/or altered by young people or to the ways in which families have traditionally used photographs and the meanings they reflect? What role do your own photo-taking practices play in drawing from and contributing to a larger culture? What further questions or speculations occur to you in this first participatory reading?

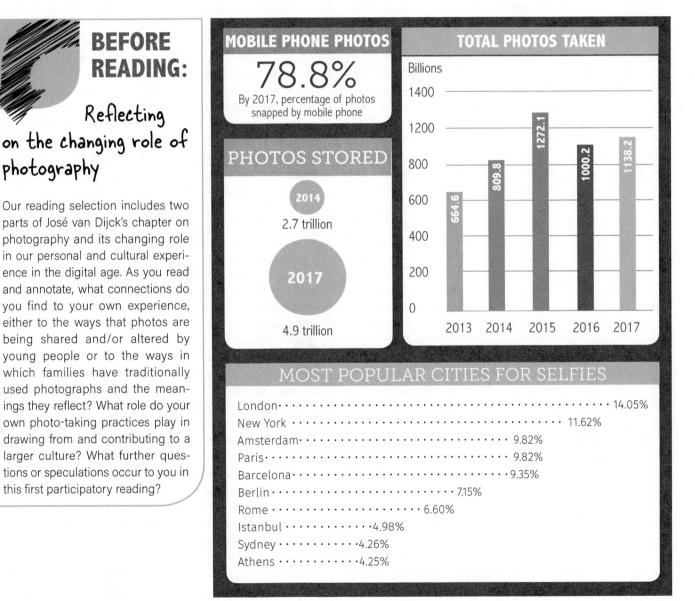

MOBILE PHONE PHOTOS

78.8%

By 2017, percentage of photos snapped by mobile phone

PHOTOS STORED

2014
2.7 trillion

2017
4.9 trillion

TOTAL PHOTOS TAKEN

Billions

- 2013: 664.6
- 2014: 809.8
- 2015: 1272.1
- 2016: 1000.2
- 2017: 1138.2

MOST POPULAR CITIES FOR SELFIES

London · 14.05%
New York · 11.62%
Amsterdam · 9.82%
Paris · 9.82%
Barcelona · 9.35%
Berlin · 7.15%
Rome · · · · · · · · · · · · · · · · · · · 6.60%
Istanbul · · · · · · · · · · · · · 4.98%
Sydney · · · · · · · · · · · · 4.26%
Athens · · · · · · · · · · · · 4.25%

Sources: http://www.statista.com/topics/2539/social-sharing/
https://www.statista.com/chart/2268/most-popular-cities-for-selfies/

Selection from
Mediated Memories in the Digital Age
by José van Dijck
Stanford University Press, 2007

Pictures of Life, Living Pictures

A student recently told me about an interesting experience. She and four friends had been hanging out in her dormitory room, telling jokes and poking fun. Her roommate had taken the student's camera phone to take a group picture of the friends lying in various relaxed positions on the couch. That same evening, the student had posted the picture on her photoblog—a blog she regularly updates to keep friends and family informed about her daily life in college. The next day, she received an e-mail from her roommate; upon opening the attached JPG file she found the same picture of herself and her friends on the couch, but now they were portrayed with dozens of empty beer cans and wine bottles piled up on the coffee table in front of them. Her dismay at this unauthorized act of photoshopping only intensified when she noticed the doctored picture was e-mailed to a long list of peers, including some people she had never met or only vaguely knew. When she confronted her roommate with the potential consequences of her action, they engaged in a heated discussion about the innocence of manipulating pictures ("everybody will see this is a joke") versus the incriminating potential of photographs ("not everyone may recognize the manipulation") and the effect of their distribution, which might have a less transitory impact than anticipated ("where do you think these pictures may show up?").

In recent years, the role and function of digital photography seem to have changed substantially. In the analog age, personal photography was first and foremost a means for autobiographical remembering, and photographs usually ended up as keepsakes in someone's album or shoebox.[1] They were typically regarded to be a person's most reliable aid for recall and for verifying life as it was, despite the fact that imagination and projection are inextricably bound up in the process of remembering.[2] Photography's functions as a tool for identity formation and as a means for communication were duly acknowledged, but they were always rated secondary to its prime purpose.[3] The recent explosion in the use of digital cameras—including cameras integrated in other communication devices—may be a reason to reconsider photography's primacy as a tool for remembering. Deployment of the digital camera is now quite commonplace, but it is a truism to say that technology has impacted the way we "picture our lives." This chapter explores how digital photography, in conjunction to a changing cognitive mindset and socio-cultural transformations, is reshaping personal cultural memory.

As the student's anecdote illustrates, digitization is often considered the culprit of photography's growing unreliability as a tool for remembrance; but in fact, history shows the camera has never been a dependable aid for storing memories, and photographs commonly have been twitched and tweaked in the process of recollection. The story above raises several intriguing questions concerning the revamped role of personal photography in contemporary digital and networked culture. First, there is the question of (digital) manipulation and cognitive editing: what is the power of digital tools in sculpting autobiographical memory and forming identity? How do we gauge new features that help us edit our pictures and make our memories picture perfect? Besides seeing photography as an extension of mental processes, we need to account for its materiality and performativity. Pixeled pictures on a computer screen have a different feel to them than their laminated precursors; photoblogs are not the equivalent of digital photo albums, as they elicit distinctly new presentational habits. And finally, we need to ask how these changes evolve along with sociocultural practices: photographs increasingly seem to be used for live communication instead of for storing moments of life for later recall. What are the implications of this transformation for our quotidian uses of personal photography?

Underlying these three questions is the recurrent issue of control versus lack of control. Part of the digital camera's popularity can be explained by an increased command over the outcome of personal pictures now that more electronic processes allow for greater manipulability. Photography in the age of digitization may indeed yield more control over someone's own pictorial identity and personal memory, and yet the flipside is that pictures can also be easily manipulated by everyone who has rudimentary software. A similar paradox can be noticed with regard to the distribution of personal pictures. Although the internet allows for quick and easy sharing of private snapshots, that same tool also renders them vulnerable to unauthorized distribution. Ironically, the picture taken by the roommate as a token of instant and ephemeral communication may live an extended life on the

READING

internet, turning up in unexpected contexts many years from now. Personal memory insidiously coils with collective memory once pictures are unleashed onto the World Wide Web. As I argue in the last section, the increased malleability of photographic images may suit our need for continuous self-remodeling, but that same flexibility may also lessen our grip on our images' future repurposing and reframing, forcing us to redefine fundamental notions of memory.

Digital Photography as Communication and Experience

When personal photography came of age in the nineteenth and twentieth centuries, it gradually emerged as a social practice that revolved around families wanting to save their memories of past experiences in material pictorial forms for future reference or communal reminiscing. Yet even in the early days of photography, social uses complementary to its primary function were already evident. Photography always also served as an act of communication and as a means to share experience. As Susan Sontag argued in 1973, the tourist's compulsion to take snapshots of foreign places reveals how taking pictures can become paramount to experiencing an event; at the same time, communicating experiences with the help of photographs is an integral part of tourist photography.[32] Notwithstanding the dominance of photography as a family tool for remembrance and reminisce, the communicative function was immanent to photography from the moment it became popular as a domestic technology. In recent years, there have been profound shifts in the balance between these various social uses: from family to individual use, from memory tools to communication devices, and from sharing (memory) objects to sharing experiences. I subsequently elucidate each of these profound shifts.

The social significance and cultural impact of personal photography grew exponentially in the past century: by the early 1970s, almost every American and western European household owned a photo camera. Long before sociologists and anthropologists began to acknowledge the significance of photography as a cultural rite of family life, Sontag took on the ethnographer's cloak and described its meaning as a tool for recording family life: "Through photographs, each family constructs a portrait chronicle of itself—a portable kit of images that bears witness to its connectedness."[33] By taking and organizing pictures, individuals articulate their connections to, and initiation into, clans and groups, emphasizing ritualized moments of aging and of coming of age. Cameras go with family life, Sontag observed: households with children are twice as likely to have at least one camera as households in which there are no children. Photography did not simply reflect but constituted family life and structured an individual's notion of belonging. Quite a number of sociological and anthropological studies have scrutinized the relationship between picture taking, organizing, and presenting photographs on the one hand and the construction of family, heritage, and kinship on the other.[34]

Over the past two decades, the individual has become the nucleus of pictorial life. In her ethnographic study of how people connect personal photographs to memory and narration, anthropologist Barbara Harrison observes that self-presentation—rather than family re-presentation—has become a major function of photographs.[35] Harrison's field study acknowledges a significant shift from personal photography as a tool bound up with memory and commemoration toward pictures as a form of identity formation; cameras are used less for the remembrance of family life and more for the affirmation of personhood and personal bonds.[36] Since the 1990s, and most distinctively since the beginning of the new millennium, cameras increasingly serve as tools for mediating quotidian experiences other than rituals or ceremonial moments. Partly a technological evolution pushed by market forces, the social and cultural stakes in this transformation cannot be underestimated. When looking at current generations of users, researchers observe a watershed between adult users, large numbers of whom are now switching from analog to digital cameras, and teenagers and young adults, who are growing up with a number of new multifunctional communication and media devices.[37] The older group generally adheres to the primacy of photography as a memory tool, particularly in the construction of family life, whereas teenagers and young adults use camera-like tools for conversation and peer-group building.

This distinctive swing in photography's use also shows up in ethnographic observations of teenagers' patterns of taking and managing pictures. One American study focusing on a group of teens between fourteen and nineteen years of age reports a remarkable incongruence between what teenagers say they value in photography and how they behave: most of them describe photos as permanent records of their lives, but their behavior reveals a preference for photography as social communication.[38] Showing pictures as part of conversation or reviewing pictures to confirm social bonds between friends appears more important than organizing photos in albums and looking at them—an activity they consider their parents' domain. Photos are shared less in the context of family and home and more in peer-group environments: schools, clubs, friends' houses. The study notes how teens regard pictures as circulating messages, an interactive exchange in which personal photographs casually mix public images, such as magazine pictures, drawings, and text.[39] In the past three years, photoblogs have become popular as an internet-based technology—a type of blog that adds photographs to text and hyperlinks in the telling of stories. Photoblogs have an entirely different function than photo albums, but they are also different from the lifelogs described in Chapter 3. Photobloggers want to promote photographs as more valuable than words, and they profile themselves in their pictures.[40]

Whereas their parents invested considerable time and effort in building up material collections of pictures for future reference, youngsters appear to take less interest in sharing photographs as *objects* than in sharing them as *experiences*.[41] The rapidly increasing popularity in the use of camera phones supports and propels this new communicative deployment of personal photography. Pictures distributed by a camera phone are used to convey a brief message, or merely to show affect. Connecting and getting in touch, rather than reality capturing and memory preservation, are there, social meanings transferred onto this type of photography. Whereas parents and/or children used to sit on the couch together flipping through photo albums, most teenagers today consider their pictures to be temporary reminders rather than permanent keepsakes. Phone photography gives rise to a cultural form reminiscent of the old-fashioned postcard: snapshots with a few words attached that are mostly valued as ritual signs of (re)connection.[42] Like postcards, camera phone pictures are meant to be discarded after they are received.

Even though photography may still capitalize on its primary function as a memory tool for documenting a person's past, we are witnessing a significant shift, especially among the younger generation, toward using it as an instrument for interaction and bonding. Digitization is not the cause of this trend; instead, the tendency to fuse photography with daily experience and communication is part of a broader cultural transformation that involves individualization and intensification of experience. ∎

AFTER READING:
Responding analytically as a reader

Van Dijck begins with an anecdote that leads to the key questions she'll explore in this chapter. How does van Dijck use her opening paragraphs to offer guidance to the reader about what will follow? What are the key questions/issues she uses her opening anecdote to raise?

Van Dijck names as one concern the need to account for photography's "materiality and performativity." Although most of her chapter is easy to follow, terms like these are aimed at a particular audience of readers in fields related to cultural and media studies. What do you make of the meanings of these terms? Can you translate them into rough working concepts of your own?

In the second excerpt, van Dijck addresses her third question, "How [do] these changes evolve along with sociocultural practices?" and she makes the case that there has been a cultural shift in the ways photographs are used, from objects of memory to "an instrument for interaction and peer bonding." She draws on the work of other researchers, bringing it into the realm of knowledge shared in turn with her readers. What research does she draw on to make her point that young people are using photos in different ways from their parents, and what evidence does that research offer? What additional evidence might you look for to support or counter her statement that this shift marks a "broader cultural transformation that involves individualization and intensification of experience"?

Building on Shared Knowledge to Explore New Understandings

We've seen that van Dijck draws on the work of other writers and researchers as she shapes and shares her new understandings. In particular, she brings in the work of Susan Sontag, whose 1977 collection of essays, *On Photography*,[6,8] remains the starting point for much serious discussion of photography and the role it plays in society. It is part of the shared cultural knowledge of people working in or writing about that medium. We can imagine van Dijck keeping a double-entry notebook as she reads, jotting down something like Figure 6.1.

From Sontag ⟶

Page 9: "Photographs ... help people to take possession of space in which they are insecure."

— "Photography develops in tandem with tourism."
— "Photographs will offer indisputable evidence that the trip was made, that the program was carried out, that fun was had."
— "Photographs document sequences of consumption carried on outside the view of family, friends, neighbors."

Possible van Dijck notes: ⟶

Photography lets people share travel experiences. But maybe it becomes the real experience?

Figure 6.1: Double-entry notes for van Dijck

Whether or not she used such a notebook, we can see how van Dijck finally shared her understanding of Sontag's words and meanings:

> As Sontag argued in 1973, the tourist's compulsion to take snapshots of foreign places reveals how taking pictures can become paramount to experiencing an event; at the same time, communicating experiences with the help of photographs is an integral part of tourist photography. (112)

The pages in Sontag's book that these notes are drawn from are included in Part I Additional Readings, and you can turn to them to explore more fully how her ideas are captured and built on as van Dijck brings them into the conversation she is having with her own readers.

To see more of how van Dijck, as a writer, moves between the ideas of others that she wants to share with her readers while building on them, look at the endnotes that go with the section of her chapter you've just read. In them, she captures the points of some who disagreed with Sontag on tourism and photography, and those who draw on Sontag's observations about photography and the family as a starting point for further work, before turning to the work of others whose more recent research on digital photography, photoblogs, and camera phones she also draws on. Just as Jake's housemate community shared cultural references and meanings, van Dijck can assume that for the community of readers interested in the role photography plays in our culture, Sontag's essays are part of their shared cultural literacy, background knowledge she can evoke and build on as she shares her own inquiry.

See Part I Additional Readings on page 185 for Dijck's endnotes.

INQUIRY

#4: Rereading with a double-entry notebook

At this point, return to van Dijck's essay and to our discussion in this chapter to create your own double-entry notes. Capture key points she makes that resonated with you and that added to your own initial thoughts as you observed the cultural references made by one of your social groups in Inquiry #2 or reflected on the role of photos in your own life in Inquiry #3. These could be points you might find useful, disagree with, question, or want to revise or clarify with your own examples. Use one column to note those points and the other to share your own thoughts in conversation with them, capturing some of this now-shared knowledge to apply to your own further inquiry. Look also at the additional commentary she includes in her endnotes. Do you find further points of contact there with your own thoughts and questions? References you might explore further at some point?

Composing
Digital Shoebox

At this point you are ready to select one of your own local communities to study. Consider the groups you associate with most frequently in a digital or partly digital context—those that contribute to an aspect of your own social identity and where some sort of knowledge is shared that connects the group to the larger culture. In Chapter 8, we'll focus on a more extended study of a local community, so you might want to choose one you'll be interested in exploring further, through other lenses. But at this point, focus on the digital tracings of the interactions of that group—the images they share on Instagram or Facebook or Twitter, the music they download, and the cultural references and posts they like and share.

WRITING MOVES ◄

Inquiring and Inventing

To begin to see how the local community you've chosen draws on the larger culture, you'll want to draw on the digital evidence you gather, and perhaps on related nondigital evidence as well. We've seen that Barry, for example, drawing from Facebook as a digital shoebox, could collect many digital references to hockey and images of hockey players shared by his teammates. But he might also decide to explore the collection shared among his family members, the images of his games that his dad shares on Facebook with a circle of coworkers, the ones of him in his uniform that his mom has shared with family and friends through Facebook and Instagram, along with a copy of an old photo of his grandfather in a hockey uniform that is framed on his bedroom wall (Figure 6.2). For Barry, the larger cultural world of hockey runs through two intersecting communities that contribute to his own social identity, and he might explore the ways in which either uses "hockey" to support its own shared meanings.

Figure 6.2: Photograph of Barry's grandfather in a hockey uniform

1 Creating a digital shoebox collection of artifacts and examples

Begin by gathering data, collecting examples of what is shared within the group you've chosen. What are some of the key areas of shared knowledge and interest within this community? If a sport is important to the group you are studying, you'll want to include sports references, images, and videos that are shared, and comments made about them. If music is a significant element of sharing, you'll want to gather music examples and references. The photos members of the group text to each other or post online might also be important to their shared meaning-making, whether they're photos of a favorite player, a favorite singer, of family members, or of one another.

2 Identifying patterns

Once you've collected your shoebox materials, you'll want to begin to group them together to find larger patterns. If you're focusing on music, you might ask what genres and artists are referenced. Does the community you're studying always listen to the same type of music? If so, in what circumstances? Or do members introduce new genres? If so, is it the same member who always introduces something new, or do all members take on the role of sharing what's new? If you're focusing on images that are shared in some way, you might ask what types of images are shared, whether they are new photos or captures of existing images, with what content, and for what apparent purposes. What's included in this collection, but also what's excluded (images of older people, images of those of a different gender or different ethnic backgrounds)? Where and how was this material shared?

You might work with a small group of others who are focused on similar scenes or objects to brainstorm as many questions as possible that you might ask in your search for significant patterns.

3 Applying concepts and considering larger meanings

Once you've collected examples and identified patterns, you'll want to consider what meaning those patterns might offer. If members of the group you're studying post Facebook images or text selfies of themselves at local restaurants and other gathering places, might it mean they take part of their personal identity from being part of this local scene? Can some of the key concepts we've been using help you to interpret what you're seeing? At this stage, be speculative about possible meanings, going back to your shoebox collection to see whether those meanings might be supported by the evidence you find there.

4 Forming a hypothesis

From the possible meanings you're exploring, you are likely to find some meanings more likely than others. At this point, you'll want to identify one or more hypotheses, questions, or tentative statements of meaning that might be tested against the evidence you've gathered. Van Dijck's larger hypothesis was that the various forms in which memories have been saved supported personal memories connected to larger cultural meanings, and that the creation and uses of those forms have been changing with digital media. Her more immediate hypothesis about digital photography comes at the end of the first paragraph of this selection: that it created "profound shifts" in several ways that she names. As you consider your hypothesis or tentative thesis based on what you've seen in this first collection of evidence, you can also allow for the possibility that adding new material to your collection or finding new patterns in what you've gathered might lead you to revise it in the future.

5 Placing your findings in conversation with the works of others

Here's the point at which your own double-entry notebook for this chapter should prove useful. Researchers always interpret and make meaning about what they're finding by placing it in the context of what others have found and said. Van Dijck draws on Sontag's observations, but she looks at evidence in the studies others have made of families and teenagers and uses their findings to test her initial hypothesis. We're not asking you to do further research on the cultural world you're focusing on at the moment, but it's likely that some of what has appeared in this chapter will resonate with what you're observing and the patterns you're finding, and making such connections will support your own meaning-making. Do the sorts of images you've placed in your collection suggest, as van Dijck finds, that your group values quick connections—perhaps even disappearing ones on sites such as Snapchat—over archived images that trace the group's history? Do the ways in which your community shares its cultural knowledge of music show how it's practicing a new form of cultural literacy, as Jake suggests is true for his community of housemates?

Drafting and Shaping

As you work from the collection of artifacts in your digital shoebox to presenting the meanings you've made from examining that collection—from finding patterns, exploring hypotheses about how and why those materials are significant to the community you're studying, and drawing on what you've read to place your own discoveries in context—you'll want to consider your readers' expectations and how you'll guide them through the composition you'll present to them.

1 Considering the context for your composition

Where and how will you present what you've discovered through your inquiry? Because you're working with materials in a digital shoebox, you're likely to want to present what you've found through a site that allows for a multimodal presentation, where you can include the photos you've collected or the Instagram pages you've captured, the screenshots of phone texts or tweets, or perhaps audio snippets of songs that appear in common on the playlists of your community and are referenced in their conversations. In this instance, deciding on a blog or wiki platform, or Prezi, PowerPoint, or video presentation, can help you determine what materials you'll be able to share directly rather than through verbal description. You might also display your collection as a Pinterest board.

2 Engaging your readers/ viewers/listeners

Van Dijck has used an anecdote of a student's experience to show how the circulation of photos is presenting new concerns in the digital world and to set up the questions she'll want to raise and the issues she'll want to talk about. The anecdote allows her to create a shared experience to build off of with her readers, and that's one effective strategy. As you look through the digital shoebox of artifacts you collected, you might find a puzzling or interesting example that points to the questions or hypothesis you're presenting. Beginning with something that invites your audience into your inquiry will prepare the ground for what follows.

3 Creating effective arrangements

As you arrange and structure your materials, you'll want to consider how to make and support your key points. But you might also consider what will make the most visual and/or auditory impact. You could, for example, move from showing individual elements of a photo or a photomontage to finally showing the whole thing, so your audience gradually comes to see the "whole picture" of how this represents the cultural group you've focused on. You'll probably play around with several arrangements as you seek the right one.

4 Structuring and drafting

Once you've used your opening to bring out your hypothesis or the key questions you'll explore, you'll also want to tell your readers how you'll go about trying to answer them: what sorts of data you've collected, what themes emerged, what evidence you'll present to answer each key question or explore each key theme. A quick outline can help you to organize this material.

In subsequent sections, you'll want to address each of your key questions or themes and show what you have learned about it from the evidence of your collection.

You'll want to conclude, then, with what you, and you hope your audience of readers, have learned from this inquiry, perhaps represented, in part, with an image or the lyrics of a song.

As you draft this material, or peer review it, you might decide to change the order of the questions/issues you address, to add or delete examples. It's helpful both to have a plan and to stay flexible until your final revision.

WRITING MOVES

Revising and Publishing

You've most likely brought an insider's knowledge to your study of the cultural meanings and connections in your shoebox collection. As you share it, you'll be able to discover whether those who are outsiders to the cultural group you studied or those who have focused on similar groups can make clear connections between the points you're making about your group and the evidence you've provided.

1 Working with possible peer response questions

- What is this composer's hypothesis about this community?
- What data has the composer examined to explore that hypothesis or to answer key questions?
- What themes or ideas have emerged from the data? Has the composer shared evidence that illustrates them effectively?
- Are there questions the composer might have asked but didn't?
- What further evidence or explanation of the evidence might you like to see?
- Has the composer taken into account the likely shared knowledge of the audience and provided new background knowledge if needed?

- Does the composer have a clear pattern of organization?
- Does the conclusion reaffirm the understandings the composer has gained from this analysis of evidence from a cultural group? Is there anything else you'd add to it?
- What other advice would you give to this composer?

2 Creating generative rubrics, revising, and reshaping

Working as a group, use your peer responses to create a generative rubric to identify key moves and strategies for organizing a digital shoebox study and to offer a general guide for revising such compositions into a final form. Use both the generative rubric and the specific peer responses you received to prepare a revised version of your composition.

Reinventing and Circulating Your Work

Here are some suggestions for extending the work of this chapter, ones that you can adapt to your own context and purposes.

➤ **Option 1: Sharing similar inquiries.** One immediate way you might extend your work with your shoebox is to compare what you've discovered with what a classmate with a similar inquiry has discovered. Does that classmate's group draw on music in the same ways (even if the music itself is different)? Does the team the classmate studied connect to similar artifacts from the national scene of the sport? Does another family take photos at the same occasions or look back at them on similar occasions? Does comparing two groups help you see any new questions to ask about your own?

➤ **Option 2: Planning a future project.** In the future, you can build on the work of this chapter to undertake a larger research project. While van Dijck sees new uses for photos as an immediate means of communication, she also explores, in subsequent chapters of her book, the idea of the digital collection or archive—collecting, in digital form, texts, photos, images of objects and artifacts, and audio elements— related to a time or place or community. While digital archives are typically hosted by libraries (e.g., the American Memory Historical Collections of the Library of Congress), digital collections can also be created by individuals or communities. Reflect on what might go into a digital archive for the community you're focusing on. These resources might contribute to a more extended archival study described in Part III of this book.

➤ **Option 3: Extending an inquiry into the changing meaning of cultural literacy.** In a 2015 article in *The Atlantic*,[6:4] Eric Liu revisited the earlier attempt to define cultural literacy by educator and literary critic Edward Hirsch (1987),[6:2] exploring what should be commonly shared knowledge in the twenty-first century to maintain a shared democratic enterprise, an increasingly diverse and multicultural America, and to allow for the ever-changing new cultural knowledge being created and shared on the internet. Turn to Liu's essay, "What Every American Should Know. Defining Cultural Literacy for an Increasingly Diverse Nation," in Part I Additional Readings. Drawing on what you've found to constitute a particular form of cultural literacy in the community you studied, how would you say we should define what every American needs to know in an era where shared knowledge is being generated, disseminated, and changed so rapidly? What might you contribute to the new set of key terms that Liu is building through crowdsourcing, drawing on the collective wisdom of his readers? What new understandings about how the full range of our cultural resources contributes to a shared identity might you add to his discussion? And how do you think the underlying concerns of the shared knowledge needed to maintain a democratic society can be addressed in the current moment?

Key Concepts

cultural lens 106	meaning-making 107
cultural literacy 108	social identity 107
cultural representation 106	visual representation 110
culture 105	

Questioning
Community Conventions

CHAPTER SEVEN

CENTRAL QUESTIONS

1 How do the literacies we use and the patterns that organize such use speak to the communities and contexts that frame our participation?

2 What can the music industry and communities built around music-making show us about how genres are created?

3 How can we question the ways in which language, style, and genre are shaped by immediate contexts and wider cultures by looking at repeated communicative acts in a particular discourse community?

Chapter Preview

In Chapter 6 we saw how local communities draw on a wider culture for some of their shared meanings, and how our practices of communicating with photos have shifted with new digital and social media tools at both a local level and in the wider culture. In this chapter, we'll continue our focus on the relationship between the local community and the wider culture, this time questioning how larger social and cultural expectations inform our local choices of language, style, and genre. Our understanding of genre as a concept derives as much from the world of music as of writing, and to examine the ways particular contexts and broader cultural scenes intersect, we'll explore how genre and language work together in popular music, how that music is situated in and reflects a larger social/cultural context, and how it defines and is defined by both performers and audiences. From this exploration, we'll look at how language, style, and genre work in particular contexts and how repeated communicative practices (genres) become central to the construction and maintenance of communities.

The communities we are a part of provide a rich picture of how culture is produced and how we build bonds within groups. By exploring the shared knowledge, purpose, and ways of these communities, we can see how communication patterns shape and inform our literacy practices and what we can accomplish with language. By questioning how genre, style, and language work together in any composition, we are fundamentally asking questions about context, audience, and how language functions in social, mediated ways.

Turning to the world of music and genre helps us consider the ways in which context shapes communication by looking to specific communicative moves. Because music genres build particular communities and audience expectations, they provide a useful avenue for thinking about how and why textual and communication genres take shape through shared ways and repeated practices. Looking to music also helps us to see how wider communities inform particular practices as we question how specific and local contexts (like particular music scenes) speak to the wider culture. Like music, in understanding the literacy practices of a community, we'll want to explore how participants use language, style, and purpose in various contexts, including digital ones, and use this knowledge to consider more deeply how we ourselves are continually producing culture through our composing.

In this chapter, we'll look at how some of our choices about language and style of communication for larger shapes and structures (genre), and even our choices of media and platforms, are affected by both our own purposes and by our senses of audience as we move between different environments. Our choices are shaped by our immediate goals and concerns, but they are also informed by wider cultural contexts that provide us with a sense of what is known and expected. By seeing our communicative choices as highly contextualized, we can look to the layers of context that inform our ways with words. All of this knowledge of **how** we communicate becomes part of our writer's toolbox, available for our own composing purposes.

Exploring
Styles of Discourse

When we talk and write, we make significant choices about not only **what** we'll say, but **how** we'll say it, depending on the context, upon **where** and how we will share our writing, and how it will reach particular audiences—about the styles and forms of discourse we use for our different communities. In informal conversations with people we know well, whether face to face or online, we tend to make decisions about what we will say and how we will say it automatically, and we are not really conscious of those choices. We mimic the shape and structure of others' tweets or follow the format set forth for a classroom essay assignment. We make our responses short or long, or structure them in particular ways, depending on the rhetorical situation, and we often use informal language or slang with friends in texts or on social media.

> ➤ Barry to a Facebook friend: "in the burg. hit me up."

We use more formal language, such as the following, in academic settings.

> ➤ Barry's Science Seminar Blue Team: "High fructose corn syrup, also known as HFCS, is an unnatural but commonly used sweetener in many of the foods we consume every day."

Or we might switch languages entirely in different conversations, or even in the same conversation, if we're bilingual. We are always making **how** we say things fit with others' expectations for speaking or writing in that setting.

Although people have always shifted between styles of language as they've moved among settings, those shifts were often associated with speaking versus writing. That is to say, although people were likely to write in casual ways in some circumstances (letters to friends, a personal diary), or speak formally in others (presentations at work, schools, churches), as a general rule, speaking was more likely to be informal with less concern for "correctness," and writing was more likely to be formalized and conventional. Now, however, much of the informal spoken communication that once took place face to face or on the phone is being carried out in writing—through digital texts where our use of informal language and style is more visible and the choices we make for different contexts become more apparent.

We see such shifts from researcher danah boyd when she addresses the same topic in two different public contexts. Here are her reflections from Paul's interview for her *New York Times* profile:

"We need to give kids the freedom to explore and experience things online that might actually help them," she added. "What scares me is that we don't want to look at the things that make us uncomfortable. So rather than see what teenagers are showing us online about bullying and suicide and the problems they're dealing with and using that information to help them, we're making ourselves blind to it."

And here are those of a research article she wrote about similar issues:

> "While we can talk about changes that are taking place, the long-term implications of being socialized into a culture rooted in networked publics are unknown. . .What we do know is that today's teens live in a society whose public life is changing rapidly. Teens need access to these publics—both mediated and unmediated—to mature, but their access is regularly restricted. Yet, this technology and networked publics are not going away."

In both cases, boyd's language is addressed to a wider public in a fairly formal way. But in speaking to a reporter for a major newspaper, her language is slightly more casual. Her sentences are shorter, and she uses terms like "kids" and shares her own emotional response to the situation the kids are in with the phrase "what scares me." In the second example, boyd uses longer and more complicated syntax and draws on terms that are commonly used by insiders in her research community: she uses concepts like "networked publics" and "mediated and unmediated." She speaks of "teens," rather than "kids," and she refrains from expressing any personal feelings she may have. Yet she adopts visual slang in the title for her article, "Why Youth (Heart) Social Network Sites,"[7:1] letting a little of her personality slip through and testing the boundaries of the genre of the research article.

The shifts we see in boyd's use of language go beyond the distinction of more and less formal. She speaks of "kids" and "what scares her" for *The New York Times* not because she can be a little less careful in that context, but because it is appropriate for that setting and for the audience she is addressing at that moment. Instead of thinking about choices of language and style in light of a language hierarchy where the most formal language is always king, we can question, instead, what is most suitable for a particular context and audience. boyd's talk of "networked publics" isn't inherently better than her comments on "bullying;" both style choices are appropriate for the audiences she addresses.

The ways in which boyd is tuned in shouldn't surprise us. We've seen from her *New York Times* profile that she's tuned in to visual style, dressing in striking ways—that she doesn't always want to present herself as a stereotypical academic researcher as she works to enter the social world of teenagers and observe their communication practices. And even as she maintains her identity in an academic research community, she plays with its boundaries so she can move across discourses and connect with the young people she studies through a process of understanding *their* shared ways of talking and writing.

The contexts we speak, write, and compose in certainly inform the decisions we make about how and what we communicate, but we also shape these contexts through the choices we make as we work within the shared genres and language and literacy practices of our communities. James Paul Gee likens our discourse, the language we use in particular settings, to an "'identity kit,' which comes complete with the appropriate costume and instructions on how to act and talk so as to take on a particular role that others will recognize."[7:2] Because our choices express our attitudes, values, and expectations as we position ourselves in the larger world, they also inform the ways in which we assert our identities. Like boyd, we choose our styles to claim different social identities at different moments, drawing on elements from the larger culture we make our own. This is not only in how we dress, the pictures we post, and the music we listen to, but also in the ways we speak and write.

We can see more about how a social identity that draws from a larger culture is reflected in choices of language and style, as well as larger patterns of interaction, by following up on a local context we first encountered in Chapter 4 with Nate Jolley's profile of the rapper Fame. Nate followed that profile with further inquiries into the local music context that Fame is part of—a group of rappers who collectively call themselves Mob Q-Records—and we learn that Nate is an insider to this group as well.

The Mob Q rappers form a discourse community, and like all discourse communities, theirs is built around shared interests and shared understandings about what to say and how to say it in their local contexts, as well as shared values. The shared ways draw from and help create a common community identity, with ever-shifting criteria for what is appropriate there. As we look more closely at what Nate tells us about exchanges in that community—about its shared knowledge, purposes, and ways—we'll see that those shared purposes are realized at three levels of communication.

❶ Level of language and style—word choice, sentence structures, etc.

❷ How these words and sentences are used in interactions to accomplish the speakers' purposes—what we'll call speech act

❸ Level of genre—the larger structures and forms that have taken shape over time

See Part I Additional Readings
for the profile of Fame and the inquiry into Mob Q's exchanges.

We'll also see that these elements are influenced by the wider music world and rap culture. And we'll see how Nate, like boyd, shifts his own discourse at each of these levels as he assumes his student identity and uses the style and speech acts and genres of academic discourse to study and write about his rapper community.

Expressing Identity through Language and Style

To begin our exploration of language and style, we can look first to the music world that Nate is part of. The world of music is a meeting and mixing place for many varieties of language, with features drawn from the contexts where different styles take shape, like the Appalachian dialects associated with country and bluegrass music, and the urban slang associated with rap and hip-hop. In a digital world, music, like other forms of composition, is widely shared. We now hear many more voices and these voices circulate far more widely than in the past. In this participatory setting, where individual musicians have more opportunities to make their work widely public, we get a richer, more robust sense of how language is actually used across communities.

As musical artists and their genres cross over and influence one another, their styles of language do, too.

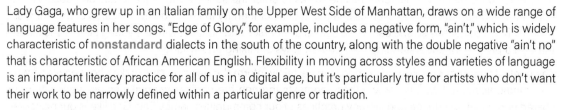

"There ain't no reason you and me should be alone tonight."
Lyric from "Edge of Glory"– Lady Gaga[7:3]

Lady Gaga, who grew up in an Italian family on the Upper West Side of Manhattan, draws on a wide range of language features in her songs. "Edge of Glory," for example, includes a negative form, "ain't," which is widely characteristic of **nonstandard** dialects in the south of the country, along with the double negative "ain't no" that is characteristic of African American English. Flexibility in moving across styles and varieties of language is an important literacy practice for all of us in a digital age, but it's particularly true for artists who don't want their work to be narrowly defined within a particular genre or tradition.

nonstandard
language dialects and practices that do not conform to and might challenge dominant ways of speaking

The forms Lady Gaga uses in this example are nonstandard from the perspective of the standard written English that's used in more formal public contexts, including academic ones. All language varieties have their own consistent rules, ones that speakers and writers understand naturally as they grow up within a community, and from a linguistic perspective, no variety is inherently better than another. In practice however, some dialects and varieties take on more **social value** than others, depending on the context. Lady Gaga's lyric above shows how different variant forms send different social signals in different contexts. Country singer Blake Shelton's line, "She likes hearin' how good she looks in them blue jeans" uses both regional pronunciation and the construction "them blue jeans" to speak to a country/western audience.[7:4] Many of our music genres arose among speakers of particular varieties of language—African American English in the world of jazz, rhythm, blues, and soul, for example—so to be an effective songwriter in those music genres, you need to use the language of the genre, the language that has the highest value for insiders in that discourse community.

social value
the weight a particular society ascribes to some sort of action, including communicative action

To get a sense of how such melding of varieties of language is happening within the discourse of current music, let's look at a blog created by students who are studying that relationship. The blog-based online journal, *Word,* created by New York University linguistics professor Renée Blake and her students, explores the structure of African American English (AAE). In this blog, on Music Mondays, students analyze the songs

that top the Billboard charts for that week, finding evidence that "many of the artists we hear on the radio are influenced by African American music and language."[7:5, L7:1]

The Lady Gaga line above appeared in this Music Monday post[L7:2] (Figure 7.1). From the link "What is AAE?" in the top navigation bar of the blog, we learn that AAE is a *variety* of English that is "**systematic** and **rule-based**. AAE is a not just a collection of words or 'slang.' . . . It has its own grammar, syntax, vocabulary, and social rules for usage." Nevertheless it has often been stigmatized as "bad English" because of "the marginalized status of many of its speakers." However,

> the idea that language and social identity are intertwined is not necessarily always a bad thing though. One of the reasons that African American English has survived for so long even with its stigmatized place in mainstream American society is the feeling of inclusiveness or 'in-group' status that speaking a nonstandard language can provide. It brings speakers together as much as it sets them apart from the mainstream, and perhaps most importantly it implies a sense of shared history and cultural roots.[7:6]

So we can see that language and social/cultural identity are closely connected and that music, as it brings the verbal elements together with other elements of sound and rhythm, allows people to perform a social identity or to listen to music that reflects one.

The choices of Lady Gaga and other singers and songwriters and the mixing of language and style in their songs are fully intentional and reflect their purposes and their understanding of their audience. These language choices demonstrate the connection between language and

Figure 7.1: Music Monday on Word

community, and they show that particular usages not only help musicians appeal to broad public audiences, but they also position them as insiders to particular groups. As they draw on a variety of languages, dialects, and styles, musicians push against the longstanding emphasis on "correct" language use and actively use different moves to expand their communicative options.

We don't have to look to the world of celebrity singers to see how such language choices play out. For Nate's local rapper friends, the features of the AAE variety of language contribute to a characteristic style—one that involves some typical features of pronunciation and syntax, but also word choice. Fame tells Nate the following in his profile interview:

> Ain't had no fans.
>
> Keep it on the down low.
>
> "I was really just chillin' with it until I met Nate and Von, and we started doin' our little freestyle thing at lunch and shit, rappin' over the phone."

And in one of Fame's own songs, "Closer to My Dreams," posted as a YouTube video as well as on SoundCloud, he tells his listeners, "I'm a let you in my brain." We can see that he uses constructions ("ain't had no," "I'm a") and pronunciation ("rappin'") that are typically characteristic of AAE, along with insider words and phrases from his community ("the down low," "chillin'") (Figure 7.2).

Figure 7.2: Public images of Fame that show his styles and social identities

Researchers have looked at the role AAE plays in African American culture, seeing it as more than a language; that is, as is true of all languages, it represents "a people's identity, culture and history."[7.7] Specific linguistic features of AAE have been carried into rap music and hip-hop culture, becoming required markers of that genre of music (even when performed by singers from other backgrounds). Sometimes these features show up more strongly in a rapper's music than in his or her ordinary spoken or written language, suggesting that they are being selected **because** they are identified with that genre of music.[7.8] Singers are always performing a social identity through their music, working within the styles of language and sound that are characteristic of a genre, even if they are pushing the genre's boundaries in their own creations. And within the larger culture of hip-hop, the choice of names like Fame or Lil' Nate highlight the idea that this is indeed an identity they are performing. The identities such artists perform are reinforced by the clothes they choose, the ways they move, and other elements we might identify in any music video. Like most of us, as they change contexts, they might shift their styles of language in the same way they change their clothes, moving fluidly through different styles and discourses.

INQUIRY

???

#1: Language styles in music

Choose a song by an artist you follow. Do you find any distinguishing features in the language used in that song? Which ones would you characterize as being a common characteristic of informal or more formal styles of language or the variety of English that might be spoken within a particular community? Are there elements of other languages as well? What do these elements contribute to the "how" of this piece of songwriting? To the ways in which the song addresses its audience and conveys its meanings? To the social identities that might be associated with it?

Speech Acts and Genres

Fame and the Mob Q rappers aren't choosing particular patterns of syntax, pronunciation, and particular words just because they are familiar. Like all rhetorical choices, these are purposeful and designed to achieve particular ends within a given rhetorical situation. These choices contribute to their **speech acts**—to the ways they are trying to act in and on the world around them through the ways they use their words. The concept of a speech act focuses our attention on the idea of rhetorical action, of doing things with our words, and using them to accomplish particular purposes. We greet people, we apologize, we joke, we express sympathy, and Nate tells us that the members of Mob Q fight and argue and "diss." They carry out these speech acts in person, in their music, and on Facebook, and they launch these verbal attacks at those within Mob Q and at those who are outsiders. Nate tells us that their motto is "Diss Anybody Records" and that "anyone who entered the group could attack anybody in the group via music, as well as any other rapper outside the group." He gives us an example of one Facebook exchange (Figure 7.3).

speech acts
repeated ways of using language to accomplish an action

Quincy Johnson Fire! !!!!!!!!!!!

March 29 at 9:11pm • Like • 2

Quincy Johnson I think that will do it !

March 29 at 9:11pm • Like • 2

Quintin Simmons Real freestyle

March 29 at 9:12pm • Like • 1

Quincy Johnson I know that man said he didn't understand the first one so I turned everything down so he can here that fire burning his ass!

March 29 at 9:15pm • Like • 2

Quincy Johnson You know me I try to make everybody happy!

March 29 at 9:16pm • Like • 2

Charlie Shaw Tru shit

March 29 at 9:19pm • Like • 3

Marquis Kingcade Man u just killed them niggas, and I can understand clearly wat ur saying.

Figure 7.3: An excerpt from the screenshot Nate included in his community analysis of Mob Q-Records

Here they're recounting a moment when Quincy Johnson (Young Q) dissed someone who was once a member of their group—their family—but proved disloyal. Young Q wrote a song that hit that ex-member with "fire," and when he said he didn't understand the first insult, the first diss, Young Q added to it "so he can hear that fire burning his ass."

Nate tells us not only why this particular speech act occurred, but that it's representative of the ways of this group—that "it just furthers the bond that they share."

> They have a saying, "If you don't diss, you don't care about the family. And if you don't care about the family, then you shouldn't be in the family." The constant ranting, the endless barrage of hurtful words, phrases and nicknames, and the seemingly never-ending comment boxes are all symbols of how this group argues to stay together.

You've probably also noted Marquis's words: you just killed them n_____s, a term Fame also used throughout his interview with Nate. This particular feature of insider discourse within the black community has been studied by researchers like linguist H. Samy Alim of Stanford University, whose work addresses the "linguistic consciousness" of Hip-Hop Nation (HHN), the speakers' "conscious use of language to construct identity." Alim tells us:

> The HHN realized that this word had various positive in-group meanings and pejorative out-group meanings, and thus felt the need to reflect the culturally-specific meanings with a new spelling (ending the word with an "a" rather than "er"). The "n-word" then becomes your main man, or one of your close companions, your homie.[7:9]

The immediate purposes of dissing vary at different moments for Mob Q, whether they are used to insult a cast-out former member or to affirm their own bonds, but the speech act remains essential to the group's identity—an affirmation of its valuing of "family." And it carries from their spoken interactions, to their music, and to their Facebook posts and comments, as they build their own Facebook post genre that looks quite different from that of Barry and his hockey friends.

What Nate finds in the interactions of Mob Q is also representative of the wider cultural scene of rap and hip-hop, and there are good reasons for that. Rap music developed from African American oral tradition, where clever wordplay was strongly valued (and from a musical heritage with an emphasis on rhythm and strong beats). A speech act of a ritual insult (with other names like "the dozens") was a part of that tradition, and dissing is a more recent manifestation. Wordplay using insider terms also allowed the shared meanings of an oppressed cultural group to be hidden from the larger society and offered a way of asserting a shared identity. Loyalty to the group, long necessary for survival, remains an essential value.

Nate tells us that their interaction

> gives each member a sense of not only who is loyal to the group, but also gives them a safety net in tough times. They know that if an event was to happen in their lives, the members of the group would be there for them, regardless if they argue or not.

As Fame, Nate, and Mob Q engage in the wordplay of the diss, they are also inventing their own versions of larger genres, writing within an established genre of rap music to which they give their own creative edge and working within the constraints of the Facebook post to comment on the raps they've composed and to continue the style of verbal exchange that so much characterizes the discourse of their community. The elements of language and style, of their speech acts and rhetorical purposes, and the larger genres that have evolved and continue to evolve around such interactions, work together as their local culture draws from hip-hop culture as one realm of a wider youth culture as well as from a black cultural identity. And as digital resources spread the music that's central to this culture around the world, these elements are reinvented and adapted to new languages and new cultural contexts.[7:10]

INQUIRY

#2: Observing speech acts, genres, and culture

???

The intersection of a local group's use of words with the related speech acts and genres of a wider culture is particularly evident in the context of rap music and hip-hop culture. But you can find parallels among other groups, who might use mock newscast or sportscaster discourse in a post or YouTube video to report on an event, as well as in your classroom where the style of language, the typical speech acts, as well as the typical genres of the academic discourse you're studying, are drawn into your class discussions and writing. Brainstorm a list, collaboratively, of such intersections and examples you have seen across settings. What can you say, at this point, about the use of these forms and styles as both larger and local expressions of a culture and how they are adapted, reused, and reinvented? Hip-hop culture shows us that the movement can go both ways, as creative members of local communities use digital means to circulate their own new words and reinvent forms back into the larger culture.

Making Connections
Genres and Context

Whatever our contexts for communication, a rich understanding of genres and how they work in those contexts is necessary for our successful participation, whether those genres are the posts of a hockey team or a rap group on Facebook, the genres of TV programs we follow and discuss, or the genres we use in our classrooms—the larger patterns and structures we draw on and adapt to our purposes in appropriate ways within our social contexts. We identify film genres (fantasy, documentary, comedy), writing genres (fiction, poetry, news), and music genres (rap, urban pop, rock). When we see or read or hear a particular example, if we're already familiar with the genre, we recognize it and bring our prior knowledge and expectations to it, easily distinguishing rap from reggae, or a discussion post from a research report. If an instance doesn't seem to fit into the genres we know, we try to figure out whether it's something substantially new, or something that fits into what others might know, even if we don't.

genre recognition
identifying familiar genres

We are always engaged in a practice of **genre recognition** that tells us much about the larger cultural contexts in which we live. If we've seen a lot of movies, or a lot of YouTube or MTV videos, we can compare what we're seeing to what we already know and identify the common elements of a particular type. If we listen to a wide variety of music, we might quickly identify a song as having elements typical of country and western, punk, or soul music, or if we listen primarily to one genre, we may have learned to distinguish more subtle features of the genre. And if we read or write a lot within one genre of writing, we might quickly identify familiar moves for opening a piece, for structuring its content, or for shaping an effective ending. When we have a lot of experience with a genre, as Nate and his friends do with rap, then we are able to work with its features, inventing and reimagining them to create our own unique compositions that both draw on shared expectations and reshape them. Becoming more finely attuned to the possibilities of a genre represents a kind of literacy whatever domain the genre is part of (and there has been much research lately on hip-hop literacies).

Genres in Popular Culture

We can develop our understandings of how genres might work—understandings that can enrich our work as writers—by considering their workings in a particular domain. And because our larger culture has provided us with a rich consciousness of music genres, we can get a clearer sense of how fine-tuning our genre recognition and use might work in other contexts, by seeing how a kind of genre-consciousness works there. In looking at music genres, we can find a rich range of examples, with much cross-fertilization among genres, and with a great deal of shared knowledge of **how** a song might be shaped within the genre and **what** one might say within that genre and what has been said before.

Music genres are also a focus of much discussion and critique among those who write about music as well as those who write music. Distribution services require that musicians place their work into genre categories, sometimes broad ("rock"), and sometimes more finely divided into subcategories (with "alternative," or "punk," or "psychedelic" among many possibilities). These genre categories shift over time. "Indie," for example, once meant that an artist recorded for an independent label, without a major studio controlling what the artist produced, so the music might be more raw or edgy. But as independent labels were bought up by larger studios, the meaning shifted to apply to any music that had what had become understood as an "indie" sound.

Music also serves as a **cultural identifier**, where genres of music like hip-hop or country, or even opera and new age, place both their performers and their fans into particular cultural groups by age, ethnicity, socio-economic status, etc. Of course, both performers and fans cross these stereotypical genre lines in practice, with white singers performing backup for Kanye West or Drake, who also have a huge following of white fans. Yet the music we listen to forms an important part of our cultural identity, and music genres can be overlaid with other cultural markers. Some have argued, for example, that "indie" is being used as a coded term for white. According to Noah Berlatsky, writing for *The New Republic:*

> There are few artists of color in the indie scene because artists of color who make what could be called "indie music" get classified as something else... White people aren't the only ones who perform country, or indie, or rock. But country and rock and indie are still iconically white—both because the default, stereotypical performer is white, and because default, stereotypical whiteness is in part defined by those genres.[7:11]

We can see then that how music is labeled—the genre categories that are applied to it—happens in a cultural context and carries broader social meaning.

In the following blog post, music industry analyst Mark Mulligan explores the ways in which changing genre categories are altering how we identify with the music we listen to. He also shows that the sense of these genres changes, with finer distinctions among more genres, as listeners become more tuned into the larger categories.

❝❝ When we have a lot of experience with a genre, as Nate and his friends do with rap, then we are able to work with its features, inventing and reimagining them to create our own unique compositions. ❞❞

cultural identifier signal about how particular individuals, actions, or symbols speak to larger cultural trends and movements

BEFORE READING:

Brainstorming genres

Brainstorm a list of the music genres you can think of quickly. Now look at the genres Mulligan names in the infographic included in his article. How does Mulligan's list speak to the one you constructed? Based on this comparison, what do you think Mulligan might offer to your own current understanding of the ways that genres work in both local and wider culture through his piece?

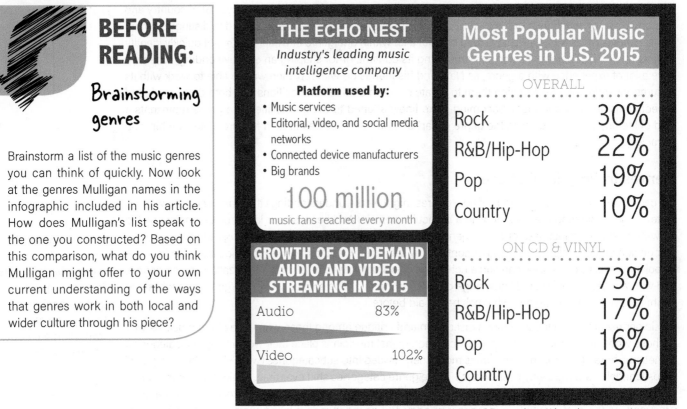

THE ECHO NEST

Industry's leading music intelligence company

Platform used by:
- Music services
- Editorial, video, and social media networks
- Connected device manufacturers
- Big brands

100 million
music fans reached every month

GROWTH OF ON-DEMAND AUDIO AND VIDEO STREAMING IN 2015

Audio	83%
Video	102%

Most Popular Music Genres in U.S. 2015

OVERALL	
Rock	30%
R&B/Hip-Hop	22%
Pop	19%
Country	10%

ON CD & VINYL	
Rock	73%
R&B/Hip-Hop	17%
Pop	16%
Country	13%

Source: Nielsen, 2015 Music Year-End Report, http://the.echonest.com/company/

READING

"How the Role of Genres Has Changed in Music Culture"[7:12]
by Mark Mulligan
Music Industry Blog, February 14, 2014

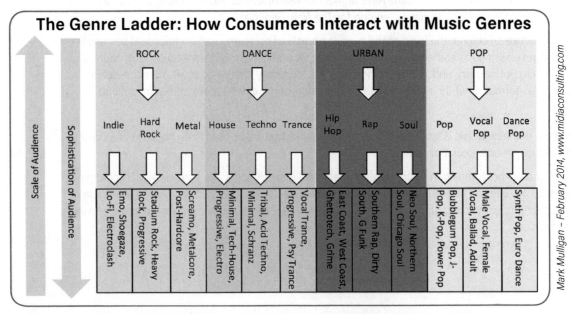

The Genre Ladder: How Consumers Interact with Music Genres

Mark Mulligan – February 2014, www.midiaconsulting.com

The Echo Nest's Paul Lamere has been doing some interesting work around age and gender music preferences which got me thinking a bit more about how the relevance of genres has changed. A school of thought that is gaining traction is that genres matter much less than they did and that they are no longer so useful for categorising* music (just look at the rise of mood based discovery from the likes of Songza and Beats Music). But as much as mood and activity are highly useful ways of programming music, genre does in fact matter just as much as it ever did, only in a different way.

Up until 20 years or so ago, music was the defining cultural reference point. Throughout prior decades it had been possible to identify people's music affinity by the clothes they wore and the style of their hair. From the leather jackets and Brylcreemed hair of rockers in the 1950's, through the mohicans and safety pins of punks in the 1970's, to the baggy trousers and hooded tops of ravers in the 1980's, musical identity was worn as much as it was played. The definition of a casual music fan was more engaged than today, with a casual fan typically every week buying a seven inch single and tuning into the charts show on the radio. Because music was the core cultural reference point the average 'music IQ' was high.

Now though, music competes with a fierce array of alternative cultural identifiers such as branded clothing, extreme sports, networked gaming etc. And of course media consumption time and wallet share are also competed for more intensely than ever before. The result is that the average mass market music fan is less engaged than in the analogue era and the overall average 'music IQ' has dropped.

This manifests itself in a greater number of mainstream consumers coalescing in the middle ground of popular music. Consequently pop music has become more amorphous, with all genres of music having strong footholds in the pop end of the spectrum. But this does not mean that genres have stopped mattering. In fact what has changed is that they have different relevance according to the sophistication of the consumer. What we have is in fact a genre ladder.

At the top of the genre ladder we have the mainstream music fan, who will think about genres in very broad terms such as rock, dance and urban, but will often have little strong preference between one or another. These are the sorts of consumers who when asked what type of music they like will most often say 'I like a bit of everything'. What they actually mean is that they like the sanitized pop end of most styles of music.

Next step down the genre ladder we get to the music fans. These are consumers that have clearly defined music tastes and will think about the genres they like in terms of broad groupings such as heavy rock or indie rock. Even at this level things start to get tribal. For example a house fan will often have little time for trance let alone metal.

The third and final step on the genre ladder is the micro genre, where the aficionados are most often found. This is where music fans think in terms of labels like Psy-Trance, Dirty South and Screamo. It is where music tastes become most tribal and in many ways behave most like they did in previous decades. Though these consumers are the smallest group they are the ones that the music industry depends upon most heavily. These are the ones that go to most gigs, that buy most merchandise, that spend most on music and are the most likely to be subscription customers.

In many ways at this end of the spectrum there is a *genre renaissance*. There has never been such granularity of styles. The digital era has enabled bands to build and reach niches on a global scale. So while genres have become more blurred at the first rung of the genre ladder, here they mean more than they ever did. ■

*Mulligan is from the United Kingdom and uses this British spelling.

AFTER READING:
Responding to an analysis of music genres

Mulligan, as a music industry analyst, is looking at trends that affect the music industry, and his audience is primarily others in that industry, yet his analysis is useful to us as well.

What is the focus of his analysis, and what are the key points he makes here? As a reader involved in this conversation, would you agree with him? Argue with him?

How does he see music genres acting as a cultural identifier, connected to other cultural identifiers, such as clothing and hairstyles, in the past and in the present?

Mulligan has provided a visual representation, an infographic, of the genre categories and subcategories he finds. What does that representation contribute to your own understanding of the points he is making?

Where would you place your own interests on this genre chart? From your own experience as a music fan, how would you alter or refine his analysis?

Artists sometimes find it hard to place their own work into such genre categories. Singer-songwriter Erika Meyer wrote about her own struggles in a blog post.

> Lately I lean towards the broad category of "rock" (or "rock n' roll"), choosing "garage", "psychedelic", or "swamp" as possible sub-genres, depending on the song or the album or my mood at any given moment. With past bands, I'd find myself waffling between two equally unsatisfactory options: "alternative" and "punk." Sometimes "alternative" and "punk" are offered sub-categories of "rock"; other times they stand next to "rock" as separate genres. The independent artist has to work with the choices offered, and those choices vary wildly from website to website. [7:13]

The songwriting process, too, differs for different genres, with "country" often composed by an individual or small groups of musicians with guitars or keyboards fiddling around together in the same room, while urban and pop genres typically involve input from producers and other songwriters, sometimes writing over a music track that's laid out first, sometimes online, and most often in collaborations with singers, producers, songwriters, and other musicians who share a close understanding of every aspect of the genre, from chord progressions to typical hooks to appropriate lyrics.

We find then that genres in music, like genres in composition, can be both useful guides to styles within a community and constraining elements that a writer might have to work against. Learning how to write within a genre is essential for the aspiring songwriter. Learning how to work creatively within the genre, opening up its boundaries, mashing it up with influences from other genres, and inventing something both familiar and new is necessary to becoming successful in the music business. But learning how to take on and resist some aspects of a genre is also central to the activity of writing and composing in more general terms. As we work in and from particular communities and contexts, we have to learn how to negotiate and work with the genres that are common to those settings.

INQUIRY

#3: Exploring your experience of music and other genres

How would you name the genre(s) of some of the music you most like to listen to, and what do you see as characteristic of those genres? What would you name as some of the conventions that listeners of that genre expect to hear, and what might have given rise to that category? Do you use genre labels to search for music you might like on iTunes or other music sites? Do you identify with a community of others who listen to the same genres?

As a composer/artist/writer/reader/listener have you ever found yourself struggling as Meyer does with the forms suggested by the way a type of activity was named or with the name itself? Do you see ways in which the naming of a genre might be helpful to those who are creating or following an area of creative work?

Style, Speech Acts, and Genres in Academic and Research Settings

What can be taken away from our discussion thus far in this chapter and applied to the writing we do in academic settings? Just as the Mob Q exchanges operate simultaneously at the levels of language variety and style, of speech acts and their rhetorical purposes, and of the larger genres those acts work within and give shape to, so do our exchanges within academic communities. And just as music fans become attuned to finer and finer points of discrimination within the genres of music they listen to, so do we all, as we make our way into new academic communities with new disciplinary orientations and acquire the moves that allow us to be full participants in the conversations of those communities.

You've had experience as a reader, and most likely as a writer as well, with the major literary genres of fiction, poetry, and drama, and some of their subgenres such as epic poetry, lyric poetry, and still more specific forms such as sonnets. You've written lab reports, research papers, and essays named by their rhetorical structures, such as comparison and contrast or argument or analysis, structures that also appear in writing for wider audiences, like Mulligan's blog post. You can name some of the moves of these genres of academic writing, understanding both in general terms and perhaps within particular disciplines what's commonly expected in introductions and conclusions, whether a thesis is presented up front or built to at the end after some evidence is considered, whether personal experience can be considered relevant to an argument or whether it should draw only on lab observations or readings, and how evidence and examples are used. You're also learning how to make those moves and adapt them to your own context and purposes. Genres are also differentiated by language and style as well as structure and purpose.

As is true for music genres, academic genres also change over time, and they may be named differently in different contexts, just as music genres may be named differently in different regions. And while textbooks name commonly used genres, the academic writer, like the original songwriter, has to learn to work comfortably and flexibly within and around genres, rather than follow a rule-bound recipe, which is why we've been emphasizing the idea of typical moves that might be carried out with different strategies, rather than fixed forms and rules.

We can see the moves Nate makes as he reframes his observations about his rap community for an academic audience. He makes larger moves like providing an introduction to that community and a description of its members, giving an example of one of their exchanges, talking about the purposes of such exchanges, and telling us how such exchanges contribute to the larger values of the community. In the process, he moves fluidly between the language variety and the casual style of the community he is studying (and that he belongs to), and the variety of Standard Written English and the more formal style used in academic settings.

> The academic writer, like the original songwriter, has to learn to work comfortably and flexibly within and around genres.

One strategy Nate uses to move between these styles is to bring in screenshots to anchor his work and provide his readers with a clear sense of the discourse drawn upon by the members of this community (Figure 7.4).

Quincy Johnson I think that will do it !

March 29 at 9:11pm • Like • 2

Quintin Simmons Real freestyle

March 29 at 9:12pm • Like • 1

Quincy Johnson I know that man said he didn't understand the first one so I turned everything down so he can here that fire burning his ass!

March 29 at 9:15pm • Like • 2

Quincy Johnson You know me I try to make everybody happy!

March 29 at 9:16pm • Like • 2

Figure 7.4: An excerpt from the screenshot Nate included in his community analysis of Mob Q-Records

Digital contexts, where we can easily share, store, and access such conversations, help make visible the rich variety of styles we have available to us as writers and language users. Writing is no longer primarily an occasion for formality, and many media platforms invite the informal banter and building on responses that we see in Nate's example. The exaggerated use of punctuation and the lack of full sentences that still communicate complete ideas ("Real freestyle") position this as a conversational encounter that is very much a rich communicative act.

As Nate comments on this conversation, he chooses at some moments to use a somewhat less formal style with capitalization to emphasize a point: "This particular conversation is also an example of one thing that is THE most important part of the Mob Q: Family," and with moments of personal commentary and explanation: "I don't mean physically being a relative of someone in the group, though in the case of some members, this is true." "I don't mean" can be read as more colloquial and conversational than might be called for in another genre or setting—in a chemistry lab report, for example—but in the context of his class's ongoing shared inquiry it fits his own rhetorical purposes and the audience he is writing for, while it also provides Nate's writing with a sense of his style, with a voice.

As Nate makes his next move—a common move in academic conversations to connect what he has discovered with what others have found—he shifts into a more traditional academic tone as he connects his thinking to the work of Nancy Baym (which we will read in Chapter 8):

Baym talks about flaming being detrimental to some groups (490), but this isn't the case for the Mob. Flaming is not only a big part of the group, but for some reason, it keeps the group together. Members of Mob Q argue and fight with each other on a day to day basis, much like siblings. But at the end of the day, the arguing is what makes their bond so strong.

Even in his move to step into a slightly more formal or academic discourse, Nate maintains his identity as a stylish language user (maybe because of his participation in the Mob Q family) as he shifts between commenting on what is "detrimental" to some communities and what "for some reason" keeps this group cohesive.

We can see that Nate is both working within the expected moves, structures, and styles of the world he's writing for and making them his own. At the same time, his class provides its own rhetorical context, with its own emergent genres that are adaptations of the more formal academic ones—genres such as informal inquiries and discussion posts.

It helps to begin, then, by being an observer of the repeated ways of writing or speaking—of composing—in academic settings, as in social or popular ones, identifying the common characteristics of what seems to make a good version of genre X in a specific setting, and inventing your own name for X as needed.

INQUIRY

#4: Seeing familiar and emergent academic genres

Genres can become central to the ways in which particular classes function. While recognizable classroom genres exist (the lecture, the Socratic method, the mini-lesson), your class has most likely developed its own way of working together, and these ways both form patterns that are central to the community itself.

In many instances, particular classroom communities create their own repeated and recognizable genres. While these patterns might speak to the common goals of academic contexts (questioning, making connections, sharing perspectives), they can suggest quite a bit about the classroom contexts they grow out of as they inform the work done in that setting. "Inquiries," for example, became central to our work in our own classrooms as we wrote this textbook and shaped much of our thinking about how to construct and build chapters (and underscore the kinds of meaning-making this text invites), and emerged as an important genre for this work.

During discussions, the emergent "response-extending question" has also become a key genre in our classes. This genre is shaped by follow-up questions meant to invite students to add to the ideas they shared during class discussion (both during class meetings and online). These follow-up questions ("What might boyd say about this?" "How does that idea connect to the discussion we had last week?", "How might your reaction to this text shape the approach you take in your profile?") serve to extend and enrich an ongoing discussion. Considering how genres like this one grow out of repeated interactions can underscore how genres, in broader terms, are constantly being created and recreated as they are negotiated, but it can also show that they speak to the goals and values of those communities that employ them.

What repeated patterns of language have emerged in your classroom? Describe one instance of this genre formation, telling how this recognizable activity is initiated, enacted, and (potentially) extended. Have you adapted and refined a familiar genre (like the Wikipedia post) to your own purposes, or invented something that seems more unique? What does this class-specific genre show about your classroom community and the shared purposes, goals, and ways that guide the work completed in this setting?

As we move into new contexts, especially academic ones, and shift to using new and more formal varieties of language within those contexts, a common fear is that unintentional "errors" will show up in our writing, or that we won't know how to use a more formal style. However, one of the most important skills of writers, as of songwriters, is their willingness to take risks with new varieties, styles, and uses of language, testing out what will work in new settings. We tend to assimilate in these ways quite naturally, but there are several strategies writers use to supplement the process—getting feedback from peers, working in a writer's group, even reading your work out loud to your dog. As we've been emphasizing in this book, such strategies are valuable literacy practices to help you understand how knowledge and language variety take shape in a community and how best to participate in that community.

> [O]ne of the most important skills of writers . . . is their willingness to take risks . . . testing out what will work in new settings.

Worries about "errors" and breaking standardized "rules" about formal English, while important, are things writers should worry about at the last stage of composing—the editing stage. Here the digital world offers many resources for the writer, from computer spellchecks and grammar highlighters to online style manuals that explain the punctuation, word forms, and grammatical fine points you are uncertain about.

Composing
Speech Pattern Analysis

Looking to patterns of language, from the repeated decisions we make at the sentence level to the speech acts and genres we return to time and time again to get things done with language, can help us understand both particular communities and the larger cultures that frame and inform their interactions. As you move through this composing section, you will turn to a community you are an insider to, one that connects at least in part using digital communications, and investigate the ways in which the wider culture informs how language is used in that setting. Though such language use is always in transition, you'll want to use examples to consider how identities (as they are negotiated by individuals and the larger community) and social scenes are constructed through language choices.

As you investigate the language patterns used by a particular group and share your findings with readers, you will actually be moving between two communities: a discourse community you have chosen to examine and a classroom community engaged in similar studies of language and the wider culture. As you present the interactions of one group to the other, you will engage in an act of translating. The following moves are helpful for moving between the set of expectations, styles, and genres established in the community you are studying and those of the classroom academic community where you will share your findings. You will have an opportunity to extend your inquiry into this community in Chapter 8.

INQUIRY

5: Exploring concerns about grammar and style

???

In Chapter 2, we introduced OWL, the Purdue University Online Writing Lab, which can be found at https://owl.english.purdue.edu/, as an editing resource. Return to it now to clarify one area of concern you have about editing your own writing. Create and share a working concept understanding of the point you explored and add it to the class's working concepts glossary.

INQUIRY

6: Examining intentional rule bending

???

Though many rules for grammar, usage, and syntax exist to be understood and applied, communities often develop their own unique, and at times, quirky usages that say more about the community itself than they show an attentiveness to more formal language conventions. Select a community you are comfortable speaking and/or writing in, and find one uncommon usage that seems specific to this group. This can be a word or term used for an unexpected purpose or in a surprising way (a group of friends saying "take it" instead of goodbye). It can be a grammatical structure used in unconventional ways (an older sibling assuring a younger brother "You cool" to provide reassurance). How did this usage come to be? What does it show about this community? How might its use be interpreted by outsiders to this group? What does it show about how language use functions in this setting?

WRITING MOVES

Inquiring and Inventing

Once you have selected a community to study, whether this is the same group you looked at as you moved through Chapter 6 or a new group, you'll want to consider the **repeated communicative patterns** central to that group's ways. You'll want to explore how those practices contribute to a social identity that's both local to the group and connected to a wider culture, and how its members use the resources of language flexibly in ways that are appropriate to the community and its purposes, but that may also speak to the interests and concerns of the wider culture.

repeated communicative patterns
ways with words used repeatedly within a specific community

1 Looking for patterns in language, style, and insider terms

As you look to the ways in which a community uses language and question what particular language choices mean, you'll need to look for patterns, things that happen repeatedly and seem to take on significance. Begin this process by looking to the terms that are used over and over in a group. These words might be insider terms (words that are created by or used in unique ways by a particular group) or common words used in exaggerated ways or with striking consistency.

Nate opens his study by turning to insider terms when he explains the divisions within the group he studies:

> One side argues that the "All Powerful" Red Side has the Mob taken over. But "The Prestigious" Blue Side claims they're "The Realest Niggas" on Mob Q.

As he introduces the Red Side (and establishes its position in the group as "All Powerful") and "The Prestigious" Blue Side, Nate not only brings us as readers into this community by providing us with a sense of both the language it uses and the way it self-organized, but he also suggests what is important to the community: a specific sense of identity. For Mob Q, that identity is enhanced by the insider names its members use.

As you turn to your own community, what specific terms seem important—nicknames, commonly used terms, terms used in unconventional ways by this group? What meaning can you make about this community based on these terms? What other characteristic patterns of language or repeated expressions do you find? For example, researcher

Amanda Ritchart has found that a style originally used by "Valley Girls" has now spread throughout Southern California. Its speakers sprinkle "like" through whatever they're saying, and they turn many statements into questions, a feature known as *uptalk*. Such uptalk shows up even when they're just stating their names (I'm Emily? I'm Sophie?).[7:14] And linguist Deborah Tannen has found characteristic differences in style between New Yorkers and Californians, between men and women, and even in the typical interactions of mothers and daughters.[7:15] Some of these patterns show up most distinctly in speaking, but they are likely to be represented in some way, even with emoticons, in texts and social media posts.

2 Identifying common speech acts

After you have listed and discussed some common insider terms, think about the ways in which this group carries out its rhetorical purposes through its speech acts, and list the speech acts that seem most central to the community. As we've seen, Nate looks to the "diss" and explains:

> Arguing and "beef" is an everyday thing in Mob Q. Sometimes individuals have their own separate problems with each other. Other times there may be arguing between The Red and Blue Sides.

This community's focus on arguing and "dissing" and their focus on "beef" stresses the competitive nature of this group, which isn't surprising for a community that taps into the larger culture tradition of competitive and performance rapping. What repeated speech acts seem central to the community you are studying? Showing encouragement and enthusiasm, perhaps? (That's great! Wonderful!)

How do those repeated communicative patterns seem to be in conversation with the concerns, ways, and practices shared by larger, more broadly defined cultural groups?

3 Naming influential genres

Nate's study makes it clear that the larger genres of rap and hip-hop shape Mob Q-Records and the ways in which this group organizes itself and its interactions. What larger, established genres seem to inform the community you are studying? Are there ways in which the genres central to a broader culture become important to this community, not only through its references to that culture (like the fringe music references we saw Jake reporting on in Chapter 6), but also through drawing on and adapting any of its genres? In what ways are these genres picked up on and reshaped by and for this community? If the group communicates through a social media platform, how do its members adapt that post genre for their own uses? How do their larger, more recognizable, nameable forms shape the ways in which this group uses language and the larger identity the group forms?

4 Considering visual indicators of style

As you study a community and the ways in which it is located in the wider culture, look to visual indicators (style choices, like those demonstrated by danah boyd or by Fame, and videos shared and commented on, like those discussed by Mob Q-Records). What do these repeated visuals suggest about the group's identity? About how this group sees itself as connected to broader cultural moments or movements?

5 Making claims and assertions

Look back at the patterns you have identified and make a claim about this group and how its group identity is tied to what it does with language. Nate does this when he says:

> As much as they argue, and as much as they diss each other continually, that arguing is central to every member who becomes a part of Mob Q-Records. They have a saying, "If you don't diss, you don't care about the family. And if you don't care about the family, then you shouldn't be in the family." The constant ranting, the endless barrage of hurtful words, phrases and nicknames, and the seemingly never-ending comment boxes are all symbols of how this group argues to stay together.

What can you say about the group you are studying? What tentative assertion can you make about how language is used in that setting? How do those language choices seem tied to a wider culture? How do those choices point to the flexible nature of language? What do they highlight about what is appropriate to and for this community?

6 Translating

Now that you have done some work looking at a community's ways of interacting through language, you will want to try to step, even if tentatively, into a more academic register, translating the characteristic style and expressions you've found in your community into those of academic writing.

WRITING MOVES

Drafting and Shaping

Once you have articulated a tentative claim, you will want to identify one speech act to analyze it in more extensive ways, as Nate does by looking at the diss. You'll want to find an example of this speech act (whether you collect that data by recording a conversation or by looking to a social media site as Nate does) and move through a careful consideration of it. Working through the following set of moves will help refine and reshape your tentative claim as you take on the style of an academic discourse community.

1 Situating the speech act

As you open your analysis, you'll want to set the scene. Because you are writing about one discourse community but speaking to another, you'll want to invite your readers in the academic community of your classroom into the world of the community you are studying. Look again at Nate's full introduction:

> It's a late Saturday night on Facebook, and 4 individuals of a rap group are going at it again. It's the classic debate on which side of the rap group is better. One side argues that the "All Powerful" Red Side has the Mob taken over. But "The Prestigious" Blue Side claims they're "The Realest Niggas" on Mob Q. And so the argument begins about not only who is better, but who actually has the most influence inside the rap group outside of Facebook.

You can see Nate drawing on the discourse of "the Mob" here in both quoted ("All Powerful") pieces of text and at other moments (for instance, when he says the members of the community are "going at it again") when he is less explicit about taking on the language of this group. At other moments, Nate's style feels more academic as he announces his focus and characterizes the interactions of this group (which he calls a "classic debate" in his second sentence).

As you introduce a speech act you will look at, you'll want to make similar moves, shifting subtly between the language of the community you are studying and an academic community in ways that might blend these discourses. You'll also want to be descriptive so your readers get a clear sense of this community in action.

2 Drawing on the voices of community insiders

To present a clear sense of what words and communicative actions make up this speech act, you'll want to bring the voices central to this community into your analysis. You can do this, as Nate does, by bringing in an actual exchange. You can also, though, tuck language from the community into your more academic sentences, as Nate does when he introduces members of Mob Q: "Truths come out on how everyone who's a part of the Red Side is only a part of that side because of the 'Killer Kid,' otherwise known as Young Q. Others call a member of the Blue Side, S Thugga 'Trashcan Sam,' which is an offensive nickname." Instead of telling readers about your community's language use, draw on their words to provide a clear sense of how communication works in this setting.

3 Weaving in academic voices

Drawing on the voices of the members of the community you are studying is central to your analysis, but pointing to the academic conversations that go on about situated language use is central to positioning your piece as a contribution to academic knowledge. Nate makes this move when he points to Baym's article (a study of an online soap opera fan community we'll read in Chapter 8):

> This particular conversation is also an example of one thing that is THE most important part of the Mob Q: Family. I don't mean physically being a relative of someone in the group, though in the case of some members, this is true. Baym talks about flaming being detrimental to some groups (490), but this isn't the case for the Mob. Flaming is not only a big part of the group, but for some reason, it keeps the group together.

By paraphrasing Baym, Nate shows he is adding to a larger discussion of how conversations work on digital sites. You'll want to summarize, quote, and paraphrase from a related article or piece in your analysis. This will help you stress the significance of your piece as you position it as picking up on and extending the work of an active academic research community.

WRITING MOVES

Revising and Publishing

Once you have a draft, you will certainly want to share it with the academic community you are working with. But you also might want to turn to the community you are studying, too, for input.

Digital Toolbox
See Part IV, Section 2

1 Sharing within your academic discourse community

Share a rough draft with your classmates in class or online, and have them consider the ways in which you present this community they are not familiar with using the following questions.

- Do I give a clear enough sense of what is discussed and accomplished through this speech act?

- Do I talk about how this repeated communicative action is accomplished in careful enough ways? What else do you want to know about how this community communicates?

- What do you understand about the purpose of this speech act? What other interpretations might I want to explore here?

- What do you notice about how I draw on multiple voices here (from my community, from a larger academic conversation)? Are there moments when I could add to this element of my analysis to shift between styles in more effective ways?

2 Getting input from your discourse community

You should also consider sharing your draft with members of the community you are studying. Ask them if you present the community in a fair and comprehensive way. Ask them if they have a different sense of why they use language in the ways they do. Ask them if there is anything else (additional examples, or explanations) you should consider including in this piece.

3 Reading your work aloud

Once you have had a chance to rework your draft and have a close-to-polished version of it, you should read it aloud to your class or to a handful of your classmates. As they listen, ask them to pay attention to the multiple voices you draw on in this piece. What can they say about the style you employ and craft here as a writer?

Reinventing and Circulating Your Work

To extend this project, you could move beyond a single example, whether by returning to your community for additional data or by working collaboratively with classmates working on similar speech acts.

➤ **Option 1: Drawing on additional examples.** One option for extending this project entails looking at a set of speech acts that are central to this community. Drawing on additional examples as you widen the scope of this analysis will help you come to richer points about this community as you present a fuller and more complete picture of it.

➤ **Option 2: Combining data.** As a composer working in a classroom context, you could find classmates analyzing similar speech acts and compile your data to make points not about specific communities, but about common or repeated speech acts themselves.

Key Concepts

cultural identifier 129
genre recognition 128
nonstandard 124

repeated communicative patterns 137
social value 124
speech acts 126

Analyzing
Discourse Communities

CHAPTER EIGHT

CENTRAL QUESTIONS

1 How are relationships and communities formed, shaped, and maintained online?

2 How might a researcher/composer make the moves of gathering information, discovering patterns, making connections, and shaping a print or digital composition that will be circulated to a wider audience, arousing its interest?

3 How can you use what you've learned about these moves to guide or extend your own academic study of a community of your choice and to create a composition, print or digital, that contributes the knowledge gained from your study to a larger conversation about the online interactions of communities?

Chapter Preview

A fundamental aspect of our human experience is that we live in communities and are constantly forming and reforming new communities with others who share some aspect of our experiences and interests, whether in sports, music, a workplace, or a dorm. We live in a web of social relationships within communities, both small and large, whether brought together initially by shared spaces or shared interests. While some communities may last a lifetime, others are more temporary, forming and dissolving as the needs and purposes of the community change. And as communities evolve, their shared interests, purposes, and ways come to reflect some of their deeper shared beliefs and values.

Because our literacy practices are very much embedded in the communities we're part of—our *discourse communities*—the study of those communities has been central to the work of scholars in composition, literacy, and rhetoric who try to identify the practices and genres that arise in different settings—whether social, academic, or public—and to the teachers who guide students in understanding how to identify and work within the practices of the communities they'll enter.

More recently, as digital communication has become more central to our lives, scholars like danah boyd have turned their attention to the communities that are formed partly or wholly online in an effort to understand more about the **changing literacies** that are emerging in these contexts. As communities increasingly add online exchanges to their ways of communicating and virtual communities proliferate, understanding more about how these communities form, how they interact, and what keeps them together (what keeps people coming back to particular online sites) has become a matter of interest not only to sociologists and discourse analysts, but to marketers, web developers, creators of social media networks, online game designers, the health care

changing literacies
reading, writing, and information management practices that are shaped and reshaped by shifting contexts and cultures

professionals who want to create support groups for those with particular health problems, or the teachers who want to create online classroom communities.

In our work thus far, but especially in Chapters 6 and 7, you've considered the literacy practices of your own local communities, how they achieve shared purposes, build shared knowledge, and draw on the shared ways required for successful communication. You've also considered how they are adapting to new digital environments. You've drawn on readings that speak to these issues. And you've worked with many of the writing moves that are common to carrying out and reporting on such inquiry. In this chapter, which completes Part I and our look at local contexts, we'll ask you to choose one community of the several you have perhaps observed or might observe, to draw together anything you've already learned about that community's digital literacy and communication practices, to look closely and systematically at an extended series of exchanges, and to compose a report—a community study—that shares what you've learned with an audience of other researchers—with your classmates and perhaps others.

Exploring
Interactions in Online Communities

What holds communities together? Historically, one important element was place. People were born in a particular area and lived in that area their entire lives. As we saw in Chapter 1, place was central to Genna May's literacy practices as she connected with several different communities, moving from her church-focused home community to a school community miles away, to a workplace community in the dairy industry. To be an active member in these communities, it was necessary for Genna May to be physically present to engage with others in each setting. In the twenty-first century we continue to move among different discourse communities like Genna May, but place, and being physically present, is no longer the central determiner of the communities we inhabit as we increasingly connect and build our communities online.

discourse communities
communities that come together around shared interests and purposes that shape shared ways of communicating

In Chapter 1 we introduced the concept of **discourse communities**—communities that come together around shared interests and purposes and that shape shared ways of communicating, including shared literacy practices. We've seen that discourse communities come in all shapes and sizes, from sisters to teammates and classmates, to large fan communities and gaming communities. They use a variety of modes of expression—gestures, body language, sound, images, emojis, and GIFs, as well as words, to build rhetorical relationships among their members, doing so using various media. Sometimes they talk in person or on the phone, sometimes they text, email, or instant message, sometimes they post photos or share music, and sometimes they write a card or a letter or publish an article. And we've observed how digital resources extend the available modes of expression in local communities, whether they have been formed in face-to-face settings or are created entirely online as **virtual communities** that depend on evolving literacy practices to compose their online exchanges. These virtual communities may be as small as just two people who interact on a regular basis and who share similar interests, purposes, and ways of communicating, or as large as a Beyoncé fan group. And smaller communities often spin off of larger ones as members find others within the larger context who share even more narrow common purposes.

virtual communities
communities formed in digital space rather than physical space

Mehdi, a freshman writer, is looking at a two-person community that is an offshoot of a large online community of Star Trek fans (Figure 8.1).

This small friendship community was formed through side conversations using an instant messenger (IM) feature on the site, and it has existed for six years. Mehdi and his friend have never met face to face. Mehdi tells us:

> The IM is the best way to find diverse people from all walks of life, where one, as what happened to me, can even find a life long friend.

Figure 8.1: Star Trek Facebook page

He gives us a picture of the larger community in which they met:

> IM users come together because of common interest. For example I met my friend via a Star Trek message board (yet another IM related literacy activity). There are many common interests that are expressed via internet message boards that range from women's rights to cooking, the list is infinite. Those common interests form a sub culture of the even wider culture of IM users.

In Mehdi's small community, he finds a wide range of shared interests that they talk about much as if they were in the same room.

> We are very close friends and our interaction has a lot of depth to it. For example, we usually will debate current events, and political issues. Sometimes if we are too divisive on an issue we may end up arguing with each other, sometimes we fight (like all close friends do) over the most trivial of things. We tell stories of what has happened to us and our family. Some of these stories range from funny to sad, to even the strange. Mostly we start off our conversation with what has happened throughout our day. We usually meet in the early morning hours at around 1 or 2 AM. We also make jokes. The jokes almost always stem from the conversation and we also use sarcasm once in while.

But there are elements to their exchanges that arise from their online medium of communication.

> Technology plays a big importance in our discourse community. As I mentioned before we interact via the Yahoo IM. This is because my friend lives in Florida and I live in Massachusetts. Of course this kind of communication could not be made possible without the invention of the personal computer and the innovation of the internet and the IM that came as a result of the computer. Consequently our conversations sometimes might be about computer and internet-related topics such as computer viruses, web design, and file sharing. E-mail is also used as a communicative tool but we both prefer to use the IM. Other uses that we use [in addition to] the IM as well as E-mail is the exchange of files such .doc, .mp3, .mpg, and .jpg/gif (documents, digital music, video files, and digital images) among other file types.
>
> As a result of using the IM's a few abbreviations that all IM users use have been formed. "brb," "g2g" or "gtg," and, "LOL," are the most commonly known abbreviations by outsiders to this community of IM users, they stand for "Be Right Back," "Got To Go," and "Laugh out Loud." Other abbreviations that might not be known to the outside community are, "ttyl," "nm," "nvrm," and "s/n," to name a few. Those stand for "Talk To You Later," "Nothing Much," "Never Mind," and "Screen Name." A screen name is what identifies IM users. My screen name is yeahhoo86.

The IM users in its own right is a culture—which me and my friend are a part of. The IM is a more personal, one on one, direct communication with a person that takes place in the present tense. It is like talking face to face to a person but pretend there is wall that separates you and your friends. The same principle applies to chat groups (a collection of several people) and e-mail.

Mehdi is also a writer in a classroom community, one where students have been looking at the shared knowledge and interests, the shared purposes, and shared ways of the communities they study—at how they draw from the wider culture, at what genres (such as arguments or stories or debates about current events) arise in their exchanges, and at the language they use. Members of that classroom community also have shared ways of interacting as they undertake inquiries, post their observations online to a class website, and read and respond to each other's writing. After this preliminary inquiry, Mehdi's classmates want to know less about the technological aspect of the internet (something that's already shared knowledge among students in this class) and more about his friendship, less about (as one student put it in posting a peer response to an early draft) "the internet as a thing" and more about (as another suggested) "the internet as a place where someone can meet people from all walks of life." Such responses tell Mehdi that, in this classroom community, the shared focus is on *why* people communicate as they do in their various communities, and not simply on the technology they use for doing so. The classroom community, too, is developing shared interests, purposes, and ways. And as Mehdi extends his inquiry through research into relevant studies, he turns his attention to larger questions about online friendships.

INQUIRY

???

#1: Selecting a community to focus on

By now you've most likely looked at several of your local communities, seeing the different kinds of literacy practices they engage in, both conventional and digital. You'll now want to choose one for a fuller community study.

Looking at other students' research on their own communities illustrates how varied the possibilities are. We've seen that Mehdi's research focused on a "community" of just two people who met on a *Star Trek* fan site. And in Chapter 7, we saw Nate Jolley move from interviewing one musician, Fame, to studying the small music community he's part of at "Mob Q-Records." Some students have also studied communities formed around online games, and you'll find an example in Part I Additional Readings, Rich Corrente's "The Dragon Court World."

Students often shift their focus as they move into a more extended study. Mehdi, for example, initially observed the exchanges among siblings in his family before turning his attention to his online friendship. You'll have the opportunity to build on this community study, if you choose, for the more extended research of Part III of this book, so it makes sense to confirm, at this point, that the community you select now is one you'd really like to focus on and one that will offer rich insights into the questions being raised by your class's larger inquiry into digital literacy practices.

As you choose one community to focus on for a fuller study, here are questions you'll want to consider.

➤ What have you learned and what might you want to learn about how digital literacy practices are shaping and being reshaped within communities? What new questions do you have at this point? Can you explore those questions with one of the communities you've already looked at, or is there another you think might offer new and richer understandings?

➤ If you've been looking at several communities (including that of your classroom), you might make a chart, listing several key points you've discovered and some further questions for each. What data have you already collected? What more might you want to collect as you work to connect

INQUIRY (continued)

the details of a community's interactions and practices to the larger patterns and meanings that shape the identity of the community in a digital world?

➤ From any earlier work or other observations, what do you already know about the exchanges of the community you're considering? Why do people engage in exchanges? What knowledge and interests bring those people together, and what do they communicate about? What have you seen about the shape of their rhetorical relationships and how they communicate—the genres and styles of their interactions, as well as the media they use? As we focus further on a community's online exchanges in this chapter and what they show about the community's beliefs and values, is there material you would incorporate and build on? What prior knowledge about the workings of local communities in digital and online environments are you now bringing to any further observations? Can that knowledge be built on most effectively by extending your prior inquiries into a community or by seeing how what you've learned might apply to or be altered in a different community?

Making Connections
Place and the Shapes of Communities

In a face-to-face community, people often first share a physical space—a neighborhood, a classroom, a dorm, or a locker room—that serves as a common location where group members can come together around a set of shared interests, purposes, beliefs, and values. Many of the local online communities we've looked at thus far have been extensions of those face-to-face communities. But the internet also makes it easy for people to build very large communities around any area of shared interest, like games, music, TV programs, movies like *Star Trek*, and even soap operas. Yet the **where** of the exchanges—the context, the number and characteristics of participants, the time period—remains important in understanding the literacy practices of these virtual communities. As we turn our attention from the practices of small online community to those of a large fan group, we'll find that the **where** continues to shape the **how** of these exchanges in ways that are both continuous with and different from the practices we've already seen.

Reading to Learn about a Community

Nancy Baym is a researcher who has been studying virtual communities as a professor at the University of Kansas, and now at Microsoft, at a lab that brings together social scientists who study social media with scholars of machine learning, computational biology, theoretical computer science, and economics. But she's also a long-term soap opera fan who learned much of what she knows about virtual communities by studying the online community of soap fans that she was part of and as an indie music fan who has also studied music fan communities.[8:1] For several years she also maintained a blog, Online Fandom.[L8:1] Unlike fan fiction communities, where members actually take on the persona of a fictional character and continue the narratives of the stories they've viewed or read, members of fan communities maintain aspects of their own identities as they come together to share ideas, images, links, and videos, to analyze plots or strategies or moves, and to express general interest in the object of their fandom, whether hockey, *Star Trek*, a music group, or as in Baym's case, a TV soap opera. In her study of that community, *Tune In, Log On: Soaps, Fandom and Online Community*,[8:2] Baym has shared some of the workings of that fan community and the discourse practices of its members as they came together as a defined subgroup on an early newsgroup site supporting discussion of the arts, rec.arts.tv.soaps or r.a.t.s. While the technology for such discussion groups, message boards, and forums has changed since Baym's study (see Part IV Digital Toolbox), the patterns of interaction she found and named continue to be seen in other studies of online communities (and her book has been cited in publications by other scholars more than 1,000 times).

link

BEFORE READING:

Evoking your prior knowledge

Before you read the following excerpt from Nancy Baym's longer work, think about what you already know about some of the shared ways of the community you are looking at and how community members build a rhetorical relationship with one another, developing shared purposes and building on their shared knowledge. Have you seen moments of disagreement? How do members and the community tend to deal with them? What specific things do members do to foster this community and the rhetorical relationships that are developing there?

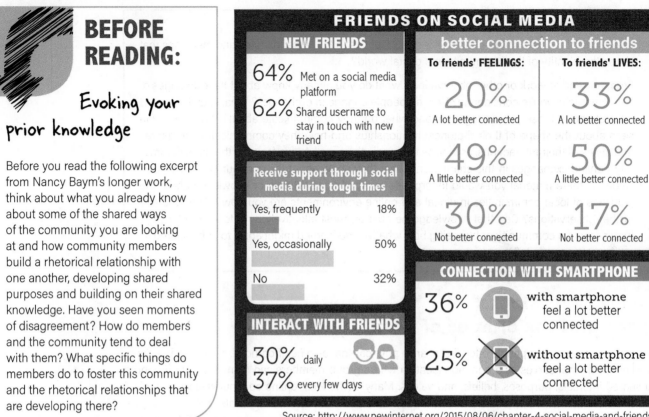

Source: http://www.pewinternet.org/2015/08/06/chapter-4-social-media-and-friendships/

"'I Think of Them as Friends,' Interpersonal Relationships in the Online Community"
by Nancy Baym
Tune In, Log On: Soaps, Fandom, and Online Community, 2000

People start to read online discussion groups because they are interested in the topics of discussion. When people first start reading rec.arts.tv.soaps (r.a.t.s.), they are attracted primarily to the wealth of information, the diversity of perspectives, and the refreshing sophistication of the soap opera discussion. Soon, however, the group reveals itself as an interpersonally complex social world, and this becomes an important appeal in its own right. For many, fellow r.a.t.s. participants come to feel like friends. Jamie's story of her involvement in the group parallels my own and reflects what several other participants describe:

> At first, I read r.a.t.s. to keep up on what was going on—again like a good book. But then you start up conversations with others. It's fascinating to see all the different points of view on such a range of topics. Then you become friends with the other posters. Pretty soon, it's like sitting down to a conversation with a bunch of close friends. Even though you've never met, you make some warm and pretty close friendships with this group. (1993 survey)

My survey question about relationships within the group—"What do you consider your relationship(s) (if any) with people on the Net to be?"—consistently elicited descriptions of the newsgroup's friendliness. This was even true of those who were new to r.a.t.s. or silent within it:

> I haven't really formed any "relationships" with anyone on the Net. I guess I view other Netters as friendly strangers, in reality. I consider myself too new to have had any real relationships with everyone, but I do think I would like to have them as friends. (Joan, 1991 survey)

> I'm a silent reader (so far:). But I think of them as friends. (Teresa, 1991 survey)

Accomplishing Friendliness

Joan and Teresa indicate that they have no one-to-one relationships with other participants. In this regard, they probably are typical of most who read r.a.t.s. regularly. After all, only a tiny minority of any Usenet group's readers actually contribute to the group; many more participants are invisible

READING

than visible. Thus, the friendly atmosphere on r.a.t.s. raises questions that are applicable to any Net group with a social atmosphere. In the case of r.a.t.s., the issue is how a group in which thousands of strangers reading what a few hundred of them write comes to see itself as an inclusive "bunch of close friends." The more general problem is how any online group comes to construct norms, in this case about what type of relationships participants share, given that most participants stay silent and there is little one-on-one interaction.

When I asked them to compare r.a.t.s. to other groups on Usenet and other networks, nearly all of my survey respondents spoke in terms of the greater friendliness of r.a.t.s., indicating how this set the group apart:

> As to other newsgroups, it doesn't compare to the other technical groups that I read. Not the same camaraderie. (Erin, 1991 survey)

> People interact in this group. It is like having a conversation. Other groups have more caustic discussions. The people I have met from this group have been really nice. It's the first group I read, and it is pleasant. (Linda, 1991 survey)

The creation of friendliness in r.a.t.s. is not a given but rather a communicative accomplishment. We already have seen a number of ways in which participants in r.a.t.s. create friendliness while addressing the topic of the soap opera. Their treatment of the soaps constructs an attractive image of the participants as intelligent and witty. The use of humor not only negotiates the problematics of participants' relationship to the soaps, it also "shows our acceptance of [the others] and our desire to please them" (Morreall, 1983, p. 115). Participants also create friendship by offering one another social support on personal issues related to the soap. . . . All of these phenomena indicate that creating friendliness is ongoing, implicit, and multifaceted. Whether consciously or not, participants orient to an ethic of friendliness when they write their messages, regardless of the particular practice in which they are engaged. In short, friendliness is something a group does rather than something a group is.

Managing Disagreement

People in r.a.t.s. are particularly aware that their sense of friendliness is demonstrated largely through a behavior they avoid. The computer often has been accused of encouraging hostile and competitive discourse. The widely noted phenomenon of flaming (i.e., attacking others) has been hypothesized to result from "a lack of shared etiquette by computer culture norms or by the impersonal and text-only form of communication" (Kiesler, Siegel, & McGuire, 1984, p. 1130). These scholars argue that rather than being mitigated, as often is the

case in face-to-face disagreements (Pomerantz, 1984), online disagreements are exaggerated. This can be a tempting argument when faced with disagreements such as the following one from a newsgroup that discusses the television show Star Trek: The Next Generation:

```
>>Just fine by me. Personally I'd like to involve
>>Lursa and her sister (the Klingons) too. Now
>>That would be a fun date.

>>—Jim Hyde

>Will you stupid jerks get a real life. Everyone
>with half a brain or more know that a human and
>a Kligon can not mate. The Klingon mating
>procedure would kill any human (except one with
>a brain like you). Stay of the net stoopid!

Oh really. Hmmmm. And I suppose Alexander and his
mom are just clones or something? If you recall,
she is half human, and Alexander if 1/4. Romulans
don't seem any more sturdy than humans, and we saw
hybrids there as well.
Looks like I'm not the one with half a brain. Check
your facts before you become the net.nazi next
time pal. This isn't just a forum for us to all bow
down and worship your opinion you know. You might
also do well for yourself to learn how to spell,
stooopid.
—Jim Hyde (rec,art,startrek,current. Apr. 12, 1993)
```

Although flaming is common online, it generally is considered bad manners. Mabry (1997) analyzed 3,000 messages collected from many forms of computer-mediated communication (CMC) and found that more "tense, antagonistic, or hostile argumentative statements" tended to be accompanied by more intense conciliatory behavior. McLaughlin, Osborne, and Smith (1995), analyzing a large corpus of messages chastising others' behavior, argue that Usenet standards discourage the wanton insulting or flaming of others. Despite this, flaming remains common in many groups. The r.a.t.s. newsgroup is not one of them, and this is inseparable from its friendliness:

> I find this to be one of the most friendly and chatty groups on Usenet. Flames are very uncommon, particularly compared to rec.arts.startrek and rec.arts.tv. (Laurie, 1991 survey)

> Comparing [r.a.t.s.] to other newsgroups: [It is] one of the nicer ones (less flame wars for the most part). (Lisa, 1991 survey)

> The group in which I find the most flame wars (thus the least friendly and supportive, in my opinion) is a local group.... I would put rec.arts.tv.soaps right under rec.pets.dogs for friendliness, support, warm[th], lack of flame wars (in Y&R [The Young and the Restless] anyway, which is the only soap I watch and read about), in general, overall enjoyment. (Teresa, 1991 survey)

This tendency to explain friendliness in terms of flaming indicates that it is easy to be friendly so long as everyone is in apparent agreement; it is in the points of disagreement that friendliness is most challenged. However, at the same time as r.a.t.s. does not want disagreement, the group is, first and foremost, in the business of maximizing interpretations, a process that inevitably leads to disagreement, especially considering how overcoded the soap operas are. Rather than considering friendliness as accomplished through behaviors that r.a.t.s. participants avoid, I look in this section to the behaviors they use to construct disagreements that attend to the ethic of friendliness.

The potential for disagreement to damage the group's sense of solidarity was enhanced in the Carter Jones discussion. This (extremely friendly) post to r.a.t.s. from Anne indicates the problem that participants faced with this story line:

```
You know I realize that whenever AMC (All My
Children) does a "heated" storyline, we all get
"heated" too! We all agree tho, it's all the
writers faults! :-)

>Man....I'm really p*ssed at those writers.
>This is too important a topic for them to give
>it the cosmetic-kissy-kiss treatment.

Oh and the cosmetics dept. too :-) I am truly
sorry to those of you that have been in an
"abused" relationship. My heart goes out to you.
I am very glad that you were smart enough to get
out of it. Applause!

I won't say what I think of men who do it. The
lowest of the low. This is just too deep a
subject to even talk about on a computer. Carter
is scum! But I guess John Wesley Shipp is ok :-)
I hope to see him a "good guy" sometime. (October
20, 1992)
```

Anne's comments that the group participants all get "heated" discussing a story line concerning subjects too deep "to even talk about on a computer" suggests that discussing this story line brought out emotions difficult to discuss even when in agreement. Such difficulty could only be enhanced when participants did not see eye-to-eye on the story line. Thus, the disagreements concerning this story line offer a revealing window into the discourse strategies that create and maintain friendliness in r.a.t.s.

Mitigating Offense

Most disagreements contained verbal components, or message features, that functioned to lessen their negative impact. Just over 40% of the disagreements used qualifiers that framed disagreements as resulting from differences in subjective opinion. Qualification leaves room for the poster

to turn out to be wrong and the other right,

From time to time, but not often, people apologize for disagreeing. This example demonstrates the apology:

```
>>Tell me, why did Brooke give Carter Jones an
>>invite to Weirdwind, & if

>She didn't INVITE him. They showed him at the
>door and the butler.

I may be wrong, but I thought Brooke did invite
Carter Jones. I actually thought he may be
covering the event as a reporter. Seeing as how
Brooke started the homeless shelter, I would
think that would give her some say in who may
attend a fund raiser. I do know she had a guest
list and showed it to Carter. That's how he
knew Galen would be there. Anyway, at the door,
he wasn't named as an invited guest, but he
identified himself as being with Tempo magazine.
(July 23, 1992)
```

```
I'm sorry, Anne my buddy, but I have to disagree
with both you and Liz... (October 19, 1992)
```

A few participants lessened the potential offense of their disagreements by explicitly framing their messages as non-offensive. This technique, used four times, is when the poster explicitly keyed her activity as something other than confrontational. In one case, this involved prefacing a contradictory assessment with "I think this is so funny." In another case, someone wrote "no offense to Knot's Landing" just before suggesting that Cape Fear had been a greater influence on the story line.

Building Affiliation

As if it were not enough to actively lessen the negative force of one's words by showing respect and backing off one's claims, as these strategies do, many disagreers articulated their disagreements in ways that actively built social alignment between the participants. For example, they frequently prefaced disagreements with partial agreements, a strategy that has been noted in face-to-face and epistolary interaction as well (Mulkay, 1985, 1986; Pomerantz, 1984). Fully 29% of the disagreements in r.a.t.s.were prefaced by partial agreements. Partial agreements generally were followed by words such as "but" and "though" or phrases such as "at the same time" that positioned what followed as disagreement. This disagreement strategy can be seen [in this example]:

"At first I'll admit I thought Nat was being very stupid too But watching her in action on Monday's show, I thought she had a good tactic. . ." (October 20, 1992).

READING

Partial agreements generally promote interpersonal harmony (Pomerantz, 1984)...

A second affiliative strategy in disagreement was the use of the other's name (used in 18% of the disagreements), as can be seen in this excerpt in which the poster makes explicit the affiliative quality of naming with the phrase "my buddy":

> **I'm sorry,** Anne my buddy, but I have to disagree with both you and Liz... (October 19, 1992)

Participants also explicitly acknowledged the perspective of the other in 12% of the disagreements.

The single most common message feature of disagreements was elaboration, which occurred in 69% of them...[for example, taking] a tangent off of the original disagreement and... moving the topic onto new ground. Offering reasoning to support the writer's perspective also was more common than any of the offense mitigators or social alignment strategies. Reasoning was given in 61% of the disagreements...

To summarize, instead of flaming, participants in r.a.t.s. attended to an ethic of friendliness by playing down the disagreement with qualifications, apologies, and reframings. They built social alignment with partial agreements, naming, and acknowledgments of the others' perspectives. They moved conversation rapidly away from the disagreement itself and back to the group's primary purpose of collaboratively interpreting the soap opera. It also is worth noting that there were relatively few disagreements over the story line—just under 10%—suggesting that one common disagreement strategy was to stay silent. The norms that protect interpretation seem to actively diffuse the force of disagreements and perhaps lead to their being voiced less often. This leads one to question to what extent a meta-text of fandom reflects genuine agreement or fans' desire to create an affiliative environment that will encourage the voicing of interpretations.

Much of what I have described is not much different from what happens in face-to-face conversation. Just as most disagreements are handled with some degree of tact in offline life, so too are they handled with an orientation toward the face of the other online. One reason that online relationships can feel like face-to-face friendships is simply that both share many of the small but essential details of human interaction used to convey warmth and respect. ■

AFTER READING:
Tracking rhetorical relationships

From reading this excerpt from Baym's book-length study of the online fan community of soap opera lovers, and entering the conversation she's initiated, what do you learn about the rhetorical relationships that have formed there?

➤ What rituals and routine ways of interacting does she describe and give examples of?

➤ What common terms do participants use in this community that others less familiar in the discourse might not know or understand in the same way?

➤ What can you say about the style of language that Baym's participants tend to use? Are there any genres or repeated forms that are particular to this discourse community?

➤ What do people, with their shared purpose of building a fan community, have to know about what to say and how to say it in building a rhetorical relationship with other participants?

In the community Baym studied, the contributions that were most valued involved humor, insight, politeness, and respect. Why were these important elements of how people communicated in that virtual community? What do you think makes contributions valued in some of the communities you focused on in your initial inquiry?

What do you learn that contributes to your own understanding of the workings of virtual communities and how they're managed and sustained through their online exchanges?

Reading as a Researcher/Writer/Composer

Baym's study is valuable to us not only because of what it tells us about the workings of an online fan community, but also as a model of the different moves a researcher makes when studying a community and then reporting their findings to an audience. We are looking at only a small selection from Baym's book, so we don't have a full account of the ways in which she worked, but we do know that one of Baym's first moves as a researcher was to choose a community to study in which she was also a participant. That gave her insider knowledge about the participants and their shared interests, as well as ongoing opportunities to observe the interactions that went on there, to look for patterns in those interactions, to collect further examples of particular types of exchanges, and to come to some larger understandings about how the community's interactions reflected their shared concerns and values. She also asked other participants about their experiences in the community (using a survey to reach its many members).

See Chapter 7
for an extended discussion of speech acts.

As Baym found patterns in the exchanges she collected, she gave names to those patterns—managing disagreement, mitigating offense—and noted some of the particular acts used to accomplish them, identifying some of their typical *speech acts*, their repeated ways of using words to act within in the community and accomplish their purposes. The concept of a speech act, which we introduced in Chapter 7, focuses our attention on the idea of rhetorical action, and speech acts like greeting, welcoming, or flaming are repeated and recognizable ways of acting in a conversation to achieve shared or sometimes conflicting or oppositional purposes. We might think of such speech acts as different strategies for accomplishing larger moves. A participant who wants to offend might use strategies of insulting or flaming, while a move of "mitigating offense" in Baym's fan community was sometimes accomplished by qualifying what the speaker was saying, and sometimes by apologizing. While the concept of *genre* helps us name some of the larger ways we engage in rhetorical action—with our discussions or debates or literacy narratives or fandom discussions—*speech acts* let us identify the smaller acts that typically contribute to these larger genres and analyze more closely both the conversational moves and the strategies that contribute to such moves in the community's exchanges.

INQUIRY

#2: Taking your initial observations further

???

Now that you have decided on a community to study, draw on Baym's model and begin to observe how communication functions in this setting in more systematic ways. If you already analyzed a speech act important to this community as you worked through Chapter 7, focus on another that helps members of this community get things done. By considering multiple speech acts, and analyzing some in more detail, you will be positioned to come to more informed conclusions about this group—to see larger patterns that will give you a richer understanding of how the members interact and the larger values and meanings these acts point to.

Begin taking notes on your observations, looking for patterns of interactions (we always find a double-entry notebook useful for recording such observations and our initial thoughts about them). Try naming some of these patterns and speech acts, and dig for further ones. Pay attention to the types of contributions central to this group and how these affect the larger workings of the community. After you have a good example, step back and freewrite about some of the larger understandings you're gaining about this community through studying these interactions.

➤ Who is involved in this speech act? Who is the speaker/writer? Who does that speaker address? What can you say about how these individuals are positioned in the larger community?

➤ Where does this speech act take place? What can you say about the context, platform, and media and how these seem to shape this speech act?

INQUIRY (continued)

➤ What is communicated? What is the content of this speech act?

➤ How is this speech act delivered? What details seem significant about how this content is communicated in this community?

➤ What purpose does this speech act seem to serve? For the speaker/writer? For the audience? For the larger community?

Once you've gathered your own detailed observations, it's a good time to return to Baym's study, to see how she has presented what she's found to a wider community of readers.

INQUIRY

#3: Analyzing Baym's moves

???

Return to the excerpt from Baym's study, rereading for **how**—for the moves she makes as a writer/composer.

➤ How does Baym work, as a writer, to bring you into the online fan community she has belonged to and studied? How does Baym provide the reader with shared knowledge about her community or evoke knowledge the reader might already have? How does she engage you as a reader?

➤ How does she work with and organize her presentation of the various types of interactions that go on in this community? Why does she suggest these elements are important to the community? Why do you think she chooses the examples she does, and how does she use her discussion of them to bring out the larger understandings she's come to about this fan group's online communication?

➤ Baym ends this portion of her community study by summarizing what she's discovered and reflecting on why these participants are able to build community in a wholly online context. Does her summary contribute to your own understanding? Do these concluding paragraphs offer a way for you to further your own thinking, as a reader, about the scholarly conversation she's brought you into?

Very often researchers will draw on the work of others, making connections between that work and their own. We can see how Baym connects to the research others have done on the speech act of "flaming" online in the following paragraph, contrasting what has been found about such behavior with the friendly behavior of her online fan group:

> Although flaming is common online, it generally is considered bad manners. Mabry (1997) analyzed 3,000 messages collected from many forms of computer-mediated communication (CMC) and found that more "tense, antagonistic, or hostile argumentative statements" tended to be accompanied by more intense conciliatory behavior. McLaughlin, Osborne, and Smith (1995), analyzing a large corpus of messages chastising others' behavior, argue that Usenet standards discourage the wanton insulting or flaming of others. Despite this, flaming remains common in many groups. The r.a.t.s. newsgroup is not one of them, and this is inseparable from its friendliness.

For connections like these, the writer will offer a brief summary or a somewhat longer paraphrase of the points made by other researchers, telling in her own words what another writer has said about a point that's relevant to her own study. There are several strategies for doing this. In this case, Baym has used a combination of *direct quoting*—drawing in an actual passage from the reading and integrating it into the flow of

Part I References and Resources
point to many other studies, some of which might be relevant to your own.

her own text—and *paraphrasing*, where she summarizes the supporting researcher in her own words. Quoting and paraphrasing from someone else's work that informs your own are important writerly moves in academic contexts—moves that help to acknowledge and build on the shared knowledge of a community whose purpose is inquiry and learning, as we saw in Chapter 5. As you compose your own community study, you'll want to look for places in Baym's or any other texts you might draw on for your study that can help you understand and explain your own findings and place those findings in the larger context of research about online discourse communities and interactions.

INQUIRY

???

#4: Connecting to Baym's research

Paraphrase a section from Nancy Baym's chapter (or another of the readings from this book or its resources), using a section you might draw on in your final community analysis. Write a paragraph in which you make connections between your study and Baym's (or another's) as you restate in your own words a key point from her text that's relevant to your own work. What has she learned, and how does it connect to what you're finding? (If you look back to Chapter 7, you can see Nate make this move as he points to Baym's discussion of flaming.)

Composing
Community Analysis

Studying communities that use digital spaces to support their extended interaction and engagement can help us come to a rich understanding about how we build and maintain relationships through words, images, and other elements of an online environment. As you further your own study of a community and report on what you've found, your own larger rhetorical purpose is to contribute to the knowledge about how digital environments are shaping the literacy practices of communities that researchers like Nancy Baym, danah boyd, and John Seely Brown have been building, and to share that new knowledge within your own classroom community and perhaps beyond.

Your study offers you an opportunity to create the rich understandings you'll share—the conclusions you will come to about the community you have been focusing on and about digital communication in broader terms, as you characterize that community, stress what is central to its use of language, its construction of a group identity, and its use of digital and networked spaces. What can others learn from a full picture of the ways of the community that will contribute to everyone's knowledge about digital literacies?

The broader points you develop about this community should be informed by the many elements you have investigated while looking at this group. One of the benefits of most informal conversations that take place online is that that they are saved in texting threads, on social media home pages, and through hashtagged posts, with associated links and images. Such archiving of conversations presents to interested researchers new opportunities to examine the shared knowledge, purpose, and ways of a community as they are reflected in that community's literacy practices. As a researcher, you will want to return to such archived moments as you frame your study by developing a specific focus.

See Chapter 18
for more information about quoting and paraphrasing research.

We'll now ask you to look more closely at another student example from our Part I Additional Readings, Hannah Morgan's study of a digital book club, "Bookworm Buddies," that was created on Goodreads. You can turn to this study and read as a composer in the process of studying a community of your own, noticing the writerly moves Hannah makes as she introduces, analyzes, and makes sense of the communicative practices central to this group, as we did with Baym's piece. We'll highlight a few examples and moves from Hannah's study, and note others from Nate's "Mob Q-Records" and from Richard's "The Dragon Court World" as we consider the moves you might make in your own composing.

INQUIRY

#5: Noting the moves Hannah makes

As you read "Bookworm Buddies," note the moves Hannah makes to engage her readers, to introduce this community, to highlight specific elements of interest in her study, and to question the importance of the language use she saw repeated. Identify at least three productive moves you see Hannah making here that you might like to emulate in your own study of a community that draws on digital resources to house and enable their interactions.

WRITING MOVES

Inquiring and Inventing

Gathering and analyzing data about a community typically involves moving back and forth between collecting material, seeing what you might learn from it, going back to get more information that will let you expand on your first insights, and finally moving into a closer analysis of what you've found. You might have been involved in this process as you moved through Chapters 6 and 7, or you might have just begun collecting data on this particular community. Researchers of discourse communities and their literacy practices find great value in looking at a community's interactions over a stretch of time. If you have been focusing on one community as you worked through the later chapters of Part I, you are most likely well positioned to make some larger points about that community. This section is meant to help you locate a larger point, theme, or question you want to develop in your study.

1 Sharing your intentions

As you bring the words or images of a group into work you'll share with your classroom community and perhaps beyond, it's important to share your intentions with members of a local community you're studying and get their permission to draw on what they've shared. Those who post publicly on Twitter or contribute to large online games or fan group discussions are already sharing their contributions with a wide audience, most often under a handle that obscures their personal identity, and they are unlikely to post anything they wouldn't want shared further, making this less of a concern. But to study participants in a private community like the two-person online friendship community, Mehdi focused on, it's important to get the participants' informed consent before bringing their words into new contexts with new audiences (and we haven't reproduced Mehdi's full study with the words of their exchanges because his friend wasn't comfortable with those words being shared beyond Mehdi's classroom).

An informal email exchange in which you explain your study and participants agree to your use of their words is probably sufficient for semiprivate

use within your classroom. But if you think you'll want to post your work for a wider public audience, you'll want to create a more formal consent form that explains the purpose and scope of your project, offers individuals the option of being referred to using a pseudonym, and makes clear how the material will be made public (and we offer an example in Chapter 18).

Once you have sufficient consent from participants, you'll want to consider how to move further into your inquiry and analysis.

2 Extending your observations

You're likely now to have an idea of the big questions that interest you about the community you've selected and what might be interesting to your readers. Hannah tells us about why she chose to study a book discussion group:

> I was interested in the group mainly because I love to read and to hold discussions with others based on the stories that I have just read. I thought that of all the places to study a community, a book discussion group would be a good choice, since it

would allow me the chance to study how people present their opinions and how they react to others' thoughts and views, whether they agree with them or not. Also, to me, meeting a bunch of strangers on the internet and planning to read the same book at the same time seems to create a strong sense of camaraderie, and I thought it would be interesting to study a community that had that.

We learn that Hannah was drawn to the group's camaraderie and wanted to see how it was achieved as members presented their opinions and responded to others. With this framing question in mind, she was able to make further observations of community interactions.

As you return to the community you're studying with your own questions in mind, you'll want to learn more about community interactions and how their content and style give shape to a rhetorical relationship. You'll want to discover how they help to support the larger beliefs, values, and purposes that are important to this community and how they are being facilitated or altered by digital media.

3 Identifying patterns and focusing on a theme

From your observations, what patterns are you beginning to see in your community's communications? What has emerged as the most important theme about your community that you'd like to show? How would you characterize this community? What kind of repeated rhetorical situations emerge there? Baym focuses on the friendliness of the online fan community she studies, Hannah on the welcoming nature of the Bookworm Buddies online book club, Nate on the competitiveness of the two groups involved with Mob Q-Records, and Richard on how well people get along with one another within a global gaming community, "Even the people you would think would be fighting, like the members of the community from Israel and the Arab states."

Hannah finds patterns that support the sense of a welcoming community. She names one move, "expressing identity," as members use different strategies for the speech act of introducing themselves. She also finds welcoming moves to greet newcomers, as well as a particular speech act of "inviting" others to take part in the discussion of a particular book in a community genre named the "Buddy Read." The members, too, she points out, have ways of dealing with differences of opinion respectfully and politely.

4 Gathering additional data and examples

What additional evidence of community interactions can you gather to show support of this characterization? Snippets from conversations, texts, or online exchanges? You might record a face-to-face conversation, draw on a digital conversation (texts, a Facebook thread, Instagram comments), or use a combination of the two. If you're considering presenting your profile in a digital format, this is a good time to gather relevant images, make audio recordings of exchanges in your community (with permission), or capture snippets of TV shows or music videos that are shared in your community and that represent their values and interests.

Digital Toolbox
See Part IV, Section 4

Hannah captures screenshot examples of Bookworm Buddies interactions. You might also look at the article on online music fandom that Baym wrote for an **online journal**,[L8:2] to see the variety of visual images that she used to capture the ways of that community.

Digital Toolbox
See Part IV, Section 5

5 Comparing observations across settings

To get a better sense of the community you are studying, you should compare it to other communities as you consider how they get things done with language. Do this by working collaboratively with your classmates to share the data you have collected. Ideally, you will be able to do this with others looking at similar communities or who might be developing related themes. What trends do you notice across settings? What distinct attributes become apparent about the community you are studying? What new realizations does a collaborative learning approach present?

6 Analyzing interactions

Begin to analyze the interactions and rhetorical situations that seem most representative of what goes on in this community. Taking notes, consider **what** is being discussed and **why**, **how**, and **where** these interactions take place.

- Where does this conversation take place, online or face to face? How do these different spaces affect community members and alter how they communicate?

- Consider what is being discussed and why this/ these topic(s) matter in this community. In online communities formed around shared interests, like Hannah's, the larger topic may be obvious (books!), but the specific choices, like the *Outlander* series of historical fiction, might say more about what the group cares about and values.

- Consider what shared knowledge members can draw on and that newcomers may not understand. The members of Baym's online fan community share detailed knowledge of episodes and plot lines, but also know one another in ways that show the tight social network that has formed in this setting. They also have an understanding of how to participate in this specific digital setting to maintain and extend the purposes of the group itself. The members of Richard's gaming community need significant shared knowledge of Dragon Court, its structure and purposes, as well as its genres—the story lines that are created, as well as the speech acts that are central to its interactions.

- Highlight special terms that members of this discourse community need to know to participate. Baym's participants, for example, use the term "TAN's" for moments when contributors go off on a tangent that's not immediately relevant to the main topic. Why might the terms you find be important in this community?

- Consider **how** people interact in this setting. Do you find patterns of repeated interactions, like the welcoming greetings Hannah finds in the book club? Other routines and rituals? Are they closely tied to particular speech acts: complimenting, persuading, gossiping, or complaining? Can you group them into categories and name those categories, those larger moves, as Baym did (for example: mitigating offense, building affiliation)? What does this repeated type of interaction suggest about this community? Do members adopt certain rhetorical stances when they contribute? Do they take on particular roles, and are those roles related to the types of interactions they engage in and how they contribute to them?

- How else would you characterize the style of language used in these acts of communication, what are its features, and what do you think this style shows? Is it carried over multiple conversations or settings? Across multiple digital platforms? Hannah finds the conversational style of the book club to be polite and relatively formal overall, but she thinks the politeness is also shown as members point out that they're only expressing an opinion, often using an informal abbreviation "imho" (in my honest opinion). Nate finds a pattern of dissing in his music group, with informal language that could be seen as insulting by outsiders, a pattern that appears in Facebook, in their music, and most likely face to face.

- Why do you think members interact in these ways? What are their immediate purposes? Their larger ones? Baym sees the types of interactions in the online fan group as immediately avoiding conflict and over time creating a community of friends. The dissing in Nate's community seems to highlight conflict, yet below that style of exchange, he finds that group argues to stay together, as "family."

Here's Hannah's analysis of the purpose of the "imho" examples she's captured:

> In both comments, Susan adds that what she writes is just "imho" or "in my honest opinion" and that it was just her opinion. In her second comment, she reacts a bit defensively, which is understandable when one takes into consideration that she just joined the group and may not be used to the way in which they interact and share their opinions. Chuck then replies in a friendly manner that he does not agree with her opinion of the book not being character driven, but he also makes sure to mention that he agrees with her point about learning a thing or two from the book. Mentioning that he agrees with at least a part of her statement is a good tactic in making sure that Susan does not feel alienated from the discussion.

Sidenote

IMHO is often defined as meaning "in my humble opinion."

WRITING MOVES

Drafting and Shaping

How do you make choices about presenting the things you've discovered about the community you've studied to others who might be interested? As writers/composers repeatedly place their own work into larger conversations, they generate common moves and styles that both draw on and adapt the genres used in a particular community. A study of an online community will inevitably have a different shape and style if it's written by someone like Baym, who is speaking to an audience of other media researchers, versus a marketing professional who wants to figure out how to advertise to such internet users. Whether you're addressing your classroom community or a larger one online, you will want to draw on your understanding of the rhetorical relationships that have formed there.

1 Considering your rhetorical situation and audience

As always in composing, you'll want to think about the **rhetorical situation** you are writing within, and this begins with paying attention to shared purposes, shared knowledge, and shared ways of a community.

> **rhetorical situation**
> the context that shapes how a composer draws upon language to accomplish something

- The audience you're composing for is one element of your composing context, or the *rhetorical situation*. In considering the rhetorical situation you'll want to think about the context your readers or viewers are coming from, **where** they'll be reading the text, **why** they might read/view/listen to what you compose, and **what** prior knowledge they are likely to have about this topic from their lives, from the media, and from their studies. What experiences and expectations are they likely to bring about **how** material like this might be presented—in what mediums, in what shapes, in what style of language?

- Your own situation as a writer/composer is another element. Your purposes in studying the community you've chosen and sharing what you've learned are your **why** and **what**, and the resources you'll draw on for presenting what you've learned in a particular form are your **how**.

- Your text or digital composition and **where** it might fit into a world of other such compositions is yet another element. Whenever you share your ideas, words, and images with others, you're placing them in the larger context of other writing about related ideas, other presentations of similar material. How has that writing (Baym's work, for

example) contributed to your own understandings, and what do you want to contribute back to that larger conversation about how communities function (to a larger body of shared knowledge about online communities)? How have the moves that writers like Nancy Baym or Hannah Morgan made contributed to your sense of how to shape your own material—what to include and where? And how have other presentations (the images or sound files included in a blog post, or Hannah's screenshots, for example) contributed to your sense of the composition you want to create?

In the end, you always want to build on what's already shared about where, why, what, and how to create a new shared space and new understandings with your intended audience. Why might they read/view/listen to what you compose, and how might their purposes overlap with your own? What might they know (what are some commonly shared understandings about your topic) or want to know (what new and interesting insights can you offer)? How might they expect you to present these new understandings, and how can you use your own sense of style, genre, rhetoric, and media to shape a presentation that will be effective in addressing shared purposes and creating new shared knowledge?

2 Orienting your readers

Where and how will you remind your readers of the shared background knowledge they're likely to bring to your study, and where will you need to provide new background information? We saw that Mehdi's readers were less interested in a lot of detail about electronic communication—something they knew a great deal about—so he could eliminate that information as he focused more on the nature of online friendship. You will need to present a rich description of your community like the ones provided by Baym, Hannah, and Nate.

How can you bring your readers into the community you're writing about in an interesting way? Good strategies might include setting the scene ("It's 2 a.m. on Thursday on the East Coast, and players from all over the world are sitting intently in front of their computers playing World of Warcraft") or beginning with a moment of interaction ("'Ready for battle?' asks Jack of Knives") and then stepping back to provide the background that will help readers to understand how such moments function in the community. Baym begins her book with a moment of her personal narrative as a player to gain her readers' involvement in a longer research study.

> My daily routine in graduate school went something like this. When I was done teaching, taking my classes, and doing the readings or whatever else had to be done that day, I curled up on my couch, rewound the videotape, and (making liberal use of the fast-forward button) watched my soaps. Later, I turned on my computer and logged on to rec.arts.tv.soaps (r.a.t.s.), a Usenet newsgroup distributed through the internet. Once "there"—in my tiny study nook with the computer before me—I read the many messages that had been posted about my soaps, sometimes sending my own. The r.a.t.s. newsgroup transformed my understanding of computers; for the first time, I saw them as social tools. The more time I spent reading and posting to r.a.t.s., the less the collection of written messages seemed like lines of glowing green text. I saw in them instead a dynamic community of people with unique voices, distinctive traditions, and enjoyable relationships. Reading r.a.t.s. began to influence me as I viewed the soap opera. I began to think of how those others would react, the types of discussion each episode would provoke, and what I might have to add. Soap viewing had become the base on which witty, sociable women and men had built an interpersonal realm rich with strong traditions and a clear group identity.

You might also begin with an image from your community—perhaps a player hunched over a controller, a screenshot, or even a video clip of a game in progress."

3 Drawing on the full range of data you've gathered

While this chapter has focused on the close analysis of typical patterns of verbal interaction, if you've looked at this community in any earlier chapters or inquiries, you've probably gathered other material, such as examples of how members use photos or texts to support their relationships or bring links and videos and music from a wider culture into their conversations. If you do have such material, consider how it fits with the interactions you're focusing on now. Focus on what else it tells you about the community and its ways and values. And include a section in your report where you tell your readers how you collected the data you're using (a "methods" section). Richard captured online exchanges in the world of Dragon Court, but he also polled participants in this global but "local" community, asking "where they came from, what age they are, and if they are male or female." (Of his respondents at that moment, 58 percent came from the United States, they averaged 21-22 years of age, and 88 percent were male.)

4 Identifying where to include key points and how to illustrate them

What are the key points you want to make about the community you're analyzing—understandings that have emerged from your observations of community interactions? And in what order? What examples will you want to include to illustrate those points? Both Baym and Hannah include examples that show how their communities remain friendly and avoid conflict, and Richard shows the same for his more global community. Mehdi eventually included actual examples of online exchanges that showed how open and supportive of each other he and his friend were.

Where will you quote from the material you've gathered? Will you want to integrate screenshots and other visual material or sound clips as part of your supporting evidence?

5 Making connections to other related studies

Have you drawn on Baym's study or other resources (including the studies of your classmates) to support your own understandings about how and why members of a community might interact in some of the ways you've found? Hannah draws on two other sources. One is an online essay by Stacy Koosel about negotiating digital identities.[8.3] The other is the blog post by danah boyd that was included in Chapter 3. Here's the connection she makes to boyd, contrasting the ways of the Bookworm Buddies community with the ways of the teens on Facebook that boyd studied:

> The inclusive attitude is also shown in the way that, unlike in dana boyd's study, the members of Bookworm Buddies do appear to communicate to only one audience; the other people who are reading the thread. While Carmen chose a particular phrase to communicate to two different audiences, none of the members of this community use any form of steganography in their comments (boyd). While they may at times send each other private messages, usually to let the person who started the thread know that they will not be able to participate in the buddy read, everything that they write in the comments is intended for others to read. What they write is what they mean, there are no hidden messages.

6 Reflecting on what you've discovered

Throughout your report on your community study, you'll be drawing on reflection—telling your readers what you think about why specific details are important and what they show about the community you are studying, leading readers to broader, more generalized points about this community, and answering the implicit question "so what?" But you might add further reflections on your new understandings or speculations or the implications of what you've learned, as Baym has done in her final paragraph:

> Much of what I have described is not much different from what happens in face-to-face conversation. Just as most disagreements are handled with some degree of tact in offline life, so too are they handled with an orientation toward the face of the other online. One reason that online relationships can feel like face-to-face friendships is simply that both share many of the small but essential details of human interaction used to convey warmth and respect.

Revising and Publishing

As with all compositions, you'll want to share your work with a peer audience, and perhaps with members of the community you're focusing on. If you're writing for two different audiences, those members as well as your classmates, your peer response group, might role-play as members of the other audience.

1 Responding to guiding questions

You can use the guiding questions below as a starting point for your peer response, adding others as you continue your conversation about audience needs and expectations and your intentions and message as composers.

- What is your initial experience of this composition? How do you enter it as a reader or viewer/listener? Retrace your reading/viewing/listening path and the moments of connection, insight, questions that arose for you.

- If the composer has completed a multimodal profile, what images strike you as most powerful? How do they support or compliment the rest of this piece? If there is audio or video used, what strikes you about the material? How do you see these modalities working together?

- How does this composer characterize this community? What kind of community is it?

- Does the composer provide the shared knowledge and background information you need about this community? What else do you want to know?

- What is the most important thing the composer is trying to show about the community? Does the composer describe that facet clearly? Where?

- What other points does the composer make about the community?

- Does the composer have a clear pattern of organization?

- Does the composer provide appropriate textual, visual, or audio evidence for the main points? Does the evidence include actual examples or images from observations of interactions or words from exchanges? Note where more evidence could be added.

- In a written text, does the conclusion reaffirm the writer's new understandings? Is there anything else you'd add to it? In a multimodal composition, do you find an effective conclusion to what the composer has discovered and shared in text, sound, or image?

- What other advice would you give to this writer/composer?

2 Responding with a template or generative rubric

Working together and drawing from your experience with the peer review questions above, create a working rubric of key elements that seem most central to effective community studies. You may want to create different versions of your rubric to take into account some of the differences between profiles prepared for print audiences and those for digital audiences.

3 Responding with ideas for presentation in different media

Thinking about how one might present a study in a different medium can provide further insight into ways in which the original presentation might be enriched.

How might the composer use different media, such as additional text, images, and sounds, to enhance the ways in which this community is introduced?

Even if the writer does not finally use another medium, these suggestions can highlight what is important to this piece.

link

4 Revising

From reviewing your own composition and those of your peer composers, what changes to your composition will most help to make your profile effective for your audience(s)? You may want to focus first on making those changes in structure, detail, clarifying additions, and deletions that will lead to a finished composition in whatever media(s) it was initially created in. However, a composition in a new medium might, in the end, better suit your audience and purpose.

5 Finishing touches

Proofreading. Have you polished a final written text? Do grammatical or surface-level features, affect the readability of this text? Have you made sure that all textual elements in a digital composition have been proofread?

Adding Works Cited. If you've referred to work by other researchers, including classmates, you'll need to add a list of Works Cited, as Hannah has done. We suggest MLA format, which you can find at the Purdue Online Writing Lab.[L8:3]

Formatting. Have you formatted a print text in an appropriate way, making it easily readable?

6 Circulating

How will you share your richly detailed and polished study with others? Will you post it to a class website as Mehdi did? Will you post it to a site for your college or university? Will you post it on a public site that accepts student submissions?

Reinventing and Circulating Your Work

If your peer response gave you ideas for translating your work into different media—a process sometimes referred to as **transmediation**—you might already have ideas for recreating your study using another medium, such as audio or video, or using a mix of digital media in a multimodal presentation.

transmediation
the process of translating a work into a different medium

Digital Toolbox
See Part IV, Section 4

➤ **Option 1: Drawing on multiple modalities.** Your profile of a community, especially a virtual community, can be enhanced in a multimedia composition. You have probably captured screenshots of interactions or images related to the community's interests. If what brings the community together involves an audio element, you can record and include that as well.

If you decide to create a digital presentation through PowerPoint or other presentation software, or on a website, wiki, or blog, you'll want to consider the following.

- What images to include (those that will provide important background knowledge and/or illustrate the points you are making)
- Where to include them
- Whether, where, and how to include audio or a video
- Whether and how to narrate your presentation (how much text to include on PowerPoint slides, for example, and whether to create a script to follow, offering key points beyond what's on those slides, for your presentation)

link

Baym also gave a talk about music fandom at a music industry event in Norway in which she used a number of visual images to help her audiences gain a richer picture of how music fan communities work. You can follow the link to that talk at her Online Fandom blog.[L8:4]

➤ **Option 2: Creating an audio profile.** Studies of communities also appear frequently in audio formats, and you might choose to create a fully audio community analysis. At the website for the National Public Radio program <u>This American Life</u>,[L8:5] for example, you can find many audio profiles of a wide range of communities, including a convention for a fan community for the TV program <u>Dark Shadows</u>.[L8:6] Listen to this audio community profile or find another that interests you and imagine your own community study produced as a podcast. What might you capture in your piece (Background sounds? The voices of community members? The voice of a narrator? Music?), and how could you arrange these elements? If you've recorded examples of exchanges in your community or other audio artifacts, you can weave them together with your own narration to bring out the key points and examples that characterize your community.

Digital Toolbox
See Part IV, Section 4

Key Concepts

changing literacies 143
discourse communities 144
rhetorical situation 158

transmediation 162
virtual communities 144

Additional **Readings**

Contents

READING 1

"Rise to Fame: Nigel Thomas"
by Nate Jolley (Student)

In this profile, Nate Jolley, a student at Coastal Carolina University, introduces us to Nigel Thomas, a rapper who goes by the name "Fame," and who uses emerging technologies to produce and distribute his music. Fame and his experiences are central to this piece, and his voice, which Nate makes prominent by quoting him directly, helps us understand him and the community that frames his rapping and lifestyle. As you read the profile, you'll find that Nate draws on Fame's characteristic ways of speaking, capturing comments like "we started doin' our little freestyle thing at lunch and shit, rappin' over the phone, battling with some of those older n____s." By using direct quotations, though, Nate differentiates this language from the academic voice he establishes for himself.

The purpose of a profile is to present a key aspect of a subject's lived experiences, and this language speaks to Fame's position in the rapping community. The linguist H. Samy Alim of Stanford University who studies the use of language in social contexts points out that the n-word has both "positive in-group meanings and pejorative out-group meanings," and suggests that participants in the world of rap and hip-hop have chosen to reflect the positive meanings with a new spelling (ending the word with an "a" rather than "er"). "The "n-word" then becomes your main man, or one of your close companions, your homie."[7,8] This is clearly the meaning that Fame intends and that Nate shares with us as readers, offering a portrait of Fame that captures his own sense of a particular aspect of his social identity and the community it is rooted in.

There are many rooms in a house. Each of these rooms hold special meaning. The kitchen is the place to be when it comes to food, cooking and snacks. The living room is the lounging area, the place where the people of the house sit and just relax. The bedroom is where many lay their heads to rest, to go to sleep after a long day of work or school. But in Nigel's house, there is one particular room that holds a special meaning. It holds more significance to him than every other room in his house.

Its original purpose was to be a typical bedroom, a place for perhaps a bed or dresser. Unfortunately, it is anything but a bedroom. There is no hint of a bed in sight when you walk in this seemingly out of place room. On the initial walk in, it feels like you step into a completely different world. The first thing you see when walking in are 3 different computer screens, each laced with projections of various parts of a music recording program. These screens sit upon a 2 leveled sturdy desk, about the size of a kitchen counter, painted black but worn from years of use. The screens sit on the first level, while a black keyboard and matching mouse sit on the desk. The keyboard has many extra keys that are not even present on a typical keyboard. The mouse has a green under glow, dimming when not in use but brightening while in use. Under the desk is the central processing unit or main hard drive, which all the peripherals of the room are connected through seemingly endless cables and where the music program itself is housed inside a dance of chips and wires. In the left corner of the room is a microphone, gleaming a chrome black when the lights are on but nearly invisible when the light is off. In front of it is a guard that prevents saliva and unwanted sounds from being recorded. Around various spots of the room, there are huge speakers that are used to project music. These speakers, which are rectangular in shape, are roughly 2 to 3 feet tall, laced with black cloth and steel, giving a durable yet elegant look. These speakers are built to project sound throughout the room, and they do their job amazingly, almost too well, sometimes blasting music throughout the house as well as the neighborhood when playing music loudly. The walls are painted red, not at all relevant to the color of the various devices of the room. Yes, this seemingly other worldly room is a home grown music studio, where a young man of 18 accomplishes things most would dream of, using the technology of today's age to create his own original sound, and then share that sound with the world though social media and music posting sites. Nigel Thomas, or more commonly known to the music community as Fame, understands that without many of the advances that technology has made in recent years, none of what he does would be possible. As Fame explains, "Technology has made my movement possible. Everything I do is because of the computers, the mics, all that." He knows that without these advances, his music would not be possible.

"Fame" was born Nigel Thomas on May 12, 1995. Growing up in the small town of Kingstree, SC, he knew since adolescence that he wanted to rap. Fame elaborates, "I started when I was little, around 12 or 13, but I never really told anyone. It was just a talent that I had. I really tried to keep it on the down low, y'know what I'm sayin', like be real low key cuz I didn't know how people was gonna react." He didn't get any true recognition from peers until he reached high school and met like-minded individuals. Fame recalls, "I was really just chillin' with it until I met Nate and Von, and we started doin' our little freestyle thing at lunch and shit, rappin' over the phone, battling with some of those older niggas." In fact, it wasn't until a year and a half later, in Florida, that he actually got to record in a studio for the first time. Fame tells me, "I never got into the studio until I moved out of the K and moved to Florida. And that's when I got my shine, and started the DMP movement and things really kicked off from there."

However, when Fame moved back, he realized that the friends he had in Florida never really promoted his music. "When I moved back to the K, I ain't had no fans, like niggas didn't even know I had bars until they heard some of my later tracks." His main priority when moving back was to grasp a true fan base, which meant getting back in the studio. Fame stares into the distance and continues, "Niggas don't understand how much technology means to this music shit. To get that fan base, that recognition, takes time, money, and technology. Those the keys to music right there." He had to rebuild a completely new fan base under a new name, and do this under his own terms. He began the process of building a home studio, using some things he brought from Florida, along with other things he either bought or had loaned to him. "I'm thankful for the people who help me set up the studio at the crib," he explains. "I show a lot of love to them for that. They helped me get on my feet, and in turn I promised them that I'd do this the right way, like represent for them on the track. And that's what I do."

With his studio finished, now came the easy part (at least to him): recording. He talks with a chuckle as he explains, "Recording a track is both easy and fun to me. It may take a minute sometimes, and sometimes be rough as hell on your body and mind, but it's easy to me cuz I love what I do." He goes on to explain the "daily grind" of making a typical song. "After writin' the bars," (lyrics) "And finding that vibe," (an instrumental) "I start workin' my magic. I start recording. Sometimes it takes a few times to get that perfect voice right, but eventually they (or I) get it good. After that, I usually edit that voice, maybe dub it or add a couple ad libs to it for a better effect. Then I keep editin' some more, maybe turn down the voice; change the equalizer, things like that." Sounds extra easy, right? A typical recording session could have Fame up until 5 a.m. doing editing alone. "It's not just a talent thing. You gotta be strong in the mind to do this. Not just rappin' or spittin', but editing too. It just comes down to a patience game sometimes." And patience is a virtue when configuring with various sound editing software. Adobe, Pro Tools, and Audacity are just a few of the programs made for the "common man," studio quality sound at a somewhat affordable price. "I love Adobe. It's great for what I do and I know how to use it. So naturally, it's the best program ever." He realizes that the programs, as well as other peripherals, such as microphones, speakers, and amps, are all necessary in his creative process.

The hard part of his music is of course, getting his name heard by other people outside his community. "Bein' known at home is all good," he says, "but I wanna be known everywhere. Like I wanna be able to just ride to another state and people be like 'Oh shit! That's Fame right there!' It's one of the things I really wanna accomplish." Social media is one of the ways he's trying to get this accomplished. He is constantly posting his musical whereabouts and happenings onto his Facebook and Twitter pages. He has even made a fan page for his rap group DMP. He smiles as I bring up the name. "DMP. I love my group. They some mad lyrical niggas that I got together and I'm almost always ridin' with them on one of my songs. Those just some lyrical niggas that I grew up with, and when I shine they shine too. That's the purpose." He tries as best as he can to promote not just himself, but the group, as well as his friends. The main way he does this is through a music site called SoundCloud. On this site, users can post and share original "sounds" that they either come across or create. Fame speaks on SoundCloud saying, "SoundCloud is life. Without it, I don't think I would be able to function, bruh. It's probably the biggest part of everything I do. Me, DMP, we live and die by that damn website. If I didn't have it…" (He pauses to think for a second) "…I'm glad I got SoundCloud, bruh."

At the end of the interview, I asked Fame how the music industry would fair without technology. He almost threw a fit. He looked me directly in my eyes and said, "There are so many reasons I could list for this question, bruh. First, technology made it possible for me to record music in the first place. All these programs and shit, the mics, the computers, all that makes us, me, possible. Second, without the Internet, we wouldn't be able to broadcast our sound at all. There would be no real way for our music to get out there, and I ain't sellin' CD's and shit out of my house. That's dead. Jay Z? That nigga pre released a whole album as an app. Who you know does somethin' like that? That's the whole point of mixing music and technology.

Technology is just an everyday part of life now, especially for this music shit. Living today, niggas can't blow up or even get heard without technology. It's everything bruh…everything." And the passion with which he said this made me understand how important technology was, and is, to his craft. He thrives off of the advances of our technological age.

And, as I suspect, he will continue to thrive off of those technologies as he continues his budding music career. ∎

Questions

❶ What moves does Nate make to introduce Fame to his readers? What do you notice about how he opens this piece? About how he moves readers through it? About the details and descriptions he uses?

❷ What moves does Nate make to create a larger sense of purpose in this piece? What is your sense of why he profiles Fame? What is his purpose for describing his experiences and quoting his words?

❸ What moves does Nate make to extend the focus of his class and of this book in his profile? What do you learn about emerging technologies and music production from this piece? What do you come to see about the community that situates Fame's experiences?

READING 2

"Mob Q-Records: More Than Music"
by Nate Jolley (Student)

In "Mob Q-Records," Nate Jolley extends the work he did introducing Fame in his profile by describing and analyzing the larger Mob Q Records rapping community as he looks to their typical and repeated communicative acts. Specifically, he examines "the diss" as a speech act, situating it in the participants typical interactions, describing the importance of this act to the Mob Q community and showing how such interactions support a family-like bond for the insiders of this group. In this instance, Nate captures a typical exchange within the group with a screenshot of a Facebook comments thread, a strategy that again allows him to represent the typical Mob Q style of language in his own academic writing. By focusing on one Facebook exchange Nate offers evidence of the ways in which the significant Mob Q speech act of dissing is carried beyond the members' face-to-face exchanges and music lyrics and into their online conversations. At the same time he draws on this example to support the larger meanings he wants to share about this community, to show how even one Facebook exchange reflects both their typical discourse practices and the larger beliefs and values that the community shares. As you read this piece, pay attention to the moves Nate makes to consider the where, what, why, and how of this conversation.

It's a late Saturday night on Facebook, and 4 individuals of a rap group are going at it again. It's the classic debate about which side of the rap group is better. One side argues that the "All Powerful" Red Side has the Mob taken over. But "The Prestigious" Blue Side claims they're "The Realest Niggas" on Mob Q. And so the argument begins about not only who is better, but who actually has the most influence inside the rap group outside of Facebook. Truths come out about how everyone who's a part of the Red Side is only a part of that side because of the "Killer Kid," otherwise known as Young Q. Others call a member of the Blue Side, S Thugga "Trashcan Sam," which is an offensive nickname. Then all of a sudden, the arguing seems to cease as one of the founders, DJ Q, tells the group of another rapper that is trying to diss Mob Q. At once they put this arguing aside and begin their coordinated attack on the individual who would dare try to come at Mob Q Records. They know the outcome, as they've been dissing people for almost a decade, so it's just a matter of who has the pride to diss these outsiders. This gives each member a sense of not only who is loyal to the group, but also gives them a safety net in tough times. They know that if an event was to happen in their lives, the members of the group would be there for them, regardless of if they argue or not.

Mob Q Records, (Mob Q or the Mob for short) is, as its name states, a music recording group. Each member of the group has, at one point or another, recorded music or has featured in a song. The group was founded by longtime best friends Marquis Kingcade and Quincy Johnson, known to the group as King Quis and DJ Q, respectively. They created this rap group back in the early to late 90's in their home town of Kingstree, SC. Upon creation, their group had the motto, "Diss Anybody Records." This implied that anyone who entered the group could attack anybody in the group via music, as well as any other rapper outside the group. They began creating music and word quickly spread in the neighborhood, as well as throughout the town that these young men were creating music, and so other people from all walks of life began to join the group. They had many members, both male and female, join the group. Many were people that the duo already knew, such as Olin Hunter (aka O), who was already living in the neighborhood DJ Q and King Quis were from. Another member, Nate Jolley (known at the time as Lil' Nate), joined the group in '08 and was the 2nd youngest member of the group. Quincy's younger cousin, Quintin Simmons, also joined the group and at the time he was only 8 years old.

The Mob is split into 2 sides: The Red Side and The Blue Side. It is best to imagine it like a high school setting. In high school there are juniors and seniors. Both are considered upper classmen, but both battle for supremacy of that particular school. The only true distinction is that the seniors have a year more experience. And in those respective classes are leaders, the individuals who have the most say so, or give an identity to that class. The Red and Blue Sides are exactly like this, with the Blue Side as the juniors and the Red Side as the seniors. The Red side has much more influential people on their side, hosting veterans such as DJ Q and Young Q. The Blue Side hosts only one veteran in King Quis, and a host of other members picked up throughout the years. Because of this, the

Red Side, for many years, had major influence in the Mob. The numbers for each side differ as well. At the Mob's peak, The Red Side had 11 members, while The Blue Side had 8 members. Total, the group contained 19 members, of which only 17 are still in the group. Don't get me wrong; each side has their own set of people who contribute greatly not only to that side, but to the Mob as a whole. But, in the end of it all, members of Mob Q have been groomed in such a way that if they had to argue with someone, they would most likely win. They argue so much that it becomes second nature to them, and they can do it with ease, regardless of the situation.

Arguing and "beef" is an everyday thing in Mob Q. Sometimes individuals have their own separate problems with each other. Other times there may be arguing between The Red and Blue Sides. Many arguments happen on the Mob Q Facebook page, which is the hub for everything that goes on in the group. If anything gets posted to the page, whether it's a video, a new song, a comment or a status update, all members are immediately notified. So this means that anything that goes up onto the page is public knowledge for everyone in the group to see.

For example, when a new song gets posted, there may be comments either arguing its significance or comments complementing or criticizing either its content or quality. Below is a typical conversation between members on a song posted to the page:

Quincy Johnson Fire! !!!!!!!!!!!
March 29 at 9:11pm · Like · 2

Quincy Johnson I think that will do it !
March 29 at 9:11pm · Like · 2

Quintin Simmons Real freestyle
March 29 at 9:12pm · Like · 1

Quincy Johnson I know that man said he didn't understand the first one so I turned everything down so he can here that fire burning his ass !
March 29 at 9:15pm · Like · 2

Quincy Johnson You know me I try to make everybody happy!
March 29 at 9:16pm · Like · 2

Charlie Shaw Tru shit
March 29 at 9:19pm · Like · 3

Marquis Kingcade Man u just killed them niggas, and i can understand clearly wat ur saying
March 29 at 9:28pm · Like · 1

Quincy Johnson I can't stop listening to this
March 29 at 9:38pm · Like · 2

Marquis Kingcade That was the death of 3mo1, them niggas dead, did u heard this mf song, yq murdered them niggas
March 30 at 4:28pm · Like · 4

Marquis Kingcade Damn!!!!!

This particular conversation is also an example of one thing that is THE most important part of the Mob Q: Family. I don't mean physically being a relative of someone in the group, though in the case of some members, this is true. Baym talks about flaming being detrimental to some groups (490), but this isn't the case for the Mob. Flaming is not only a big part of the group, but for some reason, it keeps the group together. Members of Mob Q argue and fight with each other on a day to day basis, much like siblings. But at the end of the day, the arguing is what makes their bond so strong. In the above conversation, they were discussing and commenting on how Young Q made a song about a person who decided to join Mob Q, but attempted to keep ties with his old rap group, which didn't sit too well with members of Mob Q. His loyalty was questioned and eventually, they had to diss him. He was later kicked from the group. During this time, all members of the Mob banded together to diss him, and immediately put aside any differences they had in order to attack this outsider. They considered this person a traitor to the group because they felt he didn't believe in this "family" mentality. Almost immediately

after they finished with him, not even an hour, they immediately went back to arguing, as if they had never even dissed him in the first place. This just shows that even though they argue daily, it just furthers the bond that they share when it comes to outsiders and non group members.

As much as they argue, and as much as they diss each other continually, that arguing is central to every member who becomes a part of Mob Q Records. They have a saying, "If you don't diss, you don't care about the family. And if you don't care about the family, then you shouldn't be in the family." The constant ranting, the endless barrage of hurtful words, phrases and nicknames, and the seemingly never-ending comment boxes are all symbols of how this group argues to stay together. But throughout all that, they realize that they all have one thing in common: that they were brave enough to join Mob Q "Diss Anybody" Records. ■

Questions

❶ How does Nate tend to the **where** here, to the larger contexts that shape the role dissing plays in this community? How might you pay attention to the **where** when looking to a community of your own choosing? What social and cultural contexts and platforms of communicating might be significant?

❷ How does Nate present the **what** of this conversation? What seems important about the topics this community discusses? What conclusions might you reach by looking to what members of a community you are studying discusses to their shared knowledge and interests?

❸ Why does the Mob Q-Records community engage in dissing? What sense does Nate provide of what such communicative acts mean or of how they contribute to this community? What you might be able to say about the purpose of particular patterns of communication in a community you study?

❹ What meanings does Nate construct as he looks to how this community interacts through language? What elements of interactions might you consider as you study language in action? In what ways might such work push you to increase your awareness of how you use language in a variety of settings?

READING 3

"The Dragon Court World"
by Richard Corrente (Student)

In "The Dragon Court World" Richard Corrente, a student from the University of Massachusetts Boston, introduces readers to the community built around and through the role-playing multi-user dimension (MUD) game, Dragon Court. As he explains how the community on this site interacts, Richard makes points about communication patterns and how relationships are built and maintained in the online world of gaming. Richard speaks from an insider's perspective about this community and draws on data (collected from surveys and captured conversations) to support his assertions. By providing background information, looking at particular examples of conversation, and considering how values are communicated through language, Richard is able to make points not only about this context but about online communication in general. As you read this piece, consider how Richard speaks from experience and authority, and look to see how those moves lead him to analysis in effective ways.

INTRODUCTION

The discourse community I have chosen to study is a multi-user dimension, often referred to as a MUD, called Dragon Court (Dragon Court™ v1.2 © 1997-2001, Fred's Friends, Inc.

[www.FFriends.com]), in which people from all over the world can meet each other. A discourse community is a group in which all the members share one or more things in common. Discourse communities can be anything from classrooms and groups of friends to church groups and workplaces. Ranging in membership from a few people to thousands, discourse communities come in all sizes. These communities can get together everyday or just once a month, and its members may meet in person, over the phone, or through the Internet.

Dragon Court is a Java-based role playing game, also known as an rgp, that is played online. In the game, players assume the role of an adventurer traveling through a medieval world in search of fame and treasure. In the game, players can trade items they have found and send letters to each other using the game's post office. Outside of the game, players have several other methods on communicating with each other. The ways of communicating include the forums, the chat rooms, instant messenger, and E-mail. Before looking at the ways of communicating, it is important to find out who is communicating and what is the game that brought us all together.

Dragon Court is set in a medieval world that is divided into several areas. The areas that a player can first access when they begin the game are Salamander Township and the Fields. Salamander Township is where players can save their game, buy items and equipment, and store items. The set up of the chat rooms is also based on the combination of Salamander Township and the Castle. The Fields is the first area where players can quest for treasure. As the game goes on, new areas become available to players. From the Fields, you can get to the Mounds and the Forest. The Mounds is an underground area which has several small places to quest in. The Mounds also include a place where you can fight the evil twin of the game's creator, Fred Haslam, most noted for being one of the original creators of Sim City (Sim City 2000TM © 1994-2001, Maxis, Inc. [www.maxis.com]). The Forest is another place for players to quest, and also includes a store, a place for players to practice their skills, and access to the Mountains. The Mountains offer two places to quest, as well as two shops. From Salamander Township, you can eventually access an area called the Castle. The Castle is where the post office, called DC Mail, is. The Castle also contains a place where players can join clans, special communities created by other players, and can raise their social status. Like the other areas in Dragon Court, the Castle also has places where players can quest.

PLAYERS' BACKGROUND

Knowing what the game is like is important for understanding the community of Dragon Court, but it is also important to know who the people are. As was previously stated, the players of Dragon Court come from all over the world. I polled many of the participants in the game, asking where they came from, what age they are, and if they are male or female. While the information reflects only sixty members of the community, including myself, it does provide a fairly accurate reading of what the entire community is like. Unfortunately, because not

everyone participated in my polling, not all the countries represented in Dragon Court were included in my findings. Despite that though, I was able to find out several key facts.

The most highly represented country in Dragon Court was the United States. Thirty-five of the sixty people were American, accounting for 58.3% of the total participants. The next highest country was Canada, which had eleven people making up 18.3% of the participants. 6.6% of the participants were from Great Britain, which was represented by 4 people. Australia and Norway both had two people, giving each country 3.3% of the total. The other five that were represented each had one participant, giving each of the countries 1.6% of the total. These five countries included Singapore, Belgium, Denmark, France, and Sweden. The remaining one person and 1.6% of the total went into the category "undisclosed", because that person did not give their country.

Of these sixty people, fifty-three were male. This makes up 88.3% of the people. The seven females who participated made up 11.6% of the group. Fifty-eight of the sixty people were willing to give their age. One of the undisclosed said he was "under 25, and that's all you need to know", and the other replied that she was "old enough to know better, but too young to care". For the participants who did give their age, the average ended up at about twenty to twenty-one years old. The older participant was forty-seven years old, and the youngest was only twelve. Two of the people who participated are cousins, showing that some members know each other in real life. One person had a wife who plays, one had a son who plays, and one had a brother and friend who play, but none of them participated in the poll along with the people they knew.

These different backgrounds provide the Dragon Court community with several important qualities. First, it allows for more diverse opinions in debates, and for other points of view to be explored. Second, the different languages brought in make some people more comfortable with the community, which mostly uses standard English. Third, it gives members of Dragon Court the chance to learn about other cultures. Fourth, it gives everyone something to tease each other about, like asking one of the Scottish members if he can make everyone some haggis or battling between the Americans and Canadians about who has a better country. All these different backgrounds make communication between the players more interesting.

COMMUNICATION BETWEEN PLAYERS

Players communicate using several different methods. The most common methods are the forums and the chat rooms. For more private conversations, players will use E-mail, DC Mail, and instant messenger. Each of the different ways of communicating have their own purposes, and have important functions within the community.

The forums and chat rooms have several sections to them, and require a large amount of exploring to show them. I will be designating this next section to that, but I will provide you with an overview now. The forums are divided into nine sections, each with their own specific purpose. The nine sections are the Tavern, Clan Hall, Tome of History, Trade Forum, War Stories, Peasant Forum, Congress of Nobles, House of Lords, and Bugs Forum. That chat room is made up of several small chat rooms. The central chat room is the Commons. Off of the Commons are the Market Place, Tavern, Clan hall, Adventurers' Guild, and Queen's Court. The Market Place then splits off into the Armor Shoppe, Weapon Smith, Dry Goods, and the Temple. The Tavern contains many other temporary chat rooms created by players in Dragon Court. The Adventurers' Guild has the Mage's Wing, Trader's Wing, and Warrior's Wing. Off of the Queen's Court are the Grand Ballroom, Dining Hall, House of Lords, and Council of Regents.

The other three methods players have to communicate are E-mail, DC Mail, and instant messenger. E-mail is probably the most used of these three methods. E-mail messages do not require the person receiving the message to be online when you send it. E-mail also allows you to send any form of graphic or music along with your messages, not just writing. DC Mail is probably the least used way of communication, as it takes one day for the mail to arrive at its mailbox. DC Mail also allows only small messages to be sent, two-hundred fifty-five characters long. Sometimes, it will take two or three different messages just to send one complete paragraph. The good side of using DC Mail though is that you can send mail to someone simply by knowing their name, which saves you from scouting around to find the person's E-mail or instant messenger address. Instant messenger is the easiest to use, and allows direct conversations between people. The most common instant messenger programs used are American Online Instant Messenger (America Online Instant Messenger™ v4.7 © 1996-2001, America Online, Inc. [www.aol.com]) and Microsoft Network Instant Messenger (MSN Messenger™ v4.5 ©1997-2001, Microsoft Corporation [www.microsoft.com]), both of which have almost identical functions. The down side to instant messenger is that the person must be logged into their account in order for you to send them a message. All three ways give members ways to communicate to each other in the privacy of their own, smaller communities.

IN DEPTH COMMUNICATION

Of all the ways of communicating found in Dragon Court, the forums are the most popular. These nine areas are used by most people in the game, and serve as the main way of communicating with the rest of the community. The Tavern is the place where anyone can go to talk, and is usually the main place to find polls and questions from other players. Clan Hall is based on one area in the game, where you can go to join a clan. The Clan Hall forum is where clans post advertisements about their clan and what it has to offer to potential members. The Tome of History is the main forum for poetry, and also includes many romance, adventure, and comedy stories. The continual posters in the Tome of History usually vary their style of writing. The Trade Forum is for players in the game to trade items and weapons they have found with each other. This forum is mostly controlled by the people with lots of money, such as the older players and hackers. The presence of hackers in the game is a large problem, but administration does not do much to keep them in line. The War Stories forum is mostly made up of a small group of people who post their stories and have everyone else tell them how great it is. The posts here seem less like they are trying to critique each other, and more as though they only want to be nice so the others will post kind words to them. The Peasant Forum used to be a place for members of the lower social class in Dragon Court to meet. Now, due to lack of caring on the part of the moderators, the forum is a combination of the Trading Post and Clan hall, where clans fight to buy new members who have recently joined the community. The Congress of Nobles is for the members of the middle class in Dragon Court. This forum was used mostly for talking between the middle class and for telling stories, myself being one of the storytellers there. Due to some problems the Dragon Court administration has been having with the forum, it has begun resetting itself once or twice a day, causing all the writing on the forum to erase. Once this problem has been fixed, there will hopefully be more people joining the forum again. The House of Lords is the meeting place of the upper class in Dragon Court. Because of the problem with the Congress of Nobles, I raised my social status and have begun posting in the more stable forum. I still have a middle class character who can post in the Congress once it is working right again. The Bugs Forum is where problems with the game, the forums, the chat rooms, and the hackers in the Trade Forum can be reported. Sadly enough, this seems to be one of the more popular forums among the players, but pretty much ignored by the administration.

The chat rooms work differently than the forums. The forums usually have the same groups of people in the same forums. The chat rooms usually have the same groups of people who will all go in one chat room together, but will not always meet in the same one when the group gets together again. The most popular meeting place for the groups is the Commons, which is the default room you go to when signing on to the chat rooms. The Market Place is not usually used, except for going to its Temple when players have a wedding, which is taken seriously despite the fact that it is a game. Several members who have met in Dragon Court have also gone on to get married in real life. The Clan Hall and Adventurers' Guild get almost no one in them, and it is rare to ever find one of them in use two days in a row. The Tavern and Queen's Court are two of the more frequented chat rooms. In the Tavern, players can create their own chat rooms, so this area is constantly changing. The chat rooms players can create can be open to all other people or password protected so only certain people are allowed in it. It is usually in these player made chat rooms or in the Queen's Court that online parties are held. The Queen's Court is also used by members of the middle and upper class for meeting, though its use has declined somewhat in recent months. It seems that the groups who post in the Tavern forum are the most likely to use the chat rooms. This can be seen by the larger number of "You'd have to hang out in the chat rooms to get it." remarks made by people in the Tavern who have their own insider knowledge into the chat room communities.

HOW WE TALK

Not only are there many methods for communicating within Dragon Court, but also many ways in which we talk. These ways include telling comedy and adventure stories, as well as poetry. Other ways include joking around, polling other players, bringing up questions, responding and commenting to other posts, fighting, getting angry, being polite, bringing peace, judging, introducing, and recruiting.

Of all these different ways of talking, the most common two are introducing and recruiting. Whenever someone new comes to the forums, they introduce themselves to everyone. Also, when a person moves up from the Peasant Forum to the Congress of Nobles and from the Congress of Nobles to the House of Lords they will introduce themselves so everyone else knows they are around now. Recruiting also goes on a lot, and in several different ways. Clans will recruit in Clan Hall to get new members into their groups. Storytellers, including me, will recruit people to be in new stories, which I believe makes the story more meaningful to the readers who joined. Another way of recruiting is to get people to join behind you on an idea. Sometimes people have something to they want others to help with, such as cracking down on hacking, and will recruit people to raise support for the issue.

Other speech acts are used to have fun, such as fighting and polling. Though it may seem like fighting would be hurtful to the community, it really isn't. As was stated earlier, sometimes groups from the same country will fight with groups from other countries, such as Americans verse Canadians and Irish verse English. Sometimes there will be role playing fights between everyone in a community, such as when everyone in the entire House of Lords got into a giant pie fight with everyone else. Although hitting someone with a pie isn't as funny

over the Internet as it is in real life, it was still a hilarious battle. Speech acts like this bring the community closer together.

VALUES FOUND IN SPEECH

The different speech acts and methods also are used to communicate shared values through the community. These values include a player's position on matters such as hacking, having fun, personal attacks, and cheating. Other than hackers and cheaters, the community shares the values of being against hacking and cheating. Some cheaters claim they do not like hacking, yet they have no reluctance in using the weapons and items hackers have created using cheat programs. Although hackers, cheaters, and one corrupt moderator do their best to keep the players of Dragon Court from having fun, the rest of us still hold it as an important value. The hackers, cheaters, and the corrupt moderator usually use personal attacks against members of the community to disrupt the fun, and most of the players are against this.

By looking at posts found in the forums, you see these values displayed. Having fun can be seen in the stories and poems written, in the friendly fights between players, and in jokes told around the forums. Hacking and cheating can be seen most commonly in the Trade Forum, but you can also see the fight to stop these online terrorists there. Personal attacks go on most commonly in the Trade Forum and in the Tavern, and this is also where you can see the people trying to stop them.

CONCLUSION

Despite the trouble-making made by some members of the community, there is a culture behind the game. This culture was started by people from all over the world finding a game called Dragon Court, which appealed to them. The people who came to Dragon Court met other people who shared the same interest in gaming, and they formed a community. This community has now grown to over sixty-six thousand registered characters.

This online culture has became what it is due to several factors. The first factor is the background everyone shares. People in Dragon Court have the chance to talk with people from all over the world, and have the chance to learn about the culture others have grown up in. Another factor is the many ways people have to communicate with, which helps to spread ideas and talk no matter what the conditions are. The forums and chat rooms also allow members of the community to talk to large numbers of people at one time. A third factor is the large numbers of ways the players have of talking. You can find a way that fits your idea, as well as one that fits the method you are communicating with.

When you look at the whole community, there is much that can be learned. One thing is how people get along with each other. Though there are the problem causing people, like can be found in any community, most of the players get along with each other. Even the people you would think would be fighting, like the members of the community from Israel and the Arab states, get along very well in each other's company. You also can learn that there is always someone with power who enjoys assaulting the people without it, such as the corrupt moderator. A third thing you can learn is how people separate their larger communities into smaller ones that are based on more common interests the smaller one shares than the larger one does. Overall, you learn how a community works. ∎

Questions

❶ How do the **where**, **what**, **why**, and **how** factor into this study? What points is Richard able to build as he considers these aspects of the conversations central to the Dragon Court community?

❷ What do you notice about how this piece is organized? About how you, as a reader, are both introduced to this community and walked through this study? About how and where shared knowledge is created for readers unfamiliar with this game?

❸ What strikes you about the evidence and examples used in this piece? How does Richard use details and descriptions to lead readers to broader points?

READING 4

"Bookworm Buddies"
by Hannah Morgan (Student)

In "Bookworm Buddies" Hannah Morgan, a student at Coastal Carolina University, reports on what she has learned about an online community formed around an interest in books and supported by the website goodreads.com. In this study, Hannah examines how this community is constructed and maintained through its online discussion forums as she considers how identity is expressed and managed on this particular site. Like Nate, Hannah analyzes a speech act (in this case of "inviting"), and she does this work in light of her larger focus on how members of this site interact. Despite the fact that she came to her study expecting to see members arguing about books, Hannah concludes in this study that the "Bookworm Buddies" have established a community that is welcoming to outsiders. She draws on many examples, which she presents using screenshots, to support this point, and connects her work to that of other researchers of interactions on social media sites. As you read, pay attention to the way in which Hannah moves you, as a reader, through her study. How might you organize and structure your own study to best bring your readers to key points and conclusions?

Introduction to Study

The following study has been performed in order to analyze the ways in which a particular community interacts online. Over the course of a few weeks, I have been visiting the site Bookworm Buddies, studying and analyzing the ways the members interact and communicate with each other. I began this study with the thought that there would be a considerable amount of conflict amongst the members, due to the site being dedicated to people sharing their opinions about books. However, I discovered that the members interact politely and welcomingly towards each other. They are also willing to accept new members, resulting in an almost non-existent divide between old members and new. My time spent studying the site has also shown that the members' interaction on Goodreads fits with the intended purpose of the site: to meet and interact with people who enjoy reading.

Bookworm Buddies

The community that I have chosen to study is called Bookworm Buddies. It is a group that interacts on the website Goodreads.com. On this site, people are encouraged to start a discussion thread about a particular book they are planning to read and can invite others to read along with them. Then, as each person is reading the book, they will post their opinions about the chapters they read, or about the book as a whole. The community creates an open and welcoming sense in the fact that the group is an open one and allows anyone to join, the ways the members interact with each other, and how they invite others to join in on discussions.

I was interested in the group mainly because I love to read and to hold discussion with others based on the stories that I have just read. I thought that of all the places to study a community, a book discussion group would be a good choice, since it would allow me the chance to study how people present their opinions and how they react to others' thoughts and views, whether they agree with them or not. Also, to me, meeting a bunch of strangers on the internet and planning to read the same book at the same time seems to create a strong sense of camaraderie, and I thought it would be interesting to study a community that had that.

There are two moderators of this group, one named Janie, who has the caption "Group Owner" underneath her name, and the other named Kathryn, who has the caption "Book Nerd" underneath her name. As far as I can tell, the captions are only for the moderators, and are not in any way related to how active they are on the site, since none of the other members appear to have captions underneath their names. The site starts off with the rule of "respect all people" which is the only rule in the rules section and it gives a general summary of the group: "This group is for those bookworms who like to join in buddy reads with others or start their own buddy reads. We read a wide array of genres here and love to discuss them all."

The group currently has 585 members, the majority of which are not very active. The site is split into discussion threads with each group under different headings such as: "general", "Buddy reads", "Bookworm Chatter", "Book Challenges", "Book-A-Thon", "Track Reads", "The Traveling Book", "Blog it", "Freebies/Good Deals" and "Games". (See Figure 1 below)

I went through the discussion thread labeled "Introduce yourself", since that one would most likely have been the first thread created, and noticed that the first comment, made by the Group Owner, was submitted on September 27, 2012. Since the site does not give a set date for when the group was created, I have come to the conclusion that time period is probably when the group was first made.

Bookworm Buddies also allows any member to create a new discussion thread, and not just the moderators. That would draw in more people to be active and participate in the group, since it allows people to start their own discussions instead of having to follow the discussions and whims of the group moderators. It is something that seems to have worked quite well, as most of the discussion threads were created by the members, and not the moderators.

Active Members

As part of my analysis, I went through all of the discussions threads that have been created for this group and tallied up the names of all those who started the threads. Not surprisingly, the one who starts the most discussion threads is Janie, the group creator, with thirty-eight discussion threads created. Most of the ones she starts explain what the group is about, and set the rules of the group and the how-tos, such as how to start your own discussion thread, where to place them on the site, and so forth. For the most part in her starting posts she is describing what the thread she just created is about, and can at times give people sample questions. She also gears her first post in a way that shows others how they should communicate in this particular thread. For example, she starts one particular section with: "OK guys let everyone know what you are reading right now. Do you like it? Will you be writing a review? etc., etc . . ." The way that she begins her discussion threads, and how many threads she creates, is indicative of her role in the group. Her first posts are either informative or examples of how the conversations should be, and that leadership quality that she exhibits in her posts would automatically reveal her as the creator of the group even without the caption of "group creator" beside her name.

The next person who creates the most discussion threads is the fellow moderator Kathryn, with nine discussion threads. Mainly for the discussion threads centered on talking about books, she does not phrase any of her first posts as questions, but more as one sentence descriptions of what the thread is about. For example her first post in one of the book discussions is: "Discuss Insurgent (Divergent #2) by Veronica Roth here." However, once other people start to join in on the conversation, she starts to write more. In other discussion threads, her first posts are much more conversational, such as the one starting the "2014 Resolutions" thread: "Yep! It's getting to be that time again!!!! ALREADY!!!! Lately I've been thinking about making our 2014 Resolutions thread, so I thought I'd get it started to get people thinking about the next year. What are your resolutions? Any new resolutions you hope to work on and achieve?" The fact that she is second in creating the most discussion threads, and that her starting posts take on a more commanding and explanatory manner, show her role as second in command of the group.

The third place is a tie between two members, Chuck and Victor, who both have six discussion threads. Chuck posted mainly in the Buddy Reads section, and Victor posted more in other sections. For them, as with the other members who started their own discussion threads, their first posts tend to be phrased as questions or are written in the form of "I was wondering if. . ." Unlike the posts of the two moderators of the group, the members

Discussion Board	topics: **all** | **new** | **unread**
▾ **general**	Showing 4 of 4 topics
• ****SPOILERS**** By Janie , *Group Owner & Book Addict* · 1 post · 28 views	last updated Feb 06, 2014 09:38AM
• **Guideline to posting Buddy Reads** By Janie , *Group Owner & Book Addict* · 2 posts · 432 views	last updated Sep 25, 2013 11:40AM
• **Introduce yourself!** By Janie , *Group Owner & Book Addict* · 990 posts · 382 views	last updated Mar 23, 2014 10:23AM
Updates By Janie , *Group Owner & Book Addict* · 4 posts · 17 views	last updated Mar 15, 2014 07:28AM
▾ **Buddy Reads**	Showing 20 of 168 topics — 9,342 comments total
• **Bram Stoker Award Buddy Reads Anyone?** By Chuck · 74 posts · 156 views	last updated Feb 23, 2014 12:11PM
Dracula & Incarnation May 2nd By Janie , *Group Owner & Book Addict* · 15 posts · 13 views	last updated 2 hours, 3 min ago
A late in the game "Gone Girl" buddy read. By Susan · 31 posts · 26 views	last updated 16 hours, 0 min ago

Figure 1

usually ask questions imploring others to join in a conversation. I found that the use of questions in their starter posts showed that the members are not quite as sure as the group moderators, and that they feel like they have to ask others to join in on a discussion instead of just informing them that this thread is going to be based on a discussion of a certain book.

When conversing in the discussion threads, the members will often use the term "buddy read", which refers to a group of members reading the same book at the same time. While the term is self-explanatory, it is one that I have not come across before outside of this particular group. It is usually used, by both moderators and members, in the sections concerning book reads. As of yet, I do not know if it is a term that is used only in this particular group, or if it is one that is used in other groups on Goodreads.

Expressing Identity

One of the largest discussion threads on the group is the "Introduce yourself" section, with over 990 comments. It is one of the first discussion threads added to the community, beginning in September 2012. The creator of the group starts off the thread by saying, "Tell us about yourself here guys!" In this section, new members are invited to post mini-profiles of themselves, which both allows them a chance to describe themselves and also allows others to learn more about them without having to go to their Goodreads profile.

In her paper, Koosel discusses how people can be reluctant to share their identities and personalities on a social site, for fear of backlash from those who view it (Koosel). However, an analysis of this discussion thread revealed that the restraint she noticed on Facebook is not heavily present on this particular group. One of the reasons for this different approach to expressing one's identity could be because it is not mandatory for a member to add a comment to the thread. Unlike other social sites, such as Facebook, the group does not make or pester a new member to introduce him or herself. Each member is allowed to make that choice on their own, and are not treated any differently should they choose not to.

This discussion thread takes away that nervous feeling many new members may feel when it comes to introducing themselves by giving off the appearance of a judgment free zone. For example, a lot of the members choose to line their identity up with what types of books they enjoy reading, such as Bojana in Figure 2.

Since this is a site dedicated to reading books, Bojana's decision to include the types of books she likes is a normal thing to do, but it is also an act that could open her up to an onslaught of judgment from other members. Any member could respond in disgust over the fact that she enjoys horror novels, or accuse her of living in a fantasy world for liking sci-fi and fantasy novels, or tell her that she should read non-fiction novels, but not a single member does so. Instead, the response that Bojana receives is one of welcome. This lack of judgment is shown throughout the entire thread. Not a single member expresses any kind of dislike over another member's book preferences, though they may at times write something along the lines of "I like those books/authors too!". This complete lack of judgment leads more people to feel comfortable posting their own introductions.

Another reason for the lack of restraint would be the warm welcome that each member receives when they comment on the discussion thread. While at the beginning of the

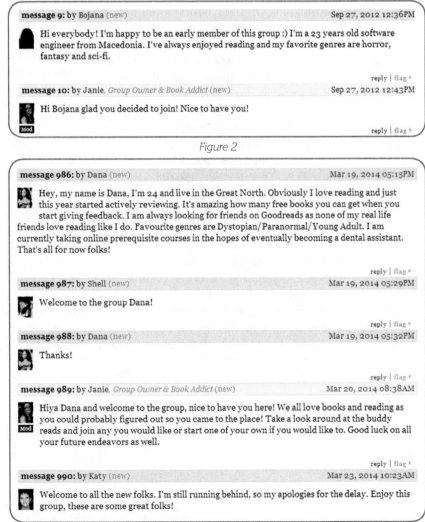

Figure 2

Figure 3

thread, Janie is the main one who chooses to welcome each new member, as the thread continues, other members take it upon themselves to welcome the newbies. An example of this is shown in Figure 3.

Both Shell and Katy, who are both regular members, choose to welcome Dana and the other new members. Katy even writes that she is "running behind" which shows that she usually makes sure to welcome every new member who adds a comment to this discussion thread. This welcoming attitude takes away the majority of the worry and discomfort that can come from posting a comment about oneself to a bunch of strangers. Not only does it take away that fear, but it can also encourage the new members to participate more in the community, since they get the sense that they are a part of it from the moment they introduce themselves.

Speech Act Analysis

Along with their welcoming speech patterns, there are also many instances where the speech act of inviting is heavily used. While studying this website, I have noticed that the members use different methods of inviting others, whether it is an invitation to join a book read, to share opinions, or to share something about themselves. This speech act can be found throughout the entire group, but for the purposes of this paper, I chose to focus on one specific example shown in Figure 4.

The setting of this particular speech act is on the discussion thread on the book *1984* by George Orwell. The discussion started February 18, 2014 at 7:41am, and it was started by a member named Jennifer. The discussion forum is open, so that anyone who wants to may join in on the conversation.

The speaker is a member called Jennifer. She is a regular member, and does not hold the status of being a moderator of the group. She is fairly new to the group, having just joined on February 10, 2014. It is revealed later on that this would be the first buddy read that she has ever participated in. The intended audience of the speech act would be fellow members who are interested in reading *1984*, though there is also the audience of members who are not interested, and since this group is not a closed group, there is also the possibility of an audience consisting of people who are not members of Bookworm Buddies.

The purpose of this particular speech act is to initiate a conversation. In her comment, Jennifer is inviting others to join in on a read with her. In the phrase "as soon as possible" she is also showing others that she is willing to start whenever they are ready to begin the read. She uses the speech act of invitation at the beginning of the discussion thread, the most logical place to put it, so that others can see it immediately.

While the comment is in the format of a question, Jennifer does not choose to end the sentence in a question mark. Instead she opts to end it in two exclamation points. This paired with the smiley face following close behind, displays her excitement, and creates an open and welcoming sense. She also uses an image of the book in the place of the title. This appears to either be a part of the Goodreads website or the group, as when other members mention the book, they show the cover instead of the title.

While Jennifer is new to the group, she does show some knowledge of how the group functions in the fact that her invitation follows an unspoken rule of this group. This speech act follows the group's norms of allowing anyone to participate in a book discussion. Jennifer uses the all-inclusive word "anyone", revealing to the audience that they are allowed to join in. Nowhere on the site, in any of the discussion threads, do the members stop certain people from joining in on a discussion. While it is not mentioned in the rules sections, it appears to be clear to all of the members that they should not refuse to let certain people into a discussion.

Interactions Between Members

The primary source of data that I chose to analyze for this paper is the discussion thread based on the book *Outlander* by Diana Gabaldon. This particular discussion thread reveals just how this community interacts with each other, and the way in which they interact with new members. It shows that the group is generally open and willing to accept and include anyone into a discussion or into the fabric of the group, no matter how new they may be to joining the group. Despite times when two or more members have varying opinions, they are able to discuss such differences in a polite and friendly manner, instead of dissolving into arguments.

The discussion thread began on September 13, 2013, and the last comment was submitted September 16, 2013. Eight people submitted comments into the discussion thread, which was created by Chuck, and consists of forty-three comments. Most of the people who are involved in the discussion have been members since late 2012, which was the year that the group was created. Only one person in this thread, Susan, joined the group in 2013. She

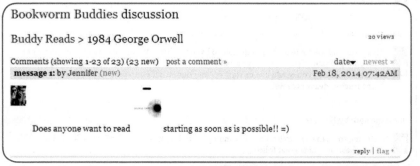

Figure 4

joined on September 15, 2013, just a few days after the discussion thread had been created. Despite being a fairly new member, she is one of the members who contributed the most comments to the thread.

Just as with the example that I studied earlier, the discussion thread was open for anyone to join. Chuck begins the thread by writing: "This is supposed to be fabulous. I'm not real big on fantasy, as I may have said once before, but I keep trying. Anyways, if anyone would like to give it a go, I'm game." Right at the beginning, it is clear that anyone is allowed to join the discussion. They do not have to have been a member for a particular amount of time, or have had to have been in a previous Buddy Read. As long as they are a member of the group, they are invited to participate in the discussion. They are also willing to start when everyone in the group is ready to begin. Even those who are not planning on joining in on the Buddy Read feel welcome to add their comments to the discussion, such as Courtney and Shell. Shell just wished them luck in her comment: "One of the ladies I work with absolutely loves this series. I'd like to give the first book a go but it's going to take me awhile to get through my current reads. Hope you guys enjoy it!"

Those that do choose to join in on reading the book, or even discussing other books, do so respectfully. They interact politely with each other, even when discussing different opinions, even going so far as making sure they specifically write that it is just their opinion. An example of this interaction would be one between Courtney, Susan, and Chuck in Figure 5.

In both comments, Susan adds that what she writes is just "imho" or "in my honest opinion" and that it was just her opinion. In her second comment, she reacts a bit defensively, which is understandable when one takes into consideration that she just joined the group and may not be used to the way in which they interact and share their opinions. Chuck then replies in a friendly manner that he does not agree with her opinion of the book not being character driven, but he also makes sure to mention that he agrees with her point about learning a thing or two from the book. Mentioning that he agrees with a least a part of her statement is a good tactic in making sure that Susan does not feel alienated from the discussion.

The inclusive attitude is also shown in the way that, unlike in danah boyd's study, the members of Bookworm Buddies do appear to communicate to only one audience; the other people who are reading the thread. While Carmen chose a particular phrase to communicate to two different audiences, none of the members of this community use any form of steganography in their comments (boyd). While they may at times send each other private messages, usually to let the person who started the thread know that they will not be able to participate in the buddy read, everything that they write in the comments is intended for others to read. What they write is what they mean, there are no hidden messages.

This polite, open, and respectful manner of conversing with each other and sharing different opinions plays back to the only written rule on the group's main page: "Respect all people's opinions". It is clear in both this example and other conversations in the group that the members take this rule to heart. Even when a new member forgets to tag the spoilers in their comments, the other members tend to not react harshly. For the most part, they will reply and ask that person to please make sure to tag any spoilers next time, and will at times go so far as to explain how to tag spoilers in comments in case the new member does not know how to do so.

Conclusion

Goodreads is a website with the purpose of having people join to find books they may want to read, discuss books with fellow books readers, and simply talk with others who share their love for reading, and the group Bookworm Buddies fulfills those goals. The members meet on this site to discuss books, suggest potential books to read, or to play games with each other, and they do so in a friendly manner. When I first began to analyze this community, I was doing so with the idea that I would come across a lot of arguments and differing opinions, and a clear divide between old members and new members.

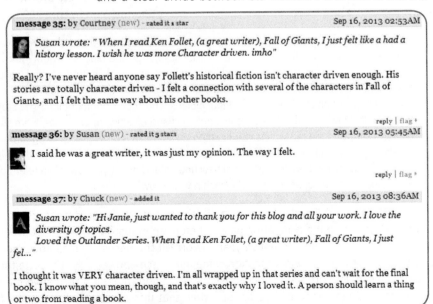

Figure 5

However, after spending a few weeks of studying this particular online community, I realized that the exact opposite was true. I have come to the conclusion that the Bookworm Buddies community is a very open and welcoming one. The members are always willing to greet any potential newcomers and immediately include them into discussions. Members, both old and new, are allowed and encouraged to begin their own discussions, and they choose to do so in a way that makes everyone welcome to join. While there is certainly the option to only allow certain people into the group, by using Goodread's option to make the group private, and to further exclude people by forming mini groups based on book preferences, there is no sign of that in this community. These facts lead me to believe that, while there are some that exist, not all internet communities are built around having members that know insider terms or have been involved in the group since it was first created or that even share the same opinions. There are some communities that are made for the sole purpose of making friends and reading really good books.

Works Cited:

boyd, danah. "Social Steganography: Learning to Hide in Plain Sight." dmlcentral. N.p., 23 Aug 2012. Web. 30 Mar 2014. <http://dmlcentral.net/blog/danah-boyd/social-steganography-learning-hide-plain-sight>.

http://www.goodreads.com/group/show/80265-bookworm-buddies

Koosel, Stacey. "Ethnographies of Social Networks: How Artists Negotiate Digital Identity." interartive. N.p., n.d. Web. 30 Mar 2014. <http://interartive.org/2013/05/ethnographies-social-networks-artist-digital-identity/>

Questions

❶ What moves does Hannah make to position her work as a scholarly undertaking? What aspects of her text (its structure, her use of evidence, the nods to other studies, the tone) feel most suited to an academic audience? What is your reaction to these elements of her writing?

❷ What moves does Hannah make to ground her work? How well does she support the points she makes throughout this study?

❸ How does Hannah move readers toward broader conclusions? How well does she build an argument here?

READING 5

"Growing Up Digital: How the Web Changes Work, Education, and the Ways People Learn"
by John Seely Brown
Change, March/April 2000

How significant is the internet in altering how we create and share knowledge? To what extent have digital learners reshaped the kinds of knowledge communities central to professional settings and places of work? John Seely Brown doesn't hesitate or qualify his stance as he argues that the web has changed how we learn and work in fundamental ways. By describing the web as a technological, social, and cultural development, he positions digital practices that have emerged from networked spaces as transformative. To illustrate his points, Brown turns to the example of technicians who repair photocopiers. The stories of such repairs, stories about troubleshooting that provide concrete information about strategies and effective approaches, were shared on a system called Eureka. Like the web, this platform supports the possibilities for creating meaning with others. According to Brown, the internet isn't important because it is a site for sharing information but because it supports the networks of relationships that allow for the collaborative gathering and sharing of new information and the construction of new understandings (a process often referred to as the "social construction of knowledge"). This, according to Brown, changes our relationship with knowledge itself.

In 1831 Michael Faraday built a small generator that produced electricity, but a generation passed before an industrial version was built, then another 25 years before all the necessary accoutrements for electrification came into place—power companies, neighborhood wiring, appliances (like light bulbs) that required electricity, and so on. But when that infrastructure finally took hold, everything changed—homes, work places, transportation, entertainment, architecture, what we ate, even when we went to bed. Worldwide, electricity became a transformative medium for social practices.

In quite the same way, the World Wide Web will be a transformative medium, as important as electricity. Here again we have a story of gradual development followed by an exploding impact. The Web's antecedents trace back to a U.S. Department of Defense project begun in the late 1960s, then to the innovations of Tim Berners-Lee and others at the Center for European Nuclear Research in the late 1980s, followed by rapid adoption in the mid- and late-1990s. Suddenly we had e-mail available, then a new way to look up information, then a remarkable way to do our shopping—but that's barely the start. The tremendous range of transformations wrought by electricity, so barely sensed by our grandparents a century ago, lie ahead of us through the Web.

No one fully knows what those transformations will be, but what we do know is that initial uses of new media have tended to mimic what came before: early photography imitated painting, the first movies the stage, etc. It took 10 to 20 years for filmmakers to discover the inherent capabilities of their new medium. They were to develop techniques now commonplace in movies, such as "fades," "dissolves," "flashbacks," "time and space folds," and "special effects," all radically different from what had been possible in the theater. So it will be for the Web. What we initially saw as an intriguing network of computers is now evolving its own genres from a mix of technological possibilities and social and market needs.

Challenging as it is, this article will try to look ahead to understand the Web's fundamental properties; see how they might create a new kind of information fabric in which learning, working, and playing co-mingle; examine the notion of distributed intelligence; ask how one might better capture and leverage naturally occurring knowledge assets; and finally get to our core topic—how all of this might fold together into a new concept of "learning ecology." Along the way, too, we'll look frequently at learning itself and ask not only how it occurs now, but how it can become ubiquitous in the future.

A New Medium

The first thing to notice is that the media we're all familiar with—from books to television—are one-way propositions: they push their content at us. The Web is two-way, push and pull. In finer point, it combines the one-way reach of broadcast with the two-way reciprocity of a mid-cast. Indeed, its user can at once be a receiver and sender of "broadcast"—a confusing property, but mind-stretching!

A second aspect of the Web is that it is the first medium that honors the notion of multiple intelligences. This past century's concept of "literacy" grew out of our intense belief in text, a focus enhanced by the power of one particular technology—the typewriter. It became a great tool for writers but a terrible one for other creative activities such as sketching, painting, notating music, or even mathematics. The typewriter prized one particular kind of intelligence, but with the Web, we suddenly have a medium that honors multiple forms of intelligence—abstract, textual, visual, musical, social, and kinesthetic.

As educators, we now have a chance to construct a medium that enables all young people to become engaged in their ideal way of learning. The Web affords the match we need between a medium and how a particular person learns.

A third and unusual aspect of the Web is that it leverages the small efforts of the many with the large efforts of the few. For example, researchers in the Maricopa County Community College system in Phoenix have found a way to link a set of senior citizens with pupils in the Longview Elementary School, as helper-mentors. It's wonderful to see—kids listen to these "grandparents" better than they do to their own parents, the mentoring really helps their teachers, and the seniors create a sense of meaning for themselves. Thus, the small efforts of the many—the seniors—complement the large efforts of the few—the teachers.

The same thing can be found in operation at Hewlett-Packard, where engineers use the Web to help kids with science or math problems. Both of these examples barely scratch the surface as we think about what's possible when we start interlacing resources with needs across a whole region

The Web has just begun to have an impact on our lives. As fascinated as we are with it today, we're still seeing it in its early forms. We've yet to see the full-motion video and audio possibilities that await the bandwidth we'll soon have through cable modems and DSL; also to come are the new Web appliances, such as the portable Web in a phone, and a host of wireless technologies. As important as any of these is the imagination, competitive drive, and capital behind a thousand companies—chased by a swelling list of dot-coms—rushing to bring new content, services, and "solutions" to offices and homes.

My belief is that not only will the Web be as fundamental to society as electrification, but that it will be subject to many of the same diffusion and absorption dynamics as that earlier medium. We're just at the bottom of the S-curve of this innovation, a curve that will have about the same shape as with electrification, but a much steeper slope than before. As this S-curve takes off, it creates huge opportunities for entrepreneurs. It will be entrepreneurs, corporate or academic, who will drive this chaotic, transformative phenomenon, who will see things differently, challenge background assumptions, and bring new possibilities into being. Our challenge and opportunity, then, is to foster an entrepreneurial spirit toward creating new learning environments—a spirit that will use the unique capabilities of the Web to leverage the natural ways that humans learn.

Digital Learners

Let's turn to today's youth, growing up digital. How are they different? This subject matters, because our young boys and girls are today's customers for schools and colleges and tomorrow's for lifelong learning. Approximately four years ago, we at Xerox's Palo Alto Research Center started hiring 15 year olds to join us as researchers. We gave them two jobs. First, they were to design the "workscape" of the future—one they'd want to work in; second, they were to design the school or "learningscape" of the future—again, with the same condition. We had an excellent opportunity to watch these adolescents, and what we saw—the ways they think, the designs they came up with—really shook us up.

For example, today's kids are always "multiprocessing"—they do several things simultaneously—listen to music, talk on the cell phone, and use the computer, all at the same time. Recently I was with a young twenty-something who had actually wired a Web browser into his eyeglasses. As he talked with me, he had his left hand in his pocket to cord in keystrokes to bring up my Web page and read about me, all the while carrying on with his part of the conversation! I was astonished that he could do all this in parallel and so unobtrusively.

People my age tend to think that kids who are multiprocessing can't be concentrating. That may not be true. Indeed, one of the things we noticed is that the attention span of the teens at PARC—often between 30 seconds and five minutes—parallels that of top managers, who operate in a world of fast context-switching. So the short attention spans of today's kids may turn out to be far from dysfunctional for future work worlds.

Let me bring together our findings by presenting a set of dimensions, and shifts along them, that describe kids in the digital age. We present these dimensions in turn, but they actually fold in on each other, creating a complex of intertwined cognitive skills.

The first dimensional shift has to do with literacy and how it is evolving. Literacy today involves not only text, but also image and screen literacy. The ability to "read" multimedia texts and to feel comfortable with new, multiple-media genres is decidedly nontrivial. We've long downplayed this ability; we tend to think that watching a movie, for example, requires no particular skill. If, however, you'd been left out of society for 10 years and then came back and saw a movie, you'd find it a very confusing, even jarring, experience. The network news shows—even the front page of your daily newspaper—are all very different from 10 years ago. Yet Web genres change in a period of months.

The new literacy, beyond text and image, is one of information navigation. The real literacy of tomorrow entails the ability to be your own personal reference librarian—to know how to navigate through confusing, complex information spaces and feel comfortable doing so. "Navigation" may well be the main form of literacy for the 21st century.

The next dimension, and shift, concerns learning. Most of us experienced formal learning in an authority-based, lecture-oriented school. Now, with incredible amounts of information available through the Web, we find a "new" kind of learning assuming pre-eminence—learning that's discovery based. We are constantly discovering new things as we browse through the emergent digital "libraries." Indeed, Web surfing fuses learning and entertainment, creating "infotainment."

But discovery-based learning, even when combined with our notion of navigation, is not so great a change, until we add a third, more subtle shift, one that pertains to forms of reasoning. Classically, reasoning has been concerned with the deductive and abstract. But our observation of kids working with digital media suggests *bricolage* to us more than abstract logic. *Bricolage*, a concept studied by Claude Lévi-Strauss more than a generation ago, relates to the concrete. It has to do with abilities to find something—an object, tool, document, a piece of code—and to use it to build something you deem important. *Judgment* is inherently critical to becoming an effective digital *bricoleur*.

How do we make good judgments? Socially, in terms of recommendations from people we trust? Cognitively, based on rational argumentation? On the reputation of a sponsoring institution? What's the mixture of ways and warrants that you end up using to decide and act? With the Web, the sheer scope and variety of resources befuddles the non-digital adult. But Web-smart kids learn to become *bricoleurs*.

The final dimension has to do with a bias toward action. It's interesting to watch how new systems get absorbed by society; with the Web, this absorption, or learning process, by young people has been quite different from the process in times past. My generation tends not to want to try things unless or until we already know how to use them. If we don't know how to use some appliance or software, our instinct is to reach for a manual or take a course or call up an expert. Believe me, hand a manual or suggest a course to 15 year olds and they think you are a dinosaur. They want to turn the thing on, get in there, muck around, and see what works. Today's kids get on the Web and link, lurk, and watch how other people are doing things, then try it themselves.

This tendency toward "action" brings us back into the same loop in which navigation, discovery, and judgment all come into play *in situ*. When, for example, have we lurked enough to try something ourselves? Once we fold action into the other dimensions, we necessarily shift our focus toward learning *in situ* with and from each other. Learning becomes situated in action; it becomes as much social as cognitive, it is concrete rather than abstract, and it becomes intertwined with judgment and exploration. As such, the Web becomes not only an informational and social resource but *a learning medium* where understandings are socially constructed and shared. In that medium, learning becomes a part of action and knowledge creation.

Creating Knowledge

To see how all these dimensions work, it's necessary to look at knowledge—its creation and sharing—from both the standard Cartesian position and that of the *bricoleur*.

Knowledge has two dimensions, the explicit and tacit. The explicit dimension deals with concepts—the "know-*whats*"—whereas the tacit deals with "know-*how*," which is best manifested in work practices and skills. Since the tacit lives in action, it comes alive in and through doing things, in participation with each other in the world. As a consequence, tacit knowledge can be distributed among people as a shared understanding that emerges from working together, a point we will return to.

The developmental psychologist Jerome Bruner made a brilliant observation years ago when he said we can teach people *about* a subject matter like physics—its concepts, conceptual frameworks, its facts—and provide them with explicit knowledge of the field, but *being* a physicist involves a lot more than getting all the answers right at the end of each chapter. To be a physicist, we must also learn the practices of the field, the tacit knowledge in the community of physicists that has to do with things like what constitutes an "interesting" question, what proof may be "good enough" or even "elegant," the rich interplay between facts and theory-formation, and so on. Learning to be a physicist (as opposed to learning about physics) requires cutting a column down the middle of the diagram, looking at the deep interplay between the tacit and explicit. That's where deep expertise lies. Acquiring this expertise requires learning the explicit knowledge of a field, the practices of its community, and the interplay between the two. And learning all this requires immersion in a community of practice, enculturation in its ways of seeing, interpreting, and acting.

The epistemic landscape is more complicated yet because both the tacit and explicit dimensions of knowledge apply not only to the individual but also to the social mind—to what we've called communities of practice. It's common for us to think that all knowledge resides in individual heads, but when we factor in the tacit dimension—especially as it relates to practices—we quickly realize how much more we can know than is bounded by our own knowledge. Much of knowing is brought forth in action, through participation—in the world, with other people, around real problems. A lot of our know-how or knowing comes into being through participating in our community(ies) of practice.

Understanding how intelligence is distributed across a broader matrix becomes increasingly critical if we want to leverage "learning to learn," because learning to learn happens most naturally when you and a participant are situated in a community of practice. Returning to Bruner's notion of learning to be, recall that it always involves processes of enculturation. Enculturation lies at the heart of learning. It also lies at the heart of knowing. Knowing has as much to do with picking up the genres of a particular profession as it does with learning its facts and concepts.

Curiously, academics' values tend to put theory at the top in importance, with the grubbiness of practice at the bottom. But think about what you do when you get a PhD. The last two years of most doctoral programs are actually spent in close work with professors, *doing* the discipline with them; these years in effect become a cognitive apprenticeship. Note that this comes after formal course work, which imparted relevant facts and conceptual frameworks. Those frameworks act as scaffolding to help structure the practice developed through the apprenticeship. So learning *in situ* and cognitive apprenticeship fold together in this notion of distributed intelligence.

I dwell on this point because each of us has various techniques, mostly invisible, that we use day in and day out to learn with and from each other *in situ*. This is seen all the time on a campus, where students develop techniques for learning that span in-class and out-of-class experiences—all of campus life is about learning how to learn. Colleges should appreciate and support such learning; the key to doing so lies in understanding the dynamic flow in our two-by-two matrix.

If we could use the Web to support the dynamics across these quadrants, we could create a new fabric for learning, for learning to learn *in situ*, for that is the essence of lifelong learning.

Repairing Photocopiers

Talk about a "two-by-two conceptual framework of distributed intelligence" can be terribly abstract; let me bring this to life, and move our argument ahead, with a story from the company where I work. When I arrived at Xerox, back in the 1980s, the company was spending millions and millions of dollars a year training its 23,000 "tech reps" around the world—the people who repair its copiers and printers. Lots of that training—it was like classroom instruction—seemed to have little effect. Xerox wanted me to come up with some intelligent-tutoring or artificial-intelligence system for teaching these people troubleshooting. Fortunately, before we did so, we hired several anthropologists to go live in their "tribe" and see how they actually worked.

What the anthropologists learned surprised us. When a tech rep got stuck by a machine, he or she didn't look at the manual or review the training; he or she called another tech rep. As the two of them stood over the problematic machine, they'd recall earlier machines and fixes, then connect those stories to a new one that explained some of the symptoms. Some fragment of the initial story would remind them of another incident, which suggested a new measurement or tweak, which reminded them of another story fragment and fix to try, and so on. Troubleshooting for these people, then, really meant construction of a narrative, one that finally explained the symptoms and test data and got the machine up and running again. Abstract, logical reasoning wasn't the way they went about it; stories were.

This example demonstrates the crucial role of tacit knowledge (in the form of stories) within a community of practice (the tech reps). But the anthropologists had more to tell us. What happened to these stories? When the reps got back to the home office, awaiting the next call, they'd sit around and play cribbage, drink coffee, and swap war stories. Amazing amounts of learning were happening in the telling and hearing of these stories. In the telling, a story got refined, added to, argued about, and stored away for use.

Today, brain scientists have helped us understand more about the architecture of the mind and how it is particularly well suited to remembering stories. That's the happy part. The sad part is that some Xerox executives thought storytelling had to be a waste of time; big posters told the reps, "Don't tell war stories!" Instead, people were sent back for more training. When people returned from it, what did they do? Tell stories about the training, of course, in attempts to transform what they'd been told into something more useful.

Let me add here that these studies convinced us that for powerful learning to occur, you had to look to both the cognitive and the social dimensions. They also led us to ask, How can we leverage this naturally occurring learning?

Our answer to that question was simple: two-way radios. We gave everybody in our tech rep "community of practice" test site a radio that was always on, with their own private network. Because the radios were always on, the reps were constantly in each other's periphery. When somebody needed help, other tech reps would hear him struggling; when one of them had an idea, he or she could move from the periphery to the (auditory) center, usually to suggest some test or part to replace, adding his or her fragment to an evolving story. Basically, we created a multiperson storytelling process running across the test site. It worked incredibly well.

In fact, it also turned out to be a powerful way to bring new technicians into this community. A novice could lurk on the periphery and hear what was going on, learn from it, maybe ask a question, and eventually make a suggestion when he or she had something to contribute. In effect, the newcomer was a cognitive apprentice, moving from lurker to contributor, very much like today's digital kids on the Web.

The trouble with this scenario is that all these story fragments were being told through the ether, and hence were lost to those reps not participating at the moment. Some of these fragments were real gems! So we needed to find a way to collect, vet, refine, and post them on a community knowledge server. Furthermore, we realized that no one person was the expert; the real expertise resided in the community mind. If we could find a way to support and tap the collective minds of the reps, we'd have a whole new way to accelerate their learning and structure the community's knowledge assets in the making. We wanted to accomplish this, too, with virtually no overhead.

The answer for us was a new, Web-based system called Eureka, which we've had in use for two years now. The interesting thing is that the tech reps, in co-designing this system to make their ideas and stories more actionable, unwittingly reinvented the sociology of science. In reality, they knew many of the ideas and story fragments that floated around were not trustworthy; they were just opinions, sometimes crazy. To transform their opinions and experiences into "warranted" beliefs, hence actionable, contributors had to submit their ideas for peer review, a process facilitated by the Web. The peers would quickly vet and refine the story, and connect it to others. In addition, the author attaches his or her name to the resulting story or tip, thus creating both intellectual capital and social capital, the latter because tech reps who create really great stories become local heroes and hence more central members of their community of practice.

This system has changed the learning curve of our tech reps by 300 percent and will save Xerox about $100 million a year. It is also, for our purposes here, a beautiful example of how the Web enables us to capture and support the social mind and naturally occurring knowledge assets. ∎

Questions

❶ What moves do you see Brown making here as he announces his argument and stance? How does he introduce and situate his thinking about the web in this piece?

❷ What do you notice about the examples Brown draws on? How compelling do you find these examples and the meaning Brown makes from them?

❸ How does Brown position other thinkers and lines of thought in this piece? How does he use this piece to extend conversations about emerging technology, new literacies, and the construction of knowledge?

❹ What moves do you see Brown making (whether these are global moves like his approach to organizing this text, or more local moves like decisions he makes about word choice) that might inform the approach you take in a text? Which of Brown's strategies might you want to try out in your own writing?

READING 6

Selection from
On Photography
by Susan Sontag
Picador, 1977

Written in 1977, *On Photography* presented Susan Sontag's reflections on photography and how we use it as a society, and has become an important part of the shared background knowledge of others interested in the subject ever since. As a later critic wrote, *On Photography* has become so deeply absorbed into this discourse that "Sontag's claims about photography, as well as her mode of argument, have become part of the rhetorical 'tool kit' that photography theorists and critics carry around in their heads."[1] In this excerpt, Sontag considers the ways in which we position ourselves behind a camera to claim a voyeuristic position rather than experience events in more complete ways, observations that speak to today's "selfie" culture. As she comments on the role photographs and the taking of photographs play in tourism, Sontag pushes readers to problematize the idea of photography as art; instead, Sontag argues, it is an activity that superimposes the real as it provides us with a ready-made defense mechanism against becoming too engaged with the cultures around us.

1. Starenko, Michael. "Sontag's Reception." After Image, vol. 25, 1998.

Recently, photography has become almost as widely practiced an amusement as sex and dancing—which means that, like every mass art form, photography is not practiced by most people as an art. It is mainly a social rite, a defense against anxiety, and a tool of power.

Memorializing the achievement of individuals considered as members of families (as well as of other groups), is the earliest popular use of photography. For at least a century, the wedding photograph has been as much a part of the ceremony as the prescribed verbal formulas. Cameras go with family life. According to a sociological study done in France, most households have a camera, but a household with children is twice as likely to have at least one camera as a household in which there are no children. Not to take pictures of one's children, particularly when they are small, is a sign on parental indifference, just as not turning up for one's graduation picture is a gesture of adolescent rebellion.

Through photographs, each family constructs as portrait-chronicle of itself—a portable kit of images that bears witness to its connectedness. It hardly matters what activities are photographed so long as photographs get taken and are cherished. Photography becomes a rite of family life just when, in the industrializing counties of Europe and America, the very institution of the family starts undergoing radical surgery. At that claustrophobic unit, the nuclear family, was being carved out of a much larger family aggregate, photography came along to memorialize, to restate symbolically, the imperiled continuity and vanishing extendedness of family life. Those ghostly traces, photographs, supply the token presence of the dispersed relatives. A family's photograph album is generally about the extended family—and, often, is all the remains of it.

As photographs give people an imaginary possession of a past that is unreal, they also help people to take possession of space in which they are insecure. Thus, photography develops in tandem with one of the most characteristic of modern activities: tourism. For the first time in history, large numbers of people regularly travel out of their habitual environments for short periods of time. It seems positively unnatural to travel for pleasure without taking a camera along. Photographs will offer indisputable evidence that the trip was made, that the program was carried out, that fun was had. Photographs document sequences of consumption carried on outside the view of family, friends, neighbors. But dependence on the camera, as the device that makes real what one is experiencing, doesn't fade when people travel more. Taking photographs fills the same need for the cosmopolitans accumulating photograph-trophies of their boat trip up the Albert Nile or their fourteen days in China as it does for lower-middle-class vacationers taking snapshots of Eiffel Tower or Niagara Falls.

A way of certifying experience, taking photographs is also a way of refusing it—by limiting experience to a search for the photogenic, by converting experience in an image, a souvenir. Travel becomes a strategy for accumulating photographs. The very activity of taking pictures is soothing, and assuages general feelings of disorientation that are likely to be exacerbated by travel. Most tourists feel compelled to put the camera between themselves and whatever is remarkable that they encounter. Unsure of other responses, they take a picture. This gives shape to experience: stop, take a photograph, and move on. The method especially appeals to people handicapped by a ruthless work ethic—Germans, Japanese, and Americans. Using a camera appeases the anxiety which the work-driven feel about not working when they are on vacation and supposed to be having fun. They have something to do that is like a friendly imitation of work: they can take pictures.

People robbed of their past seem to make the most fervent picture takers, at home and abroad. Everyone who lives in an industrialized society is obliged gradually to give up the past, but in certain countries, such as the United States and Japan, the break with the past has been particularly traumatic. In the early 1970s, the fable of the brash American tourist of the 1950s and 1960s, rich with dollars and Babbittry, was replaced by the mystery of the group-minded Japanese tourist, newly released from his island prison by the miracle of overvalued yen, who is generally armed with two cameras, one on each hip.

Photography has become one of the principal devices for experiencing something, for giving an appearance of participation. One full-page ad shows a small group of people standing pressed together, peering out of the photograph, all but one looking stunned, excited, upset. The one who wears a different expression holds a camera to his eye; he seems self-possessed, is almost smiling. While the others are passive, clearly alarmed spectators, having a camera has transformed one person into something active, a voyeur: only he has mastered the situation. What do these people see? We don't know. And it doesn't matter. It is an Event: something worth seeing—and therefore worth photographing. The ad copy, white letters across the dark lower third of the photograph like news coming over a teletype machine, consists of just six words: ". . . Prague . . . Woodstock . . . Vietnam . . . Sapporo . . . Londonderry . . . LEICA." Crushed hopes, youth antics, colonial wars, and winter sports are alike—are equalized by the camera. Taking photographs has set up a chronic voyeuristic relation to the world which levels the meaning of all events. ∎

Questions

❶ What do you notice about how Sontag makes points in this piece? How does she move readers through this piece and build upon the ideas she presents?

❷ What moves does Sontag make to ground her thinking? What specific examples or incidents does she point to here? How do those illustrations function in this text?

❸ What do you think about the ideas Sontag shares here? How relevant do you find her ideas to be to the current practice of photography and our use of photographic images in a digital environment? How have her thoughts complicated, extended, or challenged your thinking about photography and how you might take and use photographs in the future?

❹ What can you add to Sontag's thinking? How do your experiences and observations intersect with the points she makes here?

READING 7

Endnotes for the Selection from
Mediated Memories in the Digital Age
by José van Dijck
Stanford University Press, 2007

Academic writers are never working in isolation; instead they engage in a rich web of conversations that are built as writers, who are also readers, extend the meanings made in other texts. Included here are the endnotes from the reading by José van Dijck in Chapter 6 to show how she references other texts to account for the ways in which they have shaped and informed her thinking. The notes begin with references to Sontag's book *On Photography* (see Reading 6 above). Look to note 32 where she provides a direct quotation to give a sense of how Steve Garlick reacted to Sontag's dismissal of tourist photography in an article in *Cultural Studies*, an academic journal. To see how van Dijck provides a sense of how other scholars have extended Sontag's thinking about the role of photography in the family, look to the list of references she points to in note 34. Van Dijck doesn't just point to academic conversations, though; she also, in note 37, references *The New York Times* to establish that in 2003, more digital cameras were sold than film cameras. In note 38, she paraphrases the work of other researchers, Schiano, Chen, and Isaacs, on how teens take and share photos. These notes are interesting, working like links to lead readers to further material they might be interested in. They also illustrate the kind of work academic writing calls for. Note how van Dijck moves between texts, how she summarizes, paraphrases, and quotes other sources directly here.

32. In reaction to Sontag's pejorative interpretation of the touristic photographic experience, Steve Garlick argues in "Revealing the Unseen: Tourism, Art, and Photography," *Cultural Studies* 16, no.2 (2002): 289-305, that tourist photography is "a mechanism that leads the subject to engage with the world in a creative act that opens and re-opens spaces, each time people take or review their pictures" (296).

33. Sontag, *On Photography*, 8.

34. Quite a few cultural theorists and anthropologists have taken up Sontag's insights to write about photography and family. See, for instance, Marianne Hirsch, *Family Frames: Photography, Narrative, and Postmemory* (Cambridge, MA: Harvard University Press, 1997); P. Holland, "Introduction: History, Memory, and the Family Album," in *Family Snaps: The Meaning of Domestic Photography*, ed. J. Spence and P. Holland (London: Virago, 1991): 1-14; and Deborah Chambers, *Representing the Family* (London: Sage, 2001).

35. Barbara Harrison, in "Photographic Visions and Narrative Inquiry," *Narrative Inquiry* 12, no.1 (2002): 87-111, notices a recent shift in photography's social use: "Images that have a place in everyday life have become less bound up with memory or commemoration, but with forms of practice that are happening now…. Self-presentation rather than self-representation is more important in identity formation" (107). Testifying to these trends is the pin board, where private pictures are often combined with public ones and personal pictures are put on display.

36. Barbara Harrison, "Photographic Visions," 107.

37. According to *The New York Times*, American sales of digital cameras surpassed the sales of analog film cameras for the first time in March 2003. See Katie Hafner, "Recording Another Day in America, Aided by Digital Cameras," *New York Times*, May 12, 2003 www.nytimes.com.

38. Diane Schiano, Coreena Chen, and Ellen Isaacs, "How Teens Take, View, Share, and Store Photos," in *Proceedings of the Conference on Computer-Supported Co-operative Work* (New York: ACM, 2002). Interestingly, the researchers conclude that teenagers are less inclined than adults to label pictures with captions, either because they don't think it is relevant or because they put great trust in their future memory capacity; they feel confident they will always be able to remember what is in the pictures.

39. The American study is corroborated by a Japanese report identifying similar patterns among young users of digital cameras; a new preference for photography as an interpersonal tool for communication whose main function is to exchange "affective awareness" prompts hardware and software developers to redirect their framework for design. See Oliver Liechti and Tadao Ichikawa, "A Digital Photography Framework Enabling Affective Awareness in Home Communication," *Personal and Ubiquitous Computing* 4, no.1 (2000): 6-24.

40. For an incisive ethnographic study of photoblogs, see Kris Cohen, "What Does the Photoblog Want?" *Media, Culture and Society* 27, no.6 (2005): 883-901.

41. See, for instance, Tim Kindberg, Mirjana Spasojevic, Rowanne Fleck, and Abigail Sellen, "I Saw This and Thought of You: Some Social Uses of Camera Phones," *Conference on Human Factors in Computing Systems* (New York: ACM, 2005), 1545-48.

42. A field study by a group of Finnish researchers yields this interesting comparison of the pictures sent by mobile phone to postcards. See Turo-Kimmo Lehtonen, Ilpo Koskinen,

and Esko Kurvinen, "Mobile Digital Pictures—The Future of the Postcard? Findings from an Experimental Field Study," in *Postcards and Cultural Rituals,* ed. V. Laakso and J-O Ostman (Korttien Talo: Haemeenlinna, 2002), 69-96.

43. For ethnographic research on the use of camera phone pictures, see Nancy Van House, Marc Davis, and Morgan Ames, "The Uses of Personal Networked Digital Imaging: An Empirical Study of Cameraphone Photos and Sharing," *Conference on Human Factors in Computing Systems* (New York: ACM, 2005), 1853-56. ∎

Questions

❶ What moves do you notice van Dijck making as she discusses the texts that have shaped her thinking about photographs? What similar moves might you decide to draw on in your own composing?

❷ Look back at van Dijck's full text in Chapter 6. How does van Dijck position these references in her text? How does she seem to weave other sources into her writing? How does she account for the reality that many of her readers will not have read these pieces before coming to her work?

❸ Van Dijck juggles many sources here. What strategies would you find most helpful for reading, thinking through, and extending a variety of sources? What reading strategies will you draw on to make the most of your reading and meaning-making process?

READING 8

"What Every American Should Know: Defining Common Cultural Literacy for an Increasingly Diverse Nation"

by Eric Liu

The Atlantic, July 3, 2015

Eric Liu, an expert in U.S. domestic policy, provides an explanation of and response to E. D. Hirsch's *Cultural Literacy: What Every American Needs to Know* (1987). Hirsch's book connected a decrease in American intellectualism and capacity to read and understand challenging material with a lack of cultural literacy and provided, in its appendix, a list of information "every American needs to know." In this article, Liu reconsiders Hirsch's concerns from the perspective of both our diverse society and our current mediated age as he argues that the participatory nature of web culture pushes against the validity of any fixed limited list; Liu invites readers to make their own contributions to what they think Americans need currently as shared knowledge and suggests some items he'd include on his own list. In his moves to challenge (and contextualize) Hirsch and articulate a concept of cultural literacy that stresses a variety of experiences and perspectives, Liu nods to how much more complex our shared cultural literacies has become since 1987, in large part because of technological change and the greater circulation of a diverse range of cultural knowledge.

Is the culture war over?

That seems an absurd question. This is an age when Confederate monuments still stand; when white-privilege denialism is surging on social media; when legislators and educators in Arizona and Texas propose banning ethnic studies in public schools and assign textbooks euphemizing the slave trade; when fear of Hispanic and Asian immigrants remains strong enough to prevent immigration reform in Congress; when the simple assertion that #BlackLivesMatter cannot be accepted by all but is instead contested petulantly by many non-blacks as divisive, even discriminatory.

And that's looking only at race. Add gender, guns, gays, and God to the mix and the culture war seems to be raging along quite nicely.

Yet from another perspective, much of this angst can be interpreted as part of a noisy but inexorable endgame: the end of white supremacy. From this vantage point, Americanness and whiteness are fitfully, achingly, but finally becoming delinked—and like it or not, over the course of this generation, Americans are all going to have to learn a new way to be American.

Imagine that this is true; that this decades-long war is about to give way to something else. The question then arises: What? What is the story of "us" when "us" is no longer by default "white"? The answer, of course, will depend on how aware Americans are of what they are, of what their culture already (and always) has been. And that awareness demands a new kind of mirror.

It helps first to consider some recent history. In 1987, a well-regarded professor of English at the University of Virginia named E.D. Hirsch Jr. published a slim volume called *Cultural Literacy.* Most of the book was an argument—textured and subtle, not overtly polemical—about why nations need a common cultural vocabulary and why public schools should teach it and, indeed, think of their very reason for being as the teaching of that vocabulary.

At the end of the book Hirsch and two colleagues tacked on an appendix: an unannotated list of about 5,000 names, phrases, dates, and concepts that, in their view, "every American needs to know." The rest (to use a phrase that probably should've been on the list) was history.

The appendix became a sensation and propelled the book to the top of the best-seller list. Hirsch became that rare phenomenon: a celebrity intellectual. His list was debated in every serious publication and elite circles. But he also was profiled in *People* magazine and cited by pundits who would never read the book.

Hirsch's list had arrived at a ripe moment of national anxiety, when critics like Allan Bloom and Arthur Schlesinger Jr. were bemoaning the "closing of the American mind" and "the disuniting of America"; when multicultural curricula had arrived in schools, prompting challenges to the Western canon and leading Saul Bellow to ask mockingly who the Tolstoy of the Zulus was, or the Proust of the Papuans; a time when Bill Bennett first rang alarms about the "dumbing-down of America."

The culture wars were on. Into them ambled Hirsch, with his high credentials, tweedy profile, reasoned arguments, and addictively debatable list. The thing about the list, though, was that it was—by design—heavy on the deeds and words of the "dead white males" who had formed the foundations of American culture but who had by then begun to fall out of academic fashion. (From a page drawn at random: Cotton Mather, Andrew Mellon, Herman Melville).

Conservatives thus embraced Hirsch eagerly and breathlessly. He was a stout defender of the patrimony. Liberals eagerly and breathlessly attacked him with equal vigor. He was retrograde, Eurocentric, racist, sexist. His list was a last gasp (or was it a fierce counterattack?) by a fading (or was it resurgent?) white establishment.

Lost in all the crossfire, however, were two facts: First, Hirsch, a lifelong Democrat who considered himself progressive, believed his enterprise to be in service of social justice and equality. Cultural illiteracy, he argued, is most common among the poor and power-illiterate, and compounds both their poverty and powerlessness. Second: He was right.

A generation of hindsight now enables Americans to see that it is indeed necessary for a nation as far-flung and entropic as the United States, one where rising economic inequality begets worsening civic inequality, to cultivate continuously a shared cultural core. A vocabulary. A set of shared referents and symbols.

Yet that generational distance now also requires Americans to see that any such core has to be radically re-imagined if it's to be worthy of America's actual and accelerating diversity. If it isn't drastically more inclusive and empowering, what takes the place of whiteness may not in fact be progress. It may be drift and slow disunion. So, first of all, Americans do need a list. But second, it should not be Hirsch's list. And third, it should not made the way he made his. In the balance of this essay, I want to unpack and explain each of those three statements.

Let's begin with the claim that Americans do in fact need a list of what every American needs to know.

If you take the time to read the book attached to Hirsch's appendix, you'll find a rather effective argument about the nature of background knowledge and public culture. Literacy is not just a matter of decoding the strings of letters that make up words or the meaning of each word in sequence. It is a matter of decoding context: the surrounding matrix of things referred to in the text and things implied by it.

So, for instance, a statement like "One hundred and fifty years after Appomattox, our house remains deeply divided" assumes that the reader knows that Appomattox is both a place and an event; that the event signified the end of a war; that the war was the Civil War and had begun during the presidency of a man, Abraham Lincoln, who earlier had famously declared that "a house divided against itself cannot stand"; that the divisions then were in large part about slavery; and that the divisions today are over the political, social, and economic legacies of slavery and how or whether we are to respond to those legacies.

Likewise, another sentence often uttered in this anniversary year of the end of the Civil War—"Today's GOP is the party of Jefferson Davis, not of Lincoln"—assumes that the reader knows what the GOP is and what the acronym stands for, who Jefferson Davis was, how he was different from Lincoln, why it is that Republicans call themselves the Party of Lincoln, and why it is that some people, in spite of that, see in the modern Republican Party the spirit of the old Confederacy.

Hirsch, as an authority on reading and writing, is concerned with traditional texts. But his point about background knowledge and the content of shared public culture extends well beyond schoolbooks. They are applicable to the "texts" of everyday life, in commercial culture, in sports talk, in religious language, in politics. In all cases, people become literate in patterns—"schema" is the academic word Hirsch uses. They come to recognize bundles of concept and connotation like "Party of Lincoln." They perceive those patterns of meaning the same way a chess master reads an in-game chessboard or the way a great baseball manager reads an at bat. And in all cases, pattern recognition requires literacy in particulars.

Lots and lots of particulars. This isn't, or at least shouldn't be, an ideologically controversial point. After all, parents on both left and right have come to accept recent research that shows that the more spoken words an infant or toddler hears, the more rapidly she will learn and advance in school. Volume and variety matter. And what is true about the vocabulary of spoken or written English is also true, one fractal scale up, about the vocabulary of American culture.

Hirsch was taken by some critics to be a political conservative because he argued that cultural literacy is inherently a culturally conservative enterprise. It looks backwards. It tries to preserve the past. Not surprisingly, Hirsch later became a fan of the Common Core standards, which, whatever their cross-partisan political toxicity today, were intended in earnest to lay down basic categories of knowledge that every American student should learn.

But those who demonized Hirsch as a right-winger missed the point. Just because an endeavor requires fluency in the past does not make it worshipful of tradition or hostile to change. Indeed, in a notable example of the application of cultural literacy, Hirsch quoted in his book from the 1972 platform of the Black Panther Party:

> 10. WE WANT LAND, BREAD, HOUSING, EDUCATION, CLOTHING, JUSTICE, PEACE AND PEOPLE'S CONTROL OF MODERN TECHNOLOGY.
>
> When in the course of human events it becomes necessary for one people to dissolve the political bands which have connected them with another, and to assume among the powers of the earth the separate and equal station to which the laws of nature and nature's God entitle them, a decent respect to the opinions of mankind requires that they should declare the causes which impel them to the separation.

He cited another passage, from the Black Panther newspaper:

> In this land of "milk and honey," the "almighty dollar" rules supreme and is being upheld by the faithful troops who move without question in the name of "law and order." Only in this garden of hypocrisy and inequality can a murderer not be considered a murderer—only here can innocent people be charged with a crime and be taken to court with the confessed criminal testifying against them. Incredible?

These samples demonstrated for Hirsch two important points: First, that the Black Panthers, however anti-establishment, were confidently in command of American history and idiom, comfortable quoting the Declaration of Independence verbatim to make their point, happy to juxtapose language from the Bible with the catch phrases of the Nixon campaign, wholly correct in grammatical and rhetorical usage.

And second, that radicalism is made more powerful when garbed in traditionalism. As Hirsch put it: "To be conservative in the means of communication is the road to effectiveness in modern life, in whatever direction one wishes to be effective."

Hence, he argued, an education that in the name of progressivism disdains past forms, schema, concepts, figures, and symbols is an education that is in fact anti-progressive and "helps preserve the political and economic status quo." This is true. And it is made more urgently true by the changes in American demography since Hirsch gave us his list in 1987.

* * *

The new America, where people of color make up a numerical majority, is not a think-tank projection. It may well be the condition of the people born in the United States this very year. But an America where nonwhites hold a majority of the power in civic life is much farther off. If you are an immigrant to the United States—or, if you were born here but are the first in your family to go to college, and thus a socioeconomic new arrival; or, say, a black citizen in Ferguson, Missouri deciding for the first time to participate in a municipal election, and thus a civic neophyte—you have a single overriding objective shared by all immigrants at the moment of arrival: figure out how stuff really gets done here.

That means understanding what's being said in public, in the media, in colloquial conversation. It means understanding what's not being said. Literacy in the culture confers power, or at least access to power. Illiteracy, whether willful or unwitting, creates isolation from power. And so any endeavor that makes it easier for those who do not know the memes and themes of American civic life to attain them closes the opportunity gap. It is inherently progressive.

Of course, it's not just newcomers who need greater command of common knowledge. People whose families have been here ten generations are often as ignorant about American traditions, mores, history, and idioms as someone "fresh off the boat."

> The more serious challenge, for Americans new and old, is to make a common culture that's greater than the sum of our increasingly diverse parts. It's not enough for the United States to be a neutral zone where a million little niches of identity might flourish; in order to make our diversity a true asset, Americans need those niches to be able to share a vocabulary. Americans need to be able to have a broad base of common knowledge so that diversity can be most fully activated.

But why a list, one might ask? Aren't lists just the very worst form of rote learning and standardized, mechanized education? Well, yes and no. It is true that lists alone, with no teaching to bring them to life and no expectation that they be connected to a broader education, are somewhere between useless and harmful.

Lists that catalyze discussion and even debate, however, are plenty useful. If you open up Hirsch's list at random you're certain to find entries that launch deeper inquiry and learning and that are helpful to know if you want to be a capable citizen.

In fact, since I started writing this essay, dipping into the list has become a game my high-school-age daughter and I play together. Consider, from pages 204 and 205:

Sharecropping
Sherman Anti-Trust Act
Sodom and Gomorrah
Speak softly and carry a big stick
Spirit of '76 (image)
stagflation

I'll name each of those entries, she'll describe what she thinks to be its meaning. If she doesn't know, I'll explain it and give some back story. If I don't know, we'll look it up together. This of course is not a good way for her teachers to teach the main content of American history or English. But it is definitely a good way for us both to supplement what school should be giving her.

And however long we end up playing this game, it is already teaching her a meta-lesson about the importance of cultural literacy. Now anytime a reference we've discussed comes up in the news or on TV or in dinner conversation, she can claim ownership. Sometimes she does so proudly, sometimes with a knowing look. My bet is that the satisfaction of that ownership, and the value of it, will compound as the years and her education progress.

The trouble is, there are also many items on Hirsch's list that don't seem particularly necessary for entry into today's civic and economic mainstream. They seem pulled from the nineteenth-century McGuffey's Readers that Hirsch nostalgically praises, drawing from English, Latin, and Biblical references that in the 1800s seemed timeless:

Shoot, if you must, this old gray head...
Sic transit gloria mundi.
Sing a Song of Sixpence (song)
soft answer turneth away wrath., A

But it turns out items like this aren't timeless. They were displaced, as time passed, by sayings and songs of people from other places.

Which brings us back to why diversity matters. The same diversity that makes it necessary to have and to sustain a unifying cultural core demands that Americans make the core less monochromatic, more inclusive, and continuously relevant for contemporary life. A list for cultural literacy, like the Constitution, is not an antiquarian's specimen to be left untouched. It is an evolving document, amendable and ever subject to reinterpretation. Americans need a list made new with new blood. Americans are such a list.

* * *

What, then, are the 5,000 things that an American in 2015 should know?

Before we get to that, it's worth unpacking the baseline assumption of both Hirsch's original argument and the battles that erupted around it. The assumption was that multiculturalism sits in polar opposition to a traditional common culture, that the fight between multiculturalism and the common culture was zero-sum.

That's certainly how the politics and media coverage of the early culture war played out. Dead White Men against Afrocentrists. Each side's claim seen as a debit from the other's. But that was a profoundly artificial dichotomy. As scholars like Ronald Takaki made clear in books like *A Different Mirror,* the dichotomy made sense only to the extent that one imagined that nonwhite people had had no part in shaping America until they started speaking up in the second half of the twentieth century.

The truth, of course, is that since well before the formation of the United States, the United States has been shaped by nonwhites in its mores, political structures, aesthetics, slang, economic practices, cuisine, dress, song, and sensibility. Takaki's "different mirror" is kaleidoscopic, reflecting at each turn the presence and influence of peoples generally excluded from traditional histories of American life—and reflecting too the way each of those peoples, whether Apache or Chinese or Mexican or West African, influenced other peoples in America.

Yes, America is foundationally English in its language, traditions of law, social organization, market mindedness, and frames of intellectual reference. But then it is foundationally African as well—in the way African slaves changed American speech and song and civic ideals; in the way slavery itself formed and deformed every aspect of life here, from the wording of the Constitution to the forms of faith to the anxious hypocrisy of the codes of the enslavers and their descendants.

Americans are all these things and more.

As the cultural critic Albert Murray wrote in his 1970 classic *The Omni-Americans,* the essence of American life is that it relentlessly generates hybrids. American culture takes segments of DNA—genetic and cultural—from around the planet and re-splices them into something previously unimagined. The sum of this—the Omni—is as capacious as human life itself, yet found in America most fully. This is jazz and the blues. This is the mash-up. This is everything creole, mestizo, hapa. In its serious forms, multiculturalism never asserted that every racial group should have its own sealed and separate history or that each group's history was equally salient to the formation of the American experience. It simply claimed that the omni-American story—of diversity and hybridity—was the legitimate American story.

What's happened in the generation since multiculturalism first became a bugaboo to some is that a generation has passed. And as Nathan Glazer has put it (somewhat ruefully), "We are all multiculturalists now." Americans have come to see—have chosen to see—that multiculturalism is not at odds with a single common culture; it is a single common culture.

Yes, it is true that in a finite school year, say, with finite class time and books of finite heft, not everything about everyone can be taught. There are necessary trade-offs. But in practice, recognizing the true and longstanding diversity of American identity is not an either-or. Learning about the internment of Japanese Americans does not block out knowledge of D-Day or Midway. It is additive. It brings more complexity and fosters a more world-ready awareness of complexity.

Which brings us back to the list. The list, quite simply, must be the mirror for a new America. As more diverse voices attain ever more forms of reach and power we need to re-integrate and re-imagine Hirsch's list of what literate Americans ought to know.

It needs fewer English antecedents ("Trafalgar, Battle of"). It needs fewer elements of grammar ("ellipsis"). It needs fewer outmoded idioms ("tied to his mother's apron strings"). It needs nods to how the language mutates (attaching "-gate" to any scandal post-Watergate). It needs new references that illuminate how Hindus worship, how Koreans treat elders, what pieces of African custom were grafted onto what pieces of Scots-Irish custom to form what kinds of Southern folkways.

It needs more than just words, because literacy in this mediated age is not only verbal. It needs images (braceros on ranches, ballplayers in internment camps). It needs symbols ("Don't Tread On Me" flags and "99 percent" placards; quinceañera dresses and historically black sorority letters). It needs iconic sounds (Marine Corps cadence calls, a sustained Sinatra note). It needs the lingo of poor and working-class communities (Southie and Crenshaw) as much as the argot of elite precincts. It needs the most durable Internet memes (like the meme format itself), media metaphors (like "playlists" or "bookmarks"), and pop culture referents.

To be clear: A 21st-century omni-American approach to cultural literacy is not about crowding out "real" history with the perishable stuff of contemporary life. It's about drawing lines of descent from the old forms of cultural expression, however formal, to their progeny, however colloquial. As Lin-Manuel Miranda's brilliant hip-hop musical *Hamilton* reminds us, every voice contains an echo; every echo can be given new voice.

Nor is Omni-American cultural literacy about raising the "self-esteem" of the poor, nonwhite, and marginalized. It's about raising the collective knowledge of all—and recognizing that the wealthy, white, and powerful also have blind spots and swaths of ignorance so broad as to keep them dangerously isolated from their countrymen.

So we need a list. And not the list that Hirsch made in 1987. What, then, would be on your list? It's not an idle question. It turns out to be the key to rethinking how a list should even get made.

* * *

Not long after his original book came out, Hirsch published the first of several editions of a *Dictionary of Cultural Literacy*. Here the list could be supplemented with explanations and pictures. What's striking about the most recent edition, from 2002, is how multicultural it is compared to the first appendix. Where the 1987 list mentioned China but never Chinese Americans, the 2002 dictionary describes the Chinese Exclusion Act.

Still, it's notable that the 2002 dictionary was the last edition published. We've moved on. The tempo of meme creation and destruction has become too fast for one person, one book, to follow.

That's because the Internet has transformed who makes culture and how. As barriers to culture creation have fallen, orders of magnitude more citizens—amateurs—are able to shape the culture in which we must all be literate. Cat videos and *Star Trek* fan fiction may not hold up long beside Toni Morrison. But the entry of new creators leads to new claims of right: The right to be recognized. The right to be counted. The right to make the means of recognition and accounting.

And as the pool of potential culture-makers has widened, the modes of culture creation have similarly shifted away from hierarchies and institutions to webs and networks. Wikipedia is the prime embodiment of this reality, both in how the online encyclopedia is crowd-created and how every crowd-created entry contains links to other entries. (It also demonstrates that democratization can yield something much richer than a lowest-common denominator result.)

What does this mean for this omni-American cultural literacy project? For one thing, the list for these times can't be the work of one person or even one small team. It has to be everyone's work. It has to be an online, crowd-sourced, organic document that never stops changing, whose entries are added or pruned, elevated or demoted, according to the wisdom of the network.

Everyone should make his or her own list online. We can aggregate all the lists. And from that vast welter of preferences will emerge, without any single person calling it so, a prioritized list of "what every American needs to know."

It also means that every entry on this dynamic list can be a node to another list. So an entry on "robber barons" (present in the 1987 list) should open up to "malefactors of great wealth" (TR's line, not on the 1987 list) and "economic royalists" (FDR's, not there either) and "the 1 percent." There should be an entry on "Southern heritage" that links sideways to other euphemisms for white supremacy. Or an entry on "women's suffrage" that links to other suffrage movements.

This will be a list of nodes and nested networks. It will be a fractal of associations, which reflects far more than a linear list how our brains work and how we learn and create. Hirsch himself nodded to this reality in *Cultural Literacy* when he described the process he and his colleagues used for collecting items for their list, though he raised it by way of pointing out the danger of infinite regress. "Where should such associations stop?" he asked. "How many are generally known by literate people?"

His conclusion, appropriate to his times, was that you had to draw boundaries somewhere with the help of experts. My take, appropriate to our times, is that Americans can draw not boundaries so much as circles and linkages, concept sets and pathways among them.

Because 5,000 or even 500 items is too daunting a place to start, I ask here only for your top ten. What are ten things every American—newcomer or native born, affluent or indigent—should know? What ten things do you feel are both required knowledge and illuminating gateways to those unenlightened about American life? Here are my entries:

Whiteness
The Federalist Papers
The Almighty Dollar
Organized Labor
Reconstruction
Nativism
The American Dream
The Reagan Revolution
DARPA
A sucker born every minute

I chose some off-center items—Reconstruction instead of the Civil War, for instance, or the Federalist Papers instead of the Constitution—because the off-center concepts imply and necessitate command of the central ones. Others, like nativism, are both a specific historical reference and recurring motif in American politics. And "a sucker born every minute" is of course both a particular saying and a general emblem of a society that revolves around mass entertainment. What are your ten, and why? (And if you like, what are your next ten, and the next?) Share your lists with us online.[LRI.3] Argue them out with friends and family and fellow citizens. The culture wars can give way to a conversation about the culture we are. And together, over time, Americans will author a definitive, unendingly edited guide to how to read, write, speak—and be—American. ∎

Questions

❶ How does Liu position Hirch and his work in this article? How does he extend a conversation Hirsch initiated through his text?

❷ What cultural references does Liu weave throughout this piece? In what ways do those references support or detract from his points?

❸ What concepts seem most central to Liu's work? What do these terms themselves seem to suggest about cultural literacy?

❹ What does this piece suggest about the public discourse the web can support?

References, Resources, and Links

References and Resources

Chapter 1

REFERENCES

1:1 Brandt, Deborah. "Accumulating Literacy: Writing and Learning to Write in the Twentieth Century." *College English*, vol. 57, no. 6, 1996, pp. 649-51, DOI: 10.2307/378570.

1:2 Swales, John M. *Genre Analysis: English in Academic and Research Settings.* Cambridge UP, 1990.

RESOURCES

How Social Media are shaping our digital lives. (www.ted.com/playlists/26/our_digital_lives)

"Digital Nation: Life on the Virtual Frontier," *Frontline,* 2010, (www.pbs.org/wgbh/frontline/film/digitalnation/)

Chapter 2

REFERENCES

2:1 Lu, Min-Zhan. "From Silence to Words: Writing as Struggle." *College English*, vol. 49, no. 4, 1987, pp. 437-38, DOI: 10.2307/377860.

2:2 West, Kanye. "No More Parties in L.A." *The Life of Pablo,* Def Jam/G.O.O.D. Music, 2016

2:3 Flower, Linda, and John R. Hayes "A Cognitive Process Theory of Writing." *College Composition and Communication*, vol. 32, no. 4, 1981, pp. 365-87, www.jstor.org/stable/356600 doi:1.

2:4 Emig, Janet. *The Composing Processes of Twelfth Graders.* NCTE, 1971.

2:5 Herrington, Anne. "Writing to Learn: Writing across the Discipines." *College English*, vol. 43, no. 4, 1981, pp. 379-87, DOI: 10.2307/377126 Stable URL: http://www.jstor.org/stable/377126

2:6 Odell, Lee, and Dixie Goswami. "Writing in a Non-Academic Setting." *Research in the Teaching of English*, vol. 16, no. 3, 1982, pp. 201-223; www.jstor.org/stable/40170900.

2:7 Sommers, Nancy. *Revision Strategies of Student Writers and Experienced Adult Writers.* National Institute of Education, 1982.

2:8 Takayoshi, Pamela. "Short-form Writing: Studying Process in the Context of Contemporary Composing Technlogies." *Computers and Composition,* no. 37, Sept. 2015, pp. 1-13, dx.doi.org/10.1016/j.compcom.2015.04.006.

2:9 Perl, Sondra. *Felt Sense: Writing with the Body.* Boynton/Cook, 2004.

2:10 Elbow, Peter. *Writing without Teachers.* Oxford UP, 1973.

2:11 Palmeri, Jason. *Studies in Writing and Rhetoric: Remixing Composition: A History of Multimodal Writing Pedagogy.* Southern Illinois UP, 2012. *eBook Academic Collection* (EBSCOhost), 24 May 2016. .

2:12 Berthoff, Ann E. *The Making of Meaning: Metaphors, Models, and Maxims for Writing Teachers.* Boynton/Cook, 1981.

2:13 Digitales.com, digitales.us/sites/default/files/Tech4Learning%20DigiTales%20StoryKeepers.pdf.

2:14 Brandt, Deborah. *Literacy in American Lives.* Cambridge UP, 2001.

2:15 Selfe, Cynthia L., and Gail E. Hawisher, editors. *Literate Lives in the Information Age: Narratives of Literacy from the United States.* Erlbaum, 2004.

2:16 Kinloch, Valerie, Beverly J. Moss, and Elaine Richardson. "Claiming Our Place on the Flo(or): Black Women and Collaborative Literacy Narratives." ccdigitalpress.org/stories/chapters/moss/.

RESOURCES

Burns, Ken, director. *The Civil War.* PBS Broadcasting, 1990.

Brandt, Deborah. *Literacy in American Lives.* Cambridge UP, 2001.

Chapter 3

REFERENCES

3:1 Aristotle. *On Rhetoric.* Translated and edited by George A. Kennedy. Oxford UP, 1991.

3:2 Bitzer, Lloyd F. "The Rhetorical Situation." *Philosophy and Rhetoric,* vol. 1, no. 1, Jan. 1968, pp. 1-14. Stable URL www.jstor.org/stable/40236733.

3:3 Booth, Wayne. "The Rhetorical Stance." *College Composition and Communication,* vol. 14, no. 3, pp. 139-145. www.jstor.org.login.library.coastal.edu:2048/stable/355048.

3:4 Zappen, James. "Digital Rhetoric: Toward an Integrated Theory." *Technical Communication Quarterly,* vol. 14, no. 3, 2005, pp. 319-325.

3:5 boyd, danah. "Learning to Hide in Plain Sight." *Apophenia.* 23 Aug. 2010. www.zephoria.org/thoughts/archives/2010/08/23/social-steganography-learning-to-hide-in-plain-sight.html.

3:6 Wolf, Maryanne. *Proust and the Squid.* Harper Perennial, 2008.

3:7 boyd, danah. *It's Complicated: The Social Lives of Networked Teens.* Yale UP, 2014.

3:8 Hicks, Troy. *Digital Writing, Digital Teaching: Integrating New Literacies into the Teaching of Writing.* 9 Sept. 2009. hickstro.org/.

RESOURCES

danah boyd's blog. (www.zephoria.org/thoughts/archives/2010/08/23/social-steganography-learning-to-hide-in-plain-sight.html)

danah boyd. "It's Complicated. The Social Lives of Teens." *WGBH Forum.* Feb. 14, 2016. *YouTube.* (youtu.be/2yCHI8WCbDY)

Chapter 4

REFERENCES

4:1 Murphy, Kate. "We Want Privacy but Can't Stop Sharing." *The New York Times*, 4 Oct. 2014. www.nytimes.com/2014/10/05/sunday-review/we-want-privacy-but-cant-stop-sharing.html.

4:2 Scherker, Amanda. "Didn't Read Facebook's Fine Print? Here's Exactly What it Says." *The Huffington Post*, TheHuffingtonPost.com, 21 July 2014. www.huffingtonpost.com/2014/07/21/facebook-terms-condition_n_5551965.html.

4:3 Victor, Elizabeth. "How to Check Social Media Privacy Settings." *Social Media Examiner*, Socialmediaexaminer.com. 30 Oct. 2014. www.socialmediaexaminer.com/social-media-privacy-settings/.

4:4 Miller, Carolyn R. "Genre as Social Action." *Quarterly Journal of Speech*, vol. 71, no. 2, 1984, pp. 151-167, ebscohost.com.login.library.coastal.edu:2048/login.aspx?direct=true&db=cms&AN=13147541&site=ehost-live.

4:5 Berkenkotter, Carol, and Thomas N. Huckin. *Genre Knowledge in Disciplinary Communication: Cognition/ Culture/ Power.* L. Erlbaum Associates, 1995.

4:6 Schryer, Catherine. "The Lab vs. the Clinic: Sites of Competing Genres." *Genre and the New Rhetoric,* edited by Aviva Freedman and Peter Medway, Taylor & Francis, 1994, pp. 105-124.

4:7 Bazerman, Charles. "Systems of Genre and the Enactment of Social Intentions." *Genre and the New Rhetoric,* edited by Aviva Freedman and Peter Medway, Taylor & Francis, 1994, pp. 79-99.

4:8 Paul, Pamela. "Cracking Teenagers' Online Code." *New York Times.* 22 Jan. 2012. www.nytimes.com/2012/01/22/fashion/danah-boyd-cracking-teenagers-online-codes.html?pagewanted=all.

RESOURCES

Khan, Khalid S., and Sameer Chaudhry. "Systematic Review: An Evidence-based Approach to an Ancient Pursuit: Systematic Review on Converting Online Contact into a First Date." *Evidence-Based Medicine,* ebmed-2014-110101. Published Online First, 12 Feb. 2015, DOI:10.1136/ebmed-2014-110101, www.jstor.org.login.library.coastal.edu:2048/stable/355048.

Gaylor, Brett, director, "Do Not Track." *Do Not Track.* Do Not Track, 2015. donottrack-doc.com.

boyd, danah. *danah boyd.* danah.org.

boyd, danah. danah boyd/apophenia: making connections where none previously existed, www.zephoria.org/thoughts/.

"Danah Boyd." Wikipedia. Wikimedia Foundation, en.wikipedia.org/wiki/Danah_boyd.

This American Life. Chicago Public Media, www.thisamericanlife.org/.

1. *Resources about danah boyd:*

danah boyd's website: http://www.danah.org/. A briefer statement appears on danah boyd's blog, *Apophenia* (www.zephoria.org/thoughts/)

danah boyd entry, *Wikipedia* (en.wikipedia.org/wiki/Danah_boyd)

2. *Resources for Audio Profiles:*

BBC News figures (www.bbc.co.uk/programmes/b006qjz5/episodes/downloads)

Popcorntalk Network's profiles of Hollywood figures—actors, directors, etc. (popcorntalknetwork.com/category/shows/profiles-podcast/)

This American Life episode on experimental phases of young people's lives (www.thisamericanlife.org/radio-archives/episode/268/my-experimental-phase)

Chapter 5

REFERENCES

5:1 Surowiecki, James. *The Wisdom of Crowds: Why the Many Are Smarter than the Few and How Collective Wisdom Shapes Business, Economies, Societies, and Nations.* Doubleday, 2004.

5:2 Brown, John Seely. "Growing Up Digital." *Change,* vol. Mar./Apr., 2000, www.johnseelybrown.com/Growing_up_digital.pdf.

5:3 Berthoff, Ann. *The Making of Meaning.* Boynton/Cook, 1981.

5:4 Kutz, Ellie. "Part I. Overview: Digital Learners and Online Learning Communities." *UMass Boston Educational Technology Newsletter.* 26 Mar. 2012. umbedtech.wordpress.com/2012/03/26/overview-digital-learners-and-online-learning-communities/

5:5 Kutz, Ellie. "Part II. How the Web Has Changed Literacy and Learning." *UMass Boston Educational Technology Newsletter.* 26 Mar. 2012. umbedtech.wordpress.com/2012/03/26/how-the-web-has-changed-literacy-and-learning/

RESOURCES

Poe, Marshall. "The Hive." *The Atlantic,* Sept. 2006. (www.theatlantic.com/magazine/archive/2006/09/the-hive/305118/)

Chapter 6

REFERENCES

6:1 Berthoff, Ann. *The Making of Meaning.* Boynton/Cook, 1981, p. 43.

6:2 Hirsch, E. D. *Cultural Literacy: What Every American Needs to Know.* Houghton Mifflin, 1987.

6:3 Kutz, Eleanor, and Hephzibah Roskelly. *An Unquiet Pedagogy.* Heinemann Boynton/Cook, 1993.

6:4 Liu, Eric. "What Every American Should Know. Defining Cultural Literacy for an Increasingly Diverse Nation". *The Atlantic,* 3 July 2015, www.theatlantic.com/politics/archive/2015/07/what-every-american-should-know/397334.

6:5 Banks, James A. "Teaching for Social Justice, Diversity, and Citizenship in a Global World." *The Educational Forum,* 2004, pp. 289–298. depts.washington.edu/centerme/Fs04banks.pdf.

6:6 Wark, Jake. "Means and Motives." *Exploring Literacy.* Pearson/Longman, 2004, pp. 323-328.

6:7 van Dijck, Jose. "Memory and Cultural Forms." *Mediated Memories in a Digital Age.* Stanford UP, 2007, pp. 98-100, 112-114.

6:8 Sontag, Susan. *On Photography.* Picador, 1977.

RESOURCES

Popova, Maria. "The Susan Sontag Guide to Photography in the Age of Digital Culture." *Slate—Future Tense*. 11 Oct. 2013. www.slate.com/blogs/future_tense/2013/10/11/susan_sontag_photography_and_social_networking.html.

Chapter 7

REFERENCES

[7:1] boyd, danah. "Why Youth (Heart) Social Network Sites: The Role of Networked Publics in Teenage Social Life." *The John D. and Catherine T. MacArthur Foundation Series on Digital Media*, 2007, pp. 119-142.

[7:2] Gee, James P. "Literacy, Discourse and Linguistics. Introduction." *Journal of Education,* vol. 17, no. 1, 1989, pp. 5-17.

[7:3] Lady Gaga. "Edge of Glory." Streamline 2011, musicpleer.cc/#!lady+gaga+the+edge+of+glory.

[7:4] Shelton, Blake. "Doin' What She Likes." Warner 2014 , www.instamp3.co/download/blake-shelton-doin-what-she-likes.html.

[7:5] Ayeska. "Music Monday on July 4th. Can't Get No Better Than This." *Word. The Online Journal of African American English*. 4 July 2011. africanamericanenglish.com/2011/07/04/monday-music-on-july-4th-cant-get-no-better-than-this/.

[7:6] "About AAE." *Word. The Online Journal of African American English*. africanamericanenglish.com/about/.

[7:7] Smitherman, Geneva. *Word from the Mother: Language and African Americans*. Taylor & Francis, 2007, p. 145.

[7:8] Alim, H. Samy. *Roc the Mic Right: The Language of Hip Hop Culture*. Routledge, 2006.

[7:9] Alim, H. Samy. "Hip Hop Nation." *Do You Speak American*. National Public Radio, 2005. www.pbs.org/speak/words/sezwho/hiphop/reprint/.

[7:10] Alim, H. Samy, John Baugh, and Mary Bucholz. "Global Ill-Literacies: Hip Hop Cultures, Youth Identities, and the Politics of Literacy." *Review of Research in Education*, no. 35, 2011, pp. 230-246.

[7:11] Berlatsky, Noah. "Why 'Indie' Music is So Unbearably White." *The New Republic*. 4 Apr. 2015. newrepublic.com/article/121437/why-indie-music-so-unbearably-white.

[7:12] Mulligan, Mark. "How the Role of Genres has Changed in Music Culture." *Music Industry Blog*. 14 Feb. 2014. musicindustryblog.wordpress.com/2014/02/14/how-the-role-of-genres-has-changed-in-music-culture/.

[7:13] Meyer, Erika. "On the Meaninglessness of Music Genres." *Collapseboard*. 23 Jan. 2012. www.collapseboard.com/blogs/erika-meyer/on-the-meaninglessness-of-music-genre/. No longer online.

[7:14] Ghose, Tia. "Valley Girl Talk Is, Like, Everywhere in Southern California." *Live Science*. 5 Dec. 2013. www.livescience.com/41714-valley-girl-talk-is-like-everywhere.html.

[7:15] Tannen, Deborah. *Conversational Style: Analyzing Talk Among Friends*. 2nd ed. Oxford UP, 1984, 2004.

_____. *You Just Don't Understand. Men and Women in Conversation*. Ballantine, 1990.

_____. *You're Wearing THAT? Mothers and Daughters in Conversation*. Ballantine, 2006.

RESOURCES

Music Genre List (www.musicgenreslist.com/)

Music Genre Map (io9.com/a-map-showing-the-popularity-of-musical-genres-across-t-1563760391)

Chapter 8

REFERENCES

[8:1] Baym, Nancy. "The New Shape of the Online Community. The Example of Swedish Independent Music Fandom." *First Monday* vol. 12, no. 8, 6 Aug. 2007. uncommonculture.org/ojs/index.php/fm/article/view/1978/1853.

[8:2] Baym, Nancy. *Tune In, Log On: Soaps, Fandom and Online Community*. Sage, 2000, nancybaym.com/.

[8:3] Koosel, Stacey. "Ethnographies of Social Networks: How Artists Negotiate Digital Identity." *interartive*, interartive.org/2013/05/ethnographies-social-networks-artist-digital-identity/.

RESOURCES

1. Resources about Online Fandom:

Nancy Baym's blog: www.onlinefandom.com/

Baym, Nancy. *Nancybaym.com*.

2. Resources about Hockey Fandom Ethnographic Study:

Norman, Mark. "Online Community or Electronic Tribe? Exploring the Social Characteristics and Spatial Production of an Internet Hockey Fan Culture." *Mark Norman* (jss.sagepub.com/content/38/5/395.abstract)

3. Resources about Hockey Fandom Data:

fivethirtyeight.com/datalab/the-distribution-of-fandom-in-pro-leagues/

4. Resources about Google NHL Fandom Map

www.hockeyworldblog.com/2014/04/16/facebooks-fandom-map-for-the-2014-nhl-playoffs

Jacobson, Beth. "The Social Psychology of the Creation of a Sports Fan Identity." *Athletic Insight,* vol. 51, no. 2, www.athleticinsight.com/Vol5Iss2/FanDevelopment.htm.

Links

Additional Readings

LRI:1 http://www.johnseelybrown.com/Growing_up_digital.pdf

LRI:2 http://www.theatlantic.com/politics/archive/2015/07/what-every-american-should-know/397334/

LRI:3 https://www.surveymonkey.com/r/ZN5F92J?sm=dboNfDKrpW191w LbCqjWIg%3d%3d

Chapter 2

L2:1 http://www.hockeyfights.com/

L2:2 http://www.scarymommy.com/my-child-plays-with-a-tablet-at-restaurants/

L2:3 https://umbedtech.wordpress.com/2012/06/14/keynote-media-literacy-and-digital-storytelling

L2:4 https://umbedtech.wordpress.com/2012/06/14/keynote-media-literacy-and-digital-storytelling/

L2:5 https://themoth.org/

L2:6 http://www.digitales.com

L2:7 https://owl.english.purdue.edu/sitemap/

L2:8 http://www.cowbird.com

L2:9 http://daln.osu.edu

L2:10 http://ccdigitalpress.org/stories/chapters/moss

Chapter 3

L3:1 http://youtu.be/Xmzb9PlPD-Q

L3:2 http://youtu.be/Xmzb9PlPD-Q

L3:3 http://www.zephoria.org/thoughts

Chapter 4

L4:1 http://www.donottrack.com

L4:2 https://donottrack-doc.com/en/episode/3

L4:3 http://www.huffingtonpost.com/2014/07/21/facebook-terms-condition_n_5551965.html

L4:4 http://www.socialmediaexaminer.com/social-media-privacy-settings

L4:5 http://www.danah.org

L4:6 http://www.zephoria.org/thoughts

L4:7 http://en.wikipedia.org/wiki/Danah_boyd

L4:8 http://www.bbc.co.uk/programmes/b006qjz5/episodes/downloads

L4:9 http://popcorntalknetwork.com/category/shows/profiles-podcast

L4:10 http://www.thisamericanlife.org/radio-archives/episode/268/my-experimental-phase

Chapter 5

L5:1 https://umbedtech.wordpress.com/2012/03/

L5:2 https://umbedtech.wordpress.com/2012/03/26/overview-digital-learners-and-online-learning-communities/

L5:3 https://umbedtech.wordpress.com/2012/03/26/how-the-web-has-changed-literacy-and-learning/

L5:4 https://www.youtube.com/watch?v=2yCHI8WCbDY

L5:5 http://ed.ted.com/on/PBFXQpG4

Chapter 7

L7.1 https://africanamericanenglish.com/2011/07/04

L7.2 https://africanamericanenglish.com/2011/07/04/monday-music-on-july-4th-cant-get-no-better-than-this/

Chapter 8

L8:1 http://www.onlinefandom.com

L8:2 http://firstmonday.org/article/view/1978/1853

L8:3 https://owl.engish.purdue.edu/owl/resource/747/01

L8:4 http://www.onlinefandom.com/longer-writings

L8:5 http://www.thisamericanlife.org

L8:6 https://www.thisamericanlife.org/radio-archives/episode/74/conventions?act=1

Publicly Circulating Compositions

Welcome to Part II of *Writing Moves.* Here we focus our inquiry on writing in the public and increasingly global contexts that the internet now makes part of our interactive composing world. As we found for local communities in Part I, the literacy practices of these wider communities and the ways in which we engage with them are continually changing in a digital world in ways we'll explore in the chapters that follow.

In Part I we looked at how rhetorical relationships are formed, knowledge is shared, and genres and styles of interaction are created and drawn upon within local communities. Part II of this book takes that wider culture as its focus, tracing the digital contexts created by texts themselves and broadening the conversation.

In Part II we'll shift our focus beyond local discourse communities to explore the changing ways in which we communicate in the public arena, asking how rhetorical relationships work in the larger public world of the internet, how knowledge is shared and built on in a wider public conversation, and how new genres (blogs, for instance) support such knowledge-sharing and extended conversation in public contexts as texts circulate within a larger textual ecology. We'll also explore the role of multiple modalities (such as visual images) in our new public literacy practices. At the same time, we'll consider the questions people are raising about our wider emerging digital culture and the arguments they are making about both its potential and possible pitfalls. Throughout, we'll also consider where and how we can participate in these larger conversations.

The work of Part II will build on that of Part I, where we explore the personal and social literacy practices of contemporary students, and the rhetorical and knowledge-making aspects of their experiences as they unfold in online and offline spaces. There we look closely at the digital composing practices of Barry, a college student, inside and outside of his courses and explore a series of inquiries by both students and established researchers into how composing is changing in digital environments. We also introduce a number of working concepts to help us think about how literacy practices evolve in digital, multimodal, and networked environments, and how new, online contexts work to extend and expand the ways in which members of discourse communities interact. We explore the rhetorical situations these contexts give shape to and consider the importance of context (where) in shaping what gets talked about, and why and how, reflecting the shared knowledge, shared purposes, and shared ways of a community. We also explore how digital contexts position writers to take advantage of the online platforms they're working with to create multimodal compositions, such as those that draw on the visual and the auditory, to help them connect to their audience in rhetorically savvy ways. In addition, we note how the communicative practices of individuals and communities helped them shape particular social identities and draw on the wider culture in doing so.

In Part II, we expand on many of these understandings about local practices by taking the larger cultural contexts of digital media, textual production, and circulation as our main focus. While we shift our attention here to the larger scenes and cultures constructed by digital texts, we continue to think about the moves individuals make within these settings. In doing so, we'll look at the evolving ways in which writers and designers create and share compositions that are appropriate for digital environments as we question the what, how, and why of such compositions and the rhetorical situations they speak to as we look to the where, to how texts circulate across a range of media and modes. Toward this end, Part II extends the work of Part I by guiding you through the following types of explorations.

- ➤ Analyzing digital contexts, including media ecologies and textual circulation
- ➤ Drawing on design practices to analyze multimodal texts that combine various modes, such as text, image, sound, and color
- ➤ Evaluating and reviewing cultural productions
- ➤ Understanding how claims and arguments are being made for and about digital contexts in ways that showcase the concerns and the resources central to a digital age

Part II invites you to look more closely at cultural production and what it means to produce texts in a digital world. We will develop a richer understanding of textuality, context, practice, and how they intersect when texts are composed and circulated in digital networks. And you will have the opportunity to apply these new understandings to the development of rhetorical, analytical, and argumentative strategies for composing modern texts and entering the larger world of networked public debate and conversation.

Again, we consider both the writing moves made by composers who are involved in an active process of designing compositions that reflect their purposes in addressing the public and often global audiences they wish to speak to, drawing on common ways but reinventing and adapting those ways for their own purposes. But we'll significantly extend our exploration of the ways that writing now moves and circulates through wider and wider networks within a global public.

Part II invites you to research how communication is taking place in these larger public digital worlds, reading some of the public and academic writing of those who have studied these topics and contributing what you learn to those larger conversations. The smaller inquiries within chapters lead to larger projects while they engage the readings included in this section to help you enter a larger conversation about the practices and societal concerns of our rapidly changing digital environment, and they provide further possibilities for more extended and formal research studies in Part III.

Joining Public Conversations in Digital Contexts

1 How are individuals grappling with the new discourse possibilities and expectations of a larger, public "community" on the internet, and how are social media platforms that facilitate that discourse responding?

2 How are words and images being taken up, shared, and altered across platforms as they enter wide circulation, and what are the implications for how we think about ownership and creativity?

3 How do copyright issues impact composing in digital environments, and what does this mean for creativity?

4 What can you learn by tracing the circulation of a contribution you've made to a larger public discourse?

Chapter Preview

Part I focused primarily on local communities, where people share a group identity based on common purposes, interests, and practices as they interact in a variety of digital contexts. Whether through texting within a family, participating in an online book group, or posting pictures for friends on Instagram, we considered how rhetorical relationships are formed, knowledge is shared, and styles of interaction are used within those communities. We also saw how those communities drew on the wider culture and connected with a larger public world through their interests in sports or music or books.

But the interactions we explored in Part I took place primarily within the discourse spaces that these participants belonged to, where they were insiders interacting primarily with other insiders to that context, who knew **what** members of that discourse community might text or post and **why** and **how.** And while we suggested that as composers you might sometimes shift your own context, your own **where,** from addressing your immediate classroom community to circulating what you learned to a larger public, perhaps by creating a public wiki or posting to a public blog, the focus of your inquiries themselves was still on the local. But our new, digital literacies aren't just reshaping how we communicate on the local level.

As we move from the local world of familiar discourse communities to the global public world of the internet, we find that things change in surprising ways. Information and ideas are quickly shared across multiple platforms, in many forms and modes, often reaching vast audiences. Because of the fluidity of digital textuality and the ease in which we create and exchange texts, we've entered a media environment that is more interactive, participatory, global, and accumulative than it was for earlier generations.

In Part II, our focus of inquiry shifts from local discourse communities to this larger public environment, where people intentionally, and sometimes unintentionally, engage in public discourse with a potentially global audience of others who may or may not share their purposes, interests, values, and ways. What happens with this shift in context, in circulation? With the change in **where**, we find several related shifts: new rhetorical purposes as composers try to engage a more diffuse and less-known audience online and invite their participation, new topics of interest and public concern about how society is changing and what social possibilities are arising or might arise in our digital age, and new ways of sharing those interests and concerns through social media and digital genres like public blogs as users draw on digital writing tools to create more visual, multimodal, mashed-up, and remixed texts to convey meaning, and circulate those texts in a network of relationships with other texts, what we'll refer to as a *textual ecology*.

In this chapter, we'll begin our larger inquiry by looking at instances when the local and the public have clashed, when local texts have circulated beyond their intended audiences, and when others have joined the conversation in ways not envisioned by the original composer as they've shared, tweeted, and added their own meanings and purposes to an original post. In this fluid movement of texts and exchanges, words and images circulate widely and often cross over from our local communities to the broader public. New digital literacy practices of remix and mashup of copyrighted works have raised legal issues that current copyright law isn't really prepared to address. In exploring the ways meaning gets made in digital networks, we'll introduce some key concepts to help guide our inquiry into public discourse online and explore some of the new questions being raised for us as both readers and composers who participate in that public discourse.

Exploring
The Public and Digital Discourse

As we begin to consider the issues raised by the wide circulation of many sorts of compositions and texts—of music, images, words, videos, and multimodal texts drawing from all of these—within a larger public and global discourse context, we encounter a number of issues that aren't typically concerns of a local community, even when that community comes together in digital spaces. In this new **where** of public digital contexts, what can be posted and shared and altered must be negotiated across a wide public with members who have competing interests. The easy crossover of local and public spaces facilitated by the internet raises new questions of how we create shared understandings and engage in productive public discourse.

Considering What and How—Norms of Public Discourse

Exchanges within local communities are usually governed by a shared understanding of **what** and **how**—what images it's appropriate to share, what sorts of things it's appropriate to say within the **where** of that local community, and the appropriate ways to say them. The social media posts of hockey teammates or the reflections of a rapper/producer on his use of digital technology address their known audiences in ways those audiences will connect with. But when posts on social media move beyond the local context to reach a wider audience, the same words might be received in unintended ways and might elicit quite different responses from what the writer **_intended_**. When the forms of public discourse were more limited—when writing for public consumption largely appeared in controlled media, in print media like newspapers, magazines, or broadcast media like radio and TV—editors and producers controlled what went public, and even the audience response in a call-in show or a letter to the editor was monitored. Public discourse was generally expected to reflect some larger shared norms about what could be said and how to engage in even the most challenging exchanges while at least pretending to be respectful of others' opinions.

We all know that the internet has profoundly altered these expectations by facilitating the public circulation of discourse that once would have remained private and local. A New York congressman shares sexually explicit images of himself on his public Twitter account, violating implicit public norms and ruining his political career;

a cheerleader for an NFL team posts a lewd and racist photo and gets fired. Facebook develops Community Standards[L9:1] for its user community (a very broad global community of at least 1.6 billion users at the end of 2015) page to encourage respectful behavior and establish community norms about posts, addressing such concerns as nudity, hate speech, bullying and harassment, violence, sexual exploitation, and graphic content, with information about how to report, remove, or unfollow disturbing posts. Other social media sites do the same, and Twitter Rules[L9:2] and Instagram's[L9:3] and Snapchat's[L9:4] Community *Guidelines* cover similar territory.

Just like our more local discourse communities, audience and purpose continue to be central to how we think about building rhetorical relationships in this public domain. In its standards for hate speech, Facebook explicitly addresses questions of audience and purpose in considering what might be responsible discussion:

> People can use Facebook to challenge ideas, institutions, and practices. Such discussion can promote debate and greater understanding. Sometimes people share content containing someone else's hate speech for the purpose of raising awareness or educating others about that hate speech. When this is the case, we expect people to clearly indicate their purpose, which helps us better understand why they shared that content.
>
> We allow humor, satire, or social commentary related to these topics, and we believe that when people use their authentic identity, they are more responsible when they share this kind of commentary. For that reason, we ask that Page owners associate their name and Facebook Profile with any content that is insensitive, even if that content does not violate our policies. As always, we urge people to be conscious of their audience when sharing this type of content.[9:1]

Facebook's policies are a concrete example of how shared knowledge is created so actual discourse can take place between people, starting with a few basic ground rules for what's appropriate to post on their network. We can explore these ideas from a student's perspective, that of Brittany, who grapples with these questions of how people might post about their differing opinions respectfully, exploring what it means to think inside or outside of the box of societal norms and expectations. She recounts how a Facebook post by a student in one of her local communities—in her high school—was received and responded to. She tells us that the student, Akash, made a post on Facebook commenting on Caitlyn Jenner's very public sharing of her transgender experience with a cover photo on *Vanity Fair* while linking to a rather conservative article on the topic.

Brittany's concern is not to agree or disagree with Akash's position (or the stance articulated in the article he linked to), but to comment on the quality of his post and those that followed. While Brittany finds his post to be a "very thoughtful, respectful, and insightful post, linking to a website that highlighted his personal beliefs in a non-malicious way," she was disappointed by "well over a hundred comments" his post received, almost all of them slamming Akash for posting "such a thing," and to share her own response to those comments and her reflections on what happened next. Figure 9.1 is Brittany's original post.

> **Brittany Watson** This is the saddest thing I have ever read. Akash posted an article reflecting his opinion in the most respectful way. It actually shocks me how close minded society is today, people think they're accepting and open minded if they have the socially acceptable opinion, and immediately proceed to rip apart anything that differs. As soon as you start to believe people should censor their opinions and values because of yours, something is very wrong and you need to reevaluate such narcissism.
> Like · Reply · 👍 14 · June 3 at 7:54am

Figure 9.1: Brittany's Facebook post

links

Sidenote

At the end of 2015, Facebook had a global community of at least 1.6 billion users.

And here's part of her reflection on the set of posts that led to hers:

> Everyone had a box that they centered their comments around; the box, in this case, was an opinion about transgenderism. Everyone. . .ruined their points or simply did nothing with them because their focus was on feverishly arguing their opinion. Firstly, you aren't going to change anyone's opinion through a precipitate Facebook comment fueled by aggression or excitement at conflict. Secondly, if your only evidence is your opinion, and you're just reiterating what every other person says or wants to hear, newsflash, you're not achieving anything! I completely threw the box away and said hey, regardless of what anyone is speaking about, as long as it's respectful, they should be able to do so without being attacked or told to take it down. That was not an opinion about transgenderism, and do you know what? Because I had made a point that digressed so glaringly from the norm of the comments and did not concern my personal beliefs or values, it spoke to every single person reading that post, and it opened people's minds to the real problem.

Brittany soon found that her comment was circulating on Twitter (Figure 9.2).

Figure 9.2: Response to Brittany's tweet

Brittany's call for reasoned discourse rather than "slams" and the "feverish arguing" of opinions was appreciated by at least some of the wider audience her post eventually reached, and this confirmed her own position that "regardless of what anyone is speaking about, as long as it's respectful, they should be able to do so without being attacked or told to take it down."

Brittany's account echoes Facebook's statement of community standards that posts should be responsible to "promote debate and greater understanding." You can see from her example that it's challenging to everyone, not just the designers of social media platforms, but to all who use such platforms to figure out shared ways of communicating that support civic debate and maintain meaningful and respectful discourse on both the local and the public/global level. As these emerging digital environments change how texts are produced and circulated, these and other issues are ones we all need to consider.

INQUIRY

#1: The norms of social media discourse

???

What can we learn from Brittany's account? Are there parallels in your own experience of sharing or reading something that has been shared on social media? Has something you or someone you know posted circulated more widely or to a different audience than expected with unexpected results? What are your own reflections on the **how** of exchanging views on controversial issues in public spaces?

Circulating Texts: Anyone Can Become a Meme

While Akash probably did not expect his Facebook post to receive a hundred responses, and Brittany didn't expect hers to be picked up and circulated via Twitter, they were nevertheless trying to post thoughtfully and intentionally. Here's how Brittany describes her own process:

> [My post] was born from a passionate teenage girl fervidly typing into her phone, determined to free her wild thoughts into tangibility. That took about two minutes. For the next thirty eight minutes, it involved a much more tentative and calculating girl, relentlessly reading and re-reading and re-reading her work until finally, she put down the phone. Then, surprise! More re-reading. After intense consideration and seemingly minute revisions, she finally positioned her finger above the send button, closed her eyes, and quickly pushed down.

Brittany's reflection on her post illustrates how, even in a short post, she thought carefully about the potential audiences she might reach and the reaction she hoped to achieve. But many posts, responses, and tweets are more rapid and less thoughtful and intentional. And private citizens as well as celebrities may suddenly find themselves the center of public attention. A teenage boy with an after-school job at a cash register finds that he's suddenly #alexfromtarget with almost a million Twitter followers and more than two million on Instagram after a girl posted a picture she took of him surreptitiously. And teen fans of the band One Direction make a dad (@jrtoh15) famous when the dad sends a tweet saying, "I'm not a fan of One Direction being a 50 year old man and all but they can actually sing #amas" (commenting on their performance at the American Music Awards); he becomes an instant internet icon among the band's teenage fans and beyond.[9.2] When considered together, what do these events suggest about how texts and meanings circulate in digital public spaces?

➤ They show us a digital world where random moments in the lives of individuals—a photo captured at the checkout counter, a minor observation in a tweet—can suddenly go viral through social media, reaching vast audiences seemingly overnight. They become **memes**— a term drawn from the word "gene" and used to suggest that small bits of culture can replicate themselves and spread, but also evolve new forms and adapt to new contexts, growing in ways that are analogous to biological processes. So the meme of Jerry Riekert, the One Direction fan dad, not only spread among the many One Direction fans and into the Twitter universe, but when Jerry tweeted about the lamps he builds and offered to build one for One Direction, #jerrythelampbuilder was born on Twitter, while @jrtoh15 migrated to Instagram where he posted pictures of his now-famous lamps. The hashtag #alexfromtarget soon tagged a wide range of non-Alex Instagram photos, even as the original Alex maintained his own Instagram site.

memes
elements of culture that spread from person to person, often through the internet

Figure 9.3: Alex from Target Mashup

➤ Memes, as units of culture, constitute a form of **cultural production** where people participate in meaning-making activities that contribute, however briefly, to the larger culture as they use the inspiration of one small unit—an image, a text, a video—not only to share, but also to create new versions of their own. Such **mashups** and **remixes** occur when two different publicly circulating texts or ideas are combined, as when the "steal this look" fashion parody meme is brought together with the Alex from Target meme to produce the "steal Alex's look" mashup of Alex's picture plus a display of Target clothing (see Figure 9.3). Such mixes constitute an important new form of creativity in digital spaces.

cultural production
a process of drawing from and contributing to a larger culture

mashup
a text, often multimodal, that draws on more than one source to create a new cultural product

remix
an altered and reinvented piece of music or other media text

➤ Like much of what we share in the digital age, most of what gets spread as memes is cross-platform and *multimodal,* moving through social media networks from Twitter and Snapchat, to Instagram and beyond. Memes might circulate as words, images, videos, or mashups that combine several different modes, such as images with captions, or videos with links and text.

➤ As an internet meme or other circulating information moves through digital spaces it enters new contexts and new rhetorical situations where it is **recontextualized**. That is, its interplay with other elements of that new context gives it new meanings. Alex from Target might have been just a cute boy to the original girl who posted his picture, but as a circulating meme, he came to represent other meanings as his image was shared and circulated, even as an example of random internet fame. But his *New York Times* profile, with its subtitle "The Other Side of Fame,"[9.3] recontextualized his experience as it highlighted the dangers of sudden internet celebrity.

recontextualized
bringing a text into a new context, with new meanings

Memes exist within a network of texts, words, images, and sounds that can be captured and circulated with many interconnections. In that sense they represent a sort of **intertexuality** where no text really stands alone but always contains references to what has gone before, not only in a chain of tweets, but in reference to other cultural moments. Jerry's starting tweet about One Direction was initially part of a web of texts related to the American Music Awards and the band's performance there, while his story was drawn into a new network of texts about the workings of social media and about the world of teenage fandom. We can see this effect more clearly with more major cultural productions. When a new Star Wars movie was released in 2016, for example, it generated many related memes that built on not only the words ("A long time ago in a galaxy far, far away") and images (mash-ups of Jedi knights), but also the opening sound and graphics (known as the Star Wars crawl). If you do a search for Star Wars memes you'll find your own examples.

intertextuality
the interrelationship of texts as they influence and borrow from each other

Memes, practices of remix and mashup, recontextualization, multimodal texts, intertextuality—each of these key concepts points to the changing nature of how culture is produced through the texts and meanings we circulate on digital networks. Taken together, they form what we can call a **textual ecology** (see below)—the networks of human interaction, texts, and media that serve as the backdrop for our literacy practices. To think of texts and literacy as ecological is to think of our experience of literacy as flowing through a variety of contexts, situations, discourses, modes, and genres, where texts take shape, disappear, and reemerge in new texts and contexts. Textual ecologies take shape out of our social process of meaning-making as we communicate with one another, creating new understandings and perspectives on the world as we adopt, adapt, and share memes and texts. We might not know what meaning all of those who circulated comments and images related to the #alexfromtarget meme intended (although the first girl to tweet his picture, which she found somewhere on Tumblr, commented that he was cute), or why One Direction fans adopted dad Jerry, but all the contributions together create a network of circulating texts where each connects in some ways to another, creating a rich textual ecology in the process.

Textual ecology

"Ecology" is a useful concept and metaphor for understanding contemporary literacy environments. The basic meaning of the term comes from the biological sciences and describes a field of study that examines the interdependent relationships between different elements in a natural environment. For example, the ecology of a lake would include the water, the animals that live around and in the water, the vegetation, and the changing seasons. These different components of the ecology of the lake work in a dynamic and symbiotic relationship, and the health of the ecology depends on how well they work together.

> ## #2: Tracing an internet meme
>
> Choose one internet meme that has captured your attention. What can you discover about how it has circulated, what sorts of mashups and remixes it has generated, the ways in which it has moved across platforms and modes, and its connections to other texts in a textual ecology? What would you guess about the why of its circulation—the meanings contributors might have intended to share and their purposes for doing so?

People are likely to post whatever they want on social media. #Alexfromtarget wasn't asked whether he wanted his picture posted, and although he enjoyed some of the attention, much of it was negative and intrusive, according to his *New York Times* profile, and might have violated the standards Facebook is trying to establish for responsible posts. Just as the major social media platforms have developed community standards for discussion, they have also tried to set community standards related to the ownership of content and attribution, although these are as frequently violated.

We can see an example of this sort of violation in another circulating meme and the textual ecology that took shape around it. When Drake released his song "Hotline Bling" and Adele released her "Hello" in 2015, it was an obvious moment for meme-makers. Not only was each song shared on the artists' own social media sites and their music videos posted on YouTube, generating many remixes and parodies of each,[9:4] but because the two songs seemed to speak to each other, each wondering nostalgically about a past relationship, other meme mashups appeared, bringing the two artists and their songs together. One original mashup was a picture of the two singers standing together, with Drake holding his cell phone and Adele holding a retro landline phone, drawn by the artist Dave Valeza and posted to his <u>Instagram site</u>,[L9:5] where he posts new sketches almost daily, and on <u>Tumblr</u>[L9:6] and Twitter (@brainvario) with text that combined the two songs' lyrics: "I must have called a thousand times//you used to call me on my cell phone." Soon the clever piece of artwork was reposted on Drake's Instagram page (@Drake) without crediting the artist. Others noticed and tweeted, and Valeza soon reposted the image as it had appeared in Drake's Instagram, showing that his signature had been cropped out. In the end, Valeza sought legal help, and Drake removed the image from his Instagram feed. He didn't want his original picture or his subsequent posts reprinted here, perhaps because he still felt burned by what happened, but they continue to appear online, including in an MTV story by Adam Fleischer about the episode.[9:5]

Fleischer concludes his MTV article with the words of an email he received from Valeza about the incident: "The lesson here, for famous rappers or anyone that uses social media, remains the same: 'Post credit, link your sources. Just credit. There's no hard feelings. I just want credit.'"

What can we learn from this episode, and what does it tell us about how we make meaning in digital environments? Clearly the first thing is the lesson Fleischer shares. Whoever first posted Valeza's artwork, cutting out his signature and not giving him credit (whether that was Drake or someone Drake drew from) violated the terms Instagram sets forth in its Community Guidelines (Figure 9.4).

Share only photos and videos that you've taken or have the right to share.

As always, you own the content you post on Instagram. Remember to post authentic content, and don't post anything you've copied or collected from the internet that you don't have the right to post.[9:6]

Figure 9.4: Instagram's Community Guidelines

We'll return to copyright issues later in this chapter. But first there is more that this episode shows us about how a textual ecology takes shape in digital public spaces.

➤ **ABOUT *CULTURAL PRODUCTION* IN DIGITAL CONTEXTS.** Popular music artists like Drake and Adele and visual artists like Dave Valeza use Instagram and Twitter to connect with followers by posting a stream of images, videos, and updates. Aspiring artists in all media must not only master composing their music, videos, drawings, or comics. They also have to be adept at composing in various written genres and ways of distributing information creatively online. As a contemporary artist, Valeza exhibits a broad range of digital literacies. He posts his drawings on Instagram, posts and responds to comments on Twitter, and maintains a Tumblr blog where he exhibits his work and responds in greater length to his followers (currently around 3,000). Like many cultural producers, including Adele and Drake, Valeza practices and shares information about his work, and in his case, the work itself, via social media, finding inspiration in the surrounding cultural context.

➤ **ABOUT *MEANING-MAKING* IN CONTEMPORARY DIGITAL CULTURE.** As a text, image, video, or other remix changes hands and others respond, the meaning of the composition transforms to meet the needs of a new context. Memes often provide a kind of social commentary on cultural moments or events, often by parodying what others might take seriously through playful/absurdist means (as we see in the many Drake and Adele music video parodies). Having the ability to engage in such creative and inventive activity—not just by using new tools to create mashed-up images, for example, but also by knowing how to use those tools in making new meanings that will take on social significance as they circulate—reflects how our literacies, and our process of making meaning, is changing in digital public contexts.[9.7]

➤ **ABOUT *CIRCULATION* AND VIRAL CONTENT.** While Adele's and Drake's songs were circulating, and people were inventing and sharing memes related to those songs, Drake's act of posting without getting the artist's permission set off a firestorm of controversy on social media as Valeza and his followers spoke out on Instagram and Twitter. Other media outlets quickly picked up on the story, and it soon was circulating and trending online. Circulation of texts on the internet is both rapid and complex, with multiple strands to a story and multiple media sites involved in building on them, shaping them, and passing them along.

➤ **ABOUT *CONTEXT AND RECONTEXTUALIZATION*.** We might consider the what, why, and how of each of Drake's and Adele's songs in their original context—the themes and meanings they explore, their rhetorical purposes, and the ways they use resources of their respective music genres to explore those themes and achieve those purposes. But then, as each text is brought into a new context, it takes on new meanings and associations, and it is used for new purposes in new ways, altered by the new **where** of the new context. Valeza, in bringing his Adele and Drake images together in his sketch, and the words of their songs together in his caption, recontextualized their separate works in a new context that paired them, creating a new meaning in the process. In networked environments, as texts are shared and exchanged, not only do they carry with them earlier meanings, they are often borrowed and remixed by others in new texts and new contexts in just this way. The Valeza illustration is a fitting example of how a digital composition can move from context to context as others pick up and recontexualize the image for their own rhetorical purposes, creating a textual ecology in the process.

➤ **ABOUT *MULTIMODAL CREATION* AND *INTERTEXTUALITY*.** What circulates most often is not just print text or the 140-character tweet, but a mixture of different media, so it's not unusual that two artists' songs became another artist's drawing, which became TV and blog news reports that remixed these into new productions in new contexts. The Drake/Valeza episode presents another picture of a how a textual ecology can take shape in public digital contexts. Valeza's new, remixed composition was just one of many responses to Drake's and Adele's "phone" songs, and once posted and circulated online, made a notable contribution to the larger field of related texts that were emerging around the topic, initiating comments and adaptations as others shared and responded to his drawing.

Such digital contexts show how culture is produced through the creation and circulation of texts that lead to more creative production and more rhetorical situations as they move from hand to hand, context to context.

Making Connections
Creativity and Ownership in Public Digital Spaces

In the public digital space of the internet, as content circulates freely, it is easily picked up, shared, and modified, mashed up, and remixed by others. That includes the creative work of recognized artists, but also the cultural productions of ordinary people, like the photos we share on a variety of social media and photo-sharing sites, the videos we post on YouTube, the messages we send on Twitter (a fifty-year-old dad tweeting that "they [One Direction] can really sing"), and our own remixes of images and music and words from various sources. With such a flood of material, it can be hard to trace the origins of any one cultural bit, and harder still to know what is available for reuse and what is not. And although the major social media platforms try to address this in their guidelines and rules and have procedures in place for requesting removal of posts with copyrighted material, what is and isn't covered and what can be used and adapted remains murky.

Sidenote

If Drake or someone on his team had done an image search for Adele and Drake images, the original image, posted on Valeza's own sites, would have appeared.

Arguing for a Change in the Laws Governing Copyright in the Context of New Digital Practices

Copyright issues regarding sharing content on the web first came to public attention in the early 2000s, stemming from the problem of music "piracy," with file-sharing sites like Napster enabling the free downloading of music between users. The music industry reacted strongly, suing the creator of Napster for copyright infringement and initiating an aggressive practice of suing college kids who got caught downloading music without paying for it. More recently, subscription streaming services for music, such as Spotify, have offered easier access for listeners while providing a revenue stream for musicians, but file-sharing-based piracy, along with other misuses of copyrighted material, remains a problem and contested issue in our public digital society.

Legal scholar Lawrence Lessig has made a number of important public arguments that address specific legal and cultural concerns in the digital age, focusing frequently on the messy issue of copyright law. Throughout his work, Lessig uses as evidence the many cases he has researched. He finds common patterns across these cases, using their evidence to build a reasonable argument about our public digital practices. In an article for the *Wall Street Journal*, "In Defense of Piracy," Lessig uses one of those examples to argue for the need to reduce copyright restrictions that he sees as greatly inhibiting creativity.

BEFORE READING:

Evoking your prior knowledge about piracy concerns

What is your experience with online "piracy"? What do you know about copyright law as it applies to music, images, and text, and do you think you might have violated it (knowingly or unknowingly) at some point? How have you acknowledged your use of other people's work in your own textual and new media compositions?

As you read Lessig's essay, consider how your own prior knowledge, from both your experience and from our earlier discussion in this chapter, connects to the evidence and position Lessig is presenting. Make annotations or use a double-entry notebook to note those connections.

USER UPLOADS ON YOUTUBE

Uploads, deletes, and claims in a typical day — You Tube

300k video uploads
80k hours of video
24tb of data

YOUTUBE VIDEOS

3% live streams overall

15min average video size

© FIVE COPYRIGHT MYTHS

MYTH	FACT
1. Once a work is posted online it loses copyright protection.	You cannot use, copy, or post someone else's work without permission.
2. I can copy a work online if I give credit to owner or link back.	You cannot use people's work unless they give you permission.
3. If I alter the work or only use part of it I am OK.	Derivative works are still covered by Copyright.
4. If there is no copyright symbol or notice, the work can be freely used	There is no requirement to display a Copyright symbol or register any work to have protection.
5. I can use another person's work as long as I don't profit financially.	You are breaching copyright whether you make money or not.

Sources: http://www.idafrica.ng/13-youtube-facts-the-most-interesting-infographic-youll-see-today/
http://visual.ly/copyright-infringement-5-myths-vs-facts

"In Defense of Piracy"9:8
by Lawrence Lessig
The Wall Street Journal, October 11, 2008

In early February 2007, Stephanie Lenz's 13-month-old son started dancing. Pushing a walker across her kitchen floor, Holden Lenz started moving to the distinctive beat of a song by Prince, "Let's Go Crazy." He had heard the song before. The beat had obviously stuck. So when Holden heard the song again, he did what any sensible 13-month-old would do—he accepted Prince's invitation and went "crazy" to the beat. Holden's mom grabbed her camcorder and, for 29 seconds, captured the priceless image of Holden dancing, with the barely discernible Prince playing on a CD player somewhere in the background.

Ms. Lenz wanted her mother to see the film. But you can't easily email a movie. So she did what any citizen of the 21st century would do: She uploaded the file to YouTube and sent her relatives and friends the link. They watched the video scores of times. It was a perfect YouTube moment: a community of laughs around a homemade video, readily shared with

VALERIE SINCLAIR

READING

anyone who wanted to watch.

Sometime over the next four months, however, someone from Universal Music Group also watched Holden dance. Universal manages the copyrights of Prince. It fired off a letter to YouTube demanding that it remove the unauthorized "performance" of Prince's music. YouTube, to avoid liability itself, complied. A spokeswoman for YouTube declined to comment.

This sort of thing happens all the time today. Companies like YouTube are deluged with demands to remove material from their systems. No doubt a significant portion of those demands are fair and justified. Universal's demand, however, was not. The quality of the recording was terrible. No one would download Ms. Lenz's video to avoid paying Prince for his music. There was no plausible way in which Prince or Universal was being harmed by Holden Lenz.

YouTube sent Ms. Lenz a notice that it was removing her video. She wondered "Why?" What had she done wrong? She pressed that question through a number of channels until it found its way to the Electronic Frontier Foundation (on whose board I sat until the beginning of 2008). The foundation's lawyers thought this was a straightforward case of fair use. Ms. Lenz consulted with the EFF and filed a "counter-notice" to YouTube, arguing that no rights of Universal were violated by Holden's dance.

Yet Universal's lawyers insist to this day that sharing this home movie is willful copyright infringement under the laws of the United States. On their view of the law, she is liable to a fine of up to $150,000 for sharing 29 seconds of Holden dancing.

Universal declined to comment.

How is it that sensible people, people no doubt educated at some of the best universities and law schools in the country, would come to think it a sane use of corporate resources to threaten the mother of a dancing 13-month-old? What is it that allows these lawyers and executives to take a case like this seriously, to believe there's some important social or corporate reason to deploy the federal scheme of regulation called copyright to stop the spread of these images and music? "Let's Go Crazy" indeed!

All Mixed Up

People are increasingly creating something new out of the old. Here are some examples of music, art, and video built on existing songs.

It doesn't have to be like this. We could craft copyright law to encourage a wide range of both professional and amateur creativity, without threatening Prince's profits. We could

reject the notion that Internet culture must oppose profit, or that profit must destroy Internet culture. But real change will be necessary if this is to be our future—changes in law, and changes in us.

For now, trials like Ms. Lenz's are becoming increasingly common. Both professionals, such as the band Girl Talk or the artist Candice Breitz, and amateurs, including thousands creating videos posted on YouTube, are finding themselves the target of overeager lawyers. Because their creativity captures or includes the creativity of others, the owners of the original creation are increasingly invoking copyright to stop the spread of this unauthorized speech. This new work builds upon the old by in effect "quoting" the old. But while writers with words have had the freedom to quote since time immemorial, "writers" with digital technology have not yet earned this right. Instead, the lawyers insist permission is required to include the protected work in anything new.

Not all owners, of course. Viacom, for example, has effectively promised to exempt practically any amateur remix from its lawyers' concerns. But enough owners insist on permission to have touched, and hence, taint, an extraordinary range of extraordinary creativity, including remixes in the latest [2008] presidential campaign. During the Republican primary, for example, Fox News ordered John McCain's campaign to stop using a clip of Sen. McCain at a Fox News-moderated debate in an ad. And two weeks ago, Warner Music Group got YouTube to remove a video attacking Barack Obama, which used pieces of songs like the Talking Heads' "Burning Down the House." (Spokesman Will Tanous of Warner Music Group, which represents the Talking Heads, says the request came from the band's management.) Around the same time NBC asked the Obama campaign to pull an ad that remixed some NBC News footage with Tom Brokaw and Keith Olbermann.

GIRL TALK
The band, whose sole member is 26-year old Gregg Gillis, has become known for its mashups. Its fourth CD, "Feed the Animals" (due out Oct. 21 but available online now), is built on samples of about 300 songs. (myspace.com/girltalk, illegalart.net/girltalk/)

Stephanie Lenz
After Ms. Lenz posted a video of her son dancing to Prince on YouTube, it was taken down due to copyright issues. She has filed a lawsuit against Universal Music Group.

Candice Breitz
The South African-born artist staged an exhibit in London last year showing 25 John Lennon fans singing some of his songs. She's done similar exhibits of fans singing the music of Bob Marley, Michael Jackson, and Madonna. (candicebreitz.net)

Danger Mouse
In 2004, Danger Mouse put together "The Grey Album," which combined vocals from Jay-Z's "The Black Album" and samples from "The Beatles" (known as the White Album). It was leaked online but never officially released.

We are in the middle of something of a war here—what some call "the copyright wars"; what the late Jack Valenti called his own "terrorist war," where the "terrorists" are apparently our kids. But if I asked you to shut your eyes and think about these "copyright wars," your mind would not likely run to artists like Girl Talk or creators like Stephanie Lenz. Peer-to-peer file sharing is the enemy in the "copyright wars." Kids "stealing" stuff with a computer is the target. The war is not about new forms of creativity, not about artists making new art.

Yet every war has its collateral damage. These creators are this war's collateral damage. The extreme of regulation that copyright law has become makes it difficult, sometimes impossible, for a wide range of creativity that any free society—if it thought about it for just a second—would allow to exist, legally. In a state of "war," we can't be lax. We can't forgive infractions that might at a different time not even be noticed. Think "Eighty-year-old Grandma Manhandled by TSA Agents," and you're in the right frame for this war as well.

The work of these remix creators is valuable in ways that we have forgotten. It returns us to a culture that, ironically, artists a century ago feared the new technology of that day would destroy. In 1906, for example, perhaps America's then most famous musician, John Philip Sousa, warned Congress about the inevitable loss that the spread of these "infernal machines"—the record player—would cause. As he described it:

> "When I was a boy...in front of every house in the summer evenings you would find young people together singing the songs of the day or the old songs. Today you hear these infernal machines going night and day. We will not have a vocal chord left. The vocal chords will be eliminated by a process of evolution, as was the tail of man when he came from the ape."

A professional fearful that new technology would destroy the amateur. "The tide of amateurism cannot but recede," he predicted. A recession that he believed would only weaken culture.

A new generation of "infernal machines" has now reversed this trend. New technology is restoring the "vocal chords" of millions. Wikipedia is a text version of this amateur creativity. Much of YouTube is the video version. A new generation has been inspired to create in a way our generation could not imagine. And tens of thousands, maybe millions, of "young people" again get together to sing "the songs of the day or the old songs" using this technology. Not on corner streets, or in parks near their homes. But on platforms like YouTube, or MySpace, with others spread across the world, whom they never met, or never even spoke to, but whose creativity has inspired them to create in return.

READING

The return of this "remix" culture could drive extraordinary economic growth, if encouraged, and properly balanced. It could return our culture to a practice that has marked every culture in human history—save a few in the developed world for much of the 20th century—where many create as well as consume. And it could inspire a deeper, much more meaningful practice of learning for a generation that has no time to read a book, but spends scores of hours each week listening, or watching or creating, "media."

Yet our attention is not focused on these creators. It is focused instead upon "the pirates." We wage war against these "pirates"; we deploy extraordinary social and legal resources in the absolutely failed effort to get them to stop "sharing."

This war must end. It is time we recognize that we can't kill this creativity. We can only criminalize it. We can't stop our kids from using these tools to create, or make them passive. We can only drive it underground, or make them "pirates." And the question we as a society must focus on is whether this is any good. Our kids live in an age of prohibition, where more and more of what seems to them to be ordinary behavior is against the law. They recognize it as against the law. They see themselves as "criminals." They begin to get used to the idea.

That recognition is corrosive. It is corrupting of the very idea of the rule of law. And when we reckon the cost of this corruption, any losses of the content industry pale in comparison.

Copyright law must be changed. Here are just five changes that would make a world of difference:

Deregulate amateur remix: We need to restore a copyright law that leaves "amateur creativity" free from regulation. Before the 20th century, this culture flourished. The 21st century could see its return. Digital technologies have democratized the ability to create and re-create the culture around us. Where the creativity is an amateur remix, the law should leave it alone. It should deregulate amateur remix.

What happens when others profit from this creativity? Then a line has been crossed, and the remixed artists plainly ought to be paid—at least where payment is feasible. If a parent has remixed photos of his kid with a song by Gilberto Gil (as I have, many times), then when YouTube makes the amateur remix publicly available, some compensation to Mr. Gil is appropriate—just as, for example, when a community playhouse lets neighbors put on a performance consisting of a series of songs sung by neighbors, the public performance of those songs triggers a copyright obligation (usually covered by a blanket license issued to the community playhouse). There are plenty of models within the copyright law for assuring that payment. We need to be as creative as our kids in finding a model that works.

Deregulate "the copy": Copyright law is triggered every time there is a copy. In the digital age, where every use of a creative work produces a "copy," that makes as much sense as regulating breathing. The law should also give up its obsession with "the copy," and focus instead on uses—like public distributions of copyrighted work—that connect directly to the economic incentive copyright law was intended to foster.

Simplify: If copyright regulation were limited to large film studios and record companies, its complexity and inefficiency would be unfortunate, though not terribly significant. But when copyright law purports to regulate everyone with a computer, there is a special obligation to make sure this regulation is clear. It is not clear now. Tax-code complexity regulating income is bad enough; tax-code complexity regulating speech is a First Amendment nightmare.

Restore efficiency: Copyright is the most inefficient property system known to man. Now that technology makes it trivial, we should return to the system of our framers requiring at least that domestic copyright owners maintain their copyright after an automatic, 14-year initial term. It should be clear who owns what, and if it isn't, the owners should bear the burden of making it clear.

Decriminalize Gen-X: The war on peer-to-peer file-sharing is a failure. After a decade of fighting, the law has neither slowed file sharing, nor compensated artists. We should sue not kids, but for peace, and build upon a host of proposals that would assure that artists get paid for their work, without trying to stop "sharing." ∎

AFTER READING:
Understanding Lessig's argument in the context of this chapter

Lessig begins with an example of someone who has been charged with copyright violation for posting a YouTube video of her son dancing with music in the background—an instance where capturing a local moment has crossed into a public, global context. He then follows up this example with others. His thesis—the position or stance he is taking—is buried much later in the article. What argument about public discourse is he making here, and how does the evidence he presents at the beginning and throughout the article lead to and support it? What connections do you find between that argument and evidence and instances of circulating memes we explored earlier in the chapter?

Any argument about our rules of public discourse is likely to have opposing positions. What would be the opposing argument from the perspective of musicians like Prince or the Talking Heads, or of music conglomerates like Universal? How does Lessig take their argument into account?

Lessig refers to the doctrine of "Fair Use," a legal concept in U.S. Copyright Law that allows some limited uses of copyrighted material without obtaining permission from the copyright holder. Using the additional resources at the end of this chapter, try to come to your own understanding of "Fair Use" and how it might apply to Lessig's opening example. How might it apply to Drake's posting of Valeza's artwork?

> Prince held tight control over his music. Neither Pandora nor Spotify have permission to play it. David Bowie, on the other hand, had been using the internet to release music for free since the 90s, and other artists are finding new ways to sell their music and skirting the music industry.

In what ways does the practice of intertextuality conflict with practices of copyright? Do you agree that the situation of writers in "quoting the old" and that of musicians who borrow elements from other artists' music are comparable and should involve the same rules to govern their reproduction? What is your understanding of what is required for writers to be able to "quote the old" and what limitations apply?

Lessig includes images in his piece. What function do they serve? What meaning does Lessig create by drawing on the visual as a mode of communication?

Lessig ends by proposing a number of possible changes to copyright law. Do you agree with the suggestions he makes? After reading Lessig's article, how would you describe your own position about creativity, remix, "internet piracy," and the protections of copyright law?

As we try to resolve questions of how to communicate, how to access and use others' creations, and how to create and share responsibly on our public digital sites, we are often engaged in a form of argument that involves looking at examples, finding patterns, analyzing what they show, and finally taking a position and offering an answer to the question "so what?" Brittany does this on a smaller scale as she looks at the responses Akash's post received and formulates her own response—her own "guidelines" for public discourse. Lessig makes an argument about copyright law, the consequences to the public of leaving things as they are, and why therefore we should make the changes he suggests.

Finally, after nearly eight years since the case of the dancing baby video of Holden Lenz was brought to public attention, a judge ruled in favor of Stephanie Lenz in 2015. Here's how NPR's reporter Laura Wagner explained the outcome:

> Fair Use permits people to use copyrighted material in certain situations like satire or news. Now three judges on the 9th circuit say that unless Universal evaluated whether it was fair use, it may have violated

the rights of the video maker. The case is significant because critics say copyright owners like Universal abuse the take down process often at the expense of free expression.[9:9]

The decision reflects the same points that Lessig makes regarding Stephanie Lenz's video of her baby dancing to a Prince song: its use wouldn't violate the artist's interests and it falls within Fair Use guidelines. The popular "Dancing Baby" video meme should now be free to circulate.

Around the same time, a court decision finally made the Happy Birthday song publicly available, after a 1922 song book was found showing that it was old enough to be in the public domain. The Happy Birthday song, said to be the most sung song in the English language, had been a significant cultural production and circulating meme for almost a hundred years, part of our shared public cultural fabric from long before the word meme was invented. Yet, until this 2015 decision, Warner Music Group owned the rights and collected royalties from anyone who wanted to use it for public purposes.

United States Copyright Code: Fair Use Guidelines

The fair use of a copyrighted work, including such use by reproduction in copies or phonorecords or by any other means specified by that section, for purposes such as criticism, comment, news reporting, teaching (including multiple copies for classroom use), scholarship, or research, is not an infringement of copyright.

In determining whether the use made of a work in any particular case is a fair use the factors to be considered shall include—the purpose and character of the use, including whether such use is of a commercial nature or is for nonprofit educational purposes; the nature of the copyrighted work; the amount and substantiality of the portion used in relation to the copyrighted work as a whole; and the effect of the use upon the potential market for or value of the copyrighted work.

Source: 17USC Section 107

From Public Argument to Social Action

As we noted above, we produce culture through the texts we create and respond to, drawing on other texts and compositions (intertextuality) to communicate and participate in digital public culture. The resolution of two lengthy legal cases does not eliminate the conflict between ownership rights and amateur creativity that Lessig has been trying to address in support of creativity and "remix" culture. One way in which he has acted in support of a new *digital culture*—all of the productions and practices and the larger shared knowledge and understandings being shaped in a digital age—is by helping to develop an alternative to the traditional copyright system, the Creative Commons[L9:7] (CC). CC is an open and free licensing platform that aims to provide "a legal and technical infrastructure that maximizes digital creativity, sharing, and innovation." Creative Commons licenses let creators choose to protect their work with less restrictive permissions than those that are assumed under copyright, allowing for greater levels of free use and adaptation. The site also links to Google and Flickr to allow searches for materials and images whose creators have allowed for such use through Creative Commons. Lessig, too, has made much of his own work available in this way.

link

INQUIRY

#3: Going further

Visit the Creative Commons site, and explore the ways in which Lessig and his collaborators have tried to allow content creators to address the concerns he has raised in his "In Defense of Piracy" article. What further support does this site provide for his positions about what can or should be possible? What limitations might still keep those interested in creativity and sharing from pursuing licensing and copyrighting in this way? Try out the CC search feature to see whether it might prove useful to your own composing projects, particularly multimedia ones, offering music or images that creators have given you permission to draw on and/or adapt.

Composing
Cultural Production Analysis

Part II of this book pushes you to consider the culture of the web as it is constructed by public digital discourse. One productive way to do this—to question the cultures, expectations, and common practices that tend to emerge from networked and mediated spaces—is to look, as Lessig does, at one specific example and analyze the contexts of its creation to make broader points about the piece itself and what it suggests about digital culture. Lessig's points about the "Dancing Baby" video are interesting and troubling, but his move to use this video, this particular cultural production, to highlight the ways in which creativity is restricted in digital spaces by current copyright law allows him to move beyond that one instance and enter a larger conversation about sharing, regulation, and the (restricted) creative potentials of the web.

Digital Toolbox
See Part IV, Section 2 and 3

There are many conversations going on about our changing literacy practices today, as the diverse readings included in this book suggest, and you, as a student, but also as a reader, writer, and composer working within your own textual ecologies, need to find ways into such conversations. You could certainly do this on your own, but with the ease of sharing that comes with digital media, you may want to consider entering a public conversation collaboratively, working with class colleagues on the exploration of an issue and on determining where and how to circulate what you discover. Considering these elements of your turn in the conversation, the issue's what, how, why, where, and when, will increase your awareness of conversations you enter and how you are building on, extending, or pushing against what others have said.

WRITING MOVES◀

Inquiring and Inventing

Lessig focuses on an innocuous video in his article. Who could find malice in a proud parent videoing a silly moment of her child's development to share with family? This example works exceptionally well, though, because it stresses the overzealous reaction of a corporation in demanding that the "unauthorized 'performance'" of the song that invites the baby to "go crazy" be removed from the web. It is Lessig's larger critique that drives this piece, but we can assume that it's cases like Ms. Lenz's that led him to that critique, and so while his larger purpose is to share the critique, he starts with its telling. And that is where you will start, too—with identifying both an element of digital culture you would like to address and an example to analyze that can represent your questions or concerns.

1 Identifying an aspect of digital culture to explore

Are you also invested in protecting the creative potential of remix? Are you questioning the ways in which the public and the private intersect in digital spaces? What do you think about "piracy" online? Are you interested in gaming, the communities that grow out of gamers' experiences and expertise, and perhaps the recent hostile discourse directed toward some women gamers? Have you been considering the complexities about originality that fan fiction calls into question? (It's likely that

some specific examples will have generated your interest in these larger issues, and you might move freely in and out of such examples in this process.)

As a class or in a group, come up with a list of questions or concerns about digital culture. Perhaps this will be a purely generative activity, and each student will select an issue or aspect he or she would like to write about. Perhaps you will decide on a common focus as a class.

Once you have identified an aspect of digital culture to speak to, do some exploratory freewriting about it. How do others seem to be thinking about this issue?

What kinds of social and cultural concerns seem to be important? How might you step into a public debate regarding this topic?

2 Selecting a cultural production to analyze

To ground your turn in a public conversation about digital culture, you will select an example, a particular cultural production (such as our examples of a picture of a Target employee or a visual mashup that put two artists and their songs in conversation). Like Lessig, you'll want to use your example as both a way to engage your readers in your perspective and as a site for analysis related to a larger concern about digital culture.

You'll want to choose a cultural production that speaks to your own interests, that has some larger cultural significance, and that is situated in the center of a rich textual ecology, a network of related texts that it has both drawn on and inspired.

Or perhaps you'll want to create a new mashup of a circulating meme, placing your own invention into the current world of circulating texts. To do this, you can use a meme creator app such as Meme Creator or Meme Generator. As you create this mashup, you'll want to think about it as a cultural production, as a text adding meaning to an existing line of thought or conversation. Based on the work you want your meme to accomplish (the meanings you hope it suggests), make an informed decision about how and where to share it with potential viewers.

3 Mapping a textual ecology

In following a particular cultural production, you'll want to contextualize its initial creation as best as you can, and then consider how it gets recontextualized as it is shared and circulated to see how its meaning is made and remade as it enters different rhetorical situations.

By hand or by using a mapping program such as Coggle (see Part IV Digital Toolbox), map out the textual ecology of this text. What texts informed its creation? What other pieces does it speak to (compliment, echo, respond to, challenge, support)? What does this mapping suggest about the importance of where and how texts are shared? What does it show about how production and circulation work in digital spaces?

After creating a visual representation of this textual ecology, consider these questions: In what context did this text appear, or to what context will you add your own creation? What earlier contexts did it draw from? Was it recontextualized in other subsequent contexts? What shared knowledge does it depend on, and what has it built on and shared further? How has the text been shaped and newly shared? Why is the text being shared in this way? In what ways does the timing of this text, of when it was shared, seem to matter? What shared meanings seem to arise from placing this text into circulation in this context?

4 Applying concepts

Which of the concepts we've introduced in this chapter are most useful as you explore the ways in which this text works within a larger textual context? What elements of what you're finding might serve as examples of those concepts?

▶ WRITING MOVES◀

Drafting and Shaping

Now that you have selected a cultural production to analyze and have considered the textual ecology that frames its meaning, you will want to turn to the moves you can make as you compose a text that uses this example to comment on digital culture in broader terms.

1 Introducing your focus

As you open your analysis, you will want to provide your readers with a sense of your undertaking by introducing the cultural production you will analyze and the broader issue(s) it helps you better understand. What is it you will analyze in this piece? What is it you think your analysis might reveal about digital culture? You don't have to make these points in very extensive ways, but address them enough to give your readers a sense of why your analysis matters. This would be a good time to look back to Lessig's article to see how he introduces the dancing baby video and then points to the larger issues it helps us consider.

2 Analyzing a text

To begin this process, we'll turn again to some basic questions we can ask about most cultural productions.

- What: What is the cultural production? What does it communicate?

- How: How is meaning constructed through this text? What modalities does it draw upon? How does it work as a digital cultural production?

- Why: Why was this piece created? What can you assume about its most basic function? Was that purpose rewritten or overwritten as it entered a more expansive textual ecology?

To analyze a text, you should look closely at its various parts as you question their meaning.

3 Analyzing context

In addition to looking at the specific example you have taken as your focus, you should also make meaning from its textual ecology. Turn back to the map you created, and build upon your earlier analysis.

- Where: What path of circulation has this text or meme followed, and how has that path shaped its meaning or the work it has or has not accomplished? What can looking at the ways in which a text has been contextualized and recontextualized say about it? (Think back to the ways in which Valeza's drawing took on different meanings and raised new questions as it was shared beyond its intended network.)

- When: What timeline exists for this text, and how can thinking about when it was shared shape your thinking about it?

By looking to the context, you are locating meaning not only in the text itself, but also in elements that reside beyond a text.

4 Creating larger meaning out of your example

As you reflect on what you've discovered by looking both at a specific text and the textual ecology it is a part of (its context[s]), consider how this example informs your thinking about a larger aspect of digital culture. Lessig's example of Ms. Lenz's video helps us ask questions about a set of intersections (creativity/restriction, individual/corporations, copyright/Creative Commons). Brittany's post helps us think about digital conversations and norms for public discourse. #AlexfromTarget helps us think about unexpected circulation and permission. Valeza's drawing points to the importance of crediting meaning-making and creation.

What aspect of digital culture does your example help you think through?

As you analyze a particular example to come to a larger point, you might want to reread Lessig's article to see how he uses narrative (as he tells Lenz's story), analysis (of her video and similar productions of remix culture that are more intentional than hers), and explanation (of current copyright law and its enactment) to contribute to the public discourse regarding these issues.

Revising and Publishing

Now that you have shaped your own contribution to a public conversation about a concern of digital culture you will also want to turn to questions of circulation. **Where** will you share your turn in a conversation? Will you post it on social media as Brittany did? What other publication options exist? You'll also want to consider *when* you might enter a public debate. Is there a particular moment that might strengthen your contribution? By analyzing a text while looking to its context, you have worked to craft your own turn in a public conversation. Before sharing your work, you'll want to consider how it will function as a public response as you question how it might alter or inform the current conversation. This process will entail considering some of the complexities of entering the public sphere and collecting and questioning feedback from actual readers.

1 Pausing to consider what you are sharing

Brittany commented on the nature of public discourse, of the conversation we engage, extend, and shut down as we participate in discussions online. As her example shows, our contributions to such conversations often resonate with others in ways that move beyond the immediate or local conversation, but they can also prevent a productive exchange of dialogue as they move across different communities. Read your response once, from start to finish, while trying to anticipate how it might encourage or shut down further conversations. What kind of rhetorical relationship do you want to encourage? How might others read, interpret, and understand the work you are doing in this text?

At this point, you should be considering the consequences and likely outcomes of making your turn public, of entering a textual ecology yourself as you share your analysis. Lessig shows the complexities of sharing others' work in digital spaces. Do you have permission to share from the original cultural production you analyze? Are you careful to point to the original text while crediting its creator? Are you fair in how you describe, summarize, quote from, or paraphrase the original source?

In addition to being careful to fully credit others' work, there are several strategies that can help you draw on such work in public spaces.

- Consider whether what you draw into your own production is likely to be covered under the doctrine of Fair Use, which clarifies what and how much you can use from other sources in proprietarily sound ways, generally allowing some limited reproduction for purposes of criticism, comment, news reporting, teaching scholarship, or research, and considers whether the use is for commercial ventures or not. You can find some helpful advice on using images in a "Copyright and Fair Use" post in *The Social Media Examiner,*[9:10] along with other resources in Part II References and Resources.

- The original production you're working from might also be publicly available for the use you're making of it under a Creative Commons license.

- You might be able to contact the creator of the cultural production to gain permission to use it in your own public work.

- Or, if the original work is available online and your own work doesn't require you actually reproduce it in your new text, you can use the strategy of describing it and providing a link for your readers to follow.

We've used each of these strategies in composing this book.

2 Working with peer review

Getting input from readers will help you gauge how your texts will function in a public domain. As you solicit input, have your classmates consider both the text you have written and how they think a public audience might receive it. These questions can guide their work:

- Does the composer make a point about digital culture here that will contribute to a larger, more public conversation?

- Has the composer analyzed one specific cultural production to ground the points made in this piece? Is that text described and discussed in specific ways? Are enough examples used?

- Does the composer do enough to analyze both the text and the context that situates this piece?

- Is the analysis engaging? Can you follow the writer's train of thought?

- How does this piece seem to work as an example of public discourse? How do you think it will be received by the layers of readers who make up a public audience?

- What other advice would you give to the composer of the text?

Reinventing and Circulating Your Work

Many of the examples included in this chapter stress that to understand how public conversations work, we can turn to individual texts and the ways in which they are contextualized by other texts to question how they speak to public audiences.

Here are two more options for following up on these questions.

➤ **Option 1: Practicing netiquette.** As writers working to enter these webs of intertextuality and various textual ecologies, you will also want to consider how civility works in public discourse and how to build productive rhetorical relationships in the process. As Brittany points out, adding a text to a public site is not enough. As composers, we want to cultivate strategies that will allow us to enter and add productively to public debates. The term "netiquette" has been coined to capture some of these concerns and the attempts to generate shared norms for public discourse on the internet. Read the commonly accepted <u>core rules of netiquette</u>[L9.8] as framed by Virginia Shea in her book, *Netiquette,* and see how they add to or complicate your own understandings and observations about public discourse.

link 🔗 ▶

➤ **Option 2: Establishing sharing permissions.** As a composer circulating your own work in a public context, you'll want to consider what level of permissions you'll allow others to have who want to use it. Look again at the Creative Commons licensing information and decide on what feels like the most appropriate level of sharing permissions for what you've produced and the uses you'd like it to be put to.

Key Concepts

cultural production 203
intertexuality 204
mashup 203
memes 203

recontextualized 204
remix 203
textual ecology 204

Practicing Rhetoric
in Digital Spaces

CHAPTER TEN

CENTRAL QUESTIONS

1 What kinds of rhetorical moves do writers and content producers make online to successfully attract and communicate with a public audience?

2 How do rhetorical situations develop in digital environments, and how do they change as texts circulate?

3 How can developing your own rhetorical awareness help you participate and compose more effectively for larger, more public audiences?

Chapter Preview

In Chapter 3 we introduced the concept of a "rhetorical relationship"—a relationship that is formed when two or more people come together via talk, text, image, video, or other modes of communication. We looked particularly at the rhetorical relationships we create when we read and considered the different types of reading we can do to engage a text (participatory and critical). In this chapter we consider the other side of these rhetorical relationships, the ones we create as writers. While we are constantly involved in building rhetorical relationships through the texts we compose each day, in this chapter we'll take a closer look at some of the rhetorical moves writers make to attract an audience and enter a larger public conversation and how writers do so within a particular rhetorical context or situation.

Earlier, we also defined the art of rhetoric using Aristotle's classical definition "...as the faculty of observing in any given [communicative] situation the available means of persuasion" *(On Rhetoric)*.[10:1] For Aristotle, such means related directly to the arguments and style a speaker used when speaking to a live audience. In today's digital contexts, arguing well and writing with style are still important strategies for engaging audiences, but in considering rhetoric now we must also consider the newly available *ways* and *means* writers have on hand when composing with digital media in digital contexts. In this chapter we'll explore some of the ways contemporary writers try to appeal to an audience through their creative use of digital media to produce and share texts.

In the final section of the chapter you will have the opportunity to compose your own rhetorical analysis and explore how writers, audiences, texts, and technologies come together to form a rich textual ecology around a topic or issue.

Exploring
Rhetorical Relationships and Appeals

We are surrounded by attempts to attract our attention, appeal to our emotions, and persuade us, from the advertising billboards we pass on the highway to the commercials that interrupt online videos and TV. Spammers try to fill our inboxes; ads run alongside our Facebook newsfeeds; friends text and tweet and post things that urge us to click on a link to something interesting that has more links, more ads, and more attempts to grab our attention. We, in turn, share that content with other friends, helping to circulate texts and compositions through a global network of people and media. In our increasingly digital world, we find ourselves in an intensifying rhetorical environment where friends, family, companies, organizations, and content producers of all kinds persistently compete for our attention.

Attracting an Audience in a Digital World

Content creation sites like BuzzFeed, Upworthy, and Mic are establishing themselves as popular destinations for online readers. These sites specialize in creating articles and content designed specifically to attract a large audience and encourage sharing between readers. Writer and content creator Tom Barnes's article "Scientists Just Discovered Why All Pop Music Sounds Exactly the Same" is an example of this kind of content. To explore how the rhetorical situation changes when a text appears on or offline, we have provided Barnes's text for you to read first and will then provide a link for an online reading.

Global news and entertainment online

BuzzFeed

.Mic

BuzzFeed is a well-established global network for news and entertainment online. Upworthy says its mission is "to change what the world pays attention to," and it works to make the content it gathers go viral.

Mic, offering news and opinion with a focus on politics and public policy as well as style and entertainment, is run by millenials for millennial readers, and the content it creates and distributes is shaped for that audience. All writers are competing for readers' attention.

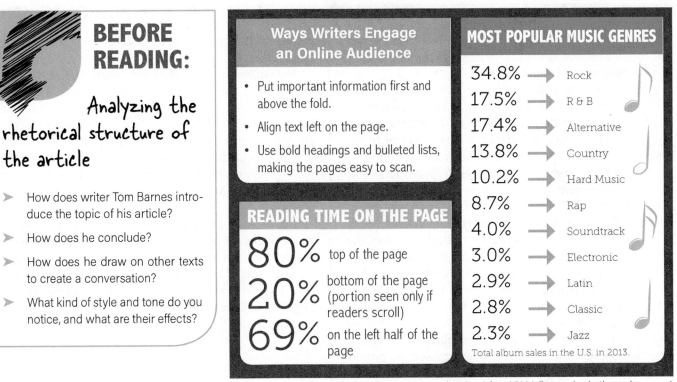

BEFORE READING:

Analyzing the rhetorical structure of the article

➤ How does writer Tom Barnes introduce the topic of his article?

➤ How does he conclude?

➤ How does he draw on other texts to create a conversation?

➤ What kind of style and tone do you notice, and what are their effects?

Ways Writers Engage an Online Audience

- Put important information first and above the fold.
- Align text left on the page.
- Use bold headings and bulleted lists, making the pages easy to scan.

READING TIME ON THE PAGE

80% top of the page

20% bottom of the page (portion seen only if readers scroll)

69% on the left half of the page

MOST POPULAR MUSIC GENRES

34.8% → Rock
17.5% → R & B
17.4% → Alternative
13.8% → Country
10.2% → Hard Music
8.7% → Rap
4.0% → Soundtrack
3.0% → Electronic
2.9% → Latin
2.8% → Classic
2.3% → Jazz

Total album sales in the U.S. in 2013.

Source: https://www.statista.com/chart/1783/album-sales-in-the-us-by-genre/

READING

"Scientists Just Discovered Why All Pop Music Sounds Exactly the Same" 10:2

by Tom Barnes
Mic, January 7, 2015

Anyone who listens to pop radio regularly has probably been hit with this realization at one point or another—a ton of pop music sounds very similar. It seems like grandpa logic, but a growing body of research confirms what we all suspect: Pop music is actually getting more and more homogeneous. And now, thanks to a new study, they know why.

A new study, surveying more than 500,000 albums, shows simplicity sells best across all music genres. As something becomes popular, it necessarily dumbs down and becomes more formulaic. So if you're wondering why the top 10 features two Meghan Trainor songs that sound exactly the same and two Taylor Swift songs that sound exactly the same, scientists think they finally have the answer.

The study: In a recent study, researchers from the Medical University of Vienna in Austria studied 15 genres and 374 sub-genres. They rated the genre's complexity over time—measured by researchers in purely quantitative aspects, such as timbre and acoustical variations—and compared that to the genre's sales. They found that in nearly every case, as genres increase in popularity, they also become more generic.

"This can be interpreted," the researchers write, "as music becoming increasingly formulaic in terms of instrumentation under increasing sales numbers due to a tendency to popularize music styles with low variety and musicians with similar skills."

So music all starts simplifying and sounding similar. Not only that, but complexity actually starts turning people off of musical styles. Alternative rock, experimental and hip-hop music are all more complex now than when they began, and each has seen their sales plummet. Startlingly few genres have retained high levels of musical complexity over their histories, according to the researchers. And ones that have—folk, folk rock and experimental music—aren't exactly big earners. Unless, of course, they fit into the Mumford & Sons/Lumineers pop-folk mold.

The findings are somewhat intuitive. Of course a genre will sell more once it forms an established sound that listeners can identify with. But the science is only proving the now-dominant truth of pop music: Record companies are only comfortable promoting things they already know will sell. And they know that now better than ever.

Record labels are pouring resources into data analysis tools, using them to predict which songs will be the next breakout hit. According to Derek Thompson at *The Atlantic*, executives can use services like Shazam and HitPredictor to see which songs will break out next with surprising accuracy.

Once a worthy song or artist emerges from the data, radio conglomerates have mechanisms in place to ensure that music will connect with an audience. Clear Channel's "On the Verge" program is one of the most talked about. When a song is dubbed "On the Verge," every station in the Clear Channel network has to play it at least 150 times—blasting it to a potential network of about 245 million listeners. This undoubtedly helped launch Iggy Azalea to incredible new heights of success, which she may not have otherwise earned with her talent alone. And her success, in turn, is spawning legions of hip-hop pop imitators whom labels will choose to blast out because their chance at success has been proven. It's a cycle.

The study is right—and it's more of a problem now than ever. Iggy Azalea may be the harbinger of hip-hop's eventual homogenization, but she is only a pawn of the larger media circuit. As reported by *The Atlantic*, "Top 40 stations last year played the 10 biggest songs almost twice as much as they did a decade ago."

Human beings crave familiarity. Numerous psychological studies show that people choose songs they're familiar with over songs that more closely match their reported music tastes. Our somewhat manipulative music industry, which chooses familiar-sounding music and pushes it to listeners in massive quantities, knows well how to capitalize on those cravings. Genres standardize over time as a way to plug into this psychology. And then we hear the same songs, over and over again.

But there's a point at which that becomes tired, and the space opens for something revolutionary—something that totally shifts the way we think about music. If we're aware of these sort of trends and practices, we can better resist what they do to our music. We can champion the genuinely original and leave aside the derivative. We can make a better musical culture.

h/t Atlantic
Tom Barnes

Tom Barnes is a staff writer and editor at Mic focused on music, activism and the intersection between the two. He's based in New York and can be reached at tom@mic.com. ■

AFTER READING:
Getting attention

Before visiting the text online, consider how Barnes attempts to capture your attention in his writing alone. What, in the style and tone of this text, seems rhetorical?

Once you have a good sense of some of the rhetorical moves Barnes is making in this print version of the text, follow the link to his original post [L10:1] online. How does your engagement with the text change? How is the digital text working differently than the print one? How is it able to attract and keep a reader's attention? What different kinds of communicative and rhetorical means do you see him using besides alphabetic text? How does he combine these elements in ways that are appealing?

As we mentioned in Chapter 3, popular discussions of rhetoric tend to focus on the persuasive (usually misleading) aspects of rhetoric rather than the "available means" a writer or speaker can draw on to engage an audience. While persuasion is certainly an important part of rhetoric, digital texts radically expand the available means that writers can draw on to compose texts. For example, Barnes's composition about pop music combines conventional alphabetic writing with links, images, and video. For everyday digital texts like this one, links, images, and video are some of the newly available means for composing. From emails, to memos, to Snapchats, street signs, tweets, billboards, and websites, the amount of texts and rhetorical situations we encounter daily has grown well beyond the practice of mere persuasion. As the means and technologies of writing evolve, so too do our rhetorical practices.

The Rhetorical Situation and Appealing to Readers

As we discussed in Chapter 3, when we engage in deliberate communication with others we step into a *rhetorical situation*. Rhetorical situations arise when there is a need or concern that must be addressed and talked about by a community, and each rhetorical situation we are a part of becomes part of the ongoing work we do together in maintaining the shared knowledge, purpose, and ways of a discourse community. Even our day-to-day exchanges with friends and family often have rhetorical elements. In this chapter, though, we are more concerned with how writers use digital media to engage in larger, public conversations online and contribute to the larger textual ecologies that form around more public conversations.

Figure 10.1 is a diagram of a basic rhetorical situation introduced in Chapter 3. When writers and audiences seek each other out, they come together around a topic and a type of text (genre), using different combinations of media in the process. In understanding the rhetorical situation between writer and audience in Barnes's text above, we could begin by considering the topic (pop music and building popular taste), the media used (digital, social), and the genre (content post on a trending topic).

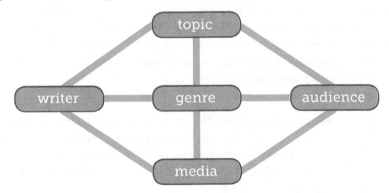

Figure 10.1: Diagram of a basic rhetorical situation

The text, and the form of genre it takes, is the cultural and social contact zone between writers and audiences. When looking at Barnes's composition, we might ask questions about the relatively new genre of the "content post." Why has this particular genre become so popular? What purposes does it serve? In what contexts? What do its current features tell us about the kinds of rhetorical situations that take place on Mic and similar sites? In considering the genre of a text, we are thinking about its shape and design and how that shape develops in response to recurring rhetorical situations that are similar. As we will see, Barnes's text is just one of several similar texts that addressed this same topic using similar rhetorical strategies. **Content posts** like Barnes's have become a common genre online as writers work to join a textual ecology around a trending conversation and generate user traffic to the sites they are writing for.

This basic version of the rhetorical situation is just a starting point for making sense of a text, of the meaning it is trying to convey, and to whom. As we think more deeply about a rhetorical situation, we also want to

content posts typically brief online articles that share some piece of content that will catch readers' attention and interest

rhetorical appeals
strategies used by writers and speakers to communicate with an audience

ethos
appeal to the credibility and ethical behavior of a writer/speaker

pathos
appeal to the audience's feelings and emotions

logos
appeal to the audience's intellect and reason

consider *how* a writer attempts to *appeal* to readers. What intentional strategies does the writer employ to connect with an audience? To get their attention and hold it? Aristotle, in the context of ancient Athens, pointed to three key **rhetorical appeals** that speakers use to appeal to live audiences—ethically, logically, and emotionally—what he referred to as *ethos, pathos,* and *logos*.

➤ **APPEALS TO CREDIBILITY (ETHOS).** Appeals to ethos invoke a writer's good reputation, credibility, and authority. Writers establish trustworthiness by being balanced and fair-minded and by treating other people's ideas fairly. By establishing that they are honest and to be trusted, that they cite sources reasonably without distortion, writers try to assure an audience that their motivations are in line with their values and beliefs.

➤ **APPEALS TO THE EMOTIONS (PATHOS).** Writers will often appeal to an audience's emotions and feelings by tapping into common beliefs and values. A writer might draw on anecdotes or personal experience to move the audience. Appeals to pathos often try to induce joy or fear in an audience. For example, insurance commercials invoke fear in viewers by exaggerating the likelihood of unforeseen accidents to produce the kind of anxiety that compels us to buy insurance.

➤ **APPEALS TO LOGIC (LOGOS).** Writers often appeal to the intellect of an audience through logic and reasoning. Logical appeals are often used in argumentative writing (see Chapter 15), where writers give evidence to support their points. Other examples of appeals to logic include the use of experts, statistics, data, and facts.

INQUIRY

#1: Appeals in contemporary culture

Use an internet search engine to conduct image searches of these three appeals. What examples come up? How do they enrich your understanding of these appeals and how they work? As a class, identify a handful of strong examples for each appeal in small groups. Share these images with your classmates (in class or on your class website), and discuss what they suggest about ethos, pathos, and logos. Based on these images, what can you say about how these appeals work in the larger contemporary culture?

These basic appeals are always overlapping. Establishing one's credibility can also serve to appeal to the reasoning and emotions of an audience. These aren't the only ways to appeal to audiences, but they are widely employed by writers and vary depending on the genre of writing. In today's competitive textual environment writers continue to develop new ways to appeal to our logic, emotions, and sense of credibility.

INQUIRY

#2: Analyzing a rhetorical situation

Using the basic rhetorical situation (Figure 10.1) as your guide, return to Barnes's post at Mic.

➤ What is Barnes's purpose in writing this text? What is he hoping readers will do?

➤ What kinds of appeals does Barnes use to attract a reader's attention? Are there appeals to the heart—to the emotions? To the intellect? How does he establish his credibility as a writer? Does the site establish it in other ways?

➤ How would you describe the genre of the composition, and how does its shape relate to the kind of media used and the topic and purpose of the text?

Expanding the Rhetorical Situation

While the basic framework for a rhetorical situation and basic appeals are a good starting point, there are additional things to consider when exploring and analyzing how rhetorical practices change in digital, networked environments.

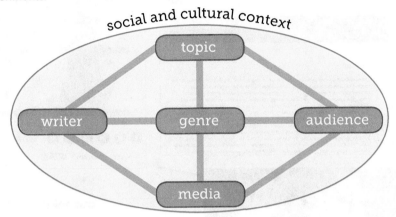

Figure 10.2: Expanded model of basic rhetorical situation

Figure 10.2 extends the basic rhetorical situation by situating it in a larger social and cultural context. The **expanded rhetorical situation** includes concepts that are in the foreground of the rhetorical moves a writer makes—the *stance, style, language, appeals,* and different *modes* used to achieve a communicative purpose.

Social and cultural context. As we've discussed throughout this book, context is a flexible term. In understanding the social and cultural aspects of a rhetorical situation, we are trying to understand the background, history, participants, and concerns that give rise to the situation and the production of a text. We can't expect to understand the entire context of a text's production, but the more background we know about a composition and the contexts in which a text is read and received, the richer our understanding will be. In trying to piece together the social and cultural context of Barnes's pop music article, we can ask questions about the textual ecology that this is a part of. What else has been written about the topic? Is there already a conversation in progress? Why is it posted on this site? What other writers are cited?

In contextualizing Barnes's piece, we can begin by doing an initial search online using a standard search engine. We could also search popular social media sites like Twitter and Instagram to see if the topic was trending at some point. A basic search using the title of Barnes's piece reveals that his was one of several texts published in early 2015 focused on precisely the same topic of why popular music sounds the same (See Figure 10.3 on the following page).

Barnes's piece was published on January 7, 2015. Two days later, Tom Whitwell wrote about the same topic at *Medium*, using a title similar to Barnes's.

Three weeks later on February 5, Rajiv Narayan published another piece on Upworthy, again using a similar title and replicating Barnes's use of a Taylor Swift banner image at the top of the text.

Devika Ohri made a similar post on February 7, 2015, at ReshareIt.com.

These are just a few of the texts written about this topic in very similar ways. What we see in this progression is how a textual ecology forms around a topic and how writers and content producers watch carefully for trending topics and use that information to attract their own audiences. And as they do so, they make similar rhetorical moves in composing their texts. As it turns out, Barnes's article wasn't actually the first to discuss the topic in 2015. He writes "h/t" (hat tip) at the bottom of his article and links to a text originally published at *The Atlantic* three days prior on January 4, 2015, by Lenika Cruz.

> **expanded rhetorical situation**
> articulation of rhetorical situation that considers the social and cultural contexts of a rhetorical situation's audience

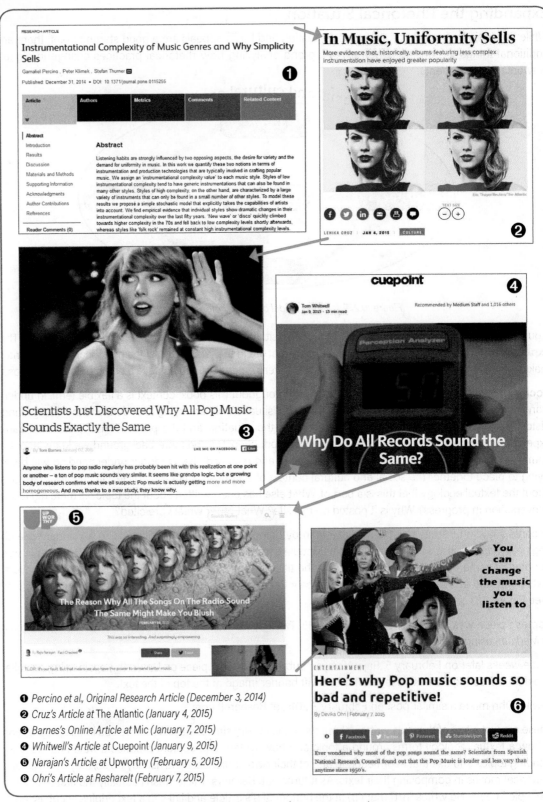

Figure 10.3: Circulation of content across sites

Once again, we see similar ways and means used in composing this text, including a link that Cruz has embedded in her introduction to the scientific research article that has been repeatedly referenced by each of the pop music writers as showing definitive proof that popular music does indeed sound the same.[10:3]

In understanding the social and cultural context of Barnes's piece, then, it's helpful to understand the various texts circulating about the topic, how they are different or similar to Barnes's text, and how they work together to create a conversation and textual ecology around current practices of making pop music.

As part of understanding the social and cultural contexts of digital texts, we also want to consider the *timeliness* of a text, what Aristotle called **kairos**. In online textual ecologies like the group of texts we see above, their dates of publication illustrate how the writers were thinking about the *when* of their text, considering the timing and urgency of the publication so they might catch some of the buzz that was starting to trend around the topic. In each case, the writers demonstrate an awareness of the rhetorical situation and current contexts in which their articles will enter and (ideally) circulate. Cruz encountered the research on pop music early and was able to get out ahead of other pieces and publish her article before the others.

kairos
the **when** of a text and its timeliness

> **INQUIRY**
>
> ### #3: Seeing rhetoric move through a textual ecology
>
> Go online and search for "why all pop music sounds the same." What other types of texts and media do you find that reference this topic? Are they part of the textual ecology we looked at above (published around the same time, linked), or part of a different one? In what ways do other texts demonstrate (or not) an awareness of kairos and the when of the rhetorical situation?

Sidenote

The step from academic research article to more popular genres is an example of how texts and ideas circulate, creating new rhetorical situations as they do.

Purpose. In Part I of this book we examined closely the **how**, **what**, **why**, and **where** of writing. Understanding these basic elements of a text are the first steps in making sense of its rhetorical purpose. Often the purpose of a text is obvious: the advertisement is trying to sell us something, and the parking ticket is dissuading us from parking illegally. In other situations, the purpose of a text may not be so clear, or it may have several purposes simultaneously, as is the case with the group of articles we've been considering. Authors write in public to participate in larger conversations and attract readers. To do so, they must appeal to the audience and do it in a compelling way. But why? What are their purposes for writing **what** they do, **how** they do it, and **when** they do it? What are they hoping readers will do beyond simply reading their text?

Barnes, as well as the authors that followed him, have several purposes in these compositions, but predictably their first priority is to attract an audience and generate traffic to the site that hosts their article. To do this, it's imperative that search engines can find the article. Thus, one of the purposes behind the "what" of the article is the strategic inclusion of key words like "pop music" and "repetition" throughout to help this page rank higher on search engines than other, similar content. Succeeding at this purpose leads to other purposes. By producers of these sites attracting an audience with content they know is trending and popular, the traffic to these sites grows and so, too, does the data they can collect about consumer habits—what topics we are reading, what we are searching for, what we share and purchase. This information can then be monetized by selling it to others, such as marketers and companies interested in knowing more about our consumption habits.

Figure 10.4: Image of Mozilla browser add-on Ghostery that shows how many different "trackers" are collecting data about our online activities

Using a browser add-on like Mozilla's "Ghostery," internet users can see how many "trackers" are being used by a particular site (Figure 10.4). Trackers are the cookies, beacons, and other technologies that are left on our computers by sites and companies interested in tracking us as we spend time online. Visitors to Mic who read Barnes's article will find that they are being tracked in 20 different ways—by the site itself to monitor site traffic, as well as marketing and advertising companies that have agreements with Mic to collect data about visitors to the site. The same holds true for other sites that replicate content to attract readers.

This, of course, is just one of many purposes behind writing these texts. When we consider the purposes behind the production of a digital text and the rhetorical moves a writer makes to achieve those purposes, we should keep in mind that multiple purposes are usually in play.

Audience. When we attend a concert or sporting event, we know who the audience is. We can see them. But when we write, the audience (the *who*) may not be so obvious. Sometimes writers are writing for multiple audiences. Other times they are writing to an audience of one (a text message). Understanding the audience(s) for a text can tell us a lot about how a text is working in context and the extent to which a writer has successfully communicated with that audience. In the case of the pop music articles, we can guess they are directed at an audience who listens to popular music and who frequently use social media for sharing. That audience, as research from the Pew Research Center has demonstrated, is primarily composed of 18- to 29-year-olds, an age group in which more than 90 percent use social media daily.[10:4] The Neilson Music Report finds that the same age group is also the largest consumer of pop music.[10:5]

Style and language. When looking at the style and language of the writing (the how) we usually begin by looking at specific instances where a writer is making an appeal. What kind of phrasing and word choice is the writer using? Is the writing style formal or informal? Informative or argumentative? What kinds of images and other design elements are used? When looking closely at Barnes's style and language, we can see he uses a combination of short and long sentences, and though his tone is more conversational, he incorporates quotes and citations from other writers to support his observations. Barnes ends his piece urging readers to "resist" the "manipulative music industry" so we can "make a better musical culture."

Mode and media. When we ask questions about the different communicative modes a writer uses, it helps to think of them in relation to media and how different media encourage different kinds of composing. Barnes's text, like all the texts in the pop music group, exemplifies digital texts intended to be circulated and shared on social media (Figure 10.5).

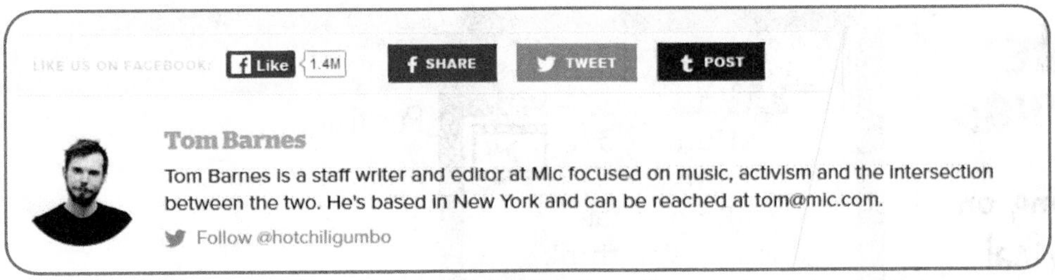

Figure 10.5: Barnes's Mic profile

In what has become a common rhetorical practice on sites like Mic, Barnes's article concludes with his image, Twitter handle, and convenient links to other social media for those readers who feel moved to share this content (Figure 10.5). When we consider the media used for a text, we also want to look at the *functionality* of the text. While traditional print texts have a certain kind of functionality, digital media and online publishing platforms are designed to encourage interaction with readers, solicit comments, make a sale, or sign up users to their service. Digital social media encourages real-time engagement and responses from readers in ways that print media cannot. When we consider the media of a text in these terms, we are asking how the functionality of an interactive text works on us rhetorically.

Modes are the different symbolic means and resources writers use to compose a text from conventional alphabetic writing to images, sound, and video (we'll look closer at modes and *visual* rhetoric in Chapter 14). Looking at the pop music pieces again, several of them use bright, colorful pictures and videos of pop stars. They use bolded headings and often include a picture of the author. Barnes, for example, intersperses his text with videos of popular bands to illustrate how the trend toward homogenization in pop music happens across music genres. All the authors integrate links to other content by changing the font color of the text to signal to readers a link to another text that, ideally, relates in some way to their overall rhetorical purposes. Analyzing the modes present in a composition can help us make sense of the different resources a writer draws on when composing a text for an audience.

INQUIRY

#4: Contextualizing a text or group of texts

???

Looking back at the pop music articles, what more can you say about the social and cultural context of these texts? How does the article genre itself seem to be shaped (and reshaped) as it takes form in each different rhetorical situation? What can you say about their purposes and how they try to realize those purposes? About their likely audience(s) and how they are being reached? And about how they use similar and different styles and language to address this purpose and audience? What is the functionality of the sites? Are some more interactive than others? More "user friendly"? Which seem to do the best at attracting and keeping readers' attention?

Making Connections
Rhetoric and Social Media

In the following article, "The Six Things That Make Stories Go Viral Will Amaze, and Maybe Infuriate, You," Maria Konnikova looks at some of the rhetorical strategies writers use to attract readers online. Using current research about online sharing practices, Konnikova modernizes Aristotle's classical appeals (ethos, pathos, logos) to explore why some content goes viral and other kinds do not. In an era when there is fierce competition for audiences, today's writers continue to develop new rhetorical strategies to attract and keep an audience.

Sources: http://www.bitrebels.com/technology/ultimate-viral-content-guide/
https://www.youtube.com/watch?v=Qk4acvdyyqo

BEFORE READING:

Reflecting on your rhetorical practices

As you read the article by Maria Konnikova, look for connections between your own rhetorical practices and the ones Konnikova points out. What kind of content is typically shared in your online communities? What kinds of content do you find yourself frequently searching for? What is it about the content that appeals to you? Do you notice yourself sharing content that is more positive (*positivity*) or provocative (*arousal*)?

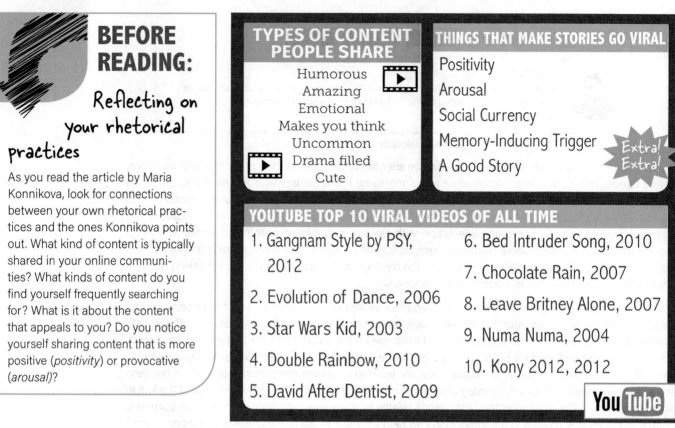

TYPES OF CONTENT PEOPLE SHARE

Humorous
Amazing
Emotional
Makes you think
Uncommon
Drama filled
Cute

THINGS THAT MAKE STORIES GO VIRAL

Positivity
Arousal
Social Currency
Memory-Inducing Trigger
A Good Story

Extra! Extra!

YOUTUBE TOP 10 VIRAL VIDEOS OF ALL TIME

1. Gangnam Style by PSY, 2012
2. Evolution of Dance, 2006
3. Star Wars Kid, 2003
4. Double Rainbow, 2010
5. David After Dentist, 2009
6. Bed Intruder Song, 2010
7. Chocolate Rain, 2007
8. Leave Britney Alone, 2007
9. Numa Numa, 2004
10. Kony 2012, 2012

You Tube

READING

"The Six Things That Make Stories Go Viral Will Amaze, and Maybe Infuriate, You"[10:6]
by Maria Konnikova
The New Yorker, January 21, 2014

When Jonah Berger was a graduate student at Stanford, in the early aughts, he would make a habit of reading page A2 of the *Wall Street Journal*, which included a list of the five most-read and the five most-shared articles of the day. "I'd go down to the library and surreptitiously cut out that page," he recalls. "I noticed that what was read and what was shared was often different, and I wondered why that would be." What was it about a piece of content—an article, a picture, a video—that took it from simply interesting to interesting and shareable? What pushes someone not only to read a story but to pass it on?

The question predates Berger's interest in it by centuries. In 350 B.C., Aristotle was already wondering what could make content—in his case, a speech—persuasive and memorable, so

that its ideas would pass from person to person. The answer, he argued, was three principles: ethos, pathos, and logos. Content should have an ethical appeal, an emotional appeal, or a logical appeal. A rhetorician strong on all three was likely to leave behind a persuaded audience. Replace rhetorician with online content creator, and Aristotle's insights seem entirely modern. Ethics, emotion, logic—it's credible and worthy, it appeals to me, it makes sense. If you look at the last few links you shared on your Facebook page or Twitter stream, or the last article you e-mailed or recommended to a friend, chances are good that they'll fit into those categories.

Aristotle's diagnosis was broad, and tweets, of course, differ from Greek oratory. So Berger, who is now a professor of marketing at the University of Pennsylvania's Wharton School,

READING

worked with another Penn professor, Katherine Milkman, to put his interest in content-sharing to an empirical test. Together, they analyzed just under seven thousand articles that had appeared in the *Times* in 2008, between August 30th and November 30th, to try to determine what distinguished pieces that made the most-emailed list. After controlling for online and print placement, timing, author popularity, author gender, length, and complexity, Berger and Milkman found that two features predictably determined an article's success: how positive its message was and how much it excited its reader. Articles that evoked some emotion did better than those that evoked none—an article with the headline "BABY POLAR BEAR'S FEEDER DIES" did better than "TEAMS PREPARE FOR THE COURTSHIP OF LEBRON JAMES." But happy emotions ("WIDE-EYED NEW ARRIVALS FALLING IN LOVE WITH THE CITY") outperformed sad ones ("WEB RUMORS TIED TO KOREAN ACTRESS'S SUICIDE").

Just how arousing each emotion was also made a difference. If an article made readers extremely angry or highly anxious—stories about a political scandal or new risk factor for cancer, for example—they became just as likely to share it as they would a feel-good story about a cuddly panda. (In this particular study, certain pieces were coded as eliciting arousing emotions; in a follow-up, arousal was further measured physiologically.)

Berger and Milkman went on to test their findings in a more controlled setting, presenting students with content and observing their propensity to pass it along. Here, too, they found the same patterns. Amusing stories that had been chosen specifically because they were positive and arousing were shared more frequently than less amusing ones. Anger-inducing stories were shared more than moderate takes on the same events. When the researchers manipulated the framing of a story to be either negative (a person is injured) or positive (an injured person is "trying to be better again"), they found that the positive framing made a piece far more popular. The findings have since been replicated by several independent research teams, who have found that videos that shock or inspire are more likely to be shared on Facebook and more likely to gain viral traction.

Positivity and arousal go a long way toward explaining the success of Web sites like Upworthy, which started in 2012 and is known for using headlines designed to make you laugh, cry, or feel righteous anger (for example, on the site right now, "A Hilarious Stand-Up Routine About How Commercials for Black People Actually Sound" and "The Struggles of Being a Woman in a Male-Dominated Field Summed Up in a Short Comic").

Even the site's tearjerker content has a positive message: "Watch a Teenager Bring His Class to Tears Just by Saying a Few Words," reads one. Despite launching less than two years ago, the site has steadily climbed the ranks of Internet popularity, ranking third in a December rating of Facebook shares, right behind BuzzFeed and the Huffington Post. Its posts are like the infamous cat videos on YouTube—funny, positive, and arousing—but taken to a new level. Still, as Berger points out, "There are lots of cat videos that don't get shared"—and lots of would-be Upworthys that never quite make it. So what characterizes the ones that do?

Since his initial foray into the nature of sharing, Berger has gone on to research and test a variety of viral-promoting factors, which he details in his new book, "Contagious: Why Things Catch On." Almost ten years in, he feels he's discovered a formula of sorts: as sites like Upworthy or BuzzFeed would likely put it, The Six Things You Need to Know to Make Your Voice Heard. While emotion and arousal still top the list, a few additional factors seem to make a big difference. First, he told me, you need to create social currency—something that makes people feel that they're not only smart but in the know. "Memes like LOLcats, I think, are a perfect example of social currency, an insider culture or handshake," Berger told me. "Your ability to pass it on and riff on it shows that you understand. It's the ultimate, subtle insider signal: I know without yelling that I know. When your mom sees an LOLcat, she has no idea what it is." When Upworthy first started, not everyone knew what it was, and the videos seemed fresh. Now they are being derided as link bait and mocked. Other sites, including the *Washington Post*, are copying their formula.

The presence of a memory-inducing trigger is also important. We share what we're thinking about—and we think about the things we can remember. This facet of sharing helps explain the appeal of list-type stories (which I wrote about in detail last month), as well as stories that stick in your mind because they are bizarre. Lists also get shared because of another feature that Berger often finds successful: the promise of practical value. "We see top-ten lists on Buzzfeed and the like all the time," he notes. "It allows people to feel like there's a nice packet of useful information that they can share with others." We want to feel smart and for others to perceive us as smart and helpful, so we craft our online image accordingly.

A final predictor of success is the quality of the story itself. "People love stories. The more you see your story as part of a broader narrative, the better," Berger says. Some cat lists are better than others, and some descriptions of crying teen-

READING

agers are more immediately poignant; the best underlying story, regardless of its trappings, will come out on top. That, in fact, is what the Upworthy editors have argued in response to their critics: the headlines may seem like link bait, but the stories, the curators promise, are worthwhile. "Coming up with catchy, curiosity-inducing headlines wasn't the reason Upworthy had those 87 million visitors," they write. "It was because millions of members of the Upworthy community watched the videos we curated and found them important, compelling, and worth sharing with their friends."

Some of these features, of course, are incompatible: a list, for the most part, isn't going to tell much of a story, and a LOLcat video or other meme isn't usually informative. But, taken together, especially with the underlying principles of arousal and positivity in mind, the guidelines can help. "I see it as a batting average," Berger says. "No one is going to hit a home run every time, but if you understand the science of hitting your batting average goes up."

The irony, of course, is that the more data we mine, and the closer we come to determining a precise calculus of sharing, the less likely it will be for what we know to remain true. If emotion and arousal are key, then, in a social application of the observer effect, we may be changing what will become popular even as we're studying it. "If everyone is perfectly implementing the best headline to pass on, it's not as effective any more," Berger says. "What used to be emotionally arousing simply isn't any longer." Those in search of evidence for this should look no further than Viralnova.com, a site that was started just eight months ago and is already the seventh most popular site on the Web, at least as measured by Facebook shares. As I type, the lead story on its front page is "Her Little Boy Has No Idea His Mother Is About To Die. What She's Doing About That Is Amazing." ∎

AFTER READING:
Analytical reading

After reading Konnikova's article, consider the following questions.

➤ What does the article suggest about how rhetorical relationships take shape online? What kinds of rhetorical appeals and strategies does she highlight that are unique to online environments? From the perspective of the writer, what kinds of rhetorical strategies is she herself using in this article?

➤ Konnikova introduces a new concept for us: **social currency**. From her discussion, what is your understanding of this term, and why might you find it useful (or not) in making sense of why some of the memes you've been considering have circulated?

➤ Konnikova's article is part of a textual ecology, connecting to a larger set of contemporary texts that have gone viral, to past cultural texts (Aristotle), and to the work of researchers on the topic. How does she use this textual ecology to support the social currency of her own text?

➤ Readers' comments form another part of this textual ecology and particular rhetorical situation. Go to the online version of Konnikova's article,[L10:2] and look over the comments that readers left. How have readers responded, and what do their responses tell us about the success or failure of Konnikova's article?

social currency
using insider knowledge when communicating with others

link

Composing
A Multimodal Rhetorical Analysis

A rhetorical analysis focuses on close analysis of specific symbolic, textual productions—from a song, to a movie, to an essay, to a blog—and looks at the *potential* work a text is trying do in relation to the audiences it attempts to address. When analyzing how rhetoric functions in a digital text, we are concerned with how relations get situated in the production of that particular piece—relations between writer, topic, audience, media, and the contexts the exchange is a part of.

To prepare you to compose your own rhetorical analysis, we turn to a student example by Alex Slotkin posted at Storify.com. In this piece, Slotkin draws on two terms we've introduced in this chapter, *pathos* and *kairos*, to explore a rhetorical situation that erupted online in response to the problem of domestic abuse in the National Football League.

▮▮ READING ▮▮

"Rhetorical Analysis of 'Get Your Game Face On'"[10:7]
by Alex Slotkin (Student)

February 15, 2014, Ray Rice, running back for the Baltimore Ravens, punched his fiancée, Janay Palmer, unconscious in an elevator while the two were arguing. Two days later, the general manager of the Baltimore Ravens said in a press conference: "Rice 'was still a big part of what we plan to do in 2014'" (qtd. in Josh Levin). It is common knowledge that Rice is not the only player in the National Football League (NFL) to commit acts of domestic violence; everyone, sports fan or not, who has ever watched the news knows that. His teammate Terrell Suggs, for instance, has had two protective orders filed against him by his wife (Levin).

But in the wake of the Ray Rice scandal, something important happened: women's rights activists, in response to how the NFL handled the controversy, took a CoverGirl ad promoting its line of NFL-inspired makeup and photoshopped a black eye onto the model's face. (Figure 10.6) You don't need to know much about football, domestic violence, or even Ray Rice to recognize that this is important. Tweets made in response to the "Get Your Game Face On" mock-NFL CoverGirl ad show a keen awareness of the opportunity of the moment—kairos—to create a persuasive argument through the use of pathos.

The edited photo was published shortly after the video capturing Rice's actions was leaked and posted online. It was initially released to discredit Rodger Goodell, the commissioner of the NFL, who chose not to obtain the video capturing the crime before handing Rice a two-game suspension (Barr). The thousand words this photo expresses, then, is best understood in this particular moment and in relation to the NFL's mismanagement of the incident.

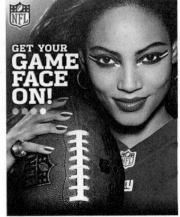

Figure 10.6: Photoshopped ad—image that started the conversation, as retweeted by E! News (top), original CoverGirl ad (bottom)

Had the photo been published at a different time, say a year in the future, it would not have been well received because it would be out of context. The context of an issue is determined by its kairos, a term used by Aristotle to capture the window of time when acting is most beneficial. This photo is a good example of the proper use of kairos because it was published a few days after the video was leaked, when the incident was fresh in our minds. In addition to kairos, it is also a good example of pathos, an appeal to emotion. CoverGirl's edited model, juxtaposed with the NFL's motto "Get Your Game Face On," sends a powerful message to her viewers, namely that the NFL condones domestic violence. It is this message, this appeal to emotion, and the timeliness of the text, that caused a flood of responses on Twitter that, in turn, used appeals of pathos and awareness of the kairotic moment to join in the conversation.

The response on Twitter testifies to the effectiveness of the mock-CoverGirl ad in raising awareness about the Ray Rice scandal. For example, the tweet below (in as poor taste as it is) demonstrates how the photoshopped "Get Your Game Face On" ad successfully appealed to its audience's emotions, made effective by the kairotic moment:

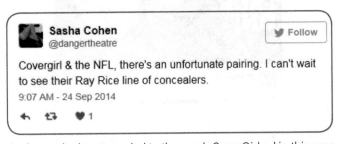

Sasha Cohen
@dangertheatre

🐦 Follow

Covergirl & the NFL, there's an unfortunate pairing. I can't wait to see their Ray Rice line of concealers.

9:07 AM - 24 Sep 2014

↩ ⇄ ♥ 1

Sasha no doubt responded to the mock-CoverGirl ad in this way because it moved and inspired her to help bring attention to the issue. Her response is timely and shows an awareness of kairos because the edited image is fresh in her readers' minds and appeals to our emotions, humor, and anger over the incident. Her point, that CoverGirl and the NFL make an unfortunate pairing, is thereby well made. The attention brought to the issue through tweets such as Sasha's help create the beginnings of a dialogue about the scandal.

This dialogue mushroomed as more and more Twitter users responded to the photoshopped ad. The New York City branch of the National Organization for Women (NOW), for example, wrote:

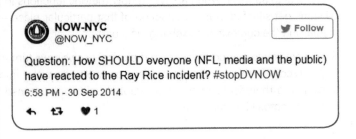

NOW-NYC
@NOW_NYC

🐦 Follow

Question: How SHOULD everyone (NFL, media and the public) have reacted to the Ray Rice incident? #stopDVNOW

6:58 PM - 30 Sep 2014

↩ ⇄ ♥ 1

Questions like this one are the beginnings of a discussion about one aspect of the issue at hand—how the controversy was handled. Other tweeters, however, decided to tackle the incident from a different angle. These writers focused their attention on Janay Palmer's decision to marry Ray Rice after he punched her unconscious. Palmer's decision to marry her abusive fiancé spurred the formation of the "Why I Stayed" and "Why I Left" campaigns.

Members of the "Why I Stayed" campaign rationalized her decision to marry Rice and posted tweets like the one below:

Sara Crisostomo
@la_gringa_loca

🐦 Follow

No one is immune to #DomesticViolence!!!! #EndDV #WhyIStayed #CoverGirlcott klou.tt/11lmcgf52ogqn

10:45 AM - 30 Sep 2014

↩ ⇄ ♥ 2

READING

Members of the "Why I Left" campaign voiced the opinion that Janay should have walked away from their marriage, posting tweets like Sarah's:

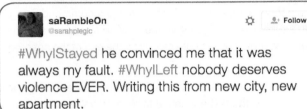

saRambleOn
@sarahplegic

⚙ ⚲ Follow

#WhyIStayed he convinced me that it was always my fault. #WhyILeft nobody deserves violence EVER. Writing this from new city, new apartment.

Both tweeters may reach different conclusions about Janay Palmer's decision to marry Ray Rice, but they both agree that domestic violence is unacceptable. By agreeing on this fundamental proposition, the two can begin to recognize where they agree to disagree. This point of mutual disagreement is known as stasis. Because the two agree that domestic violence is unacceptable, they can recognize where they disagree, thus establishing a working stasis that allows for their discussion to take place.

Rhetoric was and always will be related to persuasive language, but social media sites like Twitter and Storify have effectively changed the scale at which rhetoric is practiced. In our age of social media, anyone can spread information around the world in the blink of an eye, such as the Twitter user Fangirlfeminist.

Josie or Fangirlfeminist copied NOW NYC's post about the Ray Rice scandal, and posed her own public response on Twitter:

Josie
@fangirlfeminist

🐦 Follow

In an ideal world, what would the response to the Ray Rice scandal have been? @NOW_NYC #StopDVNOW

7:00 PM - 30 Sep 2014

↰ ⇄ ♥ 1

Reposting NOW NYC's question is a good example of the internet's version of how information spreads by "word of mouth." Josie has read a question that she finds to be important, then decides to repost it in the hopes of sharing it with her community of followers who may not have seen the question as originally tweeted by NOW NYC. Her actions mirror a child repeating something interesting he learned in school to his mother, or a business executive repeating what she thinks are the important parts of a meeting to her colleague. The Fangirlfeminist has understood the kairotic moment by sharing information with her audience that she believes will interest them.

The internet's rapid dissemination of information and abundance of texts results in the greater significance of kairos and pathos for communicating with others. While only one rhetorician can speak at a time in person, the internet is a special space where hundreds, thousands, or millions of people could conceivably talk simultaneously. Therefore, writers on the internet rely heavily on a powerful use of pathos, in accordance with kairos, to enter a public conversation and have their voices heard. In other words, internet writers try to make their posts stand out so as not to get lost in a sea of other voices. The mock-NFL CoverGirl ad, for instance, stands out from other posts relating to Ray Rice because of its strong use of pathos and the way it takes advantage of the kairotic moment created by the release of the video. As a result of its effectiveness, it helps initiate a larger conversation about the issue and expands kairos in the process for others to join in. In a space where speakers are limited to how many characters they can use—Twitter users, for example, are allowed 140 characters per tweet—social media has based much of what we say, or the photos we edit, on kairos and pathos. ∎

Inquiring and Inventing

As you begin to think about writing a rhetorical analysis, you'll want to draw on what you've discovered in the inquiries you've written and from the examples you've seen in this chapter. We recommend doing some informal writing about each different move as a way to generate ideas. Moves are intended to build on previous moves and prepare you to write your own rhetorical analysis by the end of the chapter.

1 Finding an interesting text

Find a text online that interests and challenges you. This could be a content post like Barnes's article on Mic or perhaps an image for social critique like Slotkin's. It could even take the form of a Twitter feed you follow or website you frequent.

2 Identifying the basic rhetorical situation

Once you have a possible text and you've done some preliminary thinking about its composition, try mapping out the rhetorical situation on a sheet of paper (Figure 10.7). Identify the author (or authors) and the site of the piece. What different purposes are there for composing this text? What is the concern or topic being discussed? How is it introduced? What types of audiences might the text be addressing? What is the genre of the text, and what type of media is it?

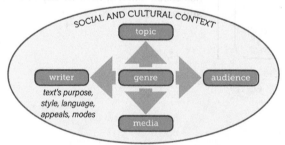

Figure 10.7: Social and cultural context

3 Exploring how the text attempts to appeal to an audience

As you are making sense of the rhetorical situation, you'll want to look closely at how the text attempts to appeal to readers, to attract their attention. How is the text appealing to readers' values and beliefs? Through their emotions, reason, or sense of credibility? Through arousal and positivity? If sources are used, how has the writer used them? How are images and other modes of communication used in the text?

As your analysis deepens and you have a good sense of the visual aspects of a text, look closely at the style and language of the writing. Is it conversational or more academic? Funny or serious? Argumentative or informative? How does the text blend conventional alphabetic text with different modes like images, video, links, and site functionality (i.e., commenting functions, social media links) to induce cooperation in readers? How are different modes used to appeal to an audience?

4 Situating the text in a textual ecology

As you become more familiar with the text you are analyzing, you'll naturally begin making connections to the culture at large. If the piece has links, follow a few to get a sense of the network of texts it is a part of. Who is cited in the text? What does this network of texts tell you about this rhetorical situation? Are there similar texts that exist? What else has been said about the topic? What cultural or historical events may have influenced the composition and content of this text? If there are comments, what do they say? Referring to Slotkin's piece, the shocking security footage posted to YouTube of NFL star Ray Rice punching his fiancée clearly hit a nerve in the public discourse and initiated a public debate around professional athletes and domestic abuse.

5 Finding a focus or theme

At this point you'll most likely have many interesting things to write about. Choose two or three rhetorical aspects of this text you find most engaging and that gives readers insight into the contexts of this text and how it is working to connect with an audience to induce their cooperation. For example, Slotkin chose to focus specifically on *kairos* (the timeliness of text) and the appeals to our emotion (*pathos*) present in the CoverGirl images.

WRITING MOVES

Drafting and Shaping

From looking closely at a text to exploring one or more aspects of its context, you are likely to have generated new understandings of its rhetorical situation, the ways it appeals to readers, and how successfully it has done so. The next step is to begin to organize your draft into a more coherent rhetorical analysis of your text within the larger cultural and social contexts of its creation and its relationship to other texts.

1 Foregrounding text and context

In analyzing rhetoric in digital contexts, one of our primary goals as writers is to help readers gain a richer understanding of how a particular text is working and the cultural and social contexts it emerges from. One way to do this is to begin with the topic the text is addressing. In Slotkin's piece on domestic abuse in the NFL, he begins by describing the incident between football player Ray Rice and his then fiancée (now wife), Janay Palmer. Establishing the context gives readers helpful background knowledge about the text and conversation he'll be analyzing. However you begin your analysis, you'll want to introduce the text you are going to look at and give readers a sense of who the author is, the context of the text, and when and where the text was published.

As always, creating a working outline can be a useful strategy to help you structure your analysis. As you draft your paper and have peers look at it, you might decide to change your original outline to add or delete sections and modify the amount of background knowledge you provide about the situation you are exploring. Again, it's helpful to have a plan but to stay flexible as you work toward a final draft.

After establishing some background and context for the rhetorical situation you are analyzing, your next goal could be to explore how this text fits into a larger conversation by looking at other texts on the topic. Slotkin cites different tweets to show some of the response on Twitter to the mock CoverGirl ad. In Slotkin's analysis, not only is he thinking about how the text is working rhetorically on audiences, he also is placing the text in the larger textual ecology and conversation that it helped generate.

2 Finding examples to support your analysis

As you narrow in on what you want to highlight in your analysis, you'll want to use strong textual evidence to support your observations. Slotkin includes the image he is analyzing so readers can see the text themselves. In analysis, you'll want to point to specific examples in the text that show your understanding. You can discuss particular rhetorical strategies the writer uses, or look at the style of the language and the tone of voice. Look for compelling quotes and examples. If the text is online and includes images or video, you might include screenshots to support your analysis, as Slotkin has done with Twitter posts. You also want people to read your work, so think about ways you can make this analysis surprising and interesting. Have you thought about your writing style? Your word choice? Your tone?

3 Integrating your examples

Once you have some textual or visual examples to work with, you'll want to think carefully about how to integrate these into your analysis in ways

Digital Toolbox
See Part IV, Section 1

that reinforce and support the observations you want to make about a text or rhetorical situation. As you work with quotes, consider how to introduce the quotations effectively by mentioning the author's name and background and when and where the example was published. There are several common ways to integrate text quotes. Using quotations, you might use the quote as its own sentence, or you can try blending the writer's words into the flow of your own sentences. If the quote is particularly long (more than four lines), then you'll want to do a *block quote* and set it off from the rest of the text by indenting it. Although Slotkin only integrates a few quotations into the flow of his text, he integrates several Twitter posts as a form of quotation. Once integrated, you'll also want to explain the meaning of the example and what it does to help us understand the situation you are analyzing. Here is an example from Slotkin's essay:

> These responses on Twitter testify to the effectiveness of the mock-CoverGirl ad in raising awareness about the Ray Rice scandal. For example, the tweet below (in as poor taste as it is) demonstrates how the photoshopped "Get Your Game Face On" ad successfully appealed to its audience's emotions, made effective by the kairotic moment:

> Sasha no doubt responded to the mock-CoverGirl ad in this way because it moved and inspired her to help bring attention to the issue. Her response was created in a moment of good kairos because

the edited image is fresh in her readers' minds and appeals to our emotions, humor, and perhaps frustration. Her point, that CoverGirl and the NFL make an unfortunate pairing, is thereby well made. The attention brought to the issue through tweets such as Sasha's help create the beginnings of a dialogue about the scandal.

> **Sasha Cohen**
> @dangertheatre   🐦 Follow
>
> Covergirl & the NFL, there's an unfortunate pairing. I can't wait to see their Ray Rice line of concealers.
> 9:07 AM - 24 Sep 2014
>
> ↩ ⇄ ♥ 1

In this example, Slotkin first introduces the tweet quote and explains that it is an example of how effective the mock CoverGirl ad has been with audiences. He then follows the tweet with further explanation, connecting the tweet back to his focus on *kairos* and *pathos*, and then explains how this tweet enters the larger textual ecology around the issue.

4 Concluding well

Conclude in a way that highlights the focus of your analysis and what you hope you and your readers can take away from it. This is also the place to re-emphasize the larger cultural concerns that this text is addressing and leave readers with something to ponder.

WRITING MOVES ◀

Revising and Publishing

If you're posting your work to a blog or a wiki, you've already made some decisions about how your text will circulate. As always, it's useful to circulate it first among knowledgeable and interested readers before posting it more publicly. Working with other writers involved in the same kind of writing can help us clarify what we think we are trying to say and to write in ways more responsive to the needs of an audience.

1 Working with peer review

Any peer review strategies that have worked for you in the past will be useful again. Here are some possible peer review questions that can guide you for preparing a rhetorical analysis text for wider circulation.

- Has the composer offered strong evidence from the text or texts he or she is analyzing to support her or his rhetorical analysis?

- Has the composer established enough background and contextual knowledge for you to understand the rhetorical situation she or he is exploring?

- How does the writer situate this text in a textual ecology?

- If the writer uses any rhetorical concepts, are they used appropriately? Are definitions provided when necessary?

- Is the analysis engaging? Can you follow the writer's train of thought? How have sources and examples been integrated into the text? Does the composer introduce them effectively? Has the writer sufficiently explained the relevance of examples and how they help to clarify the article's main purposes?

- Does the conclusion leave us something to think about?

- What other advice would you give to the composer of the text?

2 Reshaping your analysis for circulation to a larger audience

You might think about composing your analysis in a different medium beyond the printed page. In any case, first writing or typing out your analysis can serve as a foundation for composing effectively in different media.

When choosing another type of media to compose in, you'll want to think through the different benefits of each. Ask questions such as these: What kinds of meanings can I create in an alphabetic text that I can't create in a video, and vice versa? How can I combine different modes to express myself with? Each of the sample texts you read in this chapter was published online and contained images, video, and links to other content. In addition to alphabetic literacy, your rhetorical toolbox should include links, images, and video. These new literacies are today's available means of persuasion when composing with digital media. Using a combination of social media tools, you can create and circulate your writing and reach out to audiences through linking, responding, liking, and sharing.

You might also have the opportunity to present your analysis to your class. In this case, you'll want to think about the medium of speech and how best to present your work to a "live audience." If you decide to use presentation software, like PowerPoint, SlideShare, or Prezi, you'll again need to think about how to use images and text together rhetorically, but in a way that takes advantage of the visual power of presentation software. The important thing to keep in mind when choosing the medium of composition is to understand, to the best of your ability, the different rhetorical benefits of each kind.

Digital Toolbox
See Part IV, Section 6

Reinventing and Circulating Your Work

Inundated with texts as we are today, there is no shortage of opportunities to extend the work of rhetorical analysis. You could compose a rhetorical analysis on a larger work, perhaps a large website, to understand some of the rhetorical strategies that large organizations, like corporations and governments, employ in their online texts. Understanding these strategies would mean going past the surface features of the text to explore how a site functions, how organized it is, and how the site collects data on users. As the collection of pop music articles emphasized, the data users provide to online services is used, in turn, to inform rhetorical strategies designed to continually attract more users to a site.

With the rise of texting, Twitter, Snapchat, and other microcommunication platforms, we can now watch larger public conversations take place in real time. The steady stream of communications allowed by social media makes it a rich space to study rhetorical practices. For example, many of the researchers and writers we have cited in this book frequently use social media to connect with audiences (danah boyd, José van Dijck, Tom Barnes, Maria Konnikova, Lawrence Lessig). You could choose to do a rhetorical analysis of one of these writers and explore how this writer writes to situate himself or herself in larger, public conversations. You might also look at someone you currently follow online, or someone you have an interest in learning more about. In any case, you'll want to choose a person or organization that is active on social media and posts often. Look at 25–50 posts or tweets, and take notes on any rhetorical patterns you see. How personal are the posts? What kinds of things do they share? Links? Images? Once you have a sense for the content, you can begin asking questions about any rhetorical strategies you notice. Is the writer appealing to our emotions? Intellect? Is the writer trustworthy? Is the writer responding in a timely fashion? What kinds of values and beliefs does the writer invoke, and for what purpose? Is there a noticeable style in which the posts are written? Following tweets, looking at several posts on someone's wall on Facebook, combing through forum responses, following an Instagram account—all of these situations raise interesting questions about how we practice rhetoric in digital environments.

Key Concepts

content posts 225	*logos* 226
ethos 226	*pathos* 226
expanded rhetorical situation 227	rhetorical appeals 226
kairos 229	social currency 234

Building Public Knowledge
Through Online Articles

CHAPTER ELEVEN

CENTRAL QUESTIONS

1 How are twenty-first century technologies affecting the ways in which people write, read, gather, and share information?

2 How does the popular but substantial feature article, drawing on observation and reflection, function as a genre?

3 How can you use a blog platform both to explore ideas and to post a full feature article on a topic likely to interest a community of your readers?

Chapter Preview

In Chapters 9 and 10 we considered how texts circulate in and achieve new purposes in public online contexts, how they are linked within a textual ecology, and how they work toward the rhetorical purposes of public discourse. The texts we looked at were mostly informal ones—exchanges about issues of public interest posted on social media, memes that circulate through the internet, and content that's created primarily for the rhetorical purpose of getting attention and going viral. We'll build on that work in this chapter as we consider knowledge-building in public digital culture. Such cultural knowledge-building includes both the general information-sharing seen in short content articles that circulate on the internet and the more serious and extended presentation and discussion of ideas—discussion that's found on the online publication sites of established journals and in the work of those who are engaged in sustained public blogging, working in this new internet genre to carry out a new type of public conversation.

As we explore these ideas, we'll also reflect back to the work of Chapters 5 and 6, where we focused on the sharing of information, ideas, and meanings in more local sites. There we saw how knowledge from the wider culture moved from the public to the local, bringing widely circulating ideas about digital learning into a local newsletter serving a university community, and how knowledge from the wider culture—about music and uses of images—influences our local conversations and practices.

As we shift our attention from the local to the public and global, we find that our knowledge-sharing practices shift as well. As knowledge is circulated online, earlier public genres take new shapes as our literacy practices continue to change and accumulate. In this chapter, we'll consider the new ways in which we share information in public digital spaces, look at the ways in which a particular genre, the article, is evolving online, and examine how communities tap into both traditional and digital literacies to address their interests and purposes. By paying careful attention to the *where* of writing, to the ways in which it is shared and reshared, distributed and redistributed in different contexts, we will extend the definition of rhetorical situation we developed in Chapter 10 by considering how the digital production practices associated with writing for the web shape both the contexts for writing and the forms our writing tends to take. As writing contexts shift, so do the genres we associate with particular purposes and audiences, like the article and blog post.

Historically, new information and ideas have reached popular audiences through print media (newspaper, magazine, and journal articles) or broadcast media (radio and television). In the digital age, computer networks, social media, and a growing proliferation of new platforms and applications have enabled any writer/composer to share knowledge widely, to "broadcast" it in a sense. This chapter invites you to explore the various forms that knowledge-sharing and building is taking now, from the short, catchy "content articles" intended to capture a reader's attention long enough to be shared, to the extended feature article of serious thought and reflection, to the common blog post that varies in length and substance, sometimes offering less formal reflections that can lead to a more carefully shaped feature article.

Exploring
Sharing Knowledge in a Digital Age

We've already seen that the internet has profoundly altered the ways in which we share ideas and information, both in the larger world and within our immediate communities. At the same time, it has created an incessant demand for new content that people will want to share—content that reaches us whether we're looking for it or not. While readers might share links to more serious feature or news articles, much of what they send along to others is typically brief and designed primarily to attract the attention that many sites' ad-based revenue streams depend on.

Sharing Information in Informal Online Environments

If you've spent any time looking for information online, you've had articles and ads pop up that are related to what you're searching for (or that distract you from that search). On Facebook, your friends have most likely shared online content they've found interesting. On Twitter, people you follow will often tweet content they think will interest you. The internet has helped foster the growth of vast amounts of user-created content while also generating a constant demand for more, from how-to articles, to reviews of products, to news updates, to videos of almost anything we can imagine. Some of this content goes viral and transforms into memes, getting shared over and over again and often trending for at least a brief period of time.

INQUIRY

#1: Observing online content

??? Observe the content you receive online for a day or evening. What types of content and topics find their way to you via social media (Twitter, Instagram), posted on Facebook like the hockey videos we saw Barry receiving, or what kinds of content that appear on the sidebar to things you've searched for? What content do you follow up with by liking it, following a link to view it, saving it, or resharing it? As you compare your observations with those of your classmates, what do you find to be common elements in what gets shared?

Look back at Maria Konnikova's[11:1] article on what makes stories go viral in Chapter 10. Konnikova looks closely at online rhetorical practices and how writers *appeal* to readers, particularly the appeal to emotions (*pathos*) in how content is presented, especially in attention-grabbing headlines, in making content go viral. But Konnikova points to two other appeals named by Aristotle: the ethical (*ethos*) and the logical (*logos*) that shape the content in other ways. We'll want to explore those ways in this chapter.

INQUIRY #2: Beyond pathos

As you consider what has made you share or follow up on content, what besides the emotional appeal of the content or headlines has made you linger? Is the knowledge that has been shared in the content significant to you for another reason? Do the pieces that have stuck with you provide new information about a topic that's important to you, help you understand something in a new way, or speak to your values and beliefs and/or those of one of your communities? In other words, even if an amazing headline hooks you, what holds you and keeps you reading?

Reaching New Audiences with Online Content

Businesses, from restaurants to builders and plumbers, need to create interesting content to attract customers, and blogs have become a common way to do this. Advertisers want their ads to appear next to relevant and interesting content that will attract many viewers. As some of this content goes viral, getting shared and viewed over and over again, a demand is created for still more. Who provides all of this content? Posts to the blogs of major online news sites might come from paid staff, but much of it comes from freelancers—from people who get paid a certain amount for each article they write or video they create that gets accepted by a content site, most often tied to length, views, and ads that can be linked to it. As we write this, wikiHow's page[L11:1] on how to write a feature article is looking for people to write about horses, laundry and cleaning, cats, and "Rome Total War." Amazon will send free products to people in certain demographics who write frequent reviews (such as parents who review toys for toddlers). Sites such as HubPages serve as clearinghouses for writers who are invited to post articles in various general interest content categories, like entertainment and media or pets and animals. Collegemagazine.com publishes articles related to student life by student writers. And many writers who themselves make a living from the online content they provide also maintain blogs where they post articles about how to do what they do, hoping to draw enough traffic to gain attention from businesses and news sources that might hire content writers.

We're all consumers of such content, and as readers, we can come to it more thoughtfully and critically if we know more about how it is written.

Making Connections
Audiences and Contexts for Online Articles

From your brief inquiry into the world of content writing, you can see that even writers of informational, stripped-down, articles about ordinary interests are shaping their content to address certain kinds of audiences—shoppers interested in fashion or the outdoors, sports fans, dog lovers—who will most often see the articles pop up in sidebars as they search for a topic and access pages on the internet. For more serious and extended content, the question of audience and context continues to shape what's written.

Most news articles and feature articles appear online currently. All major newspapers and magazines make their print content available online, as we've seen with *The New York Times* article about danah boyd in Chapter 4, and most have their writers develop additional online content as well, often in the form of a blog.

Sidenote

Our internet searches are a big part of how companies and content producers know how to target content.

There are differences, even for the same writer, in writing content for these two digital environments. In this section, we'll look at the work of one writer, Andrew Sullivan, who has done a lot of both. Sullivan is a serious political journalist and public writer who wants to appeal to his readers' general interest in learning about the world through both logos and ethos, presenting reasoned positions about the topics he addresses and often appealing to their ethical understanding as well.

As a writer, Sullivan's work has taken two main forms, from more extended articles, like, "Why I Blog,"[11:2, L11:2] published in *The Atlantic* in both print and digital versions, and to more recent posts on his blog "The Daily Dish."[L11:3] While both the article and the blog posts appeared online, they were published in different digital contexts and were written for somewhat different audiences. Sullivan is one of the better-known bloggers in the world of news and politics, a writer who labels himself as conservative, but who takes positions across the political spectrum. He was already an established journalist and editor of a traditional print journal (now online), *The New Republic*, when he began blogging in 2000. He maintained his daily blog for fifteen years, first at *Time*, then *The Atlantic*, then *The Daily Beast,* and finally on his own website. His longer feature essay tells us much about how a serious writer works within the evolving genre of the blog post.

Sidenote

The Atlantic is one of the oldest journals of culture and opinion, started in 1857 as *The Atlantic Monthly*.

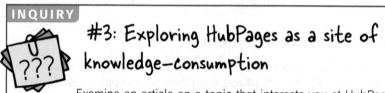

INQUIRY

#3: Exploring HubPages as a site of knowledge-consumption

Examine an article on a topic that interests you at HubPages or another online content platform, and consider what information is shared and how. Why might this article generate a lot of sharing and liking online? View the HubPages video, and read one of the how-to articles on writing for that or another such platform. What are the goals of writing at this site? What do writers do to meet those goals? From what you learn, try your hand at writing a brief article in an area of your own interest and knowledge that could potentially be submitted to such a platform (or submit it). In choosing a topic, you're likely to consider its timeliness (kairos), thinking about what's circulating and drawing interest at the moment and how you might tap into that. Share what you've learned with a group or with your class to come to broader understanding of how the articles that make up so much of our online knowledge consumption get written.

Reading a Feature Article about Blogging

One knowledge-sharing genre that has transformed in the move to digital platforms is the "feature article," an article that, while it may draw on research, is intended for a popular audience rather than experts in a field. Sometimes called a feature **essay**, or a journalistic essay, the genre has taken shape over time as a public, textual practice for thoughtful and engaged commentary on literature, culture, politics, the arts, and sciences in ways that draw on the writer's personal reflection and observation. Such articles were a standard genre for traditional print media, but we can see how they are adapted in digital environments, carrying over some traits of the traditional essay in their use of observations, research, and other evidence to support a larger understanding, while adapting to digital contexts. While feature articles still appear in print media, they have also become a common genre on blogging platforms.

essay
a genre of writing characterized by thoughtful, engaged commentary and personal reflection

The following reading is a selection from a larger piece written by Sullivan for *The Atlantic*—a feature article/essay, combining factual information with observations and reflections about his own blogging. In this essay, Sullivan says more about the genre of the essay as a provisional, exploratory form, pointing to the work of the French sixteenth-century writer, Montaigne, who first used the term, meaning "trial" or "attempt," for his writing, but applies it more directly to blogging.

Sidenote

Montaigne was the first to use the term "essay," meaning "trial" or "attempt," to describe his writing.

We can assume that when Sullivan was writing his piece, he imagined the general audience typically drawn to *The Atlantic* and the kinds of pieces published in that popular but serious journal. It is probably safe to guess that he also expected to engage general readers who followed articles on emerging technologies and their impact on print traditions.

In *The Atlantic* (see Figure 11.1), his article appeared in November 2008, along with articles by other writers on a variety of topics of potential interest to general readers, including transgender children and airline security, in a journal context created by an editor who selected and gathered these pieces into one issue (Figure 11.2).

Features

Sullivan's feature article offers new information in a genre that allows for careful structuring and revision. He's exploring an idea about his own blogging and how it's different from his other writing, but he's presenting what he has discovered in a finished essay. As you read and annotate his article, you'll want to consider first what he shares and then how he shares it.

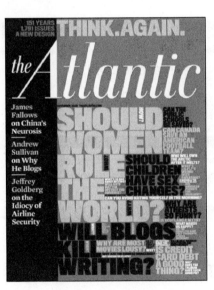

Figure 11.1: The Atlantic
November 2008 cover

A Boy's Life

What would you do if your son wanted to be a girl? Some doctors have a new and troubling answer.

HANNA ROSIN

Their Own Worst Enemy

China is stunningly bad at managing its own reputation. Here's why.

JAMES FALLOWS

The Lightning Rod

Michelle Rhee's plan to revolutionize D.C. schools

CLAY RISEN

INTERVIEWS: Michelle Rhee, the young chancellor of the D.C. public school system, talks about her career path, what makes a good teacher, and her efforts to transform a struggling school district

First Person Plural

The neuroscience of identity

PAUL BLOOM

INTERVIEWS: Psychologist Paul Bloom reflects on happiness, desire, memory, and the chaotic community that lives inside every human mind

The Things He Carried

Adventures in airport security

JEFFREY GOLDBERG

Why I Blog

The feedback is personal and brutal, but the connection with readers is intoxicating. *[Web only: Video: "Your Brain on Blog"]*

ANDREW SULLIVAN

Figure 11.2: **Feature Essays**[L11:4] *in the November 2008 issue of* The Atlantic

BEFORE READING:

Reading and annotating

Consider the following questions about the content of Sullivan's essay as you read and annotate.

- What is Sullivan's central argument in this text (his thesis)?
- What larger points about serious blogging does he want to leave his readers with?
- What information about his own experience does he share in support of the points he is making?

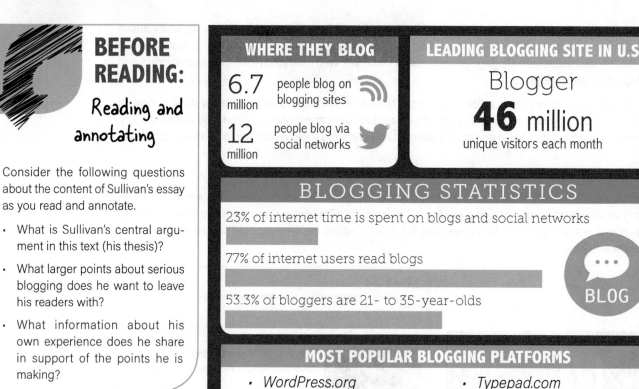

WHERE THEY BLOG

6.7 million — people blog on blogging sites

12 million — people blog via social networks

LEADING BLOGGING SITE IN U.S.

Blogger
46 million
unique visitors each month

BLOGGING STATISTICS

23% of internet time is spent on blogs and social networks

77% of internet users read blogs

53.3% of bloggers are 21- to 35-year-olds

BLOG

MOST POPULAR BLOGGING PLATFORMS

- WordPress.org
- Blogger.com
- Tumblr.com
- Typepad.com
- Wix.com

Sources: *http://www.webgranth.com/proven-expert-blogging-tips-from-experienced-bloggers*, *http://www.slideshare.net/ShellHarris1/what-is-the-best-blogging-platform-in-2016*

READING

Selection from
"Why I Blog"
by Andrew Sullivan
The Atlantic, November 2008

THE WORD *blog* is a conflation of two words: *Web* and *log*. It contains in its four letters a concise and accurate self-description: it is a log of thoughts and writing posted publicly on the World Wide Web. In the monosyllabic vernacular of the Internet, *Web log* soon became the word *blog*.

This form of instant and global self-publishing, made possible by technology widely available only for the past decade or so, allows for no retroactive editing (apart from fixing minor typos or small glitches) and removes from the act of writing any considered or lengthy review. It is the spontaneous expression of instant thought—impermanent beyond even the ephemera of daily journalism. It is accountable in immediate and unavoidable ways to readers and other bloggers, and linked via hypertext to continuously multiplying references and sources. Unlike any single piece of print journalism, its borders are extremely porous and its truth inherently transitory. The consequences of this for the act of writing are still sinking in.

A ship's log owes its name to a small wooden board, often weighted with lead, that was for centuries

Place annotations here

attached to a line and thrown over the stern. The weight of the log would keep it in the same place in the water, like a provisional anchor, while the ship moved away. By measuring the length of line used up in a set period of time, mariners could calculate the speed of their journey (the rope itself was marked by equidistant "knots" for easy measurement). As a ship's voyage progressed, the course came to be marked down in a book that was called a log . . . A log provided as accurate an account as could be gleaned in real time.

As you read a log, you have the curious sense of moving backward in time as you move forward in pages—the opposite of a book. As you piece together a narrative that was never intended as one, it seems—and is—more truthful. Logs, in this sense, were a form of human self-correction. They amended for hindsight, for the ways in which human beings order and tidy and construct the story of their lives as they look back on them. Logs require a letting-go of narrative because they do not allow for a knowledge of the ending. So they have plot as well as dramatic irony—the reader will know the ending before the writer did.

Anyone who has blogged his thoughts for an extended time will recognize this world. We bloggers have scant opportunity to collect our thoughts, to wait until events have settled and a clear pattern emerges. We blog now—as news reaches us, as facts emerge. This is partly true for all journalism, which is, as its etymology suggests, daily writing, always subject to subsequent revision. And a good columnist will adjust position and judgment and even political loyalty over time, depending on events. But a blog is not so much daily writing as hourly writing. And with that level of timeliness, the provisionality of every word is even more pressing—and the risk of error or the thrill of prescience that much greater.

No columnist or reporter or novelist will have his minute shifts or constant small contradictions exposed as mercilessly as a blogger's are. A columnist can ignore or duck a subject less noticeably than a blogger committing thoughts to pixels several times a day. A reporter can wait—must wait—until every source has confirmed. A novelist can spend months or years before committing words to the world. For bloggers, the deadline is always now. Blogging is therefore to writing what extreme sports are to athletics: more free-form, more accident-prone, less formal, more alive. It is, in many ways, writing out loud.

I remember first grappling with what to put on my blog. It was the spring of 2000 and, like many a freelance writer at the time, I had some vague notion that I needed to have a presence "online." I had no clear idea of what to do, but a friend who ran a Web-design company offered to create a site for me, and, since I was technologically clueless, he also agreed to post various essays and columns as I wrote them. Before too long, this became a chore for him, and he called me one day to say he'd found an online platform that was so simple I could henceforth post all my writing myself. The platform was called Blogger.

As I used it to post columns or links to books or old essays, it occurred to me that I could also post new writing—writing that could even be exclusive to the blog. But what? Like any new form, blogging did not start from nothing. It evolved from various journalistic traditions. In my case, I drew on my mainstream-media experience to navigate the virgin sea. I had a few early inspirations: the old Notebook section of *The New Republic*, a magazine that, under the editorial guidance of Michael Kinsley, had introduced a more English style of crisp, short commentary into what had been a more high-minded genre of American opinion writing. *The New Republic* had also pioneered a Diarist feature on the last page, which was designed to be a more personal, essayistic, first-person form of journalism. Mixing the two genres, I did what I had been trained to do—and improvised.

From the first few days of using the form, I was hooked. The simple experience of being able to directly broadcast my own words to readers was an exhilarating literary liberation. Unlike the current generation of writers, who have only ever blogged, I knew firsthand what the alternative meant. I'd edited a weekly print magazine, *The New Republic*, for five years, and written countless columns and essays for a variety of traditional outlets. And in all this, I'd often chafed, as most writers do, at the endless

Place annotations here

delays, revisions, office politics, editorial fights, and last-minute cuts for space that dead-tree publishing entails. Blogging—even to an audience of a few hundred in the early days—was intoxicatingly free in comparison. Like taking a narcotic.

It was obvious from the start that it was revolutionary. Every writer since the printing press has longed for a means to publish himself and reach—instantly—any reader on Earth. Every professional writer has paid some dues waiting for an editor's nod, or enduring a publisher's incompetence, or being ground to literary dust by a legion of fact-checkers and copy editors. If you added up the time a writer once had to spend finding an outlet, impressing editors, sucking up to proprietors, and proofreading edits, you'd find another lifetime buried in the interstices. But with one click of the Publish Now button, all these troubles evaporated.

Alas, as I soon discovered, this sudden freedom from above was immediately replaced by insurrection from below. Within minutes of my posting something, even in the earliest days, readers responded. E-mail seemed to unleash their inner beast. They were more brutal than any editor, more persnickety than any copy editor, and more emotionally unstable than any colleague.

And so blogging found its own answer to the defensive counterblast from the journalistic establishment. To the charges of inaccuracy and unprofessionalism, bloggers could point to the fierce, immediate scrutiny of their readers. Unlike newspapers, which would eventually publish corrections in a box of printed spinach far from the original error, bloggers had to walk the walk of self-correction in the same space and in the same format as the original screwup. The form was more accountable, not less, because there is nothing more conducive to professionalism than being publicly humiliated for sloppiness. Of course, a blogger could ignore an error or simply refuse to acknowledge mistakes. But if he persisted, he would be razzed by competitors and assailed by commenters and abandoned by readers. The blog remained a *superficial* medium, of course. By superficial, I mean simply that blogging rewards brevity and immediacy. No one wants to read a 9,000-word treatise online. On the Web, one-sentence links are as legitimate as thousand-word diatribes—in fact, they are often valued more. And, as Matt Drudge told me when I sought advice from the master in 2001, the key to understanding a blog is to realize that it's a broadcast, not a publication. If it stops moving, it dies. If it stops paddling, it sinks.

But the superficiality masked considerable depth—greater depth, from one perspective, than the traditional media could offer. The reason was a single technological innovation: the hyperlink. An old-school columnist can write 800 brilliant words analyzing or commenting on, say, a new think-tank report or scientific survey. But in reading it on paper, you have to take the columnist's presentation of the material on faith, or be convinced by a brief quotation (which can always be misleading out of context). Online, a hyperlink to the original source transforms the experience. Yes, a few sentences of bloggy spin may not be as satisfying as a full column, but the ability to read the primary material instantly—in as careful or shallow a fashion as you choose—can add much greater context than anything on paper. Even a blogger's chosen pull quote, unlike a columnist's, can be effortlessly checked against the original. Now this innovation, pre-dating blogs but popularized by them, is increasingly central to mainstream journalism.

A blog, therefore, bobs on the surface of the ocean but has its anchorage in waters deeper than those print media is technologically able to exploit. It disempowers the writer to that extent, of course. The blogger can get away with less and afford fewer pretensions of authority. He is—more than any writer of the past—a node among other nodes, connected but unfinished without the links and the comments and the track-backs that make the blogosphere, at its best, a conversation, rather than a production.

A writer fully aware of and at ease with the provisionality of his own work is nothing new. For centuries, writers have experimented with forms that suggest the imperfection of human thought, the inconstancy of human affairs, and the humbling, chastening passage of time. If you compare the meandering, questioning, unresolved dialogues of Plato with the definitive, logical treatises of Aristotle, you see the

READING

difference between a skeptic's spirit translated into writing and a spirit that seeks to bring some finality to the argument. Perhaps the greatest single piece of Christian apologetics, Pascal's *Pensées,* is a series of meandering, short, and incomplete stabs at arguments, observations, insights. Their lack of finish is what makes them so compelling—arguably more compelling than a polished treatise by Aquinas.

But perhaps the quintessential blogger *avant la lettre* was Montaigne. His essays were published in three major editions, each one longer and more complex than the previous. A passionate skeptic, Montaigne amended, added to, and amplified the essays for each edition, making them three-dimensional through time. In the best modern translations, each essay is annotated, sentence by sentence, paragraph by paragraph, by small letters (A, B, and C) for each major edition, helping the reader see how each rewrite added to or subverted, emphasized or ironized, the version before. Montaigne was living his skepticism, daring to show how a writer evolves, changes his mind, learns new things, shifts perspectives, grows older—and that this, far from being something that needs to be hidden behind a veneer of unchanging authority, can become a virtue, a new way of looking at the pretensions of authorship and text and truth. Montaigne, for good measure, also peppered his essays with myriads of what bloggers would call external links. His own thoughts are strewn with and complicated by the aphorisms and anecdotes of others. Scholars of the sources note that many of these "money quotes" were deliberately taken out of context, adding layers of irony to writing that was already saturated in empirical doubt.

To blog is therefore to let go of your writing in a way, to hold it at arm's length, open it to scrutiny, allow it to float in the ether for a while, and to let others, as Montaigne did, pivot you toward relative truth. A blogger will notice this almost immediately upon starting. Some e-mailers, unsurprisingly, know more about a subject than the blogger does. They will send links, stories, and facts, challenging the blogger's view of the world, sometimes outright refuting it, but more frequently adding context and nuance and complexity to an idea. The role of a blogger is not to defend against this but to embrace it. He is similar in this way to the host of a dinner party. He can provoke discussion or take a position, even passionately, but he also must create an atmosphere in which others want to participate.

What makes blogging as a form stand out is that it is rich in personality. The faux intimacy of the Web experience, the closeness of the e-mail and the instant message, seeps through. You feel as if you know bloggers as they go through their lives, experience the same things you are experiencing, and share the moment. When readers of my blog bump into me in person, they invariably address me as Andrew. Print readers don't do that. It's Mr. Sullivan to them.

On my blog, my readers and I experienced 9/11 together, in real time. I can look back and see not just how I responded to the event, but how I responded to it at 3:47 that afternoon. And at 9:46 that night. There is a vividness to this immediacy that cannot be rivaled by print. The same goes for the 2000 recount, the Iraq War, the revelations of Abu Ghraib, the death of John Paul II, or any of the other history-making events of the past decade. There is simply no way to write about them in real time without revealing a huge amount about yourself. And the intimate bond this creates with readers is unlike the bond that the *The Times,* say, develops with its readers through the same events. Alone in front of a computer, at any moment, are two people: a blogger and a reader. The proximity is palpable, the moment human—whatever authority a blogger has is derived not from the institution he works for but from the humanness he conveys. This is writing with emotion not just under but always breaking through the surface. It renders a writer and a reader not just connected but linked in a visceral, personal way. The only term that really describes this is *friendship.* And it is a relatively new thing to write for thousands and thousands of friends.

These friends, moreover, are an integral part of the blog itself—sources of solace, company, provocation, hurt, and correction. If I were to do an inventory of the material that appears on my blog, I'd estimate that a good third of it is reader-generated, and a good third of my time is spent absorbing readers' views, comments, and tips. Readers tell me of breaking stories, new perspectives, and counterarguments to prevailing assumptions. And this is what blogging, in turn, does to reporting. The traditional method involves a journalist searching for key sources, nurturing them, and sequestering them from his rivals. A blogger splashes gamely into a subject and dares the sources to come to him.

Some of this material—e-mails from soldiers on the front lines, from scientists explaining new research, from dissident Washington writers too scared to say what they think in their own partisan redoubts—might never have seen the light of day before the blogosphere. And some of it, of course, is dubious stuff. Bloggers can be spun and misled as easily as traditional writers—and the rigorous source assessment that good reporters do can't be done by e-mail. But you'd be surprised by what comes unsolicited into the in-box, and how helpful it often is.

Not all of it is mere information. Much of it is also opinion and scholarship, a knowledge base that exceeds the research department of any newspaper. A good blog is your own private Wikipedia. Indeed, the most pleasant surprise of blogging has been the number of people working in law or government or academia or rearing kids at home who have real literary talent and real knowledge, and who had no outlet—until now. There is a distinction here, of course, between the edited use of e-mailed sources by a careful blogger and the often mercurial cacophony on an unmediated comments section. But the truth is out there—and the miracle of e-mail allows it to come to you.

Fellow bloggers are always expanding this knowledge base. Eight years ago, the blogosphere felt like a handful of individual cranks fighting with one another. Today, it feels like a universe of cranks, with vast, pulsating readerships, fighting with one another. To the neophyte reader, or blogger, it can seem overwhelming. But there is a connection between the intimacy of the early years and the industry it has become today. And the connection is human individuality . . .If you think of blogging as more like talk radio or cable news than opinion magazines or daily newspapers, then this personalized emphasis is less surprising. People have a voice for radio and a face for television. For blogging, they have a sensibility.

But writing in this new form is a collective enterprise as much as it is an individual one—and the connections between bloggers are as important as the content on the blogs. The links not only drive conversation, they drive readers. The more you link, the more others will link to you, and the more traffic and readers you will get. The zero-sum game of old media—in which *Time* benefits from *Newsweek's* decline and vice versa—becomes win-win. It's great for *Time* to be linked to by *Newsweek* and the other way round. One of the most prized statistics in the blogosphere is therefore not the total number of readers or page views, but the "authority" you get by being linked to by other blogs. It's an indication of how central you are to the online conversation of humankind.

A "blogroll" is an indicator of whom you respect enough to keep in your galaxy. For many years, I kept my reading and linking habits to a relatively small coterie of fellow political bloggers. In today's blogosphere, to do this is to embrace marginality. I've since added links to religious blogs and literary ones and scientific ones and just plain weird ones. As the blogosphere has expanded beyond anyone's capacity to absorb it, I've needed an assistant and interns to scour the Web for links and stories and photographs to respond to and think about. It's a difficult balance, between your own interests and obsessions, and the knowledge, insight, and wit of others—but an immensely rich one. There are times, in fact, when a blogger feels less like a writer than an online disc jockey, mixing samples of tunes and generating new melodies through mashups while also making his own music. He is both artist and producer—and the beat always goes on.

If all this sounds postmodern, that's because it is. And blogging suffers from the same flaws as postmodernism: a failure to provide stable truth or a permanent perspective. A traditional writer is valued by readers precisely because they trust him to have thought long and hard about a subject, given it time to evolve in his head, and composed a piece of writing that is worth their time to read at length and to ponder. Bloggers don't do this and cannot do this—and that limits them far more than it does

READING

traditional long-form writing.

A blogger will air a variety of thoughts or facts on any subject in no particular order other than that dictated by the passing of time. A writer will instead use time, synthesizing these thoughts, ordering them, weighing which points count more than others, seeing how his views evolved in the writing process itself, and responding to an editor's perusal of a draft or two. The result is almost always more measured, more satisfying, and more enduring than a blizzard of posts. The triumphalist notion that blogging should somehow replace traditional writing is as foolish as it is pernicious. In some ways, blogging's gifts to our discourse make the skills of a good traditional writer much more valuable, not less. The torrent of blogospheric insights, ideas, and arguments places a greater premium on the person who can finally make sense of it all, turning it into something more solid, and lasting, and rewarding.

The points of this essay, for example, have appeared in shards and fragments on my blog for years. But being forced to order them in my head and think about them for a longer stretch has helped me understand them better, and perhaps express them more clearly. Each week, after a few hundred posts, I also write an actual newspaper column. It invariably turns out to be more considered, balanced, and evenhanded than the blog. But the blog will always inform and enrich the column, and often serve as a kind of free-form, free-associative research. And an essay like this will spawn discussion best handled on a blog. The conversation, in other words, is the point, and the different idioms used by the conversationalists all contribute something of value to it. And so, if the defenders of the old media once viscerally regarded blogging as some kind of threat, they are starting to see it more as a portal, and a spur.

There is, after all, something simply irreplaceable about reading a piece of writing at length on paper, in a chair or on a couch or in bed. To use an obvious analogy, jazz entered our civilization much later than composed, formal music. But it hasn't replaced it; and no jazz musician would ever claim that it could. Jazz merely demands a different way of playing and listening, just as blogging requires a different mode of writing and reading. Jazz and blogging are intimate, improvisational, and individual—but also inherently collective. And the audience talks over both.

The reason they talk while listening, and comment or link while reading, is that they understand that this is a kind of music that needs to be engaged rather than merely absorbed. To listen to jazz as one would listen to an aria is to miss the point. Reading at a monitor, at a desk, or on an iPhone provokes a querulous, impatient, distracted attitude, a demand for instant, usable information, that is simply not conducive to opening a novel or a favorite magazine on the couch. Reading on paper evokes a more relaxed and meditative response. The message dictates the medium. And each medium has its place—as long as one is not mistaken for the other.

In fact, for all the intense gloom surrounding the newspaper and magazine business, this is actually a golden era for journalism. The blogosphere has added a whole new idiom to the act of writing and has introduced an entirely new generation to nonfiction. It has enabled writers to write out loud in ways never seen or understood before. And yet it has exposed a hunger and need for traditional writing that, in the age of television's dominance, had seemed on the wane.

Words, of all sorts, have never seemed so now.

AFTER READING:
A writer's moves of knowledge-sharing

Look again at the moves Sullivan makes in building and sharing knowledge about blog-writing.

➤ Sullivan makes an intertextual move common to knowledge-sharing, one we saw in Chapter 5, pointing to the work of another writer and summarizing it in a way that supports his own purpose. What does he say about Montaigne, and how does he use that information?

➤ Sullivan brings up several ideas we've been exploring in this book: how the shared purposes of writers and readers take shape in specific contexts; how readers and writers contribute to a larger conversation and how that conversation is extended and circulated through links and blogrolls; and what it means to write for a larger public in a somewhat more personal, reflective genre. What do you learn from Sullivan that adds to the understandings you've been developing through our larger inquiry?

➤ Place yourself in conversation with Sullivan as a reader. To what extent do you agree with him? Which of his ideas do you find especially persuasive? Which push you to challenge his thinking? How could you build on his argument? How has reading Sullivan's article changed your thinking about the article/essay genre, blogs and what they accomplish? What can you draw from your own experiences thus far in reading and writing blogs to add to this perspective?

INQUIRY

#4: Responding to Sullivan's essay as a writer

???

Your work with this chapter will culminate in the production of a blog essay in which you'll explore your own ideas about and experience with some form of social media or digital literacy practices. What do you, a writer who will write an exploratory piece, notice about how Sullivan wrote this essay? How did he begin? What does he do to move readers through this article? What kinds of evidence does he use? What rhetorical appeals does he use? How does he position himself in this text? What strikes you as productive about how Sullivan crafted his article? What might you mirror as you write your own?

Reading a Blog in Context

As web platforms and web genres have evolved, communities of users have found them suited to particular purposes. An older social media platform, Myspace, although it started out as a general social site for friends, like Facebook, became, over time, largely a space for musicians and their followers (who then moved more of their activity to Facebook, Instagram, and Twitter). Other tools, like wikis, allow members to contribute easily to the construction of knowledge, so they prove particularly useful for sharing and working collaboratively (we've used a wiki to share our work in writing this book together while teaching at universities in different states). Blogs are set up to foreground a longer post, usually by one author, with space for others to share comments. They are also dated in reverse chronological order with the most recent post on top. While we take the commenting function for granted nowadays, having the ability to readily respond to what we read is a distinguishing feature of the blog as a writing platform. That format has led to the use of blogs for presenting content by newspapers like the *New York Times*, by individuals like Sullivan who want to reflect on and share what they read or experience, by researchers who want to share their findings, and by others who want to build an audience. In each case, the larger context shapes the specific form that a blog post takes, and the comment function allows an audience to respond more immediately to a writer, inevitably affecting the writing situation and how writers compose.

Sullivan has told us a lot about his blogging practice and the contexts he draws on, both the print context of his prior writing experience and the blog context he has discovered by reading and linking to others' blogs. His blog is wholly his own enterprise where he can post articles on whatever he personally thinks will interest his readers. And he has built a large audience of readers over time. The content of his blog, which often focuses on politics, typically draws an audience of readers who are interested in that topic, but it also draws readers who appreciate his quirky thinking and the personal life story he has threaded through his pages. Through the "blog love" blogroll on his site, he has connected himself to other bloggers writing about similar topics and established himself firmly in a textual ecology of ongoing conversations. What is evident in Sullivan's blogging practice, and in the practice of blogging in general, is the way bloggers actively connect with and spread one another's ideas.

Before we turn to Sullivan's blog, it can be useful to reflect on your expectations about what you'll find, based on what he wrote in his *The Atlantic* essay.

INQUIRY

#5: Drawing on the knowledge about blogs that Sullivan has shared

Sullivan's essay generalizes from his own blogging practices to tell his readers how he understands the act of blogging and the genre of the blog he has helped shaped. Summarize your own understanding of his blogging at this point, and then look at a post that interests you from his blog, *The Dish*. To what extent does that particular blog post confirm the understandings you gained from his essay? Do you observe anything else that he didn't comment on? From reading the information he has shared in his essay and observing his actual practice on his blog, what more might you say about how he uses the blog post? Can you and your classmates generate a working name for the type of blog post he typically writes?

In 2015, after 15 years of daily blogging, Sullivan decided to stop. Here is what Sullivan said about this decision at *The Dish* in his January 28 **"Note to My Readers."**[L11:5]

link

One of the things I've always tried to do at the Dish is to be up-front with readers. This sometimes means grotesque over-sharing; sometimes it means I write imprudent arguments I have to withdraw; sometimes it just means a monthly update on our revenues and subscriptions; and sometimes I stumble onto something actually interesting. But when you write every day for readers for years and years, as I've done, there's not much left to hide. And that's why, before our annual auto-renewals, I want to let you know I've decided to stop blogging in the near future.

Why? Two reasons. The first is one I hope anyone can understand: although it has been the most rewarding experience in my writing career, I've now been blogging daily for fifteen years straight (well kinda straight). That's long enough to do any single job. In some ways, it's as simple as that. There comes a time when you have to move on to new things, shake your world up, or recognize before you crash that burn-out does happen.

The second is that I am saturated in digital life and I want to return to the actual world again. I'm a human being before I am a writer; and a writer before I am a blogger, and although it's been a joy and a privilege to have helped pioneer a genuinely new form of writing, I yearn for other, older forms. I want to read again, slowly, carefully. I want to absorb a difficult book and walk around in my own thoughts with it for a while. I want to have an idea and let it slowly take shape, rather than be instantly blogged. I want to write long essays that can answer more deeply and subtly the many questions that the Dish years have presented to me. I want to write a book.

INQUIRY

#6: Blogs and news reports

What more do you learn about Sullivan's blogging from his post on his reasons for stopping? Does that post or his follow-up qualify his earlier statements in any way? Does it make you think differently about what's involved in maintaining a daily blog? Compare Sullivan's blog post and the *Guardian* news report. What differences do you find in these online genres? Are there commonalities as well?

Go to *The Dish*,[L11:6] and look at some other posts, both journalistic and personal. Sullivan kept his identity as a political journalist to the end of this blogging period, as can be seen in a late post on Obama's presidency, with graphs of his and earlier presidents' approval ratings. But when his readers were asked to submit their own Favorite Moments of Dishness, many of them noted those posts that were more personal and reflective. As a dog lover, for example, he often posted about his own dogs, and a series on dogs vs cats[L11:7] included extensive reader responses. What do such posts tell you about the ways in which he used his blog site and his understanding of rhetorical appeals to support an interactive community? How do you see his posts interacting with readers' comments, and what does this suggest about how knowledge is shared and built in digital environments?

#7: The blog design context

Consider the design of Sullivan's blog.

➤ Look at the design elements of this site. How is the visual page divided up, and what elements are foregrounded? What can you say about the sections that are included? About the choice of images and interplay of text and image in the header and in other areas of the page?

➤ Most blogs include an "About" section that talks about the blog writer and the blog's purpose. Sullivan's does not. What does that suggest about him and his readership?

➤ Most blogs have a "Comments" space. (You can read the comments that follow the *Washington Post's* blog article[L11:8] on Sullivan's retirement.) Sullivan chose instead to have readers email their comments to him (and his staff) and to curate them—to avoid much of the nastiness that often appears in open comments by choosing the comments that he would incorporate into his later posts. You can see how he did this by looking at any of the "Recent Threads" section of his home page. From a quick look at those threads, what more can you say about his readership and how he interacts with them?

➤ Most blog writers use hyperlinks, a significant new feature available to writers in digital contexts. The hyperlink, underlined text that takes readers directly to related information, helps writers by letting them point to additional information that would otherwise have to be included in parentheses or footnotes. And it helps readers by letting them stick with the flow of the main points and make their own decisions about whether to seek out that information. If you go back to Sullivan's "A Note to My Readers" blog post, you'll find several hyperlinked words or phrases. What does Sullivan choose to hyperlink? If you follow those links, how helpful do you find them in giving you additional information you might have been seeking?

Bringing Other Texts into the Conversation: Intertextuality

Building rhetorical relationships was a primary focus in Part I of this book as we traced digital literacy practices through various contexts, looking closely at the **what**, **why**, **how**, and **where** of composing. We'll next extend this focus on connections between writers and readers to consider the connections that are established and maintained *between* and *among* texts. Throughout our chapters so far, we have seen several examples of how writers draw on other texts, putting them in conversation with their own ideas and drawing on what Sullivan calls "money quotes." As he notes about famed French essayist Michel de Montaigne, "Montaigne, for good measure, also peppered his essays with myriads of what bloggers would call external links. His own thoughts are strewn with and complicated by the aphorisms and anecdotes of others." Sometimes a writer will use the blog post to bring a large portion of the information and ideas from another's text to a new audience for a new purpose, as Ellie did with the newsletter posts we read in Chapter 5. More often writers will offer a smaller summary of another's ideas to further their own, as Sullivan has done with Montaigne. And still more often, writers will draw in the words of others, as Sullivan tells us Montaigne has done, to complicate (and support) their own thoughts.

intertextuality
the interrelationship of texts as they influence and borrow from each other

Scholars in the field of composition refer to this intermingling of texts over time and space as **intertextuality** (introduced in Chapter 9), noting that all writing takes place within a larger textual context of what's been written before, and that the larger context shapes a new text in both explicit and implicit ways. You can begin to see how texts might be in conversation with one another by considering again both Sullivan's *The Atlantic* essay and related posts from his blog or news articles about his blogging.

Digital Toolbox
See Part IV, Section 3

INQUIRY

#8: Putting texts in conversation

Return to Sullivan's *The Atlantic* article and use it as a lens through which you read how he composes his actual blog posts, putting the article and one or more posts in conversation. Sullivan makes a number of points about blogging in his article, arguing that this emergent digital genre promotes certain unique social practices that are becoming part of our digital culture:

· instant and quick responses in communication;

· more common use of private responses to a very public audience;

· novel relationships between writers and readers;

· valuing brevity and concision; and

· altering the research and feedback loop between writers and readers.

Drawing on these and other observations, use the evidence of his own posts and/or the news posts about his blogging in the *Guardian*[11:4] or the *Washington Post*[11:5] to either support what he said in that article or to push against it.

This move, to extend your thinking about texts (in this case, both Sullivan's article and his blog posts, as well as news articles about his blog) by putting them in conversation with one another is a common move in academic writing. Now, in another move, place another blog or blogs you've read in conversation with Sullivan's. What ideas and realizations can you come to by placing Sullivan in conversation with other blogs and your own experience of reading blogs? What does this push you to realize about Sullivan's points? How does it push the conversation in one way or another? What new assertions can you make about blogging based on your understanding of how these texts interact?

Composing
Blog Article

In Chapter 5 we saw how an extended blog post in a newsletter was used to share ideas from an essay by John Seely Brown while recasting those ideas for new purposes, circulating them to a new audience of readers who might not have read the original essay. Many of Sullivan's blog posts, although written quickly, offer more extended discussions of particular points. It's time now to give you the opportunity to use a blog platform to craft a more extended post that works from, and perhaps draws in, Sullivan's ideas about blogging, and to create a text that draws from both your own experience and his to join the larger conversation about new digital writing and composing practices. Think of this kind of composing as a way to build a rhetorical relationship with an audience, a practice of knowledge-building that puts your own experiences and reflections in conversation with others' as you try to further your understanding of how digital environments change the literacy practices of individuals and communities. Echoing the title of Sullivan's essay, "Why I _____," can offer you a place to start.

The following student example is taken from an article that focuses on the effects of social media on relationships, drawing on personal experience and on research by danah boyd and others to consider how constant connectedness potentially effects our relationships.

> danah boyd, a social media scholar and researcher at Microsoft Research, wrote about this new addiction that teens have in one of her books, *It's Complicated*. According to boyd, this addiction may actually be caused by the parents. By having highly scheduled lives and parental restrictions (rules such as curfews, not going out on weeknights, etc.), teenagers lack time for face-to-face communication, resulting in them resorting to technology to make up for it (boyd). While many parents feel as if their children are too absorbed in social media and texting, danah boyd suggests that they themselves are the ones to blame for this. When using the parents as her audience, boyd explains, "Teens aren't addicted to social media. They're addicted to each other.... They're not allowed to hang out the way you and I did, so they've moved it online" (boyd). Like the Harvard survey, boyd also argues that teenagers aren't entirely to blame for their strong connection to technology. By putting together the lack of time with the biological need for social pleasure, social media is an effective option. Teenagers are always able to connect to one another in today's day in age. It is no longer necessary to talk in person in order to converse.
>
> Billie Jean Durkin, "A Dangerous Connection"

After drawing on her own experiences and observations to raise a pressing question about how technological innovations are shaping social interactions, Billie Jean enters into a conversation with danah boyd to extend her thinking, much like the way in which Ellie drew on John Seely Brown's article in Chapter 5, or Andrew Sullivan has drawn on Montaigne's ideas in his blogging essay. In her larger article, Billie Jean expresses her concern that communication technologies are detracting from our relationships, but she draws on boyd's work to suggest that the problem isn't technology alone, but is also related to the restrictions placed on teens' interactions. By engaging with boyd's research, Billie Jean is able to think about teenagers and technology in nuanced ways as she considers the multiple contexts, practices, and technologies that influence how we interact in the world.

Inquiring and Inventing

As you've read other articles, you've most likely begun to think about ideas you'd like to explore. Your own prior work is often the best source of such ideas.

1 Generating ideas

Reread some of the inquiries you have written in Part I and the other projects you've carried out as you've moved through this book. In addition, revisit any writing or posts your classmates have shared in class or online for possible topics related to new literacies, social media, and reading/writing in digital contexts you might extend through a combination of your own research, observation, and reflection. After looking through these materials and resources, make a list of all of the digital literacy practices you currently enact. Your list might look something like the following.

- I post on Snapchat.
- I respond to my classmates' ideas and posts on Moodle.
- I tweet.
- I share and caption pictures on Instagram.

Once your list is complete, pick three of the practices you've named. Start listing reasons *why* you engage in these activities, and consider what kind of insight you can glean from exploring the shape of these literacy practices. You might also do some freewriting about each to see where your thinking goes as you decide what to focus on in this blog essay.

2 Considering an audience

You'll want to consider your likely audience—other readers who will be interested in your experience and reflections. What topics are likely to be of interest to the readers you know or imagine? How might you engage their interest in this topic? We've seen also that texts in public environments can circulate in unexpected ways to unanticipated audiences. You'll also want to consider such unexpected readers, those you might not typically envision while writing a piece in which you consider your digital literacy practices. As texts circulate on the web, they often find these unexpected readers, and this invites us, as writers, to use the **where** of public texts to rethink the **what** and the **how**. What assumptions and existing understandings might these readers bring to your work? How might you anticipate their concerns, values, and ideologies as you draft this piece?

3 Developing your topic

Working from your initial inquiries or freewriting on one topic, continue on to write more about:

- the topic you're exploring and why you chose it;
- some of the observations that you and others have made that contribute to your understanding of this topic—include the words of others (from our readings, from your classmates' writing, from Sullivan's article or blog, or from this text) that contribute to your understanding;
- questions you have at this point about the topic you're exploring, or any concepts that seem confusing and need to be worked out; and
- your tentative answers or opinion.

Use a blog platform for both this exploratory post (that others can respond to) and perhaps another on the way to the final blog essay you shape. You don't need to make a separate blog post for each of these elements, but you'll move among them as you further your own thinking and develop your own stance or perspective through smaller posts that are, as Sullivan has found, "provisional" expressions of your ideas, building blocks that are more like speaking, or thinking out loud, and that lead to longer compositions.

WRITING MOVES ◄

Drafting and Shaping

1 Making connections

The thinking of other writers can contribute to your own. Bring in references to things you've read or heard or seen that help you develop your own understanding of the topic you're exploring. You can quote or paraphrase, but you also can use *hyperlinks* to let your readers follow these connections.

2 Sharing ideas through intertextuality

Create a blogroll with connections to your classmates' blogs. Read and respond to some of their posts, making connections where your thinking and observations might relate to theirs. Invite their comments on your posts, and bring some of those comments into a later post if you think they're relevant to the ideas you're working through. Make your classmates' work part of the intertextual context of your own piece by bringing in (quoting) words they've written that add to your own discussion.

3 Drafting and shaping

Drawing on the writing and thinking you've done with your informal blog posts, you are better prepared to write a longer article that presents your ideas in an extended, more organized way for an online platform. To work from material you've generated through your earlier blog posts, try the following strategies.

- Think about your audience of blog readers and beyond. What will draw them into the issues you're exploring? What will new readers need as shared knowledge, and where will you introduce it?

- Print out your posts and the comments you've received. Highlight key sentences and ideas you'll want to include in your article and create categories or clusters for them.

- Make an outline or map that includes these clusters, working toward an order that will let you put forward and support whatever ideas or positions you've come to and include most of the rich material you have at hand.

- Decide where you want to leave your readers. What have you learned from this inquiry you'd like them to take away?

4 Composing multimodally

Blogging platforms generally support the inclusion of images, video, and sound files. What other modes of composing could you draw on to make your post more compelling? Is there a particular image you might include to reinforce a point you are trying to make? Or perhaps a link to a YouTube video that enriches your post?

WRITING MOVES

Revising and Publishing

When you have a full draft of the article you're composing, you'll want to get responses from peer readers who represent a possible audience for your work.

1 Seeing reader comments as formative

We often think of peer review as an activity that takes place before we "publish" our work; it is often seen as connected to a more limited sharing that takes place as readers move through your writing in evaluative ways as they question what is working and what doesn't work in a draft. Digital articles, though, provide us with an opportunity to share work that can still be rethought, reshaped, and revised. As a result, writers can use the comments provided by readers to think through a post and consider how audiences are actually responding to our work in participatory, analytical, and evaluative ways. As you read through comments you receive (possibly from classmates, possibly from random readers on the web), consider the kinds of reading their responses construct. How might you rework your piece to extend the kinds of work and moves they are responding to? How can you use their comments to extend your approach to sharing understandings through your post? (Sullivan often incorporated his readers' responses into his own posts.)

2 Creating a generative rubric

Starting with this list of common elements of the feature article, add others you've discovered through your work with Sullivan's article and others:

- Addresses a topic of likely common interest in a community of readers

- Connects to the work of others to give a sense of a larger community exploring this topic

- Offers a sense of shared questions or inquiry and of what has been said before

- Is grounded by the writer's stance or perspective

3 Revising

Draw on your readers' posted comments and your generative rubric to prepare a final version of your blog article and post it to your own or your class's blog site.

Use this set of characteristics to consider the work you have done and to question how you are working within and against this genre.

Reinventing and Circulating Your Work

As texts circulate through the internet, there are many opportunities to make connections between your own work and a wider public conversation, as well as to see and re-see one piece of work in different media.

➤ **Option 1: Adding to an intertextual context.** Search for other blogs that address any of the issues you've explored in your blog article. Make further posts to your own blog that extend your ideas, and put them in conversation with other bloggers' ideas. Add those blogs to your blogroll.

➤ **Option 2: Reimagine your blog post in a different medium or as a vlog.** Another way to extend your thinking about your blog article is to transmediate it for another medium. Video blogs, or *vlogs*, are another way individuals are communicating with the public, crafting and sharing commentary like we see in blogs but in video form. Using your blog article as your base, is there a section you could revise into a transcription to record for an audience? For examples of popular vloggers, see the article "25 Vloggers Under 25 Who Are Owning The World Of YouTube."[L11:9]

You might also create a PowerPoint presentation that examines the same ideas as your blog post. As you transmediate, you'll want to think about what specific points to highlight and what images and visuals to use. How can you organize these points in a way that works better for oral delivery? How can you design your slides in ways that take advantage of a more visual medium and that complement (but not replace) your oral delivery?

You might also, like Sullivan, rework this piece into a more traditional article. How would that shift the approach you take and the moves you make?

link

Digital Toolbox
See Part IV, Section 6

Key Concepts

essay 246
intertextuality 258

Evaluating Cultural Productions **in a** Digital Age

CHAPTER TWELVE

CENTRAL QUESTIONS

1 What are the features of our informal reviewing activities and the reviews we read and post for wider circulation as cultural practices?

2 How do reviews take shape in particular contexts, foster larger conversations, and work within textual ecologies?

3 What effective reviewing moves can be applied when composing a review for a specific context?

Chapter Preview

In Chapter 11, we looked at the sharing of knowledge in public digital spaces, in the shorter content articles from sites like HubPages that have been set up to generate material for other users, and in the longer feature articles and blog posts written to offer readers new meanings and to contribute to an extended public conversation. On the online sites of journals of cultural commentary, like *The Atlantic,* writers engage a general (nonspecialist) audience of readers in extended thinking about topics of shared public interest, among them questions related to a digital culture. At the same time, blogs of cultural and political commentary, sometimes the work of the same writers, support a more extended conversation with a community of readers. Both typically invite reader comments, and some blog writers, like Andrew Sullivan, work with and integrate those comments into their own succeeding posts, partially erasing the line between writer and reader.

In this chapter we'll focus on another set of contexts in which we are likely to participate as writers, as well as readers, in public exchanges online: the multiple review sites that have made it easy for writers to reach a wider audience with their own impressions and experiences—their own evaluations of the quality of the movies they see, the music they hear, the food they are served. Reviewing is another way in which we, as readers and writers, are joining the public knowledge-building and knowledge-sharing activities of contemporary culture. While the world of interactive media allows more of us to become creative producers of culture, composing and playing our own music, following online tutorials on painting with social community discussion, contributing to writers' sites or fan fiction, it also allows us to share how we view others' productions.

Reviewing has become a widespread cultural practice, and much more than in the past, we're now likely to not only read reviews, but also write them for an audience of others who may be interested in our opinions of music, books, movies, restaurants, products, etc. In doing so, we're participating in new audience communities with people who share our interests and might comment on, like, or share the reviews we post. As readers and writers in these review contexts, we are engaged in a form of **cultural criticism**, focusing our attention on the various products and productions of our contemporary culture and looking carefully to see how they work and why. The wide circulation of reviews also shows how digital resources are reshaping the ways in which we share ideas and collaboratively assess cultural productions in our ordinary lives. And our digital reviewing practices intersect with other shifts in our larger culture.

....
cultural criticism
public commentary and
discussion of a cultural
production

Reviewing typically involves analysis of the sort we've been doing in the preceding chapters, but it goes beyond looking at **how** something works within a particular context to considering **how *well*** it works for its audience and purpose. A review can also be seen as a form of argument (something we'll consider more in depth in Chapter 15), one where the writer has come to a position based on experience and observation—reading a book, seeing a movie, listening to a song—and has carefully considered how and how well the work functions and now shares that position and gives evidence to support it. Such an argument about whether this book or movie or song is worth reading or seeing or hearing includes an evaluation of whatever is under review.

How do we decide not only whether something is literature or music or art, but also whether it is a "good" example of that form? Such value judgments take place within a context, sometimes within a smaller community, like a band's most loyal fans or a face-to-face book group. But in most realms of cultural production, the wider circulation of texts expands the community beyond the local toward increasingly public and global cultural exchange and a wider shared sense of what's valuable.

Exploring
The Practice of Reviewing

Within their local communities, people have always shared their opinions of the things they experience, whether simply by making a face after tasting a new food, giving a shout out to someone who's presenting at a group gathering, or clicking "like" for a Facebook post. Such responses are like mini-reviews, an opinion without any supporting reasons for it (though those could usually be added: "it's too bitter"; "she's contributed x, y, and z"; "you've used just the right words to express what many of us are feeling"). But because those opinions are shared in very familiar contexts with much shared knowledge, few words may be needed for a shared understanding. As opinions are shared with a wider audience, such shared knowledge and shared ways of conveying an opinion have to be fostered, and the unsupported opinion gradually becomes a review, with implicit or explicit expectations for both the form and substance of the review. Our reviewing practices take on new shapes and revolve around different questions in different contexts, but we can begin to discover more about this widespread online literacy practice by looking first at our most familiar settings.

Reviewing in Local and Global Contexts

In our informal local settings, we not only share quick opinions, but we also begin to turn those into informal word-of-mouth reviews. In face-to-face conversations we tell friends why they should see a particular movie or buy a particular product, and we make those friend-to-friend exchanges online as well, through posting and sharing on Snapchat, Tumblr, Twitter, or other social media platforms. These online exchanges have similar purposes and often similar content, but their shape and structure, style and tone, may be quite different.

We can think about the act of reviewing with our analytic tools of **what**, **why**, **how**, and **where**, asking

- what's being reviewed;
- why it's being reviewed (what purpose that act serves at this moment and in this community);
- how it's being reviewed (the style of language, the reviewer's stance, personal or objective, and the elements that seem to be expected within a particular community); and
- where it's being reviewed, the particular reviewing context that gives shape to these other elements.

Different communities pay attention to particular products or productions that reflect the shared interests of the community, and over time they typically develop shared criteria for what makes a good version of the things that interest them. Digital platforms make it easier to share and circulate reviews, and they also make it easier for us to see a community's interests, reviewing practices, and evaluation criteria.

INQUIRY

#1: Informal reviews within a local community

Identify texting or online exchanges in one of your immediate communities in which members share an opinion about an object of interest (a song, a movie, a TV program, etc.). Consider what makes a good version of that object of interest to members of this community. What implicit criteria do they look for (and how explicit do they make these)? How do they present their case to others, and how do others voice agreement/disagreement? Why does this sort of "reviewing" happen in this group?

Compare what you find about such informal reviewing across different communities. As you do this, note what this kind of comparison reveals about the different communities and the object of interest being reviewed. What shared assumptions, shared values, and shared ways seem to shape the sorts of things the community reviews and how?

> ❝❝ Moves are steps that have a specific communicative function within a type of exchange, ones that members of a discourse community would expect to find within a particular writing context. ❞❞

Reviewing Practices in Wider Review Contexts

More formal reviews intended to reach larger audiences traditionally appeared in print—in newspapers or magazines, or journals of criticism. Now the act of reviewing has moved online, with a broad circulation of reviews that are not only being read by wider audiences, but also written by members of these audiences as well, on general product sites (Amazon or Epinions), on movie sites (Rotten Tomatoes), and on dedicated book sites (Goodreads). Almost anything that can be reviewed now has a public platform on which it's reviewed, often building a community of repeat reviewers and readers. And some platforms, such as Amazon's, allow readers to rate reviews as helpful and to comment on their quality, giving feedback to writers.

With all of this activity, researchers have tried to discover more about the current practice of reviewing, looking at various review sites to see who posts and how often, but also **how** reviews are shaped in each reviewing context.

Scholars who study such exchanges, whether informal or formal, online or off, typically start their study of **how** with the two genre analysis concepts, **moves** and **strategies**, that we discussed in Chapter 1.[12:1] Moves (like the moves we've been pointing to in our composing section of each chapter) are steps that have a specific communicative function within a type of exchange, ones that members of a discourse community would expect to find within a particular writing context. So a typical move for reviewing a book would be to introduce that book. But writers might use different strategies for doing so: beginning by quoting a few lines, beginning by giving a brief summary of its content, or beginning by giving information about its context. In each case, the goal of such introductory moves is to build the necessary background knowledge a particular audience will need to understand what follows.

Sidenote

Criticism is a scholarly genre that has much in common with the review.

. . . .

moves
intentional steps for writing and communicating in rhetorical situations

. . . .

strategies
specific, practical uses of writing technologies for addressing specific rhetorical situations

A study of Amazon product reviews (see a sample review prompt in Figure 12.1) that were rated helpful by readers found that such reviews had a number of common moves, with several different strategies for accomplishing each.[12:2]

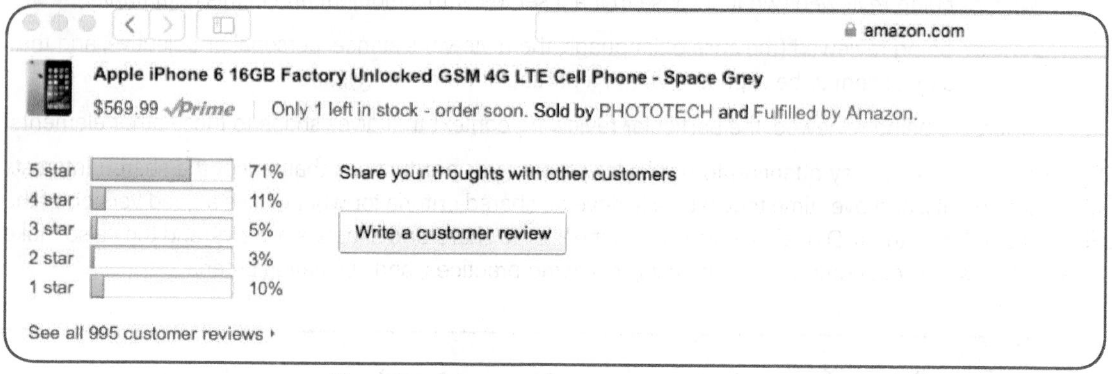

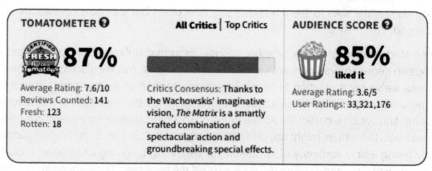

Figure 12.1: Amazon review summary and prompt

Typical moves included the following:

- Giving an evaluation of the product;

- Providing general user information about the product (a description, how it works, tips about its use); and

- Offering an account of personal experience with the product, and offering a comparison with other products.

The strategies for carrying out these moves were different, however, with some focusing directly on the writer's personal experience (with first person pronouns, "I tried. . ."), some on the readers' likely experience (with second person pronouns, "You won't. . ."), and some primarily on the product itself (with demonstrative or third person pronouns, "this product," "it"). The study found that experience-based reviews were seen as most helpful overall, but negative reviews were found to be more helpful when they focused on product comparisons rather than personal complaints. It seems that some shared criteria for good reviews have developed within the Amazon review community, and that they exclude too much complaining.

So the practice of reviewing, as it's carried out in different contexts, may include some common elements—some similar descriptive and evaluative moves. Yet the emphasis on some moves over others, and the specific strategies for accomplishing these moves, may differ significantly in the context of different interests and communities. As we know, participants in discourse communities, including more public, online communities, most often share not only areas of interest, but also background knowledge about those interests and some shared beliefs and values within that domain. They're likely to share their purposes for coming together, as well as ways of accomplishing those purposes.

Figure 12.2: Rotten Tomatoes review

For reviewing, the context includes not only the sort of thing being reviewed, but also who the reviewer is, who the imagined readers are, where the review is posted/published (including how an online platform is set up), and when. Media review sites have different priorities and concerns than product review sites (or restaurant review sites, or travel review sites) do. And, not surprisingly, there are usually differences between reviews written by professional or more experienced reviewers and those written by fans.

A study of movie reviews (see sample review in Figure 12.2), carried out much like the Amazon product review study mentioned above, looked at those written by film critics versus those written by the general public.[12:3] The researchers found common moves by both sets of reviewers. Some of these were descriptive moves.

- Giving practical information about the movie
- Describing the movie
- Placing the movie in context

Others were evaluative moves.

- Giving criticism
- Recommending the movie to the reader

But professional reviewers made more descriptive moves and rarely used first person pronouns in their criticisms and recommendations, while amateur reviewers made more evaluative moves, most often in the first person. The focus of their evaluations also suggested that professional film critics held different criteria than most ordinary viewers. This supported earlier studies showing that while ordinary viewers tend to prefer blockbuster-type movies with big stars, professional critics are more likely to favor "movies that are challenging, have abstract qualities of cinematic style, and move away from familiar settings." (This may explain why we are more often puzzled by movies with four-star ratings.)

Looking at a number of reviews from a particular context will let you discover more about how reviews in that context are typically structured, what moves are made and how, and what the typical style and tone are for amateurs or professionals writing reviews in that context. You might find and name other types of moves as well. While this particular research identified *descriptive moves* (focusing on **what** is included in the object being reviewed) and *evaluative moves* (focusing on **how well** the object works) there are also *moves of analysis* in most reviewing practices that look more carefully at **how** a cultural production works (how the elements that are included work together to make meaning), as well as **how well** it works, as we'll see below.

INQUIRY

???

#2: Finding moves made by reviewers of cultural productions in different online settings

Form groups by shared interest in a form of media: a TV program, film, music group, or book. Find online reviews by searching on review sites such as Blogcritics, Paste Magazine, Pitchfork, or Goodreads. Consider the likely audience for this site and its shared values, expectations, and interests. What descriptive, analytical, and evaluative moves are made, and how? What criteria are used to evaluate what's being reviewed? What seems to make a good review in this context?

How would you sum up the common genre practices for reviews in the setting—the typical moves that are made and how? If you've found reviews by both professional and amateur reviewers, what differences appear in the moves they make and the ways in which they make them? As you compare notes on different sites, what similarities and differences do you find? Why do you think the differences might exist?

Making Connections
Reading Reviews within a Context

Online reviews often reach a large audience and can have great power to shape opinion in ways that can make or break the success of a product or other type of cultural production. To get a sense of the ways in which reviews can circulate and review conversations can shift within one media context where there is typically widely shared public interest in a form of cultural production, we are going to begin with a particular music review and move out to consider related posts that give us a richer sense of the reviewing context for one group, one album, and its larger textual ecology. The moves we'll make could be applied to any example of a cultural production that has generated a number of reviews.

Exploring a Multifaceted Review Context

link 🔗▶

The following review appeared in *Pitchfork*,[L12:1] an online music publication that reviews independent music and that has had a large impact on what happens to that music. An article about *Pitchfork* in the *Washington Post* [12:4] describes its founder, Ryan Schreiber, as someone who started a music review blog as a new college grad with no public writing experience. It describes how his blog developed into the powerful and influential Pitchfork Media. *Pitchfork* (Figure 12.3) reviews have had the power to build a large following for musicians, or do the reverse and make them uncool to listen to.

Here's a somewhat typical review from the site, a 2012 review of Florence and the Machine's *MTV Unplugged* album. An "unplugged" performance or album refers to the unplugging of electronic instruments to create an acoustic performance, and the MTV program MTV Unplugged has been the venue for such performances and resulting albums, which typically build off of earlier "plugged" versions. In fact, the interplay of recording and performance is one more example of how cultural productions are circulated and recast in contemporary society.

Pitchfork:

❝ a guide to the underground musical wilderness ❞

❝ a hilariously snarky, oft-elitist, sometimes impenetrable but entertaining and occasionally even enlightening internet music magazine ❞

Pitchfork

THE LATEST   REVIEWS   BEST NEW MUSIC   FEATURES   ARTISTS   VIDEO   EVENTS

Figure 12.3: Pitchfork masthead

BEFORE READING:
Reading and annotating

As you read and annotate Zoladz's review, consider the following questions.

➤ Zoladz makes a number of key moves in this review. One is introducing the album and placing it in a larger context. What do you observe about her strategies for making this move and the contexts she brings in?

➤ What does she assume, you, as a reader, already know about or want to know about the program, the resulting album, and about its content—music and performances and MTV? What strategies does she use to place her readers inside this world?

➤ What other moves do you find that seem to be descriptive? Analytical? Evaluative?

➤ What seems to be the purpose of this review? What understandings about Florence and The Machine and the strengths and limitations of this example of their work does Zoladz want her readers to take away?

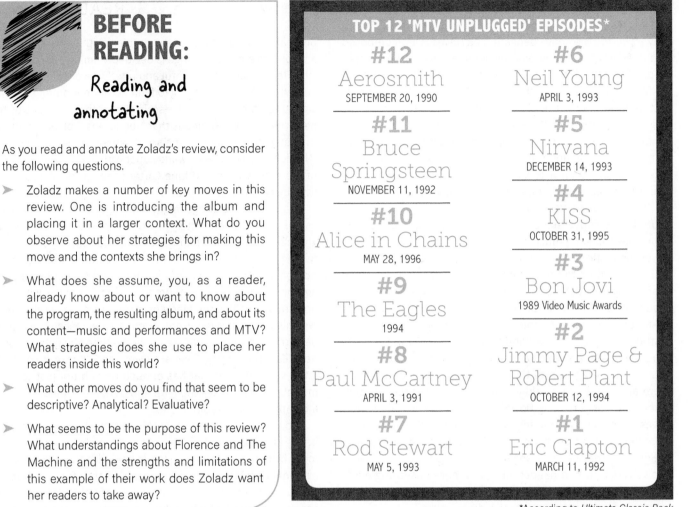

TOP 12 'MTV UNPLUGGED' EPISODES*

#12 Aerosmith SEPTEMBER 20, 1990	#6 Neil Young APRIL 3, 1993
#11 Bruce Springsteen NOVEMBER 11, 1992	#5 Nirvana DECEMBER 14, 1993
#10 Alice in Chains MAY 28, 1996	#4 KISS OCTOBER 31, 1995
#9 The Eagles 1994	#3 Bon Jovi 1989 Video Music Awards
#8 Paul McCartney APRIL 3, 1991	#2 Jimmy Page & Robert Plant OCTOBER 12, 1994
#7 Rod Stewart MAY 5, 1993	#1 Eric Clapton MARCH 11, 1992

*According to *Ultimate Classic Rock*
Source: http://ultimateclassicrock.com/top-mtv-unplugged-episodes/

READING

"Florence and the Machine: MTV Unplugged"[12:5]
by Lindsay Zoladz
Pitchfork review,[12:2] April 12, 2012

To answer your first question: Yes, they still do these. "MTV Unplugged" was once a showcase for pop culture writ impossibly large—a place where the entire world could gasp at Gene Simmons' bare face or where Kurt Cobain could introduce over five million record buyers to the Vaselines. But in recent years, the show's institutional power has fizzled, and its most recent installments have featured tepid, obligatorily low-lit performances from are-they-really-*that*-famous? acts like 30 Seconds to Mars and Young the Giant. Which is why Florence and the Machine's *Unplugged* instalment feels so promising. One of the more compelling pop acts to spring up in recent years, it's hard to imagine a voice more equipped to puff new life into the series than that of celestially soulful frontwoman Florence Welch. As on mega-hits like "Dog Days Are Over"and "Shake It Out", Welch has displayed a talent for sprawling her demons and heartbreak across canvases bigger than the sky: Every song she's ever sung has been writ large.

And occasionally, that's the problem. While her promising 2009 debut, *Lungs*, had the skittish, genre-hopping restlessness of an artist still settling into her sound, the 12 tracks on its followup, *Ceremonials*, came in only one size: gigantic. Even the ballads beat with earth-shaking percussion were gilded with epic, Greek choral background vocals and all other varieties of sonic baubles. Though Welch's voice is undeniably powerful, the songs beneath it all *seemed* well-composed and deeply felt, but their emotional impact was often blunted by producer Paul Epworth's unrelenting maximalism, ramped up from his work on Welch's debut. Which makes them perfect candidates for the classic scaled-back, stripped-down approach, right? You'd think so.

In quite a few cases, the *Unplugged* treatment does work wonders. The opening number, "Only if for a Night", is more arresting here than it is kicking off *Ceremonials,* where its haunting power (the song is about being visited in a dream by the ghost of a loved one: typical Florence stuff) was interrupted by a superfluous, glitchy beat. The *Unplugged* version gives the song much-needed room to breathe, and with fewer distractions the searing imagery of Welch's lyrics have a chance to float to the surface. "And the grass was so green against my new clothes," she trills, losing herself in the song's second verse, "And I did cartwheels in your honor dancing on tip-toes/My own secret ceremonials before the service began/In the graveyard, doing handstands." It's an oddly joyous funeral rite, but it's Welch articulating the feeling she plumbs best—deriving light from the deepest darkness and feeling more at home in the world of spirits than the corporeal one. Same goes for "Breaking Down." On *Ceremonials*, that song's edges are padded with stately chamber-pop echoes, as though to protect Welch from bruises as she wrestles her demons to the ground. The sparse arrangement of the *Unplugged* version allows Welch to find deeper and even more unsettling emotion in the song, transforming the chorus from a pop hook to something like a moaning, seasick dirge.

Some of the greatest "MTV Unplugged" moments have been somewhat unlikely covers (Maxwell doing Kate Bush! Nirvana doing Lead Belly!), and here we get Welch adding to this enduring trope with her take on "Try a Little Tenderness". It's a lovely vocal performance (she hits a note early on that will probably prompt someone to book her for an upcoming Whitney tribute),

but it also brings into focus the problem with her *Unplugged* as a whole: Its emotional range is decidedly limited. Welch's "Try a Little Tenderness" is mournful and utterly devoid of playfulness, and—though no one's going to fault her for her putting her own signature spin on a classic—so is every other moment of this performance. Which means that "Tenderness" bleeds right into the song after it, an acoustic arrangement of the power-ballad "No Light, No Light." Her twangy duet with Josh Homme, a cover of the Johnny Cash and June Carter song "Jackson", provides a little deviation, but not much.

Many of these songs might sound good on their own, but listening to them one after the other exposes their repetitions. There's only a certain number of times you can listen to Welch feeling lost in the verse and then found, transcendently, in the bombast of the chorus before it all starts to feel like a package of "Amazing Grace"-themed magnetic poetry, with each new track shuffling the elements around just so. Unlike one of Welch's songs, though, *Unplugged* is a decrescendo, and the performance runs out of steam by the time she gets to two of her best songs, "Dog Days are Over" and "Shake it Out". The latter, a torch song that has enough oomph not just to move mountains but to pick them up and punt them, peters out into a disappointingly tepid finale.

No one who listens to *Unplugged* will accuse Welch of being an untalented singer, but they might be left wanting more from the material she lends her voice to. Fans will enjoy hearing Welch's songs opened up in this format, but her *Unplugged* definitely doesn't rank among the classics of the series. The artists who have been responsible for the best and most enduring *Unplugged* albums—Nirvana, Lauryn Hill, and Jay-Z's collaboration with the Roots—all used the candle-lit stage to explore new directions in their respective sounds. For Welch, it serves the opposite end: It displays the boundlessness of her vocal talent but finds her tethered to a frustratingly limited aesthetic. ∎

AFTER READING:
A reviewer's positioning

To review a book, you have to show yourself to be a knowledgeable reader. To review music, you have to position yourself as knowledgeable about the music you're reviewing while evoking the shared background knowledge your readers bring. What strategies does Zoladz use as she positions herself as an insider to a relevant area of the world of music? In what ways does she show her knowledge and rich understandings of the world she enters through this review? What does she suggest about MTV Unplugged and its viewers? How does she anticipate the prior knowledge they bring? What does she show about herself and her values, expectations, and interests?

A review can be seen as a form of **evaluative argument,** in which the writer makes the moves of taking a position and backing it up with evidence from an analysis of what is being reviewed. Evaluating the quality of a cultural production as good, bad, or mixed suggests that the reviewer has specific criteria for making such a judgment and is measuring the work against those criteria in determining how well it works.

evaluative argument
a form of persuasion based on criteria about quality or usefulness

---

INQUIRY

#3: Responding to an evaluative argument

What position is Zoladz taking about this *MTV Unplugged* album? What seem to be her criteria for a good Unplugged performance, and how does this album match up against those criteria? What evidence does she use to support her position? Are you convinced by her argument?

Based on this evidence Zoladz offers, she gives the album a numerical rating of 5.9 out of 10. Would *Pitchfork's* often-criticized practice of assigning numerical ratings affect your own sense of the album's quality, or might you use the words of the review to come to a different judgment?

Listen to some of the group's *MTV Unplugged* album, or watch the video of their <u>MTV Unplugged performance</u>.[L12:3] Does your own experience fit with Zoladz's evaluation? What points would you agree with? Argue against?

See Chapter 15
for an extended discussion of arguments to support positions.

We've described the *Pitchfork* review context and the role that this publication plays in the music industry. And you've considered the contexts evoked by Zoladz in her review. In addition, the online platform itself affects how we understand and respond to a review, and we suggest that you now look at this review in its <u>original online context</u>.[L12:4]

INQUIRY

#4: The context of the platform

Pitchfork's online platform supports links within the text and related content around the review text. What visual/aural context is this review situated in? How does both the content of the surrounding panels and the visual appearance of the whole affect your response as a reader of this review? Within the text itself, do you find the links useful in providing further background information, or possibly distracting? What elements might you find desirable if you compose your own music review?

Placing a Review in an Intertextual Context

In the music industry, as in other areas of cultural production, there is often a rich discussion of popular work across review sites, and sometimes a discussion of those review sites themselves. The music review blog <u>Tuning Fork</u> [L12:5] was created to offer an alternative voice to *Pitchfork's* about the independent music scene. It lasted only a few years before its founder tired of the demands of maintaining a blog. An end-of-year post from 2005 comments on the quality of writing on *Pitchfork* (PFM is Pitchfork Media):[12:6]

What makes us post against Pitchfork in the first place: The PFM writers who don't fact check, those who plagiarize, those who use too many A-typical music review phrases or drop too many other band names...no less the inappropriate ones, those who offer negative opinions without backing it up with logical mature useful information, those who simply don't seem to have any real knowledge of the band they are reviewing, those who pad a review with meaningless paragraphs and there are about a million other ways a record review can go wrong so it is almost silly to try to create a list. . .

Talent aside there is occasionally a level of humor, care, unique insight, thoughtfulness and knowledge that comes across in a great piece of work and it is important to celebrate those writers too.

INQUIRY

#5: Evaluating the evaluators

Revisiting the review of the Florence and the Machine album, where do you think Tuning Fork would place this review (which came after Tuning Fork had discontinued new posts). Would it have elicited a negative Tuning Fork response for the negative qualities listed above, or would Zoladz have been one of the writers to be celebrated?

In 2013, Pitchfork Media created a print publication, with long-form feature articles (the genre we've seen from *The New Yorker* and *The Atlantic*) about the music world, while continuing the popular online review site. Now it seems that the style of the online reviews has been changing over time (and time is one dimension of context), perhaps influenced by the context of the print essays. Compare this "pitch," an excerpt from a more "pay attention" type review of rapper Kendrick Lamar's album[L12:6] (*To Pimp a Butterfly*)[12:7] with the review of Florence and the Machine. The reviewer chooses not to focus on details of any song in the album he's reviewing, but rather on placing Lamar's work within the context of the black experience, evaluating the work on how it speaks to that experience, contrasting it with the work of Kanye West, and rejecting the idea that the album should be reviewed in the usual way.

Credit: Ari Marcopoulos

Figure 12.4: Kendrick Lamar Pitchfork review

Unlike other artists whose juxtaposition of hip-hop bluster with confessional vulnerability feels like shtick, Kendrick does not do performative honesty. Rather, he performs honestly. And expertly. Do not buy it when critics will inevitably try to sell you that his work is rough or unbridled, the magic work of a hood savant. It is precise and skilled, as perfect in technical execution as it is uninhibited in content. *Butterfly* is not the recording of a natural genius. It is the record of a working artist who has been visited by genius and who has a deep and earned mastery of his form.

It is not fake, it is not afraid, and it is not accidental. Kendrick's hip-hop is not the hip-hop that allows white guys to breathe. He does not break off pieces of blackness as a hood souvenir that you can post on your wall or bump in your car in order to feel like it's all good. He doesn't even mention you at all. It is not about you. It is about him and his complete humanity. It is about the humanity of every other black person whose face is painted on the mural of this wall of sound. The question then becomes how hard and for how long will America continue to fight, deny, or ignore this humanity.

That is for you to decide when you are listening to his work in its completion. When you are alone with his words, do you hear them? Do you believe them? Or do you attempt to lump them together with whatever hackneyed and two-dimensional concept you have of "Compton?"

Rather than reviewing this album, let's review what we do with it.

Kendrick's music cannot free us. But how we respond to Kendrick's music just might.

You might also look for a *Pitchfork* review or pitch for another independent artist who interests you. Or go back to find a Tuning Fork post that responds directly to a *Pitchfork* review (usually with a link to the original review). Or read the brief *Rolling Stone*[L12:7] review and the New Musical Express (NME) review[L12:8] of Florence and the Machine's *MTV Unplugged* album to compare their approaches and evaluation. You might also want to return to the songs highlighted in any of these reviews, to see whether your own evaluation is different from what you've found in the reviews.

links

INQUIRY

#6: Learning more about a review context

As you move around, examining different reviews about different artists, or from different music review sites, what picture do you get of the conversations that go on within the community of music followers/critics and the various ways in which they work toward the same underlying purpose, discovering what's worth paying attention to in the vast world of current independent music? From your experience of these reviews as a reader, what criteria would you set for a "good" and/or "useful" review for a particular context and purpose?

Reading Advice from an Online Reviewer

While music review sites offer one context for reading a review, a more general cultural review site can provide further understanding of what effective reviews of cultural productions look like and can help both readers and writers of reviews to evaluate them. Blogcritics[L12:9] is a blog site that offers reviews of the arts and culture. Like many blogs, it has built a community of writers and readers, with more than 4,000 registered writers and more than a million monthly readers in 2014.

link

See Part II Additional Readings
for the full two-part essay on page 375.

Here's Mark Schannon's introduction to his blog essay, "So You Want to Be a Critic," which continues with a second post on "Guidelines for Writing Reviews."[12:8]

Introduction

A reviewer, regardless of the art form, has a responsibility to readers to be knowledgeable about the specific art form. Reviewers do not simply express opinions. There's a huge difference between "I **liked** *Killer Ants Devouring Lithuania*," and "*Killer Ants Devouring Lithuania* was a **good** movie."

In the former, you're only expressing a personal opinion based on your likes and dislikes. You have the right to that opinion, but as a reader, my reaction is, "who cares?" I want to know about the movie or book, not about you. In the latter, you have a set of criteria by which you can judge the work of art. Too many people fail to see or accept that distinction. If you fall into this category, you'll write lousy reviews of no interest to the reader; you'll merely be feeding your own ego by seeing your name in print.

But if you study the medium, its history and trends, if you can break a performance into its component parts to evaluate how they fit together, if you can put your review into the context of similar works, then you're offering valuable insights that will help readers decide whether to experience the art, and you're teaching them how to enhance their experience and appreciation.

Schannon goes on to talk about a number of elements (what we've been calling moves) that make up an effective review.

- The hook (the opening that draws a reader in)

- After the hook (setting the stage for what will follow, suggesting the writer's purpose)

- Other elements that will form the body of the review—the art form and its context, the genre and how this example fits into it, trends that it's part of, the criteria for judging it, and the specific artistic elements that make up the item being reviewed, such as the lighting and costumes for a play, or the quality of sound-mixing for music

- And the close, leaving the reader with a new understanding

Schannon is also part of an audience community made up of people who read and write reviews. While he's specifically addressing readers who want to become reviewers, he is also addressing the other reviewers who contribute to Blogcritics. The examples he uses come from their reviews and show both what they've done that he assesses as effective, by criteria he's naming, and what revisions he might make to their already published reviews.

INQUIRY

#7: Applying Schannon's advice to Zoladz's review

Read Schannon's essay, "So You Want to be a Critic" in Part II Additional Readings, along with his specific suggestions for writing music reviews. Schannon's advice draws on his experience as part of the Blogcritics community—a review site that draws a more general audience as compared to *Pitchfork's* narrower focus on the indie music world. How does his advice fit with what you've found in Zoladz's review? Which of his key elements appear among the moves you've found her making? Are any missing that, as a reader, you wish she'd included (or handled differently)? Are there any moves she made that could add to those Schannon discusses? What ideas about the practice of reviewing will you draw on as you work toward writing your own review of music or another genre of cultural production?

Composing
Review

In an American culture where almost everyone listens to music, reads books, goes to movies, or watches TV shows, where many review sites exist and where anyone can write a review, reviewing has become an important public genre and one way in which you can join in a larger public conversation. It is also, itself, a form of cultural production. You'll want to draw on the reviews you've explored as you think about the kind of review you'd like to write and the type of audience you'd like to reach.

WRITING MOVES

Inquiring and Inventing

Schannon talks about the importance, in reviewing, of offering a reasoned critical argument for evaluating the work you are interested in, not just giving your opinion. Some necessary preparatory moves are described below.

1 Identifying a review subject

Choose a genre of cultural production you'd like to review in an area you know something about, where you can position yourself as knowledgeable and worth listening to. Why might you be a good reviewer for this particular work in this genre? What sorts of prior knowledge and expertise do you bring to this reviewing activity? Why do you want to review this work? What is your purpose? And how might you position yourself?

2 Deciding on a review context and seeing moves typically made

Where do you find other reviews of this type of creative activity? Which review site fits best with your own sensibility, with where you'd like to add your own voice? What sort of audience would you like to connect with? (Blogcritics is a good site for

reaching an audience of readers who have a more general interest in contemporary culture.) Read some other reviews on the site you choose and see what moves are common to them—moves you're likely to want to try out in your own review.

3 Describing, analyzing, and evaluating

Researchers have identified these as different sorts of moves made in reviewing, but they're typically interwoven. You'll want to decide how much you need to describe the work (**what**), creating shared knowledge with your readers. You'll want to look carefully at **how** this cultural production works—its key elements and how they fit together to create a particular effect and convey particular meanings. And you'll want to determine the criteria you think make a work of this type effective, considering **how well** this work meets those criteria. Look at Schannon's guidelines for specific questions to consider in reviewing different genres of creative work.

WRITING MOVES

Drafting and Shaping

Reviews, like other genres, take on particular forms as they appear in specific contexts. Nevertheless, the common elements or moves that Schannon has identified from his work with Blogcritics are useful ones to draw on as you begin to give shape to your own review. Once you've worked out what you want to say in your review and why, you are ready to work with those moves.

1 Finding a hook

Reread what Schannon has said about the hook. What will capture your readers' attention? What has hooked you in the reviews you've read? And how will you follow the hook, focusing attention on the work rather than on yourself?

2 Providing context

Schannon points to several elements of context you might consider: the art form and perhaps its history and "how what's being reviewed fits or varies from that form," the other work that's being done within the genre, or the trends (societal, political, religious, artistic movements) that this piece of art references. We've seen that Zoladz, in her review, addresses several aspects of context: the MTV Unplugged program ("once a showcase for pop culture writ impossibly large") from which Florence and the Machine's *MTV Unplugged* album was drawn, the context of the singer's other work, and background about the group's usual "plugged-in" productions, providing both shared knowledge for the reader and a context for the evaluation of the specific work on this album. Zoladz sees the genre of unplugged, acoustic music as potentially offering a new opportunity to a group whose work she finds to be overproduced in the studio.

3 Drawing on your analysis of key elements of the work and how they measure up against your criteria for evaluation

Schannon reminds us that we need to pay attention to the details of the artistic production being reviewed, including questions of tone, message, pacing, timing, and especially importance: "Does this work of art set new standards, raise new questions, demand that the viewer or reader challenge his or her preconceptions?" What details and examples from the work you're reviewing can best show how it measures up to the criteria you've set? Zoladz quotes from lyrics as one way of making her points.

4 Adding other key elements, including images or audio

In *Pitchfork* reviews, links—to the group's website, to other reviews of its work, to its other albums, to performance videos on YouTube—contribute significantly to placing the work in context, and Zoladz's review uses all of these links, along with one image of the album cover. The links allow readers to listen to the songs Zoladz points to. It could be even more effective to include small audio files with snippets that exemplify the points she's making, but for a

Digital Toolbox
See Part IV, Section 4

public site, that would involve copyright concerns, with costly music permissions needed. (If you post to a private course site or are making a Prezi or PowerPoint presentation that will only be shared on a private site, you have more flexibility in bringing in actual examples.) In any event, you'll want to do as much as you can with links, images, sound, and video to bring your readers into the work you're discussing on the review site you choose. Capturing your own photos or videos of a live music, dance, or theater performance (if allowed) can give you one resource for enriching your discussion of the work.

5 Providing a closing

In your closing, you'll leave your readers with a strong final impression of the work you've been reviewing, clinching the evaluative argument you've been making about it. Here's an example Schannon gives of how he would improve the close of a published review:

> Here's a close that could have been much better had the writer just left himself out of the picture:

> "I'm sure my friends from the party are talking about my musical tastes behind my back. At forty-six, I probably should be more immersed in jazz, classical, and pop then I am. But let the mf'ers talk — so much of what we call entertainment these days is flat and boring. At least NOFX and other bands approaching middle age still have the balls to produce some very funny stuff."

Start reading from "so much of what we call entertainment. . ." and you'll see how powerful the ending could have been.

And here's Zoladz's close, contrasting what's been achieved in the best Unplugged work with what she finds in the album she's reviewing:

> The artists who have been responsible for the best and most enduring *Unplugged* albums—Nirvana, Lauryn Hill, and Jay-Z's collaboration with the Roots—all used the candle-lit stage to explore new directions in their respective sounds. For Welch, it serves the opposite end: It displays the boundlessness of her vocal talent but finds her tethered to a frustratingly limited aesthetic.

We think Schannon would approve.

WRITING MOVES

Revising and Publishing

From your initial choice of the review context you're writing for, you've already made some decisions about how and where you'd like to circulate a review. As you fine-tune your work for that site, you'll want to get feedback from others who are familiar with the site, or at least with the genre and subgenre you're reviewing.

Mark Schannon carried out a peer review process right on the Blogcritics site, posting an early version of his essay on reviewing, getting comments from his readers (many of whom were also involved in reviewing), and then revising his essay to incorporate those comments. You've read his final version. Here is his earlier introduction:

Schannon's original opening:

One of the problems trying to explain how to write a review is that there is no one way to do it. It's not like someone climbed a mountain and returned with stone tablets from "you know who" with the absolute last world on being a critic. They're more like thin layers of soft clay that keep getting crunched and missed up.

For someone just starting out, don't let all the junk here intimidate you. Read the article for the major points, and, as time goes by, you'll be able to incorporate more and more—adjusting it to your own style and tastes. For more experienced reviewers, treat the article like a refresher course. Maybe there's a gem you hadn't thought of before, or an idea that will help you better break the rules.

In his second version, after receiving readers' comments and deciding to include some of them, Schannon added the following paragraphs to his opening section, telling his readers more explicitly that the blog post is part of his ongoing effort to define effective reviews in a way that will help other writers, and that he's inviting further comments that may support further revisions.

Schannon's second version:

And just as I'm incorporating comments from people when I posted this on BC, if you see something you disagree with or that I missed, send me an e-mail. I'm always willing to revise this article.

When I posted this article on BC, Che had some excellent advice. He also wrote, "Rules are good. Breaking rules is better." He's absolutely right. I love breaking rules. But…you can't break the rules if you don't know what they are. The Picasso museum in Paris is organized chronologically. Among the paintings from his "Blue" period was this incredibly realistic painting. It was as if Picasso was saying, "Look I can paint realism, I know all the rules of composition, color, perspective, etc. I just don't want to do that anymore." But he was able to paint such incredible work because he'd learned the basics of painting.

What follows will integrate suggestions based on how most critics write reviews, and absolute, unbreakable rules that apply most of the time except when you decide to ignore them. I'll try to identify them as they appear.

Also, at the end of this article, I'll list guidelines for each art form to help you keep track of what things to consider.

For Schannon, readers' comments served as a kind of assessment of work-in-progress, offering additional perspectives or critiques for him to take into account as a writer as he worked his way toward the final two-part version, with an advice essay and a set of guidelines that now appear on the site. By that final version, the explicit reference to readers no longer appears, but their comments have led him to a more substantial revision.

Before you begin your own revision process, you might want to undertake one more inquiry, comparing the three versions of Schannon's opening section to see what you can discover about how he worked with comments on his way to a final revision. What are the significant changes that appear in the final version of his opening, and how might they reflect the sorts of understandings he shared with other reviewers? Read his words about writing a hook following this introduction. Has he accomplished what he suggests there? Would you, as a reader, have further suggestions for him as a writer?

1 Forming peer response groups by genre and possible review sites

Although you might not be part of a long-standing reviewing community in the way that Zoladz and Schannon are, you can nevertheless create your own audience community with others who are writing reviews about the same genre of cultural production and perhaps for the same review site. If Schannon's guidelines include questions for the genre you're focusing on, you can use his questions as a starting point for your peer review (or adapt them to another genre). And consider the elements he discusses: the hook, the discussion of context and analysis and evaluation of various aspects of the review object, and the closing. Depending on your course context, you might have the opportunity to post your reviews and review comments on an online class site, making it easier to capture those comments and work with them in revising.

2 Revising

Decide how to work with your reviewer's comments. If someone has offered an important new insight, you might even want to quote that person, as Schannon has done in the second version of his review essay. More likely, you'll incorporate the key points of the responses in crafting a revised version of what you've written before. And you've most likely gathered some further ideas about how you might revise your own review from being a critical reader for others' reviews. Schannon shows how changes in sentences and paragraphs can alter their impact, particularly for hooks and closings, and you might want to look again at his examples as you work through your final version.

3 Matching your review with a public review site

At this point, you'll want to make a final determination of a review site to which you'll post a public version of your review. You might find that as you've crafted a review, you've made it more suitable for one site than another. Some sites, like Blogcritics, seek new writers to post longer essay reviews about different forms of cultural production to become reviews for the site. On others, like Amazon or iTunes, you don't have to register as a writer to post a review. Amazon accepts reviews of up to 5,000 words, but you have to have purchased the book or music you're reviewing. If you've carefully crafted a review that speaks to an informed audience, you might want to post it to a dedicated review site that seeks more substantive writing, but we often find extended and useful reviews on Amazon or iTunes, as well as the many other sites you may have looked at in Inquiry #2.

4 Applying finishing touches

As always, you'll want to proofread carefully. But you'll also want to consider how else you'll present your review on its final site. If you're including links, try to make sure that they all work at the moment you post (although some will inevitably change later), and that they all actually offer rich additional context for the descriptive, analytical, and evaluative moves you are making. If you're including images, make sure they are positioned in places that will enhance the visual impact of your post. When you're done, submit your post!

Reinventing and Circulating Your Work

Now that you've contributed your own review to a larger conversation, you can follow that review context in several ways.

➤ Chances are that someone else has reviewed the particular cultural production you've reviewed. Find three other reviews (including reviews by classmates). How does this collection of reviews, including your own, speak to the quality of the work being reviewed, the shared expectations for such work within a larger audience community, and the place of that work within a segment of contemporary culture? What can you learn about the place of creative production in contemporary society from the multifaceted exploration of review conversations that this chapter has focused on?

➤ You might also want to enlarge your framework of understanding by placing the genre of work you've chosen to review within a larger industry context. Some genres of creative cultural activity, such as music and its subgenres, are driven by corporate interests as much as by the individual talent of the artists, with the industry shaping the context and forms of creative activity that get developed. Researching the history of how genres such as hip-hop or salsa have evolved and have been treated within the industry can give you a richer understanding of how contemporary genre practices have arisen and the place of a particular example in extending or challenging those practices.

➤ As you consider these different contexts, you'll want to consider **how** and **why** reviews of the same cultural product may differ, and may differ widely. What kinds of different beliefs and values emerge in different reviews? How do diverging views work in relation to one another, and what do they suggest about the context of a cultural production? At this point you might want to reinvent your own work to reflect your enriched understanding of the ways in which a multifaceted review context can shape individual reviews. What might you add to or change in your original review that addresses what you've discovered by looking at multiple reviews or at the larger industry?

Key Concepts

cultural criticism 266	moves 267
evaluative argument 273	strategies 267

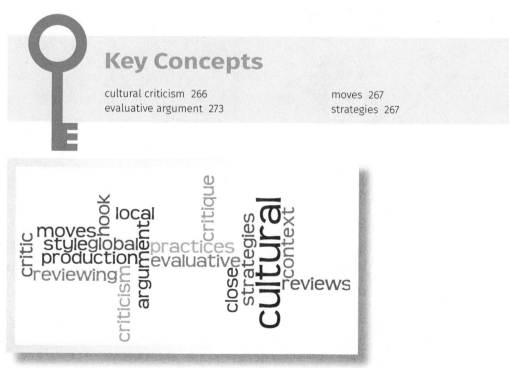

Analyzing Literature
as Cultural Critique

CHAPTER THIRTEEN

CENTRAL QUESTIONS

 How are critical perspectives on our digital culture being voiced?

2 How can we approach a piece of dystopian fiction to learn about present cultural concerns and shifting values?

3 What can our work with texts of cultural critique teach us about their larger contexts?

Chapter Preview

In this chapter, we'll turn our attention to some of the social concerns being raised as changing technologies alter many of our cultural practices, particularly those around how we communicate with one another, along with many of our beliefs and values about such fundamental issues as the right to privacy. Such cultural shifts are giving rise to much cultural critique—to a questioning of the effects these changes are having on our more fundamental human values and ways of being. That critique can take several forms. Some of it arises from what researchers are learning as they study the digital practices and related beliefs of various segments of society, especially young people, and that critique contributes to public argument based on that research. Some of it is represented visually, in the memes and images we post and circulate. It is also represented in another significant area of our cultural production: the literature we read and write.

Literature, particularly fiction, allows us to imagine the experiences of other people living in particular contexts, whether in our own time or sometime in the past or future, and to imagine societies that are both like and unlike our own. The literary genre of science fiction often imagines technological change into the future with both positive and negative effects. The utopian novel imagines better societies where present-day problems are resolved. Its counterpart, the dystopian novel, imagines worse societies, where present-day trends have negative consequences, and typically works as a form of extended cultural critique. After considering other modes of cultural critique, we'll turn our attention to an example of dystopian fiction.

Exploring
Cultural Critique

For insiders to digital culture, particularly for the "digital natives" who have grown up with digital technologies, the practices of the digital world, the ways they shape our interactions with both our local and a public/global world, and the ways they impact the larger social and economic structures of our society can seem entirely natural, and it is hard to imagine other possibilities. Culture is powerful. When we're in it, we just live it without really seeing it. We might, however, suspect that there could be other practices, other points of view, other beliefs and values, and we might note glimmers of concern about the ones we're immersed in. We can use those glimmers, those tracings, to begin to step outside of our immediate cultural experience to ask questions: What is going on? Is this the only way it can be? What are the effects of current practices, structures, and technologies? What other questions should we be asking? Stepping back in this way to question and to examine what would otherwise go unquestioned about our surrounding culture is the work of **cultural critique**, and we can begin that work by once again looking at what we post and circulate for hints of possible concerns and questions about rapid changes in our society (and in societies around the world) that are accompanying the development of new digital technologies.

cultural critique
questioning aspects of a culture

Circulating Memes and Cultural Critique

We've seen that the things that are posted and shared become memes when they circulate through large swaths of the public internet, and that they do so because they are seen as representing some shared meaning—about what's funny or cute, about the foibles of celebrities and politicians, about fandom—even if that meaning isn't explicitly stated. Increasingly what's shared hints at questions or concerns about our cultural values and practices. A search of pictures posted to Flickr with the tag "texting," for example, brings up many images of people completely involved with their devices (rather than with each other) (Figure 13.1).

Or we find images that point to different concerns, such as the public dangers inherent in the ways we're using these technologies (Figure 13.2).

Figure 13.1: Stereo texting

Figure 13.2: Texting while driving

Another implicitly **critical meme**, with many iterations, is the "wasting time" meme. Many versions of this meme circulate online, giving expression to our underlying anxiety about how or whether the use of the internet is interfering with other productive things we could be doing (Figure 13.3). That concern is reflected as well in more serious articles in business journals and advice for students on college websites. And there's a growing concern that wasting time online vs. using digital media in creative and productive ways is contributing to a new digital divide between children of higher and lower economic classes.[13:1]

Figure 13.3: A "Wasting Time" key suggests a frequent use of a keyboard

critical meme
a circulating idea or image that critiques an aspect of society

❝ Cultural critique may take different forms, but it typically involves an extended look at a social/cultural concern with supporting evidence gained by looking closely at a cultural phenomenon. ❞

Research often confirms what we've suspected—that workplace productivity is down because of internet use,[13:2] that excessive use interferes with students' success,[13:3] and even that, for some, the internet can become an addiction.[13:4] Or research can raise new concerns—about digital reading, for example, and whether the typical scanning of information on a screen may be altering our ability to read and think deeply in ways that have traditionally been supported by print text.[13:5] Often such research raises possible issues that might become the focus of *cultural critique.* Such critique may take different forms, but it typically involves an extended look at a social/cultural concern with supporting evidence gained by looking closely at a cultural phenomenon.

INQUIRY

#1: Tracing glimmers of concern

From the posts you make or encounter on social media, what glimmers of concern do you see? What posts or memes might point to an implicit questioning of some aspect of our current digital life and culture? You might also search for images related to this potential area of concern or critique. (On the Flickr site, images listed with Creative Common Attribution permissions allow you to use the image as long as you credit the person who has posted it.

With your classmates, share your collections of such moments, looking for patterns and identifying some larger questions they suggest.

From Research to Cultural Critique

Often publicly circulating "glimmers of concern" show up as themes in the data collected by researchers as well. We can see this in the case of Sherry Turkle, an MIT social psychologist who initially embraced new technologies. In the introduction to her book, *Alone Together: Why We Expect More from Technology and Less from Each Other,*[13::6] she describes her own history in studying these technologies and their effects, the "innocence" of the work she encountered at MIT, the "heady times" of seeing how people could connect in new ways to wider circles of others. But she was also an outsider, in a sense, coming as a psychologist to the world of computer science, and that shift in context led her to go beyond seeing computers as "just a tool" to observing and asking questions about how computers (and other digital technologies) are affecting us as people, as she applied the perspective of one discipline to the work going on in another, and taking a critical perspective on the world she was studying.

Turkle has discovered from her research that our constant attention to the screen is having a negative effect on our close relationships, concluding in her book that we are increasingly isolated, even when physically close. Her work has moved from research interviews to discover what people think about their uses of technology to engaging in a critique of the way in which our practices are shifting our ways of connecting with others throughout our larger culture, moving from the question "What do we expect from our technology?" to a critical position—that as we expect more from our technology, we expect less from one another, and it's harming our ability to relate to others. In the following excerpt, she focuses on the problem of attention—of how difficult it has become to get the full attention of others—and she recounts the family experiences of the young people she has interviewed.

Teenagers know that when they communicate by instant message, they compete with many other windows on a computer screen. They know how little attention they are getting because they know how little they give to the instant messages they receive. One sophomore girl at Branscomb High School compares instant messaging to being on "cruise control" or "automatic pilot." Your attention is elsewhere. A Branscomb senior says, "Even if I give my full attention to the person I am IMing . . . they are not giving full attention to me." The first thing he does when he makes a call is to gauge whether the person on the other end "is there just for me." This is one advantage of a call. When you text or instantmessage, you have no way to tell how much else is going on for the person writing you. He or she could also be on the phone, doing homework, watching TV, or in the midst of other online conversations.

Longed for here is the pleasure of full attention, coveted and rare. These teenagers grew up with parents who talked on their cell phones and scrolled through messages as they walked to the playground. Parents texted with one hand and pushed swings with the other. They glanced up at the jungle gym as they made calls. Teenagers describe childhoods with parents who were on their mobile devices while driving them to school or as the family watched Disney videos. A college freshman jokes that her father read her the Harry Potter novels, periodically interrupted by his BlackBerry. BlackBerries and laptops came on family vacations. Weekends in the country were cut short if there was no internet service in the hotel. Lon, eighteen, says when that happened, his father "called it a day." He packed up the family and went home, back to a world of connections.

From the youngest ages, these teenagers have associated technology with shared attention. Phones, before they become an essential element in a child's own life, were the competition, one that children didn't necessarily feel they could best. And things are not so different in the teenage years. Nick, seventeen, says, "My parents text while we eat. I'm used to it. My dad says it is better than his having to be at the office. I say, 'Well, maybe it could just be a short meal.' But my mom, she wants long meals. To get a long meal with a lot of courses, she has to allow the BlackBerry." Things seem at a stalemate (266–67).

In this excerpt, as in the rest of the book, Turkle has drawn on her research into people's experiences with digital technologies to build a critique of those technologies based on what she finds to be their negative effects on individuals and their relationships: as we become increasingly interconnected, we are also becoming isolated. As her critique has echoed in the media, in interviews and news articles, she has become an increasingly public figure, giving voice to current social concerns. The idea that, as Turkle writes, "our networked life allows us to hide from each other" leaving us "alone together" has become a part of our current discourse about technology and a circulating meme.

INQUIRY

#2: Your research and cultural critique

Turkle's research has led her to take a critical position about particular social developments related to digital technologies. Does her position echo any of your own concerns, or might you offer a counter-critique? From Inquiry #1 or any of your own research for prior inquiries in the context of this book, are there potential concerns that might lead you to take a critical position on some aspect of our use of digital technology? Sketch out such a position, noting the moments from your own inquiries that could support it.

In her work, Turkle also addresses the issue of privacy that has been raised so often with social media, linking a willingness to accept a lack of privacy to the same sense of aloneness that is the theme of her book.

> If you relinquish your privacy on MySpace or Facebook about everything from musical preferences to your sexual hang-ups, you are less likely to be troubled by an anonymous government agency knowing whom you call or what websites you frequent. Some are even gratified by a certain public exposure. It feels like validation, not violation. Being seen means that they are not insignificant or alone (263).

The next section considers another exploration of that theme.

Making Connections
Literature as Cultural Critique

While we can't always step out of our immediate cultural context to fully see the world from another perspective, we can nevertheless imagine other contexts and perspectives. Fiction, as a literary genre, allows us to imagine alternative worlds—to imagine the life of a child born at a different time or in a different part of the world, the life of historical figures, or of ordinary people encountering new difficulties. Both positive and negative views of the world of digital literacies and social media are also being reflected in fiction, often as part of the communicative background against which characters live their lives. One way of exploring concerns about our own society is to imagine the experience of someone being affected by those concerns, such as a young person being cyberbullied. Another is to imagine the world of the future if present trends continue, conceiving a positive, utopian world, or more often with new technology, a negative, dystopian one.

Reading Dystopian Fiction

Where the digital world becomes the context of a work of literature, that work might reflect our hopes and concerns about the near future. As a form of **cultural production**, literature often explores the tensions in a society. The popularity of a genre is also a reflection of some of those concerns manifesting themselves in literary works. One such popular subgenre of fiction today, as through much of the twentieth century, is the dystopian novel, a novel that presents not a utopian, ideal future, but a disturbing one where trends in the present society have developed in troubling ways. Dystopian stories have a long tradition, but they are often used to raise warnings or offer a counterbalance to something in the present. You may have read one

> **Sidenote**
>
> Julie Peters's young adult novel, *By The Time You Read This, I'll Be Dead*, describes cyberbullying.

cultural production
a cultural artifact produced within a society

of the famous dystopian novels of the last century, George Orwell's *1984* (1949),[13.7] in which he explores the dangers of a totalitarian state and its intrusion on individual privacy to the point of thought control; or Aldous Huxley's *Brave New World* (1932),[13.8] which explores a frightening technological future in which reproductive technologies and psychological manipulation are used to create people whose minds are conditioned to fill specific roles and classes in a new World State. Margaret Atwood's *The Handmaid's Tale* (1985)[13.9] imagines the experience of women in a U.S. dominated by a fundamentalist military government where control of their own lives has been taken away, including their choice to reproduce. More recently, the British/Japanese novelist Kazuo Ishiguro's 2005 novel, *Never Let Me Go,*[13.10] imagines a world in which children are raised in a British boarding school to become organ donors for others at the ultimate cost of their own lives (a world quite different from the boarding school fantasy fictional world of J.K. Rowling's *Harry Potter*[13.11]). Dystopian fiction is often concerned with potentially dehumanizing forces in society—forces that would take away what we believe makes us human, including our empathy, our free will, or our personal freedoms. Such concerns are reflected in other popular genres as well, and Suzanne Collins's *Hunger Games* trilogy[13.12] and the *Divergent* series by Veronica Roth[13.13] have been made into very popular films.

The Circle, by Dave Eggers (Figure 13.4), follows in the tradition of dystopian fiction, in this case raising concerns about our extreme embrace of social media and the possibility of fostering a state where all government functions are ceded to a social media corporation and all privacy disappears in the push to make the world more "transparent." Eggers has imagined a world in which a giant social media company, The Circle, run by three founders known as the Three Wise Men, has taken over the equivalents of all of today's existing companies and their functions—a company that is four generations after Google and Facebook and offers a single platform for information, sharing, shopping, monitoring health care, and using miniature, ubiquitous cameras that can be placed nearly invisibly anywhere, with an application called SeeChange, for recording and sharing almost every aspect of people's lives. The Circle's goal is to collect all possible data, to eliminate privacy and secrecy in the name of creating a better world. Politicians are expected to become transparent, having every moment of their days monitored and publicly broadcast. Members of the Circle and their millions of followers are waiting for the "moment of completion," when nothing private or secret will be left anywhere and all information will be shared and available to everyone.

Figure 13.4: The Circle
book cover
(AP Photo/Alfred A. Knopf/
McSweeney's)

We've selected a scene from halfway through the larger novel. The main character, Mae, is a young woman in her early twenties, a recent college graduate, who has landed a coveted job with The Circle through the help of her best friend, Annie. At The Circle, the more active someone is on social media, the higher they can climb in the company. Within weeks, Mae quickly becomes a top performer by engaging in a whirlwind of social media participation: posting, "zinging" (similar to liking), completing surveys, rating things, and attending events. The Circle obsessively tracks this activity at every moment so that she and all of her colleagues know not only how many followers she has, but also how much money people have spent on purchases of things she has rated (with targets for that "conversion rate" as well). It is a world where "secrets are lies" and "privacy is theft"—two key mottos of the Circle.

In this scene, Mae returns home for a visit after an intense few weeks at the Circle. The company has provided her parents with health insurance that has helped her father get treatment for his MS. A former boyfriend, Mercer, is present as well, and their views of the world quickly clash.

BEFORE READING:
Reading as a participant

With fiction, it's particularly important to read first as a participant, entering the scene that the author has created and letting yourself see the world through the eyes of its characters—as an insider to the world being portrayed. In your first reading of this scene, ask yourself the following questions.

- What is your own response to the characters, their interactions, and the points they make?

- Can you understand each of the characters' perspectives?

- What words resonate for you in some way?

- How does your own experience of social media position you as a reader of this scene?

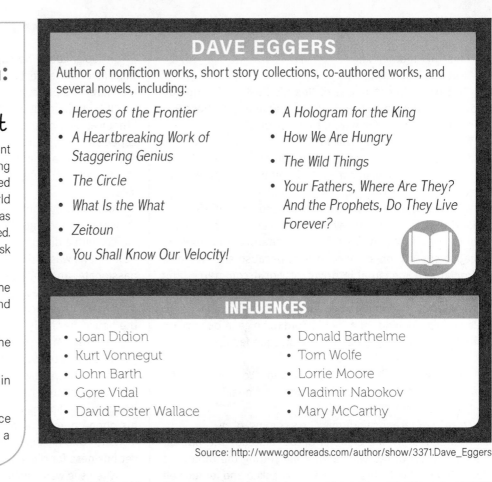

DAVE EGGERS

Author of nonfiction works, short story collections, co-authored works, and several novels, including:

- *Heroes of the Frontier*
- *A Heartbreaking Work of Staggering Genius*
- *The Circle*
- *What Is the What*
- *Zeitoun*
- *You Shall Know Our Velocity!*

- *A Hologram for the King*
- *How We Are Hungry*
- *The Wild Things*
- *Your Fathers, Where Are They? And the Prophets, Do They Live Forever?*

INFLUENCES

- Joan Didion
- Kurt Vonnegut
- John Barth
- Gore Vidal
- David Foster Wallace

- Donald Barthelme
- Tom Wolfe
- Lorrie Moore
- Vladimir Nabokov
- Mary McCarthy

Source: http://www.goodreads.com/author/show/3371.Dave_Eggers

READING

Selection from
The Circle 13:14
by David Eggers

A few nights later, on a cloudless Thursday, Mae drove home, her first time since her father's Circle insurance had taken effect. She knew her father had been feeling far better, and she was looking forward to seeing him in person, hoping, ridiculously, for some miraculous change, but knowing she would see only minor improvements. Still, her parents' voices, on the phone and in texts, had been ebullient. "Everything's different now," they'd been saying for weeks, and had been asking to have her home to celebrate. And so, looking forward to the imminent gratitude, she drove east and south and when she arrived, her father greeted her at the door, looking far stronger and, more important, more confident, more like a man—the man he once was. He held out his wrist monitor and arranged it parallel to Mae's. "Look at us. We match. You want some vino?"

Inside, the three of them arranged themselves as they always had, along the kitchen counter, and they diced, and

breaded, and they talked about the various ways the health of Mae's father had improved. Now he had his choice of doctors. Now he had no limitations on the medicines he could take; they were all covered, and there was no copay. Mae noticed, as they narrated the story of his recent health, that her mother was brighter, more buoyant. She was wearing short-shorts.

"The best thing about it," her father said, "is that now your mother has whole swaths of extra time. It's all so simple. I see the doctor and the Circle takes care of the rest. No middleman. No discussion."

"Is that what I think it is?" Mae said. Over the dining room table, there was a silver chandelier, though upon closer inspection it seemed like one of Mercer's. The silver arms were actually painted antlers. Mae had been only passingly enthusiastic about any of his work—when they were dating, she labored for kind things to say—but this one she genuinely liked.

"It is," her mother said.

"Not bad," Mae said.

"Not bad?" her father said. "It's his best work, and you know it. This thing would go for five grand in one of those San Francisco boutiques. He gave it to us for free."

Mae was impressed. "Why for free?"

"Why for free?" her mother asked. "Because he's our friend. Because he's a nice young man. And wait before you roll your eyes or come back with some witty comment."

Mae did wait, and after she'd passed on a half-dozen unkind things she could say about Mercer and had chosen silence, she found herself feeling generous toward him. Because she no longer needed him, because she was now a crucial and measurable driver of world commerce, and because she had two men at the Circle to choose from—one of them a volcanic, calligraphic enigma who climbed walls to take her from behind—she could afford to be generous toward poor Mercer, his shaggy head and grotesque fatty back.

"It's really nice," Mae said.

"Glad you think so," her mother said. "You can tell him yourself in a few minutes. He's coming for dinner."

"No," Mae said. "Please no."

"Mae," her father said firmly, "he's coming, okay?"

And she knew she couldn't argue. Instead, she poured herself a glass of red wine and, while setting the table, she downed half of it. By the time Mercer knocked and let himself in, her face was half-numb and her thoughts were vague.

"Hey Mae," he said, and gave her a tentative hug.

"Your chandelier thing is really great," she said, and even while saying the words, she saw their effect on him, so she went further. "It's really beautiful."

"Thanks," he said. He looked around to Mae's parents, as if confirming they had heard the same thing. Mae poured herself more wine.

"It really is," Mae continued. "I mean, I know you do good work." And when she said this, Mae made sure not to look at him, knowing his eyes would doubt her. "But this is the best one you've done yet. I'm so happy that you put this much into ... I'm just happy that my favorite piece of yours is in my parents' dining room."

Mae took out her camera and took a picture.

"What're you doing?" Mercer said, though he seemed pleased that she'd deem it worthy of a photograph.

"I just wanted to take a picture. Look," she said, and showed him.

Now her parents had disappeared, no doubt thinking she wanted time alone with Mercer. They were hilarious and insane.

"It looks good," he said, staring at the photo a bit longer than Mae had expected. He was not, evidently, above taking pleasure, and pride, in his own work.

"It looks incredible," she said. The wine had sent her aloft. "That was very nice of you. And I know it means a lot to them, especially now. It adds something very important here." Mae was euphoric, and it wasn't just the wine. It was release. Her family had been released. "This place has been so dark," she said.

And for a brief moment, she and Mercer seemed to find their former footing. Mae, who for years had thought about Mercer with a disappointment bordering on pity, remembered now that he was capable of great work. She knew he was compassionate, and very kind, even though his limited horizons had been exasperating. But now, seeing this—could she call it artwork? It was something like art—and the effect it had on the house, her faith in him was rekindled.

That gave Mae an idea. Under the pretense that she was going to her room to change, she excused herself and hurried upstairs. But instead, sitting on her old bed, in three minutes she'd posted her photo of the chandelier in two dozen design feeds, linking to Mercer's website—which featured just his phone number and a few pictures; he hadn't updated it in years—and his email address. If he wasn't smart enough to get business for himself, she would be happy to do it for him.

When she was finished, Mercer was sitting with her parents at the kitchen table, which was crowded with salad and stir-friend chicken and vegetables. Their eyes followed her down the stairs. "I called up there," her father said.

"We like to eat when it's hot," her mother added.

Mae hadn't heard them. "Sorry. I was just—Wow, this looks good. Dad, don't you think Mercer's chandelier is awesome?"

"I do. And I told you, and him, as much. We've been asking for one of his creations for a year now."

"I just needed the right antlers," Mercer said. "I hadn't gotten any really great ones in a while." He went on to explain his sourcing, how he bought antlers only from trusted collaborators, people he knew hadn't hunted the deer, or if they had, had been instructed to do so by Fish and Game to curb overcrowding.

"That is fascinating," her mother said. "Before I forget, I want to raise a toast ... What's that?"

Mae's phone had beeped. "Nothing," she said. "But in a second I think I'll have some good news to announce. Go on, Mom."

"I was just saying that I wanted to toast having us—"

Now it was Mercer's phone ringing.

READING

"Sorry," he said, and maneuvered his hand outside his pants, finding the off button.

"Everyone done?" her mother asked.

"Sorry Mrs. Holland," Mercer said. "Go on."

But at that moment, Mae's phone buzzed loudly again, and when Mae looked to its screen, she saw that there were thirty-seven new zings and messages.

"Something you have to attend to?" her father said.

"No, not yet," Mae said, though she was almost too excited to wait. She was proud of Mercer, and soon she'd be able to show him something about the audience he might have outside Longfield. If there were thirty-seven messages in the first few minutes, in twenty minutes there would be a hundred.

Her mother continued. "I was going to thank you, Mae, for all you've done to improve your father's health, and my own sanity. And I wanted to toast Mercer, too, as part of our family, and to thank him for his beautiful work." She paused, as if expecting a buzz to sound any moment. "Well, I'm just glad I got through that. Let's eat. The food's getting cold."

And they began to eat, but after a few minutes, Mae had head so many dings, and she'd seen her phone screen update so many times, that she couldn't wait.

"Okay, I can't stand it anymore. I posted that photo I took of your chandelier, Mercer, and people love it!" She beamed, and raised her glass. "That's what we should toast."

Mercer didn't look amused. "Wait. You posted them where?"

"That's great, Mercer," her father said, and raised his own glass.

Mercer's glass was not raised. "Where'd you post them, Mae?"

"Everywhere relevant," she said, "and the comments are amazing." She searched her screen. "Just let me read the first one. And I quote: *Wow, that is gorgeous.* That's from a pretty well-known industrial designer in Stockholm. Here's another one: *Very cool. Reminds me of something I saw in Barcelona last year.* That was from a designer in Santa Fe who has her own shop. She gave your thing three out of four stars, and had some suggestions about how you might improve it. I bet you could sell them there if you wanted to. So here's another—"

Mercer had his palms on the table. "Stop. Please."

"Why? You haven't even heard the best part. On DesignMind, you already have 122 smiles. That's an incredible amount to get so quickly. And they have a ranking there, and you're in the top fifty for today. Actually, I know how you could raise that—" At the same time, it occurred to Mae that this kind of activity would surely get her PartiRank into the 1,800s.

And if she could get enough of these people to buy the work, it would mean solid Conversion and Retail Raw numbers—

"Mae. Stop. Please stop." Mercer was staring at her, his eyes small and round. "I don't want to get loud here, in your parents' home, but either you stop or I have to walk out."

"Just hold on a sec," she said, and scrolled through her messages, looking for one that she was sure would impress him. She'd seen a message come in from Dubai, and if she found it, she knew, his resistance would fall away.

"Mae," she heard her mother say. "Mae."

But Mae couldn't locate the message. Where was it? While she scrolled, she heard the scraping of a chair. But she was so close to finding it that she didn't look up. When she did, she found Mercer gone and her parents staring at her.

"I think it's nice you want to support Mercer," her mother said, "but I just don't understand why you do this now. We're trying to enjoy a nice dinner."

Mae stared at her mother, absorbing all the disappointment and bewilderment that she could stand, then ran outside and reached Mercer as he was backing out of the driveway.

She got into the passenger seat. "Stop."

His eyes were dull, lifeless. He put the car in park and rested his hands in his lap, exhaling with all the condescension he could muster.

"What the hell is your problem, Mercer?"

"Mae, I asked you to stop, and you didn't."

"Did I hurt your feelings?"

"No. You hurt my brain. You make me think you're batshit crazy. I asked you to stop and you wouldn't."

"I wouldn't stop trying to help you."

"I didn't ask for your help. And I didn't give you permission to post a photo of my work."

"Your *work*." She heard something barbed in her voice that she knew wasn't right or productive.

"You're snide, Mae, and you're mean, and you're callous."

"What? I'm the *opposite* of callous, Mercer. I'm trying to help you because I believe in what you do."

"No you don't. Mae, you're just unable to allow anything to live inside a room. My work exists in one room. It doesn't exist anywhere else. And that's how I intend it."

"So you don't want business?"

Mercer looked through the windshield, then leaned back. "Mae, I've never felt more that there is some cult taking over the world. You know what someone tried to sell me the other day? Actually, I bet it's somehow affiliated with the Circle. Have you heard of Homie? The thing where your phone scans your house for the bar codes of every product—"

"Right. Then it orders new stuff whenever you're getting low. It's brilliant."

"You think this is okay?" Mercer said. "You know how they framed it for me? It's the usual utopian vision. This time they were saying it'll reduce waste. If stores know what their customers want, then they don't overproduce, don't overship, don't have to throw stuff away when it's not bought. I mean, like everything else you guys are pushing, it sounds perfect, sounds progressive, but it carries with it more control, more central tracking of everything we do."

"Mercer, the Circle is a group of people like me. Are you saying that somehow we're all in a room somewhere, watching you, planning world domination?"

"No. First of all, *I know* it's all people like you. And that's what's so scary. *Individually* you don't know what you're doing *collectively*. But secondly, don't presume the benevolence of your leaders. For years there was this happy time when those controlling the major internet conduits were actually decent enough people. Or at least weren't predatory and vengeful. But I always worried, what if someone was willing to use this power to punish those who challenged them?"

"What are you saying?"

"You think it's just coincidence that every time some congresswoman or blogger talks about monopoly, they suddenly become ensnared in some terrible sex-porn-witchcraft controversy? For twenty years, the internet was capable of ruining anyone in minutes, but not until your Three Wise Men, or at least one of them, was anyone willing to do it. You're saying this is news to you?"

"You're so paranoid. Your conspiracy theory brain always depressed me, Mercer. You sound so ignorant. And saying that Homie is some scary new thing, I mean, for a hundred years there were milkmen who brought you milk. They knew when you needed it. There were butchers who sold you meat, bakers who would drop off bread—"

"But the milkman wasn't scanning my house! I mean, anything with a UPC code can be scanned. Already, millions of people's phones are scanning their homes and communicating all that information out to the world."

"And so what? You don't want Charmin to know how much of their toilet paper you're using? Is Charmin oppressing you in some significant way?"

"No, Mae, it's different. That would be easier to understand. Here, though, there are no oppressors. No one's forcing you to do this. You willingly tie yourself to these leashes. And you willingly become utterly socially autistic. You no longer pick up on basic human communication clues. You're at a table with three humans, all of whom are looking at you and trying to talk to you, and you're staring at a screen, searching for strangers from Dubai."

"You're not so pure, Mercer. You have an email account. You have a website."

"Here's the thing, and it's painful to say this to you. But you're not very interesting anymore. You sit at a desk twelve hours a day and you have nothing to show for it except for some numbers that won't exist or be remembered in a week. You're leaving no evidence that you lived. There's no proof."

"Fuck you, Mercer."

"And worse, you're not *doing* anything interesting anymore. You're not seeing anything, saying anything. The weird paradox is that you think you're at the center of things, and that makes your opinions more valuable, but you yourself are becoming less vibrant. I bet you haven't done anything offscreen in months. Have you?"

"You're such a fucker, Mercer."

"Do you go outside anymore?"

"You're the interesting one, is that it? The idiot who makes chandeliers out of dead animal parts? You're the wonderboy of all that's fascinating?"

"You know what I think, Mae? I think you think that sitting at your desk, frowning and smiling somehow makes you think you're actually living some fascinating life. You comment on things, and that substitutes for doing them. You look at pictures of Nepal, push a smile button, and you think that's the same as going there. I mean, what would happen if you actually went? Your CircleJerk ratings or whatever-the-fuck would drop below an acceptable level! Mae, do you realize how incredibly boring you've become?" ∎

AFTER READING:
Sharing participatory responses

In your own first reading, you'll have noted lines of the text that resonated for you—that gave you a sense of the characters and their priorities and motivations, and that perhaps also connected to something in your own experience. Share one or two of these moments of understanding or connection with other readers (perhaps on an online site). Do you find they work together to create greater shared knowledge/understanding of the world and the characters that Eggers has portrayed? Do you find similar or different points of connection with your own experience?

Here's a response from one student, Erin, to a particular moment she connected with:

STUDENT VOICES

> Mae's every move was becoming monitored and controlled to fit the norms and the standards of *The Circle* almost to make sure that there was nothing the Circle could not do for any one circler. To establish why something like this could be so dangerous, Mercer said it perfectly when arguing with Mae, "No one's forcing you to do this. You willingly tie yourself to these leashes. And you willingly become utterly socially autistic" (Eggers pg. 262). This allowed me to see that the person I am supposed to be fully relies on the things I want to do with my own life and not the person society wants me to become. Self-realization is not about conforming to the likes of others because that is ultimately where you will lose yourself it is about finding your own path and following it.

Does anyone in your group of readers make a connection like Erin's, or like one another's, or do any personal resonances seem unique? Is Erin's response similar in any way to the responses of readers you've connected with? Did anyone else note these particular sentences, and if so, did they see them the same way, as pointing to a need for self-realization and nonconformity?

Online book sites like Goodreads support the sharing of responses and understandings by many readers of all ages and backgrounds who bring different experiences and concerns to a text. Why might such sites draw committed and active readers (like the community in Hannah Morgan's *Bookworm Buddies* study—Part I Additional Readings)?

Rereading Analytically

While literature generally lends itself to a participatory reading in the way it brings you into the world of the characters, analytical/critical reading requires that you step outside of the world of the story to see **how** it has been composed and **why** it has been composed in this particular way, and within the context—the **where**—of a particular cultural moment. With an analytical reading, you are trying to read closely and work toward an interpretation of the text, a deeper understanding of its possible meanings and how they have been shaped. The traditional discourse of **literary analysis** has involved such terms as plot, setting, character, imagery, narrator, and so forth, and we think it's useful to keep them in mind while engaging in a more open exploration. But at the same time, try to read this literary scene in much the way you would any cultural setting, paying attention to how people interact, what is said and how, and what objects are significant. These are all clues to help you make sense of the underlying beliefs and values of this small community—one that exists within a larger cultural context—and where they might be in conflict. Drawing from these observations will help you understand more about the author's purposes in constructing this world.

literary analysis
analyzing a work of literature to see how it works and why

INQUIRY

#3: Analytical reading

Return to the selection from *The Circle,* focusing first on what you've noticed and perhaps glossed in your first reading, adding to these observations and glosses in the second, and making notes and commentary. Here are some aspects of this selection to consider.

➤ Mae is returning to the world of her home from a community she has recently joined. Although she is not the narrator of her story, which is told in the third person, it's told from her narrative perspective—through what she sees and thinks and experiences. What do we learn about her as a character from her own observations and reflections?

➤ Because we see this world from Mae's perspective, the narrator tells us directly only what Mae is thinking. We learn what the others around her might think from their own words in the dialogue of their exchanges. What do you observe about what is said and how it is said by each participant in this scene? Do their words point to the different priorities, the different beliefs and values, of the different worlds they now inhabit? Do physical objects offer images that reinforce these differences?

➤ We might think of Mae and Mercer as inhabiting two different discourse communities. What do you see, from this scene, of the beliefs and values of Mae's new discourse community? What key terms are significant in that world? What are Mercer's key terms, reflecting his values? How much shared knowledge does he have of the world Mae speaks for? Of the values she thinks that world represents? Here's another student's response to this text.

STUDENT VOICES

In *The Circle*, Eggers creates a world in which a large majority of individuals attempt to quantify their worth in a different manner, a measurement of their social media interactions. Mercer, while arguing with Mae has a very insightful comment. He states "You sit at a desk twelve hours a day and you have nothing to show for it except some numbers that won't exist or be remembered in a week. You're leaving no evidence you lived. There's no proof." What lends this quote its relevance is that Mae truly believes her self worth is intrinsically associated with these numbers. (Stefan)

What do the words Stefan has chosen suggest about Mercer's understanding of Mae's work world and the values associated with it?

➤ As you place Mae's and Mercer's intentions and understandings side by side, what do you perceive about Eggers's purposes? How might the patterns you find in this episode reflect his larger meanings—his exploration of a conflict in priorities and values that he sees within contemporary society and that his readers themselves could be experiencing in a rapidly changing digital environment?

➤ What can you finally say about the interaction of **what** Eggers has included in this selection, and **how** he has crafted this portion of the novel, in contributing to the **why**—to the ideas and meanings that he is exploring here and the cultural critique he is offering through his fiction?

Composing
Literary Analysis

So far the ways in which we've looked at this excerpt from Eggers's novel aren't different from the ways we might begin to analyze any piece of literature, looking closely at the words of the text, at the ways in which the characters are portrayed, and at their dialogue and interactions. But to see a work of literature, or another cultural production, from the perspective of the cultural critique it offers, we need to consider more about its larger context—about the cultural world it draws from and imagines, about the **intertextual context** of other texts it refers to explicitly and implicitly, and about how its ideas are circulating within a larger conversation about society and its values.

As you return to this chapter's selection from Eggers's novel, or choose another section from the same work, or select another literary or other production that offers a critique of some aspect of our digital environment, you'll gain a clearer understanding of what is being critiqued and how by looking both closely at the text and more widely at these elements of context.

intertextual context
the network of texts that is evoked within any one text

textual analysis
a close analysis of the features of a text

WRITING MOVES ◄
Inquiring about Textual Analysis

If you're continuing to work with the same selection from *The Circle*, you'll have already made some of these moves, but you might revisit them to deepen your understanding of how this text is working. Because you're approaching this piece of fiction as an example of a cultural critique, you'll want your rereading to be guided also by your understanding of the author's purpose.

1 Finding a focus

Begin by generating some ideas to explore about the focus of the cultural critique of the work you have chosen. Then reread your selection with one or two of those ideas in mind, identifying textual elements and key passages that relate to that avenue of exploration.

2 Gathering data

In the analysis of a literary text or other word-based cultural production, the words of the text serve as your data and offer the examples you'll draw on in exploring your key ideas. Reread the text. As you note the words that contribute to your understanding of how the work reflects the idea you're exploring—through description, dialogue, and a character's reflections and observations—you are effectively gathering the data you'll need to support the understanding you'll come to. Glossing and annotating the text is a particularly important tool here.

3 Identifying patterns

Looking back at the places you've marked and the words you've found to be significant, what patterns do you find? In a literary text, how do words, objects, and images line up with characters, for example? What differences do you find between/among characters, at different points in a character's development, or in different settings? What do you discover about how the text works to make an implied argument about a concern of our society?

4 Considering larger meanings

Once you've found some patterns, you can begin to consider their meanings. How do these patterns reflect and contribute to the idea about the writer's explicit or implied critique of a cultural phenomenon that you set out to explore—to what you see as the author's larger meanings? Look at the following student example. Molly recontextualizes Mercer's words, connecting them with meanings about knowing and learning that have emerged in her class's discussions of *The Circle*. Are there themes from your own class discussions that connect to patterns you're finding in the reading?

The Circle is centered around being all knowing, and conflicts arise about how the company promotes knowing so much that it becomes an invasion of privacy. This concept of being omnipotent is explored by Mae, who is challenging the question by submerging herself in the company and trying to learn as much as she can. She is beginning to realize her full potential and her effort to reach that potential is evident with how hard she works. However, she is given a harsh reality by Mercer when he says, "We are not meant to know everything, Mae. Did you ever think that perhaps our minds are delicately calibrated between the known and the unknown? That our souls need the mysteries of night and the clarity of day? Young people are creating ever-present daylight, and I think it will burn us all alive. There will be no time to reflect, to sleep to cool" (Eggers 213). Here, he is telling her how we always need time to decompress and reflect on our actions or they are essentially invalid, because it is impossible to constantly be working and be on the move without having any time to rest. What Mercer says here shows a new angle on the question of "What can I know?" by focusing more on discovering how much a person should know and learning when the pursuit for knowledge becomes overbearing. By knowing ones limits and understanding their abilities, they are not hindering their learning, but rather gaining insight into what they are capable of.

contextual analysis
an analysis of the surrounding cultural context of a text or image

▶ WRITING MOVES ◀

Inquiring about Contextual Analysis

Once you've developed a rich understanding of the text and how it is working to present the critique of contemporary digital culture you see the author making, you'll want to expand your frame, taking into account several elements of context. Considering these contextual elements is likely to require that you expand your own inquiry into material beyond the text itself. If the work has been reviewed, as *The Circle* has, those reviews can help you place the work in a larger context, while themselves becoming part of the textual ecology of the work (as do reviews posted by readers like yourselves on sites like Goodreads and Amazon). We include several reviews of *The Circle* in Part II Additional Readings, and we'll draw from them here using one by Margaret Atwood for the *New York Review of Books*,[13:15] one by Ellen Ullman for the *New York Times*,[13:16] and a third by Betsy Morais for *The New Yorker*,[13:17] to see what they say about the cultural world it draws from and imagines, about the intertextual context of other texts it refers to explicitly and implicitly, and about how its ideas are circulating within a larger conversation about society and its values. (As the book becomes a movie with Tom Hanks and Emma Watson, a new cycle of textual circulation will follow.)

1 Situating a text within a cultural world

There's little question about the cultural context that Eggers is responding to: Facebook, Google, all of the Silicon Valley giants, along with Amazon, health care data providers, and apps that track our location through GPS. The dystopian novel typically builds on elements present in contemporary society, even as it presents an imagined world where those elements have gone awry. What detailed correspondences do you find between the text you are analyzing and actual elements and features of our present-day world? How effectively has the author built on those details, and how plausible is the author's extension of today's reality?

There's likely to be significant disagreement on this point. In reviewing *The Circle,* Ullman argues that Eggers adds little to what we already know about "our strange drive to display ourselves, the voracious information appetites of Google and Facebook, our lives under the constant surveillance of our own government." Morais, on the other hand, suggests that Eggers often "lands on point";

she quotes Facebook founder Zuckerberg talking about his belief in helping people share more information and points to its collection of demographic details and its tracking of online behaviors to show close correspondences between the world Eggers has invented and the actual cultural context he is drawing on. Atwood, too, points to "the 'real' world to which Eggers holds up the mirror of art in order to show us ourselves and the perils that surround us."

2 Situating a text among other texts

Writers are always working within the context of other writing, and this is particularly true with literature, where there is a long-standing historical tradition that informs present-day works directly or indirectly. What evidence do you find of that influence? You might find it harder to identify the intertextual literary context that gives shape to a work, but if you suspect some parallels or influence, you're likely to be able to find out more about them.

Eggers, in writing a dystopian novel, most clearly draws on Orwell's *1984*, echoing the slogans that were constants in Orwell's world, such as "War is peace," "Freedom is slavery," "Ignorance is strength." In the world of The Circle, these have become "Secrets are lies," "Sharing is Caring," "Privacy is theft." Such slogans represent a kind of thought control, explicit in the totalitarian state Orwell feared was coming, more implicit but just as powerful in the privacy-free and "transparent" world Eggers sees coming soon. Morais begins her review with these two sets of slogans, making the relationship of the two texts clear. Atwood, in contrast, begins her review by placing *The Circle* in the context of other work Eggers himself has written, work that explores what she sees as important ideas, before going on to trace a wide range of other literary resonances

beyond *1984*, from contemporary writing about cyber theft and cyber threats to Hans Christian Andersen's *The Snow Queen.* Ullman connects the journey into The Circle to Dante's *Inferno,* where Virgil guides Dante down into the depths of hell.

3 Locating a text within the current circulation of ideas

A writer typically draws on ideas that are circulating within contemporary society, no matter when the action takes place. Locating those ideas is another way of placing a work within a larger context, and again, this is particularly useful to understanding a work of cultural critique. You have now read other work exploring concerns about social media and privacy, for example, and can place Eggers's work in the context of others' research and other discussions. What, in the future Eggers portrays, seems supported by what others are learning in the present moment? What seems unlikely?

Each of our three reviewers addresses this context. Ullman dismissively points out that "books and tweets and blogs are already debating the issues Eggers raises"; Morais takes the concerns of the novel more seriously, connecting the "sharing is caring" goal of The Circle to work by Harvard researchers on self-disclosure; and Atwood locates this novel in "ideas about the social construction and deconstruction of privacy, and about the increasing corporate ownership of privacy, and about the effects such ownership may have on the nature of Western democracy." For each, the context of other circulating ideas that interest them shapes their sense of what's interesting and valuable (or not) in what they see Eggers trying to do.

WRITING MOVES

Drafting and Shaping

From looking closely at a text to exploring one or more aspects of its context, you are likely to have generated new understandings of the work you're focusing on, the ways it puts forth a cultural critique, and how successfully it has done so. We explored the reviewing of cultural productions in the previous chapter, and you might choose to develop your own review of *The Circle* or another work that has been the focus of your attention in this chapter. But at this moment, you'll want to give some shape to your current understandings of how a particular text of cultural critique works and how it's placed within the larger context of a cultural world, a world of other texts, and/or a world of circulating ideas, as you contribute your own ideas to this conversation.

1 Foregrounding text or context

When considering a text within a larger cultural or intertextual context, you'll want to decide which you want to foreground for your readers and to consider their likely shared knowledge of the text and its context. The convention (the commonly shared expectations of writers and readers) for essays involving the analysis of a cultural production, such as a literary text, is to assume your readers have not read or seen or heard the work in question (even if they are your classmates) and to provide a brief overview of it, as we've done for *The Circle* when it was introduced in Section II of this chapter.

With a cultural critique, where you're going beyond the close analysis of a text to place its ideas and meanings in a larger context, you'll want to think about how and where you'll address both elements.

A common structure for a typical analysis involving literature is to introduce readers to the work either with a brief summary or by taking the reader into one very small key passage at the beginning, and then moving step by step through the text, highlighting key elements and patterns, and concluding with larger observations of the patterns that have emerged and the meanings they point to. This is pretty much the structure Ullman has followed in her review.

Another common structure when that analysis is supporting a cultural critique is to begin with a larger statement of meaning, placing the text within a larger context before going on to make key points about the text and how it supports (or doesn't support) those meanings, including relevant

background knowledge along the way. Atwood puts Eggers's book in the context of Eggers's other work to show that he cares about ideas and then names what she sees as "ideas about the social construction and deconstruction of privacy." She then goes on to show how those ideas appear in the book, while connecting to other presentations of such ideas as well as to a larger literary context.

As always, creating a working outline is likely to be a useful part of your process. As you draft this material, or peer review it, you might decide to change your original structure, to add or delete textual examples, or to modify the amount of background knowledge you provide about the text. Again, it's helpful both to have a plan and to stay flexible until your final revision.

In each case, using strong textual evidence is an important part of such an analysis, and you'll want to bring significant bits of the text you're analyzing into the one you're creating. (Doing this also gives your reader the "flavor" of the text, a sense of its style, and helps to create further shared knowledge.)

2 Supporting your analysis of a cultural critique with digital resources

When you're making an argument related to a cultural context, you're likely to find many relevant resources circulating online, including images like the ones we looked at earlier, and digital platforms make it easy to draw on such images in making your own argument. If you follow the links to the reviews we've been considering, you'll see that Atwood's review[L13:1] creates context with an image

link

of Eggers (fitting her emphasis on the context of his work and ideas), and Morais's review[L13:2] simply presents the book's cover, and Ullman's review[L13:3] offers an image of a circle of smiling emoticons that become progressively unhappier toward the center, reflecting her discussion of the book's content as portraying a kind of journey into hell (Figure 13.5).

You might also create hypertext links to guide readers to a richer understanding of the cultural elements you point to in your own analysis, particularly if you're posting to a blog platform. Morais, for example, links to an article in *The Atlantic's* news blog, *The Wire*, questioning whether Eggers borrowed too much from a book by a former Facebook employee.[13:18]

You might also use a wiki for a multilayered collaborative exploration of a text like *The Circle*, creating pages that explore several aspects of the text and its context.

Figure 13.5: Images from Ullman's review

WRITING MOVES

Revising and Publishing

If you're posting your work to a blog or a wiki, you've already made some decisions about how your own text will circulate. As always, it's useful to circulate it first among knowledgeable and interested readers before posting it more publicly. These readers can play the role of insiders who have the same shared knowledge and who can step into the analytical work you are doing and help you support your interpretation of the text's meanings and purposes—perhaps clarifying those meanings and suggesting further examples of the patterns you've seen.

1 Working with peer review

Any peer review strategies that have worked for you in the past will be useful again. Here are some possible peer review questions that can guide you if you're preparing this analysis of a text as a cultural critique for wider circulation.

- In what context is the writer placing this text? How does that context contribute to an understanding of the area of cultural critique the writer is exploring?

- How does the particular text connect to and respond to that context?

- What are the larger meanings this composer has found in the work being analyzed?

- What patterns has the composer found to support those meanings?

- Has the composer offered strong textual evidence that those patterns exist? Do you see other evidence in the text that would strengthen this interpretation or that might alter it?

- Has the composer created the right amount of shared knowledge to let readers follow the interpretation without retelling the whole story?

- Is the analysis structured in a way that is easy for a reader to follow?

- Do any digital links or images work to support the composer's framing of the text's cultural context or points of critique?

- Does the analysis, by the end, leave you convinced that this is a plausible way of understanding the text within a larger context, as a form of cultural critique?

- What other advice would you give to this composer?

2 Reshaping your analysis for circulation to a larger audience

Although the audiences for the reviews of *The Circle* we've been looking at might overlap, the *New York Review of Books* publishes longer review essays, often engaging readers who are deeply steeped in both literature and current affairs, and Atwood is addressing that audience with her flowing literary allusions. Morais's discussion for *The New Yorker*, a more general interest magazine for educated readers, appears under the topic of science and technology and is likely to draw readers who are more interested in that topic than in book reviews more generally. Other publications like *Wired* and *Slate,* aimed at more technology-oriented readers, offered critical reviews that focused much more on Eggers's lack of in-depth knowledge of the Silicon Valley world he is portraying.

As you consider the wider circulation of your analysis of a work of cultural critique, you'll not only want to take into account your peers' responses to the text you've created, but also the audience community of any site where you choose to post it. The easiest public sites on which to post a discussion about a book are review sites like Goodreads (or Amazon). Look at some of the other reviews of *The Circle* on a reader review site, and see what your work might add to the discussion. Keeping in mind the advice about reviewing in Chapter 12, recast your own work for that audience.

Digital Toolbox
See Part IV, Section 3

Reinventing and Circulating Your Work

Or you might search for other discussions of *The Circle* or another text of cultural critique you've chosen to analyze, and see where these discussions appear, what their focus is, and what readership they seem to be addressing. Where might you post your own analysis if you were invited to, and how would you reshape your analysis to address the interests of this audience? If the site you've chosen accepts open submissions, you can submit your work. If not, post it on your own or a class blog site, with an introductory note about where you'd choose to make it public and how your sense of the likely audience for the site you've chosen has guided your final shaping of your work.

Here are several ways in which you might extend your work for this chapter.

➤ **Option 1: Reading further in the work you've chosen.** The primary context for a small segment of any literary work includes the whole. You can enrich your understanding of a larger work by choosing more than one section to look at closely. How does reading and analyzing a different section of the work contribute to and/or alter the understanding you gained from your first analysis?

➤ **Option 2: Comparing *The Circle* to another piece of dystopian fiction.** Other works within a genre provide part of the context within which we read a particular work. You might have read or want to read another work that explores potential problems of a society if it heads in a particular direction. How does another writer create and show the concerns of another dystopian world?

- If the work was written in a different time period (e.g., *1984*), how did the author's predictions of then-future dangers play out against the actual future? Are the concerns of that earlier work nonissues at present, or do they continue to be present for contemporary society?

- If the work looks toward the near future (e.g., Gary Shteyngart, *Super Sad True Love Story*[13:19]), how does the dystopian vision it projects compare to the one created in *The Circle*?

➤ **Option 3: Tracing the textual ecology of a work.** Search for whatever textual material you can find related to the work and circulating online—reviews, memes, images, mashups, and *transmediations* that move the work from one medium to another, as *The Circle* is being reshaped from a book to a movie. What do you discover about how the themes of critique as originally presented resonate in these new environments? How is it understood and its points highlighted, altered, or adapted in different contexts?

Digital Toolbox
See Part IV, Section 2

➤ **Option 4: Creating a composite analysis on a multipage wiki.** Where several of you have focused on the same text, you might draw from your different analyses to create a richer and more complex composite analysis. A wiki provides a useful platform for a multilayered exploration of a text that offers pages of background, summary, analysis and interpretation, and related resources, and works especially well for collaborative projects around a literary text. Here's an example of <u>a wiki created for Jane Austen's *Pride and Prejudice*</u>.[L13:4] If you and your classmates were to create such a wiki to support your analysis of *The Circle,* what pages would you create and what might they include?

➤ **Option 5: Adding your own review of *The Circle* to its larger review context.** In Chapter 12, we considered the ways reviews are shaped by the contexts in which they appear and how multiple reviews might speak to one in another. Look again at the three reviews of *The Circle* that appear in Part II Additional Readings. How do these reviews speak to the shared and differing expectations of readers of a work like this? To the place of *The Circle* within a segment of contemporary culture? Drawing on your own analysis, write a review that considers not only how, but how well Eggers has achieved his likely purposes in creating this work, and that addresses what has been said in these other reviews. What can you add to the points made in them? What would you contest? What evidence would you draw on to support your own evaluation of this work in the context of others' reviews?

Key Concepts

contextual analysis 296
critical meme 285
cultural critique 284
cultural production 287

intertextual context 295
literary analysis 293
textual analysis 295

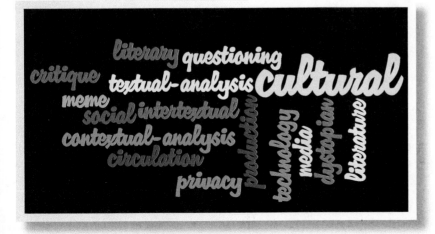

Reading
Visual Culture

CHAPTER FOURTEEN

CENTRAL QUESTIONS

1 How and why do some images proliferate in a culture? What values and beliefs do they express and gain as they circulate through new contexts?

2 What analytical tools do we need to understand how images work rhetorically?

3 What can we learn about culture and context from reading an essay about Rosie the Riveter?

4 How do we now use images and visuals to communicate, and how can we learn to *compose* creatively with images and other visual modes of writing to participate in a larger conversation around a topic or issue?

Chapter Preview

In the last several chapters, we've explored a small portion of the cultural productions that circulate through the larger public world of the internet—generally, the less serious content that circulates as memes to the more extended and reasoned content of online feature articles. We've seen how composers use rhetorical means to ensure their creations will grab the attention of viewers and go viral, but also how they might present informed and reasoned perspectives on our culture and offer cultural critiques.

As we've focused on rhetorical purposes and the available means for composing in digital spaces, we've also considered our own shifting roles as participants in digital culture, noting how *visual* modern texts are and how image-making has become a central part of how we communicate in changing contexts. In this chapter, we'll extend our analysis of visual culture and identify some analytical tools for making sense of our growing production and consumption of images. We'll consider what it means to live in an exceedingly visual world, how to work with visual resources critically, and how to see what shared beliefs and values are represented in the images we create and share.

In Part I of this book, we explored the impact of digital technologies on our ways of sharing cultural knowledge in our local communities by considering the changing uses of personal images—of photos that had moved from albums and shoeboxes onto Snapchat and Instagram and Facebook, and the changing ways (digital photography, selfie sticks) and meanings of today's "snapshot" among friends. In this chapter, we move beyond the local focus and beyond the personal snapshot to consider the means and meanings of images in the wider public arena and the rhetorical force they exert as they circulate in culture.

Exploring
Visual Texts in Contemporary Culture

As composers in the twenty-first century, we are writing and sharing more texts than ever, and our literacies are changing in the process. One of those changes has been in how images are produced and circulated. Just as corporate mass media had a monopoly on the public circulation of both written and visual texts before the digital age, today's media environment and the broad availability of image-making and image-sharing technologies have given ordinary people the means to create their own digital content and more fully participate in the production of **visual culture**. Taking pictures and video, adding text or narration, posting photos to Instagram or Facebook, editing and publishing on photo-sharing sites like Flickr, Picasa, or Shutterfly, editing videos to post on YouTube—these visual literacy practices are now a daily part of how we communicate with one another. As we post and share images or alter and adapt circulating images, we are continually involved in acts of **recontextualization**, bringing these images into new contexts for different rhetorical purposes and giving them new meanings in the process.

visual culture
culture that is expressed in visual images

recontextualization
the practice of taking a text or another cultural production that was created in one context and using it in a different context to express meaning

Images as Memes

Often familiar visuals and images go "viral" and become *memes*, ideas or cultural objects that, as we've seen in previous chapters, spread throughout the larger culture as they are taken up, posted, liked, shared, and tweeted. Sometimes we simply pass an image on to others who might be interested, and other times we might add text or use photo editing tools to change it for a different rhetorical purpose. As similar images get reused and remixed, they come to be recognized by larger audiences, sometimes for brief periods, sometimes over generations. At various moments, advertising logos like the Nike swoosh, dance styles like Korean Gagnam, and images like <u>LOLcats</u>[L14:1]

Figure 14.1: Cat meme

link

have spread and become culturally familiar across the globe (Figure 14.1). Images and videos, because they may not require words for their meanings, are particularly likely to cross language boundaries and become part of a global digital culture, proliferating rapidly and often changing meanings as other people use the image to communicate in different contexts. Even within one national setting, a **visual meme** can take on a plethora of new meanings as writers and composers adapt it for new contexts.

visual meme
a visual image that circulates through the internet

To explore how an image goes viral and becomes a meme as it circulates among contexts, let's begin with a recently popular example of a longstanding cultural meme: Rosie the Riveter.

When Beyoncé posted this image on her Instagram site (Figure 14.2), she placed it into wide public circulation. The image clearly resonated with her audience, receiving 1.4 million likes and thousands of comments. Like other circulating memes that are full of meaning for their viewers, her Instagram post generated a Twitter storm about its purpose and meanings, which in turn generated further media attention. In this visual image, Beyoncé, a twenty-first century pop culture icon, strikes a pose based on a famous image from the 1940s, the image of Rosie the Riveter. In doing so, Beyoncé is engaged in the process of recontextualization, of evoking a well-known image to express meaning in a twenty-first century cultural context.

See Chapter 9
for a more detailed discussion of memes.

Figure 14.2: Beyoncé posing as Rosie the Riveter using Instagram

Below are some other notable images of Rosie. The first is the original image of Rosie and the basic model for the Rosie meme. The second is a well-known painting by Norman Rockwell. The third and fourth are more recent examples (Figure 14.3).

Figure 14.3: Images of Rosie the Riveter

INQUIRY

#1: Tracing a visual meme

List some observations that strike you about the images in Figure 14.3. What do you know about these images? Have you seen them before? What common idea do you think the images are communicating?

What else would you need to know about its context to understand the fuller meaning of each individual image?

Go online and search for other Rosie the Riveter images. Search for Rosie the Riveter and the names of music icons or political figures or other celebrities. Or look for themes such as gay rights and Rosie the Riveter or Muslim women and Rosie the Riveter. Then look at the original poster that they're based on. What elements tend to remain constant in these recontextualizations? What sorts of changes, adaptations, and remixes do you find? What cultural meanings seem to be shared across contexts, and what meanings seem to be specific to the new context the images are part of? Why do you think this image from World War II continues to be relevant for contemporary society? And why do you think Beyoncé used it?

Images as Visual Compositions: Rosie the Riveter

As writers, we typically spend more time reading and analyzing conventional texts than images. But with the increasingly visual and multimodal nature of texts, it becomes important to our own rhetorical practices as both readers and composers that we gain some critical and analytical understandings about the production of visual culture and our participation in the circulation of meaning through the images we share and compose. Just as with verbal texts, we need to understand how visual texts work in rhetorical ways to achieve particular purposes and how they work to convey meanings that relate to the contexts in which they are realized.

We can approach a visual analysis in the way we've approached other texts, by first looking at the **what** of the text and describing its content or what we see, and **how** the various elements are arranged from a compositional perspective, focusing on the visual arrangement of the text itself. We can also look at **where** and **when**—where a visual text first appears and the historical context it emerges from, as we've begun to do above and will continue to do later in this chapter. By understanding both the text and its context, we can also come to a clearer understanding of the **why**, the likely purposes of its creator and of the shared meanings that are expressed for its viewers from a rhetorical and social perspective. In practice, these perspectives are always interacting, but we can think of them as entry points into different ways of analyzing how a visual artifact is produced and circulated, and we'll begin with the compositional perspective.

visual grammar
familiar patterns of
visual structuring

Like written compositions, visual images and hybrid texts that combine words and visuals can be seen as having a sort of **visual grammar** or commonly understood structure.[14:1] Just as a typical written essay has a common pattern, with an introduction, body, and conclusion, composing practices that use images and video have developed their own patterns of communication that have become standardized over time. As such, in analyzing a visual artifact, we can think of its production as being like that of a written text—as a product of human communication that has a specific rhetorical purpose and that is shaped by the conventions and expectations of the culture it emerges from.

In analyzing such hybrid texts, a good, generative place to begin is with description—**what** do you see? In exploring this question, we have a wealth of prior knowledge about visual communication from our own experience of living in a highly visual culture—experience we can draw on and learn to verbalize as we interpret the visual texts that surround us.

INQUIRY

???

#2: What do you know about visual composition?

Before you read on, take some time to write about some of the compositional elements you see in the Rosie pictures on the previous page.

· If you look at each image without its verbal text, what kinds of patterns do you see? What visual elements appear? How are they placed?

· What happens when words are added to an image? How are they placed? What ideas do they convey?

· How are words and images working together to create meaning in these images?

· Find a handful of similar images. These could be other images of Rosie, advertisements from different decades or in different publications, or perhaps family photos. What do you notice about how these images are composed? What kinds of conventions (repeated elements) and similarities do you see in the way the images are composed?

You've probably noted some of the more prominent features of the Rosie images: the close-in view of her face and upper body, her posture and the physical position of her arm and hand, her dress, her hair, and her expression. Even from a first glance we can glean meaning from what we see in Rosie's facial expression and body language. Our own experience of living in a human body helps us understand these images immediately because we can relate to them on a physical level. And perhaps you noted the prominence of the words, the entire width of the page. Often a first step in analyzing a visual text is to look for how words and images are working together to create meaning.

But beyond these initial observations, what other compositional elements can we observe? What kinds of practices and techniques are the composers of these images drawing on to create meaning? Here's where a few working concepts from the world of design become useful. While there are dozens of design terms we could draw on, for general composition purposes, there are five basic principles:

1. **Balance**
2. **Contrast**
3. **Repetition**
4. **Alignment**
5. **Proximity**

These terms, and the practices they describe, emerge from a long tradition of Western visual communication that emphasizes rectangular design, efficiency, realism, and hierarchies of information.[14:2] They are practices widely in use today. The terms are useful for thinking about the **arrangement** of a visual text—how each different element in a composition is placed and works with other elements to express meaning. Part of the challenge in visual analysis is to describe how these different elements work together to create meaning for an audience.

arrangement
the placement of different elements in a visual text to achieve a particular rhetorical purpose

Balance. The concept of balance refers to the way all the elements in a composition share the space of the text. Looking at the first two images of Rosie again, you'll notice how the balance of each image shifts from left to right, depending on which side of the text Rosie is on. The use of words at the top of both images creates a counter weight to the more dominant image of Rosie, keeping both images in balance and in equal importance. A sense of balance is achieved when the various elements in a composition create a sense of coherence between elements *within* the limited space of the visual text (Figure 14.4).

Figure 14.4 : Two original images of Rosie that shift balance from left to right

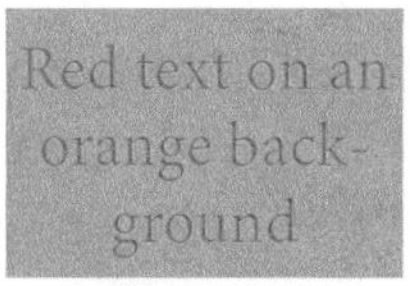

Contrast. Contrast works to emphasize how different elements in a text work together to create meaning. We often think of contrast as how colors relate to each other. For example, having red text on an orange background is difficult to read (Figure 14.5). We would say the contrast is *too low* to read it comfortably. In addition to color, though, contrast also relates to how elements in a composition interact with one another to create meaning. For example, in Norman Rockwell's depiction of Rosie, he creates a strong relationship between Rosie and the American flag rippling in the background (Figure 14.6).

Red text on an orange background

Figure 14.5: Low-contrast colors (red text on an orange background)

The effect is that Rosie and the flag have a *high* contrast, expressing two distinct visual elements that, when combined, create more meaning than each alone. Contrast signals to readers how strong or weak a relationship is between elements in a composition. In this case, Rockwell uses the flag as the patriotic background while Rosie sits in the foreground as the embodiment of that patriotism.

Repetition. Repetition isn't simply a practice of visual design; it is something we see in all facets of life, from pop songs we can't get out of our head to the change in seasons. Writers and designers use repetition in many ways, especially through their use of shape, color, font, and size of elements in a text, as well as repeating similar imagery and formatting throughout a text.

Figure 14.6 : Rockwell's high-contrast Rosie image

Figure 14.7: Screenshots of the rosietheriveter.org website

The compositional practice of repetition is a common technique at work in many websites. In Figure 14.7 there are three screenshots of the website rosietheriveter.org. As you click through the main navigation to other pages on the site, each page repeats several elements—colors, font, imagery, and overall layout. One of the effects of repetition is to create a consistent look and feel across a text.

Alignment. Figure 14.7 also exhibits the compositional practice of *alignment*. Alignment is especially useful for creating a reading path for a reader or viewer. In print documents, margins, titles, and headings have traditionally been used to bring order and balance to a text and to help make reading it easier.

Figure 14.8 shows alignment at work. The magazine's title and Rosie's word bubble are center aligned vertically and horizontally. The caption in red lettering is justified to the right, creating the appearance of an imaginary line on the right side of the page. The overall feel with this kind of alignment is that there is a frame around each element in the text, as well as the text in its entirety. We might say that everything is "lined up" right. Alignment contributes greatly to the sense of balance we feel when we see a visual text.

Figure 14.8: *Cover of* Business Week *September 2006*

Figure 14.9 complicates the standard practice of alignment. In this visual text, the elements on the page don't line up, creating different meanings between visual elements in the process.

Proximity. One of the design features in Figure 14.9 is the use of *proximity*. While the different elements in the composition aren't aligned, the even spacing between each image creates an equal relationship between each piece of the

Figure 14.9: *DIY Costume for Rosie the Riveter*

costume. No image appears to be more important than the others. At the same time, the acronym "DIY" and the word "Halloween" feel bunched and too close together, as does the text "Rosie the Riveter," which looks squished and out of alignment with other surrounding elements in the composition. The proximity of elements to one another helps define their relationship to one another.

Again, these are working concepts to help you develop your own analysis of visual texts. As we mentioned before, all writing and design concepts emerge out of the shared values and expectations of a particular culture. If many of our texts of public American culture seem to emphasize order, coherency, and functionality, it is because our culture values, and expects, these traits in our texts.

INQUIRY

#3: Revisiting an image of Rosie the Riveter as a visual composition

Revisit a Rosie image that you explored in Inquiry #2. Do any of the design concepts introduced in this chapter help you to observe aspects of the composition that you didn't notice the first time? What more can you say about the composition of the image at this point?

In discussing the concept of repetition, we used the example of several pages from the Rosietheriveter.org website. But all of these compositional elements have been applied to website design[14:3], and websites make up many of the visual compositions we encounter. We can see these concepts at work more fully if we return to examine that website more closely.

INQUIRY

#4: Applying design concepts to a website

Visit rosietheriveter.org and consider how the site uses design techniques like balance, contrast, repetition, alignment, and proximity.

How do these design elements work together to express meaning? What kind of imagery is used on the site, along with color and font? How are images and words working together?

Part of understanding the compositional and textual aspects of a digital text like a website is to also consider the structure of the site and how it organizes and presents information for readers. How does one navigate the site? Is it difficult to find information? How does the site function as you move through it, and what kinds of reading experiences is the site attempting to create (Figure 14.10)?

Figure 14.10: Home page for rosietheriveter.org

Making Connections
Cultural Contexts and Meaning-Making

Together with the compositional elements of a visual text, we can take our analysis a step further and look at the cultural context of a text's production—at **when** and **where** it is produced and circulated. Cultural perspectives on visual texts try to locate a text's composition in a place and time. We ask questions about who composed a text, what year it was composed, and where. What historical events were occurring that may have influenced the creation of a text? Does the image continue to circulate over time and continue to play a role in the production of culture?

Placing Rosie the Riveter in a Historical Context

From your exploration of these Rosie images so far, you have probably not only come to a richer understanding of these hybrid texts, but you've most likely gleaned some information about their prior cultural context. On the occasion of the death of the original model for Rosie (although whether there was an actual original Rosie is disputed), a number of articles placed the Rosie meme in a new context, including the following <u>post by Megan Garber for *The Atlantic*.</u>" L14:2

link

BEFORE READING:

Evoking your prior knowledge about Rosie the Riveter

Before you read "The Many Faces of Rosie the Riveter," reflect on what you already know or can guess from the images themselves and about the cultural context and era that produced the earliest versions of Rosie. How does Megan Garber make the story of Rosie newly relevant to her readers? Note that the online version of Garber's blog post for *The Atlantic* begins with the first of our sequence of four images, the original poster of Rosie, and then includes Rockwell's image from the *Saturday Evening Post* and Beyoncé's Instagram image.

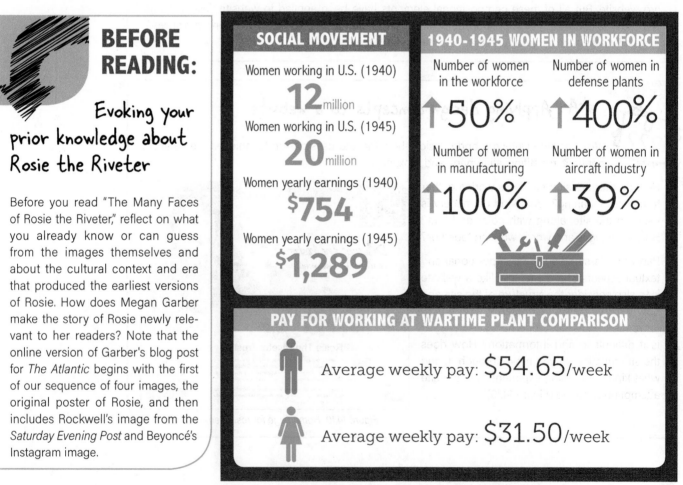

SOCIAL MOVEMENT

Women working in U.S. (1940)
12million

Women working in U.S. (1945)
20million

Women yearly earnings (1940)
$**754**

Women yearly earnings (1945)
$**1,289**

1940-1945 WOMEN IN WORKFORCE

Number of women in the workforce
↑**50%**

Number of women in defense plants
↑**400%**

Number of women in manufacturing
↑**100%**

Number of women in aircraft industry
↑**39%**

PAY FOR WORKING AT WARTIME PLANT COMPARISON

Average weekly pay: $**54.65**/week

Average weekly pay: $**31.50**/week

Source: http://infographicsmania.com/american-women-workers/

READING

"The Many Faces of Rosie the Riveter"[14:4]
by Megan Garber
The Atlantic, April 24, 2015

Mary Doyle Keefe has died. The 92-year-old was, the AP reports, the model for "Rosie the Riveter," the Norman Rockwell painting that served as the cover for the *Saturday Evening Post* in May of 1943, then as an iconic symbol for wartime solidarity and the power of labor, and then later as a token for civil rights, feminism, and institutionalized spunk.

You would be forgiven, though, for thinking that the real-life Rosie the Riveter had already passed away. Rose Will Monroe, said to have been the model for the "We Can Do It!" image commonly associated with Rosie, died in 1997. And Geraldine Doyle, who has also claimed to be the inspiration for the We Can Do It! image, via a UPI photo taken of her at work in a factory in Ann Arbor, Michigan, in 1942, died in 2010.

So who, actually, was the original Rosie? And why do so many different women claim her as their own?

The answer is in part, certainly, that Rosie belongs to all of us—and that we are all, on some level, Rosie. The images of female strength and empowerment that the images of a well-muscled female arm represent were meant at the time, and continue, to transcend the individual. They are propaganda, and as such convey their cause in the guise of a person. As an image, Rosie, in various forms, has been a first-class postage stamp. And a magazine cover model many times over. She has been displayed at the National Museum of American History. She has been refigured as tattoos. She has been used on posters supporting the election of Hillary Clinton and Sarah Palin, and supporting the influence of Michelle Obama. She has been used for marketing purposes more broadly (Clorox has used her to advertise its cleaning products). She has been made into a bobble-head doll and an action figure. She has been recreated out of jelly beans. She has been slapped onto so many different pieces of merchandise—cof-

fee mugs, t-shirts, magnets, stationery—that the *Washington Post* once dubbed her the "most over-exposed" souvenir item available in the nation's capital.

So, in part, the mysterious origins of Rosie come from that fact that everyone, in some ways,

lays claim to her. (It's fitting, in that sense, that before Rosie was an image, she was a song: "Rosie the Riveter," popular on the radio in 1943, is said to have been the basis for Rockwell's painting. Even before she had a face, she had a name.)

The other reason so many different people call themselves "Rosie," though, has to do with more basic realities—of labor, of communication, of intellectual property. There are two iconic images of Rosie the Riveter. One of them is, indeed, Rockwell's—created in 1943, printed on the cover of a popular national magazine, and based on the modeling Mary Doyle Keefe provided for the sum of $10. This is the one that actually features a factory-working woman named Rosie.

The other image is the "We Can Do It" poster. Which initially had little to do with Rosie—and, for that matter, with women at all.

This poster, the one most of us today associate with Rosie the Riveter, was created not so much to encourage women in the workforce as to encourage productivity in general. World War II coincided with the rise of labor unions in the 1930s; across the country, as factory production became war production, managers sought to build morale and minimize the frictions of the past. They did that, in part, by way of posters they displayed on factory floors, many of them bearing team-building slogans like "Keep 'Em Firing!" and "Together We Can Do It!." For optimum morale-building, the posters were rotated into and out of use.

In the early 1940s, the Westinghouse Electric Corporation commissioned the graphic artist J. Howard Miller to create a series of these inspirational posters for the company. One of these was of a woman, defiant but proud, with her work-shirt's sleeves rolled up. (There are conflicting accounts about the woman on whom Miller based his rendering: Some say it was Rose Will Monroe, who was working as a riveter at Michigan's Willow Run Bomber Plant when she was asked to star in a video series promoting war bonds; others say it was Geraldine Doyle and the UPI photo of her at work.)

On February 15, 1943, a Westinghouse factory in East Pittsburgh, Pennsylvania displayed a new poster—which was small, just 17 inches wide and 22 inches high, and one of only 1,800 or so printed for the purpose. Its caption read, "We Can Do It!"

Though it depicted a woman, feminism was likely not the poster's intended message; it was concerned much more with the outcome of labor than with the laborers themselves. Two weeks later, the poster was removed from the factory floor. And it was, for the most part, forgotten.

Then, in 1982, the *Washington Post Magazine* ran an article about propaganda posters stored in the collection of the National Archives. One of the posters it printed in its story was the "We Can Do It!" image. From there—and during a time when it would have more valence with ideas of feminism that had become widespread in the culture—the image enjoyed a renaissance, to the extent that, today, you can "Rosiefy yourself." You can buy a "Rosie the Riveter" bandana. You can make

a cocktail called "Rosé the Riveter." The now-iconic image—initially nameless, initially standing for no cause beyond work—has, through the typical avenues of cultural adoption and appropriation, taken on the mantle of progress and strength and feminism. It has taken on the name of "Rosie."

As for the other Rosie, the one painted by Rockwell and actually intended to be the face of the female war effort? Rockwell copyrighted that image, as he did with other works; after his death, his family protected that copyright. Which meant that, by law, the painting could not be modified or appropriated. So, while it gained in financial value—in 2002, it sold for nearly $5 million—it lost in cultural. The woman who announces, both to herself and to the world, that We Can Do It! may not have started life as "Rosie the Riveter," although she has, in fact, effectively become inseparable from the name. ▮

AFTER READING:
In context: cultural meanings of Rosie the Riveter

How does the information Garber provides contribute to your reading of the original two Rosie images—the Miller poster for Westinghouse and the Rockwell magazine cover?

➤ The two images are from exactly the same time period, in the midst of World War II, yet we understand that their inspiration and their rhetorical purposes were somewhat different. Can you see these differences as you look again at the images? Why do you think these two similar yet different images might have emerged, considering both the larger context of wartime America and the immediate contexts for and uses of each creation?

➤ We learn that it was the rediscovery of the Rosie poster in the National Archives in the 1980s that brought new meaning to the old image. What in the image speaks to the interests and concerns of that later context?

➤ According to Garber, how does Rosie "transcend the individual"? What does she use as evidence? Do you agree?

➤ What meanings is Beyoncé evoking with her use of the image? And why do you think Garber has made this choice out of all the current circulating versions of the Rosie meme? How does it contribute to her purpose with her essay? To the likely interests of her *The Atlantic* readers? In what ways is the Beyoncé image evidence of the process of cultural adoption and appropriation that Garber sees as the real significance to us of the Rosie story?

This history of Rosie's origin also shows us that the cultural process of texts borrowing from and building off of other texts, in what we've been referring to as *intertextuality*, applies to images as well as verbal texts. And the textual ecology of a visual text like Beyoncé's includes the images and words that have inspired her visual composition, the responses of her fans, and the sharing and circulation of the image across several social media.

To take our cultural analysis one more step, we could further contextualize Rockwell's image by noting his use of Michelangelo's classical depiction of the prophet Isaiah painted in the Sistine Chapel (1509 CE) as a model for Rosie (Figure 14.11). It's these kinds of intertextual and ecological relations that help us better understand the contexts of a text's composition and how it changes meanings as it gets picked up, altered, and used in different contexts. In understanding the circumstances of a text's production and where it circulates in time and space, we gain insight into how a text emerges from culture and how it, in turn, becomes a producer of culture as it gets shared and circulated.

Figure 14.11: Norman Rockwell's version of Rosie next to Michelangelo's painting of the Biblical prophet Isaiah in the Sistine Chapel in the Vatican, Italy

Social and Rhetorical Perspectives on Visual Texts

In addition to understanding the compositional and cultural aspects of a visual artifact, it's useful to look at the *social* and *rhetorical* aspects of a visual text, the purposes behind its composition, and the social practice of sharing images as a primary mode of communication. How far and deep does an image circulate? Why and when do people share an image? Who is the audience for a visual text? What kinds of shared meanings are being expressed in the text? And how do ordinary people draw meaning from an image and use those meanings to perform and take on new social identities?

Garber's essay has given us a sense of the original social and rhetorical purposes of the Rosie poster and Rockwell's *Post* cover. But we also want to consider **why** an image like Rosie gets taken up and circulated and remixed as a meme in our current culture.

In the final two images we introduced at the beginning of the chapter, we see the image of Rosie appropriated to create new meanings across global contexts (Figure 14.12). The first is a painting from 2010 by Chicago artist Robert Valadez. In addition to drawing on our shared knowledge of the Rosie image, Valadez builds on this meaning by using the Mexican icon of "La Adelita," a symbol from the Mexican Revolution (1910–1920), as Rosie's counterpart, and he borrows the saying "Sí Se Puede," ("Yes, it can be done") from the agrarian protests in the 1960s and 70s in California led by Cesar Chavez.[14:5] In each case, the combination of elements used by Valadez draws on several other ideas to create a new text specific to a contemporary social concern. The text borrows meanings from the original Rosie image, combined with Mexican history and lore, to express

Mexican national pride and the self-determination of Mexican women.

The second image was painted by 17-year-old artist Anat Ronen at the Avis Frank Gallery in Houston in 2014. In this image of Rosie, Ronen substitutes Malala Yousafzai, the young Pakistani human rights activist who survived a vicious gun attack by the Taliban at the age of 15. Yousafzai was awarded the Nobel Peace Prize in 2014 for her work on equal access to education for women and children around the world.[14:6] Like Mexican Rosie, Ronen's mural draws meaning from the original Rosie image but reinterprets it in a new context, further spreading Rosie and the cultural and historical meanings she carries.

Figure 14.12: Images of Rosie as "La Adelita" and Malala Yousafzai

Another important social and rhetorical aspect to consider when analyzing a visual text like Rosie is to trace how an image moves from being a shared image to a shared physical expression and enactment of the image. We can think of this type of meaning-making as **performativity**—the way, like Beyoncé, meaning-makers create shared rhetorical meaning and express themselves by photographing themselves performing Rosie. This act of performance has become especially relevant today in our highly visual world as we perform some aspect of our social identities with each photo we take and post. Often we take up cultural memes like Rosie to portray, as Beyoncé has, aspects of our identity that we want to highlight, performing an identity by taking up culturally familiar costumes, settings, poses, words, and movements.

performativity
the practice of shaping and expressing our identity through our daily acts of communication

Figure 14.13: Rosie the Riveter being performed by users on popular social media sites

At popular social media sites, such as YouTube, Pinterest, Instagram, and now-defunct Vine (Figure 14.13), one can find thousands of such Rosie performances by both ordinary and famous people as users continue to draw inspiration from Rosie for all kinds of rhetorical purposes.

#5: Seeing an image in social/rhetorical contexts

The original Rosie the Riveter poster is often called a propaganda poster. Its purpose was to convince viewers to hold a particular set of beliefs and support a set of actions that would be aligned with U.S. goals in World War II (and the later versions support other political purposes and actions). The propaganda poster is a genre of visual/hybrid art that developed to serve these rhetorical purposes, and like all genres, it developed common features that evolved from its purposes.

➤ You can place the original Rosie poster in its historical textual context by looking at other posters from the World War II Era. (You can find examples from the National Archives[L14:3] or at history.com.[L14:4])

➤ Or you can find some examples of contemporary propaganda posters[L14:5] at sites like Web Design Survivalist.

➤ Or you can work with a poster example you discovered in Inquiry #1—perhaps, for example, the image of Michelle Obama as Rosie that was originally posted at recovery.gov and was used to convey the strength of the fiscal recovery project after the economic crisis of 2008.

➤ Compare examples of propaganda posters. What kinds of compositional elements do you notice? What can you say about this genre and the ways in which it suits its purpose of persuasion? If you look at other countries' propaganda, what similarities and differences do you notice? If you've chosen an older image, is it still in use today? If so, in what other contexts has it appeared? What kinds of purposes is it used for? How is the image being reinterpreted and performed? If you've chosen a contemporary image, do you find ways in which it borrows specific visual elements from older propaganda posters?

➤ How, in the end, do composers of these posters use the compositional elements available to them to make a visual argument?

Composing
Visual Analysis

In this chapter, we've been exploring what it means to live in a world saturated with images—images created by ourselves, as well as those created by businesses and other organizations for specific rhetorical purposes. We began with a single image, an Instagram post by popular artist Beyoncé as Rosie the Riveter, then traced the roots of her image back through time to the original Rosie the Riveter propaganda poster created in 1942. In the process of exploring, we also encountered several iterations of the Rosie image as it has circulated and been picked up by other composers to create new meanings in the process. We also saw, looking at social media sites, how the visual image of Rosie has been picked up by others, in drawings, photos, tattoos, and video, as others evoke Rosie and perform her for their own social and rhetorical purposes.

It is now your turn to create your own analysis of visual culture by selecting and **curating** a group of related visual artifacts—bringing them together in a collection and then exploring the compositional, cultural, and social/rhetorical aspects of these images.

curating
the practice of selecting suitable examples based on careful study and research

WRITING MOVES ◄

Inquiring and Inventing

For this composing section, consider using an online application for curation that will help you collect and annotate any online resources (links to articles, images, and other relevant digital texts) related to an aspect of visual culture you are interested in learning more about. Some current popular apps for helping manage research online include Zotero, Diigo, Dragdis, and Instapaper. (See Part IV Digital Toolbox.) For our example here, we'll be using Diigo to demonstrate how to collect and organize images, links, and other web resources.

1 Gathering and curating relevant images

Through your inquiries in this chapter, you've had the chance to see and think about a number of visual texts and have probably begun to think about ones that interest you and why. As a first step in composing an analysis of visual culture, you could begin by choosing a visual artifact you find interesting and that has a significant presence in an area of contemporary culture that interests you. You'll want to begin with an image or visual meme that has circulated widely over time and has been used and performed in many different contexts for different rhetorical purposes. Examples can include a range of visual artifacts, from magazine ads, to superheroes, to political revolutionaries, to visual stereotypes of gender and race, to performances of the meme #looklikeaprofessor. In the example of Rosie, we started our inquiry with an image of Beyoncé performing Rosie, then built our initial collection of images around this image to explore and understand the Beyoncé image.

link 🔗 ▶

In this initial research move, the goal is to collect a large number of images to give you a broad sense of the different contexts in which this particular image is circulating in culture. You can begin with a basic image search using a variety of search engines, including Google.

Figure 14.14 is the first page of a search using "Rosie the Riveter." With an image like Rosie that is so widely present, that has spread as a meme, we could never fully explain all the different ways that Rosie is being evoked in all these different contexts. So, it's important to start simple and build your understanding of your initial image as you gather other related images. Choose images you find visually provocative, or that are using the image in novel ways. Also think about collecting images from different time periods to give you a sense of how the use of the image has changed over time. You might also consider images that have circulated as memes. A useful resource for meme images is the site **knowyourmeme.com**,[L14:6] which archives past, present, and suggestions for future memes.

Figure 14.14: Results for basic image search for "Rosie the Riveter"

For our initial image search for Rosie, we used the online application Diigo to help gather and organize our images.

Digital Toolbox
See Part IV, Section 5

Figure 14.15 shows the first round of curated Rosie images, along with the user's name (tim_wallace) and descriptive tags (rosie image) for easier searching and categorizing. Applications like Diigo let users name each image they have saved and add tags to help them organize what they find. Once you have a large group of images (15–20), the next step is to begin grouping and tagging them into different categories based on the content they depict. You'll notice in Figure 14.15 a range of images drawing on Rosie for various purposes grouped according to their different uses. The first image collection resulted in the following six categories of images.

- **Category 1:** Original Rosie images from Westinghouse and Rockwell
- **Category 2:** Pop icons using Rosie
- **Category 3:** Factory images from World War II showing women working
- **Category 4:** Rosie as political protest
- **Category 5:** Performing Rosie in culture and community
- **Category 6:** Rosie toys and apparel

2 Further curating and selecting your images

Once you have collected a good number of images and have categorized them, the next move is to curate further by going through each category and taking notes as you look closer at each image. As you do so, you'll want to look for meaningful patterns and ideas that emerge across the images you have collected. You won't be able to analyze all the categories you have discovered, so your primary goal in this stage is to begin to find a focus you can explore further. Eventually you'll want to narrow in on 4–6 main images to work with that will anchor your analysis. You can still use other images in your analysis, but having a core group of images will help you keep your analysis focused. In our exploration of the Beyoncé image for this chapter, we also examined the two original images of Rosie alongside her use as a political message, and

Figure 14.15: Screenshot of Diigo showing the first stage of collecting and curating a group of Rosie the Riveter images

the way everyday people enact and perform Rosie online and off.

3 Stepping back and reflecting on your curated collection

Before you move into a more extended cultural and visual analysis of the images you have chosen, now is a good time to step back, read through any annotations and notes you've taken, and write about some of the things you've learned in this process. What kinds of patterns and relationships have you noticed across images and websites? Are there similarities in composition? What are some of the contexts in which these images emerge and circulate? How are they shared, and what different kinds of meanings are expressed in the process? As you answer these questions, you'll want to note themes and ideas that interest you and that have potential to be extended into a more in-depth analysis of these visual artifacts.

WRITING MOVES ◄───

Drafting and Shaping

Digital Toolbox
See Part IV, Section 1

Now that you've had a chance to collect, curate, and think about an image and some of its variants, you are ready to shape and compose a longer, more sustained visual and cultural analysis of these images. You can use any number of prewriting strategies to map out your visual analysis, but one simple and effective way is to use a sheet of paper and a pen/pencil to draw visual relationships between different aspects of your analysis (often called "bubbling" or "mapping"), or use mind mapping software. The idea is to create a visual representation that can serve as a guide for your written analysis.

One way to set up your analysis is to start to map the three perspectives we've focused on in this chapter: compositional, contextual, and social/rhetorical. Figure 14.16 is the beginning of an example map for the Rosie images we've chosen to explore.

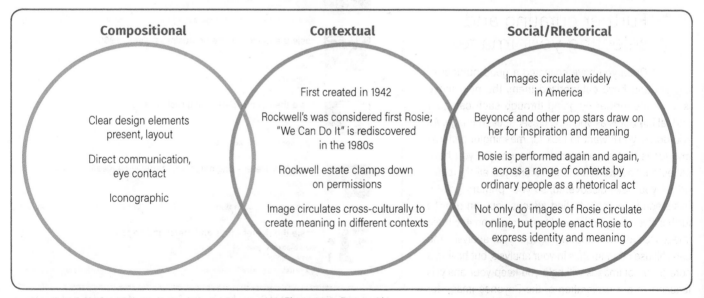

Compositional

Clear design elements present, layout

Direct communication, eye contact

Iconographic

Contextual

First created in 1942

Rockwell's was considered first Rosie; "We Can Do It" is rediscovered in the 1980s

Rockwell estate clamps down on permissions

Image circulates cross-culturally to create meaning in different contexts

Social/Rhetorical

Images circulate widely in America

Beyoncé and other pop stars draw on her for inspiration and meaning

Rosie is performed again and again, across a range of contexts by ordinary people as a rhetorical act

Not only do images of Rosie circulate online, but people enact Rosie to express identity and meaning

Figure 14.16: Perspectives map

1 Compositional analysis

As we did with the handful of Rosie images we looked at earlier, one way to begin your analysis is by looking at the **what** and **how** of the images. How are design concepts like balance, contrast, alignment, repetition, and proximity being used? How are the visual elements arranged in each example, and how are words and images working together? Do you notice any patterns or similarities across images and how they are laid out? Working through these compositional questions will help you describe what you see and provide a good base for further analysis.

2 Contextualizing the images you have chosen to analyze

When contextualizing your group of images, you are trying to understand, as much as you can, the **where** and **when** of the images' composition. What are the historical circumstances of their production? Where and when were they published? By whom? As with each of the Rosie images we chose to work with, knowing the when and where of their publication helps us understand the history and context they come from. As Megan Garber's piece demonstrates, there's an important history to the Rosie images, and that history gives us a richer sense of the meanings Rosie carries with her as she moves through different contexts. For this move, and the moves that follow, you should begin collecting relevant articles and readings you can draw on for your analysis. Again, using an application like Diigo, begin collecting and bookmarking both scholarly and more popular texts that will inform your analysis of these images (Figure 14.17).

Using your images as your starting point, search for both scholarly and more popular articles to help inform your own cultural and historical understanding of your chosen images, and bookmark those sites so you can return to them again for closer reading and note-taking. The sixth article listed in Figure 14.17, for instance, contained a helpful discussion of some of the historical/cultural contexts of the Rosie image and therefore became the reading for this chapter.

From this perspective, you'll want to ask some of the following questions.

- When and where were the earliest versions of this image created, for what purposes, and with what meanings for those who created, viewed, or circulated them at that time?

- How has the image been taken up and used in other contexts?

- Have the earlier cultural meanings been kept or altered as others have recontextualized the image and adapted it to new times, places, or uses?

- Do you find patterns in what elements are kept and evoked as an image is reshaped and remixed?

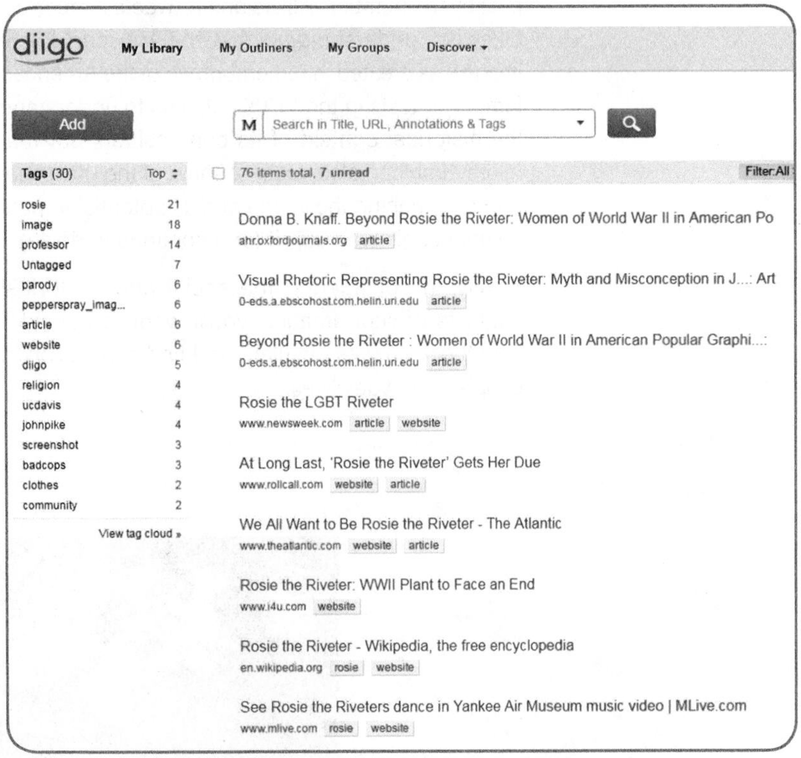

Figure 14.17: List of relevant articles for cultural and historical background on Rosie the Riveter

3 Considering the social and rhetorical aspects of the images

At this stage in your analysis, you're most likely beginning to form ideas about why the images you selected were created and for what purpose. In addition to considering the compositional and cultural aspects of your images, you'll want to also ask questions about some of the social and rhetorical purposes behind their composition. Who is the audience of these images, and how are they attempting to communicate with that audience? What values and beliefs are they expressing? As we noted with Beyoncé as Rosie, we can tell a little about how her audience favorably reacted to her post by the number of likes and retweets it received. Likewise, understanding that the Mexican Rosie image was created in remembrance of the American farmer protests in the 1970s helps us to understand the historical context of its composition, but that information can also suggest some of the rhetorical purposes behind the image and its potential impact on the people who saw it (and continue to do so).

Finally, in considering the social and rhetorical contexts of such images, you'll want to consider how these images circulate and find expression in people's everyday lives.

How are they picked up by others in different contexts? How and why do people draw meaning from these images, and how do they perform such meanings? How are others using the images to create new meanings, or, like Beyoncé, performing a particular social identity? The image in Figure 14.18 is such an example, taken in 2015 at the Rosie the Riveter World War II Home Front National Park in San Francisco, where more than 1,000 Rosie looka-likes gathered to break the *Guinness Book* world record for the most Rosies gathered in one location, surpassing the previous record of 776 Rosies set the year before in Michigan.[14.7]

4 Synthesizing your ideas

At this point, you'll want to find an interesting angle to write about. You won't be able to cover all the insights you have gained during your research process, so you'll want to focus on those things that stand out most for you. For some images, you might find that the cultural and historical meanings stand out; for others, the social and rhetorical aspects and how individuals in communities perform these images as acts of social identity may seem more relevant. In any case, your goal is to bring together a rich discussion of the compositional, cultural, and social aspects of these images in a way that sheds light on how these images express meaning and how that meaning changes as it circulates from context to context and use to use.

Figure 14.18: Women dressed as Rosie the Riveter in San Francisco, CA, 2015

WRITING MOVES ◀

Revising and Publishing

When you've finished drafting your composition, you'll want to get feedback from peer readers/viewers to see whether they've followed (and hopefully enjoyed) your analysis and to make any necessary revisions to strengthen your work.

1 Using peer response questions

Here are some peer response questions you can begin with, in addition to any you feel might be useful in helping your peer improve his or her work.

- Has the composer collected, organized, and reflected on a set of related and meaningful images?

- Has the composer analyzed the composition of one or more of these images, considering how the images are arranged and how their design communicates their intended meanings? Does the composer use that understanding to explore both what's constant and what varies across the set of images?

- How does the compositional analysis provided here lead to a larger point, a larger analysis of these images? Are there additional compositional elements that seem central to how these images function that the composer should consider?

- If working from a historical/cultural perspective, has the composer placed these images in their historical and cultural contexts, showing how they've been adapted to create new meanings as they've been recontextualized? What else might you want to know about where and how these images have circulated? What questions are you left with about the paths they traveled or what those paths suggest?

- If working from a social/rhetorical perspective, has the composer explored why and how these images are circulating, with what audiences, and for what new purposes? Has the composer explored what shared meanings and values are reflected in these images?

- Is the analysis well organized and easy to follow?

- Has the writer/composer chosen appropriate visual images and placed them effectively in the composition? Are there places where another image would be helpful or where an image is distracting and might be eliminated?

- Does the composer, by the end, leave you convinced that this is a fair and interesting analysis from which you've learned something?

- What other advice would you give to the composer of the text?

2 Revising for public circulation

You've chosen images that are already in wide public circulation. Now you'll want to consider how to place the new understandings you've gained into a public conversation. In addition to posting your full analysis to a class blog, wiki, or website, you might ask: What are some of the sites on which I've found the images I've used? Do they accept new posts or comments? Can I add particular observations to sites where they would be relevant, creating and following a plan to scatter the meanings I've come up with among the most suitable locations?

You'll want to provide source information for any images you'll post to public sites, being sure to give the appropriate credit for the original image (and you'll find the information and credits for the images we've used in this book on page 593. See also "Copyright and Fair Use: How It Works for Online Images[L14:7]). Reposting a widely circulating meme without explicit authorization from the originator has become common practice, but occasionally there are objections.

Reinventing and Circulating Your Work

Another way to approach a visual analysis is to explore how certain social identities and roles are performed visually. Twitter conversations like #ilooklikeanengineer and #ilooklikeaprofessor have been exploring the way online searches can often perpetuate certain stereotypes about different roles and identities. As Adeline Koh wrote about starting #ilooklikeaprofessor (Figure 14.19):[4;8]

Figure 14.19: Initial post from Adeline Koh and the launch of #ILookLikeAProfessor

#ILookLikeAProfessor isn't a catch-all. Rather, I'm interpreting the hashtag as a way to rally people whose bodies or orientations have been used to discriminate them and to tell them that they have no place in academia. If you teach in higher education in any way, you deserve the respect that comes with the title. Grad student, alt-ac, adjunct, contingent, tenure-track: if you teach in higher education, you deserve to say #ILookLikeAProfessor.

Figure 14.20 is a recent screenshot of a search for "professor" using Google.

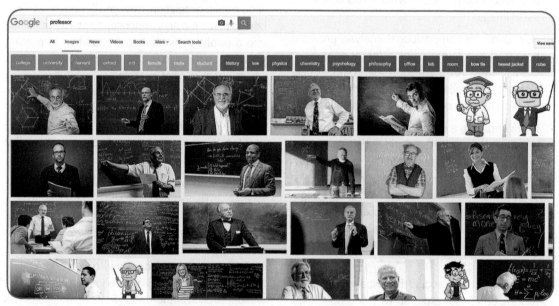

Figure 14.20: Recent screenshot of a search for "professor" using Google

Since its start in March 2015, hundreds of real professors have posted images of themselves using #ilooklikeaprofessor to show the growing diversity of professors around the country (Figure 14.21). Using the concepts from this chapter, you can explore the images themselves, the contexts that have given rise to them, and their rhetorical purposes and social meanings. How might the creative performance of a professor identity help to make strong cultural stereotypes visible and help us challenge them?

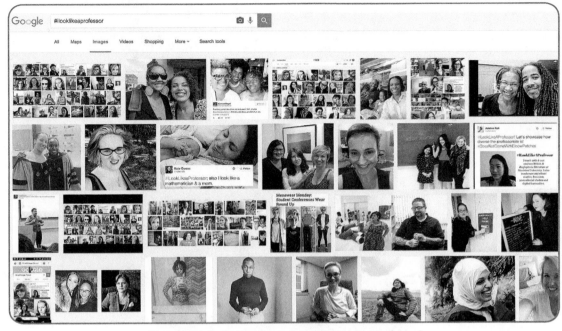

Figure 14.21: Basic image search for "#ILookLikeAProfessor"

Key Concepts

arrangement 307

curating 315

performativity 314

recontextualization 304

visual culture 304

visual grammar 306

visual meme 304

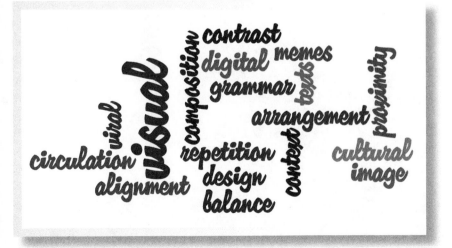

Claiming Positions
in Digital Contexts

CHAPTER FIFTEEN

CENTRAL QUESTIONS

1 What does one blog writer's position about social media and the counterarguments raised by his readers demonstrate about what claims might be convincing and how they are convincing for individuals within a particular community?

2 What does a widely circulated public argument about the broader political impact of social media contribute to our understanding of how claims about the digital world might be supported or countered?

3 What position about the impact of social media within a local or wider community might you present in a reasoned argument, and how would you present it?

Chapter Preview

We've been exploring some of the ways in which digital culture has supported wider participation in more global conversations as we find more common sites for sharing and exchange. In many of those exchanges, we find others making claims, or we make them ourselves, about what is happening in the world around us and why it might be positive or troublesome. A novelist makes an implicit claim that Silicon Valley companies are gradually eroding our privacy and could be controlling all aspects of our lives in the future. Political candidates often make outrageous claims about the risks of one another's proposals that then circulate through the internet. Our Facebook pages are filled with claims shared by friends about the benefits of health products, the behavior of celebrities, or the dangers of drones. Our conversations, and the rhetorical relationships they support, often involve an expanding cultural critique of the role the internet is playing in our lives and in our society, and often constitute an informal inquiry into the effects it might be having at both personal and societal levels.

At the same time, much of what we do on the internet helps us claim and develop stances: what we search for, what we post, what we share, and what we "like" all helps us to articulate our own positions on issues. Some of the claims we read and share are developed and backed by analysis and research. Many are put forward without real evidence. There's a difference between claiming a position and developing a reasoned position. Both are common rhetorical moves, but we'll begin to explore what's involved in the latter in this chapter.

Here, we'll focus on a recurring theme in claims about social media and their potential impact both in our individual and local settings and in more global contexts. We'll look at claims made both for and against using Facebook.

Exploring
Claims about Social Media

The internet has become the space where we make arguments about private or public concerns. Where once we might have argued for or against various positions in conversation with family or friends or through writing to a newspaper, we're now likely to take those positions through our use of social media—through what we like or share or comment on, as well as through our own posts.

Arguments, in general, are rhetorical—they are intended to persuade a particular audience to consider a specific position on an issue where there are likely to be opposing views. For example, a teenager who wants to have his curfew extended might now use Google to find evidence showing typical curfews for people his age. A community organization that wants to build a homeless shelter in a particular neighborhood might now conduct an online media campaign to present its arguments. And a president who wants the Congress to support a health care initiative might have her aides tweet links to evidence that refutes counterarguments. In each case, the proponent of the position must make some basic rhetorical moves. She must state the position and make some claims about it, present some logical reasons and evidence in support of those claims, and counter others' likely objections to those reasons or to the chain of reasoning. And doing this effectively requires understanding the audience for a particular argument and what that audience will likely respond to.

Taking and supporting a reasoned position typically involves gathering information related to that position: engaging in the sorts of analysis we've been doing to understand whether a cultural production is groundbreaking or just repetitive of earlier work, for example, or gathering data from observations or other research that shows whether texting is helping or interfering with our relationships. Indeed, most of our attempts to learn more about our digital contexts and the textual ecologies of our local and global communities involve the careful examination of claims and positions, and finding evidence that might support or refute them. In the process, we set forth our own arguments, make our own claims, and present our own evidence. As we join the larger public and research conversations about the issues and concerns we've been exploring, we are engaging in what is referred to in academic contexts as the genre of **argument**.

argument
a reasoned set of statements and evidence intended to persuade others about a claim or position

Context, Shared Knowledge, and What Makes a Good Argument

The context for a particular argument matters (the **where**). In local communities, people often have shared knowledge and are trying to come to a shared understanding about a question or issue. They may take different positions or see things in different ways. But they are taking part in a reasoned conversation with a common purpose—trying to solve a problem, to analyze a situation, or to figure out why something works as it does. Arguments are often exploratory—testing out a position or thesis. While those involved in them may hold different views, they will take into account and try to understand one another's perspectives.

Public arguments with wider audiences may or may not function in similar ways. Often, on the internet, those who put forth claims offer little support for them, yet they are widely shared and reposted. Claims made by candidates for electoral office, for example, often lack supporting evidence or are blatantly false, and various respectable fact-checking sites have arisen to address this problem. The Pulitzer Prize-winning site PolitiFact rates the claims of politicians, and the claims of others that spread virally in emails and Facebook posts, rating them on a scale from true to false to "pants on fire," for claims like the very unscientific fact that spread virally as a chain email (Figure 15.1) or false facts about Facebook's policies that spread through Facebook posts (Figure 15.2). And Snopes fact-checks urban legends, folklore, myths, rumors, and other misinformation.

Factcheck.org is another site that addresses not just political candidates' statements, but also what it calls "the viral spiral," posting information about current false claims spreading through email and the internet, and it offers a helpful video of advice about how to spot bogus claims.[L15:1]

link

Most public claims can eventually be supported or refuted, or, as the fact-checking sites often find, can be understood as half-truths. But not every claim can be so easily fact-checked. Often people take positions and make claims based on experience and opinion, and these can be harder to sort through, like the much-debated topic among individuals of whether using a particular form of social media is likely to improve your life.

CHAIN EMAIL

"Solar panels drain the sun's energy."

Don't put away that sunblock yet

Figure 15.1: PolitiFact Pants on Fire viral email

FACEBOOK POSTS

Facebook has unveiled new rules to stop their users from creating posts related in any way to religion.

— *PolitiFact National*

When satire goes viral

Figure 15.2: PolitiFact Pants on Fire Facebook post

INQUIRY

#1: Arguments for and against using social media

What are your primary ways of connecting with others online? Do you belong to Facebook, use Twitter, post to Instagram or Snapchat, or use WhatsApp? What arguments might you make in favor of your preferred medium for connecting against another medium? Are there are other members of your community who are Facebook enthusiasts or Facebook rejectors, for example? From members of your community and/or your classmates, what reasons do people give for using or not using the sites that are used most frequently? What claims get made about these sites and their advantages or disadvantages?

Facebook has been the focus of many social media arguments and of much research about its effects.[15:1] Though newer social media platforms continue to be developed, Facebook continues to be widely used by people young and old, and arguments about its advantages and disadvantages are common as people continue to decide whether to join or quit. For example, in her *Huffington Post* article, Renee Jacques, using the now-common online "list" text offers "11 Reasons You Should Quit Facebook In 2014,"[15:2, L15:2]

Sidenote

Facebook's been around for more than 10 years (a long time in the life of the internet) and has a global reach (with well more than a billion monthly users).

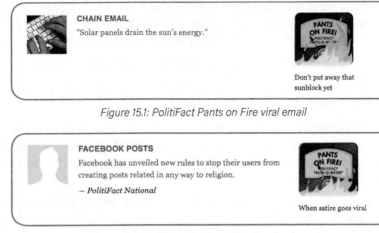

Her reasons can be grouped around several areas of concern, several claims that can be made to support an argument against using Facebook.

➤ There are problems with the platform: newer social media platforms can suit your needs better, allowing you to post photos (Instagram) or status updates (Twitter) more easily; Facebook keeps suggesting friends you don't know or want to know; it's including too many ads.

➤ There are problems with your network of friends and what they see and post (family members might learn too much about what you're doing or post photos you'd find embarrassing; you're only really interested in a small subset of those friends; you don't want to read the "good" news about their engagements).

➤ Some studies show heavy users to be less happy with their lives.

➤ There are concerns about privacy (Facebook makes it hard to keep your identity hidden, and it even tracks what you type but don't post).

This rather tongue-in-cheek list for a popular audience does reflect some real concerns about Facebook, tossing in a number of claims in no particular order. As an example of the list genre, its rhetorical purpose is to raise some provocative issues rather than making a carefully reasoned argument that takes opposing claims and evidence into account.

Here's a more careful consideration of the other side, as the journalist Gideon Lichfield, who has long taken the position for himself not to join Facebook, makes the decision to join after resisting for 10 years.

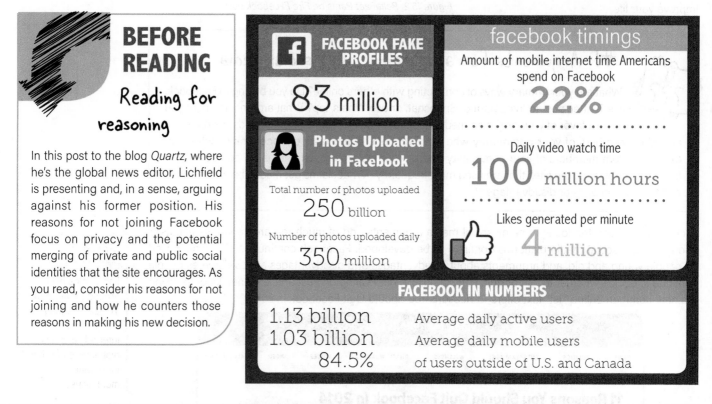

BEFORE READING

Reading for reasoning

In this post to the blog *Quartz*, where he's the global news editor, Lichfield is presenting and, in a sense, arguing against his former position. His reasons for not joining Facebook focus on privacy and the potential merging of private and public social identities that the site encourages. As you read, consider his reasons for not joining and how he counters those reasons in making his new decision.

FACEBOOK FAKE PROFILES
83 million

Photos Uploaded in Facebook
Total number of photos uploaded
250 billion
Number of photos uploaded daily
350 million

facebook timings
Amount of mobile internet time Americans spend on Facebook
22%

Daily video watch time
100 million hours

Likes generated per minute
4 million

FACEBOOK IN NUMBERS
1.13 billion — Average daily active users
1.03 billion — Average daily mobile users
84.5% — of users outside of U.S. and Canada

READING

"Why I've Finally Joined Facebook on Facebook's Tenth Anniversary" 15:3
by Gideon Lichfield
Quartz, February 4, 2014

When Facebook opened up to the general public in 2006, I was living in Jerusalem, covering the Israeli-Palestinian conflict. Before that I'd spent two years in Vladimir Putin's Russia. My work involved trying to gain the trust of groups of people who were sometimes out to kill each other. I was circumspect

and maybe a little paranoid. I got good at compartmentalizing.

Facebook was not good at compartmentalizing. At the time, there was no way to hide your friend list from people who were not on it. Mine would have included Palestinian activists, Israeli nationalists, religious Jewish settlers (perhaps

READING

my cousins among them), and a lot of gay people on both sides. What if they could all see each other? And what if the wrong person or government got hold of my friend list? For some people I knew, just being on that list might put them at risk.

Facebook's CEO, Mark Zuckerberg, offered his answer to such worries in a 2009 interview with David Kirkpatrick, author of *The Facebook Effect*:

"You have one identity… The days of you having a different image for your work friends or co-workers and for the other people you know are probably coming to an end pretty quickly… Having two identities for yourself is an example of a lack of integrity."

That seemed stupid to me (and not only to me). Only someone cocooned in a temple of reasonableness like a Harvard dorm room or a Silicon Valley tech company could be so naive. Out there where I lived, it wasn't like you could just find another job if your co-workers didn't like the company you kept. In most places, and especially in the world's less free countries, many have no choice: Life forces them to form ties with people from whom they must perforce keep secrets.

So I didn't join Facebook.

By the time I moved to New York in 2009, not being on Facebook was already exotic enough to be a kind of badge of pride. And serious people started to warn about the dangers of the network's ever-laxer privacy policy. Every time I considered joining, a new scandal or revelation deterred me.

One of them was personal. In June 2010, Facebook sent me an email telling me a friend had tagged me in a photo. Not just any photo: I was wearing drag at a gay pride march. In theory, since I wasn't on Facebook, this should have been impossible. But because several people had previously sent me invitations to join Facebook, the system knew there was an entity with my name and email address. And so, even though I had exercised the ultimate opt-out, it gave me no choice in the matter. I couldn't even untag myself, because that required logging into Facebook. I had to ask my friend to do it.

Since then, more and more prominent people have started shutting down their Facebook accounts or trimming their friend lists. They cite a lack of time, fears about privacy, Facebook's shadowy corporate governance, or its profiteering from their data. Besides, we've been told, the kids are all leaving it anyway.

So why have I just joined Facebook?

There are practical reasons. I'm missing out on invitations to things. I'm losing track of what a lot of acquaintances (especially far-flung ones) are up to, and Facebook is good way to keep up those "weak ties." There are some people with whom I want to get back in touch, and Facebook is the easiest way to find them.

But mainly it's that I'm no longer as worried as I was about privacy. This isn't because I think Facebook has become more benign; it still has a commercial incentive to not only encourage us but, as danah boyd has written, to trick us into exposing as much of ourselves as possible. Just a couple of months ago, for example, it emerged that making your friend list "private" doesn't really make it private.

No, there are two reasons I'm less worried. The first is that I've changed, partly because I've now spent five years cocooned in the temple of (relative) reasonableness that is New York City, and partly because I'm older and have less patience for other people's prejudices about who I am.

The second is that Edward Snowden's revelations about US surveillance and the steady drumbeat of stories about hackers breaching company databases have convinced me that many of my worries are moot. We all now have to live with the assumption that our privacy can be blown apart at any moment.

Such a world is not one I'd choose to live in. It's one in which I write every email, text or instant message with a little privacy devil sitting on my shoulder, whispering "What if this gets out?" But I don't have a choice. Even if governments scale back their surveillance excesses and impose tighter regulations on companies that hold our data, the sheer quantity of that data—and the things that can be exposed by a security breach or even an indiscreet friend or colleague—is still huge. Google knows more about me than I myself do. LinkedIn and Twitter know a lot. Am I really protecting myself by keeping Facebook at bay?

So I'll protect myself the way anyone should: by being careful. I won't share or "like" much; I'll use Facebook mostly passively. I'll be selective about whom I friend, and I won't friend anyone I need to protect. I'll keep the privacy settings cranked up to the max and watch out for when Facebook quietly changes them.

And when I have to win the trust of suspicious people, I may just have to earn that trust through openness instead of by concealment. And that may not be such a bad thing. ■

To support their positions, both Jacques and Lichfield point to particular examples of the extensive research that has been done on Facebook.

What they link to tells us a lot about the claims they make and how they support their positions. For example, Jacques links to a *Time* magazine article about why teenagers are leaving Facebook, as well as a scholarly article about how more frequent users of Facebook felt "that others were happier and had better lives."[15:3] Lichfield begins in a similar way, linking to articles about privacy concerns on Facebook and their data collection policies, but rather than use the articles to support why he shouldn't use Facebook, he uses them as a counterpoint to the position he is advocating, that Facebook's pros outweigh its cons.

INQUIRY

#2: Responding to claims about Facebook

After reading both articles, what is your own response to the claims made there? From your own examples, can you list some of the strongest arguments and counterarguments for and against using this form of social media?

The appeal of arguments depends on audience and context. Which reasons to join or not join Facebook are likely to be most convincing within one of your own communities? What other evidence might you seek to support a particular argument for that community?

The Huffington Post has had posts on both sides of the argument (though not in direct conversation with each other), with some tongue-in-cheek posts like Jacques's <u>list of reasons to quit Facebook</u>[L15:2] (like "It Makes Getting Over a Breakup Really Hard") and <u>another post</u>[L15:3] on the ways in which social media can benefit relationships. Would the claims offered in either of these alter the position you'd present to your community?

links

Common Forms of Position Arguments

The many writers who have taken a public position for or against joining Facebook have the likely rhetorical purposes of convincing others of its benefits or its risks. Some of these arguments fall into patterns that rhetoricians who have studied the larger genre of argument have found to recur across many positions and topics.

Types of arguments that have been used to support a position include the following.

A **causal argument**. Causal arguments, stating the position that one thing causes another, may be the most common type in public discourse. We see the argument that extensive use of the internet is altering students' reading patterns and reducing their attention span, or that the abbreviated language of texting is harming texters' ability to spell, and evidence can be found to support both sides of these positions. Many arguments against Facebook or other social media are causal.

> **causal argument**
> an argument in support of a position that one thing causes another

- Using a particular site is a bad idea because inadequate privacy controls may cause risk to users.
- Spending time on social media causes a reduction in time for maintaining face-to-face relationships.
- Spending time on social media serves as a distraction from more focused activities.

In many instances, what seems causal may just be co-occurring. If there's evidence that spelling has gotten worse since the advent of texting, it could be coincidental, or there could be other causes. If a Facebook user doesn't see friends as often, he might be otherwise busy at the times they get together. In such co-occurrence or correlation, one thing happens along with another, without necessarily being a primary cause. An article in *The Atlantic* asking "<u>Is Facebook Making us Lonely?</u>"[15:6, L15:4] points to a lack of evidence that Facebook is the cause for current loneliness, citing a study of 1,200 Facebook users by researcher Moira Burke:

link

Burke's research does not support the assertion that Facebook creates loneliness. The people who experience loneliness on Facebook are lonely away from Facebook, too, she points out; on Facebook, as everywhere else, correlation is not causation.

As a reader, it's important that you consider carefully any evidence for **causation** versus **correlation**. Arguments about the social world, for example about causes and effects related to social media, aren't likely to have definitive evidence for one side or the other, but as a writer, you'll want your causal arguments to draw on the strongest evidence you can find.

A **definition argument.** Another common type of argument in public and academic spaces attempts to define one thing in terms of another. To argue that some particular instances of online posts constitute cyberbullying, one would have to define cyberbullying and show how these examples fit that definition.

Thus a definition argument will take the form: *x* is *y*. For example, cyberbullying is the repeated posting of humiliating comments about someone online, or collecting massive amounts of data on U.S. citizens is a violation of our right to privacy (where "right to privacy" is defined). Such definitions are built into many arguments. Several of Jacques' 11 points depend on how "friend" is defined, and most definitions wouldn't include the "complete strangers" that Facebook proposes you add.

Other types of argument

Evaluative arguments involve taking a position and making claims about the quality of something, such as those made in reviews of cultural productions—a movie, a music blog, or a performance (as we saw in Chapter 12). One can also make a **proposal argument**, proposing a course of action in the world (as we saw in Chapter 9's reading, where Lawrence Lessig proposes changes to copyright law) or a proposal for a project to be carried out, as we'll describe in Chapter 17. Embedded in these arguments is the question **why**. **Why** is the proposed work needed? What evidence is there to show that? Finally, in opposition to any of these arguments are what might be termed **counter** or **rebuttal arguments**, attempting to refute or oppose an argument someone has already made, responding to the terms and claims that the arguer has proposed. Our next reading for this chapter, written by Malcolm Gladwell, also involves a counterargument, against others who would make the claim that activity on social media can cause significant political change.

The arguments that circulate often depend on more than one of these types, or perhaps others we haven't named. But the types we've named here have proven to be useful working categories for understanding the arguments that are commonly made both within and about our digital world.

Often in digital contexts arguments are made visually as well as verbally, working toward their own rhetorical purposes. For example, *Wired,* a magazine that focuses on the digital world, took the position in 2010 that "The Web is Dead,"[15:7] making that claim in bold headlines on a red background. The image quickly became a circulating meme and soon generated counterarguments and counter images. See Figure 15.3.

Because arguments are rhetorical acts, not only will you find logical reasons to believe a position (*logos*), you'll find reasons that appeal to emotions (*pathos*), as when fears about privacy concerns are invoked in anti-social-media arguments. You'll also find appeals to authority (*ethos*). Sherry Turkle, as an MIT researcher on the effects of our digital lives, is often cited by those who argue that using social media adversely affects our relationships,[15:8] while Moira Burke's research on Facebook and loneliness[15:9] is cited to support the opposite. The images of visual arguments likewise depend on these appeals.

Margin glossary

causation
when a second event is the result of a first

correlation
when a second event occurs along with a first but without evidence that one has resulted from the other

definition argument
an argument that something fits a particular definition or category

evaluative argument
an argument that takes a position about the quality of something or about how well it works

proposal argument
an argument that proposes a course of action

counter or rebuttal argument
an argument that opposes or refutes another argument

See Chapter 10 for a more detailed discussion of the the appeals.

Figure 15.3: Wired *magazine images*

INQUIRY

#3: Identifying appeals

Returning to some of the arguments you gathered for or against using Facebook or other social media in one of your own communities, what types of appeals (emotion-*pathos*, authority-*ethos*, reason-*logos*) are they based on, and what forms do they take? Do these choices reflect the particular purposes of the person making the argument within a particular context?

Making Connections
Arguments about the Power of Social Media

The posts about why to quit Facebook or why to join focus on the advantages or disadvantages of using a particular form of social media for individual users or groups of users—a primarily local concern. But arguments are being made about the global impact of social media as well. At a time when there is much concern about the ways in which social media have been used to gather recruits for ISIS and other terrorist groups, but also interest in social media as a means of engaging young people in this country in democratic political activity, there is a significant debate about the potential for the internet to impact what goes on in the world in major ways.

The article we'll turn to, by the social science journalist Malcolm Gladwell, was an early entry (2010) into an argument that continues about the potential for social media to affect large-scale political change. His article, written for *The New Yorker,* spawned a number of counterarguments at the time and has been reexamined often as newer political developments take place. We'll spend some time with Gladwell's argument before considering its later textual ecology—the ways in which it has been picked up and echoed, and its claims revisited in the context of current events. (We've reproduced major portions of his argument and summarized other sections.) Another argument essay, "Is Google Making Us Stupid?" by journalist Nicholas Carr, appears in the Additional Readings for Part II and can be explored in a similar way.

Following an Argument

As a reader, you'll want to focus your first efforts on understanding the argument being presented and the points being made to support it, even if you find yourself disagreeing and wanting to counter it in the end. As you read Gladwell's essay, note first the argument he is making.

INQUIRY

#4: Establishing context as a reader

In exploring a new topic of argument about the role of social media in creating social change, it is useful to consider what you know and how you might tentatively position yourself on this question. Before you read Malcolm Gladwell's argument for his position that such sites cannot mobilize revolutions or social change, collect your own thoughts on this issue. Can sites like Facebook or Twitter work to organize and enact social causes? What examples come to mind? Where might you find evidence to support your position?

BEFORE READING:
Reading and annotating

As you read and annotate, consider the following questions.

- What argument does Gladwell present in this article? What are his claims?

- What claims is he arguing against?

- What theories does he use to support his stance?

- What evidence does he draw on?

- What comparisons does he structure this piece around?

- What do you think of Gladwell's argument? How strong is his position?

- What can you say about the appeals of Gladwell's argument (to authority, reason, or emotion)? What effect does using a historical event from the civil rights movement as a point of comparison have on you as a reader? What sort of appeal or appeals do you find imbedded in his recounting of this event?

- How convincing do you find this piece?

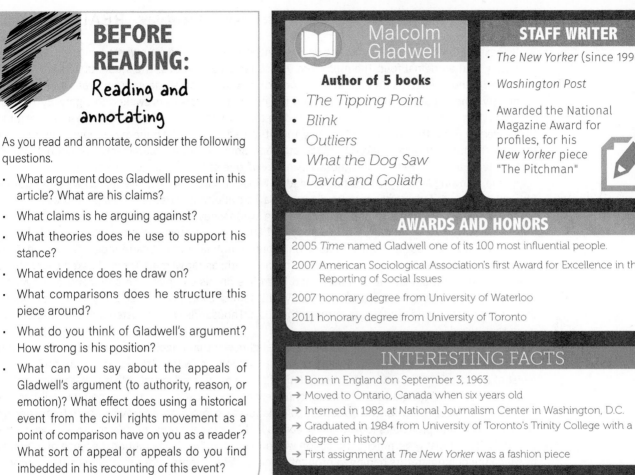

Malcolm Gladwell

Author of 5 books
- *The Tipping Point*
- *Blink*
- *Outliers*
- *What the Dog Saw*
- *David and Goliath*

STAFF WRITER
- *The New Yorker* (since 1996)
- *Washington Post*
- Awarded the National Magazine Award for profiles, for his *New Yorker* piece "The Pitchman"

AWARDS AND HONORS

2005 *Time* named Gladwell one of its 100 most influential people.

2007 American Sociological Association's first Award for Excellence in the Reporting of Social Issues

2007 honorary degree from University of Waterloo

2011 honorary degree from University of Toronto

INTERESTING FACTS

→ Born in England on September 3, 1963
→ Moved to Ontario, Canada when six years old
→ Interned in 1982 at National Journalism Center in Washington, D.C.
→ Graduated in 1984 from University of Toronto's Trinity College with a degree in history
→ First assignment at *The New Yorker* was a fashion piece

https://en.wikipedia.org/wiki/Malcolm_Gladwell

READING

Place annotations here

Selection from

"Small Change: Why the Revolution Will Not Be Tweeted" 15:10
by Malcolm Gladwell
The New Yorker, October 4, 2010

At four-thirty in the afternoon on Monday, February 1, 1960, four college students sat down at the lunch counter at the Woolworth's in downtown Greensboro, North Carolina. They were freshmen at North Carolina A. & T., a black college a mile or so away. "I'd like a cup of coffee, please," one of the four, Ezell Blair, said to the waitress. "We don't serve Negroes here," she replied.

The Woolworth's lunch counter was a long L-shaped bar that could seat sixty-six people, with a standup snack bar at one end. The seats were for whites. The snack bar was for blacks. Another employee, a black woman who worked at the steam table, approached the students and tried to warn them away. "You're acting stupid, ignorant!" she said. They didn't move. Around five-thirty, the front doors to the store were locked. The four still didn't move. Finally, they left by a side door. Outside, a small crowd had gathered, including a photographer from the Greensboro Record. "I'll be back tomorrow with A. & T. College," one of the students said.

By next morning, the protest had grown to twenty-seven men and four women, most from the same dormitory as the original four. The men were dressed in suits and ties. The students had brought their schoolwork, and studied as they sat at the counter. On Wednesday, students from Greensboro's "Negro" secondary school, Dudley High, joined in, and the number of protesters swelled to eighty. By Thursday, the protesters numbered three hundred, including three white women, from the Greensboro campus of the University of North Carolina. By Saturday, the sit-in had reached six hundred. People spilled out onto the street. White teen-agers waved Confederate flags. Someone threw a firecracker. At noon, the A. & T. football team arrived. "Here comes the wrecking crew," one of the white students shouted.

By the following Monday, sit-ins had spread to Winston-Salem, twenty-five miles away, and Durham, fifty miles away. The day after that, students at Fayetteville State Teachers College and at Johnson C. Smith College, in Charlotte, joined in, followed on Wednesday by students at St. Augustine's College and Shaw University, in Raleigh. On Thursday and Friday, the protest crossed state lines, surfacing in Hampton and Portsmouth, Virginia, in Rock Hill, South Carolina, and in Chattanooga, Tennessee. By the end of the month, there were sit-ins throughout the South, as far west as Texas. "I asked every student I met what the first day of the sit downs had been like on his campus," the political theorist Michael Walzer wrote in Dissent. "The answer was always the same: 'It was like a fever. Everyone wanted to go.' " Some seventy thousand students eventually took part. Thousands were arrested and untold thousands more radicalized.

These events in the early sixties became a civil-rights war that engulfed the South for the rest of the decade—and it happened without e-mail, texting, Facebook, or Twitter. The world, we are told, is in the midst of a revolution. The new tools of social media have reinvented social activism. With Facebook and Twitter and the like, the traditional relationship between political authority and popular will has been upended, making it easier for the powerless to collaborate, coördinate, and give voice to their concerns. When ten thousand protesters took to the streets in Moldova in the spring of 2009 to protest against their country's Communist government, the action was dubbed the Twitter Revolution, because of the means by which the demonstrators had been brought together. A few months after that, when student protests rocked Tehran, the State Department took the unusual step of asking Twitter to suspend scheduled maintenance of its Web site, because the Administration didn't want such a critical organizing tool out of service at the height of the demonstrations. "Without Twitter the people of Iran would not have felt empowered and confident to stand up for freedom and democracy," Mark Pfeifle, a former national-security adviser, later wrote, calling for Twitter to be nominated for the Nobel Peace Prize. Where activists were once defined by their causes, they are now defined by their tools. Facebook warriors go online to push for change. "You are the best hope for us all," James K. Glassman, a former senior State Department official, told a crowd of cyber activists at a recent conference sponsored by Facebook, A. T. & T., Howcast, MTV, and Google. Sites like Facebook, Glassman said, "give the U.S. a significant competitive advantage over terrorists. Some time ago, I said that Al Qaeda was 'eating our lunch on the Internet.' That is no longer the case. Al Qaeda is stuck in Web 1.0. The Internet is now about interactivity and conversation."

These are strong, and puzzling, claims. Why does it matter who is eating whose lunch on the Internet? Are people who log on to their Facebook page really the best hope for us all?

Gladwell goes on to quote several people who saw the role of social media activity in Moldova and Iran as having limited effect and suggests that innovators tend to believe that their technologies are more important than they are. He then returns to the Greensboro sit-in, noting that the core participants were college roommates, and to other civil rights activism during the Mississippi Freedom Summer Project of 1964, where the dangers were even greater (three civil rights workers were kidnapped and killed, and 37 black churches were burned, amid other violence against the protestors). He asks "What makes people capable of this kind of activism?" and cites research that showed that the difference between those who stuck with the Freedom Summer and those who dropped out was "an applicant's degree of

READING

personal connection to the civil rights movement, with more close friends who were participating, and that concluded that high risk activism is "a 'strong-tie' phenomenon."

Gladwell goes on to say:

> The kind of activism associated with social media isn't like this at all. The platforms of social media are built around weak ties. Twitter is a way of following (or being followed by) people you may never have met. Facebook is a tool for efficiently managing your acquaintances, for keeping up with the people you would not otherwise be able to stay in touch with. That's why you can have a thousand "friends" on Facebook, as you never could real life. This is in many ways a wonderful thing. There is strength in weak ties, as the sociologist Mark Granovetter has observed. Our acquaintances—not our friends—are our greatest source of new ideas and information. The Internet lets us exploit the power of these kinds of distant connections with marvellous efficiency. It's terrific at the diffusion of innovation, interdisciplinary collaboration, seamlessly matching up buyers and sellers, and the logistical functions of the dating world. But weak ties seldom lead to high-risk activism.

Gladwell then points to two examples of instances where social media has been held up as supporting effective action, one in finding a donor for a bone-marrow transplant through a network of Facebook acquaintances who eventually added 25,000 new people to a bone-marrow database and succeeded in making a rare match, and a second with the Save Darfur Coalition, which has 1,282,339 members with donations that have averaged nine cents apiece. He argues that "social networks increase participation by lessening the level of motivation that participation requires." He then returns to his Greensboro example, adding that the sit-ins were organized, with training and structure provided by the National Association for the Advancement of Colored People (NAACP) with further support from ministers, using a hierarchical organization that supports "strategic activism."

This is the second crucial distinction between traditional activism and its online variant: social media are not about this kind of hierarchical organization. Facebook and the like are tools for building networks, which are the opposite, in structure and character, of hierarchies. Unlike hierarchies, with their rules and procedures, networks aren't controlled by a single central authority. Decisions are made through consensus, and the ties that bind people to the group are loose.

This structure makes networks enormously resilient and adaptable in low-risk situations. Wikipedia is a perfect example. It doesn't have an editor, sitting in New York, who directs and corrects each entry. The effort of putting together each entry is self-organized. If every entry in Wikipedia were to be erased tomorrow, the content would swiftly be restored, because that's what happens when a network of thousands spontaneously devote their time to a task. There are many things, though, that networks don't do well. Car companies sensibly use a network to organize their hundreds of suppliers, but not to design their cars. No one believes that the articulation of a coherent design philosophy is best handled by a sprawling, leaderless organizational system. Because networks don't have a centralized leadership structure and clear lines of authority, they have real difficulty reaching consensus and setting goals. They can't think strategically; they are chronically prone to conflict and error. How do you make difficult choices about tactics or strategy or philosophical direction when everyone has an equal say?

The Palestine Liberation Organization originated as a network, and the international-relations scholars Mette Eilstrup-Sangiovanni and Calvert Jones argue in a recent essay in International Security that this is why it ran into such trouble as it grew: "Structural features typical of networks—the absence of central authority, the unchecked autonomy of rival groups, and the inability to arbitrate quarrels through formal mechanisms—made the P.L.O. excessively vulnerable to outside manipulation and internal strife."

In Germany in the nineteen-seventies, they go on, "the far more unified and successful left-wing terrorists tended to organize hierarchically, with professional management and clear divisions of labor. They were concentrated geographically in universities, where they could establish central leadership, trust, and camaraderie through regular, face-to-face meetings." They seldom betrayed their comrades in

Place annotations here

arms during police interrogations. Their counterparts on the right were organized as decentralized networks, and had no such discipline. These groups were regularly infiltrated, and members, once arrested, easily gave up their comrades. Similarly, Al Qaeda was most dangerous when it was a unified hierarchy. Now that it has dissipated into a network, it has proved far less effective.

The drawbacks of networks scarcely matter if the network isn't interested in systemic change—if it just wants to frighten or humiliate or make a splash—or if it doesn't need to think strategically. But if you're taking on a powerful and organized establishment you have to be a hierarchy. The Montgomery bus boycott required the participation of tens of thousands of people who depended on public transit to get to and from work each day. It lasted a year. In order to persuade those people to stay true to the cause, the boycott's organizers tasked each local black church with maintaining morale, and put together a free alternative private carpool service, with forty-eight dispatchers and forty-two pickup stations. Even the White Citizens Council, King later said, conceded that the carpool system moved with "military precision." By the time King came to Birmingham, for the climactic showdown with Police Commissioner Eugene (Bull) Connor, he had a budget of a million dollars, and a hundred full-time staff members on the ground, divided into operational units. The operation itself was divided into steadily escalating phases, mapped out in advance. Support was maintained through consecutive mass meetings rotating from church to church around the city.

Boycotts and sit-ins and nonviolent confrontations—which were the weapons of choice for the civil-rights movement—are high-risk strategies. They leave little room for conflict and error. The moment even one protester deviates from the script and responds to provocation, the moral legitimacy of the entire protest is compromised. Enthusiasts for social media would no doubt have us believe that King's task in Birmingham would have been made infinitely easier had he been able to communicate with his followers through Facebook, and contented himself with tweets from a Birmingham jail. But networks are messy: think of the ceaseless pattern of correction and revision, amendment and debate, that characterizes Wikipedia. If Martin Luther King, Jr., had tried to do a wiki-boycott in Montgomery, he would have been steamrollered by the white power structure. And of what use would a digital communication tool be in a town where ninety-eight per cent of the black community could be reached every Sunday morning at church? The things that King needed in Birmingham—discipline and strategy—were things that online social media cannot provide.

The bible of the social-media movement is Clay Shirky's "Here Comes Everybody." Shirky, who teaches at New York University, sets out to demonstrate the organizing power of the Internet, and he begins with the story of Evan, who worked on Wall Street, and his friend Ivanna, after she left her smart phone, an expensive Sidekick, on the back seat of a New York City taxicab. The telephone company transferred the data on Ivanna's lost phone to a new phone, whereupon she and Evan discovered that the Sidekick was now in the hands of a teen-ager from Queens, who was using it to take photographs of herself and her friends.

When Evan e-mailed the teen-ager, Sasha, asking for the phone back, she replied that his "white ass" didn't deserve to have it back. Miffed, he set up a Web page with her picture and a description of what had happened. He forwarded the link to his friends, and they forwarded it to their friends. Someone found the MySpace page of Sasha's boyfriend, and a link to it found its way onto the site. Someone found her address online and took a video of her home while driving by; Evan posted the video on the site. The story was picked up by the news filter Digg. Evan was now up to ten e-mails a minute. He created a bulletin board for his readers to share their stories, but it crashed under the weight of responses. Evan and Ivanna went to the police, but the police filed the report under "lost," rather than "stolen," which essentially closed the case. "By this point millions of readers were watching," Shirky writes, "and dozens of mainstream news outlets had covered the story." Bowing to the pressure, the N.Y.P.D. reclassified the item as "stolen." Sasha was arrested, and Evan got his friend's Sidekick back.

Shirky's argument is that this is the kind of thing that could never have happened in the pre-Internet

READING

age—and he's right. Evan could never have tracked down Sasha. The story of the Sidekick would never have been publicized. An army of people could never have been assembled to wage this fight. The police wouldn't have bowed to the pressure of a lone person who had misplaced something as trivial as a cell phone. The story, to Shirky, illustrates "the ease and speed with which a group can be mobilized for the right kind of cause" in the Internet age.

Shirky considers this model of activism an upgrade. But it is simply a form of organizing which favors the weak-tie connections that give us access to information over the strong-tie connections that help us persevere in the face of danger. It shifts our energies from organizations that promote strategic and disciplined activity and toward those which promote resilience and adaptability. It makes it easier for activists to express themselves, and harder for that expression to have any impact. The instruments of social media are well suited to making the existing social order more efficient. They are not a natural enemy of the status quo. If you are of the opinion that all the world needs is a little buffing around the edges, this should not trouble you. But if you think that there are still lunch counters out there that need integrating it ought to give you pause.

Shirky ends the story of the lost Sidekick by asking, portentously, "What happens next?"—no doubt imagining future waves of digital protesters. But he has already answered the question. What happens next is more of the same. A networked, weak-tie world is good at things like helping Wall Streeters get phones back from teen-age girls. Viva la revolución. ∎

Place annotations here

AFTER READING:
Responding to Gladwell's argument

What is your first response to Gladwell's claims? Do you agree that successful activism requires strong ties and a hierarchical structure? Do you see ways in which social media might contribute to strong ties as well as weak ones? Do you see ways it might contribute to the sort of hierarchical organization Gladwell sees as needed to accomplish significant results in the larger social world?

Write a response to Gladwell's position based on your own experiences and on those frequently reported. What connections do you see as existing between media and social action? Can sites like Facebook or Twitter work to organize and enact social causes? What potentials do you find in these social networking sites for such action? Do other forms of media seem better suited for such organizing? Where might you find evidence to support your position?

INQUIRY

#5: Seeing the moves of a counterargument

Who does Gladwell seem to see as being on the other side? What are the specific claims he presents as being made by that side—the side that sees social networking as helping to support revolutionary change—the side he is opposing here? How do the claims he attributes to them match up against the claims he is making against the power of social media?

Seeing an Argument in Context

Throughout Part II, we've been exploring the various ways in which context shapes how we read an individual text, and there are several contexts that intersect to affect our understanding of this text and of the larger conversation circulating around it. One is the context in which you are reading and responding to his text—the historical/cultural context of relevant events that are happening in the world around you at the time you are reading, the larger context your classmates bring into your exchanges. A second is the intertextual context that Gladwell himself brings in—the connections between his own inquiry and the other research he refers to, the other writers and social media experts he is drawing from or responding to. And a third is the larger textual ecology beyond the text itself and your immediate discussion—not only what has been written before that Gladwell addresses, but how his text has circulated and how his claims have been taken up and responded to (see Figure 15.5 on page 340).

❶ **The reader's context.** As a reader, you've brought some prior knowledge and ideas to your encounter with Gladwell's essay. Now that you've read his argument, it's likely to resonate with other experiences you've had or events and ideas you've read about. The additional knowledge you bring to his text offers you a richer framework of understanding for exploring and responding to the argument Gladwell is making. And a significant part of such additional knowledge in a classroom context includes what has been shared by your classmates in class discussion, online or off.

The student discussion below took place just after one of our too-common tragedies as a nation, when a gunman killed nine people—members of a Bible study group, including a state senator, and their pastor—at the historic Emanuel African Methodist Episcopal Church in Charleston, South Carolina, in June 2015. The context of those events and the role social media played in the aftermath shaped the responses of these students to Gladwell's claims about the role of social media. As you read these students' posts, consider how the dual context of external events and what others have to say contributes to their larger conversation about the ideas of Gladwell's essay.

Excerpts from Online Discussion of Gladwell's Essay

STUDENT VOICES

Jordan: Maybe the larger issue here is that we as a society expect our social media to reflect our society when it doesn't any more than our personal profiles really reflect ourselves. There are kernels of truth, but there is some artificial construction...a show if you will for a larger public. Changing the language and rallying people on social media changes what is happening on social media, it doesn't change what is happening in our society.

Megan: This article was very interesting to me, especially since it spoke about civil rights events which is something I'm particularly passionate about. I loved reading about all the sit-ins and protests of brave college students and how word spread across the south so quickly. However, I am an avid Twitter user and rely on it for lots of news breaks and other gossips locally and nationally. I heard about the Charleston shooting on Twitter over any news outlet or any other source. It seemed like the news spread like wildfire with links to live pictures and video footage from Charleston. Twitter was also a source that gave me live updates of President Obama's eulogy from inside the arena the funeral of the senator was held. It is true that social media is not a necessity for news to hit people all over the world, but it is the most easy and accessible source to stay updated consistently and quickly.

McLean: Like Jordan, I would caution us against relying on social media as a substitute for real life, much less real activism, which requires what Gladwell refers to as "strong-tie" relationships. Like Megan, my mind also went to the recent church shooting in Charleston as I was reading this article. That there was an abundance of social media discussion regarding this event is undeniable. And this communication is a good thing. However, the scenes of native Charlestonians and visitors gathered together side by side in the aftermath is what gave a true voice to the victims. The power was in the physical, tangible unity of real people, flesh and blood. As Gladwell points out, there's a big difference between being actively committed to a cause and simply participating in it. Platforms like Facebook and Twitter make online organizing relatively quick and convenient, but motivating people to come out into the streets and join the fight is an entirely different hing.

INQUIRY

#6: Resituating an argument in a new context

In their online discussion, these students pick up on and extend central points Gladwell makes in "Small Changes." They consider his claim about social media's weak ties versus the strong ties he sees as supporting social activism as they look to one recent event they read about on Twitter. How do they bring together their own social media experiences, the contemporary Charleston events, and one another's contributions in responding to Gladwell's claims?

Investigators later found that Dylann Roof, the shooter in Charleston, had created a website with a racist manifesto and photos of himself in paraphernalia with Nazi associations at Confederate heritage sites, and that he wrote that he had been radicalized through what he learned on the internet. What might this knowledge have added to these students' responses to Gladwell's essay?

Do any recent events form part of your context as you respond to Gladwell's argument? Social media experiences? Points made by classmates? How does the rich context surrounding your reading of Gladwell's essay contribute to your own understanding and to your evolving response to arguments about the potential offered by social media in the larger world?

❷ **The writer's intertextual context.** In all of our composing activity we are continuing some aspect of an ongoing conversation; our ideas are always informed by what we've heard and read, and we make that process more visible in our public and academic writing. Gladwell, in distinguishing between traditional and online activism, draws on research by sociologist Mark Granovetter (who identified the importance of weak ties in social networks in a 1973 paper[15:11] looking at job-seekers' networks) that has influenced a lot of more recent research into the social effects of internet use (such as Ellison et al. 2007).[15:12] Although Granovetter's work had already been gaining in circulation before 2010, Gladwell's essay brought new attention to it. The following graph (Figure 15.4) showing citations of work by others, lets us see that an increasing number of other writers cited Granovetter's work as it was brought into new arguments about social media.

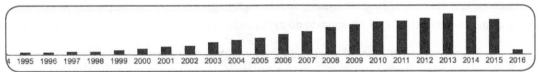

Figure 15.4: Google Scholar citation graph

Gladwell acknowledges what Granovetter showed about weak ties—"There is strength in weak ties, as the sociologist Mark Granovetter has observed." But, as we've seen, he makes the claims that both strong ties and a hierarchical organization are central to traditional activism and thus to actually accomplishing significant change, arguing that because they are organized around weak ties, social networking sites cannot become catalysts for social action. (Lichfield picks up on the same "weak tie" idea, arguing that in his situation, having worked in many parts of the world, it's keeping up with "far-flung acquaintances" that is an advantage to joining Facebook.)

Gladwell makes brief references to the work of other researchers (and you can follow the link to his full article[L15:5]), but he hones in specifically on the work of Clay Shirky, discussing an example from Shirky's book, *Here Comes Everybody* (2008)[15:13] at some length.

INQUIRY

#7: Considering the writer's intertextual context

Where does Gladwell draw on the weak tie research of Granovetter? How does he use it in relation to his own claims? Why do you think he brings it in, when he's arguing for the importance of strong ties and a hierarchical organization for social activism? Why do you think he has chosen to make such brief reference to this work?

Gladwell spends more time (several paragraphs versus a sentence) with the work of Clay Shirky. How does he use Shirky's example to support the claims he is making? Why do you think he spends so much time with it? What do you see as Gladwell's larger purpose, and how does this choice of writer and example support it?

While you're thinking about the Shirky example, you might also consider what it tells us about the circulation of texts and the ways particular content goes viral on the internet. What is your own response to this example of social media use and the activity it can generate?

⑧ **The context of circulation.** Gladwell's essay for the *The New Yorker* was written in 2010, before a number of events in which social media played a role, including significant revolutionary events in the Middle East and in the Ukraine, the Occupy Wall Street movement, protests across the United States in response to the deaths of unarmed black men at the hands of police, and the increasing use of social media for ISIS and other terrorist recruiting efforts. Since then there have been several articles that have explicitly responded to Gladwell's position and a number of studies of social media and their role in revolution. For example, one article from *The Huffington Post* uses the title, "Tweeting the Revolution"[15:14] (a conscious echo of Gladwell's title). That article draws on real-time data about the use of social media in protests in the Ukraine in February 2014 that was collected at the Social Media and Political Participation Lab[L15:6] at New York University. In this article, which is included in the Additional Readings for Part II, the researchers Pablo Barberá and Megan Metzger first set the context, pointing out that the three previous days were the most violent in recent Ukrainian history, with more than 70 protesters reported to have been killed. They then explain that they have been collecting Twitter and Facebook data related to key protest hashtags and analyzing those data, which seem to counter Gladwell's position.

links

> Our findings suggest that social media, as it has throughout these protests, continues to be a pivotal organization tool for those in Kiev and also the most relevant mechanism for disseminating and exchanging information both within Ukraine and abroad. . . . What social media has shown over the last few days. . .is its flexibility as a tool. As needed, and in response to dramatically shifting events on the ground, Twitter and Facebook have been effective means to convey messages about the violence to the international community, to organize those willing to get involved in the protests, and to coordinate resources for the injured and those in need in Maidan square.

#8: Exploring the context of circulation

To see how Gladwell's ideas have been taken up and responded to, circulating through many posts of all sorts on the internet, search for "Tweet and Revolution" (or Twitter, Facebook, or social media and revolution). What are some of the events for which arguments about the power of social media have played out since Gladwell wrote his piece? From your quick survey of what's online, do you see other articles like the one from the NYU researchers that directly echo his work? Do you think Gladwell took a position in an argument that was already circulating and would have circulated without him? Or did his widely circulated essay frame a discussion that might have pushed others to take their own positions or to look more closely at the role of social media in other contexts where activity directed toward social and political change was taking place?

To see more about how the NYU research data speaks to claims about social media and revolution, turn to the full article in Part II Additional Readings. As you follow the evidence presented, are you inclined to adjust the position you've come to through your reading thus far?

Composing
Position Argument

While an argument like the one Gladwell makes is built around the statement of a position, it most likely began as an inquiry. Perhaps Gladwell heard a Silicon Valley guru speak about the powers of social media and thought to himself, *I wonder if that's right?* Or perhaps he read the example he points to from Shirky's book and thought, *No, I don't think that's real social activism of the sort that will produce significant changes in our society.* Before most serious journalists, like Gladwell, take on a position, they try to discover all they can about a question, about the claims that might be made and the evidence that might support those claims.

Gladwell's strategy of comparing current examples of political action to the civil rights movement offers a useful method of inquiry, as does his research into what different authorities have said about the role of social media in recent situations and about the ways in which social media work. Does his essay offer you, as a reader, a sense of a real inquiry into a complex issue? Do you think he might he have done more to bring his readers into an authentic and open inquiry into the question of whether social media are contributing to major social and political change?

By now, as you've read, thought about, and conducted your own inquiries into the ways in which digital media are affecting our lives, both locally and in a changing global culture, you have probably begun to identify some claims you think seem convincing but that you would want to explore further—or some positions you're starting to hold, tentatively, and want to examine. Perhaps you'd like to jump right into the debates about social media we've explored in this chapter, considering its potential value or limitations on either a personal or a social level. You might start out believing in a position, but as you gather supporting evidence and take into account the opposing position, you are likely to see more complexities and nuances, leaving room for questions and uncertainties.

WRITING MOVES

Inquiring and Inventing

In preparing to add your voice to an ongoing argument with many voices, you'll first need to discover what arguments interest you and what those other voices are saying.

Digital Toolbox
See Part IV, Section 5

links

1 Reflecting on the context

What claims for or concerns about our digital environment seem significant to you at the moment? What events or experiences in a global or local context seem to speak to the issues and concerns that have emerged through your reading and discussion? What points have you wanted to engage with? What claims have you wanted to think through more carefully? Where do you find a position represented that you might want to learn about, take up, or argue with, entering a larger conversation? Who makes up the likely audience for this area of concern, and how might you finally reach that audience?

2 Deciding on an independent or a collaborative inquiry

Although we most often see individuals presenting their sides of an argument, many debated concerns about our digital world lend themselves to collaborative inquiry. If several of your classmates are interested in the same question or issue, you might work in a group to present two sides of an argument (and assign sides without reference to the positions members initially hold). Debating teams often work in this way.

3 Exploring the territory of the current debate

What are some of the voices that are relevant to the issue you're focusing on? Gladwell doesn't make his own claims. He sees what others are saying and engages in that discussion. If you decide to take on the argument about the potential of social media to enact social and political change, you already have Gladwell's piece to work with. A quick Google search with his title, or with the terms "tweeting" and "revolution," will bring up a number of direct and indirect responses to his essay and give you a sense of the discussion it stimulated and some of the supporting and counter evidence that was offered. You might also look at Shirky's response to Gladwell[15:15, L15:7] (or a **subsequent exchange**[L15:8] between them[15:16] or a reassessment of their positions in *Wired*[15:17, L15:9] a year after Gladwell's article). Your classroom discussion site can also offer a sense of what others think and why on this or other issues. Or you might look for information about the role of social media in other protests that have taken place in the last several years, such as the 2013 Gezi Park protests in Turkey, for example; an analysis of **the use of social media in those protests**[15:18, L15:10] explores some of the territory covered in the Gladwell-Shirky debate but asks whether there's a social-media-fueled protest style and considers the visual images that were circulated.

Likewise, Turkle's concerns about the impact of our current technologies on our social interactions, which she sees as leaving us "alone together," has generated much debate you can begin to discover with a quick search, while the concerns Eggers raised in *The Circle* about where the increasing collection of our data might lead and whether or not we should be concerned are also topics of ongoing discussion. From your own exploration of a question that concerns you, you can begin to see where you want to place yourself in an ongoing debate.

4 Identifying others' claims and counterclaims

From your inquiry, what positions do you find people taking on the issue you're exploring? What claims and counterclaims are being made? What sorts of appeals are being used on each side? What moves do people make in support of their claims? What evidence is being offered? Where do you now want to position yourself, what counterclaims do you want to argue against, and what claims do you want to make?

5 Finding compelling examples and evidence to refute others' claims and support your own

Gladwell, in making his claim that strong ties and hierarchical organization are needed for effective social action, draws on the example of the civil rights movement to show what those elements looked like in a time before the internet. His account of that movement, when matched up against Shirky's lost phone example, is much more compelling. But the example of how protesters used social media for organization in the Ukraine might be a more compelling counterexample to refute Gladwell's idea that "the revolution won't be tweeted." What compelling example(s) and evidence, for yourself and your readers, can you draw on to support the claims you're making? How can you counter the most compelling evidence from the other side?

Consider also the role of visual evidence in supporting your claims, both images and visual displays of data (see Chapters 14 and 16).

WRITING MOVES ◄

Drafting and Shaping

When you're ready to add your own voice to the larger public conversation about the issue you're focusing on—to put forth your position and respond to the claims of others—you'll want to consider the following moves.

1 Framing your argument

We've seen that Gladwell frames his argument with an account of the Greensboro lunch counter sit-in and that Shirky, in the book Gladwell is countering as "the bible" of the social media movement (Shirky 2008[15:19]) frames his with the lost cell phone story. Each of them is ordering the reader's experience and expectations by these choices of a beginning, involving the reader before setting forth any claims or counterclaims. While sometimes it's useful to state your position almost immediately ("Social media advocates think X is true, but I'm going to show Y is true for the following reasons"), a structure you've probably used before and that's implicit underneath many arguments, more often you'll want to use a compelling scene or example to bring your reader into the territory of the argument you'll be making, to set that argument up, and then to state the position you're arguing for or against. For Gladwell, the "against" doesn't come until the fifth paragraph ("The world, we are told, is in the midst of a revolution").

2 Setting forth the counterclaims and your own claims

You've already lined up the claims and counterclaims others are making and decided what you want to argue for and which claims and evidence you think will be most powerful. Now you want to think about the most effective order for these, typically presenting the claims for the other side and countering each with your own, and moving toward the strongest claim you can make for your own position. But we can see that Gladwell has brought us into an example that speaks for his own argument first. And his final paragraphs focus on Shirky's example for the side he is countering, using it to state his version of Shirky's position in a way that would lead his readers away from embracing it: "A networked, weak-tie world is good at things like helping Wall Streeters get phones back from teen-age girls." Whatever order you decide on, it's important to take your readers through a sequence of reasoning that will bring them with you to your conclusion: For Gladwell, strong ties are needed for engaged social activism, social media support weak ties, therefore the revolution won't be tweeted.

3 Presenting others' evidence and your own

Once you've determined the sequencing of your claims and counterclaims, you're ready to present the strongest evidence you can for each of them—to show why you've come to see the claims of the other side as less right than those on the side you're arguing for. Of course putting it this way makes it sound clear and simple. In reality, all arguments about the social world are messy. Gladwell's argument for his position works fine if indeed social media can't support strong ties and hierarchies, but less well if they can. The point of exploring arguments about the digital world is not to beat down the other side, but to gain a richer understanding of what's going on, and finding that something is still an open question, or that there's a stronger middle ground between two apparently opposite claims often makes a more useful contribution to a larger conversation.

As you present your evidence, consider also how you might use visual evidence. Most contemporary protest activity takes place across several social media platforms and includes a variety of images, posters, and other icons as well as photos of events. The New York University researchers, in examining the role of Facebook in the protests in Ukraine, found that the most widely shared posts on Facebook were "images of police violence, injured protesters, or individuals acting bravely." Such images are part of the argument protesters are making in support of resistance. And graphic images displaying data on Twitter or Facebook usage contribute to an argument about the role of social media in this situation. In turn, your own argument might draw on such images, on sound, and on videos. Drawing on the concepts from Chapter 14, you might also use the visual analysis of protest or other images to support claims you might make about how social media are being used.

WRITING MOVES ◄
Revising and Publishing

In adding to any conversation about our larger social world, you'll most likely want to circulate your own contribution locally before doing so more globally on public media. The effectiveness of your argument essay can be measured by how well your audience is convinced of the position it presents. For an argument in which a series of claims are made with relevant evidence in support of the position, you'll want to know whether your readers could follow the reasoning you've presented, whether they agree that your position can be supported by the evidence you've presented, and whether you've adequately countered the likely claims of the opposing side.

1 Getting local response from peers

Whether you've worked on your argument independently or by preparing arguments and counterarguments in debate team fashion, you'll want to present that argument to your peers, with questions designed to elicit the feedback you want. Here are some possible questions to start with.

- What argument is being made? Where do you find the clearest statement of position?

- Create a sketch of the argument: of the position being put forward, of the claims that support it and the evidence for those claims, of the opposing position, claims, and counter evidence being refuted.

- Do the composer's claims fit logically with the position being presented?

- Does the evidence the composer has provided offer convincing support for the position the composer presents?

- Has the composer provided convincing evidence against the opposing view?

- What further evidence or explanation of the evidence might you like to see?

- Has the composer taken into account the likely shared knowledge of the audience and provided new background knowledge if needed?

- Does the composer have a clear pattern of organization?

- Does the conclusion leave you convinced of this position (or with a clearer understanding why someone would hold it)? Is there anything else you'd add to it?

- What other advice would you give to this composer?

- Use these responses to revise or reshape your argument and prepare it for larger public circulation.

2 Entering the public conversation

It's not always easy to insert your claims into a larger public conversation and get a response to them. You can make your argument public by posting to a public class blog or website, or to another site you've identified. Or you might add parts of your own argument to ongoing threads of readers' comments on other sites where a discussion of the topic is going on. Or you might post and then tweet a link to the post with some hashtags that will bring it up in a relevant topic area. Or you might create a video of a classroom debate and post it to YouTube. Plan, with your classmates, some social media strategies for adding your voices to the voices of others in a public arena, and then keep track of any activity that shows your work being shared, liked, retweeted, or any direct comments from readers, reflecting on the success of the strategies you've tried and how any response you've received contributes to your own understanding.

Reinventing and Circulating Your Work

One possibility for extending your work for this chapter is to move beyond Gladwell in examining the role of Twitter.

With his title, Gladwell's article focused attention on one social media platform above others. Biz Stone, the co-founder of Twitter, in a response to Gladwell in *The Atlantic* (2010), not surprisingly picked up on the challenge about Twitter and looked at how it was being used in political and protest activity in China, Kenya, and Moldova. But there's been more recent attention to its role as well, and if you search on "Twitter and Activism," or on "Twitter" and key words that address any recent political activity, you'll find further discussion of its role. Look at some of the ways in which Twitter is being used for social and political causes. (One recent presidential candidate used Twitter as his primary platform, tweeting his thoughts constantly.) What do you find about its role in more recent events that adds to or alters your sense of its possibilities? How might you use it to organize a multifaceted campaign about an area of your own concern?

Key Concepts

Putting Data
to Work

CHAPTER SIXTEEN

CENTRAL QUESTIONS

1 What possibilities and potential problems does "big data" collection present?

2 What are the characteristics of effective data presentation and visualization?

3 How can we draw on these understandings to create effective presentations that explore a hypothesis and build an argument from small data and with relevant big data?

Chapter Preview

In Chapter 15, we considered some of the arguments and claims being made for and against the value of social media for particular uses at both the personal/local and the public/global level. In this chapter, we extend this exploration to examine critically both the potential and the limitations of digital tools for communicating in ways that can help a society reflect common beliefs and values.

As we try to sort out how to build and maintain shared values in more public contexts, we continue to identify new areas of concern and new questions to explore through argument and inquiry. One of those concerns is the massive production of data we now create when we go online, via any kind of electronic device, and the wide-scale collection and analysis of this data—what is often called **big data**. We saw in Chapter 13 how author Dave Eggers imaginatively explored a future where personal privacy was no longer considered important and where everyone was encouraged to produce and consume as much data as possible. Today, we find ourselves in a big data world that is changing some of our fundamental notions about both our public and private lives. Large-scale data production alters what we can learn about our world and how, and it's providing information that can help us understand, and perhaps act on, a range of public concerns. It's also changing the work of researchers who endeavor to study and learn about the growing complexity of the digital world. Big data changes how researchers think about and use data, big and small, to build shared knowledge and make sense of the world around us.

Researchers working with both big and small data are also engaging in a form of argument—not the sort of top-down argument that involves setting forth a position and finding examples and evidence to support it—the kind of argument we saw with Malcolm Gladwell in Chapter 15—but what we might call a

> **big data**
> the massive amount of data that can be collected electronically and that requires computer analysis

bottom-up argument
an argument that
begins with data
and examples and
moves to a position or
hypothesis that can
explain them

bottom-up argument. A bottom-up argument *begins* with collecting data, finding patterns in the data that point to possible interpretations, and working from those observations to make informed claims and take positions based on what you've researched.

Here again, argument is used as a means of inquiry—to ask questions, work out new understandings, and build a stance on a topic—this time based on a close examination of *data*. Data, in their simplest form, are types of evidence that support an idea or hypothesis we have about the world. Data can be observations, records, statistics, or surveys—any kind of information used to make reasonable judgments that can lead to valid arguments.

Exploring
Big Data

The production and collection of data continues to grow, providing researchers with more data than ever for studying all aspects of our world. Faster computers and networks, along with growing storage capacity, have helped expand the amount and type of data that is collected in our current culture of information. Increasingly, not only are sites like Google, Facebook, and Twitter collecting data about users and citizens, "big data" collection is becoming standard practice in business, health care, education, and government for managing our complex, modern societies. Every time we do an online search, it is big data technology that spits out an instantaneous result. Individual researchers and journalists are also drawing on big data to build new understandings and shape new arguments. Big data is thus an exaggerated term to describe the use of digital, electronic computing and very large data sets to study and understand the world in new ways.

As we saw in Chapter 13, there are significant critiques of the role of big data in contemporary life as more and more data is collected about individuals. This ability to monitor and save information about citizens and consumers is raising serious concerns about and challenging our shared understandings about work, money, information, and privacy. In his in-depth analysis of Facebook, "What Facebook Knows,"[16:1, L16:1] Tom Simonite writes that

link

> If Facebook were a country, a conceit that founder Mark Zuckerberg has entertained in public, its 900 million members would make it the third largest in the world. It would far outstrip any regime past or present in how intimately it records the lives of its citizens. Private conversations, family photos, and records of road trips, births, marriages, and deaths all stream into the company's servers and lodge there. Facebook has collected the most extensive data set ever assembled on human social behavior. Some of your personal information is probably part of it. (44)

Such large-scale data collection about users raises important concerns about privacy and technologies that can be used intrusively for surveillance purposes. Facebook is just one of many businesses and institutions that specialize in collecting and analyzing user data for all kinds of purposes, ranging from academic studies on why we share online content to understanding how to better entice users to click a link.

The world of big data collection is a newly emerging one, and we are currently living through its earliest stages. Schools, courts, and governments are in the process of understanding how to manage and legislate big data practices. As users and citizens, it will be necessary for us to ensure there is adequate oversight and that data is used ethically, transparently, and in ways that do not infringe on our rights as citizens.

At the same time, the capability of collecting and analyzing such digital data can contribute greatly to our building of shared public knowledge in many areas. Whether or not writers learn to do the work of data analysis themselves, much research and many public arguments will draw on the results of such analysis, and it is increasingly important to take our growing use of big data into account when thinking about how public arguments are made and how shared knowledge is created.

Big Data for Shared Knowledge

Big data isn't simply a potential violation of privacy—it is also helping researchers understand new aspects of both the natural and social worlds we inhabit. Social media companies like Twitter, Instagram, and Facebook use big data to see and understand all kinds of new patterns and phenomena about our communication practices that we couldn't see before. Twitter, for example, is an important source of communication data, collecting more than 500 million tweets (micromessages) a day. Twitter data is commonly used by media corporations, government, and academic researchers to learn everything from where earthquakes might be occurring based on the occurrence of many short tweets at once with "earthquake?"[L16:2] to the dietary habits of a population.[L16:3]

The U.S. Census Bureau is one of the oldest collectors of big data, collecting information about U.S. citizens and residents since 1790. What's new now is 1) the ability to collect and analyze information faster and in more volume to produce census results within one year instead of 10, and 2) the ease of sharing digital data, which can be easily accessed and analyzed by other researchers. Data USA[L16:4] is one site that draws on data gathered by the U.S. Census Bureau to report on such topics as the demographics of U.S. cities and the average salaries earned by college graduates in various majors, information you might find valuable in thinking about your own future.

Using other large data sets, a reporter can discover what's happening to music sales in different formats, finding, for example, that downloads of MP3s plummeted in 2014 while sales for streaming music sites and vinyl records went up.[16:2] The data for such reports is collected through Nielsen SoundScan,[L16:5] a company that collects and analyzes music sales data from around the world. Big data collection like this has become an important resource for musicians and producers alike for tracking the popularity of a song and providing a basis for calculating the royalties each should receive.

Some big data inquiries can provide a larger context for the more local themes we explored in Part I, such as the role that fandom plays in contributing to an individual's social identity and the connections it can draw between a local community and a wider culture. For example, Seth Stephens-Davidowitz, in a *New York Times* feature article, "They Hook You When You're Young,"[16:3] used big data to ask a new question about baseball fandom: Does a team's record during a person's childhood shape his or her team preferences as an adult? Here's what he says about his use of data from Facebook:

> From Facebook's publicly available advertising platform, I downloaded data on how many fans every baseball team has, broken out by gender and age. (Facebook estimates whether someone is a fan of a team based on both "likes" and posts.)
>
> This data is not perfect, but it does correlate pretty well with previous polling. According to Facebook, the most popular teams are the Yankees, Red Sox, Mets, Cardinals and Braves; there are 1.65 Yankees fans for every Mets fan.
>
> Facebook data can reveal patterns that polls generally do not have large enough sample sizes to detect. For example, Facebook tells us that among men, the ratio of Yankees fans to Mets fans fluctuates enormously depending on when those men were born. The Mets are popular among an unusually high number of men born in 1961 and 1978. (Interestingly, women's fandom depends much less on when they were born.)
>
> These huge swings appear to be driven by winning over young boys with on-the-field success. Fans born in 1961 and 1978 were both 8 years old when the Mets won the World Series. Fandom is determined by a huge number of factors, like what team your father supports, but winning when boys are young stands out clearly in the data.

Stephens-Davidowitz goes on to connect the pattern he finds in these data with his own experience as a Mets fan, noting that he was a young boy when the Mets won the World Series in 1986. In this case, Stephens-Davidowitz began his inquiry from the bottom up, noting how his personal experience as a fan led him to ask larger questions about this experience. He notes several other interesting questions others are asking of such large data sets, including the long-term effects that events from our childhoods might have on our political and economic outlooks, with evidence, for example, that "if you grew up in bad economic times, you are more risk averse as an adult." (You can find his full article in Part II Additional Readings.)

INQUIRY

1: Generating big data questions

Researchers use big data to answer questions any of us might ask. What questions have arisen in your work with this book that big data might help to answer? Generate a common list with your classmates and do a quick Google search to see whether some of them have been addressed, and if so, using what data. What questions about local trends, such as college students' dating behavior, or public concerns, such as the effects of climate change, are being studied, and how? How does this research connect to more local practices?

Visualizing Data

Along with the growth in the use of big data to study and make sense of the world has come a need to make those data easier to understand for larger public audiences. Big data arguments are often accompanied by visual representations of those data. The ability to read, use, and compose charts, graphs, and **infographics**—visual representations of information representing data and information like those that appear in this book's chapters—has become an important literacy in a digital, big data age.

infographics
visual representations
of information

The article on "Tweeting the Revolution" (in Part II Additional Readings) includes several examples of data-driven visualization, including graphs for social media use in the Ukrainian protests of 2014 (Figures 16.1, 16.2, and 16.3).

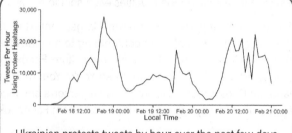

Ukrainian protests tweets by hour over the past few days (Data: NYU Social Media and Political Participation (smapp.nyu.edu) Lab; Figure: Pablo Barberá and Megan Metzger)

Figure 16.1: Ukranian Protest Activity Graph 1 – Tweets by the hour

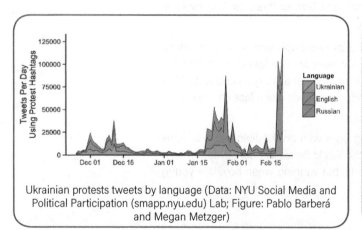

Ukrainian protests tweets by language (Data: NYU Social Media and Political Participation (smapp.nyu.edu) Lab; Figure: Pablo Barberá and Megan Metzger)

Figure 16.2: Ukranian Protest Activity Graph 2 – Tweets by language

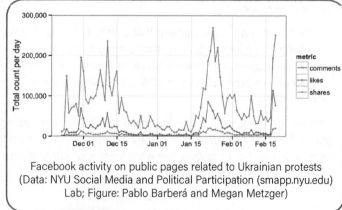

Facebook activity on public pages related to Ukrainian protests (Data: NYU Social Media and Political Participation (smapp.nyu.edu) Lab; Figure: Pablo Barberá and Megan Metzger)

Figure 16.3: Ukranian Protest Activity Graph 3 – Facebook

Examples include a simple one-line timeline graph of tweets per hour on different days that were related to the Euromaidan protests (#Euromaidan), a colored graph breaking up that same information into the different languages (English, Ukrainian, Russian) used in these tweets (and showing a shift to more English as the protests went on and received more international attention), and a three-color graph of Facebook activity over the same days, showing likes, shares, and comments, with increased activity as violence around the protests increased. The visual images allow us to see these changes in activity easily, helping us to make sense of the supporting data for the verbal claims being made in the article. Moreover, using big data, researchers are able to make claims about communication behavior across a larger number of people.

Stephens-Davidowitz likewise uses graphs that let readers visualize what he has learned about baseball fandom. The first offers a combination of a timeline and notes and shows how the ratios of Yankees fans to Mets fans vary by how old the fans were when the Mets had a winning season (Figure 16.4).

The second visual uses a bar graph to convey, in a striking way, the relationship between a boy's age at the time of a World Series championship win and the likelihood of lifelong fandom (Figure 16.5).

Or we can consider again what's happening in the music industry and how to visualize the changes that have been taking place, as in the infographic "Social Sound Bytes" (Figure 16.6 on page 352). This particular image combines several forms of data display to show what's been happening in the music industry as music listeners have shifted from vinyl LPs to digital MP3s over time. It shows information on MP3 music sales in 2009, showing what proportions of downloaded and streaming media were bought from different sales sources, and more. Such infographics have become a common genre and contribute greatly to our shared understanding of the changes occurring in our digital society.

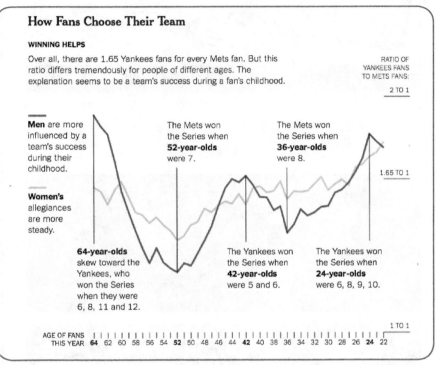

Figure 16.4: Fan Data Graph 1 – Men and women by age

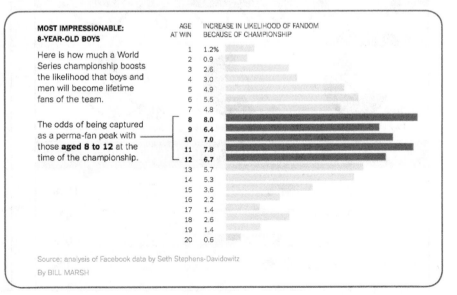

Figure 16.5: Fan Data Graph 2 – Fandom and age at championship

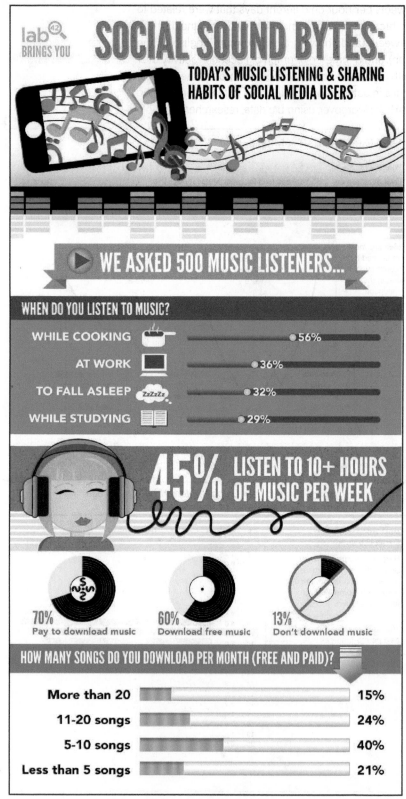

Figure 16.6: Social Sound Bytes infographic

#2: Working with visual information

Look at the visualizations of data and information about the protests in the Ukraine and for baseball fandom and then at the full articles in Part II Additional Readings. What do the visualizations add to your understanding of the points being made in each article? How explanatory would you find the visual image on its own? The written text on its own? How effective do you find such multimodal compositions for the presentation of such information and interpretation of data? You might also look at the visualizations created from census data at Data USA to see how they contribute to the various stories being found in the data.

Look also at the "Social Sound Bytes" infographic about music listening and sharing habits of social media users, with its several different display formats. In this case, the composer has most likely drawn information from different sources to create one visual presentation. Which elements do you find most helpful in understanding the information presented? What do think about the arrangement of these elements? If you were composing an infographic with these elements, are there any changes you might make?

Have any of the infographics in this book seemed particularly useful in providing additional information about the chapter topics? Have any proved visually interesting as a model for an infographic you might create? Beyond this book, what other infographics have you encountered recently? Are there any you find particularly compelling? Why? Have you become more aware of their presence online and the role they're playing in the public sharing of knowledge? Why do you think such infographics have become so common?

Interacting With Data for Research and the Public Good

Social media giants make the data they collect available for marketing (and thus for their own profit-making), but also for researchers who are trying to address questions related to the public good. Twitter, for example, has created a blog that has posted about research being done with Twitter data (see "Twitter Data for Research"[16:4, L16:6]) and has also created the account @twitterforgood with tweets about good works the company is supporting. The hashtag #twitterforgood is being used to share information about uses of Twitter for the public good—for example, a link[L16:7] to a *Guardian* article about how tweeting flood information became a "civic duty" in Jakarta, Indonesia (see Figure 16.7).[16:5]

 links

Beyond reading others' analyses of big data to explain things that are happening in the world and drawing on visualizations that offer supporting evidence for the arguments others are making, there are also ways in which we can consciously contribute our small data points to areas where we want to see our own attitudes and behavior (attitudes toward race, practices related to health) in a larger public/global context.

Figure 16.7: Tweet about Jakarta flood tweeting

One of the benefits of modern data collection technologies is their ability to collect *and* analyze more data in real time, giving us new understandings of the world at various scales. One example of using big data both to offer such understandings and to present an implicit argument can be found at slaveryfootprint.org. Slaveryfootprint.org is a nonprofit organization that works to inform the public about the problem of modern-day slavery in the global economy (Figure 16.8). The site uses a series of infographics to explain how such slavery works and where and how it appears, as well as a blog that provides updated information about actions being taken to combat such slavery.

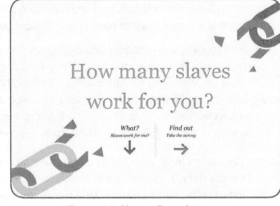

Figure 16.8. Slavery Footprint survey

INQUIRY

#3: Using big data to see your consumption footprint

Visit the site slaveryfootprint.org[L16:8] and take the "survey." In addition to considering the implications of your consumption practices, write about the ways slaveryfootprint.org collects data and how they use the data to present an argument. How do they justify the results they come up with after a user takes the survey? Are you convinced? Why or why not?

Consider also the rhetorical effectiveness of the website with its linked elements and infographics. How does the site design work toward its purposes of educating people and moving them toward action? Have the designers succeeded in engaging you and raising your awareness of this global social problem?

 links

Here are the reflections of one student, Hayden:

"I have to admit, the survey at slaveryfootprint.org really stunned me. I rarely think about how my consumption affects workers from other countries, and I haven't thought much about where my phone and computer came from. And it's not just phones—it all electronics combined—old ipods, ereaders, tablets, gaming consoles. In any case, it took me about 20 minutes to take the survey. It is a very visual and interactive site. After you enter details about your different levels of consumption (food, gas, electricity, water, clothes, cosmetics, etc), slaveryfootprint uses a special algorithm to calculate how many "slaves" (workers with no or little wages) might actually be supporting your consumption. I can't really say I completely understand how they come up with a number, but they claim to use data from labor statistics from around the world to make a very convincing argument."

Making Connections
Big Data and Small Data

While many researchers and activists are using big data to explore questions that interest them, others continue to use small data, the sorts of local data that you've been gathering through observing your own local digital communities or in public digital environments and the collections you've been making of texts and images you've found there. Analyzing big data and small data can be complementary approaches to studying a question or problem, and one can often give us further understanding of the other. Researchers danah boyd and Kate Crawford have raised "critical questions about big data,"[16:6] pointing out that

> Big Data triggers both utopian and dystopian rhetoric. On one hand, Big Data is seen as a powerful tool to address various societal ills, offering the potential of new insights into areas as diverse as cancer research, terrorism, and climate change. On the other, Big Data is seen as a troubling manifestation of Big Brother, enabling invasions of privacy, decreased civil freedoms, and increased state and corporate control. As with all socio-technical phenomena, the currents of hope and fear often obscure the more nuanced and subtle shifts that are underway. (663–64)

In their discussion, boyd and Crawford make several points about how we might think about big data, among them that big data is changing the definition of how we understand knowledge, human networks, and community; that we need a **conceptual framework** (a set of interrelated key concepts like the ones related to digital literacies we've been using in this book) in order to interpret and make sense of the huge amounts of knowledge and information available to us; that, taken out of context, big data can lose its meaning; and that "it is increasingly important to recognize the value of 'small data'" and the richness it provides on the level of individual and local experience.

conceptual framework
a set of key concepts that work together to support interpretation and analysis

Boyd and Crawford stress that working with data, big or small, involves the very sort of analytical work we've been doing throughout our inquiries. Whether data is processed on a large scale with computer algorithms or on a small scale by our efforts to sort out what we've collected and find patterns in what we've gathered, our effective use of data depends on analyzing and interpreting what we find.

The marketing and branding consultant Martin Lindstrom makes similar points in his recent book *Small DATA: The Tiny Clues That Uncover Huge Trends* (2016)[16:7] in which he considers the important uses of small data in a big data world, making his own argument to a public audience. Often those who use small data begin their reports with examples from those data and build from them to lay out a larger position, and Lindstrom proceeds in precisely this way. Throughout his book, he tells the stories of the many specific instances in which he was able to discover a branding strategy for a particular company using the small data of his close observations of particular people, settings, and contexts. These stories support a larger claim that small data can tell us things that big data can miss. The following excerpt is from his introduction.[16:7]

BEFORE READING:

Reflecting on the appeal of Lego

In this excerpt, Lindstrom begins with the story of Lego's successful rebranding strategy and how a small data moment led him and the company to see the appeal of Legos in a different way. Before you read, consider for a moment your own thoughts about Legos, about why they might have appealed to you (and maybe still do) or to others around you. As you read, what do you learn about how Lindstrom defines the appeal and what led him to that understanding? About the sort of small data he focuses on in his work and on why he does so? About the larger claims he is making with the examples he chooses?

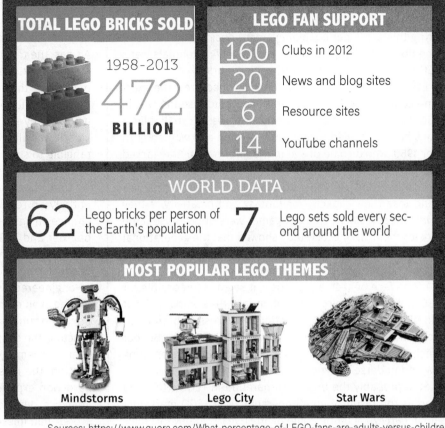

Sources: https://www.quora.com/What-percentage-of-LEGO-fans-are-adults-versus-children
http://www.thebrickfan.com/lego-related-sites/
http://gizmodo.com/5019797/everything-you-always-wanted-to-know-about-lego

READING

Selection from

Small DATA: The Tiny Clues that Uncover Huge Trends
by Martin Lindstrom
St. Martin's Press, 2016

The solution to LEGO's problems—the thing that may have rescued it from potential bankruptcy—lay in an old pair of sneakers.

It was early 2003, and the company was in trouble, having lost 30 per cent of its turnover over the past year. In 2004, another 10 per cent vanished. As Jørgen Vig Knudstorp, LEGO's CEO, put it, "We are on a burning platform, losing money with negative cash flow, and a real risk of debt default which could lead to a break-up of the company."

How had the Danish toymaker fallen so far so fast? Arguably, the company's problems could be traced back to 1981, when the world's first handheld game, Donkey Kong, came to market, inspiring a debate within the pages of LEGO's internal magazine, Klodshans, about what so-called "side-scrolling platform games" meant for the future of construction toys. The consensus: platforms like Atari and Nintendo were fads—which turned out to be true, at least until the advent of computer games for PCs launched their wildly successful second wind.

I had begun advising LEGO in 2004 when the company asked me to develop its overall branding strategy. I didn't want the company to move away from what it had been doing well for so long, but no one could deny the increasing everywhere-ness of all things digital. From the mid-1990s on, LEGO began moving away from its core product, i.e. building blocks, and focusing instead on its loosely knit empire of theme parks, children's clothing lines, video games, books, magazines, television programs and retail stores. Somewhere during this same period, management decided that considering how impatient, impulsive and fidgety millennials were, LEGO should begin manufacturing bigger bricks.

Every big data study LEGO commissioned drew the exact same conclusions: future generations would lose interest in LEGO. LEGO would go the way of jackstraws, stickball, blindman's bluff. So-called Digital Natives—men and women born after 1980, who'd come of age in the Information Era—lacked the time, and the patience, for LEGO, and would quickly run out of ideas and storylines to build around. Digital natives would lose their capacity for fantasy and creativity, if they hadn't already, since computer games were doing most of the work for them. Each LEGO study showed that the generational need for instant gratification was more potent than any building block could ever hope to overcome.

In the face of such a prognosis, it seemed impossible for LEGO to turn things around—but, in fact, the company did. It sold off its theme parks. It continued successful brand alliances with the Harry Potter, Star Wars and Bob the Builder franchises. It reduced the number of products while entering new and underserved global markets.

Still, probably the biggest turnaround in LEGO's thinking came as the result of an ethnographic visit LEGO marketers paid in early 2004 to the home of an 11-year-old boy in a mid-sized German city. Their mission? To figure out what really made LEGO stand out. What executives found out that day was that everything they thought they knew, or had been told, about late twentieth—and early twenty-first-century children and their new digital behaviors—including the need for time compression and instantaneous results –was wrong.

In addition to being a LEGO aficionado, the 11-year-old German boy was also a passionate skateboarder. Asked at one point which of his possessions he was the most proud of, he pointed to a pair of beat-up Adidas sneakers with ridges and nooks along one side. Those sneakers were his trophy, he said. They were his gold medal. They were his masterpiece. More than that, they were evidence. Holding them up so everyone in the room could see and admire them, he explained that one side was worn down and abraded at precisely the right angle. The heels were scuffed and planed in an unmistakable way. The entire look of the sneakers, and the impression they conveyed to the world, was perfect; it signaled to him, to his friends and to the rest of the world that he was one of the best skateboarders in the city.

At that moment, it all came together for the LEGO team. Those theories about time compression and instant gratification? They seemed to be off base. Inspired by what an 11-year-old German boy had told them about an old pair of Adidas, the team realized that children attain social currency among their peers by playing and achieving a high level of mastery at their chosen skill, whatever that skill happens to be. If the skill is valuable, and worthwhile, they will stick with it until they get it right, never mind how long it takes. For kids, it was all about paying your dues and having something tangible to show for it in the end—in this case, a pair of tumbledown Adidas that most adults would never look at twice.

Until that point, LEGO's decision-making was predicated entirely on reams of big data. Yet ultimately it was a small, chance insight—a pair of sneakers belonging to a skateboarder and LEGO lover—that helped propel the company's turnaround. From that point on, LEGO refocused on its core product, and even upped the ante. The company not only re-engineered its bricks back to their normal size, it began adding even more, and smaller, bricks inside their boxes. The bricks became more detailed, the instruction manuals more exacting, the construction challenges more labor intensive.For users, it seemed, LEGO was all about the summons, the provocation, the mastery, the craftsmanship and, not least, the hard-won experience—a conclusion that complex predictive analytics, despite their remarkable ability to parse "average" scores, had missed.

Cut to 10 years later when, during the first half of 2014, in the wake of the worldwide success of The LEGO Movie and sales of related merchandise, LEGO's sales rose 11 percent to exceed $2 billion. For the first time ever, LEGO had surpassed Mattel to become the world's largest toymaker.

Believe it or not, almost every insight I come up with as a global branding consultant happens just this way. I might be developing a new car key for Porsche owners, designing a credit card for billionaires, creating a newfangled innovation for a weight loss organization, helping reverse the fortunes of a stumbling American supermarket chain or trying to position the Chinese automotive industry to compete globally. There's a well-known quote that says if you want to understand how animals live, you don't go to the zoo, you go to the jungle. And so I do. In nearly every instance, after conducting what I call Subtext Research (which I occasionally shorten to Subtexting), a detailed process that involves visiting consumers in their homes, gathering small data offline and online, and crunching, or Small Mining, these clues with observations and insights taken from around the world, there almost always comes a moment where I uncover an unmet or unacknowledged desire that forms the foundation of a new brand, product innovation or business.

READING

The people I study and interview could be teenaged girls living in a Brazilian favela; merchant bankers in the Czech Republic; housewives in Southern California; sex workers in Hungary; mothers-in-law in India; or sports-obsessed fathers in Geneva, Beijing, Kyoto, Liverpool or Barcelona. Sometimes I go so far as to move inside people's houses or apartments where, with the owners' permission, I make myself at home. The families and I fraternize, listen to music, watch television and eat all our meals together. During these visits—again, with permission—I go through refrigerators, open desk drawers and kitchen cabinets, scour books, magazines, music and movie collections and downloads, inspect purses, wallets, online search histories, Facebook pages, Twitter feeds, emoji usage and Instagram and Snapchat accounts. In the search for what I call small data, almost nothing is off-limits. I've gone so far as to interview consumers through text-messaging—a study shows that people lie less frequently in texts—though I'm far more likely to take people by surprise by inspecting their microwave ovens and glass and plastic recycling cans. I see myself as a forensic investigator of small data, or emotional DNA—a hunter, almost, of desire. [5]

Do any of us really know how we come across to other people? Are we aware of the haphazard sequence of small data we leave behind us every day—the rituals, habits, gestures and preferences that coalesce to expose who we really are inside? Most of the time, the answer is no. What we snack on, how we choreograph our Facebook page, what we tweet, whether we chew cinnamon gum or nicotine lozenges—all these slight gestures may at first seem indiscriminate, undirected and too small to have much bearing on our identities. But when we begin to see life through the new and unfamiliar lens of small data, we also come across revealing clues about the people closest to us, including ourselves.

Small data could show up in how a family's shoe collection is arrayed in a hallway, or in the scrambled letters and numbers that make up a person's computer password. In the course of doing Subtexting, I dig through garbage cans, past squeezed-out toothpaste tubes and ripped candy wrappers and expired coupons, searching for that one thing that will solve the puzzle, or provide the answer I need, even when I'm not sure what the puzzle consists of, or what it is exactly that I'm looking for. A lone piece of small data is almost never meaningful enough to build a case or create a hypothesis, but blended with other insights and observations gathered from around the world, the data eventually comes together to create a solution that forms the foundation of a future brand or business. [8-9]

In-person observation, and a preoccupation with small data, is what sets apart what I do in a world preoccupied by big data. Most of us judge practically everything in seconds, or minutes at most. We've become spontaneous seekers and instant responders. As more and more products and services migrate online, and technology helps us understand human behaviour in real time at granular levels, many people have come to believe that human observations and interaction are old-fashioned and even irrelevant. I couldn't disagree more. A source who works at Google once confessed to me that despite the almost 3 billion humans who are online, and the 70 per cent of online shoppers who go onto Facebook daily, and the 300 hours of videos on YouTube (which is owned by Google) uploaded every minute, and the fact that 90 per cent of all the world's data has been generated over the last two years, Google ultimately has only limited information about consumers. Yes, search engines can detect unusual correlations (as opposed to causations). With 70 per cent accuracy, my source tells me, software can assess how people feel based on the way they type, and the number of typos they make. With 79 per cent precision, software can determine a user's credit rating based on the degree to which they write in ALL CAPS. Yet even with all these stats, Google has come to realize it knows almost nothing about humans and what really drives us, and it is now bringing in consultants to do what small data researchers have been doing for decades. As one analyst once told me, "Considering that management doesn't know what to do with big data, everyone is searching for what is post big data—and the answer is small data." [12-13]

The integration of online and offline data—that is to say, the marriage of big data and small data—is a crucial ingredient of marketing survival and success in the 21st century... We're living in an era in which our online behaviors and communications are haunted by subtext and obfuscation. The German word *maskenfreiheit* can be translated into "the freedom conferred by masks", and anyone who has ever spent time online knows that the ability to customise our digital selves, and our occasional online anonymity, creates personae that bear only a loose resemblance to the people we actually are, and the lives we actually live, when we're offline. You might say that thanks to technology, we are all at least two people, with at least two residences: a bricks-and-mortar home and a home page. Sometimes they overlap, but often they don't.

Nor can we say we are any more "ourselves" when we surf the web anonymously. Without a name, or a face, or an identity, we become primitive versions of ourselves, a phenomenon some experts attribute to a lack of empathy that comes from communicating laptop to laptop, and that is also familiar to anyone who has ever flipped off a pedestrian, or worse, while driving a car....This is the paradox of online behavior. We're never truly ourselves on social media, and when we communicate anonymously, the result lacks any context that our offline lives might provide and enrich. Online, what we leave behind is largely considered and strategic, whereas the insides of our refrigerators and dresser drawers are not, as they were never intended for public exhibition.

This is why, in my opinion, the best, closest approximation of who we are as humans comes from mixing our online and offline selves, and from combining big data with small data. Considering that 90 per cent of what people give off in conversation are non-verbal signals, our truest identities can be found by studying who we are in our real lives, cultures and countries. [13-14] ■

AFTER READING:
Revisiting Lindstrom's method and claims

Lindstrom offers a number of specific details about the sorts of small data he gathers, telling us "nothing is off limits." He suggests that he searches without a guiding hypothesis or question, without a particular conceptual framework to give shape to what he collects, beyond the search for "an unmet need or an unacknowledged desire." Yet, as a marketing consultant, he is working within a defined context, usually of an existing product or brand, and that context inevitably informs and guides the activities he might pay attention to (an 11-year-old boy), and even the artifacts he might "collect" (sneakers used in a form of play). What more do you learn about his research methods and the understandings that guide his collecting of small data? Do you think he might describe his process differently if he were writing for other researchers rather than to the larger business world? (And with our concerns about online invasion of privacy, do you think that concern might apply to offline data-gathering as well?)

In building to a position in support of small data, Lindstrom makes a number of related claims about people and their desires and rewards, but also about the characteristics of our online world and how our online selves relate to our offline selves. What are some of his specific claims? How do they contribute to his larger position? From your own gathering of small data through various inquiries, are there any of his claims you would disagree with or modify?

Lindstrom's stories offer rich examples to support the continuing value of small data—data that provide the rich details of context that can help us understand human behavior on a local level and make meaning from the big data swirling around us. He's making an argument for the vital importance of small data in the world of marketing that has, like many industries, turned to big data for market research. Occasionally his claims are misleading, as when he writes that "Google has come to realize it knows almost nothing about humans and what really drives us." Google isn't necessarily in the business of studying all the data they collect, but they are in the business of selling that data to marketing and advertising agencies who do study the data on consumers. Big data may not tell us much about our individual selves, but that's not its intention.

Big data is useful for what it can tell us, in aggregate, about ourselves, but small data give us a different kind of insight, especially on the local level. We can return to the example of census taking. The census is one of the original "big data" problems. Modern electronic computing on a large scale began in 1880, when the first tabulating machine was used for the U.S. census. The census tells us very little about individuals, but it does give us insight into larger patterns and demographic trends taking shape in the country. And understanding those demographic trends, as well as what motivates an 11-year-old boy, might offer understandings that marketers, and other researchers, need to make more informed decisions.

After considering what big data can and can't do, Lindstrom ends with a call for the integration of online and offline data in marketing. Yet he seems to finally conflate what's online with big data and what's offline with small data. Reread his last several paragraphs. How do his claims and his position line up? Might you clarify, modify, add to, or otherwise refine the moves he makes here?

Composing
Data-Driven Argument

Increasingly researchers who are exploring the effects of digital environments on our lives find themselves working with both small and big data. Those studying children's play but not working for Lego tend to do as Lindstrom says and look at both their offline and online worlds, and at both small and big data. The conceptual framework of key concepts and understandings about "play" bridge both worlds. So the small data they collect includes what takes place in the communities and interactions of both their offline and their digital worlds. Here's what one group of researchers had to say about their use of data in a study of young teens (tweens) participating in online play in the virtual town of Whyville:[16:9]

> Where do we see the benefits of big data in what we have learned? Understanding patterns and trends in participation over large numbers of people and over extended periods of time provided a bird's-eye perspective that is difficult to obtain while standing on the ground amid hundreds and thousands of participants. Where do we see the benefits of small data? The ethnographic approach gave us a lens through which to study the norms and practices that shape play in Whyville, what it means to look cool, how to talk, and what to do (139).

While working with both sorts of data might be desirable for many purposes, individual researchers working with small data can still contribute to the big picture. While it's important to take big data into account, to see what big data studies might contribute to your understanding of questions you're exploring and help to place your own discoveries in a larger context, begin first with some of the small data you've been collecting.

For this final composing activity of Part II, further your own understanding about how small data you've collected can contribute to the big picture of how digital environments are contributing to the shape of our communities, our literacy practices, and how we build shared beliefs and values in a wide range of local contexts, online and off, as well as in wider, public, and often global contexts. What big picture questions might you want to explore, and how can any of the small data you've considered so far (observations, interviews, shoebox collections, circulating images and memes, blog posts and articles, etc.) contribute to that exploration? As you seek or revisit patterns in these data, what might you look for? What tentative hypotheses can you make or positions might you build to? Part III of this book will ask you to revisit, build on, and add to some of your earlier work as part of a formal research process. This composing activity is intended to potentially contribute to your thinking for that work.

WRITING MOVES

Inquiring and Inventing

As readers and writers working in networked spaces that generate lots of data, you can draw on those data—both what you've gathered and what others have collected and analyzed—to inform your thinking on a variety of research questions and to make new discoveries. Articulating your argument or tentative position as the starting point of your inquiry (the process we saw Gladwell using in Chapter 15) can define but potentially restrict the kinds of evidence and sources you draw on in your work. Exploring a question, testing out a hypothesis, and composing a tentative argument from the bottom up with data is typically a more open-ended process than starting with a position, making claims, and then determining how to support it. Starting with your data invites a very different process of meaning-making. As you enter public conversations and address broad audiences on the web, working from data can help you arrive at unexpected insights and conclusions.

As you prepare to compose your own bottom-up argument from data you or others have collected, you'll want to work flexibly with the following moves, going back and forth to match up small data, a big picture question, and possible big data analyses, and to find patterns in these data, moving back and forth between the data you've collected and the larger understandings you believe those data can support as evidence.

1 Identifying topics, questions, and relevant data

Before you start to work with data, big or small, and begin looking for trends and patterns, you will need to consider what topics and questions you might want to explore further and what data you've already collected that can help you explore them. Have you already been gathering data about the Instagram posts, circulating memes, sports or music fan practices, music reviewing or book discussions, or Facebook discourse strategies in one of your communities? Any such data offers a good starting point for your further inquiry. And you can add to these data with quick online surveys of community participants. You are also likely to find that others have collected big data that's relevant to your focus. If you're focusing on sports fandom, Stephens-Davidowitz's article might lead you to ask new questions of your own fan community about when they became fans and what role significant team successes might have played. Or you might consider what information you can find in your own Facebook friends' likes and shares. Or perhaps you want to extend a project from Part I of this book and collect a complete set of text messages exchanged

within one community to better understand the ways of using words central to that group. Maybe you want to use data to complicate your thinking about a Part II project, such as an analysis of *The Circle* or another piece of utopian or dystopian literature about the digital age, by looking at the data set created by Amazon reviews of the novel. Data can take many forms and can be located in a variety of places. Try to consider as many sources of data as you can. Your most basic goal is to pull together different sorts of related data you can consider and come to new understandings in the process.

2 Locating patterns and trends

Once you have decided on a set of data to examine, you will want to use it not just to locate evidence, but also to see what it shows or suggests about a topic. Throughout much of our schooling, we are trained to look for discrete pieces of evidence to support a preconceived point or our existing understandings. This process should feel different. As you approach your data, allow it to direct your inquiry. You can do this by tending carefully to this data. One good example of this process can be found in the reading for Chapter 8, the excerpt from Nancy Baym's study of her online soap opera fan

Digital Toolbox
See Part IV, Section 5

community, *Tune In, Log On: Soaps, Fandom and Online Community*, and if you haven't read it, or you haven't read it recently, you might want to review it now.

- Read your data looking for trends. What is repeated? What patterns do you see forming? Name these repeating patterns. Nancy Baym, for example, started finding patterns in the ways in which members of her online soap opera fan group interacted with one another in moments when they seemed to try to avoid offending others or to back off disagreements.

- Code your data. Coding your data is similar to the process of tagging—organizing and categorizing your data based on the patterns and trends you see. Once you have read for patterns and named some of your findings, return to this dataset again, and notate each and every repeated trend. Baym started to use the labels "mitigating offense" and "building affiliation" for two of the patterns she was finding.

- Count what you are seeing. Once you have created some categories to make sense of your data and have identified when and how those moves are repeated, count them. Quantifying your data can help you see more significant trends and think about how to represent this information and the types of reasonable claims you might make. Baym found that "Fully 29 percent of the disagreements in r.a.t.s. [her online community] were prefaced by partial agreements" and in 18 percent of disagreements, the person disagreeing included the other person's name, leading her to identify these moves as two major strategies for building affiliation.

3 Reviewing your small data and gathering more

Once you have located some trends and patterns, you can take stock of the understandings your data suggest. Allow these realizations to inform your tentative stance. At this point, you'll want to question your data: Does it provide you with a rich enough picture of your inquiry? Would drawing on additional data help you contextualize or extend your thinking?

4 Finding a big picture question

After "cooking" your data—spending time working it, reading it with different questions in mind, and annotating it as you try to identify patterns, you should have a sense of both what it can tell you and why that information is important. What big picture questions does your data suggest? At this point, you might want to do some exploratory freewriting about what you've been seeing and the questions that interest you, and begin articulating the stance your data seems to be leading you to claim. Baym's big picture understandings are about the role of friendliness and the use of gendered discourse patterns that maintain a friendly atmosphere in this mostly female online community, but she also sees this friendliness as "just one example of the general tendency of ongoing computer-mediated groups to develop behavioral norms."

5 Finding related big data

At this point, you might want to look for some big data studies that could contribute to a big picture question you'll explore with your small data. Such studies can often provide a much wider context for something you've observed locally. If you're interested in the role social media play for a particular fan group, you might see whether others have collected relevant data (in the way Stephens-Davidowitz did for baseball fans). If you're considering what might attract members of one of your online communities to circulating memes, look for big data studies about what makes memes circulate. If you've become interested in how a local community group is using social networking to accomplish a public good, you might find big data evidence for similar concerns at sites such as the Twitter research blog or at @twitterforgood. You could also look for infographics and other works that draw on big data to address questions similar to your own. You might not find an exact match between the small data you're focusing on and the big data that's available, but big data studies can often help you locate your small data in a larger context. Baym's online community was one of many using Usenet, an online system for discussion boards, and so in the first chapter of her book,[16:9] she drew on statistical data about Usenet to contextualize her own study—to locate the group she was studying among the "high traffic" groups of users (and to suggest that the findings about her fan group might be relevant to others).

The most popular of Usenet's groups always have been those that discuss recreational and social issues. This is demonstrated by statistics gathered by Brian Reid through 1994 and posted to Usenet. In the 20 most *read* discussion groups in March 1993, for example, his figures show that a quarter of the messages (4,629) were in groups discussing

social issues ranging from political activism to Indian culture. Nearly a fifth of the messages were in groups discussing sex. If figures on readership tap users' curiosities, then figures on the number of messages each group generates tap users' creative investments. In the highest *volume* discussion groups, half of the messages (24,983) were about social issues such as Indian culture, abortion, homosexuality, and guns. Another two fifths of the messages (20,025) in these high-traffic groups were in fan groups that discussed sports, television shows, and movies (7–8).

WRITING MOVES ◀

Drafting and Shaping

Once you've worked out a big picture argument you can contribute to from the patterns you've found in your small data and any big data you've found, you're ready to turn your attention to structuring and shaping your presentation of those data and the claims you might make from them in support of a larger position.

1 Considering context and audience

Context includes the audience you'll address, the form your presentation will take, and the platform you'll use. Oftentimes writers must consider different levels of audience. For example, Stephens-Davidowitz was writing for a general public audience—readers of the *New York Times,* so he could imagine that his audience includes other baseball fans but also people who are interested in what we can learn from social media data. In his article about Lego, Lindstrom addresses a general business audience. He most likely intends his book to reach not only marketing professionals, but also a larger audience of people who have an interest in the uses of large and small data for research. In both cases, the authors use data to tell an interesting story about human experience and behavior that is likely to engage a wider audience.

While you might choose a blog platform or a traditional print format, this sort of bottom-up use of small data for big picture exploration lends itself to presentation formats that encourage visual display, exchange, and collaboration, such as a PowerPoint or Prezi presentation for a classroom

or for a community group website, or to post on an online site (with voice-over narration). Because trying to answer big picture questions can get complicated as more data are considered, collaborating with others on these questions can help you bring together pieces of a larger puzzle. Digital tools like Google Docs, wikis, or a content management application like Diigo are all highly useful for collecting, organizing, and sharing multiple pieces, including original data.

Digital Toolbox
See Part IV, Section 1

2 Organizing your presentation—telling a story

As always, a map, outline, sketch, or storyboard is helpful in structuring the information you'll present, whatever your mode of presentation. It's most likely that you'll want to take your audience on a journey with you, from the bottom up, telling them a story through your data and showing how particular moments in your data have led to the larger question you are exploring, the claims you might make, and the exploratory argument you might put forth about

Digital Toolbox
See Part IV, Section 6

some aspect of the big picture of our digital world.

Your compositional arrangement will depend on your data, the writing application you choose, and on how you want to structure your argument. A ground-up argument often builds toward the strongest examples of evidence. As you compose a multimedia argument, you'll also want to be thinking visually about rhetorical ways of using images, color, typeface, and other design elements.

3 Experimenting with infographics

This is a good moment to think about how to integrate any relevant infographics you have found or created. Infographics aren't just for big data, but can be used to make key points about small data as well. Do an image search using the search terms "infographic and social media," "infographic and the music industry," and "infographic" and another search term. You're likely to find any number of existing infographics that can contribute to the points you want to make. You'll also find infographics creators (included in Part IV Digital Toolbox) that work much like meme creators to guide your own infographic construction.

Digital Toolbox
See Part IV, Section 6

To the right is an infographic showing the results of a large study of how sports fans interact with social media, one that could serve as a model for your own infographic about how members of a community you're studying interact about a topic through social media (Figure 16.9).

4 Creating a full draft

As you create your full presentation, whether in print form or in a multimodal presentation, you'll want to present the data and examples that are most compelling and that give your audience a rich picture of your research without overwhelming them. And you'll want to work to convince them, in the end, that your larger argument, your big picture claim, is plausible, or even likely, based on what you've shown them.

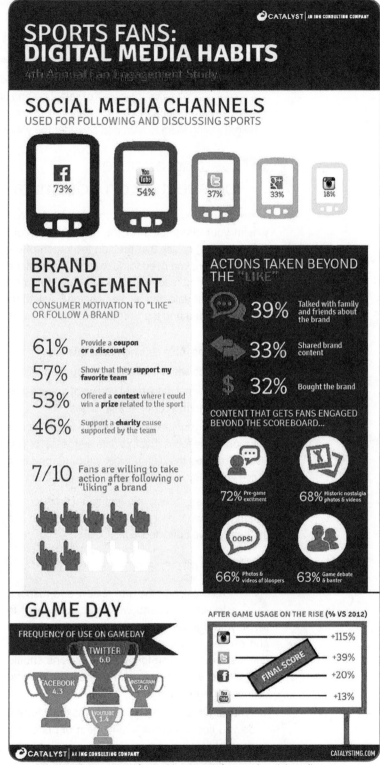

Figure 16.9: Infographic—Sports fans and social media

WRITING MOVES

Revising and Publishing

For a bottom-up argument, where the position follows from the data, it is useful to get a sense of whether a reader can follow your process of selecting and analyzing data and whether they agree that the position you take can be supported by the data you've presented. It can be very useful to share your data with others before asking them to read and consider the ways in which you have written about it.

1 Getting another perspective on your data

Though you won't want to completely overwhelm your classmates (or the members of your writing group) or ask that they do too much of the analytical work you need to do to really understand your data, asking readers to look at a representative sample of your data can be really helpful. Ask them to read this data and then respond to the following questions.

- What seems most striking about this data?
- What trends seem to emerge as you read it?
- What additional data might you want access to in order to enrich your understandings?

Then talk with your readers and share your big picture question or the focus that this data suggests for you. Have them read the data against your interpretation to see what they see.

How does this process, this additional perspective, enrich your own thinking about this information and the data you've collected?

2 Sharing and revising

After asking others to review and respond to your data, you will most likely want to revisit your draft. Once you have a nearly complete and revised piece, you will want to share it with readers for input. The following questions should help you get a rich sense of how others are reading your bottom-up argument.

- What argument is this composer making? Where do you find the clearest statement of his or her position?
- What data has the composer used to show how he/she has arrived at that position?
- Does the evidence adequately support the position the composer comes to?

- What further evidence or explanation of the evidence might you like to see?
- Has the composer taken into account the likely shared knowledge of the audience and provided any new needed background knowledge?
- What is the story being told about this data? Does the composer have a recognizable pattern of organization?
- Does the conclusion make a convincing statement of the argument the composer has built? Is there anything else you'd add to it?
- What other advice would you give to this composer?

You might also, in a group, use your peer responses to create a generative rubric to identify key elements of a ground-up argument and to shape a general guide for revising such compositions into a final form. Use both the generative rubric and the specific peer responses you received to prepare a revised version of your composition. And as always, remember to do careful editing and proofreading.

3 Circulating your work to a public audience

By now you most likely have a sense of some online sites, whether within your college or university context or beyond, where you could find an audience for the study you've shaped, where people will be interested in the connections between the big data picture and what your small data study has shown about the literacy practices of the digital world. How are essays presented on the site you chose? As you prepare to post your work, what elements of design and presentation will you take into account? How will you work with the platform you chose to present your own work in the most effective way possible?

Reinventing and Circulating Your Work

As we've seen, infographics have become a popular way to communicate large amounts of data and their relationships in more visual ways. News media sites like *The New York Times* and *The Huffington Post* commonly use infographics with other compositional elements when composing online articles and arguments. Other sites, like infogr.am[L16:9] and Daily Infographic[L16:10], are sites for creating and sharing infographics.

Another way to place your own work in a larger context is to discover and analyze the infographics that others have created about related topics. You may have drawn on or composed an infographic to support your own study. But finding a number of infographics on a topic can allow you to see both the circulation context for information about the topic and the different ways in which infographic writers have worked with typical elements of information.

Search for infographic images on a topic you've been exploring. Where do they appear, and what audiences do they address? How do they differ in the information presented? In design? And how do the elements of the information presented and the design of that presentation work toward the likely rhetorical purposes of each presentation context? How does the infographic support the argument being made?

As a conclusion to your consideration of big data and what it contributes to our understanding of a digital world, share your infographics and your analysis of how they work with others in your own classroom community and perhaps beyond.

Key Concepts

big data 347	conceptual framework 354
bottom-up argument 348	infographics 350

Additional Readings

Contents

READING 1

"The Hashtag Revolution"
by Danielle Small (Student)

This essay was written in response to Malcom Gladwell's article "Small Change: Why The Revolution Will Not Be Tweeted" (featured in Chapter 15). In this well-known article, Gladwell argues that social media alone, in particular Twitter, cannot create lasting social change. Using the Greensboro lunch counter sit-ins as his example, he shows how deeply invested these communities were in making social change and how this depended on face-to-face relationships and a willingness to encounter violence. Danielle responds in her essay by first acknowledging Gladwell's main point, that social change has always needed great investment by individuals and communities, but she shows, citing activist hashtags like #blacklivesmatter and #LoveWins, how social media can actually play a very large role in making social change. She notes that after the 2015 Supreme Court ruling on marriage equality, over 6.2 billion tweets used #LoveWins, "making it the most tweeted hashtag in history" (4). Without dismissing Gladwell's argument, Danielle convincingly argues that, while social media has limitations, it has become a vital tool for organizing activist movements in a more globalized, digitized world.

President Obama ✔
@POTUS
Follow

Today is a big step in our march toward equality. Gay and lesbian couples now have the right to marry, just like anyone else. #LoveWins 💙

RETWEETS FAVORITES
261,793 206,154

7:10 AM - 26 Jun 2015

KANYE WEST ✔
@kanyewest
Following

600,000 people rallied for justice on Dec. 13th #blacklivesmatter

umair haque ✔
@umairh
Follow

Tanks. Military police. Occupation. Media blackout. No fly zone. In...a suburb. This is America in 2014. #Ferguson

Reply Retweet Favorite More

RETWEETS FAVORITES
919 338

2:20 AM - 13 Aug 2014

deray mckesson ✔
@deray
Follow

There is no rank order to injustice.

We fight for #Mizzou, #PrayForParis, and seek justice for #SandraBland -- at the same time.

RETWEETS LIKES
4,142 4,419

2:41 AM - 14 Nov 2015

As I absorbed the meticulously written article "Small Change: Why The Revolution Won't Be Tweeted" by Malcolm Gladwell, I couldn't help but see the above images in my head. I thought about the hundreds upon thousands of hashtags that flooded my dashboard over the past few years, and the majority of them were activist movements. I can still feel the joy and positivity that was emulated through my screen as I opened Twitter the morning the Supreme Court came to a verdict on marriage equality. While at the same time, seeing footage of an unarmed black man being choked to death for questioning his "stop and frisk" and thinking, is this really happening? Such strong feelings of merriment and outrage conjured by presumed entertainment platforms couldn't be a farce. I feel that as our society becomes more adept in understand the power that social media platforms can hold, they begin seeing them more as opportunities to spread awareness and change, rather than gossip and menial topics. A subtle yet important shift of mindset for today's society, one I feel was not displayed in Gladwell's article.

"The Revolution Will Not Be Tweeted" is a bold statement for Gladwell to make, for his words disprove themselves with time. As you can see on the timestamps, several revolutions were occurring simultaneously just a few years subsequent of his claim. The above tweets are just a handful of the hashtags created to achieve social justice, something I feel he seemed to ignore in his statements which focused mostly on political revolts. I was intrigued by the sociological perspective he brought to the table when discussing his opinion on the "Then and Now" structures of revolutions. Yet, when contrasting both in detail he neglected to compare their similarities. Even more so, he denied the fact that they could ever coexist, painting them as separate entities. That is where I disagree with his point.

Throughout the article there is an underlying context that social media networks alone are not enough to cultivate strong relationships, and therefore impactful activism. Although I agree that social media is a tool that is easily abused by those who obtain it, I feel we should not place the blame on the platform, but rather those people who are misusing it. In Gladwell's view, "activists were once defined by their causes, they are now defined by their tools" and I have mixed feelings about it. On one hand I can see how the tool of social media may obstruct the humility that comes along with in-person activism. It may seem that it is removing the emotional connotation connected with activists' cause. But, I still insist that we should not blame that on social media as an entity. Just as it was in the 1960's, it's the activists' responsibility to ensure their cause is vouched for. Activists who know how to properly use the tool they're working with will be able to establish all of the same rhetori-

cal appeals online as they would in person. Not only that, but reach a more diverse community at the same time.

The historical anecdote used as an example of strong tie revolution unintentionally portrays racial inequality as a thing of the past. Understandably, Gladwell's article needed a specific focus and direction. As a member of the African American community, Malcolm Gladwell has expressed his awareness of the modern day injustices regarding race in America in his other pieces. It's clear that he's not ignorant about its relevance, though for this specific article he ultimately chose to not incorporate it for the sake of his succinct argument. To be clear, my intention is to not blame the author for his lack of acknowledgment of the topic in 2010. With that being said, we undoubtedly base our knowledge of what is relevant in our society based on social media influx and trends. As affirmed in Gladwell's piece: "There is strength in weak ties, as the sociologist Mark Granovetter has observed. Our acquaintances—not our friends—are our greatest source of new ideas and information." One of the most powerful tactics of organizations like Black Lives Matter is uploading video footage from social media users who experience situations of bias everyday. I presume if we were to ask Gladwell now to comment on similar topics from his article in 2010, it'd be impossible to ignore the "Black Lives Matter" Movement for it is continually prevalent on social media. By including the topic of police brutality to his argument, not only would it've strengthened his depth, but perhaps shifted his perception of the benefits social media provides for modern day activism.

Deray McKesson is an established member of the Movement for Black Lives, who is most recognized for his activism on Twitter, as seen above. He has a degree in government and legal studies from Bowdoin College and participated in several protests in turbulent areas like Ferguson and Baltimore. He is a perfect candidate of how an activist can use the resources available to him while still participating in "high-risk activism" which Gladwell downplays. In his view, "It doesn't involve financial or personal risk; it doesn't mean spending a summer being chased by armed men in pickup trucks. It doesn't require that you confront socially entrenched norms and practices." Basically, Gladwell is proposing the idea that social media activism removes the danger that was a direct consequence of protesting during the civil rights movement. In this regard, how would he classify the events of Ferguson, Missouri? As seen in the photo below, police forces approached the protests militarized. Driving MRAP Mine Resistant Ambush Protected Vehicles and clad in riot gear and shields. They bore machine gun rifles and used tear gas on the protesters. The image alone refutes Gladwell's point that there is no personal risk in today's activism. But to renounce his claim verbatim, on August 10th,

2015 protesters were being chased by militarily armed police officers, in ambush resistant army vehicles because they were confronting the socially entrenched norm of police brutality and racially biased practices in our justice system.

Business insider

Celebrity and grassroots activists alike are advocating for their causes, and the results are substantial. Gladwell belittles the potential impact social media has by believing that:

"The drawbacks of networks scarcely matter if the network isn't interested in systemic change—if it just wants to frighten or humiliate or make a splash—or if it doesn't need to think strategically. But if you're taking on a powerful and organized establishment you have to be a hierarchy." Malcolm Gladwell

Let's take that statement and apply it to marriage equality, shall we? According to statistics revealed by the Associated Press, In 2010, only five states in the nation granted same-sex marriage licenses. Within the past five years, social network platforms have become the face of the LGBT community. YouTube has over 36,000 "coming out" videos uploaded to date and Facebook has had equality (2013) and gay pride (2015) filters available for users' profile pictures. So much media attention sparked an uprising in the fight for equality, and the activists seized on their chance. By 2015, social media propelled the issue of marriage equality to the Supreme Court, and on June 26th of that year it was deemed a constitutional right by the majority of the Justices. President Barack Obama, alongside 6.2 billion other tweets used "#LoveWins" six hours after the ruling, officially making it the most tweeted hashtag in history. A perfect example of how social network platforms played a significant role in achieving systemic change. This proves that a network can be "resilient and adaptable" and also maintain a "strategic and disciplined" structure to achieve change. It counteracts his claim that an organization must be a hierarchy if it wants to implement a serious transformation. The United States Government and the Constitution are an organized establishment and relatively powerful, Mr. Gladwell.

Never once did Gladwell consider the possibility of integrating the two structures of revolution. Doing so would create a hybrid, stronger and more efficient way than ever imagined when the two stood alone. In terms of social media, I agree with Gladwell when he says that there can be a misconstrued understanding of the responsibility a true activist undertakes.

Coming from someone who is a part of "Generation Z" I can attest that this is true, but I think his explanation is slightly off. He feels like we're being manipulated and defined by our tools, yet I think we define ourselves on how we're perceived. Luke O'Neil summarizes my point best in an article he wrote for *Esquire*. "When we're reminded that our friends are watching us, we're more likely to do what we think is the right thing. Civic engagement isn't its own reward for young people, but being perceived as being civically engaged is." And social media's very foundation is perception. When we can choose everything that we want to be seen by our friends, it's easier to come across well. By default, with our millennial desire to be seen as an active member in society, we're also subconsciously becoming aware and educated on important issues. The personal connection to the cause is vague because anyone has access to the information and it lacks the courage that change needs to be successful. Yet, within the flaw we see it's biggest strength. Finally, people can access relatively unbiased, factual information and form an opinion of their own instead of being given one by biased television networks. These issues can be brought to entire populations of people it may not have reached fifty (or even five) some-odd years ago. The outreach and accessibility social networks provide are crucial in spreading awareness of a cause, as well as recruitment.

The mode of revolution used before social media also provides a vital aspect: relationships. Gladwell was right in his belief that strong ties keep activism alive and thriving. Knowing someone in the movement holds you to the responsibility that social media lacks. It promotes loyalty to the cause and an opportunity for dialogue and discussion that isn't misinterpreted by noting all perspectives equally. To build a revolution, you must start from the ground up, starting small and using the tools at one's disposal to spread awareness and a call to action. I believe that if people are personally invested and share their passion for change with hundreds of acquaintances who adopt that same drive, it creates a mobilization that results in effective revolution. ■

Questions

❶ For this assignment, Danielle was asked to have a written conversation with Gladwell. What kinds of writerly moves does she make to have this conversation?

❷ What is Danielle's larger point she is making? What smaller points does she make to support her larger point? Find specific passages to support your answers.

❸ If you haven't read Gladwell's article at this point, take a look at it in Chapter 15. After reading the piece, does your reading of Danielle's piece change? Are there other aspects from your experience of social media and political activism you could add to this conversation?

READING 2

"Breaking the Mold Like a Girl"
by Erin Gaglias (Student)

In this cultural and visual analysis written for a first-year writing course, Erin analyzes the compositional, cultural, and rhetorical aspects of the Always #LikeAGirl advertising campaign that first appeared as a 60-second ad [LRII:1] during Superbowl XLIX (2015). Gaglias breaks down the visual look of the video, how it is filmed, and how it uses sound to enhance the effect of the message. She explains how several females of all ages were asked what it means to "run like a girl" or "throw like a girl." The young girls who haven't been exposed to such gender stereotypes tended to run and throw as fiercely as young boys, while older females, 12 and above, initially performed (mockingly) weak-wristed throws or dainty running when asked the same questions. Erin then turns to Twitter and looks at some of the posts that were made in response to #LikeAGirl, including the start of #LikeABoy. She makes the observation that the many negative responses on Twitter towards the commercial demonstrate that the negative stereotypes of "like a girl" continue to exist in modern society, and social media often shows how widespread hurtful stereotypes can be.

The advertising industry as a whole is ubiquitous; as consumers, sometimes we're aware of its multi-million dollar impact, distracted by the eye-catching effects, annoying jingles, and repetitive air time. More frequently however, we maintain our innocence and go about our daily lives relatively unsuspecting of the nearly 700 ads we're exposed to every day (American Association of Advertising Agencies). But what if these advertising ploys actually have a message? In this era of transparency, can marketing strategies extend beyond the realm of promoting a product, and simultaneously build a brand and a conversation? That's exactly what Proctor and Gamble's *Always* #LikeAGirl campaign seeks to achieve with its 60-second commercial spot for Superbowl XLIX in February 2015. Although it comes with the territory that branding strategies are profit driven, they evidently still have the power to create a productive conversation about culture; in this case, the rhetorical weight falls upon gender stereotyping. Through engaging compositional techniques and the exploration of a provocative message, the #LikeAGirl commercial effectively portrays the social and cultural issues prompted by this age-old question: What does it mean to be like a girl?

Directed by Lauren Greenfield, the #LikeAGirl commercial depicts the confusion that young girls experience while growing up with gender stereotyping. The commercial opens with a casting audition; young adults are posed with a series of questions, such as what does it look like to run or throw like a girl. The individuals unanimously convey that doing an action 'like a girl' is uncoordinated and weak; when the same questions are posed to younger girls around the age of 10, their movements reflect confidence and athleticism (Condon).

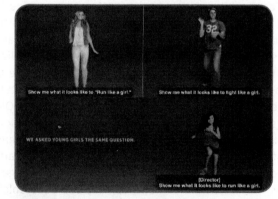

When Greenfield asks the young adults how they would think the negative connotation of their responses would affect young girls, the audience is prompted to reflect upon the destructive nature that gender stereotyping has on young girls'

self-esteem as they move through middle school and high school. They're asked to show what it looks like to run and throw 'like a girl' again, which is met by stronger and more athletic responses.

The commercial ends with a statement describing how Always wants to help young girls improve their self-esteem and confidence as they grow up, reclaiming what it means to be like a girl as a positive remark rather than an insult.

Often the first aspect of a video text that an audience concentrates on is the compositional value, or the elements that make up the structure of the commercial. Much of the #LikeAGirl commercial demonstrates uniformity; the shots are centered with a solid blue background, the individuals are filmed portrait-style, and all words that appear are in a block-lettered font with no elaborate graphics. Because the featured individuals are being interviewed, the commercial is largely unscripted which accounts for the documentary-like format of the visual text as a whole. Sensory contrast is also employed with the distinction of no background music for a majority of the commercial except during the last interview responses at the end. The music itself is layered and rounded while remaining at mid-tempo, creating a dramatic effect while still being soft enough to avoid overpowering the dialogue of the commercial. This provides a point of reference in the interviews where the young adults are starting to realize and reevaluate how negative their initial responses were, placing emphasis on the central message that being 'like a girl' should be empowering instead of insulting. Ultimately, the raw, stripped down compositional approach stylistically emphasizes the honesty and transparency of the unscripted discourse that revolves around the social impacts associated with gender stereotyping.

Although the original #LikeAGirl commercial was released in June 2014 at 3 minutes and 30 seconds, it was rereleased for a 60-second spot during Superbowl XLIX. Met with over 61 million views on YouTube, a #1 ranking for "Best Superbowl Spots" on Adweek, top honors at the Webby Awards, and an Emmy award for best commercial, the ad was produced and directed by acclaimed documentarian and filmmaker Lauren Greenfield (Diaz). Most well known for her award-winning projects that examine youth culture and social issues, Greenfield explains in an interview with Always "When the words 'like a girl' are used to mean something bad, it is profoundly disempowering... I am excited to be a part of the movement to redefine 'like a girl' into a positive affirmation". The commercial itself also fulfilled the ultimate goal of every branding strategy: it went viral. While the commercial does subtly convey feministic themes, it doesn't "throw" feminism at the audience and instead strategically focuses on the one question at hand. The release of the #LikeAGirl campaign seems to involve some deliberate timing as well; the commercial was actively aired in the same time frame as the rise of Ronda Rousey and the U.S. Women's Soccer team's World Cup victory, both garnering female attention in male dominated sports and adding to the cultural relevance of the campaign's message. The commercial was also aired during a televised event with a primarily male viewership, creating the opportunistic conditions to call attention to a conversation about female empowerment that traditionally is met with little interest from the male demographic.

Always has presented its audience with a rhetorically saturated visual text that's clearly capable of generating a rich social response. Much of the response in question results from the prominent use of contrast across age groups and genders throughout the commercial , including the male vs. female and child vs. young adult perceptions. The uninhibited reactions elicited from the featured individuals absolutely enhance the pathos of the principal message of the ad, or what it means to be 'like a girl'. In turn, this contrast strengthens the persuasive power of the commercial through the simultaneous reflection of both the speaking subjects and the audience, again marked by the introduction of background music. Because of the commercial's 'narrativity', or one of the three matrices of power that describes the storytelling ability of a visual text, the #LikeAGirl message was readily received by viewers (Scholes).

Granting that this could very possibly be a strategic composition choice by Lauren Greenfield, the audience's consequential questioning of social norms is no mistake. With Twitter as the seemingly most popular form of social media during Superbowl XLIX as a result of its uncanny proclivity for broadcasting personal opinions, much of the commercial's positive responses were met with those of a negative nature. Contact reporter Beth Kassab of the Orlando Sentinel dictated it best: "If anybody questions whether a campaign to boost girls' confidence is needed today, all you need to know is that moments after the ad aired on Sunday night the hashtag "like a boy" was trending on Twitter." (Figure 1)

In true Twitter fashion, Clapback ensued; not only from female users but from males as well. This distinction from the primarily male #LikeABoy tweeters is an interesting observation that adds greater weight to the gender stereotyping dispute because it proves that this issue yields cultural value because of its challenging social impact. Furthermore, this Twitter 'war' reflects a microcosm of this debate as a whole; despite the argumentative sentiments, the productive conversation it creates definitely fulfilled the social objectives of the commercial.

Ultimately Proctor and Gamble's Always has presented its audience with a social experiment, one of utmost cultural relevance that generated a rich societal response. One of the most unique components of the #LikeAGirl commercial is that the actual brand name is barely mentioned: the message of the commercial sells itself through the composition of the visual text and the response it generated. Branding strategies such as this one are moving towards the growth of a new genre of commercials, one that provokes a conversation about the reality of feminism that has been answered by other companies such as Nike and Verizon. It's a movement in the name of reflection, discussion, and empowerment; what does 'like a girl' truly mean?

That's a good question. ■

Figure 1

Questions

❶ Before watching the video, answer the following questions.

- What is Erin's main point in this essay? What does she suggest about the rhetorical purpose of the commercial?

- If a reader of this piece hasn't seen the commercial, could they still understand Erin's analysis? What kinds of writerly moves does she make to create this understanding? To structure her analysis?

❷ Find the video on YouTube and watch it.[LRII:1] Read some of the comments that have been posted. If you were going to build on Erin's work in any way, what would you add?

READING 3

"Stereotypes Oppressing Women: A Cultural Analysis Linking Greek Life and the Workforce"
by Mary Rufo (Student)

This essay focuses on the systematic oppression of women in modern American culture and looks to the ways in which members of sororities use social media to rewrite traditional disempowered representations of women. Mary looks to particular Facebook groups and hashtags that stress the academic and community commitments of sorority members and argues that these kinds of cultural representations push back on a larger social trend of inequality. In this piece, Mary takes on a historical context of oppression to show the potential of the digital sphere. As she draws on her own experiences, the activities of the Coastal Carolina University chapter of Gamma Phi Beta, and secondary sources that take issues like sorority sisterhood and wage inequality as their focus, Mary positions herself as an informed writer who takes on social causes by analyzing a local cultural context.

Women have been scrutinized and discriminated against from the early history of society onwards. Even today in 2016 women are still being held down by the glass ceiling hovering over the workplace. A smaller scale example of this is the scrutinization of sorority women. Sororities have deeper values than the presumable superficial priorities of partying and boys. The values that each sorority was founded on is central to their mission and goals, but something which is universal is the driving force to better their chapter, their community, and the world. Tabloids and newspapers are eager to exploit the mistakes and poor decisions of individual sorority sisters, continuing the generalization that all sorority members are party girls and heavy drinkers. Exploiting and perpetuating these stereotypes is just another example of how society puts women down to increase the status and power of men. Just as women work extremely hard fighting for their equality in the work place, sorority members work tremendously hard to eliminate their degrading stereotype and better their community. One way they try to eradicate this stereotype is by sharing their hard work and service on social media. By sharing photos on Facebook, Instagram, or Twitter they are able to give visual representation of their hard work and dedication to bettering their communities. Photos of community service and academic achievements are common examples. Attaching hashtags allows sororities and non sorority members to see these photos and connect with them on a deeper level. Just as sorority members are fighting for a good reputation, women are still fighting for equality in society.

Since 1874 women have been gathering together for a supportive and intellectually challenging environment that they were not finding in regular society. Before the 19th amendment women were ostracized and excluded from the work place and most higher forms of education. In 1874 four courageous women at Syracuse University coined the word "sorority" when they founded Gamma Phi Beta. Despite women's lower status in society these women realized their higher potential. They founded Gamma Phi Beta in order to form an environment where women would have the opportunity to intellectually express themselves, be professional and respected. They decided on the four core values of love, loyalty, labor, and learning. Love and loyalty are essential components to form a life long bond with your sisters and the organization. Not only were members expected to have love and loyalty for each other, but for Gamma Phi Beta, their chapter, and all members of their community. Their labor would happen through work in the classroom and through community service. Learning, which is why they attended Syracuse, was extremely important and their studies they made a top priority. These would guide the group as well as "aspire the highest type of womanhood", which is the sorority's motto (The History of Gamma Phi Beta).

All of these aspirations would hopefully open the eyes of men and force them to realize women have the capability to be academic and professional, just as men could.

Greek life is constantly being scrutinized in the media and online for its bad reputations surrounding partying and hazing. Most of the time when sororities are mentioned in the news it is about scandals involving hazing or out of control parties. Sororities have even been banned at some Universities in fear of their negative effects on campus. Swarthmore College, located in Swarthmore Pennsylvania is just one example of a campus who banned sorority life. The ban had been in place since the 1930's and finally after 80 years without sororities the campus relinquished it, with the hopes of creating a promising and respectable organization to promote relationships between diverse women (Ann Schnoebelen). Many schools unlike Swarthmore still have bans on Greek life or have just refused to allow it on campus because of the bad reputations these organizations have. Sororities and fraternities work hard to counteract the stereotypes.

Posting on social media is allowing them to tell people there is more to sororities than meets the eye. Social media is an easy way to share these values with large numbers of people. The sororities' pages as well as sisters' social media accounts are both filled with information and experiences involving their values. Helping outsiders understand their mission and the beauty of their community is important, and certain hashtags allows them to elaborate on those ideas.

Gamma Phi Beta, a sorority here on Coastal Carolina's campus has a Facebook account, Instagram account, Twitter page and website, which are all regularly updated to share their hard work and dedication. One prominent hashtag that circulates most of those sites is #whygammaphiwednesday. On Wednesdays members are encouraged to post pictures on all media platforms with other members and caption them with #whygammaphiwednesday and add their personal stories or reasons for why they chose to join Gamma Phi Beta. By allowing members from all different chapters of Gamma Phi Beta, across the United States and Canada, to relate to one another because of their shared values, everyone can connect and talk about the events they all share or they individually have as a chapter. This also allows for the group to see that every sister and every chapter is different. These posts help express the four core values, but also appreciates and celebrates the differences each member has. Another hashtag used is #gammaphibeta, and is often tagged for pictures of certain accomplishments or community service projects. Gamma Phi Beta's national philanthropy is an organization called Girls on the Run, an organization that works to inspire and build strong ambitious girls, while also keeping them physically active. While fundraising for this group, Gamma Phi Beta also hosts events like 5k's or parties for the girls and their families. Additional community service events include regular beach sweeps, The Myrtle Beach Heart Walk, and Relay for Life. Other photographs that share this hashtag are academic accomplishments, like making the Dean's or President's list. With the access to this online community, they are constantly learning from each other and from other Greek organizations and organizations on campus or in the community. Society only focuses on and publicizes the personal mistakes of sorority members and puts the blame on Greek life as a whole, and because of this sororities and fraternities must publicize the good they do to restore their reputation. Each photograph with one these hashtags is helping to eliminate the stereotype's society has labeled them with.

From the founding of America, women have been thought of as inferior to men. This has lead to the cultural perception that women are not as capable workers as men. For many decades women were exiled from working or going to higher forms of education, so instead they were forced to stay home and do domestic chores. This is because society perceived them as something they were not. The first time women debuted in the work place was during World War II, and only because most men were at war. During this time about five million more women got a chance to work and perform well, but sadly when the men returned many women lost their jobs and the few who kept them were often demoted (Women in the Workforce). Sadly this gender gap is still happening today. Although women have entered the work force in high numbers, there was still about twenty percent more reported men working in 2014 than there was women (Ratio of Female to Male Labor Force Participation Rate). Although in 2016 there has been a great amount of progress made from the early 1900's when most women did not work, there is still more progress needed. Even today there is still a gender wage gap. According to the Women's International Network News "[w]omen earned an average of $14,761 less than men in public doctoral-granting institutions and $13,239

less than men in private doctoral-granting institutions" (Usa: Huge Pay Gaps Between Women And Men At Us Universities). Something so trivial as gender is costing women money and respect in the work place, just as sororities are loosing respect and pride because of their affiliation.

Sororities are punished because of society's poor opinion of them, just as women are punished because they are assumed to be less capable than men. Both of these stereotypes are hurting the societal progression of women. Although sororities tend to have higher GPA's than the rest of campus, are major fund raisers for many philanthropies across the world, and donate millions of hours of community service each year, they are still pulled down by their party girl stereotype (Fraternity Statistics). Women stepped up after World War II and proved they were capable of working like men only to be pushed back down, and in 2016 have yet to reach equality in the work place. Both groups have and continue to work exceptionally hard to prove themselves and alleviate their stereotypes, now it is society's turn to open their eyes and appreciate their hard work.

Works Cited

Fraternity Statistics. North American Interfraternity Conference. NIC Standards Compliance Report, 2014. Web. 10 Feb. 2016.

Ratio of Female to Male Labor Force Participation Rate (%) (modeled ILO Estimate). Data. World Bank Group. Web. 10 Feb. 2016.

Schnoebelen, Ann. "After A Ban Of 80 Years, Sisterhood Takes Hold At Swarthmore." Chronicle Of Higher Education 59.38 (2013): A16-A17. Academic Search Complete. Web. 10 Feb. 2016.

The History of Gamma Phi Beta. To Inspire the Highest Type of Womanhood—History of Gamma Phi Beta. Gamma Phi Beta. Web. 11 Feb. 2016.

"USA: Huge Pay Gaps Between Women And Men At US Universities." Women's International Network News 28.3 (2002): 63. Academic Search Complete. Web. 10 Feb. 2016.

Women in the Workforce. NebraskaStudies.Org. Net Learning Services, n.d. Web. 10 Feb. 2016.

Questions

❶ How does Mary draw on and position examples in this text? What do you notice about the range of examples she pulls from in this essay?

❷ What do you think of Mary's larger point? What moves of analysis does she draw on as she builds her position? What critical moves do you see Mary making?

❸ What do you notice about how Mary structures this text, how she moves between local and public contexts throughout this piece? What can you learn from this essay about options for organizing your own work?

READING 4

"So You Want to Be a Critic"[LRII:2]
by Mark Schannon
Blogcritics, April 13, 2006

Mark Schannon might be called an amateur critic, someone who has made his living in another sphere (consulting, public relations), but who has engaged seriously over time with the work of writing reviews, for his own pleasure and to be part of an online community of those interested in the arts. His essay, "So You Want to Be a Critic," along with his "Guidelines for Writing Reviews" appeared on *Blogcritics*—a site for reviews of various cultural productions, such as books, games, and films. The process he used when writing this piece shows he was fully involved with this community as he shaped his final essay. He first drafted and posted one longer essay, asked for readers' comments, noted their individual suggestions in a second draft, which he also posted, and then created the third draft, which more deeply incorporates those suggestions into his own revised essay—the one that appears on the site now. In that revision process, he also broke out specific questions reviewers of various genres might ask and put them into the separate "Guidelines" post. His essay has been noted by other *Blogcritics* reviewers, who have drawn on his advice or pointed out differences in their own approaches. It speaks to those who have tried on or want to try on the critic's role.

Introduction

A reviewer, regardless of the art form, has a responsibility to readers to be knowledgeable about the specific art form. Reviewers do not simply express opinions. There's a huge difference between "I **liked** *Killer Ants Devouring Lithuania*," and "*Killer Ants Devouring Lithuania* was a **good** movie."

In the former, you're only expressing a personal opinion based on your likes and dislikes. You have the right to that opinion, but as a reader, my reaction is, "who cares?" I want to know about the movie or book, not about you. In the latter, you have a set of criteria by which you can judge the work of art. Too many people fail to see or accept that distinction. If you fall into this category, you'll write lousy reviews of no interest to the reader; you'll merely be feeding your own ego by seeing your name in print.

But if you study the medium, its history and trends, if you can break a performance into its component parts to evaluate how they fit together, if you can put your review into the context of similar works, then you're offering valuable insights that will help readers decide whether to experience the art, and you're teaching them how to enhance their experience and appreciation.

Here's where it gets messy. These criteria are not completely objective nor are they totally subjective. They lie somewhere in between. But if you deny the criteria and claim that all opinions are subjective, why bother to review anything at all? Your opinion carries no more weight than a three-year-old watching the same movie.

What follows are standards used by professional critics, and few people have the time to engross themselves this thoroughly in an art form. Don't be overwhelmed by the complexity; rather, use this article as a starting point, adopting ideas and concepts that make sense and recognizing that, to become a good critic, you never stop studying the medium.

It's also important to emphasize that while there's not one right way to write a review, there are essential elements that make it either a good or bad one.

Elements of a Review: The Hook

Like all good writing, a review has to have a "hook," an opening sentence or paragraph that draws in the reader. Rarely, if ever, should that hook include the word "I," which tells the reader "it's all about me." Most will stop reading and move on to another article. Another trap to avoid is being obvious while attempting to be profound. For example, comments about short stories, poetry, or essays not getting the kind of attention they deserve insult your readers' intelligence.

Here's the opening sentence of a book review on BC: "Harvey Pekar writes autobiographical comic books for grown-ups, and he is rather prone to grumpiness." (Except for the word "rather," it's a great set up. Remember adjectives and adverbs are weak words; nouns and verbs are strong words.) Regardless, look at the juxtaposition of *autobiographical*, *comic books*, and *grumpiness*. How could you not want to read on?

Here's another from a BC review: "David Jones came from humble beginnings and worked his way up to CEO of a successful British retail company. And he did so without telling anyone that he had Parkinson's Disease for most of his tenure." Personally, I'd eliminate the period after "company" and substitute a comma. But the surprise of the Parkinson's compels the reader to keep going.

One doesn't have to be formal and rigid with a hook. Consider the opening of this BC book review: "Okay guys, listen up. Because it's time to Man Up. And who better to teach the finer points—the ins and outs if you will—of being a 'man's man' than veteran mob guy character actor Frank Vincent?" I don't even know who Vincent is, but I read the review.

Hook 'em. It's just like fishing. You put a worm or a lure on the hook, not a picture of yourself or a treatise demonstrating your deep wisdom.

Elements of a Review: After the Hook

You've captured my interest with a solid hook. Now increase that interest by continuing to be provocative. Don't wander off into parts unknown...yet. If you're going to do that, you'll have time.

1. "*Matrix IX* is a really interesting movie with great special effects. I was captivated from the first moment."
2. In what seems to be a never-ending raising of the technological bar, *Matrix IX* once again demonstrated that there seems to be no limit to how mind-boggling special effects can get.
3. *Matrix IX* continues a series of mechanical performances by actors who could just as easily been replaced by some computer generated figures.
4. I could barely keep my eyes open during the most boring *Matrix* movie yet, *Matrix IX*.

See the difference? Numbers 1 & 4 are all about "me." 2 & 3 are about the movie. It should be easy to see how to expand these topic sentences for a longer paragraph explaining what you mean.

Elements of a Review: The Rest

Earlier, I wrote that reviewers have a responsibility to be knowledgeable about the art form they're reviewing. What does that mean? This list isn't intended as a straightjacket; quite the opposite, this part of the review is where you can bring in not only comments about other works of art, you can carefully express your own opinions within each of the elements, below. Also, while everything in this list doesn't need to be included or in this order, reviewers should be or become knowledgeable about:

- The art form and how what's being reviewed fits or varies from that form.
- The history of that art form and others to be able to give the reader some context in which to judge what's being reviewed. What in the past is similar to what you're reviewing? What's dissimilar?
- The genre in which whatever's being reviewed fits. Is it just more of the same, or is the artist breaking new ground within the genre? What other works of art can you cite that will give the reader a better understanding of the work in question?

- The trends, i.e. the societal, political, religious, artistic, etc. movements, that this piece of art references.
- The criteria for judging a specific work of art. This part is perhaps the hardest because knowledgeable people can disagree, but a reviewer needs to be able to comment on issue such as *tone* (is it consistent throughout), *message* (is it clear or confused...perhaps intentionally confusing,) *pacing and timing*, and *importance* (does this work of art set new standards, raise new questions, demand that the viewer or reader challenge his or her preconceptions, etc.)
- (Most important) The specific artistic elements that make up the item being reviewed. For example, in a play or movie, the set, the lighting, the costumes, how well the director manages the artists' performances and their movements (called *blocking*), the writing, the music, the actors' interpretations, and the actors' interactions, to name a few. In music, how well the sound is mixed, the quality of the lyrics or band, and the variation in the selection of music to create a complete experience.

This knowledge base is what allows a reviewer to form a judgment that something is aesthetically *good* or *bad* as opposed to offering a personal opinion. One doesn't always have to cover all of these points—sometimes it's not relevant, but you can't ignore them all either.

Interspersed among the above are the reviewer's judgments about the acting, singing, story line, whatever. It's how you continue to engage readers by offering insight into what kind of experience they're likely to have.

Elements of Review: The Close

Just as the *hook* grabs the readers' attention, the close is where you create something memorable so that your review stays with them. Unfortunately, it's just as difficult to write as a good hook.

By now, you should be done with the details, but you want to remind the reader why this art is a piece of gold or...clay. For example, if you're reviewing a fantasy book, and you're a Tolkien fanatic, here's one suggestion: "Many years ago when I put down the final volume of Tolkien's *Lord of the Rings*, I knew I had found a gem the likes of which I'd probably never again uncover. *Dragons Don't Have Teeth* may not be the Hope Diamond, but it comes as close to Tolkien as you're likely to get."

The use of "I" works because of the reference to one of the most beloved fantasies of all time. People will see the Tolkien reference and understand completely what you mean by getting close without being distracted by your opinion.

Here's a close that could have been much better had the writer just left himself out of the picture:

I'm sure my friends from the party are talking about my

musical tastes behind my back. At forty-six, I probably should be more immersed in jazz, classical, and pop then I am. But let the mf'ers talk—so much of what we call entertainment these days is flat and boring. At least NOFX and other bands approaching middle age still have the balls to produce some very funny stuff.

Start reading from "So much of what we call entertainment..." and you'll see how powerful the ending could have been.

Here's an almost perfect close that sums up quickly the essence of an album:

It's a relative impossibility that Queensryche could ever surpass the brilliance it created the first time around. Too much time has passed: Whereas the original likely sprung from a magical, collective inspiration, the band's musical ideas are now conceived and planned. Still, there is no denying that the band's latest release is the best work it has done in more than a decade. An appropriate sequel to their best-ever work, Operation Mindcrime II delivers as most had hoped it would.

I can't help but be an editor. The only problem is too many words. Here's the same close tightened up:

It's impossible that Queensryche could surpass its original brilliance—too much time has passed. Where the original sprung from a magical, collective inspiration, the musical ideas are now conceived and planned. Still, the band's latest release is its best work in over a decade. An appropriate sequel to their best-ever work, Operation Mindcrime II delivers as most had hoped it would.

A few more good closes:

The band sounds good, and the power of Dio's voice does come around eventually, but the bulk of the appealing CD here (disc 1) is plagued by the most raspy, unpowerful voice you'll ever hear from Ronnie James Dio. Says it all, and leaves the reader with a clear picture.

Eh, but who cares about bad acting and moral lessons anyway? We're here to see Karloff's Monster lurch and grunt and beat people up, and that's what we get. And as an added

bonus, he cries. What more can you ask for from a monster? A memorable close and a great last line.

Conclusion

If the point hasn't been driven home by now, let's make it simple: Being a critic is hard work, it requires study and analysis, but if you're just starting out, this article should be consider inspirational rather than a foundation you have to build before you can proceed.

Being a critic means sitting in a theater or music hall with a notepad on your lap, trying to capture everything going on around you without losing the essence of the experience. It also means divorcing yourself from what you're experiencing so you can make the statement, "I didn't like it but it's a great work."

For example, I hate, despise, and can't bear "Romeo & Juliet," but I can't deny that it's a great play. Slasher movies scare the shit out of me, so I'm totally incapable of making any aesthetic judgment about them.

When I was a theater reviewer many years ago, friends who'd accompany me would ask, "How can you enjoy the play when you're always taking notes and tearing it apart like that?" Hence the "like" vs. "good" issue. Critics enjoy the work more because they understand how difficult it is to get all the elements to come together in a masterpiece, or they can see which elements failed and which caused the piece to not be a masterpiece. Ask yourself, who would appreciate a jazz album more, Thelonius Monk or your five-year-old? (Note, I didn't say "enjoy." *Appreciating* is an aesthetic experience; *enjoying* is a personal one.

If you review books, read constantly. If you review plays or movies, try to go three or four times a week. If you review music, you should be listening to everything you can get your hands on. And you should be reading reviews written by the top reviewers in the field to get a feel for what they do.

Being a critic can be one of the most satisfying things you'll ever do—but you'll only succeed if you know what the hell you're doing. ■

READING 5

"Guidelines for Writing Reviews"[LRII:3]
by Mark Schannon
Blogcritics, May 23, 2006

HOOK GUIDELINES:

- How can I surprise the reader with something unexpected?
- Did I capture something unusual, profound, funny, tragic, or unexpected in the first sentence?
- Am I coming up with interesting new ways to say things or am I relying on tired old clichés?
- Does my next sentence play off the first in a logical, compelling way or did I just introduce a totally new idea which will confuse the hell out of the reader?
- Does the hook serve as an introduction to the rest of the review, or did I wander off into clever-land without realizing that it has nothing to do with what I'm reviewing?

BODY GUIDELINES:

For a book:

- What was your reaction when you finished the book? If it was powerfully positive or negative, that may be a good place to begin.
- What is the writer trying to accomplish? It's different for each genre: thrillers, romance, literary fiction, sci fi, etc. Does it work or not, and why? (Sometimes the idea is great but the mechanics are so bad that it has no power—see a list of the mechanics, below.)
- It could be the narrative—a story so compelling that you can't put it down or so vapid that you found yourself flipping pages just to get through.
- The characters may be so powerfully drawn that what happens to them becomes your primary concern... or they could be so two-dimensional or trite that if one dies, you don't even notice—or care.
- How does the writer handle dialogue? Does it flow easily, sounding natural, or is it stale with too many adverbs describing the characters' mood. Remember the goal in fiction is to show not tell.
- What about how the artist describes surroundings and people. Again, too many adjectives and adverbs create weak writing. Is there too much needless description that just interferes with the narrative flow?
- All books have to create some kind of tension leading to a climax and then a resolution. How does the author create or fail to create that tension. Is the ending anti-climactic—telegraphed well in advance? Were you surprised in a good or bad sense.
- Does the storyline hold together or does it feel that the author is using too many coincidences and tricks to hide what is really a flawed plot?
- Even in fiction, the theme or philosophy behind the story may be the dominant feature—either well or poorly done.
- How does this book fit in the overall work of the artist? Does he or she use common themes throughout or is every book a surprise—an exploration of an entirely new idea?
- Is there anything about the author's personal life that's relevant?
- For non-fiction, what is the author's central thesis and how well is it explained and argued?
- Or, for non-fiction, is there something besides the central thesis that dominates—which is usually a bad thing—and distracts from what the author's trying to say.
- Maybe this is just another in a hundred other books on "Parenting for Teenage Mutant Ninja Turtles." It's all been written before, so why bother to write another?
- Does the book break new ground in some way? Combining two genres (humor/thriller or romance/sci-fi) or doing something revolutionary or evolutionary with a genre?
- How does the book compare to similar books in the same category? Why is it better or worse? How can you talk about other books and the category in a way that educates your reader?
- If non-fiction and controversial, are there other books or articles that support or criticize the position taken by the author? Do you have any expertise to add your own point of view or should you just let the experts fight it out?
- Finally, after examining all the pieces, is this an important book? You may begin your review with your assessment, but you're going to have to support that judgment with critical analysis.

For a music CD:

- What was your overall reaction when listening? If it was powerfully positive or negative, that may be a good place to begin if that wasn't already in your hook.
- Is there an overall theme that is explored through each song? Is it compelling, making you stop and think about important issues...or is it trite, becoming mind-dulling by the end. (You can integrate both good/bad and like/dislike here, but remember that the good/bad usually comes first—that creates the context into which you can introduce your personal opinions.)

- If there's a broad social theme (anti-war, love & relationships, society), does the music say something new and different? Does it make you consider these themes in a new way? Or is just another social commentary you've heard before.
- How does this CD fit within the history of the group's other CDs or music? Is their music always within the same format and formula? Are they breaking new ground? Going back to tried and true formulas that are interesting and fun but not particularly noteworthy?
- Which songs blew your mind (and why—be analytical even though you're talking about an emotional experience) and which made you want to blow your brains out?
- Compare the musical genre to similar artists and the kind of work they're doing? Be critical and analytical in your judgments. Explain why one is better than the other (although this is a place where you can also talk about what you personally like.)
- The order of songs is always important as artists try to create an overall impression. Does it work or not and why?
- Given the genre, how good is the music and what makes it that way? What about the lyrics? Are they powerful, traditional, inane...and again, why?
- How well does the band play together? Is it a seamless, tight performance where the musicians are in synch—or is it ragged and almost amateurish? Is there one musician who is particularly good or bad?
- How are the production values, the mixing, the sound quality?
- Is there anything about the musicians' personal lives that's relevant? Is the first CD in a long time? Why? Do they have a new member in the band, and what effect did that have on the overall performance?
- Is there anything about when the band goes on tour that's relevant to this CD?
- Finally, after examining all the pieces, is this an important CD? You may begin your review with your assessment, but you're going to have to support that judgment with critical analysis.

For a movie:

- What was your reaction when the movie was over? If it was powerfully positive or negative, that may be a good place to begin.
- What is the director trying to accomplish? It's different for each genre: thrillers, romance, drama, sci fi, etc. Does it work or not, and why? (Sometimes the idea is great but the mechanics are so bad that it has no power—see a list of the mechanics, below.)
- Is the theme so powerful that it makes up for problems in other parts of the movie?

- Are there social, cultural, political, religious issues that the director is drawing your attention to? How does he do it? Is it subtle, heavy handed, clever, compelling, annoying, etc.?
- It could be the narrative—a story so compelling that you're drawn into the world of the movie and lose all sense of place and time . . . or it's so boring that you can hear every squeak in every seat in the movie house.
- The characters may be so powerfully created that what happens to them becomes your primary concern... or they could be so two-dimensional or trite that if one dies, you don't even notice—or care. Are the characters appropriate for the genre? Do you have people in the year 3203 speaking like we do today with the same slang?
- Which of the actors should you highlight? What about their performances is particularly noteworthy or ragged? Can you tell if it's bad directing or just a bad actor (or vice versa?)
- How does the writer handle dialogue? Does it flow easily, sounding natural, or is it stale and trite making it impossible to get to know the characters.
- How does the lighting or set enhance or distract from the movie?
- If there are special effects, how well are they done and how well are they integrated into the movie? Or is it just a movie to show really cool special effects?
- All movies have to create some kind of tension leading to a climax and then a resolution. How does the director create or fail to create that tension? Is the ending anti-climactic—telegraphed well in advance? Were you surprised in a good or bad sense.
- Does the storyline hold together or does it feel that the director is using too many coincidences and tricks to hide what is really a flawed plot?
- How does this movie fit in the overall work of the director? Does he or she use common themes throughout or is every movie a surprise—an exploration of an entirely new idea?
- How well does this movie either fit its genre or break new ground or rely on tired old clichés? What other movies can you compare the various elements to?
- Does the director's work remind you of other directors? Is that good or bad?

For television:

Television can be a very difficult medium to review. Sitcoms, police shows, and even most dramas are basically the same show week after week, so how much new analysis or criticism can you come up with? Some shows, such as *House*, introduce so many varied issues—medical, philosophical, religious, personal—every week that it stands out as an exception. Compare that to *CSI*—an interesting show that's convinced me to give up my life of crime, but so much the same every week that there's virtually no character development. (Although I have to confess I don't watch a lot of TV.) That being said, here are some suggestions:

- Does the show lend itself to weekly reviews or should you be doing periodic updates?
- Is there an ongoing story line that threads through all or most of the episodes? How does it play out? When is it successful and why? Or not?
- Do the characters evolve through each episode or over a season? Does the evolution make sense? What about the characters in general—three dimensional, complex, interesting, or cardboard cutouts of the tough cop, the corporate lawyer, the wise-guy.

- The narrative, although I know some people want a lot and others a little. You have to find a proper balance.
- Issues, trends, and societal themes the show explores. Are they well-examined, fairly explored, compelling, dramatic?
- What's the genre and how well does this show stack up to others?
- Consider doing a genre review of the week—looking at four or five cop, comedy, drama, or (shudder) reality TV shows and comparing them.
- Specials, documentaries, made-for-TV movies can be reviewed like movies—check out those guidelines.
- Behind the scenes stories about a show, a network, actors, writers, etc. ■

Questions

❶ In his essay, "So You Want to Be a Critic," Schannon says, "Use this article as a starting point, adopting ideas and concepts that make sense and recognizing that, to become a good critic, you never stop studying the medium." What advice seems most helpful to you, as a potential cultural critic? How does it fit with what you've seen in other reviews you've read? How does it fit with your own thoughts about reviewing as you've read through and worked with reviews in Chapter 12?

❷ Schannon identifies key elements of a review, which suggest moves reviewers make. Do his examples help you see different strategies for working with these elements or making these moves? Do his examples help you think about the elements of a review?

❸ Schannon suggests a larger context—the genre, the history, the trends—helps to shape the criteria you'll use to talk about elements within the work. How much of the reviews you've read or written depends on this larger context?

❹ Look at Schannon's specific guidelines for writing reviews of different genres of work. Do his questions offer closer guidance for a particular type of review that you're interested in writing? What might you add to or alter about the suggestions he makes for a genre you pay attention to?

INTRODUCTION TO READINGS 6-8

Reviews for
The Circle by Dave Eggers

In Chapter 12 we saw that reviewers have both common moves and different strategies as they examine both how and how well a cultural production works. Here we've included three reviews of Dave Eggers' *The Circle*, which we approached as cultural critique in Chapter 13. Each reviewer presents a different evaluation of the work, and each proceeds in a different way to support that evaluation. Yet you'll find in each the moves that Schannon suggests to Blogcritics reviewers—including a hook, providing context, analyzing how elements

work, creating a close—and you can see something about these different reviewers' approaches and likely purposes by identifying the strategies they use for these common moves. We suggest that you read the three reviews as a set, considering not only how the writers use the moves of the review genre to their own purposes but also what further light each sheds on Eggers' likely purpose, methods, and the cultural critique he offers. ■

READING 6

"Ring of Power"LRII:4
by Ellen Ullman
The New York Times, November 3, 2013

Ellen Ullman is a writer and computer programmer who has written about that experience in fiction and in nonfiction, including an article LRII:15 for *The New York Times* on the experience of being a woman programmer. Her review of *The Circle* appeared in the weekly book review section of *The New York Times*—that is, for an educated newspaper audience with general rather than literary interests. Her readers are most likely to be interested in Eggers's portrayal of Silicon Valley culture and his take on the concerns of our current technological directions, and so her review evaluates his work from that point of view as well as in terms of its literary quality. With so much discussion of these social concerns in all media, she is asking, implicitly, "What does Eggers add that's new?" And she seems to think, "Not much." And if he's not offering new ideas, is there any other reason her readers might be interested in this novel?

Mae Holland, a woman in her 20s, arrives for her first day of work at a company called the Circle. She marvels at the beautiful campus, the fountain, the tennis and volleyball courts, the squeals of children from the day care center "weaving like water." The first line in the book is: "'My God,' Mae thought. 'It's heaven.'"

And so we know that the Circle in Dave Eggers's new novel, "The Circle," will be a hell.

The time is somewhere in the not-too-distant future—the Three Wise Men who own and rule the Circle are recognizable as individuals living today. The company demands transparency in all things; two of its many slogans are SECRETS ARE LIES and PRIVACY IS THEFT. Anonymity is banished; everyone's past is revealed; everyone's present may be broadcast live in video and sound. Nothing recorded will ever be erased. The Circle's goal is to have all aspects of human existence—from voting to love affairs—flow through its portal, the sole such portal in the world.

This potential dystopia should sound familiar. Books and tweets and blogs are already debating the issues Eggers raises: the tyranny of transparency, personhood defined as perpetual presence in social networks, our strange drive to display ourselves, the voracious information appetites of Google and Facebook, our lives under the constant surveillance of our own government.

"The Circle" adds little of substance to the debate. Eggers re-frames the discussion as a fable, a tale meant to be instructive. His instructors include a Gang of 40, a Transparent Man, a shadowy figure who may be a hero or a villain, a Wise Man with a secret chamber and a smiling legion of true-believing company employees. The novel has the flavor of a comic book: light, entertaining, undemanding.

Readers who enter the Circle's potential Inferno do not have the benefit of Virgil, Dante's guide through hell and purgatory, but they do have Mae, a naive girl with the sensibility of a compulsive iPhone FaceTime chatterer. (Oddly, Mae does not lead us through the ranks of programmers—let alone offer a glimpse of a woman programmer—a strange omission in a book purporting to be about technology.)

Mae has been introduced to the Circle by her friend and former roommate Annie, who is close to the Three Wise Men. She begins work in lowly Customer Experience, providing boilerplate answers to client questions and complaints. Her performance is tabulated after every interaction, her ratings displayed for all to see.

Mae is an eager competitor, earning a record score on her first day. Soon she is a champion Circler, moving ever closer to the company's inner rings. Eventually she becomes as transparent as a person can be within the realm of the Circle: wired for the broadcasting of her every waking move. In the bathroom, for instance, she can turn off the audio, but the camera stays on, focused on the back of the stall door. (If she is silent for too long, her followers send urgent messages asking if she is OK.)

At each advance into "participation" (or descent into hell, as the case may be), Mae is a tail-wagging puppy waiting for the next reward: a better rating, millions of viewers. Far from resisting, she finds each new electronic demand "delicious" and "exhilarating." Now and then, she briefly feels a black "tear" opening inside her, but the feeling comes at improbable moments and in such overheated prose as to parody emotion: "a scream muffled by fathomless waters, that high-pitched scream of a million drowned voices."

Can anything prevent Mae's fall into the depths of the Circle? Enter the mysterious Kalden. While everyone else lives in the clear light of transparency, Kalden emerges from the shadows. Everyone working at the Circle can be located, but Kalden's name appears nowhere; Mae experiences his invisibility as "aggressive." Everyone inside the Circle is young and healthy; the outside is for the old and ill. And here is Kalden, who has gray hair yet looks young. The symbolism—is he a vibrant Circler or an old man from the dark outside?—is all too obvious.

At their second meeting, Mae follows Kalden down long corridors, through underground tunnels, down and down and down. What she sees in this netherworld is a metallic red box the size of a bus, wrapped in tentacles of "gleaming silver pipes." Kalden tells her it stores the experiences of the Transparent Man, who for five years has recorded everything he has seen and heard. Kalden makes some excuse for the box's huge size, but his technical explanation is ridiculous. There just happens to be a mattress in an alcove, where Mae and Kalden have sex—she thrills as he breathes "fire into her ear." Later Kalden will say the Circle is in fact a "totalitarian nightmare," as if a reader did not know this from the start.

Like Kalden, alas, Eggers tends to over explain. An example of what might have been a fine scene: Mae is with her ex-boyfriend, Mercer, who makes chandeliers out of deer antlers. (Eggers has not been kind to Mercer in giving him this occupation.) Mae takes out her digital device and, without Mercer's asking, starts reciting negative online reviews of his work. He begs her to stop. But Mae reads another: "All those poor deer antlers died for this?" The scene, having established Mae's casual cruelty, should have ended there. Instead it continues for five more pages, during which Mae and Mercer debate the effects of social media. The words "author's message" flash above the scene, as they do above too many others.

Do we even care about Mae? What remains of her life outside the Circle—Mercer, her family, her father's multiple sclerosis—she relentlessly (and blithely) draws inside the power ring of the company, to disastrous and tragic effect. And finally Annie, the onetime friend who drew her into the Circle: Mae wants to triumph over her and push her out, again to disastrous effect. A sense of horror finally arrives near the end of the book, coming not through Mae's eyes but through the power of Eggers's writing, which we have been waiting for all along. The final scene is chilling.

Mae, then, is not a victim but a dull villain. Her motivations are teenage-Internet petty: getting the highest ratings, moving into the center of the Circle, being popular. She presents a plan that will enclose the world within the Circle's reach, but she exhibits no complex desire for power, only a longing for the approval of the Wise Men. She is more a high school mean girl than an evil opponent. Perhaps this is what Eggers wants to say: that evil in the future will look more like the trivial Mae than it will the hovering dark eye of Big Brother. If so, he should have worked much harder to express this profound thought. The characters need substance; Mae must be more than a cartoon.

There is an early scene in which Mae could have become a rounded character, one we might worry about. It is her first day on the job. All information on her digital devices has been transferred to the Circle's system. During the introductory formalities, she is asked if she would like to hand over her old laptop for responsible recycling. But Mae hesitates. "Maybe tomorrow," she says. "I want to say goodbye."

If there was ever a need for a pause in the narrative, it is after that "goodbye." In the opening of a white space, we might imagine Mae's feelings as she holds the device containing her private experiences. We might linger over what it means to surrender—voluntarily, even eagerly—the last shreds of one's personal life. ∎

Questions

1. What context does Ullman establish for her review? What intertextual connections does she make, even briefly, that offer a backdrop to her evaluation?

2. How does Ullman characterize Eggers's work? How does she describe it in terms of genre? What criteria does she seem to have for such work?

3. What are some of her specific criticisms of the work he has created?

4. As a reader, how would you evaluate her review as a review? What does she offer to hook you? What moments and pieces of evidence interested you, engaged you, maybe even convinced you? Does her close follow from the evaluative argument she is making here, reinforcing the sense of the work that you've gotten from her review?

READING 7

"Sharing Is Caring Is Sharing"[LRII:6]
by Betsy Morais
The New Yorker, October 30, 2013

Betsy Morais is a journalist and editor who writes general interest articles for magazines like *The Atlantic* and *The New Yorker* that present essays on a wide range of topics. Here she is writing for *The New Yorker*, for a general, educated audience but perhaps with a somewhat more literary/artsy inclination than *New York Times* newspaper readers. In her writing, while she has explored such non-tech and non-review topics as how coyotes are captured in New York city, she has also written reviews—for example, of an exhibit of the photography of Annie Liebovitz[LRII:7] which considers the influence of Liebovitz's partner Susan Sontag, and of another on the art of emoji[LRII:8]—but also on other technology topics, including a site that lets people explore connections among various texts, supporting the sort of cultural literacy for reading that Eric Liu[LRII:9] (Part I Additional Readings) addresses. Morais' review of *The Circle* is categorized under technology rather than books, so she is at least partly concerned with how Eggers is addressing the social concerns our technology raises along with the quality of his work as a piece of literature.

War is peace. Freedom is slavery. Ignorance is strength.
—*George Orwell, "1984"*
Secrets are lies. Sharing is Caring. Privacy is theft.
—*Dave Eggers, "The Circle"*

The construction begs for comparison, and yet "The Circle" is no "1984." In the future, according to Dave Eggers, one mega social-network corporation, the namesake of his new novel, has become the technological architect of daily life—arranging conversations, restocking pantries, making payments, and ranking human beings. The company's leaders wear zip-up hoodies, of course, and enjoy surfing, yet they are known with reverent remove as the Three Wise Men. It's serious business—so serious that even the parties are work, since attendance is monitored by your boss—and Eggers emulates this sobriety in his writing, which plods across the corporate campus resentfully. New hire Mae Holland, the novel's protagonist, bounds forth into the communal ethos of her overlords, embracing her first assignment, answering e-mails that provide a "human experience" to small advertisers. Eggers seems bored by the task—Oh, must we spend another day at the Customer Experience desk, minutiae un-inspected, e-mails unread? He doesn't want to be in the grind, or even playfully tease it. Disclosure is the story of "The Circle," yet Eggers hardly tells enough.

But even without the searing wit of "1984," the book is capable of landing on point—when it's at its most irksome. Where "1984" has the vigilant Police Patrol and Thought Police, "The Circle" has SeeChange and Clarification. Surveillance isn't a bad word; it's a gift, even a human right. "I truly believe that if we have no path but the right path, the best path, then that would present a kind of ultimate and all-encompassing relief," Wise Man Eamon Bailey, standing in for the role of Internet missionary, tells Mae. "We can cure any disease, end hunger, everything, because we won't be dragged down by all our weaknesses, our petty secrets, our hoarding of information and knowledge. We will finally reach our full potential."

The speech has a familiar ring: in September, 2006, Mark Zuckerberg wrote an open letter about the launch of News Feed, and the note resurfaced with this week's unveiling of The Zuckerberg Files, an archive of his every public utterance cataloged by Michael Zimmer and a small team at the University of Wisconsin-Milwaukee's Digital Commons. (Zuckerberg, the social wizard who likes to keep to himself, has fittingly been made all the more transparent now that his transcripts have been neatly collected for viewing.) "When I made Facebook two years ago my goal was to help people understand what was going on in their world a little better," Zuckerberg wrote. "I wanted to create an environment where people could share whatever information they wanted, but also have control over whom they shared that information with." He also said that a week prior, "I created a group called Free Flow of Information on the Internet, because that's what I believe in—helping people share information with the people they want to share it with."

Katherine Losse, Facebook employee number fifty-one and the author of "The Boy Kings"—which, she has unsatisfactorily argued, Eggers ripped off—worked in customer support before becoming Zuckerberg's speechwriter. By 2009, as Losse was writing e-mails on behalf of her boss, Facebook was working on adjusting its privacy settings. "We are pushing the world in the direction of making it a more open and transparent place," she quoted Zuckerberg as saying in meetings. So, too, transparency is the guiding principle of the Circle; the company's mantra is "ALL THAT HAPPENS MUST BE KNOWN." (Deletion is outlawed.) But Mae, unlike Losse, is not quite a skeptic. Rather, she's an earnest wannabe who divulges more and more over time, with less and less apprehension. Though Mae occasionally has impure thoughts about whether to keep to herself instead of hopping into the Circle, as employees are expected to do—with feeling!—she strives to post more. In doing so, she "feels a profound sense of accomplishment and possibility."

Last year, Diana Tamir and Jason Mitchell, of Harvard's department of psychology, published a paper titled "Disclosing information about the self is intrinsically rewarding." As part of their study, they asked participants to undergo fMRI scans while stating opinions. The researchers found that "humans so willingly self-disclose because doing so represents an event with intrinsic value, in the same way as with primary rewards such as food and sex."

"The sites make the process so easy, and people see their friends sharing, and that encourages them," Jessica Vitak, an assistant professor at the University of Maryland College of Information Studies, told me. "So it's kind of like 'Hey, join this party.'" In research released last week, to be presented at a conference in February, Vitak and her co-author, Jinyoung Kim, followed Facebook users as they decided what to post. They found that, through "an often-complex thought process," users weigh the pros and cons in deciding what to share, as a way of replicating the boundaries of offline conversation. As one participant, Zara, reflected of facing her invisible audience:

> If you post this, are you okay with people, everyone seeing this? Is that okay with you? I think twice about it. And if I think it's not a big deal, then I'll go ahead and do it. But if I'm thinking about the repercussions of it; if I can think of a few, then I won't do it.

Among American adults on Facebook, forty-four per cent update their status at least weekly, fifty-three per cent comment on a friend's status, and forty-eight per cent comment on a photo. Sites that tell users they've only filled out a limited percentage of their personal pages—Where did you go to high school? Are you in a relationship?—encourage more disclosure, no matter how seemingly mundane. "Any piece of information that people share benefits these sites, because it gives Facebook, or whatever company, a more accurate profile of the user," Vitak said. "They say there's no such thing as bad publicity. Well, there's no such thing as bad information, in their mind. It's adding information that's valuable to them."

That data collection, of demographic details, is only half of the equation; Facebook also tracks behaviors. On Tuesday, the company announced that it would start monitoring stats like how long your cursor hovers over something on the site, or whether your News Feed is visible on your screen at any particular moment. There's no opportunity to pause for self-censorship here, it's just seamless sharing, along the lines of an automatic Foursquare check-in or a Google Now update to let people know you're running late. More passive modes of personal data-gathering turn up in "The Circle" more subtly, as in a silver bracelet Mae is given at the health clinic, where a message is engraved in steel above the cabinets: "TO HEAL WE MUST KNOW. TO KNOW WE MUST SHARE." The band monitors her heart rate, blood pressure, caloric intake, digestive efficiency, and so on. Elsewhere, in the ChildTrack lab, biochemists are working out a way to implant a chip into children's bones, a permanent G.P.S. (They succeed.)

Not everyone in the Eggers dystopian near-future wants to be sucked up into the social vortex. Mae's ex-boyfriend Mercer does what he can to stay off the grid, so he can focus on his antler-chandelier business. The novel's extremes are laid out in the dialogue between the two characters. Condensed highlights from one scene:

> Mercer: "Mae, I've never felt more that there is some cult taking over the world."

> Mae: "You're so paranoid."

> Mercer: "I think you think that sitting at your desk, frowning and smiling somehow makes you think you're actually living some fascinating life. You comment on things, and that substitutes for doing them."

The Circle is as much Google as it is Facebook (though it officially stands in for neither, as the Circle is supposed to have succeeded them). Google's motto, "Don't be evil," is upended in Eggers's telling: these companies may not have started out as the clubhouses of moustache-twirling villains, but, he writes, in a return to Orwell, "We're closing the circle around everyone— it's a totalitarian nightmare." *The Wall Street Journal* compared "The Circle" to "The Jungle," with the caveat that the former is "not great literature. But it is a great warning." Other critics, including Losse, have pointed out that Eggers can't be held up as the revelatory chronicler of an industry that he isn't immersed in; his ominous depiction isn't backed up by thorough inquiry. It's a novel, though, his novel, with his anxieties. It's the account of an observer, not a participant: maybe even the kind who comments on things, which substitutes for doing them.

Losse wrote, "We film and we post and read social media constantly in order to capture something, some exciting moment or feeling or experience that we are afraid to miss, but the things about life that we most want to capture may not be, in the end, capturable." Whether it's a status update or a novel, the good ones can grasp hold of their subject—if not with the completion of a circle, then at least by delivering an essential sliver of truth. ∎

Questions

❶ How does Morais hook her readers? What context does her opening set and how does that literary context frame what you expect from this review and from Eggers' novel?

❷ As she moves through her discussion of Eggers' novel, Morais brings in other references that create a context beyond the literary one. What shared knowledge does she seek to create with her readers and what does that suggest about her focus and purpose with this review? How does she see *The Circle* within that context? By what terms does she evaluate it?

❸ How would you evaluate this review from the perspective of its usefulness to you as a reader? How would you compare it to Ulman's review? What does it add to your picture of how effectively Eggers has created a piece of fiction that addresses critical questions about our digital world?

READING 8

Selection from
"When Privacy Is Theft" LRII:10
by Margaret Atwood
The New York Review of Books, November 21, 2013

Margaret Atwood is a prize-winning Canadian novelist, poet, and literary critic. She is interested in what she calls "speculative fiction"—fiction that represents a world that is possible within our contemporary situation, as opposed to science fiction, which is usually set in a technologically altered future. And she has written her own dystopian novel, *The Handmaid's Tale* (1985), in which she imagines a totalitarian dictatorship ruled by Christian religious fundamentalists, who take power by staging a terrorist attack and blaming it on Islamic militants and who immediately restrict human rights, especially for women, who lose even the right to read. Writing for *The New York Review of Books,* Atwood addresses an audience interested in long critical essays about books covering the full range of politics, current events, history, fiction, and more. In her very long review of *The Circle* (which we have excerpted), Atwood approaches Eggers's novel, not from the perspective of how detailed his knowledge is of the world of technology companies or even of the stylistic quality of his sentences, but from how effective his speculation is about the potential dangers to society if present events take a particular course.

The Circle is Dave Eggers's tenth work of fiction, and a fascinating item it is.

Eggers's first major book was the much-acclaimed semi-fictional memoir *A Heartbreaking Work of Staggering Genius* (2000), which recounts the struggles of Eggers to raise his younger brother after the death of their parents. By that time he was already active in the underground worlds of comic strip writing, small-magazine founding, and columnizing in the then-embryonic realm of online magazines. He has continued along a multi-branched road that has included the founding of *McSweeney's* magazine and publishing house, and an associated monthly, *The Believer*; of 826 Valencia, a youth literacy charity; and of ScholarMatch, connecting non-rich college-age kids in the San Francisco Bay Area with donors.

Then there's the writing: the screenplays, the journalism, and, of course, the books. These include two unflinching looks at man's inhumanity to man, in Africa and America respectively—*What Is the What* and *Zeitoun*—and the novel *A Hologram for the King*, which glances at the decline of America's international clout through the eyes of a sad sales-man. Eggers appears to run on pure adrenaline, and has as many ideas pouring out of him as the entrepreneurs pitching their inventions in *The Circle*.

The outpouring of ideas is central to *The Circle*, as it is in part a novel of ideas. What sort of ideas? Ideas about the social construction and deconstruction of privacy, and about the increasing corporate ownership of privacy, and about the effects such ownership may have on the nature of Western democracy. Dissemination of information is power, as the old yellow-journalism newspaper proprietors knew so well. What is withheld can be as potent as what is disclosed, and who can lie publicly and get away with it is determined by gatekeepers: thus, in the Internet age, code-owners have the keys to the kingdom.

Marshall McLuhan was among the first to probe the effects of different kinds of media on our collective consciousness with *The Gutenberg Galaxy* (1962) and *Understanding Media* (1964). Even then, before interactive technologies, he pointed out that "the global village" could be an unpleasant and claustrophobic place. As far back as 1835,

Toqueville's *Democracy in America* predicted the tyranny of public opinion, a tyranny that can be amplified immeasurably via the Internet.

The concerns that underlie *The Circle* are therefore of long standing, but have been much discussed recently, not only in newspapers and magazines both online and off, but in books. Misha Glenny has written eloquently about cybertheft and cybercrime in *McMafia* and *DarkMarket*, and, in *Black Code*, Ronald Deibert has detailed various cyberthreats to democracy and privacy. In *The Boy Kings*, a 2012 memoir that chronicles the early days of Facebook, Katherine Losse questioned the desirability of making personal information public.

The Circle takes its name most immediately from a fictional West Coast social media corporation that has subsumed all earlier iterations such as Google, Facebook, and Twitter. It traces the rise and rise within this company of its female protagonist, Maebelline, a name that closely resembles that of a brand of mascara, thus hinting at masks and acting. (Names matter in *The Circle* because they matter both to its author and to its characters, some of whom go so far as to pick out new ones for themselves from the Internet.) Maebelline is commonly called "Mae," and this nickname is then expanded by a coworker who's bringing Mae up to speed on her Circle duties. She's opened a "Zing" account for Mae—zinging being an amalgamation of tweeting, texting, and pinging. "I made up a name for you," says Gina.

"MaeDay. Like the war holiday. Isn't that cool?"

Mae wasn't so sure about the name, and couldn't remember a holiday by that name.

Clever Mr. Eggers. There is no real war holiday called MaeDay, but "Mayday"—from the French *m'aidez*—is a venerable distress signal. May Day was once a pagan springtime celebration, but was adopted in the nineteenth century as a workers' holiday. It was then appropriated for military parades during Stalinism, a period noted for its hyperactive secret police, and satirized in Orwell's *1984*, a work that is echoed more than once in *The Circle*. Maebelline, Zing-christened as MaeDay: a makeup accessory, a distress signal, a totalitarian power-show. The reader feels a pricking of the thumbs.

At first Mae is winsomely innocuous. She's recently been an Everygirl stuck in her own version of purgatory, the humiliating McJob in the gas and energy utility of her small hometown in California that she took out of the need to pay off her crushing college debts. Now she's called back from the living dead by her college roommate turned Circle higher-up, Annie. Annie too is significantly named: Annies get their guns, being competitive, perky sharpshooting tomboys; they're Orphan Annies, brave and adventurous and protected by Daddy Warbucks, who uses his wealth for Good. This Annie is a golden-girl scatter-brained "doofus" who slouched around at college in men's flannel trousers, but then, after a Stanford MBA, was recruited into the Circle and has been soaring like a helium balloon, adored by all.

Annie comes from money and family class—Mayflower rather than MaeDay—not that eye-rolling Annie claims to take her aristocratic descent seriously. None of her privilege has been lost on second-fiddle Mae, who, as she enters the Circle, is suffused with gratitude toward Annie and wonderment at being actually *there*, part of "the only company that really mattered at all"; but as the reader may anticipate, an *All About Eve* girl-on-girl mud-wrestling glint soon flickers in her star-bedazzled eyes.

Eggers sets forth the players and ground of his novel right at the beginning, like a gamer setting up the board. The Circle, we learn, is run by a triumvirate known as the Three Wise Men. Like Melville's Pequod and Stephen King's Overlook Hotel, the Circle is a combination of physical container, financial system, spiritual state, and dramatis personae, intended to represent America, or at least a powerful segment of it; so these three, like Melville's three harpooners, are emblematic.

Next comes the physical layout or "campus," described in lavish, enchanting detail: readers of lifestyle sections will salivate over the adjectives, and are sure to make comparisons between what's on offer here and what real life has already provided on other such company "campuses." The Circle's security walls enclose a paradise of green spaces, buildings, fountains, artworks, and game spaces, with luxurious dormitories for those who may wish to work late and stay overnight, not that there's any pressure, mind you. The restaurants dish up gourmet but virtuous food, the parties are übercool, and there's a sample room full of products that their manufacturers are dying to have the trend-setting Circlers adopt.

The different buildings are named after historical periods: the Dark Ages, the Renaissance, and the like. (He who controls the past controls the future and he who controls the present controls the past, as 1984 puts it.) Artists, both starving and otherwise, are brought in to entertain, like the troubadours in the Middle Ages or Voltaire at the court of Frederick the Great; for such corporations are the modern equivalent of kingdoms and Renaissance dukedoms.

The palatial buildings are made of glass, ostensibly to underline the Circle's mantra of "transparency"—everyone should be open to everyone else in all ways, a goal within the Circle's reach thanks to the ingenious schemes and doodads cooked up by its collective brain trust: the tiny "SeeChange" cameras that can be planted everywhere (no more rapes and atrocities!), the scheme to embed tracking chips in children's bones (no more kidnapping!). Why wouldn't any sane person want those things? People who live in glass houses not only shouldn't throw stones—they can't throw them! Isn't that a good thing? And if you have nothing to hide, why get paranoid?

As the story advances, our view of the Circle moves from bright to dark to darker. At first, viewed through Mae's eyes, the place seems wondrous:

The rest of America...seemed like some chaotic mess in the developing world. Outside the walls of the Circle, all was noise and struggle, failure and filth. But here, all had been perfected. The best people had made the best systems and the best systems had reaped funds, unlimited funds, that made possible this, the best place to work. And it was natural that it was so, Mae thought. Who else but utopians could make utopia?

But if this is utopia, why is Mae so anxious most of the time? True, her workload in "Customer Experience" is crushing, as she answers questions, sends "smiles" and "frowns"—the Circle equivalent of Likes and Dislikes and Favorites—to other websites and accounts, fields an avalanche of messages and invitations from other Circlers, and is under increasing pressure to spend all her time "participating." But her main terror is being cast out of the Circle: she'll do almost anything to stay inside, and worries constantly about what sort of impression she's making. Is she getting enough approval, a substance she measures by messages, Zings, "smiles," and online watchers? Is she making the grade?

The Circlers' social etiquette is as finely calibrated as anything in Jane Austen: how fast you return a Zing or your tone of voice when saying "Yup" can matter deeply, and missing someone's themed party is a lethal snub. Every choice is tracked and evaluated, every "aesthetic" ruthlessly judged. The nineteenth-century art critic John Ruskin—who famously said, "Tell me what you like and I'll tell you who you are"—viewed bad taste as a moral offense, and the young Circlers subscribe to this dogma: nothing gets you the brushoff more quickly than a

pair of uncool jeans. Utopia, it seems, is an awful lot like high school, but with even more homework.

Eggers treats his material with admirable inventiveness and gusto. The plot capers along, the trap doors open underfoot, the language ripples and morphs. Why has he not been headhunted by some corporation specializing in new brand names? Better than reality, some of these, and all too plausible. But don't look to *The Circle* for Chekhovian nuance or thoroughly rounded characters with many-layered inwardness: it isn't "literary fiction" of that kind. It's an entertainment, but a challenging one: it demands that the reader think its positions through in the same way that the characters must. Some of its incidents are funny, some of them are appalling, and some of them are both at once, like a nightmare in which you find yourself making a speech with no clothes on.

But apart from the moments of almost farcical discovery—among them the discovery by the characters themselves that there is indeed such a thing as TMI, or Too Much Information—Eggers has a serious purpose, or several. One of them is to remind us that we can be led down the primrose path much more blindly by our good intentions than by our bad ones. (He's entitled to speak about good intentions, having manifested so many of them himself, in his various other lives.) A second may be to examine the nature of looking and being looked at.

Publication on social media is in part a performance, as is everything "social" that human beings do; but what happens when that brightly lit arena expands so much that there is no green room in which the mascara can be removed, no cluttered, imperfect back stage where we can be "'ourselves'? What happens to us if we must be "on" all the time? Then we're in the twenty-four-hour glare of the supervised prison. To live entirely in public is a form of solitary confinement. ■

Questions

❶ What is Atwood's hook, and what context does she present as most significant for approaching Eggers's present work? What does she add to that context as she works through her review, and why do you think she works in this way? What does she seem to imagine as the range of shared background knowledge her readers will bring—their cultural literacy?

❷ How does she draw on readers' assumed shared knowledge to suggest how we might see Eggers's work? What are the criteria by which she finally evaluates it, and how does she see it in relation to those criteria?

❸ Atwood considers *The Circle* to be serious entertainment, demanding "that the reader think its positions through in the same way that the characters must" as it presents its critique of our present culture. Does her close support the ways in which she has evaluated Eggers's work? How does her reading compare to those of Morais and Ullman? What does her review add to your own perspective on Eggers's work, from your own reading and analysis of the excerpt included in Chapter 13?

Selection from

"Is Google Making Us Stupid?"^{LRII:11}

by Nicholas Carr

The Atlantic, July/August 2008

In his cover story for *The Atlantic,* journalist Nicholas Carr explores the impact of the internet on how we read, write, and think. Carr begins by reflecting on how his own thinking has changed after a decade of writing and researching online. He writes that he has trouble finishing a longer text, that he no longer has the patience to read a novel. He draws on current research on brain plasticity and reading to argue that, because our brains, especially our frontal lobes and language centers, are so malleable, they are particularly susceptible to media technologies. In a world of print where genres like newspapers, books, and magazines dominated, Carr argues, texts tended to be more word-based with fewer images and encouraged more introspective reading. In contrast, digital texts and media seem to foster a different kind of literacy, one that values media multitasking and skimming—skills that, according to Carr, erode those encouraged by print. He concludes that, for better or worse, digital media and the time we spend online is having profound effects on how we read and write.

"Dave, stop. Stop, will you? Stop, Dave. Will you stop, Dave?" So the supercomputer HAL pleads with the implacable astronaut Dave Bowman in a famous and weirdly poignant scene toward the end of Stanley Kubrick's *2001: A Space Odyssey.* Bowman, having nearly been sent to a deep-space death by the malfunctioning machine, is calmly, coldly disconnecting the memory circuits that control its artificial brain. "Dave, my mind is going," HAL says, forlornly. "I can feel it. I can feel it."

I can feel it, too. Over the past few years I've had an uncomfortable sense that someone, or something, has been tinkering with my brain, remapping the neural circuitry, reprogramming the memory. My mind isn't going—so far as I can tell—but it's changing. I'm not thinking the way I used to think. I can feel it most strongly when I'm reading. Immersing myself in a book or a lengthy article used to be easy. My mind would get caught up in the narrative or the turns of the argument, and I'd spend hours strolling through long stretches of prose. That's rarely the case anymore. Now my concentration often starts to drift after two or three pages. I get fidgety, lose the thread, begin looking for something else to do. I feel as if I'm always dragging my wayward brain back to the text. The deep reading that used to come naturally has become a struggle.

I think I know what's going on. For more than a decade now, I've been spending a lot of time online, searching and surfing and sometimes adding to the great databases of the Internet. The Web has been a godsend to me as a writer. Research that once required days in the stacks or periodical rooms of libraries can now be done in minutes. A few Google searches, some quick clicks on hyperlinks, and I've got the telltale fact or pithy quote I was after. Even when I'm not working, I'm as likely as not to be foraging in the Web's info-thickets—reading and writing e-mails, scanning headlines and blog posts, watching videos and listening to podcasts, or just tripping from link to link to link. (Unlike footnotes, to which they're sometimes likened, hyperlinks don't merely point to related works; they propel you toward them.)

For me, as for others, the Net is becoming a universal medium, the conduit for most of the information that flows through my eyes and ears and into my mind. The advantages of having immediate access to such an incredibly rich store of information are many, and they've been widely described and duly applauded. "The perfect recall of silicon memory," *Wired's* Clive Thompson has written, "can be an enormous boon to thinking." But that boon comes at a price. As the media theorist Marshall McLuhan pointed out in the 1960s, media are not just passive channels of information. They supply the stuff of thought, but they also shape the process of thought. And what the Net seems to be doing is chipping away my capacity for concentration and contemplation. My mind now expects to take in information the way the Net distributes it: in a swiftly moving stream of particles. Once I was a scuba diver in the sea of words. Now I zip along the surface like a guy on a Jet Ski.

I'm not the only one. When I mention my troubles with reading to friends and acquaintances—literary types, most of them—many say they're having similar experiences. The more they use the Web, the more they have to fight to stay focused on long pieces of writing. Some of the bloggers I follow have also begun mentioning the phenomenon. Scott Karp, who writes a blog about online media, recently confessed that he has stopped reading books altogether. "I was a lit major in college, and used to be [a] voracious book reader," he wrote. "What happened?" He speculates on the answer: "What if I do all my reading on the web not so much because the way I read has changed, i.e. I'm just seeking convenience, but because the way I THINK has changed?"

Bruce Friedman, who blogs regularly about the use of computers in medicine, also has described how the Internet has altered his mental habits. "I now have almost totally lost the ability to read and absorb a longish article on the web or in print," he wrote earlier this year. A pathologist who has long been on the faculty of the University of Michigan Medical School, Friedman elaborated on his comment in a telephone conversation with me. His thinking, he said, has taken on a "staccato" quality, reflecting the way he quickly scans short passages of text from many sources online. "I can't read *War and Peace* anymore," he admitted. "I've lost the ability to do that. Even a blog post of more than three or four paragraphs is too much to absorb. I skim it."

Anecdotes alone don't prove much. And we still await the long-term neurological and psychological experiments that will provide a definitive picture of how Internet use affects cognition. But a recently published study of online research habits, conducted by scholars from University College London, suggests that we may well be in the midst of a sea change in the way we read and think. As part of the five-year research program, the scholars examined computer logs documenting the behavior of visitors to two popular research sites, one operated by the British Library and one by a U.K. educational consortium, that provide access to journal articles, e-books, and other sources of written information. They found that people using the sites exhibited "a form of skimming activity," hopping from one source to another and rarely returning to any source they'd already visited. They typically read no more than one or two pages of an article or book before they would "bounce" out to another site. Sometimes they'd save a long article, but there's no evidence that they ever went back and actually read it. The authors of the study report:

> It is clear that users are not reading online in the tradi-
> tional sense; indeed there are signs that new forms of
> "reading" are emerging as users "power browse" horizon-
> tally through titles, contents pages and abstracts going for
> quick wins. It almost seems that they go online to avoid
> reading in the traditional sense.

Thanks to the ubiquity of text on the Internet, not to mention the popularity of text-messaging on cell phones, we may well be reading more today than we did in the 1970s or 1980s, when television was our medium of choice. But it's a different kind of reading, and behind it lies a different kind of thinking—perhaps even a new sense of the self. "We are not only what we read," says Maryanne Wolf, a developmental psychologist at Tufts University and the author of *Proust and the Squid: The Story and Science of the Reading Brain*. "We are how we read." Wolf worries that the style of reading promoted by the Net, a style that puts "efficiency" and "immediacy" above all else, may be weakening our capacity for the kind of deep reading that emerged when an earlier technology, the printing press, made long and complex works of prose commonplace. When we read online, she says, we tend to become "mere decoders of information." Our ability to interpret text, to make the rich mental connections that form when we read deeply and without distraction, remains largely disengaged.

Reading, explains Wolf, is not an instinctive skill for human beings. It's not etched into our genes the way speech is. We have to teach our minds how to translate the symbolic characters we see into the language we understand. And the media or other technologies we use in learning and practicing the craft of reading play an important part in shaping the neural circuits inside our brains. Experiments demonstrate that readers of ideograms, such as the Chinese, develop a mental circuitry for reading that is very different from the circuitry found in those of us whose written language employs an alphabet. The variations extend across many regions of the brain, including those that govern such essential cognitive functions as memory and the interpretation of visual and auditory stimuli. We can expect as well that the circuits woven by our use of the Net will be different from those woven by our reading of books and other printed works.

The human brain is almost infinitely malleable. People used to think that our mental meshwork, the dense connections formed among the 100 billion or so neurons inside our skulls, was largely fixed by the time we reached adulthood. But brain researchers have discovered that that's not the case. James Olds, a professor of neuroscience who directs the Krasnow Institute for Advanced Study at George Mason University, says that even the adult mind "is very plastic." Nerve cells routinely break old connections and form new ones. "The brain," according to Olds, "has the ability to reprogram itself on the fly, altering the way it functions."

As we use what the sociologist Daniel Bell has called our "intellectual technologies"—the tools that extend our mental rather than our physical capacities—we inevitably begin to take on the qualities of those technologies. The mechanical clock, which came into common use in the 14th century, provides a compelling example. In *Technics and Civilization*, the historian and cultural critic Lewis Mumford described how the clock "disassociated time from human events and helped create the belief in an independent world of mathematically measurable sequences." The "abstract framework of divided time" became "the point of reference for both action and thought."

The clock's methodical ticking helped bring into being the scientific mind and the scientific man. But it also took something away. As the late MIT computer scientist Joseph Weizenbaum observed in his 1976 book, *Computer Power and Human Reason: From Judgment to Calculation*, the conception of the world that emerged from the widespread use of timekeeping instruments "remains an impoverished version of the older one, for it rests on a rejection of those direct experiences that formed the basis for, and indeed constituted, the old reality." In deciding when to eat, to work, to sleep, to rise, we stopped listening to our senses and started obeying the clock.

The process of adapting to new intellectual technologies is reflected in the changing metaphors we use to explain ourselves to ourselves. When the mechanical clock arrived, people began thinking of their brains as operating "like clockwork." Today, in the age of software, we have come to think of them as operating "like computers." But the changes, neuroscience tells us, go much deeper than metaphor. Thanks to our brain's plasticity, the adaptation occurs also at a biological level.

The Internet promises to have particularly far-reaching effects on cognition. In a paper published in 1936, the British mathematician Alan Turing proved that a digital computer, which at the time existed only as a theoretical machine, could be programmed to perform the function of any other information-processing device. And that's what we're seeing today. The Internet, an immeasurably powerful computing system, is subsuming most of our other intellectual technologies. It's becoming our map and our clock, our printing press and our typewriter, our calculator and our telephone, and our radio and TV.

When the Net absorbs a medium, that medium is re-created in the Net's image. It injects the medium's content with hyperlinks, blinking ads, and other digital gewgaws, and it surrounds the content with the content of all the other media it has absorbed. A new e-mail message, for instance, may announce its arrival as we're glancing over the latest headlines at a newspaper's site. The result is to scatter our attention and diffuse our concentration.

The Net's influence doesn't end at the edges of a computer screen, either. As people's minds become attuned to the crazy quilt of Internet media, traditional media have to adapt to the audience's new expectations. Television programs add text crawls and pop-up ads, and magazines and newspapers shorten their articles, introduce capsule summaries, and crowd their pages with easy-to-browse info-snippets. When, in March of this year, *The New York Times* decided to devote the second and third pages of every edition to article abstracts, its design director, Tom Bodkin, explained that the "shortcuts" would give harried readers a quick "taste" of the day's news, sparing them the "less efficient" method of actually turning the pages and reading the articles.

Old media have little choice but to play by the new-media rules.

Never has a communications system played so many roles in our lives—or exerted such broad influence over our thoughts—as the Internet does today. Yet, for all that's been written about the Net, there's been little consideration of how, exactly, it's reprogramming us. The Net's intellectual ethic remains obscure.

The goal, as Taylor defined it in his celebrated 1911 treatise, The Principles of Scientific Management, was to identify and adopt, for every job, the "one best method" of work and thereby to effect "the gradual substitution of science for rule of thumb throughout the mechanic arts." Once his system was applied to all acts of manual labor, Taylor assured his followers, it would bring about a restructuring not only of industry but of society, creating a utopia of perfect efficiency. "In the past the man has been first," he declared; "In the future the system must be first."

Google's headquarters, in Mountain View, California—the Googleplex—is the Internet's high church. Google, says its chief executive, Eric Schmidt, is "a company that's founded around the science of measurement," and it is striving to "systematize everything" it does. Drawing on the terabytes of behavioral data it collects through its search engine and other sites, it carries out thousands of experiments a day, according to the *Harvard Business Review,* and it uses the results to refine the algorithms that increasingly control how people find information and extract meaning from it. What Taylor did for the work of the hand, Google is doing for the work of the mind.

The company has declared that its mission is "to organize the world's information and make it universally accessible and useful." It seeks to develop "the perfect search engine," which it defines as something that "understands exactly what you mean and gives you back exactly what you want." In Google's view, information is a kind of commodity, a utilitarian resource that can be mined and processed with industrial efficiency. The more pieces of information we can "access" and the faster we can extract their gist, the more productive we become as thinkers.

Where does it end? Sergey Brin and Larry Page, the gifted young men who founded Google while pursuing doctoral degrees in computer science at Stanford, speak frequently of their desire to turn their search engine into an artificial intelligence, HAL-like machine that might be connected directly to our brains. "The ultimate search engine is something as smart as people—or smarter," Page said in a speech a few years back. "For us, working on search is a way to work on artificial intelligence." In a 2004 interview with *Newsweek,* Brin said, "Certainly if you had all the world's information directly attached to your brain, or an artificial brain that was smarter than your brain, you'd be better off." Last year, Page told a convention of scientists that Google is "really trying to build artificial intelligence and to do it on a large scale."

Such an ambition is a natural one, even an admirable one, for a pair of math whizzes with vast quantities of cash at their disposal and a small army of computer scientists in their employ. A fundamentally scientific enterprise, Google is motivated by a desire to use technology, in Eric Schmidt's words, "to solve problems that have never been solved before," and artificial intelligence is the hardest problem out there. Why wouldn't Brin and Page want to be the ones to crack it?

Still, their easy assumption that we'd all "be better off" if our brains were supplemented, or even replaced, by an artificial intelligence is unsettling. It suggests a belief that intelligence is the output of a mechanical process, a series of discrete steps that can be isolated, measured, and optimized. In Google's world, the world we enter when we go online, there's little place for the fuzziness of contemplation. Ambiguity is not an opening for insight but a bug to be fixed. The human brain is just an outdated computer that needs a faster processor and a bigger hard drive.

The idea that our minds should operate as high-speed data-processing machines is not only built into the workings of the Internet, it is the network's reigning business model as well. The faster we surf across the Web—the more links we click and pages we view—the more opportunities Google and other companies gain to collect information about us and to feed us advertisements. Most of the proprietors of the commercial Internet have a financial stake in collecting the crumbs of data we leave behind as we flit from link to link—the more crumbs, the better. The last thing these companies want is to encourage leisurely reading or slow, concentrated thought. It's in their economic interest to drive us to distraction.

Maybe I'm just a worrywart. Just as there's a tendency to glorify technological progress, there's a counter tendency to expect the worst of every new tool or machine. In Plato's *Phaedrus*, Socrates bemoaned the development of writing. He feared that, as people came to rely on the written word as a substitute for the knowledge they used to carry inside their heads, they would, in the words of one of the dialogue's characters, "cease to exercise their memory and become forgetful." And because they would be able to "receive a quantity of information without proper instruction," they would "be thought very knowledgeable when they are for the most part quite ignorant." They would be "filled with the conceit of wisdom instead of real wisdom." Socrates wasn't wrong—the new technology did often have the effects he feared—but he was shortsighted. He couldn't foresee the many ways that writing and reading would serve to spread information, spur fresh ideas, and expand human knowledge (if not wisdom).

The arrival of Gutenberg's printing press, in the 15th century, set off another round of teeth gnashing. The Italian humanist Hieronimo Squarciafico worried that the easy availability of books would lead to intellectual laziness, making men "less studious" and weakening their minds. Others argued that cheaply printed books and broadsheets would undermine religious authority, demean the work of scholars and scribes, and

spread sedition and debauchery. As New York University professor Clay Shirky notes, "Most of the arguments made against the printing press were correct, even prescient." But, again, the doomsayers were unable to imagine the myriad blessings that the printed word would deliver.

So, yes, you should be skeptical of my skepticism. Perhaps those who dismiss critics of the Internet as Luddites or nostalgists will be proved correct, and from our hyperactive, data-stoked minds will spring a golden age of intellectual discovery and universal wisdom. Then again, the Net isn't the alphabet, and although it may replace the printing press, it produces something altogether different. The kind of deep reading that a sequence of printed pages promotes is valuable not just for the knowledge we acquire from the author's words but for the intellectual vibrations those words set off within our own minds. In the quiet spaces opened up by the sustained, undistracted reading of a book, or by any other act of contemplation, for that matter, we make our own associations, draw our own inferences and analogies, foster our own ideas. Deep reading, as Maryanne Wolf argues, is indistinguishable from deep thinking.

If we lose those quiet spaces, or fill them up with "content," we will sacrifice something important not only in our selves but in our culture. In a recent essay, the playwright Richard Foreman eloquently described what's at stake:

> I come from a tradition of Western culture, in which the ideal (my ideal) was the complex, dense and "cathedral-like" structure of the highly educated and articulate personality—a man or woman who carried inside themselves a personally constructed and unique version of the entire heritage of the West. [But now] I see within us all (myself included) the replacement of complex inner density with a new kind of self—evolving under the pressure of information overload and the technology of the "instantly available."

As we are drained of our "inner repertory of dense cultural inheritance," Foreman concluded, we risk turning into "'pancake people'—spread wide and thin as we connect with that vast network of information accessed by the mere touch of a button."

I'm haunted by that scene in *2001*. What makes it so poignant, and so weird, is the computer's emotional response to the disassembly of its mind: its despair as one circuit after another goes dark, its childlike pleading with the astronaut—"I can feel it. I can feel it. I'm afraid"—and its final reversion to what can only be called a state of innocence. HAL's outpouring of feeling contrasts with the emotionlessness that characterizes the human figures in the film, who go about their business with an almost robotic efficiency. Their thoughts and actions feel scripted, as if they're following the steps of an algorithm.

In the world of *2001*, people have become so machinelike that the most human character turns out to be a machine. That's the essence of Kubrick's dark prophecy: as we come to rely on computers to mediate our understanding of the world, it is our own intelligence that flattens into artificial intelligence. ■

Questions

❶ How does Carr begin and end his article? What do you think his purpose was in beginning and ending in these ways?

❷ Carr draws on several other resources to support the points he's trying to make. What kinds of experts does he draw on, how does he integrate their work into his text, and for what purpose?

❸ Carr wrote this article several years ago. Are his concerns still relevant? In what ways do they persist and in what ways have they changed?

READING 10

"They Hook You When You're Young"[LRII:12]
by Seth Stephens-Davidowitz
New York Times, April 19, 2014

Op-ed writer for the *New York Times* Seth Stephens-Davidowitz begins this article with the intriguing question, "How do events in our childhood shape our adult preferences?" Using a large data set from Facebook, the author explores this question as it relates to baseball fandom, wondering, what some of the factors are that influence the choice of a favorite team. In his analysis, Stephens-Davidowitz shows that "the most important year in a boy's baseball life is indeed 8." According to Facebook data, if a team wins a championship around the time when a fan is eight years old, there is a greater chance that he will remain a fan as an adult. What Stephens-Davidowitz found was a correlation between when a baseball team wins a championship and when a person becomes a fan. This was true only for males; females didn't show the same correlation. He then combines this data with other data on the kind of revenues teams generate, showing how teams that win generate more revenue, and teams that win a championship can expect to have higher revenues the following year. But such revenue drops off if a team stops winning. In light of this data, Stephens-Davidowitz makes the point that, although teams have to continue to win to earn high revenues, when they do win, especially championships, they tend to create lifelong fans out 5-15 year old boys.

How do events from our childhood shape our adult preferences?

I recently studied this question using a classic American example: baseball. I tested how a team's performance at every age of our childhood affects which team we root for as adults. From Facebook's publicly available advertising platform, I downloaded data on how many fans every baseball team has, broken out by gender and age. (Facebook estimates whether someone is a fan of a team based on both "likes" and posts.)

This data is not perfect, but it does correlate pretty well with previous polling. According to Facebook, the most popular teams are the Yankees, Red Sox, Mets, Cardinals and Braves; there are 1.65 Yankees fans for every Mets fan.

Facebook data can reveal patterns that polls generally do not have large enough sample sizes to detect. For example, Facebook tells us that among men, the ratio of Yankees fans to Mets fans fluctuates enormously depending on when those men were born. The Mets are popular among an unusually high number of men born in 1961 and 1978. (Interestingly, women's fandom depends much less on when they were born.)

These huge swings appear to be driven by winning over young boys with on-the-field success. Fans born in 1961 and 1978 were both 8 years old when the Mets won the World Series. Fandom is determined by a huge number of factors, like what team your father supports, but winning when boys are young stands out clearly in the data.

This effect can be quantified more rigorously. I used data on all 17 current Major League franchises that had been established in their current city by 1965. I modeled the probability of an adult's supporting a team today based on the adult's age and gender, the team and how good the team was at every year of his or her childhood. Note that this model takes into account the fact that some teams, like the Yankees and the Red Sox, are more popular at all ages. And it takes into account the fact that baseball fandom, at least as expressed on Facebook, differs by age.

Let's look at men. The model's results were striking. They show that the years before a boy's birth and the first couple of years of his life are, as you would expect, statistically irrelevant to his adult fandom. But then things start to matter in a big way.

The most important year in a boy's baseball life is indeed age 8. If a team wins a World Series when a boy is 8, it increases the probability that he will support the team as an adult by about 8 percent. Remember, this is independent of how good the team was every other year of this guy's life. Things start falling off pretty fast after the age of about 14. A championship when a man is 20 is only one-eighth as likely to create an adult fan as a championship when a boy is 8. Just winning games also matters, with a similar age pattern. But the data shows that there seems to be something really special about winning championships.

These results mean a successful team leaves a huge imprint long after all the players are retired. Consider a team like the St. Louis Cardinals. In a five-year period in the 1940s, led by Stan Musial, the Cardinals averaged more than 100 wins a season and won three championships. According to my model, roughly 20 percent of 80-year-old male Cardinals fans today would either support another team or not be a baseball fan if not for Musial and his teammates' epic run.

Of course, winning is not all that matters for fandom. Long-suffering teams like the Cubs have plenty of fans. But winning helps in a big way, and the Cubs would have far more fans if they had won more.

What about women? In general, the patterns were less precise and less concentrated on particular ages. It seems that female fans of all teams are about equally likely to be won over at different points in their lives.

There is a broader implication here for baseball. Winning is much more valuable than economists previously thought. The traditional methodology to value winning is as follows: Measure how a team performs in a given year, and see how much more beer and how many more tickets and hot dogs it sells that year and perhaps the following year.

I did this analysis with data posted by the sports economist Rodney Fort of the University of Michigan. On average, if a team wins an additional 10 games in a season, it can expect about a 12 percent increase in attendance that year. But the effects die off completely the following year. Winning a World Series does increase attendance by about 12 percent the following year, but the effects die off shortly after. The long-term effects on hooking young boys, in other words, aren't captured in the traditional data.

In 2012, the San Francisco Giants won 94 games and the World Series. That year, they made $129 million in gate revenues. The traditional analysis would say, relative to a .500

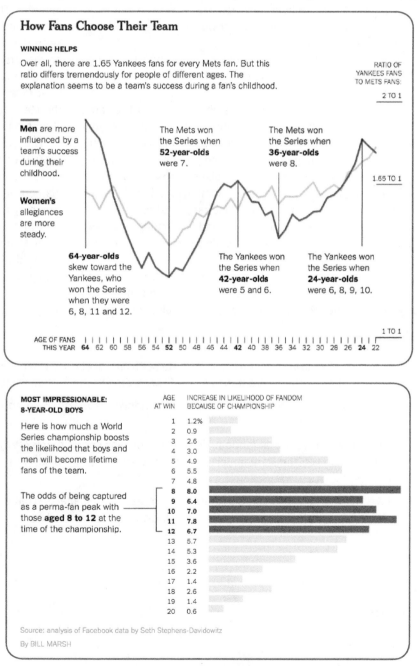

How Fans Choose Their Team

WINNING HELPS

Over all, there are 1.65 Yankees fans for every Mets fan. But this ratio differs tremendously for people of different ages. The explanation seems to be a team's success during a fan's childhood.

RATIO OF YANKEES FANS TO METS FANS:

2 TO 1

Men are more influenced by a team's success during their childhood.

Women's allegiances are more steady.

The Mets won the Series when **52-year-olds** were 7.

The Mets won the Series when **36-year-olds** were 8.

1.65 TO 1

64-year-olds skew toward the Yankees, who won the Series when they were 6, 8, 11 and 12.

The Yankees won the Series when **42-year-olds** were 5 and 6.

The Yankees won the Series when **24-year-olds** were 6, 8, 9, 10.

1 TO 1

AGE OF FANS THIS YEAR   64 62 60 58 56 54 **52** 50 48 46 44 **42** 40 38 36 34 32 30 28 26 **24** 22

MOST IMPRESSIONABLE: 8-YEAR-OLD BOYS	AGE AT WIN	INCREASE IN LIKELIHOOD OF FANDOM BECAUSE OF CHAMPIONSHIP
Here is how much a World Series championship boosts the likelihood that boys and men will become lifetime fans of the team.	1	1.2%
	2	0.9
	3	2.6
	4	3.0
	5	4.9
	6	5.5
	7	4.8
The odds of being captured as a perma-fan peak with those **aged 8 to 12** at the time of the championship.	8	8.0
	9	6.4
	10	7.0
	11	7.8
	12	6.7
	13	5.7
	14	5.3
	15	3.6
	16	2.2
	17	1.4
	18	2.6
	19	1.4
	20	0.6

Source: analysis of Facebook data by Seth Stephens-Davidowitz

By BILL MARSH

season, that the Giants' 2012 run made them about $33 million in gate revenues—about $18 million from increased attendance during the pennant race and $15 million from more excited fans the following year.

But my model suggests that among 5- to 15-year-olds in 2012, 5 percent more fans will root for the Giants for the rest of their lives. Assume spending on baseball increases at roughly the rate of interest. And assume that these fans spend about as much as the average fan. The Giants can expect about $33 million, in net present value, from here on out, from their 2012 season, just from the boys they won over.

A championship season, in other words, is at least twice as valuable as we previously thought.

OK., this is only baseball, hardly the most important arena of life. What are the implications of this research outside of sports?

The explosion of big data sets should lead to the rapid development of precise insights into how events at every year of our childhood affect how we think as adults. We can learn a lot about the formation of tastes and preferences, both trivial and fundamental. Do you like Coke or Pepsi as an adult? Cheerios or Raisin Bran? Obama or Romney? All these answers can now be compared to things that happened to us as children. Already, some scholars have found fascinating long-term effects of events that happened while we were young on our political and economic outlooks.

The economists Ebonya Washington of Yale University and Sendhil Mullainathan of Harvard University found that if you are just old enough to vote in a presidential election, you will be more likely years later to be a partisan of the party you voted for than if you were slightly too young to vote in that election. Another pair of economists, Ulrike Malmendier, at the University of California, Berkeley, and Stefan Nagel, at the University of Michigan, found that if you grew up in bad economic times, you are more risk averse as an adult.

There is also a less serious implication of this study. It gives me ammunition for one of my favorite activities: whining.

I am obsessed with the Mets and this obsession, I suspect, plays a large part in my persistent disappointment with adult life. The Mets of the Dwight Gooden-Darryl Strawberry era hooked me as a boy, dangling in front of me the diving plays of Keith Hernandez at first, the dramatic escapes of Jesse Orosco on the mound and the surprising power of Howard Johnson at third. I assumed that being a Mets fan meant a lifetime of pennant races and championships. But after I became an adult, the Mets delivered more losses than wins and no additional championships.

The data shows that if I had just been born 10 years earlier or 10 years later, I would be significantly less likely to be in this mess. I could be out celebrating Derek Jeter's farewell tour, instead of lying by my radio, listening to another Mets loss, clutching my Rey Ordóñez-signed mitt.

You could say this is my fault and nothing to complain about. I am a grown man and can choose whatever baseball team I'd like. But data analysis makes it clear that fandom is highly influenced by events in our childhood. If something captures us in our formative years, it often has us hooked for life. ∎

Questions

❶ Stephens-Davidowitz draws on a large data set from Facebook—what is often called "big data" in the popular press. How is this "big data" different from "small data"? According to the author, what are the benefits of using such large data sets?

❷ What is the main argument that Stephens-Davidowitz is making? How does he build this argument using data and personal experience?

❸ Thinking about your own fandom, do you support any sports teams? Why are you a fan of a particular team? What other factors do you think are important when choosing a team to support beyond following a winning team when you are younger?

❹ Take a closer look at the infographics that are used in this piece. What do they contribute to the rhetorical purposes of the author? Do you feel they contribute to your own understanding?

READING 11

"Tweeting the Revolution: Social Media Use[LRII:13] and the #Euromaidan Protests"

by Pablo Barberá and Megan Metzger

The Huffington Post Blog, February 21, 2014

The question of how much impact social media can have on political events and social change has been much debated in recent years. After Malcolm Gladwell argued against its potential power in "Can the Revolution be Tweeted?" (Chapter 15), others have explored the question in different ways. In a *Huffington Post* article, "Tweeting the Revolution," which echoes Gladwell's title, New York University graduate students Pablo Barberá and Megan Metzger, present data that was collected at the Social Media and Political Participation Lab[LRI:4] at New York University in the winter of 2014. The Lab works with the sort of big data about vast numbers of social media users that is now routinely collected by sites like Facebook and Twitter, and its researchers draw on the data for a variety of academic and public reports. In this case, Barberá and Metzger analyzed real-time data about the use of social media in protests in the Ukraine in early 2014. There, in Maidan (Independence) square, protests took place against the government of then-president Viktor Yanukovych, who was seen as being corrupt, heavy-handed, and too aligned with Russia. The protesters wanted more freedoms and a closer alignment with Europe (and used the hashtag #Euromaidan). Although the protesters were met with violence with at least 82 people killed and over a thousand injured in mid-February, in the end President Yanukovych fled the country and was impeached and replaced by an interim government. Yet it's still not clear if all of the reform that protesters were seeking will be achieved and maintained.

The past three days have been the most violent in recent Ukrainian history. Over 70 people are reported to have died since violence erupted on Tuesday, including following the reemergence of violence on Wednesday after the collapse of a truce between the government and protesters. Thursday, the EU formally announced that it will impose sanctions on those it deems responsible for the violence, marking the first active international intervention since the beginning of protests in November. As in other events of collective actions in the past few years, social media appears to be playing a prominent role in organizing and motivating Ukrainian protesters.

At the Social Media and Political Participation lab at NYU we have been closely following social media activity related to the protests since they began in November, collecting Twitter and Facebook data related to key protest hashtags. Our findings suggest that social media, as it has throughout these protests, continues to be a pivotal organization tool for those in Kiev and also the most relevant mechanism for disseminating and exchanging information both within Ukraine and abroad. Furthermore, as the graph below [below left] shows, activity on social media is incredibly responsive to events on the ground.

The number of tweets mentioning the main hashtag used by protesters, #Euromaidan (and its translation to Ukrainian and Russian), steadily increased over the day on February 18th as protests in the square became more violent. The activity peaked in the late evening as the police encourage women and children to evacuate, leading to the most violent period of the day. Today, we have observed a similar pattern. Activity decreased over night, to then steadily rise throughout the day as the situation became increasingly violent. The overall volume of activity is also significantly higher than at any other point in the protest. Over 250,000 tweets using the protest hashtags have been sent in the past 24 hours. Previously, the highest volume of tweets per hour was about 10,000 but today we have seen volume as high as 30,000. The graph below gives some insight into what is driving these shifts in activity.

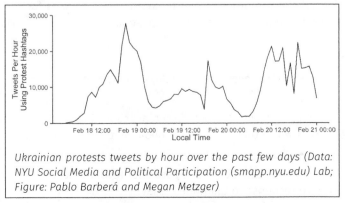

Ukrainian protests tweets by hour over the past few days (Data: NYU Social Media and Political Participation (smapp.nyu.edu) Lab; Figure: Pablo Barberá and Megan Metzger)

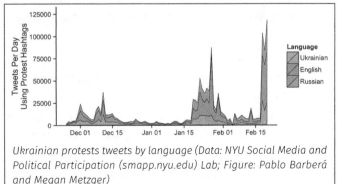

Ukrainian protests tweets by language (Data: NYU Social Media and Political Participation (smapp.nyu.edu) Lab; Figure: Pablo Barberá and Megan Metzger)

This figure shows that the dominant language on Twitter is currently English, but that was not always the case. Earlier in the protests, language use was more evenly distributed. However, over the past few days, the proportion of tweets in English has gone up dramatically, from 44 to 53%. Our numbers do not suggest that Ukrainians are tweeting less than during other high-volume days, but instead that their numbers are being augmented by a much larger population of users from the international community. Another possible explanation for the increased activity could be a concerted effort by supporters of the protest to engage the international community, that is, Ukrainians tweeting in English to prompt this increase in participation on the part of those outside the country. Perhaps the images of violence coming out of Kiev over the past few days are extreme enough to capture the attention of even those generally less aware of international affairs. Maybe violence, particularly in Europe, mobilizes international attention in a way that mass protest alone simply can't.

The story on Facebook is quite different, with the main EuroMaidan Facebook page operating almost entirely in Ukrainian. Facebook is more obviously being used to serve the dual purpose of spreading information and operating as a logistical tool for those on the ground. Shared documents have been distributed for people to volunteer to man shifts at hospitals, and, poignantly, to gather information on the dead and any needs their families may have. There are Facebook pages specifically established for emergencies and assisting people in getting medical care. There are calls to action, as well as specific requests. Further, there is now a page, almost entirely in English devoted to spreading information more widely. The EuroMaidanPR Facebook page bills itself as the "Facebook page of the Official International Public Relations Secretariat for Headquarters of the National Resistance in Kyiv Ukraine."

Data from the main EuroMaidan Facebook page indicates that this medium also responds, in terms of volume of activity, to events on the ground. The chart [at top right] shows numbers of likes, shares, and comments over time on the main page. It's clear that activity increases dramatically, particularly likes and shares, during major incidents such as the violence over the past couple days, as well as the brief, lower-level violence in January.

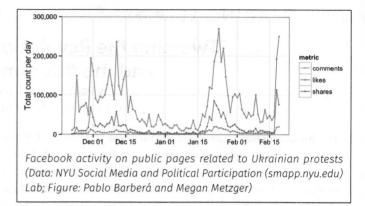

Facebook activity on public pages related to Ukrainian protests (Data: NYU Social Media and Political Participation (smapp.nyu.edu) Lab; Figure: Pablo Barberá and Megan Metzger)

The most widely shared posts on Facebook over the past days are images of police violence, injured protesters or individuals acting bravely, such as images of medics coming in to assist the wounded, which serve as crowd-sourced narratives of the events in Maidan square, and motivate the protesters to resist despite police violence. The Facebook page, however, also contains an incredible amount of information ranging from news updates, to individual accounts and experiences, links to live streams of the protests, and as mentioned above information coordinating action.

While there are obviously downsides to the massive amount of information that social media creates (it can be hard, at times, to sort through everything and to assess the accuracy of the information that is shared), we have also seen that the availability of these platforms gives protesters a loud voice internationally, independent of traditional media structures and of the government, and provides a space for organization outside of the square itself. We found similar dynamics in Turkey, particularly during periods where the mainstream media locally did not cover the protests. We did not, however, observe the level of violent conflict in Turkey that is currently happening in Ukraine. What social media has shown over the last few days, however, is its flexibility as a tool. As needed, and in response to dramatically shifting events on the ground, Twitter and Facebook have been effective means to convey messages about the violence to the international community, to organize those willing to get involved in the protests, and to coordinate resources for the injured and those in need in Maidan square. ∎

Questions

❶ What data do the researchers present about the use of Twitter and Facebook over these few days? What patterns do they find for tweets and posts?

❷ What do they infer from their observations: About moments of increased activity? About likely reasons for the more frequent choice of a particular language? About the different ways in which these two social media platforms seem to be being used?

❸ What do they conclude from their very focused small study of the use of social media at a particular revolutionary moment? Does any of the evidence they present contribute to your own response to Gladwell's essay?

References, Resources, and Links

References and Resources

Chapter 9

REFERENCES

9:1 "Encouraging Respectful Behavior." Facebook Community Standards. www.facebook.com/communitystandards#.

9:2 Scherker, Amanda. "One Direction Fans Can Make Anyone Famous—And They Chose Jerry The Lamp Builder." *The Huffington Post*, 25 Nov. 2014, www.huffingtonpost.com/2014/11/25/one-direction-twitter-dad_n_6218892.html.

9:3 Bilton, Nick. "Alex from Target: The Other Side of Fame." *The New York Times*, 12 Nov. 2014, www.nytimes.com/2014/11/13/style/alex-from-target-the-other-side-of-fame.html?_r=0.

9:4 Jackson, Vannessa. "Adele's "Hello" and Drake's "Hotline Bling Have Parodies Every Fan Needs To See but Which Has The Best Parodies?" *Bustle*, 4 Dec. 2015, www.bustle.com/articles/127785-adeles-hello-drakes-hotline-bling-have-parodies-every-fan-needs-to-see-but-which-has.

9:5 Fleischer, Adam. "Drake Reposted this Artist's Drawing on Instagram Without Permission: 'No Hard Feelings, I Just Want Credit.' *MTV News*, 23 Nov. 2015, www.mtv.com/news/2547881/drake-adele-drawing-instagram-reposted-without-credit/.

9:6 Instagram Community Guidelines, help.instagram.com/477434105621119/.

9:7 Knobel, Michele, and Colin Lankshear. "Online Memes, Affinities, and Cultural Production." *New Literacies Sampler,* edited by Knobel and Lankshear, Peter Lang, 2007.

9:8 Lessig, Lawrence. "In Defense of Piracy." *The Wall Street Journal,* 11 Oct. 2008. www.wsj.com/articles/SB122367645363324303.

9:9 Wagner, Laura. "'Dancing Baby' Wins Copyright Case." *The Two-Way.* National Public Radio. 14 Sept. 2015. www.npr.org/sections/the-two-way/2015/09/14/440363919/dancing-baby-wins-copyright-case.

9:10 Hawkins, Sara. "Copyright Fair Use and How It Works for Online Images." *Social Media Examiner,* 23 Nov. 2011, www.socialmediaexaminer.com/copyright-fair-use-and-how-it-works-for-online-images/.

RESOURCES

Dunn, Thom. "Thanks to U.S. Copyright Laws, Nothing has Entered the Public Domain in Nearly 40 Years." *Upworthy,* 5 Jan. 2016, www.upworthy.com/thanks-to-us-copyright-laws-nothing-has-entered-the-public-domain-in-nearly-40-years?c=reccon1.

"The 'Fair Use' Rule: When Use of Copyrighted Material is Acceptable" NOLO, www.nolo.com/legal-encyclopedia/fair-use-rule-copyright-material-30100.html.

U.S. Copyright Office Fair Use Index, www.copyright.gov/fls/fl102.html.

Lawrence Lessig's March 2007 TED (Technology, Entertainment, and Design conference) talk on "Laws that Choke Creativity." www.ted.com/talks/larry_lessig_says_the_law_is_strangling_creativity?language=en.

Chapter 10

REFERENCES

10:1 Aristotle. *On Rhetoric.* Translated and edited by George A. Kennedy, Oxford UP, 1991.

10:2 Barnes, Tom. "Scientists Just Discovered Why All Pop Music Sounds Exactly the Same." *Mic,* 7 Jan. 2015. mic.com/articles/107896/scientists-finally-prove-why-pop-music-all-sounds-the-same#.JEJWFRC0O.

10:3 Percino, Gamaliel, Peter Klimek, and Stefan Thurner. "Instrumental Complexity of Music Genres and Why Simplicity Sells." *PLoS ONE,* vol. 9 no. 12, 31 Dec. 2014, journals.plos.org/plosone/search?q=Instrumental+complexity+of+music+genres&filterJournals=PLoSONE.

10:4 Pew Research Report. "Social Networking Use." 2015. www.pewresearch.org/data-trend/media-and-technology/social-networking-use/.

10:5 2015 Neilsen Music U.S. Report. www.nielsen.com/us/en/insights/reports/2016/2015-music-us-year-end-report.html.

10:6 Konnikova, Maria. "The Six Things That Make Stories Go Viral Will Amaze, and Maybe Infuriate, You." *The New Yorker,* 21 Jan. 2014. www.newyorker.com/tech/elements/the-six-things-that-make-stories-go-viral-will-amaze-and-maybe-infuriate-you.

10:7 Slotkin, Alex (Student). "'Get Your Game Face On' A Rhetorical Analysis. Understanding the rhetoric surrounding the mock-NFL CoverGirl ad." storify.com/AlexSlotkin/get-your-game-face-on-a-rhetorical-analysis.

RESOURCES

Cruz, Lenika. "In Music, Uniformity Sells." *The Atlantic.* 4 Jan. 2015. www.theatlantic.com/entertainment/archive/2015/01/in-music-uniformity-sells/384181/.

Ohri, Devika. "Here's Why Pop Music Sounds So Bad and Repetitive." *Reshareit*, 7 Feb. 2015, www.reshareit.com/heres-pop-music-sounds-bad-repetitive/.

Whitwell, Tom. "Why Do All Records Sound the Same?" *Cuepoint*. 9 Jan. 2015, medium.com/cuepoint/why-do-all-records-sound-the-same-830ba863203#.ddq826c4k.

"Listen Up: Music and the Multicultural Consumer." *Neilsen*, 2014. www.nielsen.com/us/en/insights/reports/2014/listen-up-music-and-the-multicultural-consumer.html.

Chapter 11

REFERENCES

11:1 Konnikova, Maria. "The Six Things That Make Stories Go Viral Will Amaze, and Maybe Infuriate, You." *The New Yorker*, 21 July 2014, www.newyorker.com/tech/elements/the-six-things-that-make-stories-go-viral-will-amaze-and-maybe-infuriate-you.

11:2 Sullivan, Andrew. "Why I Blog." *The Atlantic*. The Atlantic, Nov. 2008, www.theatlantic.com/magazine/archive/2008/11/why-i-blog/307060/.

11:3 Sullivan, Andrew. "A Note To My Readers." *The Dish*. Andrew Sullivan, 28 Jan. 2015, dish.andrewsullivan.com/2015/01/28/a-note-to-my-readers/.

11:4 Dean, Michelle. "Andrew Sullivan Stops Writing at The Dish: It's the End of a Blogging Era." *The Guardian*. The Guardian, 28 Jan. 2015, www.theguardian.com/media/2015/jan/28/andrew-sullivan-dish-post-blog-era.

11:5 Farhi, Paul. "Andrew Sullivan, Blogger Extraordinaire, Decides That It's Time to Stop Dishing." *Washington Post*, 28 Jan. 2015, www.washingtonpost.com/lifestyle/style/andrew-sullivan-blogger-extraordinaire-decides-that-its-time-to-stop-dishing/2015/01/28/681ad5d2-a72e-11e4-a06b-9df2002b86a0_story.html.

11:6 Samuelson, Kate. "25 Vloggers Under 25 Who Are Owning The World Of YouTube." *The Huffington Post*, 26 Dec. 2014, www.huffingtonpost.co.uk/2014/12/17/25-vloggers-under-25-who-are-owning-the-world-of-youtube_n_6340280.html.

RESOURCES

"Why I Blog: A Conversation with *The Atlantic's* Andrew Sullivan." Interviewed by Ta-Nehisi Coates. *The Aspen Institute*. 1 July 2009, www.youtube.com/watch?v=QvhcYKyeAJs.

Cillizza, Chris. "Andrew Sullivan is going to stop blogging. No, blogging isn't dead." *Washington Post*. 28 Jan. 2015, www.washingtonpost.com/news/the-fix/wp/2015/01/28/andrew-sullivan-is-going-to-stop-blogging-no-blogging-isnt-dead/

Chapter 12

REFERENCES

12:1 Swales, John M. *Genre Analysis: English in Academic and Research Settings*. Cambridge UP, 1990.

12:2 Skalicky, Stephen. "Was this analysis helpful? A genre of the Amazon.com discourse community and its "most helpful" product reviews." *Discourse, Context & Media*, Vol. 2, No. 2, June 2013, pp. 84–93.

12:3 de Jong, Ilona K.E. and Christian Burgers. "Do consumer critics write differently than professional critics? A genre analysis of online film reviews." *Discourse, Context & Media*, Vol. 2, No 2, June 2013, pp. 75-83.

12:4 Du Lac, J. Freedom. "Giving Indie Acts A Plug, or Pulling It." *Washington Post*. 30 Apr. 2006, www.washingtonpost.com/wp-dyn/content/article/2006/04/28/AR2006042800457.html.

12:5 Zoladz, Lindsay. "Florence and the Machine: *MTV Unplugged*." *Pitchfork*, 12 Apr. 2012, pitchfork.com/reviews/albums/16480-florence-the-machine-mtv-unplugged/.

12:6 "A Year in Review: 2005." *Tuning Fork*, 19 Dec. 2005, tuningforkmedia.blogspot.com/2005/12/year-in-review-2005.html.

12:7 "Kendrick Lamar and Black Humanity." *Pitchfork*, 19 Mar. 2015, pitchfork.com/thepitch/704-on-kendrick-lamar-and-black-humanity/.

12:8 Schannon, Mark. "So You Want To Be A Critic." *Blogcritics*, 13 Apr. 2006, blogcritics.org/so-you-want-to-be-a/.

12:9 Schannon, Mark. "Guidelines For Writing Reviews." *Blogcritics*, 23 May 2006, blogcritics.org/guidelines-for-writing-reviews.

RESOURCES

Media Review Sites: blogcritics.org, www.televisionwithoutpity.com, www.pastemagazine.com/, pitchfork.com, www.goodreads.com/, tuningforkmedia.blogspot.com

Video of Florence and the Machine's MTV Unplugged Performance. www.youtube.com/watch?v=PuGWZgpI_pQ

Rolling Stone Review of Florence and the Machine's *MTV Unplugged* Album, www.rollingstone.com/music/albumreviews/mtv-unplugged-20120410

NME Review of Florence and the Machine's *MTV Unplugged* Album, www.nme.com/reviews/florence-and-the-machine/13011

Chapter 13

REFERENCES

13:1 Richtel, Matt. "Wasting Time is New Divide in Digital Era." *The New York Times*, 29 May 2015, www.nytimes.com/2012/05/30/us/new-digital-divide-seen-in-wasting-time-online.html.

13:2 "Cyberloafing." University of Texas at San Antonio. "How to increase productivity by stopping cyberloafing: Giving employees a say has a huge impact on stopping wasteful Internet surfing." *ScienceDaily*, ScienceDaily, 20 Jan. 2016, www.sciencedaily.com/releases/2016/01/160120111527.htm.

13:3 Jacobsen, Wade, and Renata Forste. "The Wired Generation: Academic and Social Outcomes of Electronic Media Use Among University Students." *Cyberpsychology, Behavior, and Social Networking*, vol. 14, no. 5, 2011

13:4 DeAngelis, Tori. "Is Internet Addiction Real?" *Journal of the American Psychological Association*, vol. 31, no. 4, Apr. 2000, p.24.

13:5 Wolf, Maryanne. *Proust and the Squid: The Story and Science of the Reading Brain*. Harper, 2007.

13:6 Turkle, Sherry. *Alone Together: Why We Expect More From Technology and Less From Each Other*. Basic Books, 2011.

13:7 Orwell, George. *1984*. Penguin, 1949.

13:8 Huxley, Aldous. *Brave New World*. Penguin, 1975.

13:9 Atwood, Margaret. *The Handmaid's Tale*. Anchor, 1998.

13:10 Ishiguro, Kazuo. *Never Let Me Go*. Vintage, 2010.

13:11 Rowling, J.K. *Harry Potter and the Sorcerer's Stone*. Scholastic, 2003.

13:12 Collins, Suzanne. *The Hunger Games*. Scholastic, 2008.

13:13 Roth, Veronica. *Divergent*. Harper Collins, 2011.

13:14 Eggers, Dave. *The Circle*. McSweeney's, 2013, pp. 253-63.

13:15 Atwood, Margaret. "When Privacy is Theft." Review of *The Circle* by David Eggers. *The New York Review of Books*, 21 Nov. 2013, www.nybooks.com/articles/archives/2013/nov/21/eggers-circle-when-privacy-is-theft/.

13:16 Ullman, Ellen. "Ring of Power." Review of *The Circle* by David Eggers. *New York Times Sunday Book Review*, 1 Nov. 2013, www.nytimes.com/2013/11/03/books/review/the-circle-by-daveeggers.html?_r=0.

13:17 Morais, Betsy. "Sharing Is Caring Is Sharing." Review of *The Circle* by David Eggers. *The New Yorker*, 30 Oct. 2013, www.newyorker.com/tech/elements/sharing-is-caring-is-sharing.

13:18 Greenfield, Rebecca. "Did Dave Eggers 'Rewrite' Kate Losse's Book?" *The Wire. News from The Atlantic.* 19 Sept. 2013, https://www.theatlantic.com/technology/archive/2013/09/did-dave-eggers-rewrite-kate-losses-book/310824/.

13:19 Shteyngart, Gary. *Super Sad True Love Story.* Random House, 2010.

RESOURCES

2014 Wasting Time at Work Survey, Salary.com www.salary.com/2014-wasting-time-at-work/

Pride and Prejudice Wiki. humanscience.wikia.com/wiki/Pride_and_Prejudice

Chapter 14
REFERENCES

14:1 Kress, Gunther R., and Theo van Leeuwen. *Reading Images: The Grammar of Visual Design.* Routledge 2nd Ed., 2006.

14:2 Wysocki, Anne Frances, Johndan Johnson-Eilola, Cynthia L. Selfe, and Geoffrey Sirc. *Writing New Media: Theory and Applications for Expanding the Teaching of Composition.* Utah State UP, 2004.

14:3 Williams, Robin, and John Tollett. *The Non-Designer's Web Book: An Easy Guide to Creating, Designing, and Posting Your Own Web Site* 3rd Ed., Peachpit, 2006.

14:4 Garber, Megan. "The Many Faces of Rosie the Riveter." *The Atlantic* 24 Apr. 2015, www.theatlantic.com/entertainment/archive/2015/04/the-many-faces-of-rosie-the-riveter/391364/.

14:5 "History of ¡Si, Se Puede!" *United Farm Workers*, www.ufw.org/_board.php?mode=view&b_code=cc_his_research&b_no=5970.

14:6 Leiby, Michele Langevine. "Malala Yousafzai: From a Schoolgirl to a Nobel Peace Prize Winner." *Washington Post*, 9 Dec. 2014, www.washingtonpost.com/news/worldviews/wp/2014/12/09/malala-yousafzai-from-a-schoolgirl-to-a-nobel-peace-prize-winner/.

14:7 DeVille, Nancy. "Rosie the Riveter – Still Inspiring Women in Richmond." *Richmond Pulse,* 25 Aug. 2015, richmondpulse.org/2015/08/25/rosie-the-riveter-still-inspiring-women-in-richmond/.

14:8 Koh, Adeline. "Who Gets To Say #ILookLikeAProfessor? And Who Would Want To?" *Medium,* 9 Aug. 2015, medium.com/synapse/who-gets-to-say-ilooklikeaprofessor-and-who-would-want-to-568fbe698198.

RESOURCES

"Rosie The Riveter Trust - National Park Nonprofit Supporter Richmond CA," www.rosietheriveter.org.

"Powers of Persuasion." National Archives and Records Administration, www.archives.gov/exhibits/powers_of_persuasion/powers_of_persuasion_intro.html.

"World War 2 Posters." History.com, www.history.com/topics/world-war-ii/world-war-history/pictures/world-war-ii-posters/recruitment-poster-by-tom-woodburn.

Gleick, James. "What Defines a Meme?" Smithsonian.com, May 2011, Internet Archive: Digital Library of Free Books, www.smithsonianmag.com/arts-culture/what-defines-a-meme-1904778/?no-ist.

Bartlett, Jamie. "Viral Memes Are Ruining Our Politics. Share If You Agree." *The Telegraph.* Telegraph Media Group, 27 Apr. 2015, www.telegraph.co.uk/news/general-election-2015/politics-blog/11565661/Viral-memes-are-ruining-our-politics.-Share-if-you-agree.html.

Know Your Meme. CheezBurger, knowyourmeme.com/.

Kress, Gunther, and Theo van Leeuwen. *Reading Images: The Grammar of Visual Design* 2nd Ed., Routledge, 2006

Scholes, Robert. "On Reading a Video Text." *Center for Media Literacy,* www.medialit.org/reading-room/reading-video-text.

Chapter 15
REFERENCES

15:1 Wilson, Robert E., Samuel D. Gosling, and Lindsay T. Graham. "A Review of Facebook Research in the Social Sciences." *Perspectives on Psychological Science , vol. 7, no. 3, 2012, pp. 203-220* pps.sagepub.com/content/7/3/203 to http://pps.sagepub.com/content/7/3/203.abstract.

15:2 Jacques, Renee. "11 Reasons You Should Quit Facebook in 2014." *The Huffington Post,* 23 Jan. 2014, www.huffingtonpost.com/2013/12/30/reasons-quit-facebook_n_4493791.html.

15:3 Lichfield, Gideon. "Why I've Finally Joined Facebook on Facebook's Tenth Anniversary," *Quartz.* 4 Feb. 2014, qz.com/173093/why-im-finally-joining-facebook-on-facebooks-tenth-anniversary/.

15:4 Chou, Hui-Tzu Grace, and Nicholas Edge. "'They Are Happier and Having Better Lives than I Am': The Impact of Using Facebook on Perceptions of Others' Lives." *Cyberpsychology, Behavior, and Social Networking,* vol. 15, no. 2, Feb. 2012, pp. 117-121, DOI:10.1089/cyber.2011.0324.

15:5 Marche, Stephen. "Is Facebook Making us Lonely?" *The Atlantic,* May 2012, www.theatlantic.com/magazine/archive/2012/05/is-facebook-making-us-lonely/308930/.

15:6 Anderson, Chris, and Michael Wolff. "The Web is Dead. Long Live the Internet." *Wired,* 17 Aug. 2010, www.wired.com/2010/08/ff_webrip/.

15:7 Turkle, Sherry. *Alone Together: Why We Expect More from Technology and Less from Each Other.* Basic Books, 2011.

15:8 Burke, Moira, and Robert Kraut. "Growing Closer on Facebook: Changes in Tie Strength Through Site Use." ACM Conference on Human Factors in Computing (CHI), 26 Apr. 2014, https://research.facebook.com/publications/growing-closer-on-facebook-changes-in-tie-strength-through-site-use/

15:9 Gladwell, Malcolm. "Small Change: Why The Revolution Will Not Be Tweeted." *The New Yorker,* 4 Oct. 2010, www.newyorker.com/magazine/2010/10/04/small-change-malcolm-gladwell.

15:10 Granovetter, Mark S. "The Strength of Weak Ties. "*The American Journal of Sociology,* vol. 78, no. 6, May 1973, pp. 1360–1380, sociology.stanford.edu/sites/default/files/publications/the_strength_of_weak_ties_and_exch_w-gans.pdf.

15:11 Ellison, Nicole B., Charles Steinfield, and Cliff Lampe. "The Benefits of Facebook 'Friends': Social Capital and College Students' Use of Online Social Network Sites." *Journal of Computer-Mediated Communication*, no. 12, 2007, pp. 1143–1168, DOI: 10.1111/j.1083-6101.2007.00367.

15:12 Shirky, Clay. *Here Comes Everybody: The Power of Organizing without Organizations.* Penguin, 2008.

15:13 Barberá, Pablo, and Megan Metzger. "Tweeting the Revolution: Social Media Use and the #Euromaidan Protests." *The Huffington Post Blog*, 21 Feb. 2014 and 23 Apr. 2014, www.huffingtonpost.com/pablo-barbera/tweeting-the-revolution-s_b_4831104.html.

15:14 Shirky, Clay. "The Political Power of Social Media," *Foreign Affairs*, Jan./Feb. 2011, www.foreignaffairs.com/articles/2010-12-20/political-power-social-media.

15:15 Gladwell, Malcolm, and Clay Shirky. "From Innovation to Revolution. Do Social Media Make Protests Possible?" *Foreign Affairs*, Mar./Apr. 2011, www.foreignaffairs.com/articles/2011-01-19/innovation-revolution.

15:16 Wasik, Bill. "Gladwell vs. Shirky: A Year Later, Scoring the Debate over Social Media Revolutions." *Wired*, 27 Dec. 2011, www.wired.com/2011/12/gladwell-vs-shirky/.

15:17 Tufekci, Zeynep. "Is There a Social-Media Fueled Protest Style? An Analysis From #jan25 to #geziparki." *Technosociology*, 1 June 2013, technosociology.org/?p=1255.

RESOURCES

Koifman, Natasha. "Can Social Media Actually Benefit Relationships?" *The Huffington Post*, 17 Oct. 2013, www.huffingtonpost.ca/natasha-koifman/social-media-and-relationships_b_4115588.html.

Stone, Biz. "Exclusive: Biz Stone on Twitter and Activism." *The Atlantic*, 19 Oct. 2010. www.theatlantic.com/technology/archive/2010/10/exclusive-biz-stone-on-twitter-and-activism/64772/.

McAdam, Doug. "Revisiting the U.S. Civil Rights Movement: Toward a More Synthetic Understanding of the Origins of Contention." *Center for Research on Social Organization Working Paper Series*, Sept. 1999, deepblue.lib.umich.edu/bitstream/handle/2027.42/51352/588.pdf?sequence=1.

"Revolution Will Not Be Televised." (Song) www.youtube.com/watch?v=vwSRqaZGsPw.

Data collection on the protests in the Ukraine by the Social Media and Political Participation Lab at New York University, smapp.nyu.edu/.

Chapter 16

REFERENCES

16:1 Simonite, Tom. "What Facebook Knows." *MIT Technology Review*, 13 June 2012, www.technologyreview.com/s/428150/what-facebook-knows/.

16:2 Smith, Ethan. "Music Downloads Plummet in U.S., but Sales of Vinyl Records and Streaming Surge." *The Wall Street Journal*, 1 Jan. 2015, www.wsj.com/articles/music-downloads-plummet-in-u-s-but-sales-of-vinyl-records-and-streaming-surge-1420092579.

16:3 Stephens-Davidowitz, Seth. "They Hook You When You're Young." *New York Times Sunday Review*, 19 Apr. 2014, www.nytimes.com/2014/04/20/opinion/sunday/they-hook-you-when-youre-young.html?_r=0.

16:4 Baker, Brett. "Twitter Data for Research: From Understanding Relationships to Spotting the Aurora Borealis." *Twitter Blog*, 30 July 2015, blog.twitter.com/2015/twitter-data-research.

16:5 Holderness, Tomas, and Etienne Turpin. "How Tweeting about Floods Became a Civic Duty in Jakarta." *The Guardian*, 25 Jan. 2016, www.theguardian.com/public-leaders-network/2016/jan/25/floods-jakarta-indonesia-twitter-petajakarta.org.

16:6 boyd, danah, and Kate Crawford. "Critical Questions for Big Data." *Information, Communication, and Society*, vol. 15, no. 5, May 2012, DOI: 10.1080/1369118X.2012.678878.

16:7 Lindstrom, Martin. *Small Data: The Tiny Clues that Uncover Huge Trends.* St. Martin's, 2016.

16:8 Kafai, Yasmin B., and Deborah A. Fields. *Connected Play: Tweens in a Virtual World.* The MIT Press, 2013.

16:9 Baym, Nancy. *Tune In, Log On: Soaps, Fandom and Online Community.* Sage, 2000.

RESOURCES

"Social Networking Websites." www.ebizmba.com/articles/social-networking-websites

Thompson, Clive. "The Surprising History of the Infographic." *Smithsonian Magazine*, July 2016, www.smithsonianmag.com/history/surprising-history-infographic-180959563/.

Links

Additional Readings

LRII:1 www.youtube.com/watch?v=F_Ep0O5fWN4

LRII:2 http://blogcritics.org/so-you-want-to-be-a/

LRII:3 http://blogcritics.org/guidelines-for-writing-reviews

LRII:4 www.nytimes.com/2013/11/03/books/review/the-circle-by-dave-eggers.html?_r=0

LRII:5 http://www.nytimes.com/2013/05/19/opinion/sunday/how-to-be-a-woman-programmer.html

LRII:6 www.newyorker.com/tech/elements/sharing-is-caring-is-sharing

LRII:7 http://www.theatlantic.com/entertainment/archive/2012/01/an-annie-leibovitz-exhibit-with-shots-of-niagara-falls

LRII:8 http://www.newyorker.com/tech/elements/do-you-speak-emoji

LRII:9 http://www.theatlantic.com/politics/archive/2015/07/what-every-american-should-know/397334/

LRII:10 http://www.nybooks.com/articles/2013/11/21/eggers-circle-when-privacy-is-theft/

LRII:11 http://www.theatlantic.com/magazine/archive/2008/07/is-google-making-us-stupid/306868/

LRII:12 www.nytimes.com/2014/04/20/opinion/sunday/they-hook-you-when-youre-young.html?_r=0

LRII:13 www.huffingtonpost.com/pablo-barbera/tweeting-the-revolution-s_b_4831104.html

LRII:14 http://smapp.nyu.edu/

Chapter 9

L9:1 https://www.facebook.com/communitystandards

L9:2 https://support.twitter.com/articles/18311

L9:3 https://help.instagram.com/477434105621119

L9:4 https://support.snapchat.com/en-US/a/guidelines

L9:5 https://www.instagram.com/p/9T8RSMsL-0/

L9:6 http://davevaleza.tumblr.com/post/132095393166

L9:7 http://creativecommons.org/

L9:8 http://www.albion.com/netiquette/corerules.html

Chapter 10

L10:1 http://mic.com/articles/107896/scientists-finally-prove-why-pop-music-all-sounds-the-same#.7t897kHki

L10:2 http://www.newyorker.com/tech/elements/the-six-things-that-make-stories-go-viral-will-amaze-and-maybe-infuriate-you

Chapter 11

L11:1 http://www.wikihow.com/Write-a-Feature-Article

L11:2 http://www.theatlantic.com/magazine/archive/2008/11/why-i-blog/307060/

L11:3 http://dish.andrewsullivan.com/

L11:4 http://www.theatlantic.com/magazine/toc/2008/11

L11:5 http://dish.andrewsullivan.com/2015/01/28/a-note-to-my-readers

L11:6 http://dish.andrewsullivan.com

L11:7 http://dish.andrewsullivan.com/?s=dogs+vs+cat

L11:8 http://www.washingtonpost.com/blogs/the-fix/wp/2015/01/28/andrew-sullivan-is-going-to-stop-blogging-no-blogging-isnt-dead/

L11:9 http://www.huffingtonpost.co.uk/2014/12/17/25-vloggers-under-25-who-are-owning-the-world-of-youtube_n_6340280.html

Chapter 12

L12:1 http://www.pitchfork.com

L12:2 https://www.youtube.com/watch?v=PuGWZgpl_pQ

L12:3 http://pitchfork.com/reviews/albums/16480-florence-the-machine-mtv-unplugged

L12:4 http://tuningforkmedia.blogspot.com

L12:5 http://pitchfork.com/thepitch/704-on-kendrick-lamar-and-black-humanity

L12:6 http://www.rollingstone.com/music/albumreviews/mtv-unplugged-20120410

L12:7 http://www.nme.com/reviews/florence-and-the-machine/13011

L12:8 http://www.blogcritics.org

Chapter 13

L13:1 http://www.nybooks.com/articles/archives/2013/nov/21/eggers-circle-when-privacy-is-theft/

L13:2 http://www.newyorker.com/tech/elements/sharing-is-caring-is-sharing

L13:3 http://www.nytimes.com/2013/11/03/books/review/the-circle-by-dave-eggers.html?_r=0

L13:4 http://humanscience.wikia.com/wiki/Pride_and_Prejudice

Chapter 14

L14:1 https://en.wikipedia.org/wiki/Lolcat

L14:2 http://www.theatlantic.com/entertainment/archive/2015/04/the-many-faces-of-rosie-the-riveter/391364/

L14:3 https://www.archives.gov/exhibits/powers_of_persuasion/powers_of_persuasion_home.html

L14:4 http://www.history.com/topics/world-war-ii/world-war-ii-history/pictures/world-war-ii-posters/recruitment-poster-by-tom-woodburn

L14:5 http://webdesignsurvivalist.com/inspiration/inspiration-30-modern-propaganda-posters

L14:6 knowyourmeme.com

L14:7 http://www socialmediaexaminer com/ copyright-fair-use-and-how-it-works-for-online-images/

Chapter 15

L15:1 www.politifact.com; www.snopes.com; http://www.factcheck.org/hot-topics

L15:2 http://www.huffingtonpost.com/2013/12/30/reasons-quit-face-book_n_4493791.html

L15:3 http://www.huffingtonpost.ca/natasha-koifman/social-me-dia-and-relationships_b_4115588.html

L15:4 http://www.theatlantic.com/magazine/archive/2012/05/is-facebook-making-us-lonely/308930

L15:5 http://www.newyorker.com/magazine/2010/10/04/small-change-malcolm-gladwell

L15:6 http://smapp.nyu.edu

L15:7 https://www.foreignaffairs.com/articles/2010-12-20/political-power-social-media

L15:8 https://www.foreignaffairs.com/articles/2011-01-19/innovation-revolution

L15:9 http://www.wired.com/2011/12/gladwell-vs-shirky/

L15:10 http://technosociology.org/?p=1255

Chapter 16

L16:1 https://www.technologyreview.com/s/428150/what-facebook-knows

L16:2 https://blog.twitter.com/2015/usgs-twitter-data-earthquake-detection

L16:3 http://www.jmir.org/2013/6/e125/

L16:4 https://datausa.io

L16:5 http://www.nielsen.com/us/en/solutions/measurement/music-sales-measurement.html

L16:6 https://blog.twitter.com/2015/twitter-data-research

L16:7 https://www.theguardian.com/public-leaders-network/2016/jan/25/floods-jakarta-indonesia-twitter-petajakarta-org

L16:8 http://slaveryfootprint.org

L16:9 https://infogr.am/

L16:10 www.dailyinfographic.com

Researching in Context

In Part III of *Writing Moves*, we shift our focus from the local communities of Part I and the public and often global contexts of Part II to the academic communities that you're entering through your current work. As was true for the communities discussed earlier in the book, the literacy practices of the academic world—of students, teachers, and researchers—are being altered in an environment of digital communication, affecting both what is studied and how it is studied and shared in the scholarly work central to colleges and universities.

We've already seen some evidence of the what—of the questions being asked and the discoveries being made by the researchers in several disciplines whose work we've drawn on in earlier chapters—questions you've also been exploring with your own inquiries. In this part of *Writing Moves*, we'll look more closely at the how—at the tools available to researchers in the twenty-first century and the ways in which those digital tools are both facilitating and reshaping the research process. While most of us have become skilled digital researchers in local and public settings—as we find answers to many questions with ease through a Google search and learn about individuals and groups by investigating their presence on social media—academic research demands both a slower, more deliberate scholarly process and the careful presentation of that work.

The conversations of the academic world, like those of local and public communities, depend on shared purposes as well as shared interests and shared ways. In this case, the larger shared purpose is to further knowledge and understanding within and across academic disciplines. Those disciplines can be seen as communities of practice—a term we introduced in Chapter 5 for communities both inside and outside of the academic world where participants are involved in a shared knowledge-creating enterprise and where members learn by being immersed in the practices of the community. Such communities can also be found in workplaces (as in the Xerox example in Chapter 5) and in public spaces where writers and journalists are engaging in inquiry and sharing what they learn with dedicated readers. But it is in academic settings, including the classrooms that introduce students to academic work, that sustained learning communities focused on particular areas of knowledge and discovery can most often be found.

While those who ask related questions and use similar methods do tend to form such communities within the academic world, and those communities are most closely tied to academic disciplines, those communities don't have rigid borders but instead shift and change as new questions and problems emerge and new discoveries are made. We define our own larger academic community of practice as "composition," attending that field's conferences and publishing in its journals. But like other members of this disciplinary community, we draw from related work being done in other disciplines—in different areas of the social sciences, in media studies—forming new communities with those who share our interest in the ways in which the digital world is reshaping not only our literacy practices but many other areas of our lives.

In Part III, as we look at how academic communities share knowledge and build on prior knowledge in making new discoveries, we'll turn to the scholarly articles, blogs, and books that make the sort of work we've been exploring in this book potentially available to a wide audience, and we'll move beyond the public web of Google and other such search engines to explore the scholarly databases that catalog academic work so that others can find it. We'll also consider how you can understand and find your own way into ongoing scholarly conversations by questioning who contributes to them, how such contributions are shaped, and where to find relevant and credible sources. This unit also invites you to contribute to this scholarly process of meaning-making as you step into the academic genres of the proposal and the annotated bibliography, and as you move through your own ethnographic, archival, or literature-review-based project. You will also consider how to collect, organize, and present your work in a professional portfolio.

As you work through these academic genres, you will once again focus on writing moves to extend the work you began as you worked through Part I and/or Part II of this book. This section invites you to consider moves central to academic endeavors, such as the following.

- Moves to establish a conversation: drawing your readers into a particular focus as you establish the significance of your work

- Moves to enter an existing conversation: summarizing, paraphrasing, and acknowledging the work of other scholars to create a strong sense of ethos in your own work

- Moves to extend a conversation: synthesizing sources to generate and articulate your own realizations and conclusions (no matter how tentative those might be)

- Moves to reflect on, share, and present the understandings you've gained throughout your work

Part III invites you into the academic research process in ways that will support your work not only in your composition class, but across courses. Specializing in a particular major involves understanding and, ideally, joining the academic conversation central to an academic or professional field. The following chapters are intended to help you understand more about the process of entering the conversations of academic discourse communities—not only those of composition and literacy and media studies, but other fields as well, and we encourage you to return to them as you do work across your campus.

Planning Research
in Context

CHAPTER SEVENTEEN

CENTRAL QUESTIONS

1 How have shifting digital literacy practices reshaped approaches to research?

2 How can we draw on the potentials of networked and mediated digital spaces as we carve out a research project and agenda?

3 How can composing a research proposal help us think through a particular project and imagine its significance to our own learning? How might we, as researchers, see ourselves contributing to a larger conversation through our work?

Chapter Preview

The digital world has had profound effects on the ways in which we search for information, making it easy to find quick answers to questions that arise in daily life. But this ease raises concerns about how we approach more serious and academic research projects. According to a <u>Pew Research Center Report</u>[17:1, L17:1] on technology and education, teachers find that "'doing research' has shifted from a relatively slow process of intellectual curiosity and discovery to a fast-paced, short-term exercise aimed at locating just enough information to complete an assignment." This chapter encourages you to resist the immediate pressure of such "just enough" research and helps you develop strategies to foster and extend your own sense of intellectual curiosity as you plan a research project. With this chapter you will articulate a focus for a systematic and contextualized research undertaking, work that you'll build on in the next two chapters.

An important part of conducting research is establishing a clear sense of what you want to study, why your project is significant, and how to move through your process in productive and generative ways. While the research process is often messy (much messier than our quick Google searches suggest), taking time to question your intentions (even when they are in response to a fairly specific assignment) can help you think through your process more fully, to go beyond completing an assignment to see your work as a moment for making meaning. In this chapter, we'll ask you to reflect on what you know about doing serious research in a digital context, consider how you can build on the skills you've developed from your ordinary quick online searches to support an extended discovery process, explore what an effective research process looks like in today's academic environment, and to compose a proposal for a research study that will let you find a foothold in the academic conversation this book has been drawing on.

Exploring
The Research Process in a Digital Environment

link

In Nicholas Carr's 2008 essay for *The Atlantic*, "Is Google Making Us Stupid?"[17:2] (in Part II Additional Readings), he describes the advantages he finds, as a writer, to using internet search engines:

> The Web has been a godsend to me as a writer. Research that once required days in the stacks or periodical rooms of libraries can now be done in minutes. A few Google searches, some quick clicks on hyperlinks, and I've got the telltale fact or pithy quote I was after. Even when I'm not working, I'm as likely as not to be foraging in the Web's info-thickets reading and writing e-mails, scanning headlines and blog posts, watching videos and listening to podcasts, or just tripping from link to link to link.

At the same time, Carr cites research showing that online users of major research libraries "exhibited 'a form of skimming activity,' hopping from one source to another and rarely returning to any source they'd already visited. They typically read no more than one or two pages of an article or book before they would 'bounce' out to another site," and he wonders whether, as we spread our attention out across the digital landscape, we are losing the ability to read and think deeply.

Like Carr, and like most people today, you probably use the internet for research frequently in your daily life, using Google and other search engines to find quick answers to questions that arise about current or historical events, about games or movies, about singers and bands, as well as about topics you're exploring for school projects. These quick searches might not actually feel much like research, but they do show us how we relate to information—how we seek it out and how we interpret it.

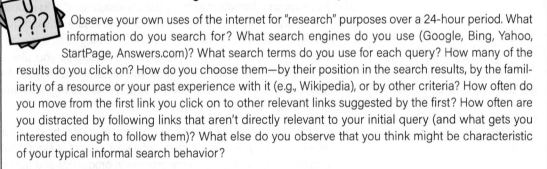

INQUIRY

#1: Considering casual research practices

Observe your own uses of the internet for "research" purposes over a 24-hour period. What information do you search for? What search engines do you use (Google, Bing, Yahoo, StartPage, Answers.com)? What search terms do you use for each query? How many of the results do you click on? How do you choose them—by their position in the search results, by the familiarity of a resource or your past experience with it (e.g., Wikipedia), or by other criteria? How often do you move from the first link you click on to other relevant links suggested by the first? How often are you distracted by following links that aren't directly relevant to your initial query (and what gets you interested enough to follow them)? What else do you observe that you think might be characteristic of your typical informal search behavior?

Observing your casual, everyday "research" process gives you a starting point to think about how you might approach a more intentional and sustained topic-focused inquiry.

#2: Stepping into a more focused process

For this inquiry, you'll want to set aside whatever you think might be the "right way" to search online and just do whatever seems right to you at the moment. Begin your exploration by identifying a question related to our inquiry into digital literacies. Trace your process for that inquiry. Does your search behavior change from your casual search practices?

Making notes about your own thoughts as you proceed, try to find two informative and useful blog or website posts related to your inquiry. What do you use as search terms? Once your search generates pages of results, how do you decide which to pursue? As you go to specific sites, make notes about your own interaction with each site and how you decide whether to linger and make the site one of the two you'll choose. What captures your attention? What holds your interest? How does your interaction with the sites in this more focused and intentional search differ from how you looked at sites when searching more casually? What makes you feel that the information on this site might be reliable (or not)?

Then compare notes about your own processes with your classmates', looking for common elements in your search behaviors. What do the patterns you identify tell you about your most-used search practices and skills? What might you build on as you take on a larger academic research project? What might you alter? Did the different focuses and purposes of your searches affect your processes?

Evaluating Site Credibility

In considering your online research practices, you'll want to step back and think about how you interact with content online (Figure 17.1). What did you find that you look for when a casual search lands you at an online site? Do you grab the information and run, or do you linger and poke around a bit, trying to work out how much you can rely on the information you've found? What informal strategies do you use in your everyday searches for information to find online content you can trust? Once you've reached possible sites for information, how do you decide whether to spend time with them or move on? If you do linger, how do you decide whether to trust the information you find there?

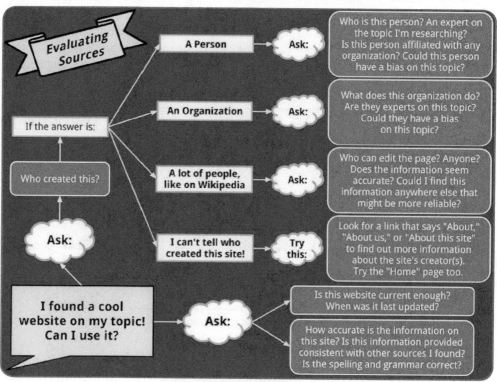

Figure 17.1: Evaluating sources

The question of how people find information online they feel they can trust has been of concern to researchers in a number of fields from health care to marketing. There seem to be four elements that contribute to a sense of site credibility:

❶ Position in search engine results, with the first results seen as pointing to more credible sites, even when the top links were marked as paid for.[17:3] (Unfortunately, search result positioning is related to many factors—as can be seen by the controversy that erupts every time Google changes its algorithm for generating these results, and position is not a good determiner of site credibility.)

❷ The visual appearance of the website: the interface design, including fonts, organization, and attention to detail.[17:4]

❸ The content: accuracy, relevance, and who posted it.[17:4]

❹ How the information on one site compares to that on others.[17:3]

Other studies have shown that people searching for information about a particular topic online typically start with a rapid screening of their search results before focusing on a few in more depth. Once some promising sites have been found, searchers use several criteria to decide whether to trust the content. Those searching for medical information, for example, looked for the expertise behind the site (reputable medical organizations), how accessible the information was (FAQs helped foster trust), and whether they could identify personally with what was presented (with familiar language and more personalized content).[17:5] Other factors may also contribute to your sense of whether a site is to be trusted.

Increasingly, websites are tied into a larger textual ecology of linked sites and related social media, and information about both the site and its textual context becomes important to evaluating site credibility. Most university libraries offer information about how to evaluate websites for scholarly purposes, asking questions about audience and purpose, the website's authority (whether it has an institutional home like a university or government agency, for example) and that of any author, the accuracy and objectivity of the content, and its timeliness (look to see if your library provides such a resource). EasyBib, an online application for creating a bibliography, has created a visual guide to determining whether websites are credible[L17:2] (Figure 17.2).

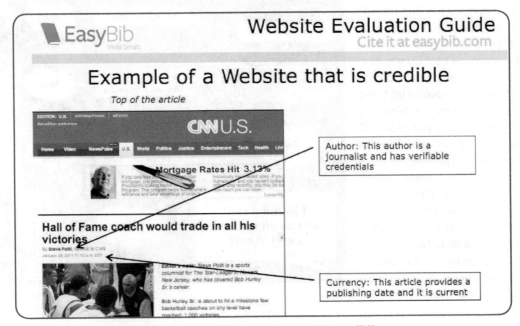

Figure 17.2: EasyBib comments on website credibility

Andrew Walsh, an academic librarian, describes on his website his own additional criteria for evaluation of sites for more casual/personal purposes.[17:6] He notes three important elements in his evaluation: how the authors introduce themselves; whether (if the author is affiliated with a commercial enterprise) the author's comments come across as "personal, honest observations or recycled corporate sales copy;" and whether and how an author uses social media:

> Also, are there social sharing buttons on the website's individual posts? How many times have they been retweeted, shared on Facebook or Google +1'ed across the web? Is it easy to leave comments, and do the authors respond to their readers?

INQUIRY

#3: Evaluating online site credibility

??? How do these ways that others have found to determine site credibility compare with your own informal processes? How important were the following elements to you?

➤ Position in search results

➤ Visual appearance and accessibility of information

➤ Content and apparent expertise

➤ How information compared across sites

➤ How much you could personally identify with what was presented

What would you now list as some elements to consider in determining whether to trust content you find online? As you look back at the posts you chose in Inquiry #2, how would you now evaluate their credibility for seeking general information in a casual search? For more focused but preliminary searches related to the research topic you'll pursue? Would you add any elements that you hadn't considered before? Can you create a rubric to guide others' evaluation of this sort of post (or the composer's revision of it)?

Working Systematically and Using a Research Platform

As you move from informal queries to sustained research it becomes important not only to evaluate the credibility of the sites you visit and the information they cover, but also to become systematic in collecting and organizing the information you gather and the resources you use. Considering how to do this from the beginning will help you to keep track of everything you need in the complex process of researching, from thinking about a topic to revising a final paper. It also positions you to be more intentional about your process and how you are thinking about your focus.

A research platform, a central online location like a blog or wiki that helps you organize your process, can support an intentional approach. Before deciding on a platform, you need to consider what you'll do with it. An effective platform should allow you to carry out two main functions.

1. Thinking and meaning-making: reflecting on possible topics, initial questions, how you're proceeding, what you're learning from data you collect and sources you consult, and how your own thinking about the topic changes as you go along.

2. Gathering and organizing relevant information: recording your process and methods, collecting data that can help you answer and refine your initial questions and can show you what others have learned from similar inquiries, taking notes from your sources, keeping track of the important information about those sources.

Both gathering information and thinking/reflecting/making your own meaning from that information are essential aspects of the research process, and researchers often distinguish between keeping a research diary or log for information and data-gathering and a research journal for thinking/reflecting. However, we'll combine both in our discussion of a **digital research journal**—a journal in which you'll move between one function and the other in much the way we suggested in Chapter 5 for using a double-entry notebook.

You can do all of your note-taking and reflection with paper and pencil, of course (or on the index cards that were traditionally used in such projects), but it makes sense, in the context of our larger inquiry into new literacies and the practices made possible by new technologies, to use a digital platform. There is more information about digital platforms in the Part IV Digital Toolbox, and your class might have access to others that will enhance or constrain your choices. Whatever you use, you'll want to be sure it supports the dual activities of information-gathering and reflection.

As both Nicholas Carr and the Pew Research Center Report we cite in this chapter suggest, slowing down your research is important, and a digital research journal can help you do that by creating a space to collect ideas and materials and reflect on them. This will help you move beyond "just tripping from link to link to link" as you engage "a relatively slow process of intellectual curiosity and discovery."

Digital Toolbox
See Part IV, Section 1

INQUIRY

#4: Starting a digital research journal

Consider platforms that are familiar from your earlier work and their strengths and weaknesses for collecting data, recording notes from resources, making key connections/understandings, and reflecting on your process and the information you're gathering. Based on your earlier work, generate a list of questions about what you think you'll want in a digital research journal, and then compare the platforms available to you. How easy might it be to organize your information/reflections using each platform? Does the platform support sharing your work in progress and gathering responses from others? Does it let you upload relevant documents? Is it familiar to you and easy to work with (or not) from your earlier experience with it? You might create a comparison chart for the platforms you're considering, with the features you most value.

While we and our students have used blogs, wikis, Google Docs, and the journaling options in different online course platforms like Blackboard, Canvas, and Moodle, our personal favorite for the sort of collaborative research and writing that went into this book is a wiki because it allows us to upload materials, share and comment easily, while adding new pages and changing the organization as a project takes shape. Here, for example, is a student's project proposal page for a project in one of our courses (Figure 17.3).

Digital Toolbox
See Part IV, Section 2

Unit 2 Project Proposal

✏ Edit 💬 1 🕓 3 ...

🔍 Search

Proposal Paragraph

I plan on reading Chapters 8 and 9 of L&L to give me a jumping-off point and then examining the following literary works:

Jamaica Kincaid's <u>Girl</u>

Leslie Marmon Silko's <u>Storyteller</u>

Tony Cade Bambara's <u>The Lesson</u>

Although I chose the "Language and school contexts" option, it is more the "lesson-learning contexts" that I will be focusing on, instead of the "school context". None of these three texts are typical school environments, there are certainly strong lessons learned in all three and that's what I want to focus on. I plan on juxtaposing the purpose of "lesson-learning" with the different purposes within each story. I will examine the different uses of languages and dialects, paying special attention to why the different types of variant forms of langues are used in each of the different stories and situations. I plan on using the following lenses:

Home

Unit Two Project
Introduction
Excerpt 1
Excerpt 2
Excerpt 3
Conclusion
Bibliography

Unit Two Research Journal
Exploration
Proposal Paragraph

Research Journal

Figure 17.3: A student's project proposal page on a wiki

You can see from the sidebar navigation that she has integrated her proposal and her research journal pages with all the other elements of her project, while using the main part of the page to describe her proposal.

Reflecting on Prior Knowledge and New Questions

Although there are many, many questions you could ask related to the themes of this book, it's generally a good idea to follow up on a topic you've already begun to explore through your earlier inquiries. That way, you can build on your own prior knowledge, adding to it as you focus on a new or related question. Whatever process of data-gathering and/or analysis contributed to the understandings you've developed so far, as you further your research, you'll want to take into account what others have learned about the topic. Perhaps the Facebook examples in our early chapters and/or a community profile study that drew on your friends' use of Facebook has made you want to learn more about the use of Facebook among college students, for example. If so, you'll want at this point to consider what you've already learned that's relevant to this topic, what resources you've already found, and what more you want to discover.

INQUIRY

#5: Preliminary research journal reflection

Consider your own earlier inquiries into new literacies, social media, textual ecologies, and composing in local and global digital environments as you've collected data and composed reflections, analyses, and arguments. Identify one area in which your own work would be enriched by a deeper understanding of what others have discovered about this topic. What new questions have emerged through your earlier research that you might explore through the work of others, as well as, perhaps, through gathering new data? Why do you want to explore this topic? Do you think it will contribute to the knowledge of your larger community? Are others in your classroom community interested in related topics, opening up the possibility of collaborative research where you each explore a common topic from different angles? Post this first reflection to your choice of research platform.

Considering Common Research Genres: The Ethnographic Study, the Archival Study, the Literature Review

There are many shapes and forms that the design of research and reporting on that research can take. We'll focus on three common genres in the academic world, two of which you've probably been working with in your earlier projects: the ethnographic study, the archival study, and the literature review. As we work through these chapters, we'll draw on an example of a student's community profile project from our Part I readings, "Bookworm Buddies" by Hannah Morgan, showing how Hannah might build on it as she expands her research.

INQUIRY

#6: Reading as a researcher

Read quickly through Hannah's community profile to get a sense of the online book group she has been studying and what she's discovered thus far about their interactions. How has she collected data? What patterns has she found? What has she learned from this study, and what questions might she explore with further research?

> **primary research**
> a process of inquiry grounded by sources that you identify, seek, and collect yourself
>
> **secondary research**
> a process of inquiry shaped by what others have published on the topic you are considering (in books and articles, for instance)

A distinction is often made between **primary research**, where you are making observations, gathering data, and doing analysis yourself, and **secondary research**, where you are drawing on and synthesizing the primary research and analysis that others have done. While ethnographic and archival studies are considered primary research, they typically draw on others' research as well, so a brief version of the literature review, surveying earlier research on your topic, is likely to be a component of these first two genres, as well as a stand-alone research genre. Other common methods of primary research (outside of science labs) include observation, gathering artifacts, such as photos, and texts, such as social media posts, interviews, and surveys; if you collect data in these ways, you'll also want to point to the research literature that has been published about your topic.

The ethnographic study

Ethnographic research focuses on the study of communities, the objects that are important to life in a community, and people's roles and relationships, their common activities and practices, ways of interacting, their discourse, their arts—everything that can be observed about their lives. Such research was shaped first within the field of anthropology, where often researchers went, as outsiders, to study distant cultures in far parts of the world. But gradually the methods of ethnographic research were focused, not just on distant cultures, but on all sorts of communities in the contemporary world—in workplaces, educational settings, prisons, churches, and online gaming communities. And the methods are now shared across the social sciences and in the fields of composition and literacy studies, with the researcher often in the role of an **insider participant observer**.

Ethnographic research allows us to study the communicative practices of communities in a rich cultural context. For that reason, it has contributed important understandings to the fields of composition and literacy studies and to the study of how people interact in digital environments. Many of the studies you've read and projects you've undertaken in the context of Part I of this book, including those of Deborah Brandt, danah boyd, and Nancy Baym, have drawn on ethnographic methods.

If you decide to expand an earlier community profile or begin a new one, you'll want to gather your data on acts of communication in the community in systematic ways.

- Keeping an observation notebook as part of your research journal, noting the **where**, the context, and connecting the details of **what** you observe in any interactions or posts and with your reflections on **how** it's carried out and **why** it takes place in these ways. A double-entry notebook format, first introduced in Chapter 5, with one column for observations and the other for reflections, is particularly useful for this purpose.

- Capturing the data of posts and exchanges with screenshots (as Hannah has done) or audio or video recordings. Again you'll want to make notes about the context, the **where**, for these instances, and the **what**, **why**, and **how**, and you'll want to transcribe any audio segments you'll focus on for closer analysis.

- Interviewing. Once you've gathered data and developed some preliminary questions and hypotheses about what's going on and why in your setting, you might want to get the perspectives of participants (or additional participants) in that setting. If you have a way to contact them individually, you might ask them to participate in an interview, online (using FaceTime or Skype) or face to face. You can also ask them to provide written responses to questions, but a real-time exchange allows you to ask follow-up questions or open up more exploratory discourse into related areas you hadn't thought of before.

- Surveying. You can also get the perspectives of participants by asking them to respond to an online survey that you can easily construct with a tool like SurveyMonkey. Surveys aren't flexible like interviews, and they are less connected to the original communicative context, but they can nevertheless be a quick way of getting information about the perspectives of a larger group of participants. For Hannah's study of a large online book group, a survey asking questions about when members chose to join in a conversation and why might offer additional support for patterns she's already seen or new possibilities she hasn't thought of.

insider participant observer
a researcher who studies a community he or she also takes part in

Archival research

When a community, a group, or an individual gathers materials of any sort (including digital materials), those materials become available as resources to tell us more about past or present ways and meanings. Libraries may be the holders of archival collections of historical documents, the unpublished work and letters of a writer, and collections of historical photographs. Government entities typically have their own archives, such as the U.S. National Archives and Records Administration,[L17:3] and the Library of Congress.[L17:4] Universities often have archives related to their location and mission. University of Massachusetts Boston's Archives and Special Collections,[L17:5] for example, contain a wealth of documents and photographs and oral history interviews related to local community history and culture. Many such collections have been digitized, allowing easy internet access and searching, and the UMass Boston digital collection includes photos and stories shared by ordinary people around the state as part of an ongoing Mass. Memories Road Show.[L17:6] Your own college or university library may have similar collections that can support your own primary research project.

You might also have your personal or family collection of papers and/or photographs that can provide resources for an archival study. A digital collection, such as photos posted to Instagram, Picasa, Pinterest, or Facebook, can also be used as archives. In Chapter 6, we suggested some ways in which such resources could be used to engage in cultural analysis, and we considered José van Dijck's argument that photographs are being used in different ways and have different meanings for young people in a digital age. Materials you may have gathered and questions that may have arisen in that project can lend themselves to a fuller archival study. Or you might have gathered a collection of memes that have circulated in a particular context in your work for Part II and be interested in understanding that collection in relation to other research on memes and why they circulate.

Hannah's interest in her current book group might lead her to shift gears and do an archival study, gathering artifacts related to her own earlier reading experiences that might have involved childhood digital literacy or that might be contrasted to the digital experiences of a younger sibling or acquaintance. She could gather favorite childhood books she might have kept, her own early book-writing efforts for school, book reports she wrote in high school, photos of reading or being read to as a child at home or in a classroom, along with examples of the online reading activities she or a young friend was involved in as a child. Archival collections often include oral histories, and she might want to record the digital literacy memories of her parents or siblings. Or she might treat her present library (physical or digital) as an archive, exploring the relationship between the fuller representation of her own reading and the portion that's represented in online discussions.

The literature review

When we think of a typical college-level library research project (whether we access materials in the library or online), it's most often the literature review we have in mind. This research genre focuses on discovering what others have learned about a particular topic (research that's secondary to you because you're not collecting the primary ethnographic data or working with the primary documents in an archive), and it involves drawing on their studies to answer your own questions and carry out your own explorations. It attempts to answer the question "What is the current state of knowledge about this topic?" A literature review component that quickly summarizes the most important, relevant recent work is typically included in other research studies, including ethnographic and archival studies. But the literature review often stands alone as well. If you have become interested in a question you might not be able to explore easily through your own primary research, such as how the use of digital media affects young children's development over the preschool years, you'll need to rely wholly on the work of other researchers (starting perhaps with the 2014 Harvard Family Research Spotlight Report: "Families and Digital Media in Young Children's Learning"[17:7]). Almost any question we've begun to explore in the context of this book can lead to a rich literature review study.

If she continues her ethnographic research, Hannah will search for literature related to online book groups, and perhaps other online groups like fan groups (she's already noted that some of the patterns she has observed echo those found by Nancy Baym). An archival study of earlier literacy artifacts might lead her to studies of children's literacy, or a study of her own print/digital library archive might lead her to learn more about what other studies show about why people choose digital or print formats, or about the recent history of changing reading patterns. Or she might become interested in the question of whether online book clubs can support the reading of middle and high school students, a topic she can't gather direct data for at this moment, but can explore with a more extended literature review.

We discuss the **how** of each of these research genres in more detail in Chapter 19, but you'll want to consider which will work best for the questions you want to explore as you begin to plan your work.

We've seen several examples of studies using ethnographic methods: Deborah Brandt's study of Genna May's early twentieth century literacy in Chapter 1, danah boyd's blog report on how Carmen hides her real concerns from her mother in her Facebook posts in Chapter 3, Nancy Baym's study of the interactions of her online fan community in Chapter 8, and Martin Lindstrom's exploration of what children valued that might keep them involved with Legos from Chapter 16. Archival studies including José van Dijck's use of digital and "shoebox" archives of photos to study how uses of such artifacts are changing in a digital age (Chapter 6), and the various archives of Rosie the Riveter, both in the Library of Congress and on various websites and Pinterest boards (Chapter 14), offered a model for curating your own archival collection. Many of the larger books or articles from which we've drawn readings also include literature reviews.

INQUIRY

#7: Considering common research genres

Consider the features of ethnographic, archival, and literature review approaches and how they might fit your research interests and questions. Are your questions likely to be answered by gathering further data about a group in the ways you've done in many earlier inquiries (the ethnographic study)? Might they be answered by creating and working with a personal or community digital collection/archive of artifacts or by working with a collection held by a library (the archival study)? In each case, consider other examples we've looked at and notice how the writers have brought in other relevant studies, connecting to some of the research literature that already exists on this topic.

Alternatively, can your own questions be pursued wholly by focusing on the existing research literature or by putting that research literature together with data you've already gathered? In that case, you might choose to carry out a more extensive literature review. Explore the advantages and disadvantages of each type of study for answering the tentative questions you want to research.

INQUIRY

#8: Gathering more primary data

If your study will focus, in part, on primary data you've gathered, you may want to gather more as you begin to see what other research has been done that's related to your topic. Take a few minutes to describe what you've collected from earlier projects about the community and the question you want to study. Are there other sorts of data you might collect to give you a fuller picture?

Addressing Ethical Concerns

In gathering data, whether online or face to face, it's important to protect the identities of those you're studying unless they have chosen to make them public. We've gotten permission from students whose posts or studies we've included in this book, but we've also intentionally used pseudonyms in examples of students' Facebook or other online posts, and for other writing if a student has requested anonymity. When a large group is included (as in a book group with more than 500 participants), full names aren't given and more personal information isn't shared, so there's less likelihood of a privacy concern. Ethical concerns about the use of online information when the writer doesn't know what he or she has posted might be used outside of the original context have been the subject of much discussion among researchers. We list a useful guide to ethics for social media researchers in the chapter resources.

For your own research purposes and in classroom contexts, it's generally safe to assume you can use material that has been made available to the public, on any platform, as long as you credit the composer of any original material. But sometimes people accidentally post publicly something they had only intended for private sharing, so it's important to check with friends and family members before using material that seems to include anything personal. If you're gathering unpublished writing or photos or friendship circle posts or audio files, you should ask permission to use them, specifying whether they'll be shared only in your immediate research context or perhaps on a blog or website that will be made public, and whether the person would prefer to be identified with a pseudonym.

> **INQUIRY**
>
> ### #9: Considering the need for permissions
>
> If you plan to propose an ethnographic or archival study, this is a good time to review the material you've gathered or will gather, to make sure you are in a position to share it. Make a list of any materials for which you might need permissions and add to it as you go along. Create a simple form to use when permissions are needed, specifying what will be used and how. An email response is acceptable. See example in Figure 17.4.

I give permission to (your name) to use my Facebook posts of (dates) or my Instagram photo (description and date) for a course research project. This material may be shared

___ with members of the classroom community only.

___ on a closed online site within the college or university.

___ on a publically accessible site.

I prefer to be

___ acknowledged with my real name.

___ identified with a pseudonym.

Signed: _____

Date: _____

Figure 17.4: Sample permission form

Making Connections
Locating the Relevant Conversations

Once you've identified a topic you'd like to explore in more detail, considered the type of study that will help you examine your focus in close and careful ways, and have generated some initial questions, you can begin to explore what other research has been done that might relate to the topic. You'll want to find out where the conversations addressing the topic occur and what general understandings exist about the topic. In Chapter 18, we will focus more on how you can find specific sources of information and evaluate those sources as you consider new perspectives, but this chapter focuses on how you can learn more about your research project by locating your topic in a larger ongoing conversation. As you come to a richer sense of what you want to say, you should work to get an idea of what has been said before.

The Process of Seeking and Finding New Information

We conduct research and collect sources in informal ways quite often. When we meet a new friend, we explore her photos on Facebook; when we want to find a new restaurant to try, we read reviews. And our informal processes of finding information and evaluating what we find offer practice for doing the same in more formal ways in academic contexts.

> **INQUIRY**
>
> ### #10: Building on your existing research strategies
>
> Go back to your observations of your own "research" at the start of this chapter. What do these informal undertakings show about finding information, coming to a sense of consensus, evaluating sources, and allowing new perspectives to shape your understandings? What moves or strategies can you take from those experiences as you approach a more systematic research undertaking?

We hope you can see that these major moves of research are already part of your daily repertoire outside of the academic world. Nevertheless, it can feel overwhelming at first to make the transition from real-life research, and even high school research, to what's expected within the academic discourse communities of a college or university. Studies of freshman researchers have shown both that they have some useful strategies to draw on as they carry out a research project and that they find some things about their new context overwhelming. Like much else about learning, the experience of students as researchers has been studied, and the following excerpt from a 2013 study of almost 2,000 first-year college students at six different schools offers a sense of their concerns as they work through this process.

BEFORE READING:
"Learning the Ropes"

As you read the following excerpt from the research report, annotate and comment on the elements that represent your own concerns, things you'd like to know more about, and things you feel pretty confident about at this point.

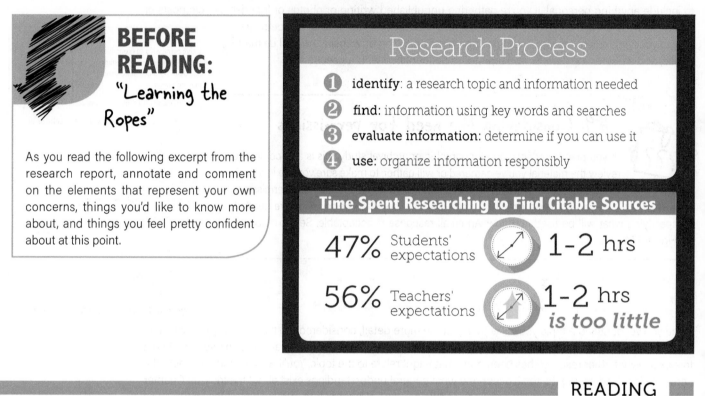

Research Process

1. **identify**: a research topic and information needed
2. **find**: information using key words and searches
3. **evaluate information**: determine if you can use it
4. **use**: organize information responsibly

Time Spent Researching to Find Citable Sources

47% Students' expectations ⟋ **1-2** hrs

56% Teachers' expectations ⟋ **1-2** hrs *is too little*

Place annotations here

READING

Selection from
"Learning the Ropes: How Freshmen Conduct Course Research Once They Enter College"[17:8]
by Alison Head
Project Information Literacy, December 4, 2013

Here's how the college research process is defined in the report:

The college research process involves interpreting, evaluating, and synthesizing the information sources that have been found. Through this discovery process, students become more knowledgeable about a topic. They are expected to make inferences and formulate an original proposition, argument, or what some students refer to as their "thesis." The expected depth of investigation combined with using primary sources makes college research time-consuming.

A critical part of college-level research setting it apart from high school research is the necessity of "re-researching" a topic. Like photographers, students need to focus on their subject and then adjust and readjust the focus, as needed, as the discovery process unfolds.

READING

The expected depth of investigation combined with using primary sources makes college research time-consuming. It usually takes skill to integrate scholarly sources and infer a broader meaning from them. It takes curiosity and a desire to learn something new. It also takes keen organizational skills to keep track of and document everything that has been found.

And here are some students' reflections on their research process, grouped by the areas of concern the researchers found. If you've been experiencing any of these difficulties, you'll find you are not alone.

Difficulties with the College Research Process

1) Formulating effective and efficient online searches. A large majority said they were challenged by figuring out key words for unlocking the wealth of academic sources available to them through their campus library's portal. Some said they used Google in a two-step workaround. In the first step, these students did a Google search to see what key words popped up, and then they placed some of these terms in a library database's search engine. Others grappled with finding a preconceived idea of a "perfect source" they needed. These students often had trouble translating their perfect sources into key words that met the precise syntax library databases require:

> We had to do a paper about something that affects children in a negative way and I chose how moving affects children and their development and how they socialize with other people. It took me an hour to know what words to use. I was sitting there using my laptop and it was really hard because I was typing 'families that move a lot' and I saw nomads come up, and I thought, maybe nomads would be something, like 'nomadic families,' but that had nothing to do with it. It's that anxiety when you type in words and none of the words match the results and you're like, okay, let me try this, and you have a limited amount of time—that's a problem.

Grinding through endless screens and trying to cull relevant material was another frustrating part of search, according to many of the freshmen we interviewed. These students said if they could "crank down"—narrow—their search queries beforehand, they were more likely to reap useful results. But for many, searching on library database interfaces was entirely new, and it was difficult to figure out how different search engines worked. After spending years defaulting to Google searches for finding information, others said they were lost when it came to incorporating Boolean operators and faceted searching into their strategies:

> You have to really put in the right words into the academic search engine. Sometimes I'd put in a word like I'd do in a Google search and it pulls up things that I'm not looking for. The librarian came to our class and told us how to do this certain search logic, and so when you use that it is a lot easier to find the sources you're looking for. But, I've noticed that if you try to use an academic search engine like you'd use a Google search, it won't work as effectively, so it takes knowing how to different search engines work.

2) Identifying, selecting, and locating sources. A majority of freshmen in our sample said they were overwhelmed by the variety, quantity, and newness of potential sources available through their campus library:

> So, I'd go onto the Internet, click on library, click on e-sources, and, there would be all these different types of subcategories, and I was like, 'What do I use?' Do I use EBSCO or do I use Britannica or all these other things? That is what made it difficult, because I really didn't know which link to click on.

Unlike high school work, college-level research seemed to have an infinite number of ways to find sources, according to the interviewees. First-term freshmen often described having floors of books, portals full of library databases, and scientific findings and sources from the public Web they could access for college-level research assignments. Some students were confused by the practice of combining

Place annotations here

Place annotations here

familiar sources (e.g., books, Google) with unfamiliar sources (e.g., PubMed, JSTOR).

In other cases, some students had a hard time keeping track of notes, articles, and quotes from the different kinds of online and print sources they had found. In their words, hunting down print sources from a list of citations could be "tedious," "full of surprises," "unpredictable," and "confusing." Even though some said finding sources was easy for them, many often learned otherwise once they tried to locate specific sources:

> One of the criteria was to gather an outside source on your own and then a source that Deborah Tannen cites in her book. So, at first, it was kind of a challenge to go through the whole list of sources and try to find one of the sources here. Some of them were books and some of them were articles. I would find a book but then realize the library has access through some other library on the other side of the state and they could have gotten it but it would have taken weeks, and it wouldn't really help. Then, I found some articles with reviews, but it wasn't the full article, just some review. Some were here, but not here and were at different libraries on campus.

3) Reading, comprehending, and summarizing materials. Once they had some trusted sources in hand, about a third of the freshmen said they floundered with reading different formats and making sense of what they had found. Many had never seen, let alone read a journal article or an abstract before. At the same time, students wrestled with understanding what authors meant, given their lack of familiarity with scholarly language and writing style. A few students mentioned that they used an online dictionary as they read to help them understand the terminology in journal articles...about a third of the freshmen said they floundered with reading different formats and making sense of what they had found.

> It's the reading, deciphering what you've found that's most difficult. So, I used an online dictionary to figure out words meant for my paper on nanotechnology. I mean I read three sentences and I would need to go look up seven words out of those three sentences! It worked for me, I learned a lot from reading like this. It's the only way to understand what they are saying, I mean if you are not reading with a dictionary then you won't be able to get it. It's just what it takes.

Some freshmen we interviewed said they had trouble with selecting meaningful passages and tying it all together. In their words, they had problems "connecting the dots," "figuring out the hook," and "discerning what you're going to use." They purposely selected sources from the results page that had a common thesis or similar interpretation of the same set of facts, as a way of gauging the credibility. As one student explained, "I know if it's printed several places, then it's true and I can use it." In other cases, students had trouble selecting which quotes to include in their papers:

> How do you read a 30-page article and pick out a few meaningful quotes? I mean what is the right, exact quote to select and use? I am just kind of picking from here and picking from here and there for this paper. I just don't know. I mean is the writing I do in my composition course representative of the rest of the writing I do in college? ■

Boolean operators
the terms used to connect two or more words in a search (AND, OR, NOT, or AND NOT)

faceted search
type of search that lets you choose or rule out categories of materials, such as articles versus books

AFTER READING:
Taking stock of your own experiences and understandings

How does the description of the research process offered in this report compare with your own understanding? How has your own prior research experience prepared you for such work? What strengths, understandings, and prior knowledge do you bring to the research you're undertaking, and what more do you hope to learn about the process as you pursue your topic? As you read this report, did you find that some terms, such as "**Boolean operators**" and "**faceted search**," were new to you? Generate a group or class list of search process questions and areas in which you'd like more guidance.

INQUIRY

#11: An informal online exploration

Drawing on one of your new questions about your research topic, begin an informal online exploration of relevant resources, keeping notes in your research journal about your process and strategies.

One way to keep track of relevant resources is to take screenshots of them and save them in a digital folder (which you can upload to your blog or wiki). Once you have taken and filed shots of 10 or 12 possible sources, look back at them. What do they seem to focus on? Who do they seem to address? What can you say about the images they draw on? The points they make? Based on this informal exploration, come to some tentative conclusions about your research focus. What might this suggest about where to turn from here?

Once you have completed and reflected on this informal search, share your findings with your classmates. You could do this by sharing your actual sources or just the notes you took about them. As a group, what conclusions can you come to about the research process after pooling your experiences and resources? What does this suggest about digital research on the free web? What strategies does it push you toward as you begin a more formal and systematic approach to your inquiry?

Digital Toolbox
See Part IV, Section 5

Chapter 18 will guide you through a more formal search process that involves the scholarly databases that the students in the "Learning the Ropes" report were concerned with. But for the moment, focus on your own "discovery process," and approach your research in an exploratory way, drawing first on your own prior knowledge and strategies.

Disciplinary Perspectives: Who Studies Related Topics and Questions?

Scholarly research is mostly discipline-specific. If you're interested in how and why college students use Facebook, for example, you'll find some studies in journals from the field of psychology and other behavioral sciences, some in computer and technology journals, some in journals in the field of education, and some in composition journals. General search strategies can offer useful material, and common resources like Wikipedia and Google can be used critically as a "preresearch" starting point.

Wikipedia offers general background information about a vast array of topics, but rarely for the sorts of combinations you might need to pursue. If you're interested in a question about "college students" and "Facebook," for example, you won't find an entry combining those terms, but you can get a lot of background information about Facebook, as well as a list of suggested related topics that include "social media." The social media entry addresses a number of topics, like loneliness or social media in the classroom, that could potentially be useful to you. Most Wikipedia articles are footnoted with references at the end, and the social media entry includes some sources that are included in our own readings, including the Gladwell essay on social media and revolutions. Such footnotes can offer a starting point for authoritative articles about your topic, even if the entry itself is the product of a more collaborative endeavor that may or may not have such authorities as contributors.

A search on Google using its general search engine (we'll discuss Google Scholar in the next chapter) is likely to bring up more short news articles and blog posts, but often these more popular texts reference academic research studies. A search on college students and Facebook can bring up news articles about students' use of this form of social media (and whether it's declining), about classroom uses, as well as Facebook pages from student groups at different colleges. A 2015 *Huffington Post* article[17:9] reports on a study showing that while college students from different backgrounds spend about the same amount of time on Facebook, those from lower socio-economic backgrounds use it less for connecting and communication. The article links to the original study and points out other relevant research, making even this popular news source a potentially valuable resource for some inquiries. Doing a search for the authors of research articles is also a way of determining how much of an authority someone is likely to be on the topic.

INQUIRY

#12: Searching the popular web

Use Wikipedia as a starting point for a search related to your topic. What topic searches provide useful background information? Do any entries point you to useful research reports or scholarly articles you might want to follow up on? With a general Google search do you find articles that suggest where you might find further information? Check on the information you get through Google about one or two of the authors or researchers Wikipedia or your general Google searches point you to. Do you find information that leads you to think that their work might be authoritative and reliable sources for your own study?

Beyond the popular web, you can find an easily accessible search engine for scholars. Hidden behind the "more" tab on Google, you'll find a "still more" tab that will lead you to Google Scholar. (This is true on a computer screen, but not on a tablet, where you'll have to put in the URL scholar.google.com.) Google Scholar is, as its name suggests, is a wonderful resource for scholars, allowing a quick and easy search for a vast array of academic scholarship and research. Many of the articles that a search will bring up will appear in subscription-only journals, but those are often journals your library subscribes to in an online form, and your college or university library may provide a direct link from Google Scholar to those articles when you sign into the library portal.

One tool this search engine provides is the ability to see who has cited a source. This provides a sense of how a piece is situated in the larger conversations that go on around issues. If you were to search the key words "composition" and "circulation" on Google Scholar, you might notice that one of the texts listed—Kathleen Yancey's article "Made Not Only in Words"—has been cited by 129 other pieces or more. From that, you can tell this piece is important to many people's thinking about this topic.

Once you've found some useful articles through any of these resources, you can use the links that appear in them, their lists of works cited and references, and tools like "Cited by" to get a sense of how communities of readers form around topics.

INQUIRY

#13: Using Google Scholar to consider communities of readers

To explore the community of readers and scholars who might be involved with your topic, conduct a search on Google Scholar and select one source that speaks to your research interest. What other sources are linked to from this source? (If it is a digital text, it might contain links.) Who is cited? By whom is it cited? Does the journal it appears in (and/or the pattern of citations) link it to a particular disciplinary field? Who is invested in this issue? What scholarly community might you be addressing with your own study?

> **INQUIRY**
>
> **#14: Reflecting on possible audiences in your research journal**
>
> Based on your investigation thus far, what can you say about the audience you might envision as you work through your research? What communities might be interested in your inquiry? What academic or professional disciplines might you be addressing? Depending on the direction she chooses for her further research, Hannah might imagine an audience of her online book group participants or those who might consider joining, or other researchers of communication in digital environments (including her classmates), or educators interested in supporting the development of literacy in digital environments.

Composing
Research Proposal

Now that you've done some preliminary thinking about what you know and might build on in your own study—the general topic you'd like to pursue and some questions about it—and you've started to see what kinds of research others have done that's related to your topic, you can begin to define your own project more clearly in a research proposal. As a researcher who will propose your own study, you'll want to consider both the type of project you'll undertake and the elements of the proposal genre. In your proposal you'll sketch out **what** you plan to study, **how** you'll go about it (your methods), and **why**—your purpose in carrying out this research and what you hope to learn and contribute to the shared knowledge about this field.

Research proposals are tentative plans of inquiry. Your proposal will offer a preliminary map for the project you are undertaking and contain your starting questions or hypotheses, the methods you'll use in trying to answer those questions, the data you've gathered or will gather, and what others have learned that's related to your inquiry. The typical research proposal includes all of these elements, although they may be addressed in different ways.

WRITING MOVES ◄

Inquiring and Inventing

Although research proposals are often seen as an impersonal genre, you may place yourself, as a researcher, within your research frame. You've chosen a topic that interests you, focusing perhaps on a cultural group or a digital setting or a set of artifacts, such as digital photos or videos; you've conducted a preliminary inquiry or have done some preliminary reading related to your topic in the course of your work for the semester; and you've begun to discover a little about what studies have been done that relate to your topic (and you've been recording your progress in your research journal). All of that provides a rich foundation for your proposal: the context for its specific details.

1 Freewriting about your research undertaking

Before you begin to shape a formal proposal, do some freewriting about its context—about what you already know about this topic, why you want to go forward with this project, what interests you about it, a moment or quotation that led you to some questions, and what you think now that you've begun to find other sources of information. Some of this will most likely make its way into your introduction, but for the moment, just explore these thoughts freely, recording your thinking in your research journal.

2 Considering your investment in this process

After you have taken some time to compose some generative writing about your topic, consider what it is you are drawn to about this project in more specific terms. How are you positioned to research and write about your topic? What specialized knowledge or relevant experience do you bring to this project? How might your investment or involvement in this topic be reflected in your writing and design?

WRITING MOVES

Drafting and Shaping

The research proposal has several purposes: it gives you an opportunity to plan and order your research; it gives you a chance to take stock of what you know, where you're going, and how you expect to get there; and it allows you to get feedback and guidance about your plan at an early stage. You'll be doing more extended versions of this work in your major field, and the proposals you write then will be shaped to fit the expectations of that discipline. Here we'll focus on what's common to most proposals.

1 Compiling common proposal elements

An introduction (**what**). Here you'll want to create the context, share your initial questions and hypotheses about your topic (which may well change as you carry out further research) and what you know to start, and tell your readers what type of study you plan to carry out.

A statement of purpose (**why**). What are your goals as you carry out this work? What do you hope to learn? Why do you think it might be important? Who might you share it with?

A description of methods (**how**). How do you plan to go about answering your initial questions? Here, if you're drawing on primary data you've already gathered, you'll describe what you gathered and how, and what you'll seek if you gather more. If you will only work with secondary material—with studies that others have already done—your methods will focus only on that effort, but in each case your methods will include seeking out particular strands of others' research that can help you to answer your own questions.

A preliminary literature review. At this early proposal stage you can't say much about what you'll find as you dig into the scholarly literature on your topic. But you can point briefly to what you've found in your early searching and from any of the semester's readings to say something about what you know at this point.

A conclusion. Here you can say or restate what you hope to learn as you go about this research in these ways.

2 Outlining a proposal

For this highly structured genre, it can be particularly useful to create an outline to work from. Here's an outline for a proposal that Nancy Baym might have written as a student researcher just beginning to study her community of soap opera fans.

- **Introduction.** Background about the soap opera I watch and the online fan site that lets us discuss the story we're following. My questions about why and how people are involved in the site: I've noticed that people join our discussion at first because they're just interested in the topic. But they seem to become friends over time. Do aspects of their online interaction contribute to their becoming friends and forming a community?

- **Purpose.** I hope to learn more about how people form friendships and a community when they can only connect online and not face to face. I think this knowledge will help me to be a more effective member of this group, and it might contribute to general knowledge about how such online fan groups work.

- **Methods.** I've already collected transcripts of many of our interactions on the discussion site. I'll focus on those, and maybe collect some more that seem to show particular moves toward friendship, and I'll analyze them to see what specific moves participants make. I'll also carry out a review of the literature on the topics of fan groups and other online groups. I think there are differences between the ways men and women interact online, and since most soap opera fans are women, I'll see what I can find about those gender differences in communication. And since some of the interactions are negative— "Flaming"—I'll see what I can find about that topic.

- **Literature review.** So far I've found literature related to my topic in a journal on communication, so I'm thinking that I should search for more sources in that field, and maybe in psychology. From my preliminary search, I've found a couple of sources that might be useful. One is an article on "Making Friends in Cyberspace" (published in the *Journal of Communication*[17:10]) that talks about types of interactions that support friendship. The other one is about gender and style in online groups, in which the researchers studied discussion groups and found some differences. (This one, titled "Gender language style in group composition in Internet discussion groups," was published in the *Journal of Computer-Mediated Communication*[17:11]). I actually hadn't thought about the issue of gender until I saw this article, but now I think it's an important thing to consider.

- **Conclusion.** From my research so far, I think I can learn more about how communication and forming friendships in online groups are related. Now that I see that gender may play a role in this communication, I might revise my initial question to focus more specifically on how women use their communication to build friendships and create community online.

Drawing on the imagined proposal we constructed for Baym, create an outline for your own proposal.

Did you have to adapt these elements to fit what you are imagining you'll do?

With a good outline, you should be able to move on through a draft of your full proposal. The full proposal should let you formulate your own plan more clearly and use it to get feedback from peer researchers.

3 Defining your research question or focus

A strong proposal provides readers with a clear sense of **what** is being explored or investigated. As you explain your research focus, you can also work to narrow your topic and, as a result, the scope of your project. It can also be generative to frame your focus as a question you hope to address through your research, whether you are working with primary or secondary data.

4 Nodding to your purpose

Once you have explained your research focus, you should also consider and address the **why** driving this undertaking in your proposal. What do you hope to learn as you work through this inquiry? What new ideas or understandings do you hope to offer your readers? What will your project contribute to what is already known about a topic, setting, or conceptual question?

5 Describing your methods

In your proposal, you will want to give readers a sense of **how** you will address the research question you have articulated. How will you collect data? What kinds of sources will you draw on? How do you plan to arrive at new ideas in this piece? As you describe your methods, you should give your readers a clear sense of how you will move through this research project (though, of course, this plan will most likely change as you conduct your research).

6 Providing a sense of what others have said about this topic

By previewing other sources that examine similar research questions, you will be able to situate your work for your readers. So, by showing what others have said about your topic, you will help define a starting point for yourself. Think of this literature review as a place to say, "Here is what has already been said, and here is what I hope to add to this conversation."

7 Concluding your proposal

Your conclusion is a nice place to explain what you have learned from writing your proposal; it can be a moment when you show how the beginnings of your research process have shaped the plans you are making for this piece. This is also a nice place to point to the significance of your research, to explain why this is an important project, and why it is work worth doing.

● WRITING MOVES ◀

Revising and Publishing

As you work on your proposal, you will most likely want other readers to have a look so you can discuss the what, why, and how of your project. Use these questions to guide that discussion.

1 Inviting feedback

Ask a classmate to read your drafted proposal and comment on it using the following questions as a guide.

- Does the writer offer a clear line of inquiry, addressing all of the proposal elements?

- Does the study seem doable—are the questions defined carefully enough that it can be done in the amount of time available for this project? If not, how would you suggest focusing it more?

- Are there other aspects to the question the writer might want to consider?

- Are there other data or resources that the writer could use?

- What other recommendations would you make to the writer at this point?

2 Revising your proposal

Use the feedback you've received to revise your proposal. This is an opportunity to revisit and refine your plan, although you may want to refine it further as you begin a serious search through the scholarly literature, which will be the focus of the next chapter. You might also have discovered that others are planning to research closely related topics. In that case, you might invite some your classmates to also be co-searchers. Consider drawing on their findings as you revise your own project proposal, or consider working through a multipart project together.

Key Concepts

Finding and Evaluating Sources in Media-Rich Settings

CHAPTER EIGHTEEN

Chapter Preview

As Chapter 17 underscores, we use digital research strategies regularly, often to find information or resources quickly. Academic research, though, demands a different approach to collecting, managing, and synthesizing sources and information. This slow, deliberative process can feel antiquated in this digital age, but it is central to academic work and to careful, critical thinking. Stepping into such a process can feel foreign or overwhelming, especially if this isn't how you are used to conducting research. Students who were interviewed for the "Learning the Ropes"[18:1] study discussed in Chapter 17 described three major areas of concern: formulating effective online searches, identifying and locating sources—scholarly articles that related to their own topic and questions, and reading and understanding what they found. Their concerns echoed those of many students, and in this chapter, we'll discuss those concerns in more detail.

As you worked through Chapter 17, you used the free web to gather sources in informal ways. In this chapter, we will highlight how you can use the scholarly web to continue this process and extend those skills you have already acquired by examining how to find, store, and analyze the sources you locate when you move through academic inquiries. The questions you're exploring have been studied before, and your own research will bring your work into conversation with the work of others, an academic conversation that takes place within the textual ecology of a scholarly community.

In your research proposal, you articulated what you hope to study and how you plan to collect information about a given topic; in this chapter, we'll investigate the **annotated bibliography** as another research tool that will help you make sense of the sources that inform and shape your thinking.

. . . .
annotated bibliography
a common academic genre that consists of annotated citations of secondary sources

Exploring
The Scholarly Web

The research proposal in Chapter 17 invited you to articulate the basics of a project: what you will investigate, how you will undertake this investigation, why this inquiry matters, and what it might contribute to current shared understandings. Actively working through that research, however, probably won't be as neat a process as your proposal made it sound, and you're likely to adjust your proposed topic as you move through this chapter.

Now that you have an idea of what you hope to discover, you will look to see what others have said about your topic. If you are working through an ethnographic or archival project, you will do this to contextualize your work, to show what others have found when looking at similar communities or artifacts, or to follow up on themes you discover. If you are working through a literature review, this exploration of what others have found will be central to your undertaking. Your goal is to see what has been said before about your topic. This process, though, this seeing what others have said, will most likely shift what it is you are interested in and will most likely help you refine your focus even further.

Seeking Sources: Using Library Databases

The academic libraries of colleges and universities serve as sites of communication about a vast world of knowledge that is accessed through databases. We'll begin to explore their place in the research process by considering what shared knowledge they represent and what shared purposes might be served in guiding you to make use of them, before we turn to more specifics of how to use them most effectively.

What is an academic database?

A database is a collection of information—of data—that's organized so it can be searched, managed, and updated easily. With vast amounts of data being generated and collected in every area of life, electronic databases that manage that information—whether health records or credit card transactions—have become essential to the functioning of modern society. **Academic databases** focus on the information that's most useful to researchers—particularly the information in scholarly books and journal articles, but also primary documents—and they are organized (often within disciplinary areas, such as the sciences or social sciences) so this information can be searched and accessed by users.

> **academic databases**
> a collection of academic publications commonly used in scholarly research

Academic libraries subscribe to databases that collect vast amounts of scholarship across disciplines in a searchable form. Such databases, which are only available to subscribers, form a layer of the deep web as opposed to the free, surface web of the public internet. The infographic in Figure 18.1 offers a visualization of the layers of information available on the internet, starting near the surface of the internet and moving down below to the deepest of the deep web.

Databases catalog or index an enormous amount of information that's not easily found on the free web (although Google Scholar points to some of it), and they typically allow paid subscribers to access full articles (Google Scholar can take you only to the access point for a lot of content, where you'll still have to pay). College and university libraries pay for access to these databases and the journals they index, and they make all of this content freely available to their students and faculty. So the place to start any serious research project is with your own school's library.

> **Sidenote**
>
> The original image (Figure 18.1) is interactive, with links to further information at each yellow button. You can explore the original at cnn.com.[L18:1]

On your school library's website you will find links to general academic databases like *Academic OneFile*, or *Academic Search Complete*, and *JSTOR*, as well as more discipline-specific databases, such as *ERIC*, which is used by educators, *PsycINFO* for Psychology, *ProQuest Nursing & Allied Health Source,* or *ScienceDirect* (which includes journals related to computer science and indexes an important journal for us, *Computers and Composition).* Or your library might offer its own academic search engine that takes you to the resources of these databases.

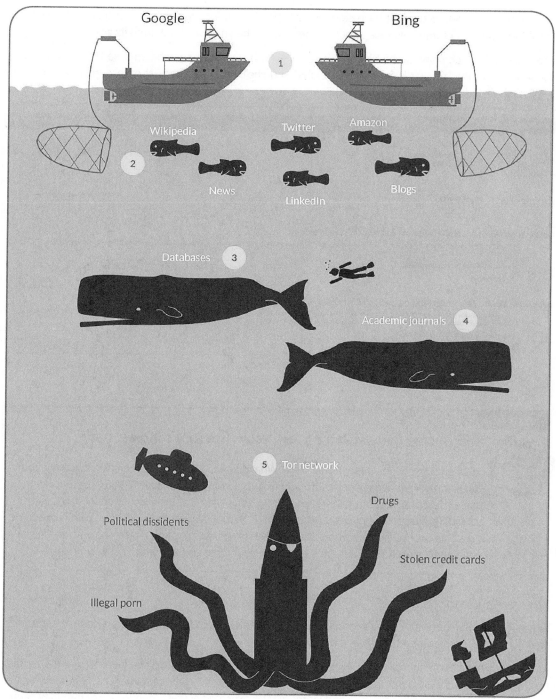

Figure 18.1: A CNN infographic of the deep web

Hannah's search

In Chapter 17, we saw Hannah using the public web to search for information that would contribute to her study of the online community of a book club. The starting place for the next phase of Hannah's search is the library web page at her university (the Kimbel Library at Coastal Carolina University[L18:2]), which supports research by offering an easy entry point called *Discover!* It offers a simultaneous search of the catalog of materials owned by the library, journals the library subscribes to, and databases (typically divided by discipline) that index what's available in these materials.

Your own library's website might have several entry points to these materials, rather than just one, but it should also offer you some guidance about the best way to begin your search from its site.

The *Discover!* search point at The Kimbel Library offers a box to enter search terms, so Hannah can begin her search with the key words "online book clubs," and she'll receive a long list of resources (a whopping 5,902 hits) related to those terms (Figure 18.2).

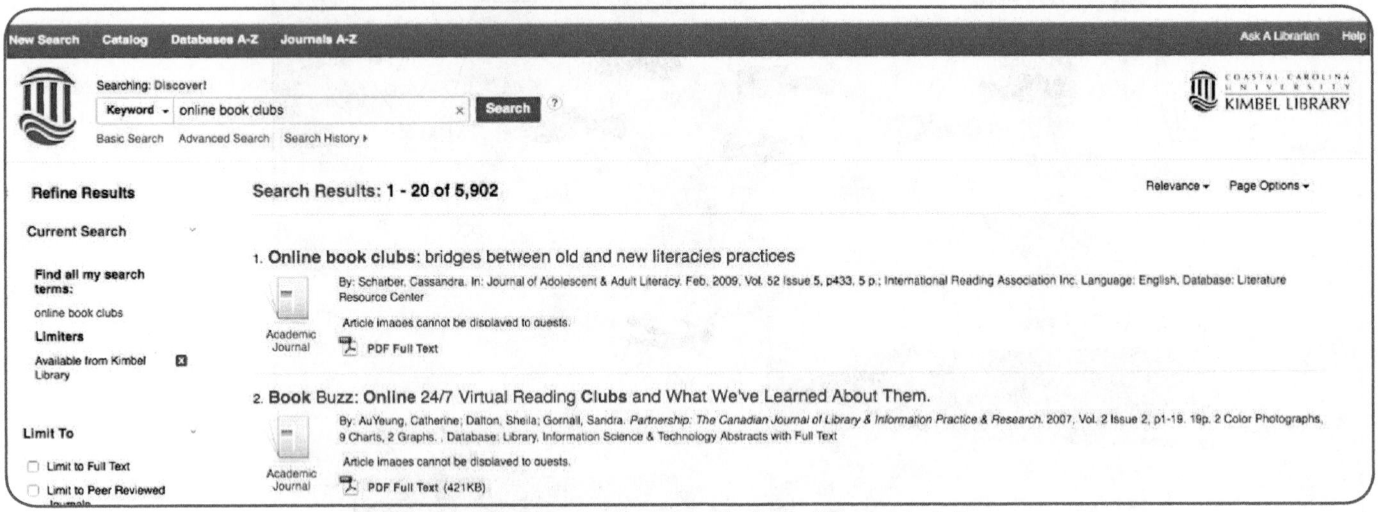

Image 18.2: A Discover! search on the Kimbel Library's website

---

INQUIRY

#1: Getting started on your library's home page

Go to your school's library home page. What guidance do you find there for beginning your research? What access points do you find to academic databases? Your institution most likely subscribes to both general academic databases that include important work across disciplines, such as *Academic OneFile,* and databases that allow you to dig deeper within specific disciplines, such as *SocINDEX* or *Communication & Mass Media Complete.* Beginning with a general database, enter some starting search terms related to your topic and see what results you get.

Why use a library database?

Why might Hannah turn to a library's database search engine rather than Google at this point in her search, or why might her professor require her to do so?

As college writers, Hannah and her classmates are writing to enter communities of learners—whether they are the communities of students and scholars central to her university (a community she'll gradually join as she works through composition courses and learns what is expected of that group) or the community central to a given discipline, of biologists, or journalists, or mathematicians. They will become insiders to a group organized around shared interests and ways of learning and talking about those interests. Using scholarly databases, which are usually prominent on universities' and colleges' library websites, brings them into the work of those communities and helps them enter a conversation that those in academic disciplines have been engaged in for a long period of time.

The sources included in these databases are typically articles published in academic journals that reflect the ongoing scholarly conversations of various fields. And each academic field is a discourse community in its own right, so these conversations provide a significant sense of the shared knowledge, understandings, and ways that are important to a given field (or a subset of a field). As you become further invested in a given field (and develop a sense of what is expected of and known by insiders to a field), you will most likely come to know its key journals (as compositionists, we often turn to journals like *College Composition and Communication, Computers and Composition*, and *Composition Studies*) and will use these as a starting point to see what others in your community have said about a topic or issue.

The first three hits that came up for Hannah's *Discover!* search were pieces published in the following journals: *The Journal of Adolescent & Adult Literacy, Partnership: The Canadian Journal of Library and Information Practice and Research,* and *The International Journal of the Book.* The first of these journals is from the field of literacy studies, while the next two are from the area of library science. Often a larger topic, like online book clubs, will be approached by scholars from different disciplines, using different methods and pursuing different aspects of the topic. As you collect academic sources, consider the disciplines that seem to address the research topic you are studying by noting the journals publishing this work. That will help you contextualize your topic a bit as you consider who thinks about it and why. You will begin to get a sense of the larger **textual ecology** related to that topic—the various journals where the topic is being addressed, the fields they're connected to, and some of the specific articles—which will often cross-reference one another.

A search of Hannah's topic in *JSTOR*, a general database that is particularly strong in indexing articles related to the larger general area of language and literature, brings up the same article from *The Journal of Adolescent & Adult Literacy* and two others from library science journals in the top results, but also returns two articles from *The English Journal* about working with online book clubs in an English class. And the database *Communication & Mass Media Complete,* because it indexes different journals, brings up a different set of articles, including several from *Publishing Research Quarterly,* but also one from a conference of the *International Communication Association* about coercive control in online book clubs. As you conduct your research, use different databases and see what these results can show about disciplinary conversations.

Sidenote

It might be helpful to map out some of these sources as you consider the fields interested in this line of inquiry and to add to that map as you go along.

textual ecology
the networks of human interaction, texts, and media that serve as the backdrop for our literacy practices

See Chapter 9 for an extensive discussion of textual ecologies.

Hannah's Scholarly Search

Initial search term	Library databases used	Journals accessed (sample)	Articles found (sample)
"Online book clubs"	Discover!	*The Journal of Adolescent & Adult Literacy*	"Online Book Clubs: Bridges Between Old and New Practices"
		Partnership: The Canadian Journal of Library and Information Practice and Research	"Book Buzz: Online 24/7 Virtual Reading and What We've Learned About Them"
		International Journal of the book	"Forming Online Innovative Communities in the Book Publishing World"
		The Journal of Adolescent & Adult Literacy	"Online Book Clubs: Bridges Between Old and New Practices"
	JSTOR	*Middle School Journal*	"Research into Practice: Digital Collaborative Literacy: Using Wikis to Promote Social learning and Literacy Development"
		The English Journal	"Wiki, Wiki, Wiki—What? Assessing Online Collaborative Writing"
	Communication & Mass Media Complete	*International Communication Association*	"Invoking the Power of Book Club: An Investigation of Concertive Control in an Online Community"
		Publishing Research Quarterly	"From Obscurity to Bestseller: Examining the Impact of Oprah's Book Club Selections"
		Information, Communication & Society	"Richard and Judy's Book Club and 'Canada Reads' Readers, Books, and Cultural Programming in the Digital Era"

Not all of these articles will be relevant to Hannah's interests, and she'll want to refine her questions and search terms, but seeing what research might be available can help her see that she's most interested in the social dynamics of these online groups.

Articles published in academic journals like these have most often gone through a peer review process, which is, in many ways, similar to the peer review you have used in your writing course. Scholars compose articles that contribute to a larger conversation in a field and submit them to journals that have published other pieces focusing on similar lines of inquiry, questions, or methods. After an editor decides that a particular submission would be a good fit for a given journal (and often pieces are rejected because they aren't good fits and the writers need to find a better "home" for them), the draft is then sent on to a group of reviewers—insiders and experts in the field who read the piece and offer responses and revision suggestions for the writer(s). This process grounds these pieces firmly within the conversations of a larger disciplinary-specific discourse community as the reviewers read submissions in light of what has been published before and in light of what a larger group of academics might expect from a piece.

If we look for internet researcher danah boyd's work on teenagers' uses of social media, we'll find that she has published on this larger topic in a number of different journals across several disciplines: those focusing on research about communication and new media (*New Media & Society*[18:2]), others focusing on research about young people (*Journal of Youth Studies*,[18:3] *Journal of Children and Media*[18:4]), and still others focusing on legal and policy concerns (*Policy & Internet*,[18:5] *Surveillance & Society*[18:6]), among others. In each instance, the journal brings her work into a specific type of conversation, even as she uses her underlying data to address the concerns of that discipline. But her work is most firmly anchored within the larger area of the social sciences, and much of it is available on the *Social Science Research Network* database.

Undertaking academic research, then, is a gradual entry into a research community. As you read more about how others have approached similar threads of inquiry, you will learn more about your topic, but you will also learn how others in the field pose questions, collect data, present results, and position their work in light of what has come before. This kind of research helps you become familiar with the discourse central to an academic community and with the processes central to how that group makes meaning.

INQUIRY

#2: Exploring a disciplinary database

???

While your topic might bridge disciplines, you can often find useful resources by beginning with a disciplinary database. Choose a database from a discipline that might be relevant to your topic, and use your same search terms to see what sorts of articles from which journals it shows you. If you have trouble identifying an appropriate database, contact a librarian for help. At many colleges and universities, librarians can be reached over email, by phone, or (at times) over text.

See Part I Additional Readings for the full text of "Bookworm Buddies."

At this point, Hannah might take a few minutes to explore her initial findings before she gets too far along in her research. Maybe she would decide that much of what shows up in this first general search doesn't address her real interest of how new members are welcomed into existing online communities, a topic she also points to in her earlier community profile of "Bookworm Buddies." So, while the project she outlines in her research proposal might be a bit different than the line of inquiry she actually investigates, she might actually be more invested in the new direction her research has suggested.

As you collect and read sources of information about your topic, you will most likely come to understand the points you want to make in richer ways, but you might also have to rethink your research topic or question in light of what research already exists or doesn't exist. Like the research you engage in on a day-to-day basis more informally, the more academic approach you use when collecting sources for a paper should still be a flexible process. You want to allow what you are finding (or, in some cases, what you can't seem to find) to shape your topic as you continue to refine your project.

Collecting Sources

One of the challenges identified by the students interviewed for "Learning the Ropes" was "formulating effective and efficient online searches."[18:1] Their real challenge was coming up with the key words that would lead them to the kinds of sources they needed. In fact, many of them started with Google to find the key words that would lead to more relevant sources on academic databases. While this might seem like an unnecessary amount of work—searching on Google to find the precise language to build a search around—it was most likely, for some of these students at least, a productive process. While your initial key terms might not be as precise as you might hope (Hannah's search phrase "online book clubs" serves as an example), they can offer a starting point. By refining your key words as you search (by noting how others have named the topic or phenomenon you are considering), you will find new sources as you create the opportunity to reshape the ways you think about a topic. Here are a few useful research strategies.

- **Formulating a research question.** A question or set of linked questions can help you to move beyond your initial broad topic. (e.g., Why do people join online book clubs? How do people communicate in them? How are topics introduced and managed? Do online book clubs share patterns of interaction with other online groups?)

- **Using your question/s to generate some key words.** In this case, "online groups," "communication," and "social interaction." You can pair key words with quotation marks, so that instead of bringing up articles with the key word "online" and articles with the key word "groups," you get only those that combine the two terms. And you can keep adding to your possible key words as you go along.

- **Using quotation marks.** By putting quotation marks around "book clubs" in her initial search, Hannah could have narrowed down her results by about one-fifth (Figure 18.3).

- **Nesting multiple phrases within parentheses and combining terms with the word AND.** For example, search "online groups" AND communication to bring up articles that address both topics. (AND, OR, and AND NOT are referred to as *Boolean operators.* Be sure to capitalize them.) You can learn more about them and other ways of thinking about your search terms with these search tips[18:3] from UMass Boston's Healey Library. By searching for "book clubs" AND "reading clubs" Hannah can find sources that use either term (see Figure 18.4 on next page).

- **Using the tools provided by the databases themselves.**

  - Using JSTOR to search "online book clubs," Hannah can find 4,181 results (Figure 18.5).

  - By selecting the "Journals" tab, she can narrow those results to 3,754. She could also modify her results by choosing a particular date range for articles, or particular journal names.

- **Seeking help from a librarian to find the best strategies.** Librarians are experts in the discourse of searching, and helping others find information is an important part of their role. You can usually call, chat, or email a question if a face-to-face meeting is impossible.

New Search   Catalog   Databases A-Z   Journals A-Z   Ask A Librarian   Help

Searching: Discover!

Keyword ▾ | online "book clubs"   ✕ | Search ⑦

Basic Search   Advanced Search   Search History ▸

COASTAL CAROLINA UNIVERSITY
KIMBEL LIBRARY

«   **Refine Results**   Search Results: 1 - 20 of 1,321   Relevance ▾   Page Options ▾

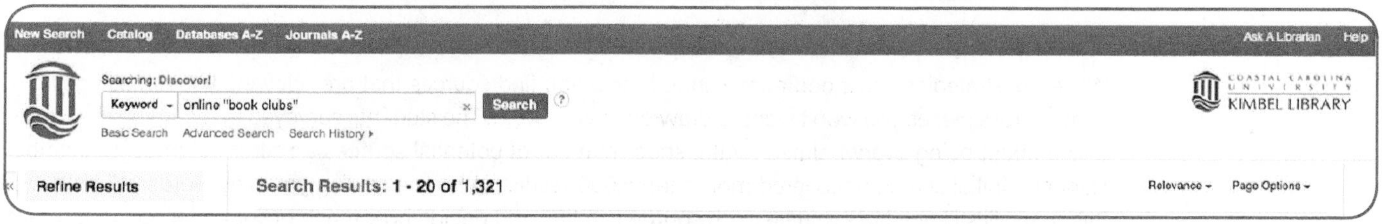

Figure 18.3: A search utilizing quotation marks

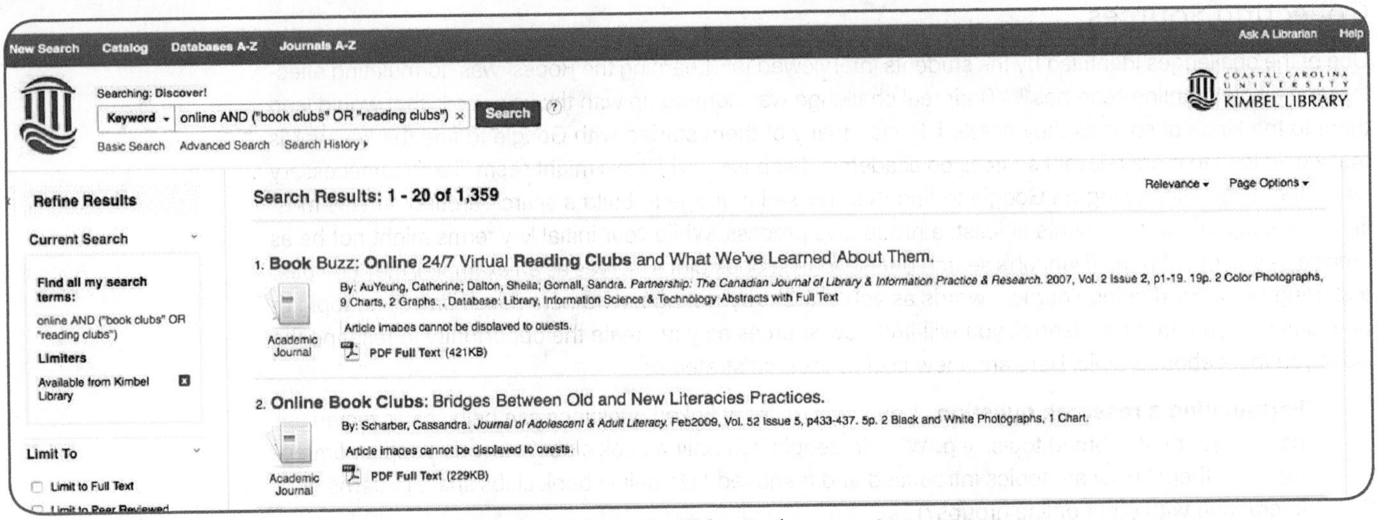

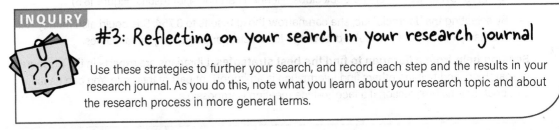

Figure 18.4: A search utilizing Boolean operators

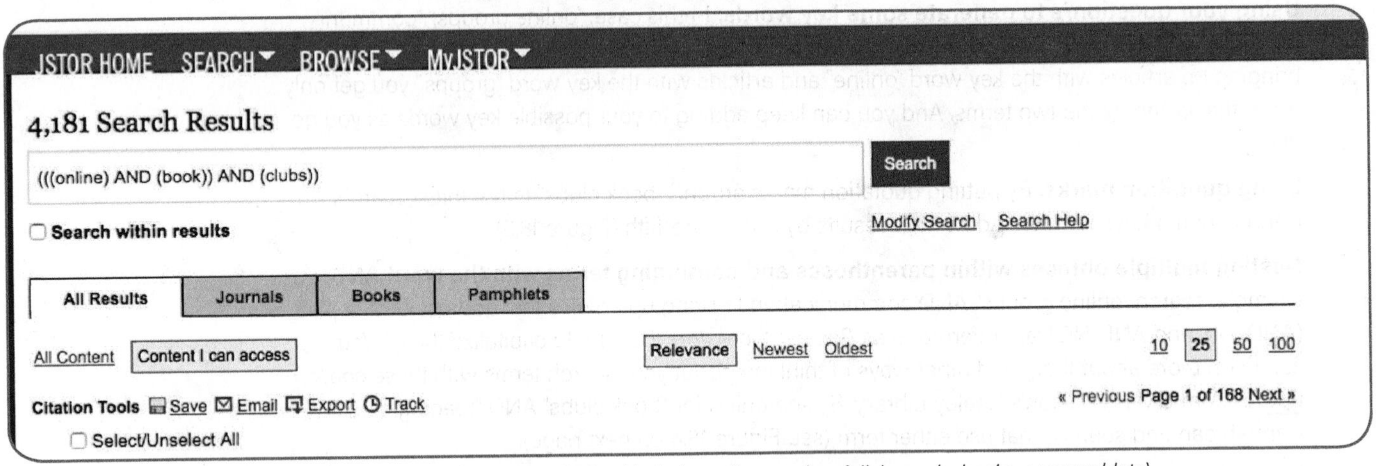

Figure 18.5: In JSTOR, you can control what kind of results you view (all, journals, books, or pamphlets)

INQUIRY

#3: Reflecting on your search in your research journal

Use these strategies to further your search, and record each step and the results in your research journal. As you do this, note what you learn about your research topic and about the research process in more general terms.

Evaluating Sources

While the strategies described above should help you find sources that are relevant, you are still going to come across pieces you won't want to draw on in your work. The students surveyed in "Learning the Ropes" talked about being overwhelmed by the sheer number of potential sources a search returned. Remember, Hannah's initial search uncovered more than 5,000 results! While narrowing your key words will help with this, you will still need to evaluate each source you find and decide how much of your attention it deserves.

- Your first step will be to give each of the most promising sources a quick look to see if it is worth saving. Read the title and, if there is an abstract (a brief overview of the article), read that as well.

  Let's turn again to Hannah's initial search of "online book clubs" (Figure 18.6).

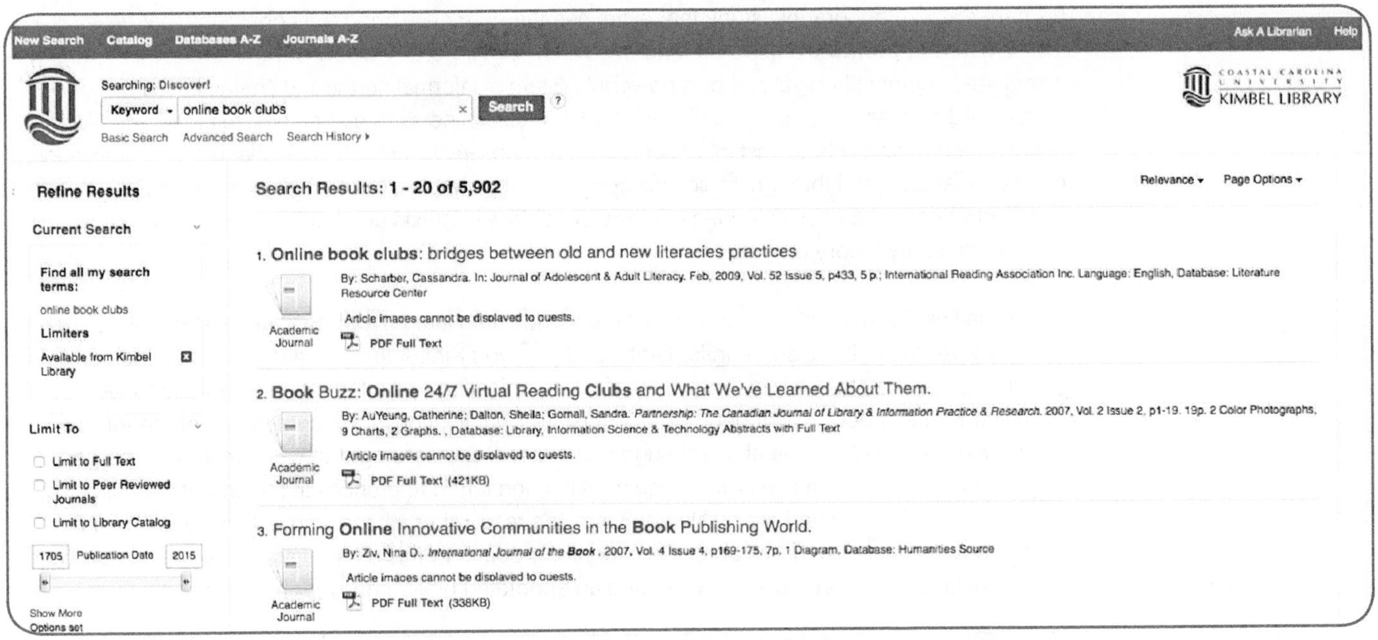

Figure 18.6: Discover! search results for "online book clubs"

- Even just after a quick glance, it seems like the first article that initial search returned is promising. The title, "Online Book Clubs: Bridges Between Old and New Literacies Practices," speaks to Hannah's interests in clear ways, and the fact that it is an academic article published in a journal that focuses on literacy also suggests that this is a strong fit for her interests. The third result, though also an academic article, seems like less of a fit. Hannah is more interested in reading communities than she is in the world of publishing, so she might not want to investigate that source further.

- As you read through abstracts, you will also want to evaluate the relevance and credibility of the sources you have come across. Do this by looking to these elements.

  - **The authors.** Do they seem knowledgeable? Trustworthy?

  - **Site of publication.** Is it reputable?

  - **The information.** Does it match up with the information presented in other sources?

  - **Citations.** Do they cite other relevant sources?

You will also want to question the "authority" represented in your sources. If your article has been published in a peer-reviewed scholarly journal, you can assume that its authors speak with authority about their subject. But you might find potentially useful material that you are uncertain about. By doing a web search on the author's name, you should quickly be able to find more information about his/her background and credentials.

Hannah's source

Hannah can find one potentially useful source, "Invoking the Power of Book Club,"[18:7] on the *Communication & Mass Media Complete* database, but it's a conference paper rather than a published article, so she might be less certain about its authority. Although conference paper proposals are usually peer-reviewed, the process is not as rigorous as it is for articles.

The abstract notes that this is an ethnographic study and that it focuses on the interactions of an online community in which the participants refer to themselves as a book club. The abstract points to familiar types of interaction, and although the "theory of concertive control" is unfamiliar, overall the abstract suggests that the paper will be both understandable and relevant:

This paper is an ethnographic study that examines the normative control mechanisms that develop in a self-organizing **online** women's community. The findings portray **Book Club** as a close-knit, highly personalized community regulated by a powerful system of informal norms and characterized by concertive control. Members engaged in collective forms of discipline such as pile-ons, reinforcing collective memory through posts about past infractions, building consensus through back-channel communication, and unobtrusive control through ironic appropriations of technology. The findings reveal that the theory of concertive control can be extended to nonwork, **online** contexts and have implications for CMC and **online** community theory as well.

The database link doesn't include the name of the author, but Hannah can do a web search for the paper's title and discover the authors are Jennifer Gibbs and Heewon Kim. A further search on those names shows that Jennifer Gibbs is a professor in the School of Communication and Information at Rutgers University, and that Heewon Kim is a doctoral student there. The site of publication is the conference of the *International Communication Association.* The abstract suggests that the content might fit with what has emerged from other studies of online communities, and a quick skimming of the references at the end of the paper shows that several of the articles cited are by Nancy Baym, the researcher whose study of online fan communities was excerpted in Chapter 8 of this book. So everything points to this as a relevant and reliable source for Hannah to include as she works toward creating an annotated bibliography for her research.

INQUIRY

#4: Evaluating sources

Using Hannah's steps as a guide, evaluate several of the sources you've found. What can you say about how reliable these sources seem?

Managing Sources

Once you have found some useful and reliable sources, you need to think carefully about how to keep track of them and of what you're learning from them as you mine them for information and organize your research materials. You will be crafting careful summaries of your sources that examine your own thinking, and there are several tools available to you for organizing this sometimes messy process.

➤ **Bookmarking tools.** Delicious, Diigo, and Zotero are resources that allow you to bookmark references you find and might want to come back to. You can use tags to categorize a resource in several ways.

The "Invoking the Power of Book Clubs" paper can be tagged with the words "book clubs," "online communities," "online interactions," and any other terms that might be useful for retrieving the information later.

- **Delicious** lets you share these resources with others.

- **Diigo** allows you not only to bookmark and tag and share resources, but also to annotate the resources you find and to organize your material.

- **Zotero** allows you to do these things and keeps your references in a form that allows you to create correctly formatted bibliographies easily.

All of these tools save your materials in the cloud, so you can access them from any computer.

Digital Toolbox
See Part IV, Section 5

➤ **Bibliographic tools.** Zotero, EasyBib, and EndNote are commonly used tools that can help you create citations. EasyBib, as the name suggests, makes it especially easy to enter the bibliographic information for the works you are citing and to generate a correctly formatted bibliography, and the MLA version for the format that's most often used in the humanities is free. Be sure to double-check the citations you create using these tools, though, to be sure they are formatted correctly.

➤ **Writing and organizing tools.** As you develop your thinking about a project, you're likely to want a tool that lets you keep adding and reorganizing pages as you work. This becomes even more important if you are working collaboratively, researching and writing with a team. Using an organizational tool, like a wiki, to store notes and ideas in a form that's easily shared can help streamline your research process. Wikis, like Wikispaces (Figure 18.7) or the PBWorks wiki, allow you to create a variety of self-designed pages. Using these to organize ideas, possible sources, guiding questions, and digital resources, for instance, can help you organize and reorganize your thinking, either on your own or collaboratively.

Digital Toolbox
See Part IV, Section 1

➤ **Document storage and retrieval tools.** You can save Word files on your computer or a memory stick, but it can be convenient to keep them and share them on an online site, like Dropbox.

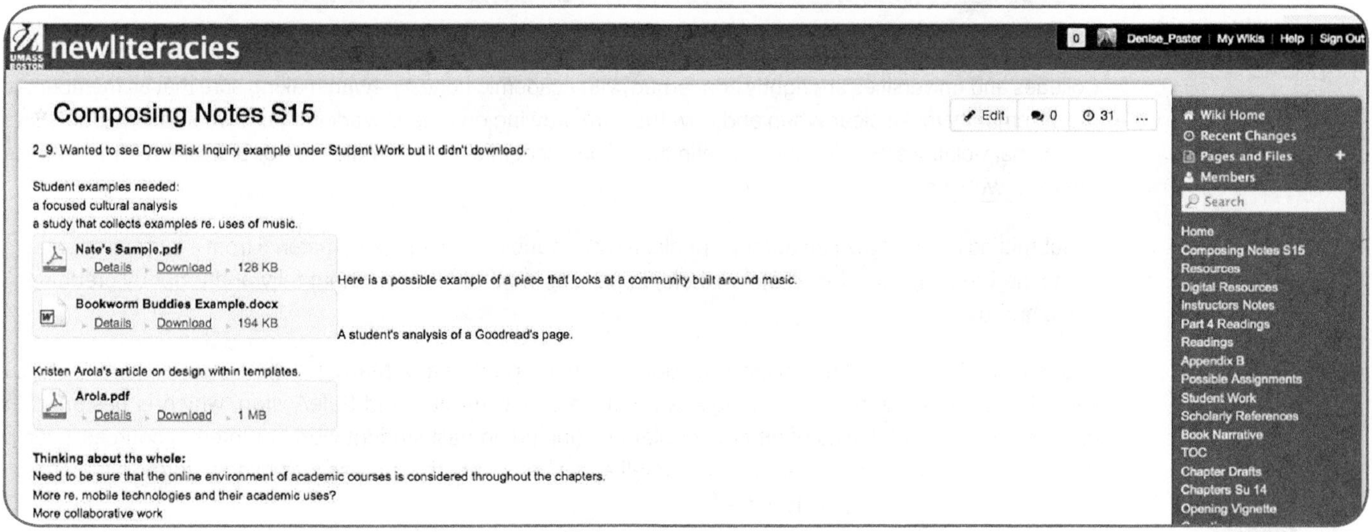

Figure 18.7: An example of process notes shared on a wiki

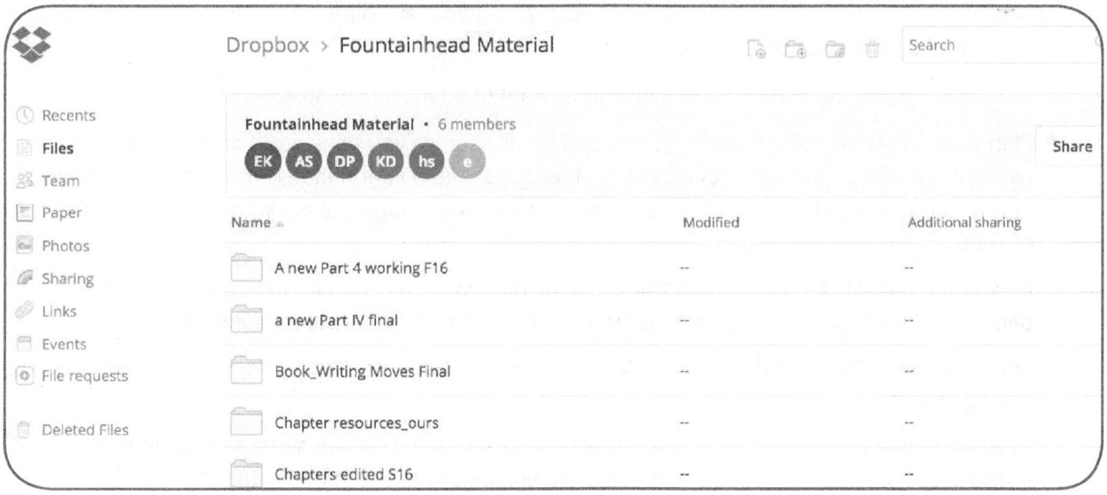

Figure 18.8: Dropbox allows you to create and share folders on the cloud

#5: Reflecting on information management strategies

Share information management strategies that work for you with your classmates. Once you find something useful on the web or on a database, how do you catalog it? Where do you "put" things you want to be able to find later? Where and how do you organize notes you put on texts? How will you capture the full bibliographic information for an article so you can use it for your own citations and references?

Researchers are continually perfecting and rethinking ways to manage sources. What works well about how you approach this process? What might you want to try as you work through this inquiry? Make a plan for how you, individually or collaboratively, will proceed, and include it in your research journal.

Avoiding Plagiarism Through Planning and Organization

Colleges and universities are rightly concerned with academic honesty—with making sure that all members of the community make clear when and how they are drawing on others' work in their own and with punishing intentional violations. Here's a typical definition of an academic honesty violation—or plagiarism—from <u>UMass Boston's website</u>:[L18:4]

> Submitting as one's own an author's published or unpublished work (e.g., material from a journal, internet site, newspaper, encyclopedia), in whole, in part, or in paraphrase, without fully and properly crediting the author.

The internet has made the policing of such violations pretty easy. Many teachers now require that you submit your papers through antiplagiarism software, like Turnitin and SafeAssign, which is designed to catch any unattributed uses of others' scholarship (including past student work) or internet sources. Even a quick Google search on a phrase is likely to tell a teacher where that phrase was used before. So intentional plagiarism is increasingly likely to be found.

Digital Toolbox
See Part IV, Section 5

But much unacknowledged borrowing isn't intentional. Sometimes it's just careless, and there are some specific strategies you can use to avoid accidental plagiarism, working carefully with your sources from the start. Other times it arises from uncertainty about how exactly to integrate others' words and ideas into your own work, and we'll discuss that below. (You can read more about avoiding plagiarism in digital contexts in <u>"Addressing Plagiarism in a Digital Age."</u>[18:8, L18:5])

In the information-gathering stage of your work you'll want to do the following.

- Plan ahead, keeping clear citation information for all sources you think you'll draw on (since writers who are pressed for time are more likely to have gaps where information is missing). Save this information, either in an electronic file or by printing your source pages, along with the URL and the date of printing.

- Keep a separate file for information from each electronic source, putting material you might quote or paraphrase into that file, rather than cutting and pasting information straight into an essay.

- Keep your own writing drafts and the files of information from your sources separate throughout the writing process.

- Keep notes on your own process in a research journal or log. This can serve as a source trail, allowing you to reconstruct your own path from sources, to notes, to drafts, to revisions.

INQUIRY

#6: Reflecting on strategies for avoiding plagiarism

Reflect on how your organizational tools and strategies will help you to keep track of citation information and the words and ideas that come from your sources. What "best practices" seem most helpful to you as a researcher and writer?

Making Connections
Entering the Conversation

As the students quoted in the "Learning the Ropes"[18:1] study make clear, locating, evaluating, and managing sources is a time-consuming and complex process, but it is well worth your attention because the time you spend with these texts will help you extend and contextualize your thinking about your research topic or question. By seeing how other writers have approached a given topic (by paying attention to the questions they pose, the kinds of evidence they collect and analyze, the language they use to talk about a topic, and the conclusions they come to), you will feel ready to add to this "conversation," to share your own ideas, perspectives, and conclusions. In fact, this process of connecting to and mining sources is central to the construction of new meaning.

Taking on the ways of communicating that are central to a community you are entering or coming to new ideas by critically examining what others have said will not happen unless you question the **what**, **why**, **how**, and **where** of the sources you collect. Most of us are used to quickly scanning texts for information—especially those pieces we read on the screen. But quickly scanning is mostly useful for determining whether or not a source is potentially valuable to your project. Reading for understanding and to make connections takes time and attention.

Reading Research Articles

The students interviewed in "Learning the Ropes"[18:1] noted that "It's the reading, deciphering what you've found that's most difficult." Reading is difficult, in many cases, because students are reading texts written for insiders to communities they are just entering (as, for instance, they write about internet privacy for an ethics class and try to react and respond to texts written by and for accomplished philosophers).

Chances are, you will collect sources that are a bit beyond your grasp. Most academic texts are written for other scholars in a field, and these texts will most likely use terminology and language that can be hard to follow. The authors of these texts might assume a lot of shared knowledge—familiarity with a field that you just don't yet have or references to other studies you haven't read. But even if you struggle with a text, even if you can't follow some sections, you can still read for general understanding of the whole, for connections with your own work, and for links to other resources. What you want to keep in mind is that you are reading to learn more about your topic; you are reading as a writer who is looking for ideas to build on in your own text.

Digital Toolbox
See Part IV, Section 1

INQUIRY

#7: Reading for exploration

Here are some steps you should find helpful as you begin this exploratory reading:

➤ **GETTING STARTED.** Select one source you have found that seems a bit foreign to you but that you think will be potentially useful. If possible, choose an article that represents the type of research project you are engaged in—an ethnographic study, an archival study, or a literature review—so you can see from the ways in which this article is structured how you might structure your own report. Begin by reading the abstract, if there is one, or the opening paragraphs if there isn't. What do you learn about the focus of this article, the questions being explored, and how the writer(s) will proceed?

➤ **MAKING YOUR MARK.** As you begin working with this source, decide how you will "mark" it. Will you make notes in the margins? Will you keep notes in a separate notebook or file? Will you insert digital comments (using, for instance, a PDF reader)? You'll want to mark both the points you do understand and might use, and those you need to make sense of, including unfamiliar terms.

➤ **LOOKING AT ALL TITLES AND HEADINGS.** What do these titles and headings tell you about what is included in this piece? What do they show about how the text is organized? What do these pointers to particular sections suggest about what you, as a reader, might be interested in and might bring to a reading about this topic?

➤ **READING THE FIRST PARAGRAPH IN EACH SECTION.** What does each initial paragraph tell you about the central elements of this presentation of research? About the progress of the writer's argument? What are the main conclusions the writer brings you to?

➤ **FINDING CONNECTIONS.** Look at the citations made throughout this text. Do they point to other sources you are familiar with? If so, how does the writer seem to use them? If not, are there any additional sources you should track down to enrich your understanding of this topic?

➤ **CONSIDERING EVIDENCE.** Now that you have a sense of what this piece is about and the kinds of claims made in it, question how they are supported. What kinds of evidence do the writers use? What points does the evidence support?

➤ **MINING THE SOURCE.** Return to your source for a careful rereading. What might you use from this source in your own work? Pull out key terms you might draw on and quotations you might use in your own text, and mark them in clear ways. (The double-entry notebook introduced in Chapter 7 is particularly useful for this purpose.) Then comment on these. What do they contribute to your thinking or the points you are being drawn to as you work through your own research process?

Hannah's choice of article

The conference paper on "Invoking the Power of Book Club"[18:7] can be explored with these strategies. It includes an abstract, which gives enough information to suggest its usefulness for Hannah's purposes, including the fact that it is an ethnographic study, like Hannah's own. Following the abstract is a list of key words—terms the writers have selected as key concepts that others might use to have this paper come up in their searches: computer-mediated communication, concertive control, social norms, online communities, unobtrusive control.

The article's title makes it an obvious possibility for inclusion in Hannah's list of resources, and its headings and subheadings show how these writers have structured their presentation. These include the following.

➤ Introduction (with a review of relevant literature)

➤ Norms in Online Contexts (with a review of specific studies that address how groups create shared norms for behavior in these contexts)

➤ Methods (ethnographic with participant observation—becoming a member of the group, and textual analysis—the analysis of the words posted online)

➤ Findings—including several italicized subheadings that highlight major points or ways in which members of this group work together to exercise control of participants' interactions:

- Concertive (collaborative) discipline through pile-ons (which they define, on page 24, as "a recurring genre of posts designed to build and reinforce collective memory of a shared history")
- Building/reinforcing collective memory
- Building consensus through backchannel communication (communicating through private messages)
- Unobtrusive control through appropriation of technology (e.g. using emoticons)

➤ Discussion

- Theoretical implications (where they focus on "concertive control")
- Limitations and future research directions

Reading the first paragraph of each of these sections gives readers an idea of what will be discussed there. For example, the first paragraph of the section on Norms in Online Contexts points out that researchers saw evidence of shared social norms as a sign that a community had been created, and that earlier studies documented this. Hannah can be pretty sure that the rest of what follows in this section will be a review of these earlier studies.

The writers of this article make a number of points that connect to what Hannah has discovered in her "Bookworm Buddies" study: she has already noticed that the structure of the group might influence its interactions, that group members might or might not be judgmental, and that there are both explicit and implicit rules for interactions. Gibbs and Kim make points that reinforce and provide additional support for what Hannah has found, and they point to new elements, such as some specific ways in which the members collaborate to shape the discourse, which Hannah might look for if she returns to gather more data or do more analysis.

The evidence the writers have offered for concertive control (peer control based on the group's shared understanding of implicit rules and values and ways to enforce them) includes specific examples of the four ways they saw this control being exercised, the four categories of interaction. This evidence not only supports their argument, but also can show Hannah the sorts of interactions she might look for when she returns to her own data.

Finally, there is much that Hannah might pull from this article for her own work. For example:

- She might **quote** the definition of concertive control, being careful to copy the writers' words exactly and to place them in quotation marks:

> According to Gibbs and Kim, "Concertive control is a form of peer influence that arises in participatory, flat structures without formal leadership in which members collaborate and work 'in concert' to reach a 'negotiated consensus' on the ideas, norms, and rules that will guide their activity and work processes" (4).

quote
drawing on another's words directly and marking them with quotation marks and in-text documentation

paraphrase
putting another's ideas in your own words, marking them with a clear introduction and in-text citation

- She might **paraphrase** Gibbs and Kim's summary of other research about norms in online communities, putting much of what they say into her own words:

ORIGINAL: Although these studies are about online communities in general, they clearly illustrate that social norms emerge through online interaction and play a significant part in building and managing communities. In particular, they describe both newly developed technological norms and existing social norms imported from offline society that are used to control people's behavior online (pp. 7–8).

PARAPHRASE: Studies of online communities have shown that they develop social norms through their online interaction, drawing on social norms from other offline communities and new norms that are shaped by the new technology to control participants' online behavior (Gibbs and Kim 7–8).

summarize
succinctly articulating the main gist or central point of another's work

- She might **summarize** what the writers say about Baym's integrative model of online community (itself a summary). Like a paraphrase, a summary involves putting the writers' ideas into one's own words, attempting to capture all the main points in a sorter form.

ORIGINAL: The integrative model of online community by Baym (1995, 1998) provides a better understanding of unique aspects of online social norms. First she describes not only explicit but also implicit online social norms as a property of online communities. According to Baym, normative conventions are constructed through group interactions; moreover, norms are continually reinforced by creating structural and social sanctions against people who abuse those norms. Also she argues that norms are manifest in a group's language patterns based on her analysis of agreements and disagreements (Baym, 1996).

SUMMARY: Gibbs and Kim draw on Baym's (1995, 1998) integrative model of online community for understanding online social norms, noting that she describes these communities as having both explicit and implicit social norms, that the norms are constructed through group interactions, that they are reinforced through sanctions, and that they can be identified through language patterns.

She might briefly reference a finding that either echoes or contrasts with what she has found:

In the online book club that Gibbs and Kim studied, members worked together to discipline violators of social norms in ways that were often "quite harsh," with many members "run off" because of their violations. In contrast, the group I studied was consistently welcoming and respectful.

Hannah has already made some of these moves in her earlier "Bookworm Buddies" study. There she has drawn on two sources: danah boyd's "Learning to Hide in Plain Sight," our reading from Chapter 3; and an article she's found by Stacey Koosel, "Ethnographies of Social Networks."[18;9] She *summarizes* Koosel's main point before noting the contrast to what she has found:

"Koosel discussed how people can be reluctant to share their identities and personalities on a social site, for fear of backlash from those who view it."

And, assuming her readers' shared knowledge of danah boyd's article, she points to a contrast between boyd's finding and her own:

"None of the members of this community use any form of steganography in their comments (boyd). While they may at times send each other private messages, usually to let the person who started the thread know that they will not be able to participate in the buddy read, everything that they write in the comments is intended for others to read. What they write is what they mean, there are no hidden messages."

As you work with the sources you've found useful, you'll want to draw on them carefully in these ways.

#8: Working with other texts

Following Hannah's model, interact with some of your own sources in careful ways. Be sure to summarize, paraphrase, and quote from your sources as you show how they intersect with your thinking about your topic.

Mining Sources while Avoiding Plagiarism

When you are entering a new scholarly conversation (by finding and reading a set of sources about a topic), a new field, and a new setting (as you write for college courses), it can be hard to stake your own ground in a text and claim enough authority to write from your own perspective and position. Working with others' words is a necessary step in learning the discourse of a field, and others' words and ideas are essential to your own research as you use those ideas to support or expand your own thinking, or use your own work to challenge what others have said. But bringing others' work into your own writing requires careful attention to how to use them appropriately and how to credit your sources, showing exactly when and how you are building on others' thinking.

One way to think about the process of building on the ideas of others is to use the analogy of music, as Wayne Rhodes has done in his essay, "Love and Theft: Borrowing to Sound More Like Yourself" (in Part III Additional Readings). Rhodes, who is both an English professor and a musician, considers how the blues tradition has worked for musicians like Muddy Waters, who heard songs from the cotton field and songs from other singers until his own song "fell into his head."

> The blues tradition or "folk method" Waters describes is what drives creativity and innovation in popular music. Go to YouTube and listen to the Chiffons singing "He's so Fine," and then go to George Harrison's "My Sweet Lord." Listen to "Who's Been Talkin," by Howlin' Wolf, and then to Carlos Santana playing "Black Magic Woman." For something more recent, listen to Articolo 31's "Come una Pietra Scalciata" which builds a new song around Bob Dylan's "Like a Rolling Stone," or to The Grey Album, by Danger Mouse, which takes the Beatles' The White Album and remixes it with vocals from Jay-Z's The Black Album.

> Clearly, the later songs are influenced by the earlier ones. Yet, each song is distinct, a new creation built upon what came before. Depending upon the artist's skills, the "copy" may be as indispensable as, or even more significant than, the "original." And just as the old song made the new one possible, the new one provides fertile ground for what will follow.

Drawing on the work of Lawrence Lessig (Chapter 9), Rhodes goes on to talk about how a similar process of drawing on earlier work for a new and creative "remix" occurs in other fields—in medicine or especially in law, where legal briefs are built on earlier cases, remixing those prior cases to make an argument that is new—a necessary process for creating new knowledge. He ends by explaining what he wants for his students:

> I want my classroom to copy the fashion designers, lawyers, and musicians. I want to tell my students to go ahead—be Woody, sing his songs, stand in his boots, adopt his accent and his biography, smoke his brand of cigarettes, pose like he does in photos. That's not theft—that's love . . .

> Later, when student writers have nearly finished their project, before the official release or publication or evaluation, they can see their work as being just like Muddy Waters' blues. Now they can take their Alan Lomax readers on a tour of the cotton field where it all came from, the place where they heard it, learned it, made it. Documentation now takes on new meaning and significance. Let me show you how I did this thing I'm so proud of.

So Hannah can "remix" the ideas she gathers from her sources, mixing a little from here and a little from there (she might now draw on Baym, as well as Gibbs and Kim) and adding her own new understandings, until she has something that builds on the work of others and yet remains wholly her own. But she still has to acknowledge them and her use of them, just as musicians must do, crediting and paying earlier songwriters for the work they cover or the familiar hook they incorporate (and thus avoiding copyright violations). And to be more than a cover band, they must use what they borrow to create something new.

With a mix of quotation, summary, and paraphrase, Hannah can weave the understandings she's gained from her sources into her own work, being careful always to cite those sources and to include them in her final list of works cited or references. Creating an annotated bibliography from the most useful sources she's discovered, in the ways suggested in the Composing section of this chapter, will help her to find the right balance.

In addition, if her school has a license for SafeAssign or Turnitin, she can submit a draft, when she's ready, to see what matches to others' work the software finds—to see whether she's inadvertently used another's phrasing without marking a direct quote, whether she's relied too heavily on one or two sources, or whether the density of her use of others' words, even if correctly quoted, paraphrased, and cited, outweighs what she's adding to the mix. And she can review the report with others, to see whether the software has highlighted phrases that are common in the field and don't need specific citations, like *discourse community* or *digital literacy*, and what she might want to change or add.

Sidenote

Highlighting common phrases as if they were plagiarized is a frequent problem with plagiarism software.

Digital Toolbox
See Part IV, Section 5

INQUIRY

#9: Using plagiarism software as a revision tool

Submit some of your preliminary writing about one of your sources to SafeAssign or Turnitin in draft mode and see what information you get back. Work in small groups to interpret these responses and to think about how to avoid any indications of plagiarism. If your college doesn't subscribe to these tools, work through one another's paragraphs to see what your own examples tell you and where more careful work with a source might be required.

Composing
An Annotated Bibliography

What is an annotated bibliography, and why is it useful to your research? It's a bibliography, a list of citations for books, articles, and other sources, but it goes beyond a simple list; each citation is accompanied by a brief annotation that both describes the content of the work and suggests something about its usefulness in relation to the writer's larger research purpose. It's often used to show that you're familiar with the key research literature about a topic, but it's also a useful way of keeping track of the key points of sources you've found and reminding yourself of how those points might contribute to your own work. Two people's annotations for the same article are likely to differ, depending on their own projects and purposes.

Hannah's Annotation

Here is an annotation Hannah could write about the conference presentation we describe earlier in this chapter. As you read this example, try to name some of the moves Hannah could make while commenting on this source. How does she draw on Gibbs and Kim's ideas and words by summarizing, paraphrasing, and quoting? How does she evaluate or critique this source? How does she describe and represent their work? How does she put it in conversation with her own study? With other ethnographies of online communities? How does she question its authority? Comment on its relevance? Also, notice how this annotation helps Hannah think through this source in careful ways.

MLA FORMAT:

Gibbs, Jennifer and Heewon Kim. "Invoking The Power Of Book Club: An Investigation Of Concertive Control In An Online Community." *Conference Papers—International Communication Association*, 2011, pp. 1-30. *Communication and Mass Media Complete*.

APA FORMAT:

Gibbs, J. & Kim, H. "Invoking the power of book club: An investigation of concertive control in an online community." (2011). *Conference Papers—International Communication Association*, 1–30.

This ethnographic study focuses on the interactions of an online community, which the participants refer to as a book club. By examining how the members of this close-knit community establish and maintain community standards, the presenters are able to analyze how this women's message board community functions. In my own study, I plan to question how roles, topics, and relationships are negotiated in an online discussion of books, so this presentation provides me with a rich model as it gives me a clearer sense of the kinds of conclusions other ethnographers arrive at as they study online communities built around an interest in books.

While this is not an academic article (which would have been peer reviewed), the presenters are credible and authoritative sources: Jennifer Gibbs is a professor in the School of Communication and Information at Rutgers University and Heewon Kim seems to be one of her doctoral students.

One of their main findings is that members are shown how to act on this site through "concertive control," which Gibbs and Kim define as "a form of peer influence that arises in participatory, flat structures without formal leadership in which members collaborate and work "in concert" to reach a "negotiated consensus" on the ideas, norms, and rules that will guide their activity and work processes" (4). So, in this online book club, members worked together to discipline violators of social norms in ways that were often "quite harsh," with many members "run off" because of their violations. In contrast, the group I studied was consistently welcoming and respectful. What does it mean that in the online community I am studying "concertive control" was not needed to establish a sense of how to participate in the group?

In addition to conducting an ethnographic study, Gibbs and Kim also provide an extensive literature review in this presentation. In fact, they cite Nancy Baym (whose work we read this semester). They explain that studies of online communities have shown that they develop social norms through their online interaction, drawing on social norms from other offline communities and new norms that are shaped by the new technology to control participants' online behavior (7–8). This pushes me to question whether the nature of the community I am studying, the "Bookworm Buddies," is a result of its digital nature, or if this online community is extending the shared ways of more traditional book clubs.

Creating an annotated bibliography allows you to pay attention to the conversation you are entering as you read, consider, and write about each of the sources that informs your thinking about your topic and research undertaking. Depending on the size and scope of your project, you'll want to select and annotate at least five to 10 of the most promising sources you've found. You'll want to select sources you think will be useful in showing what work has been done that's relevant to your research, that can complement and further your own understanding, or that you might want to counter with your own work.

WRITING MOVES

Inquiring and Inventing

As we stressed in Chapter 17, an academic research process should allow for time. Instead of jumping quickly from source to source, as we often do while executing more informal research tasks, you should slow down your reading as you carefully question what and how each source contributes to your thinking about your topic. That is, you should "listen" to each source carefully and with intention. To do this, you will want to consider the general goal (or project) central to each source as you narrow in on the particular points or specifics that seem especially meaningful to your own thinking. You can see each of these moves underlying the "Hannah's Source" example above. We can turn to another article that looked promising from Hannah's search to see them more clearly.

Scharber, Cassandra. "Online Book Clubs: Bridges Between Old and New Literacies Practices." *Journal of Adolescent & Adult Literacy* 52.5 (2009): 443–437. Discover! Web. 15 June 2015.

1 Articulating the bigger picture

To provide a broad sense of what each source is working to accomplish, comment on the **where**, **what**, the **how**, and the **why**.

- The where: Where was this piece published? What does this publication venue suggest about its intended audience and/or the academic conversation it engages and works to extend?

- The what: What argument, point, or position is central to this piece?

- The how: How was the research carried out, and how does it support the argument, points, or position established? What do you notice about how this piece is composed?

- The why: Why do you think this work is presented in the ways that it is? For what audience and purpose?

As you describe a source's means of distribution (its where) and main focus (its what), nod to how it is composed (its how), and consider its purpose (its why), you will most likely compose a solid summary of it. Including such a summary in each annotation is important, as this is a key way to introduce each of your sources to your readers.

Where: Published in the *Journal of Adolescent & Adult Literacy* in 2009, "Online Book Clubs: Bridges Between Old and New Literacies Practices" engages an audience of professionals interested in teaching reading strategies. This fairly recent article's focus on a digital book club helps readers (including teachers) to consider how social interactions around reading can be supported on the web.

What: Scharber argues that book clubs, which promote reading as "social engagement," can encourage a generation that is reading less to read voluntarily (433).

She also suggests that book clubs that occupy digital spaces can use emerging technologies, which are often connected to a decrease in reading, to encourage reading in digital natives.

How: She conducted research on online book clubs hosted by a public library and showed that the participants liked the social activity supported by chats on the site (hosted on the learning management system, Moodle).

Why: She is addressing those interested in adolescent and adult literacy, using what's been learned in public library settings to show the value of online book clubs and to suggest they could support literacy in school settings as well.

2 Tending to the specifics

As you continue to listen to each source, move beyond a general description and pay attention to some of the more focused points made that speak to your research interests and questions. To do this, you might paraphrase particular points by putting them in your own words. When you paraphrase, you pay attention to an idea presented in another's writing as you share that thinking using your own words and voice. You will want to be sure to cite the page number you draw from and to be sure to introduce it (by saying something like, "According to Gibbs and Kim") to make it clear that this is another's idea you are working with.

When you want to maintain the voice, style, or phrasing of one of your sources, you will quote specific points made. By drawing someone else's actual words into your annotation, you can do interesting things with the rhythm and pace of your writing as you move between your voice and another writer's. As with paraphrases, be sure to introduce and cite quotations to move readers in and out of them in smooth ways.

> Scharber found that "The club members did not know one another prior to the club, and they found the chat to be a place to get to know the other kids and make 'e-friends.'" (435)

3 Evaluating each turn in the conversation

Once you have presented both the big picture and discussed more nuanced points through paraphrasing and quoting each of your sources, you will also want to evaluate them. How helpful do you find a source? What hesitations do you have about drawing on it? What seems especially intriguing or interesting about it? Use your annotations as a place to consider the value of each source as you question how each speaks to your concerns, interests, and undertaking as a researcher.

> The book clubs Scharber studied were different in nature from the thread I investigated on Goodreads, but her finding that the preteen girls she studied liked the online chats and became "e-friends" seems to support my conclusions about the welcoming nature of book discussions.

> Otherwise, Scharber's study was not as useful as others, because she presented very limited data about this online book group. She gave some examples of the girls' interactions but didn't analyze their exchanges.

WRITING MOVES

Drafting and Shaping

At this point, you have described your sources, considering what they accomplish and how they inform your thinking. To question how they work together to provide you with a larger sense of how scholars, researchers, and academics consider your topic, you will want to think about how they work as a set. So, you'll want to return to each source and consider how it contributes to the larger textual ecology made up of your sources.

1 Synthesizing sources

How do your sources seem to speak to one another? In what ways do they extend one another? Where do they seem contradictory? In what ways can they complicate or enrich points made when they are read together?

At this point, you'll want to return to your annotations and consider what points you might come to by establishing some connections among your sources. How (and where) might you be able to put sources in conversation by looking to intersecting notions, examples, and implications they suggest?

Hannah can find such connections between these new articles, Nancy Baym's study of an online fan group (Chapter 8), and the study by Koosel[18:8] that she cited in her earlier "Bookworm Buddies" paper (Part I Additional Readings).

> Both Gibbs and Kim's and Scharber's studies show that a friendly environment is an important element that keeps people involved in book-club-type spaces. Baym, too, found that the online fan group she studied was maintained in part through a welcoming and friendly atmosphere. Sharing some personal information seemed to help maintain that environment in each case. Koosel found that artists also shared such information online in building a Facebook community.

2 Stepping into the conversation

At this point, you will most likely feel a bit more comfortable speaking with (and possibly back to) your sources. By commenting more on what each source contributes to your developing stance, you can figure out your role in this larger, ongoing conversation you are entering. How does each source shape your thinking about and approach to this topic? How do you see yourself using these sources in your text? In what ways do they fit into the picture of your research?

Koosel, in her study of how artists negotiate their digital identities on Facebook, found that the artists she interviewed said they changed the way they interacted with others over time: "posting content that was deemed appropriate and fun to share in the beginning, became more censored, less personal and, professionally oriented in the end." So it might be the case that what participants contribute to maintaining an online community over time might be different on different sites, or with different purposes. That suggests a new aspect of the "bookworms buddies" interaction to explore.

Though your individual annotations should focus on your sources, you can also add to your annotated bibliography, using it as a place to begin to tease out the ways in which your thinking is developing and bringing in the connections you see and the questions they might prompt you to ask.

3 Including complete bibliographic information

As you compose your annotations, be sure they follow the conventions of this genre. Have you followed a particular citation style (such as MLA, APA, or Chicago Manual of Style)? Do you introduce and cite all paraphrases and quotations? Have you organized your entries alphabetically? Do you provide all bibliographic information for each source your discuss?

WRITING MOVES ◀

Revising and Publishing

Sharing your annotated bibliography with others provides you with an opportunity to consider additional perspectives, to get a sense of what others might notice about the conversation these sources construct.

1 Following conventions

Before sharing your annotated bibliography, be sure it follows the conventions of this genre. Have you followed a particular citation style (such as MLA, APA, or Chicago Manual of Style)? Do you introduce and cite all paraphrases and quotations? Have you organized your entries alphabetically?

2 Asking for input

As you solicit input, have your classmates consider both the ways in which you present your

Sidenote

MLA style was revised in 2016, and you'll find citations in both the previous MLA 7 and the newer MLA 8.

sources and how you seem to pay attention to the larger conversation they construct.

- Is each source summarized?
- Are specific points considered in careful ways?
- Does the writer move between sources, synthesizing their ideas to see how they speak to one another?
- Is the writer's stance discussed throughout these annotations? Is a sense of how the writer will join and contribute to this conversation provided through annotations?
- What else might this writer need to know about this topic? What might round out the conversation formed by this textual ecology?

3 Final annotation

Here is a final annotation for Scharber's article, with careful attention to the points made in that piece in relation to Hannah's own line of inquiry.

In this brief article, an entry in the "Digital Literacies" column of the *Journal of Adolescent & Adult Literacy*, Scharber argues that book clubs, which promote reading as "social engagement," can encourage a generation that is reading less to read voluntarily (433). Further, she suggests that book clubs that occupy digital spaces can use emerging technologies, which are often connected to a decrease in reading, to encourage reading in digital natives. Based on research she conducted on online book clubs hosted by a public library, Scharber argues that the participants liked the social activity supported by chats on the site (hosted on the learning management system, Moodle); she also claims that digital book clubs would work well in school settings. While the book clubs Scharber studied were different in nature from the thread I investigated on Goodreads, she also found that "The club members did not know one another prior to the club, and they found the chat to be a place to get to know the other kids and make 'e-friends.'"(435). This seems to support my conclusions about the welcoming nature of book discussions.

An added reflection on the connections between sources and the new questions they might pose would bring in both the synthesis of what Hannah was finding in Move 1 of "Putting Sources into Conversation" above and her own entry into the conversation in Move 2.

This careful conversation with sources will provide the underpinnings for the work of shaping and synthesizing research that we address in the next chapter.

Key Concepts

academic databases 428
annotated bibliography 427
paraphrase 442

quote 441
summarize 442
textual ecology 431

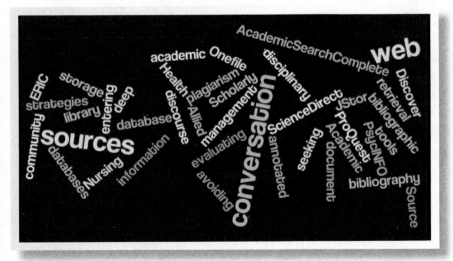

Shaping and Synthesizing Research

CHAPTER NINETEEN

CENTRAL QUESTIONS

1 What do you need to know about how research study genres are being reshaped for understanding and working in a digital world?

2 How can you draw upon and possibly reshape elements of these research genres as you step into them?

3 How can considering the **what**, **why**, **how**, and **where** of your research undertaking help you make informed decisions as you enter academic conversations?

Chapter Preview

In the last two chapters, we've focused on general research strategies that are useful for any type of project. In this chapter, we'll focus more specifically on the types of projects we're highlighting in this book: the ethnographic study, the archival study, and the literature review. Why have we chosen these research genres? Because these genres are consistently used across a range of disciplines and media platforms to help researchers study culture and community in ways that are highly valued in modern American society.

Genres are adaptable textual forms and practices that take shape as people repeat particular ways of communicating that are appropriate for a recurring communicative need. As traditional **research genres** are being applied to the study of digital environments, they are taking on new and often blended forms. At the same time, research practices within these genres are being reshaped by the changing composing practices emerging in a digital world. In practice, distinctions between these types of projects are often blurred—an ethnographic study of a community might draw on an "archive" of saved exchanges—of emails, texts, IMs, and social media posts among family members, for example, and it might also include a literature review. While these types of studies take on different shapes in different disciplines, they are ideal genres for pursuing inquiry-based research and data collection, even as the ways of carrying out such studies are rapidly changing in our digital world.

> **research genres**
> document types specifically developed for academic research

Project Type 1
The Ethnographic Study

Ethnography literally means the study of a nation or group. Ethnographic research methods and the resulting genre of the ethnographic report originated within the field of anthropology

> **ethnography**
> research that focuses on the shared ways of a particular community

in the early twentieth century to guide the study of indigenous cultures—their customs, language, history, etc. Over time, such methods have been adapted by other disciplines to study culture and community around the world, including turning the lens on ourselves to study our own culture. The fields of composition and literacy studies have found ethnographic genres of research quite suitable for studying the shared literacy practices and culture of discourse communities. And as we have seen in many examples throughout this text, such methods are proving to be very useful for the study of online communication and new media literacies. If you're following up on data you've gathered about the digital literacy practices of a community, you'll be engaging in ethnographic work (Figure 19.1).

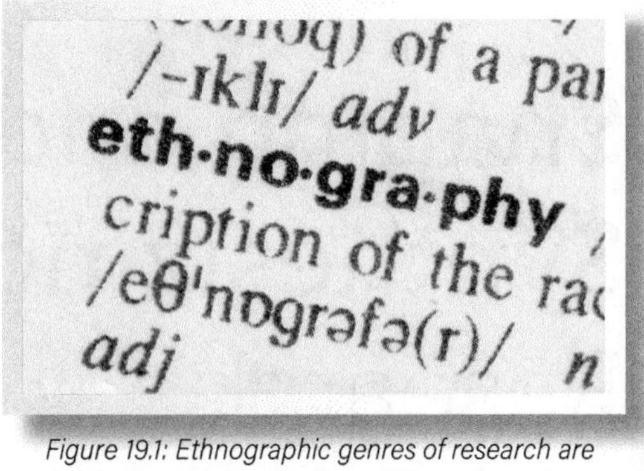

Figure 19.1: Ethnographic genres of research are suitable for studying the shared literacy practices of discourse communities

Ethnography in a Digital World: Digital Ethnography

digital ethnography
a set of research methods for studying of culture and community in the digital world

Many of the researchers whose work we've included in our readings have not only drawn on ethnographic methods, but they also try to redefine these methods for research in digital settings. **Digital ethnography**, also called "internet ethnography" or "virtual ethnography" involves looking, at least in part, at online data, trying to understand the practices and purposes of participants in online settings. It also involves a close consideration of the contexts in which digital texts arise—the participants' values and beliefs, the historical moment, the genres that are taking shape, and the kinds of writing tools and media in use.

Writing about her research on the mediated lives of modern teenagers, danah boyd states that "Internet ethnography is not about the technology—it is about the people, their practices, and the cultures they form."[19:1] And José van Dijck, in considering the ethnographic research focus on context, points to the ways in which platforms themselves shape our online experiences: "Algorithms, protocols, and defaults profoundly shape the cultural experiences of people active on social media platforms" and are "profoundly altering the nature of our connections, creations, and interaction."[19:2] She notes, in particular, the idea that on social media sites, "buttons that impose 'sharing' and 'following' as social values have effects in cultural practices." So one way to think about "digital ethnography" is as a set of research methods for the study of culture and community in the digital world.

Another facet of digital ethnography is the collection of new resources and tools now available for ethnographic study—what can be collected and analyzed with digital resources, from big data analysis of Facebook use during a political conflict in the Middle East, to visual and sound data, like video or podcasts posted by members of a particular community. And still another way is to consider the resources available for presenting and sharing ethnographic research, including slideware, infographics, blogs, tweets, and Instagrams.

Doing high-level, sophisticated digital ethnographies like some of the ones we have read in this book involves time, skills, and resources that are beyond what most undergraduate students can draw on, but they're useful as models for how to approach your own ethnographic research. Ethnography Matters[L19:1]—an ethnography research blog—features researchers exploring the intersection between ethnographic methods and the digital world. The researchers at *Ethnography Matters* (Figure 19.2) believe that "ethnographic research—with its focus on human experiences in context—is critical for countering the trend towards treating people as numbers, as digits, as data and as markets,"[19:3] and they're exploring ways of using digital tools while staying attuned to cultural meanings. In our Part III Resources, we've included links to the posts of one Ph.D. researcher, Wendy Hsu, on her digital methods for studying the culture of a Taiwanese punk band and its followers around the world.[L19:2]

links

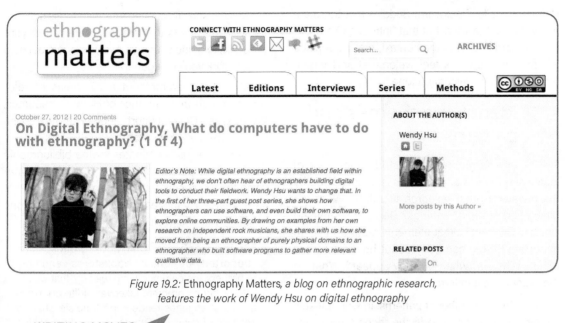

Figure 19.2: Ethnography Matters, *a blog on ethnographic research, features the work of Wendy Hsu on digital ethnography*

WRITING MOVES

Inquiring and Inventing

At this point, you've already conducted much of your research for this study, both by collecting data from the participants and setting you've studied and by finding relevant work from other researchers that connects to your own. As you prepare to report on what you've learned, here are the moves you'll want to make.

1 Selecting and using primary data

You've probably gathered quite a bit of evidence from observations, Facebook or Twitter posts, texts or IM exchanges, fan blog posts, play lists or other archives, and perhaps follow-up conversations or interviews with participants in the community you're studying. For a larger study, you might try to use as much as possible of your data and keep collecting more (and there is special software, such as Ethnograph and NVivo, to help advanced researchers handle large amounts of qualitative data). But for a small study, you'll want to pull out the small excerpts and examples that seem most representative and that relate most clearly to your questions and hypotheses.

If you turn back to Hannah Morgan's "Bookworm Buddies" profile in Part I Additional Readings you can see that, from all of the possible posts by its 585 members, she has chosen a few strands, showing the role the group's leader plays and how members interact as they discuss a particular book. Her focus thus far has been on the group's interactions, and she can build on that work. She might at this point place the discussions she's already analyzed in the larger context of other Bookworm Buddies discussions, seeing whether the patterns of interactions vary by book being discussed, for example.

2 Considering the context

The exchanges and practices of any group are shaped by the context in which they take place, and that is particularly true when they occur online on Twitter, Facebook, or even a site like Yelp. The Goodreads site where the Bookworm Buddies group meets uses the format of discussion threads with numbered messages, giving a particular shape to the exchanges that go on there. But the context also includes the participants, the reasons they come together, their interests and concerns, and anything else about the world they're participating in.

See Part I Additional Readings
for the full text of Hannah Morgan's "Bookworm Buddies."

Hannah finds for Bookworm Buddies that there are many different threads, but that "Introduce Yourself" is an important part of the context, making a place where new members feel welcomed and where others can set a welcoming tone.

3 Identifying themes and patterns

In a larger research study, the work of identifying themes and patterns is often guided by the review of other research literature. What did others find in similar settings? Do I see something similar? Different? What elements recur and seem important? What can I say about how often they recur? Why and when do they appear? What do they seem to mean to members of the group?

Hannah finds a number of patterns: in who initiates the most discussion threads, the second most, etc.; in the content of those initial posts; in what they suggest about how to participate; and in the style of posts by different contributors. She also identifies specific insider terminology for the group ("buddy read"), insider ways in which people are welcomed to the group, etc. She also looks for a pattern that showed up in other research, of a reluctance to share much of a personal identity on some social sites, but doesn't find that to be true here.

4 Drawing on secondary resources for interpretation and analysis

For your annotated bibliography, you provided a brief summary of the most useful sources you've found. At this point you'll want to work with those sources in two ways:

❶ Synthesizing what's been found about your topic. What important points have emerged that you need to consider as you work with your own data? If you completed an annotated bibliography as described in Chapter 18, you'll have begun to synthesize your sources and put them in conversation with one another, work that you can continue and refine as you begin to compose a final report on your study.

❷ Making specific connections with those sources, with the points that are most relevant to your study, to guide your own analysis, again building on work you've begun in Chapter 18.

Here's a brief example of a synthesis of relevant research from another of Hannah's sources, "Reading as a Contact Sport," another study of online book clubs by a research librarian.[19:4] Its author, Barbara Fister, uses endnotes for the bibliographic details of the studies she refers to while summarizing two perspectives on popular book clubs that have emerged in the research she's drawing on, one negative and one positive.

> Some critics worry that book groups, often supported by chain bookstores and big publishers, are commodifying reading, that we are witnessing a corporate takeover of literary practices that engages readers in formulaic, shallow analysis of texts. (2) Others see the burgeoning of reading groups as a grassroots appreciation of books that can teach us much about the relationship of readers and texts. Hall has noted that "the classroom study of literature sometimes dims the joy of reading," and popular literacy practices encouraged by Oprah offered attractions that academics should take seriously. (3) Striphas has found in Oprah's invitation to relate books to everyday lives a feminist reclamation of reading as an act of transformation. (4)

2. Dennis Barron, "I Teach English—and I Hate Reader's Guides," *Chronicle of Higher Education* 49, no. 6 (2002): B5; William McGinley and Katanna Conley, "Literary Retailing and the (Re)Making of Popular Reading," *Journal of Popular Culture* 35, no. 2 (2001): 207–21.

3. R. Mark Hall, "The 'Oprafication' of Literacy: Reading 'Oprah's Book Club'," *College English* 65, no. 6 (2003): 665.

4. Ted Striphas, "A Dialectic with the Everyday: Communication and Cultural Politics on Oprah Winfrey's Book Club," *Critical Studies in Media Communication* 20, no. 3 (2003): 295–316.

As you add to your secondary sources, you'll want to continue to gather important information about them in your research notebook, noting their focus, summarizing them, highlighting their key points/key findings, noting their methods, and commenting on their relevance to your own study. Where you find points that are particularly relevant to your study, copy the passage into your notes, with page numbers, so you can use this as a quote or paraphrase to support your work.

WRITING MOVES

Drafting and Shaping

1 Making connections

For an ethnographic or archival study where you're working with primary data, you'll be using your secondary sources partly to show what others have learned that's relevant to your study, as Fister has done in the example above, and partly to connect what's been learned to your efforts to understand and interpret your own data. Hannah does this with a study she discovered while writing her community profile, a study by Stacy Koosel[19:5] on how artists negotiate online social identities. She finds a significant difference between what Koosel's research showed and what she is finding:

> In her paper, Koosel discussed how people can be reluctant to share their identities and personalities on a social site, for fear of backlash from those who view it (Koosel). However, an analysis of this discussion thread revealed that the restraint she noticed on Facebook is not heavily present on this particular group. One of the reasons for this different approach to expressing one's identity could be because it is not mandatory for a member to add a comment to the thread. Unlike other social sites, such as Facebook, the group does not make or pester a new member to introduce him or herself. Each member is allowed to make that choice on their own, and are not treated any differently should they choose not to.

2 Structuring the ethnographic report

At this point, you're ready to use all of the material of your research notebook inquiries in constructing a final report on your ethnographic study. As with all composing, you'll want to balance the expectations of your audience and what key elements will capture their attention with a presentation of your own inquiry and the understandings you've gained. Because there are several ways you could organize such a report, you might find mapping or outlining to be helpful at this point, both for structuring your paper and for generating some headings that will make that structure evident to a reader while highlighting some key points.

These are the elements (also represented in your research proposal) that you'll want to include.

- An introduction that introduces the community you're studying, why you have chosen to study it, and your initial questions/hypotheses about that community

- The context in which this community's interactions take place—its purpose, its members, its online platform (if it's online), and any other background information that will provide your readers with a richer understanding of this community and your research

- The research context—a summary and synthesis of some relevant research that has helped you to think about your own data

- The larger themes and patterns that have emerged from your study, with specific examples that illustrate them. (These might be used as headings for different sections in which you talk about each)

- The connections you've found between what you've discovered and what other research has shown

- A conclusion in which you share the understandings you've gained and point to further questions/areas of research that could follow

- Citations and references used in the ways described under Project 3—the Literature Review

Digital Toolbox
See Part IV, Section 1

Project Type 2
The Archival Study

Like the ethnographic study, the archival study aims to explore cultural contexts, but it does so by examining the **documentary** traces of lives and events. While the ethnographic study focuses on gathering all types of primary data from the present life of individuals and communities, often through direct observation and the real-time recording of daily interactions and practices, the archival study focuses on primary texts and artifacts that have been collected and saved from different eras, including the recent past: letters, various sorts of documents, images such as those we saw for Rosie the Riveter in Chapter 14, and sound recordings of music or oral histories (Figure 19.3). Like the ethnography, the archival study aims to understand more about human activities in their social and cultural contexts, but often such archived materials are far removed from their context of origin, and reconstructing that relationship will yield new understandings about the artifacts themselves, the contexts in which they were created, and the meanings that make them relevant to a local community or a wider public.

documentary
a collection of documents or artifacts

See Chapter 6
for van Dijck's discussion of shoeboxes.

Libraries have long acted as repositories for primary source documents, images, and artifacts, while personal collections have often existed, as José van Dijck says, in "shoeboxes." Archival studies began largely within the field of history with the use of primary documents related to historical events—U.S. immigration records, soldiers' letters from the Civil War, photographs of urban life in the 1920s. Collecting and studying these texts and artifacts became a vital part of understanding past events and time periods. The U.S. Library of Congress defines primary sources as "the raw materials of history"—original documents and

Figure 19.3: In the past, archival materials were housed in filing cabinets and warehouses; now, many archives are preserved digitally

objects that were created during the time under study. Anything that can be recorded and saved in any media can be archived—photographs, music, memoirs, letters, video—and rich resources of such materials reside at the Library of Congress in Washington, D.C. and in other libraries, but also in the personal collections of individuals and families. Projects like the Mass. Memories Road Show[L19:3] at the University of Massachusetts in Boston aim to bring more of those personal collections into shared archives (Figure 19.4).

link

Open Archives: Digital Collections
at the University of Massachusetts Boston

| Open Archives Home | Browse the Road Show Collection | About the Road Show | Open Archives News | Rights and Reproductions |

Search [   ] **Search** Advanced Search

Home » Mass. Memories Road Show

Mass. Memories Road Show

YOUR PHOTO HERE

About this collection

The Mass. Memories Road Show (MMRS) at UMass Boston is an event-based public history project that digitizes family photos and memories shared by the people of Massachusetts. University Archives staff work with local planning teams to organize free public events where residents are invited to bring family photos to be scanned and included in this digital archive. Contributors are invited to share "the story behind the photos" on video, have their own "keepsake photo" taken, and receive advice from professional archivists and historians on dating and caring for their family photos.

Figure 19.4: The Mass. Memories Road Show website shows how personal pieces inform public memory

Archival Study and Digital Resources

Digital technologies and databases have made archives, in particular media archives, much more available for study. You don't have to travel to Washington, D.C. to explore the resources of the Library of Congress; you can just go online to www.loc.gov[L19:4] to access the library's immense store of media artifacts, including the digitization of old images, books, film, and sound recordings from the nineteenth and twentieth centuries (Figure 19.5). Another rich online archive of cultural artifacts, the Internet Archive, at archive.org.[L19:5] Founded in 1996, the Internet Archive is open access, and it now stores millions of digital cultural texts and artifacts freely available to the general public. Scholars working in the area of the digital humanities are using new methods and digital tools to reimagine the study of art, history, literature, and related fields in the digital era. Some of this work involves digitizing and archiving resources about a literary period, such as Romanticism. Other work might look at new forms of digital literature or studying a large corpus of digitized texts from a particular era, looking for the use of key words and phrases.

Figure 19.5: The Library of Congress website

With the advent of digital, networked technologies, saving and archiving every text and piece of media that we create has become a daily reality, one that brings with it its own cultural and social complications. The vast majority of the texts and media now created are digital. Research done by information scientists shows that "[j]ust 1% of the world's capacity to store information was in digital format in 1986" while "explod[ing] to 97% of the world's storage capacity by 2007."[19:6] While digital media have brought great conveniences, there is a question of how permanent digital texts and artifacts can be. Texts online change frequently or disappear. Documents that would once have been preserved on paper might now exist only digitally, in a format that will be as unreadable in a few years as the five-inch floppy disks of the 1980s are now. The personal archives of families and individuals are also at risk of being lost, both because they may exist only in a perishable hard copy, and because their digital versions may not be saved in a way that will allow them to be accessed and used.

The problem of what to save and how to access it also applies to personal digital archives. While there might still be shoeboxes or albums of photos, memory boxes, or scrapbooks somewhere in your life, much of what we gather now, we gather and keep online, creating problems of organizing and accessing all of that material. And because digital materials don't use up our physical space, we tend to keep more of them; how many more photos do you save than you can actually look at? Facebook has become a default archival site for many people, with its stores of photos, its personal timeline, and its creation of "your year in review" that help with organization and presentation.

Digital resources also provide new means of organizing, synthesizing, and presenting archival materials, however, that make them much more usable, accessible, and meaningful. Primary materials from various institutional collections are now used in multimodal and multidisciplinary productions, like this one on Politics, Literary Culture, & Theatrical Media in London: 1625-1725,[L19:6] the collaborative work of an English scholar, a historian, and their students, drawing on primary texts, maps, period illustrations, and audio files to create a coherent integration of a wide range of resources (Figure 19.6).

Individuals are also using personal archives from families and friends to create multimedia presentations—often for a significant birthday, a wedding, or a funeral. Public sharing of some personal archival resources takes place on sites such as Cowbird, where recent brief stories with photos and/or documents have told of a search for family history[L19:7] (Yesterday>Today), the artifacts a grandmother saved[L19:8] (Yesterday's Hard Copy), and the diary and war photos[L19:9] of a father, found after his death (A Young Man's War Diary). Students' digital stories also draw sometimes on family archives, including the bottom one at this University of Wisconsin Whitewater site[L19:10] about the generation gap between Hmong children and parents.

Digital Toolbox
See Part IV, Section 4

Figure 19.6: The Politics, Literary Culture, & Theatrical Media in London: 1625-1725 is an example of a digital archival project

Inquiring and Inventing

While you're likely to encounter archival projects in other areas of your studies, such as history or American studies, the same research process can be applied to your personal archive. That's what we'll focus on here. Hannah could have chosen to follow up her work in "Bookworm Buddies" with an archival study of her own childhood literacy experience compared to the digital experience of a younger relative, and in that case she might describe what's been saved from her childhood to set the larger context but choose a few representative examples to analyze in more detail, along with contemporary digital examples.

1 Finding and selecting primary documents and artifacts

If you've chosen to do an archival project, you've probably already discovered some artifacts—photos, documents, music—you want to use. But you might find supplemental documents that can enrich your study—photos of a particular time period in your community, newspaper accounts of the events of a historical period—and these materials are likely to be found in the local archives of your state or college/university or perhaps in the Library of Congress,[L19:11] the National Archives,[L19:12] the World Digital Library[L19:13] (with significant primary materials from all countries and cultures), or the Digital Public Library of America[L19:14] (bringing together materials from U.S. libraries, archives, and museums). Remember that adding any of the following words to a search query will help you access archival materials in general searches: papers, diaries, correspondence, records, and manuscripts.

2 Locating primary documents in a time and place (the context)

Whatever you've located in your personal archives can be better understood and interpreted if located within a larger context—historical or cultural or even digital. A Hmong student studying his family's photographs places them in the context of events that were taking place in Southeast Asia in the period before Hmong immigration to the United States. The man remembering a small piece of his family history in Yesterday>Today tries to establish a context of place by revisiting the town he grew up in, interviewing those who still live there, and photographing the buildings he remembers.

If Hannah had decided on a personal archive project related to her own literacy history, she might have searched for a book she remembered (with suggestions for finding children's books "Looking for a Book?" on Old Children's Books website[L19:15]), looked for information about other books published in the same period (to see how the genres commonly available compared with what she read), looked at Newbery Medal winners[L19:16] for the period, or checked local library archives for news accounts or pictures from literacy events such as Story Time (the Huntington Beach, CA library, for example, has both in its archives). She could also have created her own digital archive with images from these materials, photos of the covers of books she still owns, or screenshots of digital versions now available.

3 Identifying themes and patterns

As with the data from an ethnographic study, your archival data can be analyzed to find particular themes and patterns related to your questions or hypotheses, often drawing ideas from the secondary resources you've discovered. Archival studies also draw on the analysis of primary materials, considering the following questions.

❶ Who was the author/speaker/creator?

❷ When was it written or created?

❸ What kind of perspective does it represent? What biases or limitations does the source reflect?

④ Who was its intended audience?

⑤ Why was the document produced? What sort of function did it serve? Was it perhaps created in response to a particular kind of problem? If you suspect that it was, what might the problem have been?

⑥ What can the primary source tell us about the society at the time it was written? What can it tell us about social norms and expectations of the time of its composition?

⑦ How does the source add to/change/challenge your understanding of the period and the context?

Hannah would find a number of scholarly studies of gender bias in children's books that would cover the late 1980s and early 1990s, a period in which some of her favorite books were published. That

might lead her to examine one or more of the books from her personal archive to see how gender was portrayed, and then consider other artifacts from her childhood—such as toys or children's records (perhaps her parents played for her the 1972 record by Marlo Thomas, "Free to Be You and Me" that explicitly challenged traditional gender biases). She would also find studies showing that gender bias continues to show up in educational software for young children.[19:7]

4 Using secondary sources to support analysis and interpretation

As with an ethnographic study, you'll want, in an archival study, to synthesize the information from different sources and make specific connections to them.

WRITING MOVES ◀

Drafting and Shaping

1 Synthesizing and summarizing prior research

Here's an example of a summary of prior research, noting key themes that have emerged, from a 2014 study, "The Gender Journey in Children's Picture Books" by April Maddox and Michelle Sobolak.[19:8]

> As Sunderland (2011) explains, while gender was not completely ignored as an aspect of children's literature prior to the modern Women's Movement in the late 1960s, the topic rose to prominence after that sociocultural shift (p. 9). Early explorations into gender in children's literature (e.g., Fisher, 1970; Stewig & Higgs, 1973) found that female characters were more sparsely represented; when they were depicted, it was in more subservient ways that ranged from "dull to degrading to invisible" (Fisher, as cited in Sunderland, 2011, p. 10). Since then, studies in children's literature have continued to show two distinct trends: 1) girls are portrayed less often than boys in children's stories (Knowles & Malmkjaer, 1996; Singh, 1998), and 2) females and males tend to be depicted in stereotypical terms: "girls are represented as sweet, naive, conforming and dependent, while boys are

> typically described as strong, adventurous, independent, and capable" (Jett-Simpson & Masland, 1993, as cited in Singh, 1998, p. 2). Perhaps the most important message that we can take away from this research is that how gender is portrayed in children's books "contributes to the image children develop of their own role and that of their gender in society" (Singh, 1998, p. 2). Our purpose here is to look at best-selling children's picture books from the past 40 years to trace any changes in the ways boys and girls are depicted, but also to examine the types of gender role models that best-selling children's picture books showcase.

Hannah might prepare a similar summary of the research she draws on. And, as with an ethnographic study, she'd go on to show how she is drawing on this prior research in her own inquiry, showing how it's relevant to her questions and her data.

2 Making connections

As with an ethnographic study, you'll want to make connections between what you've found in others' research and what you're seeing in your own primary data. If your archive includes photographs, for example, you might want to draw on what van Dijck has found in our selection from *Mediated Memories* (Chapter 6), about earlier and current uses of photo collections. How do her understandings help you to see and interpret material from your own archive?

Maddox and Sobolak[19:8] go on to examine children's picture books drawn from the *New York Times* best seller list that were published at 10-year intervals, looking for how often books had primary female characters, how often males versus females were portrayed with images of strength, and how often females were portrayed in stereotypical female roles, finding that there was a shift in each of these elements over time toward more positive inclusion of female characters.

Hannah might see, if she examines her favorites from her personal children's book collection, whether these features also characterize those books and whether they vary, depending on the date of publication, recording the connections she finds and quoting Maddox and Sobolak[19:8] in her research journal. She might even go on to turn the lens of gender stereotyping back onto the books that Bookworm Buddies are discussing in the digital world.

3 Structuring your archival study

At this point, you're ready to use all of the material of your research journal inquiries in constructing a final report on your archival study. Again, you'll want to balance concerns about your audience (their expectations for key elements of such a study and what will gain their interest) with a presentation of your own inquiry and the understandings you've gained, so you might organize these elements in different ways. You'll find a map or outline to be helpful at this point, both for structuring your paper and for generating some headings that will make that structure evident to a reader while highlighting some key points.

These are the elements (also represented in your research proposal) that you'll want to include.

- An introduction that tells what collection of materials you're studying and why, and your initial questions/hypotheses about them.

- The context for this collection—whatever you've been able to discover about who gathered the collection and/or created its materials; their purpose and how and when they were originally used, of information you've been able to gather about them and about the larger social/cultural/historical context in which they were created or used; and any other background information that will help your readers understand what you've come to understand.

- The research context—a summary/synthesis of some relevant research that has helped you to think about your own data.

- The larger themes and patterns that have emerged from your study, with specific examples that illustrate them. These might be used as headings for different sections in which you talk about each.

- The connections you've found between what you've discovered and what other research has shown.

- A conclusion in which you share the understandings you've gained, in the end, and that might point to further questions/areas of research that could follow.

You'll also want to work with citations and references in the ways described under Project 3: The Literature Review.

Digital Toolbox
See Part IV, Section 1

Project Type 3
The Literature Review

The literature review arose from a need, across disciplines, to sum up and synthesize earlier research and scholarship as scholars undertook new projects. At this point, you have seen how to use the scholarly tools of the digital world for your own research, and you've collected relevant sources for exploring your own topic and questions. You've also seen examples of how a review of relevant literature—the scholarship related to a particular topic or question—is used in studies focused on working with primary data, the ethnographic or archival study.

The literature review, a separate research genre, focuses on the secondary materials of other scholars' studies, offering a fuller look at what has been learned about a question or topic. Literature reviews typically address audiences of other scholars, both those who are undertaking their own research on the topic and those who simply want to be informed about the topic, whether or not they are doing research that's directly related to it. The literature review answers the question: What do we know about x, and how have we come to know it? What do we know about how the use of social media affects face-to-face interactions? About how reading children's books on an iPad versus in print affects the development of literacy in early childhood? About what young people know about searching for information on the internet?

See Chapter 9
for Lawrence Lessig's article.

A literature review can also serve as the basis for your own argument about a topic. Once you've reviewed the studies of children's digital versus print reading, you might find yourself convinced about whether reading on screens harms or helps their development of literacy, and you can use the research you've reviewed to support an argument related to their use of computers or tablets—whether to integrate tablet-based reading into the home or a preschool program, for example.

Often literature reviews are prepared for research centers, to represent the state of knowledge about an area. For example, a report from Gasser and other researchers at the Berkman Klein Center for Internet & Society at Harvard University (also a scholarly home for Lawrence Lessig) on *Youth and Digital Media*[19:9] summarizes various strands of research on how young people do research on the internet. Literature reviews can also help with planning future research by showing what's been addressed and perhaps also where there are gaps or unanswered questions.

The Literature Review in Digital Contexts

The form of the literature review has changed little in digital settings. It continues to function much the same way it has traditionally and to serve much the same purposes of pulling together and finding patterns in what has been found. But because the literature review project generally involves gathering many more sources and synthesizing their information, the digital research management tools we've seen in the last few chapters, from searchable electronic databases, to note-taking and bibliographic reference tools like EndNote or Zotero (which we discuss further in Part IV—Digital Toolbox), have allowed researchers to access vast amounts of the research being done by others and to make this information-gathering process more manageable. What's important in preparing a more limited literature review is the combination of: 1) accessing but also filtering the results in an electronic database to find the most valuable ones for the topic and questions you are pursuing, and 2) managing the information you find.

Digital Toolbox
See Part IV, Section 5

Researching and Reporting

See Chapter 18
and its discussion of gathering research materials relevant to your topic.

Once you've gathered articles that are relevant to your topic in the ways we explored in Chapter 18, you'll begin to take stock of what you've found. You can draw on the model of other literature reviews related to your topic (and you can search for these by adding the term "review" or "literature review" to a search). Some reviews will be quite narrowly focused, while others will be large and comprehensive. Both seek to find patterns in the literature—groupings of materials around particular questions or themes.

For example, a 2012 review of "Facebook Research in the Social Sciences"[19:10] found 226 articles that could be grouped around the following questions.

- Who is using Facebook, and what are users doing while on Facebook?
- Why do people use Facebook?
- How are people presenting themselves on Facebook?
- How is Facebook affecting relationships among groups and individuals?
- Why are people disclosing personal information on Facebook despite potential risks?

The researchers summarized what was learned about each of these questions. They found that the research literature showed that why people use Facebook was tied to external and internal motivations. Here's their summary of research about internal motivation:

The most common internal motivation discussed in the literature was users' desire to keep in touch with friends (Ellison, Steinfield, & Lampe, 2006; Joinson, 2008; Lampe, Ellison, & Steinfield, 2006; Saleh, Jani, Marzouqi, Khajeh, & Rajan, 2011; Sheldon, 2008).

Expanding on these findings, researchers have explored the underlying influence of "social capital," which refers to the benefits received from relationships with other people (Steinfield, Ellison, & Lampe, 2008). To understand the connections between social capital and Facebook relationships, researchers have distinguished between strong and weak ties among Facebook friends (Granovetter, 1973). A typical Facebook user will directly communicate with a small core group of friends by posting comments or messages, indicating strong ties, and then follow the majority of friends through passive means such as viewing the news feed and browsing, indicating weak ties (Burke, Marlow, & Lento, 2010). Research has shown that users are able to cultivate weak ties in an informal manner, and Facebook use may help maintain previous relationships and crystallize otherwise ephemeral relationships (Ellison, Steinfield, & Lampe, 2007; J. Lewis & West, 2009).

> **See Chapter 15**
> and its discussion of social media's role in political change.

The article ends by identifying some areas where more research is needed, including research on the topic we addressed in Chapter 15, the role of social media in organizing grassroots activism toward political change. Although it doesn't include Gladwell's essay on whether the revolution will be tweeted, since that was an article in a magazine for a popular readership, it does include the research he drew on about strong and weak ties in social media.

From just this summary and excerpt from the Facebook literature review, you can see some typical elements of this genre.

- A grouping of studies into categories around particular questions or topics
- A summary of what was found by each of the key studies in this category
- A synthesis of what has been found related to each question or topic

At this point, you're ready to use all of the material of your research journal inquiries in constructing a final literature review. Again, you'll want to balance concerns about your audience (their expectations for key elements of such a study and what will gain their interest) with a presentation of your own inquiry and the understandings you've gained, so you might organize these elements in different ways. You'll find a map or outline to be helpful at this point, both for structuring your paper and for generating some headings that will make that structure evident to a reader while highlighting some key points.

See Chapter 18
for more about how
and why to create an
annotated bibliography.

WRITING MOVES ◄

Inquiring and Inventing

Let's start with the moves we saw in the Facebook literature review to provide a sense of how to shape this kind of work.

1 Grouping studies into categories around particular questions or topics

What themes or issues connect your sources to one another? What questions have they helped you to answer? What perspectives do they represent (e.g., the importance of internal motivation versus the importance of external motivation for Facebook users)?

2 Summarizing what was found by each of the key studies in this category

Your summary will usually include information about how the study was carried out, its key points, as well as what it showed that's most relevant to your inquiry, information that you gathered as you prepared your annotated bibliography.

3 Synthesizing what has been found related to each question or topic

What did each study or cluster of studies find that contributes to your understanding of that topic? Do the studies all reinforce one another, or are there some that show different or conflicting findings? What remains to be explored, through looking at a broader range of studies or through primary research?

4 Structuring your literature-based study

These are the structural elements you'll want to include.

- An introduction that tells what topic you're pursuing and why, and your initial questions/hypotheses about the topic

- Your purposes for carrying out this literature review—what you hope to contribute with it to the ongoing conversation about the topic

- The method of your review—what disciplines did you focus on, and how did you select the sources you finally decided to include?

- The categories or groupings of your studies around particular themes or subtopics (These might be used as headings for different sections in which you present your synthesis of what's been learned about that topic)

- The position the evidence from your review of the literature leads you to take (if you're exploring a contested issue)

- A conclusion in which you share the understandings you've gained, in the end, and that might point to further questions/areas of research that could follow

WRITING MOVES

Drafting and Shaping

Once you have shaped the report of your research, addressing the key elements of the genre you're working in, you are in a position to refine it. We've seen earlier that groups in local discourse contexts, using social media sites like Facebook, have generated certain expected ways of entering the conversations that take place there, and that the public discourse contexts entered by blog writers and reviewers and those who would present arguments about the power of social media have expected ways—an expected style—as well. So, too, do the discourse contexts of academic fields, with some common expectations across disciplines as well as the discipline-specific styles you've begun to find as you've explored the research literature on your topic. You've probably absorbed some of the ways of entering an academic conversation from your reading and research, and from the composing and sharing you've been doing throughout your work with this book.

The moves discussed in this section will help you to review your presentation of your work and help you to consider what's characteristic of the typical public/academic and mediated conversation you're entering with that work—the rhetorical context you're participating in.

1 Entering the conversation

As you make rhetorical decisions about how to refine your presentation of your work, you can consider the following moves.

- **Situating your turn.** Considering what it means to contribute to what others have said and are saying about a topic can help you decide how to position your turn in a conversation. One really productive way to do this, to situate not only what you are saying, but also why you are saying it, is to create a sense that your writing isn't just filling up space but addresses a real need as it makes a new contribution. You can do this by nodding to what has come before as you explain how your work extends, complements, or challenges others' thinking. So, Hannah could say something like, "Though book clubs (both analog and web-mediated) have been examined before in light of community formation, my study provides a careful consideration of how online introduction can work to support and maintain a sense of belonging." As you craft your title and introductory sections, you will certainly want to grab your readers' attention, but you will also want to orient them by positioning your work as a larger turn in a conversation as you highlight why your turn is important.

- **Weaving other voices into the conversation.** As this chapter stresses, you can bring other voices into your composition in a variety of ways as you draw on ethnographic work, archival analysis, and existing published accounts through a literature review. As you shape your research, think carefully about how you weave between these voices and your own in your work. Do you introduce questions and paraphrases, letting readers know why and how you are extending your thinking by turning to others? Do you move between your voice and others' to create richness and texture in your writing? Do you bring a variety of perspectives together as you represent others' thinking about the topic you are examining? Have you included the voices of your peer researchers who are studying related topics where their findings complement or challenge your own? And, for an ethnographic study, how do you weave in the voices of those being studied?

- **Commenting on your turn as a turn.** Concluding a research project can be overwhelming; you have moved through an extensive project and have most likely come to think about your focus (a community, a set of texts or artifacts, a line of inquiry) in new ways, but once you are presenting this work to others, you might not know what larger ideas to point to as you conclude your work. Thinking about your project as a turn in a conversation can help you decide how to highlight the richness and value of your research. How has your work contributed to what others have said before? How might it invite other new turns in the larger, ongoing conversation? How might it work to invite others to think with you about this or connected topics? Commenting on your work as a turn in a conversation can help you articulate its significance in pragmatic and conceptual terms as you consider how your work might shape what others do and how they think.

2 Using citations to archive others' turns

As you draw on others' published or publicly shared work that speaks to your topic, you will want to be sure to handle your citations with care. As you do this, you will need to follow the guidelines associated with the style of citation your class uses. There are several major styles that are used in different disciplines.

- **MLA (Modern Language Association) style.** This style is typically used in the humanities, and it is the style normally expected in English courses. It is the style we use throughout this book.

- **APA (American Psychological Association) style.** This style is typically used in the social sciences and education and is generally expected in courses in those areas. It stresses dates of publication.

- **CMS (Chicago Manual of Style) style.** This style is used in history and other areas of arts and sciences.

- **CBE (Council of Biology Editors) style.** This style is drawn upon in many of the natural sciences.

All of these styles are supplemented with guidelines for citing online sources from the internet through COS (Columbia Online Style). These styles represent an already established **shared how** you will want to tend to with care as you take on an academic community's ways of working with other texts. You'll find guides to MLA, APA, and COS style for common types of citations and references on the Purdue OWL website.

- **Citing sources within a document.** Though each citation style handles this a bit differently, you will need to be sure you cite each intertextual move you make in your piece. So, when you draw on others' ideas and words (as you paraphrase or quote them), you will need to be sure to show exactly when you begin to represent another's work and then provide a sense of how to find that work in your Works Cited or References list. As we make clear in Chapters 17 and 18, we create a textual ecology as we collect and draw on sources as researchers. You will want to make sure you give your readers access to that web of texts by clearly showing when you are drawing on them.

- **Preparing a list of works cited.** Using a resource like the Purdue OWL website, create a list of works cited (if you are using MLA) or references (if you are using APA). While part of this process will focus on tending to the style-specific conventions for creating such a list, you should also consider the conversation you are drawing on and extending through your work.

WRITING MOVES

Revising and Publishing

Once you've completed a full research draft that includes all elements expected in a report on the type of research you've done, and that incorporates the shared ways of engaging in an academic conversation, you'll want to prepare to share your work with your peers and in the wider academic world.

Digital Toolbox
See Part IV, Section 4

1 Considering multimodal possibilities

As you think about sharing your work, consider the possibilities for making it multimodal. As with all of the composing projects we've

suggested in this book, we would argue that your work will be enhanced if you use more than one mode of expression. What images of sites you've studied or artifacts you've analyzed, what sounds of voices you've recorded can you include as examples in your report on your study, both to engage your readers and to help them to see what you've seen, hear what you've heard, and better understand why you've come to the understandings you're sharing?

2 Inviting peer review

As you invite readers to engage and respond to your nearly final research paper, you might ask them to share what they find with you by writing you a letter as a more extended response. As they comment on how you have shaped your research, how to synthesize multiple sources, have them comment explicitly on how you join and contribute to a larger conversation. The following questions can guide that work.

- How have I, as a writer, represented what has already been said about my topic? How do I add to that existing conversation?

- Have I made a clear presentation of the understandings I've come to and how I came to them with all of the elements of the type of study I've carried out?

- How do I draw on other voices in my work? Do I do enough to introduce, analyze, and extend others' thinking here?

3 Revising and editing

Drawing on your peer review feedback, you'll want to prepare a final version of your report. At this point, you'll also want to do a careful final editing, both of your text and of the format for your citations.

Reinventing and Circulating Your Work

Although the research you have created as you have moved through Part III probably won't engage the public audience we focus on in Part II, writers in academic contexts have many platforms for publications for making their contributions to an academic conversation, and some of these are available to student researchers.

Your campus might house publications that distribute student research; at Coastal Carolina University, for instance, *Bridges Journal* is a publication for undergraduate research. *Young Scholars in Writing: Undergraduate Research in Writing and Rhetoric* (http://arc.lib.montana.edu/ojs/index.php/Young-Scholars-In-Writing/index) is also a great venue.

Alternatively you might set up a wiki or website on which you group and share related studies, with introductions to each set suggesting how the work collectively contributes to our understanding of and shared knowledge about how we are practicing our new literacies in digital contexts.

Key Concepts

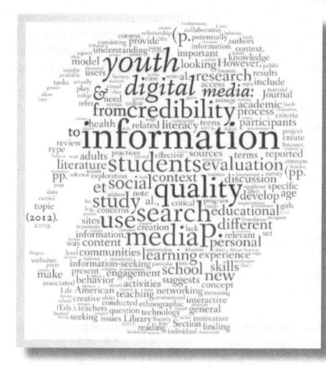

Constructing
a Portfolio

CHAPTER TWENTY

CENTRAL QUESTIONS

1 What different types and purposes are there for creating a writing portfolio?

2 How do writers go about curating, preparing, and reflecting on their work for a portfolio?

3 What tools and techniques can you draw on to compose a digital portfolio that can be shared online?

Chapter Preview

In print culture, writers, designers, and artists of all kinds create *portfolios* to showcase their work. They share these collections of representative texts (pieces of writing, art, images, and projects) with employers or customers, or others producing similar pieces or working in similar contexts. The portfolio has become a common practice for professional writers and artists as it allows them to collect and share their work with potential audiences. The digital turn at the beginning of the twenty-first century has expanded the ways in which such print portfolios are constructed and shared. Digital media, cloud computing, and an increase in sharing technologies create more possibilities for the circulation of portfolios and, in turn, make the act of portfolio creation an important cultural practice, especially for writers and artists trying to establish an online presence. We've seen that constructing and performing an online identity is important in a digital, networked world where information about one another can be easily searched for and shared. Digital portfolios provide an opportunity for individuals to construct an intentional, public, and professional identity tied to a collection of work and interests. Not surprisingly, portfolios are also becoming increasingly common in college, where students are asked to pull together the work they have completed over a semester, year, or college career in order to reflect on their work and its development over time, and to share that work with a larger audience.

As a writer, preparing a portfolio offers you an opportunity to collect, reflect on, and share your work as you come to larger understandings of the texts you have produced over a span of time and question what you have learned during that process. While portfolios often take the shape of a final product intended for a specific context and audience, they also invite a careful consideration of your composing process as you look back on the decisions you've made about a set of texts. And digital portfolios let you easily include and highlight digital and multimodal compositions. In this chapter, we'll consider the types and purposes behind both professional portfolios and the portfolio you might create for the writing course you are currently taking.

Exploring
The Purposes and Uses of Portfolios

Portfolio creation, like all composing, is guided by specific contexts and purposes. You might be constructing a portfolio because you are completing a composition or writing course, because you are graduating soon and one is required for your major or university, or because you want to show a collection of your work to prospective employers. Portfolio building is similar to the process we go through when we carefully gather and curate informational resources in an organized collection of texts, images, or links. We can begin to think about what's involved in more formal portfolio building by reflecting on what we do informally.

Reflecting on Informal Collecting

As we've mentioned in previous chapters, much informal collecting takes place online, on sites like Pinterest.

Figure 20.1: Pinterest post

Figure 20.1 is a screenshot of a Pinterest board Ashley Canter created while working through her digital literacy narrative (discussed in Chapter 2) about how she and her sister use texting to support their relationship. Just a quick look at this board shows that Ashley created it thematically, as she collected and archived images and quotations about sisters. In making this collection, Ashley drew on her implicit and explicit understandings of visual design as she used the application to support the written composition of her literacy narrative. Creating such collections has become an important way to manage the constant flow of information in our digital world. In fact, applications like Pinterest, Diigo, Instagram, and Flickr (to name a small few) are specifically designed to help people manage and share their digital lives. Pinterest, for example, serves as a digital bulletin board where people can pin images and links they want to keep track of, making separate collections for places to go, recipes to try, ski boots to consider, or as Ashley has done, images and quotations related to themes they want to explore about their lives or the world.

As people go beyond collecting to considering the meanings of their collections and how to select from them and organize them to bring out those meanings, they are involved in a process of *curation*. Traditionally we've thought of curation as the work of art museum curators, experts who consider what a museum owns in a particular area, such as contemporary art, and decide what's appropriate to display for an exhibit, around what themes, in what order, with what captions—the purpose being to create a meaningful experience for museum goers, or of archivists and historians who do similar work with collections of other materials. But with the vast amount of content circulating on the internet, curation is becoming a necessary literacy practice. As Sue Waters, editor of The Edublogger,[L20:1] reminds teachers and students (and everyone else): "It's no longer just about creating content. We are living in an era of content abundance. It's now about finding and putting content into a context, in a meaningful and organised way, around specific topics." With so much information swirling around us, we all have to act as informal curators as "we collect, manage and collate the best, most relevant content, on a specific topic or theme, for ourselves and to share with others."[20:1]

Waters uses the term **digital curation** to point to the fact that both the materials being collected and the tools being used to organize them are digital, even at this level of individual activity. But the need for effective digital curation is also a challenge facing contemporary society, as we consider both what's worth preserving into the future and how to manage and archive a vast array of materials in ever-changing digital formats.

Pinterest is one site that helps individuals like Ashley with this process, whatever their focus or interests, and in Part IV of this book we'll consider other digital resources that can help with managing and organizing the growing abundance of the digital artifacts we create, save, and share.

> **digital curation**
> the thoughtful collecting and organizing of digital materials with digital tools

> ❝ It's no longer just about creating content. We are living in an era of content abundance. It's now about finding and putting content into a context, in a meaningful and organised way, around specific topics. ❞

INQUIRY

#1: Curating digital content

Find an example of digital curation. Maybe you will look to a Pinterest page you have created of a collection of materials (images, texts, songs, movies) that someone else has composed and shared. What is important here is just that you find an example of a purposeful digital collection of artifacts. Looking at this collection consider the what, how, where, and why of the collection. What is included in this collection? What sorts of texts, artifacts, or materials have been brought together? How have these things been collected? How are they organized? How are they being presented? Where is this collection housed? Who might come across, find, and use this collection? And, finally, why have these materials been curated? What purpose does this digital collection seem to serve?

Curating More Formally: Professional Portfolios

Thinking about the curation process that underlies any collection is one way to prepare for creating your own portfolio, and collecting is the first step you take when pulling together a portfolio of your work. Another useful step for preparing a portfolio is to look at the portfolios of professional writers to get a sense of the realm of possibilities. In today's digital, cloud-based writing environments, creating and presenting online portfolios has become a common tool for professional and freelance writers. Such portfolios come in a lot of different shapes, and getting a sense of this variety can help you see how to present and share your work as you make informed decisions about how to best display it to potential viewers. Here are a couple of examples of writers who are using online writing portfolios as a way to introduce themselves and their work (Figure 20.2).

> **Sidenote**
>
> As you begin to think about creating your own digital portfolio of your work, what new understandings can you take from this example about what you will include in your portfolio, how you might construct it, where you might house it, and the significance of this undertaking? Reflect on these ideas as you work through the rest of this chapter.

Figure 20.2: Portfolio home page for freelance writer Ximena Vengoechea [L20:2]

Ximena is just beginning her career as a freelance writer. Like many freelance writers, Ximena has a day job, working on a research team at Twitter. On her portfolio site, she tells us a little about that job and presents portfolio pages with examples of her design/illustration work and her writings about personal growth, culture, and technology, including articles on contemporary topics, such as one on internet dating for *The Huffington Post.*[20:2]

And then there's Jeff Bartlett (Figure 20.3). Jeff Bartlett introduces himself as an adventure photographer/writer and that "My biggest passions—cycling, skiing, and hiking—are synonymous with active travel, so I use my craft to tell compelling stories about mountain life and culture." His portfolio home page shows some of his photography, with announcements for workshops he's offering, and has links to his blog and to his portfolio with collections of both his photography and his writing about mountain biking, skiing, and chasing after wildlife, all with the goal of "getting people outside to explore." Jeff situates his portfolio within a textual ecology of social media, inviting his viewers/readers to connect with him via Facebook, Instagram, and more. For Jeff, the portfolio is a piece of his larger professional strategy.

 *Figure 20.3: Portfolio home page for professional writer/photographer Jeff Bartlett*[L20:3]

Note that while we refer to writers' portfolios, they often include more than written text. Ximena's includes her sketches and illustrations from a variety of design projects. And Jeff's photographs offer a visual representation of his adventurous life while showcasing his work as a photographer as well as a writer.

INQUIRY

#2: Learning from professional writing portfolios

Looking at these or other freelance writers' portfolios, what do you find that can guide your own process of creating a portfolio? Follow the links and move through the pages. What elements/pages do these writers include? What do you learn (and where) about who they are as writers and their purposes for presenting their work in this way? About the look and design of their site and the ways in which they've organized their portfolios? About the different kinds of work they've included?

Curating for the Classroom and Beyond: Student Portfolios

In addition to looking at the portfolios of professional writers, looking at other student writing portfolios will be even more relevant in planning your own portfolio. At John Jay College of Criminal Justice in New York City, freshman and sophomore students prepare digital portfolios under the guidance of Professor Carmen Kynard. You can find several examples at johnjay.digication.com,[20:3] and we recommend you look at the portfolio of Christian Nunes titled "My World in My Words" (Figure 20.4).[20:4]

Figure 20.4: Portfolio home page for student writer Christian Nunes[L20:4]

Christian's world is New York City, and he makes that clear with the image of the city skyline on his home page. We can see that he includes both an About page and a Visual Statement that says something about his design choices for the portfolio. And he includes shorter pieces he has written—a research study on social media and youth culture, and reflections on the pieces he's included, as well as one about the e-portfolio itself. Christian created his portfolio as the culminating project for his first-year writing course.

Another example is from a recent graduate of the Master of Arts in Writing program at Coastal Carolina University, Laurie J. Jackson (Figure 20.5).[20:5]

Like Christian, Laurie has chosen a particular theme and style for her portfolio that she feels represents her identity and work in some way. She also includes an About page and a link to her portfolio of writing samples. While Christian has chosen work completed in a single class, Laurie, as a student preparing for graduation, selected work from across several courses and years, including works of fiction, nonfiction, technical writing, and her master's thesis. She also has included a main link to her resume.

Figure 20.5: Portfolio home page for graduate student writer Laurie J. Jackson[L20:5]

INQUIRY

#3: Learning from student writing portfolios

Looking at these student portfolios, what do you find that is similar to but also perhaps different from the professional portfolios you've just examined? What first impression do their home pages give you? Follow the links for one or two and move around a bit. What have they included, and how have they organized their collection? How might their rhetorical purposes, the why and where of their projects as students at different points in their college careers, differ and lead to different choices in what they include and how they present this material?

As you explore other portfolios you find online, begin your own informal process of collecting and bookmarking, or even pinning on Pinterest, any portfolio sites you may want to return to for inspiration as you create your own.

Purposeful Collecting and Curating

Once you have a good sense of how others have constructed their collections/portfolios and have considered different ways you could present your own collection of work, you're ready to begin gathering your materials. If, like Christian, you're creating a portfolio for one course, most likely you've already started this process and have been saving the writing and multimodal composing you have been doing for your course work in a folder on your computer or on a remote server in the cloud. The next step is to look over this work, as well as other writing and related work you have completed during the course, and potentially digitize (by typing it up or taking a picture) any handwritten work (maps, sketches, freewrites) you have done that you feel should be included in your writing portfolio. If, like Laurie, you're creating a portfolio that represents a wider range of your work, you'll nevertheless begin by gathering materials you could potentially include, but we'll focus first on the course-based portfolio.

As you go through this process of collecting and curating, you'll want to think rhetorically and consider the purpose of your portfolio, who the intended audience is, and what type of media to use to present your work. You'll then want to select and organize, from the full range of your work, the pieces you feel to be most relevant and significant to your purposes.

Gathering your work

As you begin to curate your work, it's useful to start simply and gather any relevant documents you want to consider in a folder, one that can be shared with others. You can certainly do this in a physical folder, and your instructor may ask you to do so, but we also suggest you do this digitally using any online, cloud-based platform that allows you to readily share your work with others (Dropbox, Google Docs, etc.). A basic process portfolio might look something like this (Figure 20.6).

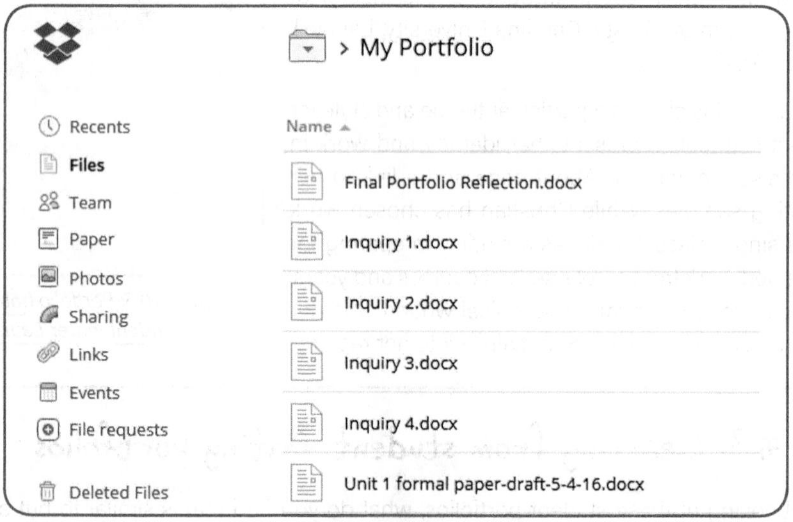

Figure 20.6: Online collection of writings from a first-year writing course using Dropbox

In this example for a first-year writing course, the student has gathered several inquiries, both rough and final drafts of formal papers, and a final reflection. You can think of this initial process of collection as stepping back to get a larger sense of the *amount and diversity of writing you have done this semester.* Depending on the specific details of your portfolio assignment, you may want to add other texts, such as instructor and peer feedback, discussion posts, and other pieces you've written outside of the course, to capture a rich sense of how you have engaged in the writing process over the semester. You might also decide to include examples of work you completed outside of the course context that drew on composing skills you were developing over this period, such as contributions to a team website. How you organize these pieces will be up to you, ultimately, but for starters it's useful to put these texts in chronological order, starting with what you wrote first. Having your collection online makes it easy to share with potential audiences, which may include other instructors, advisors, and peers.

Reviewing your materials

Once you have these texts in a folder, spend some time reading through your collection of texts, taking notes on the following questions.

- What common themes, interests, or concerns are central to these texts, images, and other materials?
- What do they show about your development as a writer and composer? What shifts do you see that showcase what you learned throughout this semester?
- What pieces offer the best examples of the themes or patterns you've found? What pieces best fit your purposes in creating this portfolio? Select these pieces for further curating and reflection.

Reflecting on your purpose

As you begin to reflect, consider your purpose (as an individual or as a member of your class) for creating a portfolio. What do you want to show about your body of work? What themes and patterns have you identified and now hope to showcase by compiling a set of finished pieces? Do any pieces need to be revised to better show what you hope to show? What theme about yourself, your writing and composing, college writing, or new literacies do you hope to develop? What audience (your professor, your classmates, the public) will you be addressing? Who will read, view, and have access to this portfolio? Reflect on the scope of materials that would suit this purpose and audience.

An immediate purpose for your own collection might be provided by a course assignment: to show how you have developed as a writer/reader/designer over time, to showcase the strongest work you have produced over a semester, to create a thematic approach to a subject. Beyond an assignment, there is also value in looking closely at all of the pieces you have composed over the course of a semester in a more open inquiry process. By organizing the work you've done, and then reading these texts with the purpose of understanding the progression of your writing and thinking over the semester, your goal is to arrive at some interesting realizations about the work you've completed and the learning process you've been through.

Sharing your collection with a reader

Once you have read through your collection and noted your observations, exchange your working portfolio with a classmate or other reader and move through each other's collected pieces. Each of you should note what you observe and then compose a letter that summarizes your observations. Unlike most peer review activities, you aren't reading your classmate's work to make suggestions for revision; rather, you are trying to help each other clarify what this collection of work shows about your development as composers or about the texts you have created based on all (or most) of the pieces you have produced this semester.

Ask your reader to address these questions.

- What do you notice about my texts?
- How do they seem to develop?
- How do they seem to respond to specific contexts and purposes?

- Where I've used multimodal resources, what do you see about my choices and how I've made use of them?

- What can you, after reading this collection, say about my style, approach, voice, strengths, quirks, design sense, and/or other characteristics?

- What do you notice as you "read" my semester as it is represented through these pieces?

- Which pieces do you think best represent my work?

- Which pieces seem to best suit the purpose(s) of this collection?

In looking through your work, what strengths and characteristics does your reader find to be most strongly represented and in what pieces? Ask your reader to write a draft of an introduction to your work, telling its story. What is that story, as seen in this collection, and what can other readers/viewers expect to find there?

WRITING MOVES ◄

Inquiring and Inventing

reflection
considering work you have completed in order to come to a deeper understanding of yourself and your learning process

At this point in the portfolio process you should have a folder (print, digital, or both) of relevant texts and generative notes on this collection from yourself and your peers. As you have done this work, you have initiated the reflective process about your purpose. Now it is time to extend this **reflection** and consider both your process of production and the pieces you have composed. A reflective frame (a piece of writing often requested in portfolios required for classes) provides you with a time and place to comment on your work and to guide the ways in which your readers and viewers might consider your portfolio as a whole and as a collection of smaller pieces. The following are specific reflective moves to consider as you compose your portfolio reflection.

1 Reflecting on your work and the progress it highlights

Reflecting on your work and how you created it is central to the creation of a portfolio, and making this analysis and reflection explicit is typically required in student portfolios. Reflecting on your work to see what you can learn from it typically involves an analysis of what you find there. And it should also include considering your work as a highly situated literate activity—an activity very much shaped by its context.

Any consideration of what your work shows and how you've worked as a writer and composer will involve a close analysis of the texts you've produced. There are many angles you can take, but your ultimate goal in writing a portfolio reflection is to demonstrate to an audience that you can thoughtfully reflect on and assess your development as a writer and learner.

Turning to a student example, Brian Santoro chose to include several inquiries he had created for the course, along with drafts and teacher and peer comments. As Brian wrote in his final reflection:

Something that I tried to take away from this semester that demonstrated my growth was really integrating examples and quotes into all my work. This work was not only essays, but it was also inquiries, and reading texts. This was first done by annotating texts in close detail and picking out the most relevant information to include in the essay or inquiry. After the fact, I would focus on working the example into my paper and making sure it fit correctly. I worked on this skill throughout the semester and continued to get better at it. In other words, I would make sure to elaborate on the quote or example, set it up beforehand and then transition smoothly into the next sentence etc.

As Brian read through the writing he did for the semester, he started to make connections between different writing assignments and see his progression as he became more comfortable with the reading and writing skills he was asked to try in the course.

Ashley (who we first met in Chapter 2) also reflected on the work she completed in her composition class. As she looked back on her experiences as a first-year college writer, she wrote:

> During this class, I feel that I have acquired a more full and nontraditional understanding of important concepts like "literacy." Also, during my time in the course, I feel that I have improved greatly as a writer. The work in the very beginning of the semester allowed me to learn more about certain terms like "new literacies" and discover new writing techniques that I would later employ. My rough draft of the first paper we wrote was phrased well and grammatically correct, however the structure was a bit boring and formulaic. Over the course of writing each paper, I feel like my writing became increasingly complex and more interesting to the reader. The most valuable technique or skill I have acquired in my writing throughout this course is the ability to make even academic and research papers interesting and creative. Academically, I feel that this skill will help me write well in all my course, inside or outside of the English classroom...Publicly, I now have the ability to write and speak in a way that is professional, but still personal and innovative.

When organizing their portfolios, Brian and Ashley could highlight these developments in their writing, selecting pieces of their work that show where they have effectively brought others' words into new conversations or have been making academic papers "interesting and creative," organizing them to show their progress in doing these things, and commenting on the patterns and changes they now find in them. They are essentially involved in a process of curating their collection. This kind of work helps you do more than make a case for your writing (or justify a good grade as you complete a class); it provides you with an opportunity to take stock of your experiences and understandings.

As you reread your work, highlight sections that point to understandings you have come to about your writing process, literacy, or about digital culture and the circulation of texts in broader terms. Do you see any relation between your writing and the feedback you received from your teacher and peers? What kinds of changes and revisions did you make from draft to draft, from inquiry to draft? Once you have marked such instances, comment

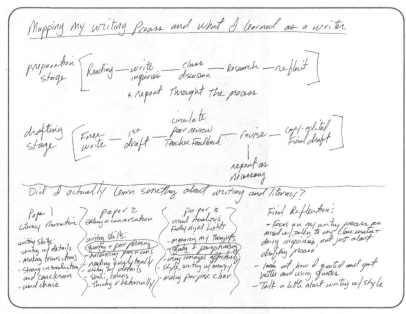

Figure 20.7: Visual mapping of Brian's writing process and writing skills practiced during the course

on them as you explain what they show about the texts you have composed and your development. Using pen and paper, try to map out how your writing has progressed. Ashley could map out the ways in which her academic writing has become more "interesting and creative," and then mark and comment on places where she has found this to be true (Figure 20.7).

Digital Toolbox
See Part IV, Section 1

2 Choosing specific examples and highlighting writerly moves

As you focus on this process of learning, you'll want to note specific areas of your work that highlight this learning. To do this, mark places where you see yourself making moves you are proud of: the ways in which you work with other texts and quotations, your ability to make connections and read critically, the ways in which you organize your ideas or demonstrate rhetorical awareness, and the ways you work with multimodal resources. In Brian's reflection, one area he chose to focus on was the ability to quote from other texts.

One important skill I have really worked on this semester is how to enter a written conversation. In the second paper, we had to choose amongst two articles we read and have a "conversation" with the writer. This was a challenge for me because most of the writing I've done in school didn't ask for my opinion. I really had to break down the article and actually understand what it meant first, before I could state my own view. Before writing the full essay, we did an inquiry where we picked out one single passage we liked and responded by first introducing the quote, adding the actual quote, and explaining the meaning of the quote. I took this same approach into my longer essay, a response to Nicholas Carr's article, "Is Google Making Us Stupid." In my final essay, here is one example of how I tried to work in a quote in this way:

Overtime technology has been transformed from the printing press, to the typewriter, and now to the modern day computer. However, each generation had a different way of reading along with writing. For instance, in "Is Google Making Us Stupid?" written by Nicholas Carr, he tries to explain what the internet is doing to his brain, "I feel as if I'm always dragging my wayward brain back to the text. The deep reading that used to come naturally has become a struggle." Carr is trying to understand how his time online is effecting his ability to concentrate. He goes on to add, "My mind isn't going – so far as I can tell – but it's changing. I'm not thinking the way I used to" (57). Carr takes the position that reading on a screen has made him not as avid a reader as he may have been in years past. I, for one, agree with this statement. When reading on a computer or an iPhone, not many people take the time to read several pages all at once. This would not only take too long, but one's eyes start to hurt from staring at the screen for too long. Some may say that the technological progress overtime has improved the way people think and learn; others argue that too much exposure to rapid growth of technology has ultimately and negatively affected our brains.

In this example I was able to introduce two interesting quotes from Carr by breaking up a larger one, and kind of interrupt his idea with my own. After the quote, I set up my response with "I, for one, agree with this statement" as a way to explore my own thoughts about the subject and build on Carr's point. I think if I did another draft, I might add more details about the positives of technology. The thought of entering a conversation was a new way of writing that I discovered to make one's argument more effective and persuasive by making it more of a conversation.

As you can see in Brian's example, he was able to find a concrete example in his paper that demonstrated his growing competency with quoting and engaging in a written conversation with another author.

Your ultimate goal in making this move is to find textual proof to support the patterns and growth you see. Once you have a group of different examples (3–5), analyze them. What do these examples suggest about your writing or about this collection of texts? What common characteristics do you see across multiple drafts? What do they show about your development and about what you value in writing? What do they suggest about your writing process?

3 Examining the importance of community

This is a move to **contextualize** the work of your portfolio, to place it in the social setting in which it was produced. As we've stressed throughout this book, writing always takes place in a discourse community. Embedding this work in a context is an important aspect to reflection and to understanding the very social nature of learning. By stepping back and locating this writing in a context, we are able to draw connections between our individual experience of learning and its relation to the people and technology it is a part of.

As you make this move, you'll want to explore what your work shows about the community you are in. What does your work show about the shared expectations, ways, and values central to this community? What does it suggest about your awareness of this community as audience?

In Brian's final reflection, he points specifically to the idea of a *discourse community* and how writers must be aware of the **what**, **how**, and **why** of a writing situation if they want to understand an audience:

For instance, discourse community knowledge makes connections between a discourse

contextualize
situating a text in a
time and place

community's goals, its typical rhetorical situations, its genres and writing processes, and its expectations for "good" or effective writing. Discourse community knowledge also contributes to ongoing written conversations by engaging the ideas and texts of others too. An example of a discourse community is a certain group who is really passionate about football and likes to follow the game in depth, which may include statistics, players, coaches, etc. Understanding the discourse of a community is important because it helps writers understand their audience. There were several inquiries we completed that asked us to explain the shared knowledge of a group (what), their shared purposes (why), and their shared ways of communicating (how). These three points are fundamental to understanding a discourse community and how to write to them.

By describing the context in which you composed the pieces you include in your portfolio, you can consider the ways this context influenced the pieces you wrote for your portfolio.

4 Building on a theme or structure

As you go through this reflective process, begin considering a memorable way to present this work to your audience. Remember, your ultimate goal in creating and reflecting on your portfolio is to show your developing competence as a writer and thinker. Not only can this be done through the observations you make about your work, but it will also come through in how you approach and organize your reflection. As you start to make sense of the bigger picture of your development as a writer during the course, you might also consider other questions to help you. Did the work you produce make you rethink literacy and your own literacy practices? Did it impact your ideas about what you hope to study and investigate in the coming years? Did it incite you to revisit your thoughts on writing or about college in more general terms? Ashley's realization that she has "acquired a more full and nontraditional understanding of important concepts like 'literacy'" offers a theme she could explore further as she curates her portfolio, giving her a larger theme to use in structuring her final reflection. For Brian, his larger themes were developing rhetorical awareness and seeing writing as a conversation carried out in a community context.

5 Finding a metaphor

Thinking with a metaphor can help you organize your reflection. Another student, Tom, for example, used the metaphor of working out in the gym as a way to talk about his growth as a writer:

> Writing well is like going to the gym, it's like working-out. It's impossible to get in shape and get stronger if you don't exercise consistently. Not only that, you can hurt yourself if you don't go through the right steps. You might not hurt yourself if you try to take short cuts in your writing, but it's going to be impossible to get better at writing without practicing it consistently and going through the proper steps.

What Tom has done is create a connection between his experience of writing and that of working out as a way to express a more meaningful and personal description of his learning. That is, he is able to capture the journey of his learning by making explicit connections to a personal activity in his own life.

In his Final Thoughts for his electronic portfolio, Christian uses metaphorical thinking as he explains what writing means to him: "Picking up a pencil is sort of a bridge for my thoughts. At one end of this bridge is my mind. At the other end is a piece of paper. The mind can only hold so much. . .but the blank pieces of paper provide an endless amount of space for your thoughts." Whether you choose to make metaphorical connections like these or not, your main purpose in using a guiding theme for your reflection is to demonstrate your development as a writer in both the content of your piece and in the shape and style of it.

6 Considering the whole

Your portfolio will be read as a collection, so you will want to consider how the whole functions rather than considering only specific pieces. Portfolios are meant to make a point or an argument about your work, the choices you made as a writer, and your ability to identify and explain your writing process. Because your audience can't be sitting by you each time you sit down to write, your final reflection should help them understand your writing process more clearly.

> ❝ Essentially, in writing a portfolio reflection, you are trying to build a persuasive argument about your growing competence as a writer in both the form and content of your piece. ❞

WRITING MOVES ◀

Drafting and Shaping

Creating a portfolio of work that can be shared with others may be as simple as creating a file and sharing it through any number of cloud-based applications (Google Docs, Dropbox, iCloud, etc.) as Brian did for his course assignment. But a final presentation of your work will more often involve a richer digital platform, one that allows you to exhibit your work in effective ways for a wider audience. Your college or university might have its own platform for creating e-portfolios, along with blog and wiki applications.

Digital Toolbox
See Part IV, Section 3

1 Choosing a digital platform and planning a portfolio

There are any number of digital platforms you could choose to create an online portfolio. If you are familiar with HTML and web design, you could build your own site from scratch (as Jeff Bartlett in our first example did). You could also seek out an online platform for publishing your portfolio using any number of free blogging sites, like Blogger, Medium, and WordPress. Whatever platform you choose, you'll want to choose based on your rhetorical purpose and your level of expertise in designing for the web. Most platforms allow you to keep your work private as you design and construct a portfolio, and you'll want to use those privacy or limited-sharing controls.

Looking again at Laurie's presentation portfolio, she used Wix, a site with easy-to-use templates (some free, others for pay) that can be used for building an e-portfolio (Figure 20.8).[20:6]

Template and website building tools like Wix are quite common online. Other popular platforms include Weebly, Seesaw, Squarespace, and Digication. They provide a service for ordinary users to create attractive, functional sites without having to have a deep knowledge of website development. Such templates have their pros and cons, but more and more student and professional writers are turning to them as a practical way to present their portfolios online.

All such sites will generally have hundreds of templates to choose from. Templates provide a basic structure and arrangement for a portfolio, so some of the rhetorical choices regarding design and layout have already been made for you. However, with the visual nature of the web and the common use of images in our day-to-day communications, understanding and composing with these templates will require you to think rhetorically about what images, colors, links, and other design features you'll want to incorporate in presenting your work online. There might be some trial and error as you familiarize yourself with different platforms. As you do so, note the different affordances and limitations of each platform. Eventually you'll want to choose a platform that best suits the purposes of your portfolio.

Photography Portfolio · Outdoor Photography · Illustrator Portfolio

Figure 20.8: Different types of portfolio templates at Wix.com

2 Considering audience(s)

In looking back at Christian and Laurie's digital portfolios, we can tell by the content they have included on their sites who their primary audiences are. Christian includes work he did over one semester, along with some reflective writing and a visual statement. His portfolio looks more like a process portfolio primarily intended for an audience of his course instructor and classmates, but since it is posted online, it is also trying to appeal to a larger audience. We can include ourselves in this audience now, an audience that Christian may not have anticipated, but one that nevertheless is looking at and analyzing his work. He has chosen to make his work public and available to a wider audience (and he convinced many of his classmates to do the same), and he has given permission for us to share it with our readers as we bring it into a new conversation about composing and digital contexts. While you won't be able to plan for every kind of audience, you want to at least be aware that, especially with digital texts, your portfolio may be viewed by unanticipated audiences.

Figures 20.9: Portfolio home pages for Christian Nunes and Laurie J. Jackson

Laurie's portfolio (Figure 20.9) developed at a different point in her college career, and she has a different intended audience. She designed the site using a template from Wix shortly before she graduated with her master's degree in writing. Her specific purpose was to create an online presence for herself and to showcase her work for potential employers. Rather than include a reflective piece on her writing, Laurie has instead included a direct link to her resume. Both Christian and Laurie demonstrate audience awareness in the texts they choose to share and how they share them.

3 Selecting your artifacts

Understanding who your audience is will help guide other choices you make about your presentation portfolio. Like Christian's audience, it may be small and more local, but, like Laurie, you may have to do some research on your audience by looking at other similar portfolios with similar purposes. Looking back over each of the portfolios we've been considering in this chapter, each composer has selected a different group of texts based on her or his intended audience. Christian has selected pieces from a single course, while Laurie has chosen work across her college career. The same holds true for a more established writer like Jeff Bartlett, who includes published pieces, blog posts, and direct links to pieces he has published. You'll want to choose examples of your work that you feel are your strongest and that would appeal best to your prospective audiences.

4 Considering the visual look of your digital portfolio

When using a template, as suggested in Move 1, the layout and basic page design is already done for you. While users are limited in layout changes, they have more control over other design components, like images, color, and font. It is these visual elements you'll have to think through, depending on your audience and the kind of meaning you want to express about yourself in connection with the work you choose to post here. As we've noted, Christian decided on a darker site with white text, creating excellent contrast between text and background and making the text easy to read. Laurie has reversed these colors, using the standard black lettering on a white background.

Visually, Christian has integrated a black and white image of New York City, along with a graphic on the home page, "My Writing" rendered in a graffiti artist font. He explains on his Visual Statement page, which includes more images of New York City (Figure 20.10):

> For my ePortfolio, The color scheme I chose was black, white, and a small hint on green. I chose these colors because black is my favorite color and it is a sleek color. I think bright colors

Figure 20.10: Christian Nunes's Visual Statement page with images of his daily life in New York City

are annoying and somewhat ostentatious. The banner I chose was a black and white picture of manhattan. The reason why I chose this picture because the city is a brand new lifestyle to me... My ePortfolio banner and title do have a connection. I enjoy writing about both positive and negative emotions that I may have at a given time. For example, living in the city of new york, it is very exciting. Being in a beautiful school, towering skyscrapers rising above me, and the diverse community is something I really look forward to. I feel that I can easily write a poem on this new change of lifestyle!

Christian chooses darker colors because they are "sleek" and avoids bright colors because they are "annoying" and "ostentatious." Although he is still working through how to articulate his choice of images and color, he does have an intuitive sense of audience and the meanings he wants to convey by using these different visual modes.

When considering the visual appeal of your portfolio, you'll want to consider the different composing modes you draw upon in this text as you question the ways in which they invite viewers and readers to experience your work. Laurie talked about the importance of multimodality in her portfolio as she reflected on her decision-making process:

> The combination of text and image involves more senses and creates a stronger meaning for readers. I furthered this idea of involving more senses for the viewers by adding sound to my home page. Now, the viewers can scroll through photographs

I've taken, read about the website, and write themselves (if they want to reach out and contact me), all while listening to music. I picked a song that would work with the banner image and my about page, expressing this idea of taking chances and discovering what's out there in the world. Once, the viewer leaves the home, about, and contact pages for the portfolio and resume pages, the music stops. It gives the viewer a break as they reach pages that are more text based and at the heart of the portfolio. The viewer gets to decide whether they want to click play in the reflection section, which creates more of a personal interaction between the viewer and myself.

Laurie drew on work she had done in a variety of contexts as she created her portfolio, including art classes she had taken in the past. She also drew on her own personal sense of style in design as she reshaped and remixed the original template that she began with as she constructed her website:

> Everyone has their color, and mine revolves around blues and greens. I knew my photographs would express that, so I left the gold and hot pink makeup smears as my background image for contrast. It reminded me of smearing paint on a canvas. It was the only image from the original site I worked from. The header text is called Lulo Clean, which creates an easy, clean-cut title font. The paragraph fonts are Linotype Didot, which creates a cursive feel, without being cursive. The subtitle on the homepage is Libre Baskerville. Usually it is recommended to use two fonts at most because too many can make the pages look tacky, for lack of a better word. However, I didn't want my initials to compete with the subtitle. The punctuation marks at the end of the titles for each page become an image, bringing the gold background color to the text. The LJJ punctuation mark is a blue-green color because that's my color, and it ties into the color of the footer. I then layered the LJJ punctuation mark with the play button for the music, so viewers could pause the music if they wanted. I looked at design through functionality.

Like Christian's observations, Laurie explains how her use of different modes, like text, image, color, and font, were all meant to convey a site that was visually inviting and engaging.

5 Considering the layout of your digital portfolio

In addition to elements like images, color, and font, the great majority of templates come with a basic page layout that incorporates the five design elements we introduced in Chapter 14: balance, alignment, proximity, contrast, and repetition. Each of the portfolios we have seen in this chapter all demonstrate these different design elements to a greater or lesser degree. Just a quick glance at a page of templates from a content management application like Wix gives us a good sense of how fundamental these design aspects are to modern digital texts (Figure 20.11).

In Laurie's case, she chose a colorful, abstract image with bright smudges of makeup in two opposite corners. No matter what page you go to in the portfolio, a similar page will appear. If you click on the About page, you'll see the image behind an image of Laurie and a friend scuba diving. Like Christian, Laurie is using repeating elements to give her portfolio a sense of coherence and consistency throughout the site. This same consistency can be seen in the range of colors they choose (often called a color scheme) and their choice of font (Figure 20.12).

As you design your own portfolio online you'll want to consider each of these visual elements rhetorically and how to compose your digital portfolio in a way that is engaging and purposeful for your intended audiences. What color scheme will you use? Are you using too many colors, or are they clashing in some way? What kind of images and graphics can you use, and for what purpose? Do you use more abstract images, landscape images, or personal ones? How are images and text working together to express meaning? What font, or fonts, should you use, and why? Drawing on the design elements of balance, alignment, contrast, proximity, and repetition that we discussed in Chapter 14 will help you think through some of these composing questions.

6 Navigation, social media, and search engines

For an online presentation portfolio you will also want to consider how your readers will navigate the collection you have compiled. A navigation menu is an essential function for all websites, and it acts as a central organizing element that is usually repeated on every page and helps determine how visitors will move through a site. As we've mentioned already, any template you use will come with a predesigned navigation menu. You just have to choose the most fitting links for your purpose, based on what you know about your audience's expectations. For Christian's portfolio, his primary audience included his instructor and classmates, so he decided on a basic navigation function that pointed directly to each piece of formal writing he did for his course (Figure 20.13).

Digital Toolbox
See Part IV, Section 3

Figure 20.11: Portfolio template designs from Wix exhibiting basic design principles

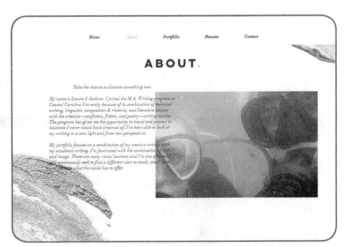

Figure 20.12: Laurie J. Jackson's About page on her portfolio site

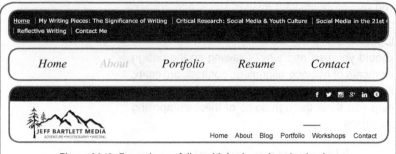

Figure 20.13: Example portfolios with horizontal navigation bar

Figure 20.14: Example of vertical navigation bar

Figure 20.15: Links to social media from portfolio site

Laurie's navigation is broader and includes more standard links found in presentation portfolios (Figure 20.13). Professional writer Jeff Bartlett's navigation menu has some overlap with Laurie's, but he has added a "Blog" and a "Workshops" link (Figure 20.13).

Typically, navigation menus run horizontally across the top of a site or vertically in a column on the right or left side of a site's pages. This is one of those design choices you'll want to make when you choose a template to work with (Figure 20.14).

In addition to considering navigation, you may also want to consider the where of your portfolio and how you will use social media to attract and network with audiences. You'll notice both Laurie and Jeff Bartlett have included icon links to Twitter, Instagram, and LinkedIn. As you design your site, you'll want to decide which social media tools to use and for what purpose, and how you might drive viewer traffic to your portfolio site (Figure 20.15).

As you consider circulation, you'll also want to think like a search engine. In addition to sharing links to your site using social media, you may also want to attract a larger audience for your work. Because search engines are the first place people go to find things online, you'll want the content of your site—your formal writing examples as well as the content of your basic pages—to have a number of key words that search engines can find. Search engines find and rank sites based on their titles, headings, content, and links. In order for viewers to find your site, you'll want to imagine what words they might search for—professional writer, content producer, designer, etc. This kind of rhetorical awareness is often called *search engine optimization* (SEO) by web developers. For more information on designing your site for SEO, see Part IV.

As you think through the visual look of your digital portfolio, consider these questions: What experience do you hope to create for your readers as they make their way through your portfolio? How can you use the navigation possibilities of your platform to guide your readers on a path that tells the story you'd like them to take away? Try sketching out a plan for navigation, locate the pieces you'll use on appropriate pages, think about key words, and then create the relevant navigational elements on your platform.

Revising and Publishing

Whether you are doing a reflection on a progress portfolio or a presentation portfolio, you'll want to get feedback from your peers. Ask a classmate to read your reflection and portfolio now that you have it arranged or designed as you like. Instead of commenting on pieces individually, ask them to articulate the story you seem to be telling or the argument you seem to be making using these texts and with the design you have chosen. This will help you get a sense of how readers will experience your portfolio.

1 Peer reviewing a portfolio reflection

As you read through your peer's reflection, comment on the following components.

- Is there an inviting introduction to the portfolio reflection and the pieces that are included? Has the writer explained or demonstrated in some way why these texts were included? Do you have a sense of how they work together here?

- Does the portfolio and reflection demonstrate a level of awareness about the materials included and the journey of the writer/composer over time? Does it help readers understand the writer's progress by highlighting what is significant about the moves made in the portfolio?

- Has the writer constructed an organized theme or structure that points to a rich exploration of the work that's included?

2 Peer reviewing a presentation portfolio

To review the portfolio of a peer, perform the following steps.

- **Visit your peer's portfolio online.** What is your immediate impression of the home page? Is it confusing? Inviting? What kinds of visual and design elements do you notice?
- **Explore the site.** Click on each link to see what kind of content is there. What is it like to navigate the site? Is it easy to find things? How is the site laid out? How does the site function?
- **Look closer at the visual design of the site.** What kinds of images and other visual elements, like color and font, has the writer chosen? Do they seem appropriate for the intended audience of the portfolio? Has the writer incorporated basic design elements, like balance, alignment, proximity, contrast, and repetition? How are words and other visual elements working together on the site?

- **Think about the layout of the portfolio.** Has the writer designed the portfolio in a way that highlights his or her strengths as a writer and a designer?

If the platform you're working with supports comments, invite comments from readers in your target audience. You can additionally take such comments into consideration in a final version of your reflection(s).

3 Going live

The platform you've used for your portfolio will have allowed you to password-protect or otherwise keep your portfolio offline or unavailable to a public audience until you are ready to publish it. Before making your portfolio public, if you choose to do so, consider again the concerns about privacy we've raised in earlier chapters. How much personal information have you included? What are the privacy policies of the platform you are using? What is done with your personal information, and could that information be used for identity theft or to find your physical address? Professional writers like Jeff Bartlett and Ximena Vengoechea (and soon Laurie Jackson) often create dedicated Facebook, Instagram, and Twitter accounts for their professional work to keep it separate from their private social worlds, and if you're including social media links, you might do the same. And your platform most likely allows you to keep some pages private, even as you publish others. When you're ready to go live and place your portfolio into a larger public and global conversation, be sure to do so cautiously, with a full awareness of what you want to share beyond your local context.

Reinventing and Circulating Your Work

A digital portfolio you share with others offers one mode of presentation in itself. But you might also have the opportunity to give an oral presentation of your work to others, perhaps to classmates. In preparing such a presentation, you'll want to identify those aspects of your portfolio that you feel best demonstrate your work and your development over time. If you are sharing the process you went through in creating an online presentation portfolio, you may want to use different screenshots of your process to show how the site and your thinking developed over time. In either case you'll want to consider the following.

➤ What you want to say about the content of your portfolio, the rhetorical choices you've made, and what you've discovered about your work and about yourself as a writer/composer through this process

➤ What you want to say about your process of creating an e-portfolio and the kinds of design decisions you made in creating it

➤ What highlights from your portfolio will engage your audience

➤ What balance of text, image, and perhaps audio will keep your audience's attention

➤ How to time and edit your presentation to be effective in the time you're allotted

It is common today when making presentations to use digital presentation tools, like PowerPoint, Keynote, and Prezi. While we encourage you to use one of these tools for presenting your portfolio, we also think it can be helpful to step away from the computer at times to conceptualize how you might approach your presentation. To learn more about planning a presentation, you can find an excerpt from *Presentation Zen*, Chapter 2, "Planning Analog," along with a student example in the Additional Readings.

Key Concepts

contextualize 478
digital curation 471
reflection 476

Looking Ahead

Throughout this book we've explored literacy as a dynamic, social, and highly contextualized activity, and we've invited you to join a larger, ongoing conversation about literacy practices as participants and researchers in a digital world. In the first part of the book, we looked closely at our local literacy practices and how we use digital media to build shared knowledge together. We considered the question of context and how context is shaped by the what, why, how, and where of our daily acts of literacy, and we looked at how we build rhetorical relationships with others through our reading and writing. In Part II, we placed our local communities in the broader culture of a public and global internet and looked at the ways in which digital networks create global communities around common local issues. We considered the growing visual and multimodal nature of our communication and how traditional rhetorical practices like participating in civic debate, creating an argument, or engaging in cultural critique are changing in a digital world. In Part III we delved into what it means to research today and manage the research expectations of academic writing. We looked at how to evaluate both print and digital resources and how to navigate the research process and the many texts that inform a systematic inquiry. We considered three different types of research studies (ethnography, archival, literature review) and, finally, we focused on how to best archive and share your work by constructing a portfolio in the last chapter you just read to stress how creating such a collection can help you reflect on your writing and compositions.

As you look back on the work you have done here, we hope you'll find that you've gained some insight into your own evolving literacy practices and how these vary across contexts, communities, and cultures. As you look ahead to the writing you'll do in local, public, and academic contexts in the future, we hope you'll draw on the discoveries you've made here. When you enter new communicative contexts, we hope you pause to consider not only how participants join in—by drawing on particular moves and strategies—the conversations that shape these settings, but that you also question why they work in these ways. Considering the where, what, how, and why of language use in different contexts will guide your work as you create and share knowledge with others. We hope that this book has helped you grow as a writer and reader, as a rhetorical being who will engage critically in an ever-expanding digital landscape.

Additional **Readings**

Contents

READING 1

Selection from
"Annotated Bibliography"
by Zacharie Loveless (Student)

Zacharie Loveless composed an annotated bibliography as he collected, read, and reflected on sources for a literature review on the ways in which emerging technologies are shaping the music industry. This excerpt from his work provides a clear sense of how Zacharie used the process of crafting annotations to consider his sources in specific ways and to reflect on how he would use them in his own paper. In his annotations, Zacharie tends to the *what* (what each source is about), the *who* (who wrote them and their credentials), and the *where* (where they were published and how that publication venue positions a source in terms of credibility), as he comments on why each of them is important to his own thinking about his topic. As you read these annotations, notice how he uses this genre to think through the sources he has collected as well as his own research undertaking of composing a literature review.

Cayari, C. "The YouTube effect: How YouTube has Provided New Ways to Consume, Create, and Share Music." International Journal of Education & the Arts, 12.6 (2011): 1-30. Web. 19 April 2016.

The first part of this case study focuses on how and why people use YouTube and also how YouTube affects its users. The second part of the study is when they actually do the experiment involving an up-and-coming music artist, Wade Johnston, who uploads his original music and covers to YouTube. Johnston made a statement: "[YouTube] makes me try harder. It makes me want to write songs more. It makes me want to be a better musician. I want this to be my ticket to the real deal. It makes me want to try so hard (W. Johnston, interview, May 11, 2009)." That reflects one of the main topics the first part of the study explains. This quote shows one of the effects of YouTube on its music artists and it makes them want to post more music for their followers.

The author of this study, Christopher Cayari is a K-12 music specialist at John Hill Magnet School. Cayari received his M.M.Ed from the University of Illinois. The study was also published in the *International Journal of Education & the Arts*. This gives the study a high authority because it comes from a reliable author with a college degree and from being published in an internationally recognized journal. This study refers back to my topic of how technology effects the music industry well because it follows a highly used technology resource and how it can affect a new artist.

This will be one of my main sources for my research paper because it relates back to my topic so well. The first part of the source will help me with background information of other studies and articles pertaining to the effect of YouTube on music. This in turn reflects my topic of how technology affects the music industry. The second part also reflects on my topic because it is an actual study of how YouTube affects an artist and how it allowed him to grow and become a known artist.

Duchêne, Anne, and Patrick Waelbroeck. "The Legal and Technological Battle in the Music Industry: Information-push versus Information-pull Technologies." *International Review of Law and Economics* 26.4 (2006): 565-80. Web. 19 Apr. 2016

The main topic of this source is the explanation of how the music industry may be effected by new changes in copyright laws, which are caused by technology used by piracy websites and music sharing websites. Another topic is the differences between information-push and information-pull technologies. The source also uses mathematical equations to show the effect of these different technologies on the music industry. The authors of this source are Anne Duchêne and Patrick Waelbroeck. Duchêne is currently an economics lecturer at the University of Pennsylvania. She received her PhD from Ecole Nationale des Ponts et Chaussees in Paris. Waelbroeck is currently an associate professor of industrial economics and econometrics at Télécom ParisTech - Ecole nationale supérieure des télécommunications. He earned his PhD from the University of Paris La Sorbonne. He also holds an M.A. from Yale University and is a Fulbright alumnus. This gives the source a very high authority and reliability because both authors have PhDs and are working at recognized establishments. The source was also published in the Journal of *International Review of Law and Economics*. This raises the reliability of the source because it is an international recognized journal, which is reviewed and edited by a committee with members that also have good credentials.

This source is somewhere in between useful and not useful. What I find not useful about this source is that it is confusing to read and when the authors add in the equations the confusion increases. This is also a weakness because some people who read this source will not fully understand why the equations are used. I do not know how to interpret some of the equations because they are so complex. The strength of this source comes from how they set up the evidence in paragraphs. In the model section of the source, the authors separate the paragraphs with different headings. The different headings represent the different aspects of how music is protected and shared. They come to the conclusion that an increase in copyright protection will negatively affect the music industry because the listeners and the buyers of the music will not want to pay for something they don't know they like.

Even though this source is not blatantly about how technology affects the music industry, there are still some components that correspond to my topic. The aspects from the source that I will find useful are the sections about music sharing technology. Theses sections show how technology is partly positive and partly negative. The positive side of the argument is that music sharing technologies allow listeners to sample the music that they would want to buy. This leads to an increase in sales of the music because the consumer knows what they are getting and what it sounds like. On the negative side, music sharing technology is causing record companies to contemplate whether or not to increase their copyright protection. This is negative because it hinders the listeners from finding out how the music sounds and if they actually like it. This can cause the listeners to not want to buy the music, which in turn lowers sales. So this source can be used to explain the pros and cons of new technologies and music. ■

Questions

❶ What do these excerpted annotations show about the annotated bibliography as a genre? What do they suggest about how you might use this writing task to engage an academic research process?

❷ What repeated moves do you see Zacharie making here as he discusses two sources? What additional moves might have been useful for him to make as he thought about his own research undertaking?

❸ How is the work Zacharie does here similar to and different from the work he would most likely do with sources in a final essay? How do you see him preparing to do that kind of work here?

❹ How will you consider the what, where, why, and how as you compose your own annotations?

READING 2

SAMPLE LITERATURE REVIEW

"Digital Fitness: Online Forums for Physical Activity"
by Razz Green (Student)

In this sample student research paper, Razz Green considers how social media sites (and the communities built on and through such platforms) support increased physical activity and fitness. In this section of his paper, Razz points to a variety of sources to show that we are becoming increasingly active online and that the social interactions common on the internet can be used to increase physical activity. In his paper, Razz introduces the sources he works with and draws on them through paraphrases, block quotations, short quotations, and summaries. While this literature review could be (and was) central to Razz's inquiry into this topic, it also might have provided a nice platform for a more focused study of a particular online fitness community (in the form of an ethnography) or an analysis of documents, such as Pinterest boards focusing on fitness (in the form of an archival project).

Over the last 16 years, computer and internet access have increased greatly. According to the publication, "Computer and Internet Use" from the U.S. census, in 2000, about 45.1 percent of the U.S. population had access to the internet, but in a little over a decade the percent of Americans with access to the internet jumped to 74.8 in 2012. With the rise in internet access, people have the ability to reach out for support and to socialize with others over fitness more than ever. Physical activity participation has increased with access to online social forums. Online fitness forums create a welcoming environment that promotes well being and support through socialization.

Online fitness forums have recently begun to grow along with the increased attention on changing America's obesity problem. The forums provide access to workouts, dieting, and tips from professionals. In the article "Online Fitness Networks: A Link to Hybrid Training?" written by author and fitness technologist Biray Alsac, she states:

> When you think of Myspace or Facebook, you think of online social communities where members are able to create profiles, connect with friends, join interest groups and contribute to forum discussions. But lately we are seeing niche networks evolve, some specifically launching with health- and fitness-related themes. (28)

In recent years far more fitness sites have begun to bring people together to find common fitness goals such as weight loss, powerlifting, and bodybuilding. These sites allow people to converse on public forums to get feedback and support and share ideas with other fellow fitness enthusiasts or even fitness beginners. Not every person around you is a fitness guru or trainer, so online access to forums gives people the opportunity to get tips and training without having to search hard or hire a personal trainer.

The world is full of individuals looking to be inspired and motivated. Online fitness forums can become the support group for a person who otherwise would not exercise. In a study done by the Center for Disease Control (CDC), they found

that the one of the main reasons there was a barrier to exercising for individuals, was due to lack of support from family members and friends. The CDC said "The social support provided through the discussion forums of these networks and the ability to connect with users online likely increases physical activity; the existing literature supports that having one friend to exercise with increases the likelihood of doing so by 45%". Having support is very important when a person decides to make a life change and begin working out. Lack of support from the people closest to an individual can be detrimental to a person's growth or willingness to participate in anything, let alone working out. The support can come in many forms from words of encouragement to giving tips for workouts to even working out with the person.

Socialization is a motivating factor when it comes to getting people to become physically active. Individuals are more likely to participate in physical fitness if they have a companion to accompany them. Sports can be a huge ingredient to tag team with online fitness communities to get people to be physically active. In the article experiment, "A Qualitative Study to Examine Feasibility and Design of an Online Social Networking Intervention to Increase Physical Activity in Teenage Girls," professors Gisela Van Kessel, Madeleine Kavanagh, and Carol Maher tested teenage girls in Australia to find out how to market physical activity through social media. They found that the majority of the girls found physical activity advertisement more appealing when it was focused on sports and socialization. When interviewed, one of the test subjects read "I enjoy the social side of things and I prefer to do a sport like a team sport over having to run on my own. Like, I find being with other people motivates me" (5). Through athletics, physical activity is made more fun and more appealing. If social media sites such as twitter or Facebook promote physical activity, it can bring "followers" or "friends" together to become more physically active and fit. Online forums that promote physical activity through socialization and sports can help increase the number of participants. This idea connects back to the idea that lack of support from family and friends can decrease the chances a person actually works out. The experiment depicted first hand that people, especially teenagers, find physical activity more enjoyable and are more willing to workout when they have support, which can be found in online forums and social media.

Works Cited

Alsac, Biray. "Online Fitness Networks: A Link to Hybrid Training?" *IDEA Trainer Success* 5.4 (2008): 25-29. *SPORTDiscus with Full Text.* Web. 17 Apr. 2016.

"Computer and Internet Use." *Publications About Computer and Internet Use.* Census Bureau for the Bureau of Labor Statistics, n.d. Web. 25 Apr. 2016.

Nakhasi, Atul, Album Xiaotian Shen, Ralph Joseph Passarella, Lawrence J. Appel, and Cheryl A. M. Anderson. "Online Social Networks That Connect Users to Physical Activity Partners: A Review and Descriptive Analysis." *Journal of Medical Internet Research* 16.6 (2014): 61-74. *PsycINFO.* Web. 17 Apr. 2016.

Rn, Butler, Davis R, Lewis Cb, Nelson Me, and Strauss E. "Physical Fitness: How to Help Older Patients Live Stronger and Longer. Part I of a Roundtable Discussion." *Geriatrics* 53.9 (1998): 26-40 7p. *Ccm.* Web. 17 Apr. 2016.

Van Kessel, Gisela, Madeleine Kavanagh, and Carol Maher. "A Qualitative Study to Examine Feasibility and Design of an Online Social Networking Intervention to Increase Physical Activity in Teenage Girls."*PLoS ONE* 11.3 (2016): 1-11. *Academic Search Complete.* Web. 17 Apr. 2016.   ∎

Questions

❶ What strong moves does Razz make as he draws on secondary sources to discuss the ways in which social media (and web 2.0 technologies in broader terms) impact fitness? What additional moves could he have made to do more nuanced work with the sources he points to in this piece?

❷ How might Razz have done more evaluative or analytical work here? How might he have done more to put his sources in conversation (or to synthesize their main findings)?

❸ What moves does Razz make to address an audience of his classmates in this piece? How might your considerations of audience shape the approach you take as you weave sources into your writing?

❹ What will you take from this piece as you prepare to compose a research paper that involves a literature review? What goals can you set for yourself as you point to others' voices and ideas in your own work by drawing on and carefully considering your sources?

READING 3

SAMPLE LITERATURE REVIEW

Selection from

"Reading Revolutions: Online Digital Text and Implications for Reading in Academe"[LRIII:1]

by Barry W. Cull

First Monday, June 6, 2011

In this literature review, Barry Cull (an Information Services Librarian who is invested in familiarizing students with academic approaches to research) questions how reading online differs from reading print texts by turning to research completed on that topic grounded in a variety of disciplines. As he discusses sources that consider social, behavioral, and technical aspects of reading digital texts, Cull focuses his inquiry on the habits of college students. In this excerpt, taken from a section of his larger review titled "Online Research and Reading Behaviour," Cull draws from a variety of sources to make points about typical online research practices and then ends by suggesting that these aren't so dissimilar from traditional academic research strategies, as the starting and stopping we do as we read online can provide an opportunity for reflection. Throughout this review, Cull handles sources with ease, summarizing them, quoting from them, and synthesizing them. This helps him create an ethos of authority and positions him as exceedingly knowledgeable about this topic. His article appeared in the online peer-reviewed journal *First Monday*. He uses MLA formatting for his in-text citations.

Spending time online does not automatically lead to the development of online research or advanced reading skills. Sociological research of the digital divide has suggested online research skills are often not well developed among people who are online (Hargittai, 2002). When it comes to university students, especially beginning undergraduates, they are typically content to make do with simplistic "good enough" information search strategies — ease of access to information often continues to be more important than the accuracy of that information (Currie, et al., 2010; De Rosa, et al., 2006; Nicholas, et al., 2009; Weiler, 2005). There is a relationship between this low level of information literacy skill and academic performance — low-performing students typically have low information literacy skills.

This path-of-least-resistance research behaviour is not distinctive only of students. Within academe, everyone — from first-year undergraduates, to practitioners, to professors — are exhibiting a similar tendency to search "horizontally" instead of "vertically," skimming information and bouncing quickly from place to place:

The average times that users spend on e-book and e-journal sites are very short: typically four and eight minutes respectively. It is clear that users are not reading online in the traditional sense, indeed there are signs that new forms of "reading" are emerging as users "power browse" horizontally through titles, contents pages and abstracts going for quick wins. It almost seems that they go online to avoid reading in the traditional sense. (Rowlands, et al. 2008)

Indeed, Web site designers know very well that people generally do not read much online. Web site users tend to browse pages rapidly, and read only about 20 percent of the text on an average page (Nielsen, 2008; Weinreich, et al., 2008).

A typical "screen-based reading behaviour" is emerging, characterized by more time spent on "browsing and scanning, key word spotting, one-time reading, non-linear reading, and reading more selectively", while less time is spent on in-depth reading, and concentrated reading. When online, people switch between two poor kinds of reading — "tunnel vision" reading in which one reads a single bit of text without a sense of the context, and "marginal distraction", which happens, for example, when a person reads textual feeds on the sidebar of a Web site such as a blog (A. Liu, et al., 2009).

Yet it is an over-simplification to suggest that this sort of bouncing happens exclusively online. A recent study of academic staff at one university suggests that the "immersive reflective" reading done by these expert scholars is typically discontinuous even when done on paper:

Experts seldom read a scholarly article or book from beginning to end, but rather in parts, and certainly out of order, actively using hands and fingers in flicking back and forth, underlining and annotating, often connecting their reading to their writing, and usually spreading pieces of paper around their desk (Hillesund, 2010). ■

Works Cited

Alan Liu, Sandra Aamodt, Maryanne Wolf, David Gelernter, and Gloria Mark, 2009. "Does the brain like e-books?" *New York Times* (14 October), at http://roomfordebate.blogs.nytimes.com/2009/10/14/does-the-brain-like-e-books/, accessed 26 November 2010.

Terje Hillesund, 2010. "Digital reading spaces: How expert readers handle books, the Web and electronic paper," *First Monday*, volume 15, number 4, at http://firstmonday.org/htbin/cgiwrap/bin/ojs/index.php/fm/article/view/2762/2504, accessed 26 November 2010.

Ian Rowlands, David Nicholas, Peter Williams, Paul Huntington, Maggie Fieldhouse, Barrie Gunter, Richard Withey, Hamid R. Jamali, Tom Dobrowolski, and Carol Tenopir, 2008. "The Google generation: The information behaviour of the researcher of the future," *Aslib Proceedings*, volume 60, number 4, pp. 290–310, and at http://www.emeraldinsight.com/journals.htm?articleid=1733495&show=abstract, accessed 29 November 2010.

Harald Weinreich, Hartmut Obendorf, Eelco Herder, and Matthias Mayer, 2008. "Not quite the average: An empirical study of Web use," *ACM Transactions on the Web*, volume 2, number 1, pp. 5.1–5.31, at http://portal.acm.org/citation.cfm?id=1326566&coll=ACM&dl=ACM&retn=1#Fulltext, accessed 29 November 2010.

SAMPLE LITERATURE REVIEW

Selection from

"Youth and Digital Media: From Credibility to Information Quality" [LRIII:2]

by Urs Gasser, Sandra Cortesi, Momin Malik, and Ashley Lee

The Berkman Center for Internet & Society, July 17, 2015

Another literature review, "Youth and Digital Media: From Credibility to Information Quality," published by the Berkman Center for Internet & Society at Harvard University, also looks to teenagers' digital literacy practices, but the emphasis of this review is specifically on information literacies as it questions how teens find, evaluate, and create knowledge online as they question how out-of-school approaches do or do not extend to the classroom. While it does include quotations, this excerpt stresses just how effective paraphrasing can be when trying to represent and synthesize others' thinking about a topic. The many paraphrases and summaries provided here allow the authors of this piece to maintain a unified voice in this text while nodding to a plethora of sources. In the two brief sections provided here, the authors of this literature review turn to existing research to consider how writing and collaboration skills are developed through teens' online literacy practices.

6.3.2 Writing and Language Skills

Youth today may be producing more texts than ever as they communicate using email, instant messaging, blogs, social networking sites, and other Web services (Pew Internet/Lenhart et al., 2008). While there is a widespread concern that the quality of writing is deteriorating as young people become lax about grammar and spelling when communicating online (Pew Internet/Lenhart et al.,2008), a growing body of literature suggests that online spaces such as blogs and fanfiction sites help youth develop language and writing skills.

Moving beyond the traditional use of computers as simple editing tools, these sites allow participants to take advantage of networked communities of readers and writers. Students who participate in networked spaces can discuss their writing with a variety of readers ranging from peers to experts throughout the writing process (Black, 2005a, p. 127). The sense of immediacy that is created by interacting with the audience in real time further motivates young people to write (Drexler, Dawson, & Ferdig, 2007, p. 140; Black, 2005a). Through such participation, students learn to write with purpose and address specific audiences (Black, 2005a, p. 127). Commenting and hyperlinking features in these sites can further serve as powerful learning tools by helping youth situate knowledge in a wider context and allowing them to build a relational understanding of knowledge and knowledge-making processes (Ferdig and Trammell, 2004). Moreover, students gain digital and visual literacy skills that are needed {87} in social, academic and professional contexts (Lankshear & Knobel,2003). Writing in the context of online communities can help students develop critical, analytical and associational thinking skills (Drexler et al., 2007, p.141).

Black (2005a) finds that English language learning (ELL) students were actively participating in a fanfiction site to present their stories written in English, interact with their audience, and obtain feedback on their writing and language ability. In another study that conducted a blogging collaboration between preservice teachers and third-grade students, Drexler et al. (2007, p. 140) finds that collaborative blogging was an effective way to improve students' writing and to encourage positive attitudes towards writing.

6.3.3 Social/Collaborative Skills (collaborative knowledge building, problem solving, etc.)

Recognizing that reading and writing are "dialogic meaning-making processes that are acquired and embedded in specific social contexts" (Black, 2005a, p. 120), and that the writing and language skills discussed above are social in nature, we also look specifically at social skills.

The Internet presents opportunities for youth to get involved in collaborative content creation and dissemination processes. Many online activities have social dimensions and demand group work from participants. In the genre of participation of "geeking out" (Ito et al., 2010, p. 2), many young people seek out specialized knowledge groups on the Web to develop their expertise in a particular area and build their reputation among peers. In these groups, adults and youth meet and interact on an equal footing as expert peers, sharing and building knowledge using discussion forums, mailing lists, community websites, etc. By engaging in this kind of serious play, young people may develop skills in collaborative knowledge building and group problem solving.

Lange and Ito (2010) looked into how amateur subtitlers, or "fansubbers," collaborate together to translate and subtitle anime that is distributed to a worldwide audience on the Internet. Fansub groups are comprised of people who volunteer in various capacities as translators, editors, typesetters, etc.

Working on tight deadlines with a short turnaround time, fansubbers show surprising efficiency and productivity that surpass professionals (Lange & Ito, 2010; Ito et al., 2010, p. 30).

A major context for social interaction online is gaming, which has received attention from researchers as a platform for learning (Lyman, Billings, Ellinger, Finn, & Perkel, 2004; Squire, 2008; Gee, 2007a; 2007b). Researchers are actively exploring how games might teach young people technological, social and collaborative skills that are essential for the workplace and society. In a highly collaborative process, gamers often form a complex social structure for collective action. In many networked games such as MMORPGs, social communication and interaction are integral to the game experience (Johnson et al., 2009). As a team, youth exercise decision-making and leadership skills when organizing and implementing game action plans. Players systematically organize themselves to accomplish difficult tasks, such as defeating a powerful monster (Ito et al., 2010, p. 30). Digital games can be the source of establishing a strong sense of community among young people, and youth derive a sense of group membership when playing games that require collaboration with their peers (Lyman et al., 2004, p. 14). Gamer communities also form around games to facilitate the discussion of gaming experience and exchange of information. Youth interact with expert teenagers and adults around the world to share cheats, strategies, and custom modifications ("mods") (Lyman et al., 2004, p. 13).

From pages 86-88

Works Cited

Black, R. W. (2005a, March). Online fanfiction: What technology and popular culture can teach us about writing and literacy instruction. *New Horizons for Learning Online Journal*, 11(2). http://www.newhorizons.org/strategies/literacy/black.htm

Drexler, W., Dawson, K., & Ferdig, E. F. (2007). Collaborative blogging as a means to develop elementary expository writing skills. *Electronic Journal for the Integration of Technology in Education*, 6, 140-160

Gee, J. P. (2007a). *What video games have to teach us about learning and literacy*. New York, NY: Palgrave Macmillan.

Gee, J. P. (2007b). *Good video games and good learning: Collected essays on video games, learning and literacy*. New York, NY: Peter Lang

Ito, M., Baumer, S., Bittanti, M., boyd, d., Cody, R., Herr-Stephenson, B., Horst, H. A., Lange, P. G., Mahendran, D., Martinez, K. Z., Pascoe, C. J., Perkel, D., Robinson, L. Sims, C., & Tripp, L. (2010). *Hanging out, messing around, and geeking out: Kids living and learning with new media*. Cambridge, MA: The MIT Press.

Johnson, N., Xu, C., Zhao, Z., Ducheneaut, N., Yee, N., Tita, G., & Hui, P. (2009). Human group formation in online guilds and offline gangs driven by a common team dynamic. *Physical Review* E, 79, 066117.

Lange, P. G., & Ito, M. (2010). Creative production. In M. Ito, S. Baumer, M. Bittanti, d. boyd, R. Cody, B. Herr-Stephenson, H. A. Horst, P. G. Lange, D. Mahendran, K. Z. Martinez, C. J. Pascoe, D. Perkel, L. Robinson, C. Sims and L. Tripp, *Hanging out, messing around, and geeking out: Kids living and learning with new media* (pp. 243-294). Cambridge, MA: The MIT Press.

Lenhart, A., Arafeh, S., Smith, A., & Macgill, A. (2008, April 24). Writing, technology, and teens. *Pew Internet & American Life Project*. http://www.pewinternet.org/Reports/2008/Writing-Technology-and-Teens.aspx

Lenhart, A., Arafeh, S., Smith, A., & Rankin, A. (2008, September 16). Teens, video games, and civics. *Pew Internet & American Life Project*. http://www.pewinternet.org/Reports/2008/Teens-Video-Games-and-Civics.aspx

Lyman, P., with Billings, A., Ellinger, S., Finn, M., & Perkel,D. (2004). *Literature review: Digital-mediated experiences and youth' informal learning*. White paper for the MacArthur Foundation. San Francisco: Exploratorium. http://www.exploratorium.edu/research/digitalkids/Lyman_DigitalKids.pdf

Squire, K. (2008). Video-game literacy: A literacy of expertise. In J. Coiro, M. Knobel, C. Lankshear& D. J. Leu (Eds.), *Handbook of research on new literacies* (pp. 635-670). New York, NY: Lawrence Erlbaum Associates Taylor and Francis Group, LLC.

Questions

❶ What does looking at both of these sample literature reviews show you about this academic genre? What do you notice about the work the authors do with sources? List the different ways sources are referred to in these pieces.

❷ How is authority constructed through these literature reviews? What kind of ethos are these authors able to establish? How are they able to position themselves in these ways?

❸ What strategies can you borrow from these pieces?

"Love and Theft: Borrowing to Sound More Like Yourself"LRIII:3
by Wayne Rhodes

Kutz, Eleanor, Wayne Rhodes, Stephen Sutherland, Vivian Zamel. "Addressing Plagiarism in A Digital Age." *Human Architecture: Journal of the Sociology of Self-Knowledge*, vol. 9, no. 3, 2011.

Plagiarism has been a vexing concern for both faculty and their students, and it has become more so as digital resources make it easier to "borrow" the work of others. In this essay, part of a longer collaborative article on "Addressing Plagiarism in a Digital Age," by several faculty members at UMass Boston, Wayne Rhodes draws on the ideas about remix that have been applied to discussions of copyright by Lawrence Lessig (see Chapter 9). As a musician as well as an English teacher, Rhodes brings those two worlds together, reflecting on what creativity means for songwriters and for writers, the ways in which new work builds on what has come before, and on what the implications of creative borrowing and remixing might be for how students can draw on the work of others, appropriating language "to establish group membership, to grow, and to define themselves in new ways" (Hull and Rose).

In an article about Bob Dylan and plagiarism, Jonathan Lethem quotes from an interview where Alan Lomax asks Muddy Waters how he wrote the song "Country Blues." Waters says he "made it up," that the song "fell into" his mind, that previously there had been "some blues played like that," that the song "came from the cotton field," that Robert Johnson had "put the record out," and that he'd "learned" how to play it from Son House. Because of my experience inside the music community, such talk doesn't surprise me. Yet in my other life teaching Freshman English, it makes me wonder. What if my students talked like that? *It came from the Internet. I saw some papers written like that. Someone put it out in a magazine once. My mother helped me write it.*

Though Waters claims authorship, his language acknowledges that the song didn't come out of nowhere. It already existed in multiple contexts and forms. You might ask, "How could he write a song that already exists?" Jazz critic Kevin Whitehead, speaking of saxophonist Lucky Thompson's tendency to copy the styles of other greats, explains it this way:

> Thompson used all that inspiration to sound more like himself, to expand the expressive qualities he had already. I think that's why saxophonists love him. He shows how to fold influences into a well-rounded style of your own.

Lethem attributes similar qualities to Bob Dylan, someone who is often accused of plagiarism. Early on, Dylan copied his hero Woody Guthrie so closely that he became Guthrie's spitting image (the cheathouse.com version). Eventually, though, Dylan became an expert at influence folding, an origami master. Lethem calls Dylan's appropriations an example of "the ecstasy of influence," pointing out that though Dylan has copied much over his long career, still, "Dylan's originality and his appropriations are one." A good example of this is the way Dylan took the traditional song "No More Auction Block" and turned it into "Blowin' in the Wind."

The blues tradition or "folk method" Waters describes is what drives creativity and innovation in popular music. Go to YouTube and listen to the Chiffons singing "He's so Fine," and then go to George Harrison's "My Sweet Lord." Listen to "Who's Been Talkin'," by Howlin' Wolf, and then to Carlos Santana playing "Black Magic Woman." For something more recent, listen to Articolo 31's "Come una Pietra Scalciata" which builds a new song around Bob Dylan's "Like a Rolling Stone," or to *The Grey Album*, by Danger Mouse, which takes the Beatles' *The White Album* and remixes it with vocals from Jay-Z's *The Black Album*.

Clearly, the later songs are copies of the earlier ones. In another sense, however, each song is distinct, a new creation built upon what came before. Depending upon the artist's skills, the "copy" may be as indispensible as, or even more significant than, the "original." And just as the old song made the new one possible, the new one provides fertile ground for what will follow.

"But all that copying is just musicians," you might say. "It doesn't apply to writing essays in school." If you look around, though, you'll see similar methods used in other fields. Robert Polito compares Bob Dylan's musical borrowings to Picasso's "modernist collages," where he took artifacts he didn't "create" and mixed them together to make something new. Lawrence Lessig writes about Andy Warhol taking preexisting designs (like soup cans) and presenting them in ways that Lessig describes as "distinctly Warhol." Fashion designer Johanna Blakley claims that her industry's "culture of copying" is a sign of its health because it forces designers to "up [their] game" and spurs them to invent "signature styles."

"Okay, but that's the arts," you might say. "Bad example." Well, keep looking. Examples of the "folk method" show up in science, medicine, and law as well. Legal scholar Lawrence Lessig argues that too much restriction on copying and "re-use" suppresses innovation and new ideas. For an example of how essential "second use" can be, Jonathan Lethem cites library and information science researcher Don Swanson who, through what he calls "text-mining," made an important discovery about Raynaud's Syndrome. Here's how Swanson describes it:

...I was struck by lightning and have never recovered. I encountered, partly by accident, two pieces of information from two different articles in the medical literature that together suggested an answer to a question for which I could find no single article that provided an answer. It seemed I might have found out something that no one else knew and that the medical literature might be full of such undiscovered connections.

Using old material, Swanson came up with insights that a new study might never uncover. Lessig's "second use" principle could also be applied to Matt Friedman's "discovery" of a "missing link" in the fossil record. Friedman didn't set off for exotic locales to dig up the fossils as you might suspect. Instead, he "unearthed" his evidence while digging through dusty museum basements and forgotten file drawers to sort through previous researchers' mislabeled, misfiled, and neglected work.

In law, says Lessig, the spirit of Muddy Waters and the methods of Don Swanson are in full swing:

A great brief seems to say nothing on its own. Everything is drawn from cases that went before, presented as if the argument now presented is in fact nothing new. Here again, the words of others are used to make a point the others didn't directly make. The old cases are remixed. The remix is meant to do something new (52).

To make a point the others didn't directly make. This is the lawyer version of the cotton field. This is what makes Muddy Waters distinct from Robert Johnson or Son House, Bob Dylan distinct from Woody Guthrie, and Lucky Thompson more than some dude who lifts riffs from Stan Getz and John Coltrane. Lessig, the creator of Creative Commons, argues that all disciplines need the same type of open source "commons" those musicians used—not just so we can produce new songs, but so we can produce new knowledge.

As essential as it may be, copying makes people jumpy. The academic community and popular press reaction to cases of student plagiarism mirrors the press reaction to Bob Dylan's borrowings. After Dylan called attention to his own "thefts" with his 2001 album, *"Love and Theft"* (quotation marks, Dylan), a flurry of articles followed, most expressing dismay and outrage. In recent works, Dylan has "plagiarized" from *Huck Finn, The Great Gatsby*, Muddy Waters, Confederate poet Henry Timrod, Japanese novelist Junichi Saga, Ovid, and Virgil, among many others, and the list is still growing.

Some writers, though, take a different view and use Dylan's "thefts" to examine the role of influence and appropriation in the world of ideas. Polito uses "modernist collage" and "sampling" to describe what Dylan is doing. Richard Thomas examines the importance of "intertexts" in Dylan's art and seeks to distinguish plagiarism from "creative reuse." Jonathan Lethem's "The Ecstasy of Influence: A Plagiarism," plagiarizes numerous sources in order to demonstrate as well as explain Dylan's composing methods.

Jason Johnson, a former educator turned information technology consultant, also seeks to distinguish between plagiarism and creative use, not for music, but for education. In his Washington Post article, he resists the typical laments: Kids these days! Darn that Internet! and What's this world coming to? Instead, he examines the policing/detection model teachers use and wonders "if that's really what teachers should be doing." Focusing on detection diverts attention from more essential concerns. One of the article's commentators, "jdresner," elaborates on what teachers can do to mitigate the problem through revamping "assignment design," through working in "stages" "rather than simply having one big due date," and through "juxtaposing works [not] usually connected." As Johanna Blakley might say, teachers need to make like fashion designers. They need to up their game.

One way to do that, says Lessig, is to use a different "architecture." Citing the computer software terms RO (read only) vs. RW (read and write) to make his point, Lessig examines the transition from the RO/analog age of record players, where listeners could only listen, to the RW/digital age of CDs and MP3s, where listeners hold the power to be music makers, too. Educators have relied for too long, he believes, on RO-style models in the classroom:

When students come to law school, most come from an essentially RO education. For four years (or more), they've sat in large lecture halls, with a professor at the front essentially reading the same lectures she's given year after year after year. 'Any questions?' usually elicits points of order, not substance. 'Do we have to read chapter 5?' 'Will the subjunctive be on the exam?' (85-86)

Law school, however, is a RW environment, where a class session takes the form of an "argument." The "structure demands that [students] create as they participate in the instruction" (86). Lessig's call for law school-type RW architectures allows room for writing instruction and writing assignments to follow models similar to those of the fashion designers and the blues singers. Just as he argues for fewer copyright restrictions in music in order to encourage more innovation and less policing (the very thing Blakley claims helps her field thrive), he calls for similar changes in the classroom.

Under traditional architectures in the classroom, accompanied now by a strong detection ethic, students experience mostly the anxiety of influence and rarely the ecstasy that fuels someone like Waters or Dylan or Blakley or Lethem. Dylan raises the "Love and Theft" question to make a statement about the indispensable role of influence in the creative process. In the RO/"cult of originality" world where most education systems live, however, that message can't get through. The opportunity for theft still exists, but love, that's not even on the syllabus. Ecstasy? Better look elsewhere.

Essentially, Waters' and Dylan's methods resemble what English teachers call "patch writing," where passages are copied, altered, and mixed in various ways. Though seen as plagiarism when undocumented, as Johnson noted, the "skills" involved deserve attention. Glynda Hull and Mike Rose, after "wrestling" with their concerns over this issue with a particular student, say,

> it struck us that something profoundly literate is going on here. A fundamental social and psychological reality about discourse—oral or written—is human beings continually appropriate each other's language to establish group membership, to grow, and to define themselves in new ways. . . .

"A powerful pedagogic next move," they suggest, "would be temporarily to suspend concern about error and pursue, full tilt, her impulse to don the written language of another" (151). Of patchwriting, Rebecca Moore Howard says,

> Often it is a form of writing that learners employ when they are unfamiliar with the words and ideas about which they are writing. In this situation, patchwriting can actually help the learner begin to understand the unfamiliar material. Yet it is a transitional writing form; it is never acceptable for final-draft academic writing, for it demonstrates that the writer does not fully understand the source from which he or she is patchwriting. Because patchwriting can result from a student's inexperience with conventions of academic writing, instruction in quotation and source attribution and a request for subsequent revision of the paper may be an appropriate response for the instructor. But because patchwriting often results from a student's unfamiliarity with the words and ideas of a source text, instruction in the material discussed in the source and a request for subsequent revision of the paper is even more frequently the appropriate response (799).

Based on the sources cited here, a RW classroom might include parameters such as these on the syllabus:

- Sharing and collaboration
- Asking new questions
- Working in stages
  - Introducing unexpected (even spontaneous) sources from a variety of fields (and provided by students as well as teachers)
- Connecting disparate elements (such as using the metaphor of a record player as an analogy for education)
- Promoting "second use" through imitation with modification
- "Assembling other people's ideas" to discover new insights and perhaps happen upon "undiscovered public knowledge"
- Viewing mistakes as potential opportunities

This kind of design frees student writers from the anxiety of influence (and their teachers from the anxiety of enforcement) and creates the conditions for experiencing the ecstasy of influence instead. Like Waters, students can learn what it's like to write a song that already exists and somehow make it new. Like Thompson, they can learn how to copy in order to sound more like themselves and also, in Lessig's words, "to make a point the others didn't directly make."

As a teacher, I don't want to play meter maid or traffic cop. I want my classroom to copy the fashion designers, lawyers, and musicians. I want to tell my students to go ahead—be Woody, sing his songs, stand in his boots, adopt his accent and his biography, smoke his brand of cigarettes, pose like he does in photos. That's not theft—that's love. It's language acquisition. It's "adopting and embracing of filiations, communities, and discourses," says Lethem (using a phrase "lifted" from George L. Dillon). Teachers need to realize that some of the thefts they see are not thefts, but what Susan McCarthy calls "an early stage of a journey toward grace, competence, and comprehension" (x). In a collaborative environment, a student can learn, in music critic Paul Williams' words, "to reach beyond his or her present abilities, beyond what he's sure he can do and into the unknown" (85). The classroom becomes New York's Café Wha?, circa 1961, or the Mississippi Delta in the 1920s and 30s—a collaborative, teeming reef of ideas and creativity.

Later, when student writers have nearly finished their project, before the official release or publication or evaluation, they can see their work as being just like Muddy Waters' blues. Now they can take their Alan Lomax readers on a tour of the cotton field where it all came from, the place where they heard it, learned it, made it. Documentation now takes on new meaning and significance. Let me show you how I did this thing I'm so proud of. See? Here's how you can do similar things yourself. Here, student writers become teachers, translating for those poor, uninitiated folks who've never visited Gerde's Folk City, The Gaslight Cafe, or 1920s' New Orleans. Classmates are collaborators even at these final stages, making up a kind of open source community help desk where they share influences and offer advice to each other on how to use their sources more effectively and make them more open and accessible to all. Students become invested in the work, not just the grade, and when you are invested in the work, the work gets better.

Assignments are no longer a pressure-packed one-shot deal. The incentives to cheat evaporate. Why sweat it? We're going to write this again. We're going to find new things to add, things we haven't discovered yet. And we don't have to do it alone. We'll have lots of help. After we work like that for a while, our admittedly derivative work will evolve into its remixed or hybrid form, something that from there just might turn into some as yet unforeseen brand new thing, where our originality and our appropriations finally become one. "No More Auction Block" recedes, and "Blowin' in the Wind" is born.

In such a setting, English compositions, term papers, and research projects have an opportunity to become more than just requirement-fulfilling, forgettable, who-gives-a-damn exercises, the kind that create little more than the ideal conditions for dishonesty. In an ecstasy of influence environment, students, much like Swanson, stand at least a fighting chance of getting struck by lightning.

Works Cited

Blakley, Johanna. "Lessons from Fashion's Free Culture." *TED: Ideas Worth Spreading*, April 2010. Web. May 2010.

"Flatfish Fossils Fill in a Missing Link." *University of Chicago News*. July 9, 2008. Web. < http://news.uchicago.edu/article/2008/07/09/flatfish-fossils-fill-missing-link>.

Howard, Rebecca Moore. "Plagiarisms, Authorships, and the Academic Death Penalty." *College English* 57.7 (Nov. 1995): 708-36. Print.

Hull, Glynda and Mike Rose. "Rethinking Remediation: Toward a Social-Cognitive Understanding of Problematic Reading and Writing." *Written Communication* 6 (1989): 139-54. Print.

Johnson, Jason. "Cut-and-Paste Is a Skill Too," *Washington Post*, March 25, 2007. Web. <http://www.washingtonpost.com/wp-dyn/content/article/2007/03/23/AR2007032301612.html>.

Lessig, Lawrence. *Remix: Making Art and Commerce Thrive in the Hybrid Economy.* New York: Penguin, 2008. Print.

Lethem, Jonathan. "The Ecstasy of Influence: A Plagiarism." *Harper's*. February, 2007. Web. <http://www.harpers.org/archive/2007/02/0081387>

McCarthy, Susan. *Becoming a Tiger: How Baby Animals Learn to Live in the Wild.* New York: Harper Collins, 2004. Print.

Polito, Robert. "Bob Dylan: Henry Timrod Revisited." *Poetry Foundation.* 2007. Web. <http://www.poetryfoundation.org/article/178703>.

Swanson, Don R. "On the Fragmentation of Knowledge, the Connection Explosion, and Assembling Other People's Ideas." *Bulletin of the American Society for Information Science and Technology.* Vol. 27, No. 3 February/March 2001. Web. http://www.asis.org/Bulletin/Mar-01/swanson.html.

Thomas, Richard F. "The Streets of Rome: The Classical Dylan." *Oral Tradition*, 22/1 (2007): 30-56. Web. <http://journal.oraltradition.org/issues/22i/Thomas>.

Waters, Muddy. "Interview No. 1," by Alan Lomax. *The Complete Plantation Recordings.* Chess Records, 1993. CD.

Whitehead, Kevin. Review of "Sax in the City." *Fresh Air.* Host Terry Gross. Natl. Public Radio, 3 June, 2009. *NPR.org.* Web. <http://www.npr.org/templates/story/story.php?storyId=104871379>.

Williams, Paul. *Bob Dylan: Performing Artist 1960-1973.* London: Omnibus, 1994. Print.

Questions

1 Does Rhodes's extended discussion of how borrowing and remix have worked in the world of music give you a perspective on the creative process and how the new might build on what has gone before, in writing as well as in music?

2 Rhodes suggests that students need to "learn what it's like to write a song that already exists and somehow make it new," and that teachers should encourage "imitation with modification," assembling other people's ideas to discover new insights, and viewing mistakes as potential opportunities. Have you found any of these moves to be present in your own work?

3 However, Rhodes is not suggesting borrowing others' ideas and words without giving appropriate credit. Rather, he would have students complete their work by taking their readers "on a tour of the cotton field where it all came from, the place where they heard it, learned it, made it." Imagine providing such a tour for an example of your own writing. How would you, as tour guide, show what influenced your work, what you borrowed, what you remixed? What would a narrative account, as opposed to only a list of citations, look like?

"Realistic Expectations About Anti-Plagiarism Software"LRIII:3
by Eleanor Kutz

Kutz, Eleanor, Wayne Rhodes, Stephen Sutherland, Vivian Zamel. "Addressing Plagiarism in A Digital Age." *Human Architecture: Journal of the Sociology of Self-Knowledge*, vol. 9, no. 3, 2011.

Anti-plagiarism software like SafeAssign and Turnitin promises to eliminate the problem of plagiarism by catching every possible instance of it in the papers students submit. In this section of a larger article, Eleanor (Ellie) Kutz describes how she undertook her own inquiry into how and how well such software works, first by observing her students' experience with it, and then reviewing the research that others have done on it. Such programs appear helpful—certainly to teachers as they cut down on potential time spent "catching" plagiarists but also to students, as they can be used during the drafting process to help students become more critical of how they are working with sources. But Kutz cautions that they can also get in the way of a writing process in which students step into and become confident using repeated language patterns. Because students are penalized by taking on recognizable ways with words, programs such as these can actually prevent students from learning the conventions and insider terms and ways that are central to a professional or academic community. Kutz concludes that anti-plagiarism software should be used to increase students' awareness of their linguistic strategies and writing moves rather than to police students' writing.

All teachers would love to have an easy solution to one of the more troublesome aspects of teaching—the problem of whether students are indeed doing their own writing and thinking or instead just using the words and ideas of others without working them into their own argument, and without attribution. And anti-plagiarism software looks, at first, like that easy solution:

> This is going to be great. It should save me hours because it will trawl through thousands of pages of material on the databases and find spots where text has been lifted. I hope it will be a quick and relatively thorough means of finding out where students plagiarise and highlight those spots for me. It takes me so long at the moment and even though I can spend a couple of hours checking suspect papers, I'm never really convinced that I've got everyone. This could be the answer (Australian faculty member quoted in Sutherland-Smith and Carr, 96).

In my own teaching, I have long tried to learn what motivates the ways in which my students work with sources and to guide their practices with all research, online or off; toward this end I've guided their own inquiries into the discourse practices of both non-academic and academic discourse communities so that they could see what was involved in their own processes of appropriating and internalizing new discourses (Kutz). I felt that the writing assignments I created were sufficiently individualized, not easily lending themselves to plagiarism. But I've also been working with other faculty on using educational technology and trying to learn more about the tools that they were interested in. Since increasing numbers of our faculty were requesting SafeAssign (available to UMass faculty through the Blackboard learning management system), I decided I needed to try it out in my own teaching, find out

how others were using it, and discover what research had been done into the accuracy of anti-plagiarism software. As a member of the English department and long-time teacher of both freshman writing and of graduate students who are or will become teachers of writing in high schools and colleges, I wanted to know, for my own students and colleagues, what's important to understand about how these tools work, what safeguards are needed, when and how to implement them effectively, and how to shape a larger pedagogical context that will help our students understand and care about authority and authorship.

I started by adding the SafeAssign option to my Blackboard site for a graduate course I was teaching on "Teaching English with Technology"—a course that enrolls many teachers and prospective teachers. SafeAssign will check papers and provide a report to a teacher. But it also offers a draft mode in which students can submit their own papers and receive their own reports. For either mode, any material that has been drawn from another source (including correctly quoted and cited material) will be highlighted, with a link to where the material can be found. Teachers also have the option of having student work be added to an institutional database, so that future student submissions will be checked against prior ones.

I asked my graduate students to try out SafeAssign by choosing a piece of their writing from any class to submit in draft mode and then reporting on the results and what they learned. They generally found the software to be useful in highlighting material that came from other sources. Brittany Wadbrook, an English MA student who is currently teaching freshman writing at UMass, offered a typical response on her course blog:

I got 4% and it only highlighted one sentence, which was a sentence in quotes. It highlights the quote and provides the website where the highlighted material was detected. Then, I can click on the website where the information came from. This is great if the material is not cited, because then I can see what types of sources my students are reading and selecting from. Also, I can click on the highlighted material itself, and it will show me how much the text matches (in my case 91% which makes sense for a direct quote) and then you don't even need to navigate away from SafeAssign because it shows you the uploaded manuscript text and the Internet Source side-by-side so you don't even need to search the website for [the] place where the student copied data from! This, I think, is great.

Brittany also submitted a heavily plagiarized text and again received appropriate results.

So SafeAssign did seem to catch significant copying of other texts. But did that make it a useful pedagogical tool, one that would help me give my students better guidance in their work with sources rather than just doing a better job of policing what they did? To try to figure this out, I submitted some early drafts of research papers done by some of my former freshman students, and I received interesting and more complicated results. For example, one student who had followed her ethnographic study of a nonacademic community (a nightclub where she worked) with research into an issue related to that community (in this case, prostitution) had relied heavily on quoted material in her draft, and this material was flagged/highlighted, but the accuracy of the quotations varied from 100% down to 68%, showing that she often wasn't quoting her sources accurately. At the same time, some material that the student had paraphrased showed a closer match to the original (72%) than some of what she had presented as direct quotations. The extent of highlighted material also made it clear just how heavily her reliance on her sources was in this early draft. I had addressed that issue with her in subsequent revisions, and her final paper had been more strongly shaped around her own argument, with a much more judicious choice of supporting evidence from her sources. But, judging from the SafeAssign reports I now had at hand, I can see that previously I hadn't caught the fact that she was quoting her sources inaccurately, and I didn't give her as much help as she needed in learning how to paraphrase. Would having a SafeAssign report have helped both of us to see these issues more clearly? I now believe it would have.

The next phase of my own inquiry was to find out what others had discovered about plagiarism software and what lessons I might take away from their endeavors. Other faculty and librarians have been running their own informal experiments with these sites, constructing heavily plagiarized essays and submitting them for review. Results seem to vary, depending on the source materials used, but typically, some instances of copying are missed. Catherine Pellegrino, a librarian at St. Mary's College, reports on one such experiment in her academic blog, in which she found that SafeAssign identified 10 out of 15 copied passages (using Google allowed her to find 8 of them). SafeAssign did better at identifying paraphrased passages, while Google did better with content from JSTOR and Project Muse. But SafeAssign most often pointed to website sources, even when the content had originally been drawn from licensed databases. Similar experiments suggest that SafeAssign is particularly helpful for identifying the web content that students are most likely to draw on, but it isn't foolproof. From this information I've drawn *Lesson #1. The most commonly used software (Turnitin and SafeAssign) does not identify all cases of plagiarism.*

Beyond informal inquiries, there have been several carefully researched studies, including one carried out at the University of Texas (Gillis et al.). The researchers submitted 356 freshman essays (typical 10-page research papers with 8-10 sources) to both Turnitin and SafeAssign, following up with a careful analysis of a random sample of 40 essays. Both tools showed that the full sample of 356 essays fell into a range that suggested what the software showed as "low risk" of plagiarism (with less than 24% of the text showing a match with other sources). Both flagged material from web sources and student sources (the institutional database of student work) but not from print materials. There were some differences in what the two tools showed (in the percentage of instances flagged, the percentage of instances that were citation errors, and the number of sources flagged). SafeAssign showed all matches it found with other text, whether correctly quoted and cited or not. SafeAssign flagged fewer matches to the student database, and where it did so, papers were sometimes flagged based on students citing the same source—for example, a student's discussion of three different topics related to birth control was flagged because all three cited a link to the website of Planned Parenthood. From this study, I've drawn lesson *Lesson #2. Much of what is identified as a match to materials on the web or in institutional databases of student work has other explanations besides intentional plagiarism.*

For their closer analysis, after eliminating all correctly cited text (which is flagged by both programs), Gillis et al. began by asking "*what* the marked text rhetorically represents," looking carefully at the context in which it appeared. They found that 70% of the text marked by Turnitin and 83% by SafeAassign fell into four categories: the use of a *topic term* (such as global warming); a *topic phrase* (e.g., "global warming is a serious problem"); a *commonly used phrase* (e.g., "there are many risks associated with global warming"; "researchers have found that

___"); and *jargon* (words typically attached to discussions of a specific topic such as "global surface temperature," "climate model," "global dimming"). The remaining matches were actual citation errors—which could have been either accidental or intentional.

In the end, Gillis et al. did not recommend the adoption of either tool at the University of Texas. They were concerned that students, in their attempts to avoid "plagiarism" by using the common terms and phrases of a field's discourse, would be likely to turn to quick fixes like the thesaurus and end up avoiding the "expert, insider prose," they should have been acquiring, writing instead to the software. Their conclusion? "The applications' approach to writing is inconsistent with WAC [Writing Across the Curriculum] pedagogy. That is, in lieu of good pedagogy, the applications often penalize students for doing exactly what we want them to do: learn the basic language structures used by people who are writing about a common topic in a given discipline" (52). As Wayne Rhodes has suggested above, drawing on such structures is not necessarily an act of theft, but is often an essential aspect of embracing and trying out new discourses. And that leads me to *Lesson #3. The use of such software in identifying actual plagiarism requires careful instructor interpretation of the results.*

Nevertheless, I've come to believe that, with a clear understanding of what the software does and does not do, it can be useful as a learning tool for students if they are given the opportunity to learn about its capabilities and limitations in an appropriate teaching context. In such a context, students could, for example,

- Be given the opportunity to submit their essays as drafts;
- Be taught what the individual reports show, including the ways in which the appropriate use of common terms and phrases may be flagged;
- Be given the opportunity to change their work for resubmission (where they have actually paraphrased inadequately or missed a citation);
- Be asked to provide a narrative account of what in their work should stand as it is.

The faculty interviewed by Sutherland-Smith and Carr in their study at South Coast University in Australia reached similar conclusions. While they were disappointed to find that the software they were using (Turnitin) would not prove to be a foolproof and simple tool for addressing all plagiarism, they came to believe that "it could perform a useful function in heightening awareness of plagiarism as an issue of academic integrity, where subject-specific exercises were developed and students were invited to submit their own work" (101).

My own conclusions: I am very concerned with helping students develop the range of literacies they need to be suc-cessful in academic settings. As those settings have drawn increasingly on educational technology (including the use of learning management systems and other online resources to create a virtual classroom environment), I have seen it as my responsibility when teaching first year students to prepare them as readers and writers for such an environment. And if tools like SafeAssign are likely to be used in their other courses, I would want them to understand how these tools work, and what they can learn from them.

If I were currently teaching undergraduates, I'd not only show them how to submit drafts of assignments but I'd have them work in peer response groups to a) review their drafts and the SafeAssign reports; b) identify the reasons for any "matches" that appeared, using the terms suggested by Gillis et al. for the sorts of typical academic discourse that are often picked up as "matches"—*topic terms, topic phrases, commonly used phrases* and *disciplinary jargon*—as well as instances of problems with paraphrase and citation; and c) decide on appropriate changes—not so much to get a wholly clean report but to get a report they could explain and defend. Since every user seems to agree that the SafeAssign reports need to be interpreted, we need to teach students how to interpret them also. But above all, I'd want to engage them with larger questions about why and when they borrow the words of others, and what it means to do so creatively and originally, making something of their own from what they've found. And tools like SafeAssign, while they can show students where their borrowings are likely to violate academic norms, won't, by themselves, give students a richer picture of ways to work as writers. Those ways are typically much more complicated than any plagiarism-checker can begin to suggest.

Works Cited

Gillis, Kathleen, Susan Lang, Monica Norris and Laura Palmer. "Electronic Plagiarism Checkers: Barriers to Developing an Academic Voice." *The WAC Journal 20*, November 2009, 51-62. Web. 30 June, 2011 <http://wac.colostate.edu/journal/vol20/gillis.pdf >.

Kutz, Eleanor. Exploring Literacy. *A Guide to Reading, Writing, and Research*. New York: Longman, 2004.

Pellegrino, Catherine. "SafeAssign vs. Google for Plagiarism Detection." *Spurious Tuples: Flapping the Unflappable Since 1996*. Web. March 30, 2010. <http://www.spurioustuples.net/?p=384>.

Sutherland-Smith, Wendy and Rodney Carr. "Turnitin.com: Teachers' Perspectives of Anti-Plagiarism Software in Raising Issues of Educational Integrity." *Journal of University Teaching and Learning Practice* 2 (3), 2005, 92-101. Web. 30 June, 2011 <http://ro.uow.edu.au/jutlp/vol2/iss3/10 >

Wadbrook, Brittany. "Journal Week 3, Activity 2." English 613 Blog, June 20, 2010. Web. 30 June, 2011. <http://brwadbrook.tumblr.com/page/2>.

Questions

① What has Kutz found, from her own inquiry and the research of others, about the strengths and limitations of anti-plagiarism software? What material is most likely to be flagged if borrowed too closely?

② What has been your own experience with such software? If you currently have access to Turnitin or SafeAssign, submit a piece of your current work in draft mode, and see what you can learn from the report you receive. You should find matches for work you quoted and cited correctly. Is anything else highlighted as a match with other existing text? If so, can the match be explained as common topic terms and phrases that anyone discussing the topic would be likely to use, or key terms and phrases (jargon) often associated with that topic, like "academic discourse community"? If you gave a "tour of the cotton field" of your work, to use Rhodes' analogy, how would it fit with what the software shows? Do you find instances in which the feedback it gives you can also help you find missed citations or material you drew on too closely without quoting it?

READING 7

Selection from
Presentation Zen
by Garr Reynolds
New Riders, 2008, pp. 45; 85-89.

In this chapter from *Presentation Zen* by Garr Reynolds, Reynolds explains how "slideware" like PowerPoint and Keynote actually steers users to make really boring presentations with too much text and awkward, template backgrounds. Rather than starting with slideware when planning a presentation, he suggests we begin by "planning analog" by using simpler technologies like pen and paper, or white boards, to better tap into our creativity in the initial planning stages for a presentation. He also suggests that presenters need to be thinking about audience more and design presentations that consider how to engage a live audience by taking full advantage of the visual affordances of slideware, using more imagery and less text. He concludes the chapter with a helpful, succinct four-step guide for preparing a presentation that audiences will find worth their time.

One of the most important things you can do in the initial stage of preparing for your presentation is to get away from your computer. A fundamental mistake people make is spending almost the entire time thinking about their talk and preparing their content while sitting in front of a computer screen. Before you design your presentation, you need to see the big picture and identify your core messages—or the single core message. This can be difficult unless you create a stillness of mind for yourself, something which is hard to do while puttering around in slideware.

Right from the start, most people plan their presentation using software tools. In fact, the software makers encourage this, but I don't recommend it. There's just something about paper and pen and sketching out rough ideas in the "analog world" in the early stages that seems to lead to more clarity and better, more creative results when we finally get down to representing our ideas digitally. Since you will be making your presentation accompanied by PowerPoint or Keynote, you will be spending plenty of time in front of a computer later. I call preparing the presentation away from the computer "going analog," as opposed to "going digital" at the computer.

The Process

The problem with slideware applications—PowerPoint, in particular, since it's been around longer and influenced a generation—is that they have, by default, guided users toward presenting in outline form with subject titles ad bullet points grouped under each topic heading. This is similar to the ol' topic sentence in the high school composition class. Seems logical enough, but it is a structure that makes the delivery of the content utterly forgettable for the audience. Storyboarding can help. If you take the time in this part of the preparation stage and set your ideas up in a logical fashion in storyboard format, you can then visualize the sequential movement of your content narrative and the overall flow and "feel" of the presentation.

Since you have already identified your core message away from the computer, you can now begin to create a storyboard that will begin to give shape to the story of your short presentation. Storyboards have their origins in the movie industry, but are used often in business, particularly in the field of marketing and advertising.

One of the simplest and most useful features of PowerPoint and Keynote is the Slide Sorter view (Light Table view in Keynote). You can take your notes and sketches and create a storyboard directly in PowerPoint or Keynote, or you can remain "analog" a bit longer and draft a storyboard on paper or by using Post-its or a whiteboard, etc.

Each situation and each individual is different, and there are indeed many paths to better presentations, including better preparation. My personal approach moving from rough analog sketches to digital slides is not uncommon at all. Many people take a similar approach. I have been surprised, however, that for the most part today individual professionals, entrepreneurs, and students usually just open up PowerPoint and type about a dozen subject slides and then fill them with talking points. This is not an effective approach, nor is it a method I recommend, although it is common.

Below is the four-step approach I usually take. I sometimes skip the third step, but I find it works well when a group is planning the presentation. For students working on a group presentation, Step 3 is vital.

Step 1

Brainstorming. Step back, go analog, get away from the computer, tap into the right brain and brainstorm ideas. I do not edit ideas much here; the aim is to just let it flow. I explore. It may be messy. That's OK. What I'm trying to do—whether I am working alone or leading a group—is to see the issue from all sides. But to do that, you have to take a step back and see the big picture. When I work with a client, I listen carefully and ask questions. I listen far more than I speak. The listening is the important part. I'll look for themes in Step 2, although if clear themes are emerging as I listen and probe, then I'll begin to group items as I go.

Step 2

Grouping & identifying the core. In this step, I look to identify the one key idea that is central (and memorable) from the point of view of the audience. What is the "it" that I want them to get? I use "chunking" to group similar ideas while looking for a unifying theme. The presentation may be organized into three pars, so first I look for the central theme that will be the thread running through the presentation. There is no rule that says your presentation should have three sections or three "acts" from the world of drama. However, three is a good number to aim for because it is a manageable constraint and generally provides a memorable structure. Regardless of how many sections I use, there is only one theme. It all comes back to supporting that key message. The supporting structure—the three parts—is there to back up the core message and the story.

Step 3

Storyboarding off the computer. I take the ideas sketched out on paper n Step 2 and lay them out with Post-it notes. The advantage of this method (compare to the Slide Sorter view in PowerPoint or the Light Table view in Keynote) is that I can easily add content by writing on an additional Post-it and sticking it under the appropriate section without ever losing sight of the structure and flow. In software I have to switch to Slide mode to type or add an image directly on a slide and then go back to the Slide Sorter mode to the big-picture structure. Alternatively—and this is very popular with my Japanese business students—you can print out blank slides, 12 slides per sheet, which gives you essentially a larger version of a Moleskine Storyboard. If you want larger slides, you can print out nine slides or six. You can then tape these to the wall or spread them out on the desk, keeping them in a notebook when you're done. You can sketch your visuals and write down your key points in a printed version of slideware notes.

Step 4

Storyboarding in Slide Sorter/Light Table view. If you have a clear sense of your structure, you can skip Step 3 and start building the flow of your presentation directly in slideware. Create a blank slide using a template of your choosing (or the simplest version of your company's template if you must use it). I usually choose a blank slide and then place a simple text box inside it with the size and font I'll use most often. (You can create multiple master slides in PowerPoint and Keynote.) Then I duplicate several of these slides, since they will contain the visual content of my presentation, short sentences or singles words, images, quotes, charts & graphs, etc. The section slides—what presentations guru Jerry Weismann calls *bumper slides*—should be a different color with enough contrast that they stand out when you see them in the slide sorter view. You can have these slides hidden so that you see them only when planning in Slide Sorter view if you prefer; however, in my case, these slides will serve to give visual closure to one section and open the next section.

Now that I have a simple structure in the Slide Sorter view, I can add visuals that support my narrative. I have an introduction where I introduce the issue or the "the pain" and introduce the core message. I then use the next three sections to support my assertions or "solve the pain" in a way that is interesting and informative but that never loses sight of the simple core message.

For detailed advice about creating your story using the Slide Sorter view, I recommend Cliff Atkinson's *Beyond Bullet Points* (Microsoft Press).

Questions

1 Do you agree with Reynolds about how boring most presentations that use slideware are? What do you think makes a presentation "boring" versus interesting? Come up with a list of traits that you feel make up a good presentation.

2 Explain the point that Reynolds is trying to make with the "bicycle of your mind" metaphor. How does such a metaphor work rhetorically for Reynolds?

3 Although Reynolds never uses the word "literacy" in this piece, what kinds of literacies is he encouraging us to use? How does this connect with the ways you've thought about literacy throughout *Writing Moves*, and what does it suggest about literacy today?

READING 8

"Final Reflection"
by Brian Santoro (Student)

For this paper, Brian was asked to reflect on his growth as a writer in his first-semester writing course. He starts out his final reflection with a quote by Ben Franklin to set up the main theme of the paper—learning to write well takes time and patience. He focuses on three key things he learned throughout the semester—understanding audience, defining your purpose when you write, and entering a written conversation. He stresses the importance of knowing that, when we write, we rarely just write for ourselves. Instead, we write because there is a purpose to write, and part of that purpose is to connect with an audience. He notes that, in finding your purpose for writing, prewriting activities like double-entry notes and annotating a text help prepare you to write with more detail and more feeling. At each step along the way, Brian considers some of the challenges that he faced, explains some of the confusion he experienced in working through the course, and discusses how tolerating this struggle helped him grow as a writer.

Ben Franklin once stated, "Tell me and I forget. Teach me and I remember. Involve me and I learn." Expository writing was embedded on Ben Franklin's words of advice in that the course taught new objectives, involved a different approach to writing, and even helped students learn how to participate effectively while in class. The beginning of the semester started off a little shaky. I didn't comprehend the material as much as I should of and my grades reflected this. However, I was able to pick myself up and use the comments the professor was giving me as constructive criticism to help me later on. After completing this class, expository writing has given me the knowledge of addressing audience, having a certain purpose, and entering a conversation throughout the semester.

One of the most important elements of this course was learning what audience is truly about. A specific example in how our class learned to think about audience was writing a literacy narrative. In this unit students had the task of trying to come up with a story in their lives that related to what the definition of literacy actually was. At the same time, the students had to focus on their audience. In other words, they had to keep in mind that no one but themselves knew what they were talking about, in which case they had to make the story understandable for an audience to comprehend. This was a challenging assignment because it was difficult to relate a real life story and flip it into a literacy narrative while keeping audience in mind. Another example in how audience was addressed throughout the curriculum was reading "The Source of Bad Writing." In this article, written by Steven Pinker, he provides input on how some people have difficulties teaching a concept when they have "too much knowledge," on a particular subject matter. Pinker writes, "Pseudo-intellectuals spout obscure verbiage to hide the fact that they have nothing to say, hoping to bamboozle their audiences with highfalutin gobble-dygook." Pinker means that individuals who are so bright on a topic will not actually address a question being asked by someone else who doesn't know the material well. This is why knowing how to talk to an audience is such an important skill that can be used not only in writing but in other aspects of life.

Having a purpose when you write is crucial to being able to put your thoughts into words. When it comes to purpose I learned that following directions is vital to writing a successful paper. An example in how purpose was portrayed through some of my work throughout the semester was the inquiries done for readings, forums, and short essays. The inquiries were a great way to allow students to follow a purpose of their own choice. At first I struggled a bit with this idea because I wasn't following directions, my thoughts were a bit sporadic, and not much elaboration was going on. However, after completing several inquires it became a bit easier and by the end of the semester my responses would range between two and three hundred words. The inquiries became so comfortable for me that I would even restate the question in my response and then answer it completely often times giving my own input on a specific situation or topic.

Another part of writing that helped me understand my purpose was double entry journal note taking. This is a technique for taking notes that we learned in class to help arrange people's thoughts, ideas, and questions in an organized fashion. I liked this technique because two columns were set up, one side was a section labeled "Passages, quotes, phrases, and questions," the other side was titled "Thoughts, responses, and suggestions." The idea behind double entry notes is to address the purpose of a reading that you just finished. The professor did a tremendous job in teaching students how to address the purpose of a reading through asking questions, underlining areas that were confusing, annotating important phrases, and even taking side notes from time to time. These elements were put into the double entry journal notes in an easy way to understand and grasp.

Another area of expository writing that helped me understand purpose was the rhetorical appeals of ethos, logos, and pathos. These Aristotle terms were used in other objectives of the course, but seemed to fit most appropriately in defining what purpose truly represented. For instance, ethos is the concept of credibility, pathos represents emotion, and logos represents logic/reasoning. In order to have an effective rhetorical purpose, one can draw on each of these appeals. I learned that by using these appeals in my writing, it made my papers more appealing, more interesting to follow, and even more credible. Learning about purpose and the rhetorical appeals has helped me become a better writer in that it allows me to emphasize key points, while at the same time describe how I am feeling about a topic.

The last point I got out of this class was how to enter a written conversation. This component was focused especially in the second paper. For instance, the assignment was to choose amongst two articles that we read and annotated in class and discuss how you felt about it. In addition to this, the professor emphasized that we should first develop our own opinions on a specific topic and "enter the conversation" at the right time. This was a challenging feature because students had to be able to break down an article and actually understand what it meant first, before stating their own view. For example, in my unit two essay, I would say phrases such as, "Carr takes on an interesting perspective mentioning," and then stating, "I, for one agree with this statement." I was careful to set up a quote in the correct way, and then give my own take on what the author was trying to depict. Another part of the class that helped me realize what entering a conversation involved was the chapter we read titled "Entering a Conversation." An important part of this piece is when it mentions, "What makes writers masters of their trade is not only their ability to express interesting thoughts but their mastery of an inventory of basic moves that they probably picked up by reading a wide range of other accomplished writers" (Graff and Birkenstein 1). I found this statement interesting in that, in order to enter a conversation effectively, one must have prior knowledge by engaging in other conversations in other work to sound more credible and reliable with their points they are trying to make. The thought of entering a conversation was a new way of writing that I discovered to make one's argument more effective and persuasive about a topic.

Expository writing has been an impactful class on me. I say this because the objectives and units stretched my limits and made me think and explain myself on a whole new level. All the homework assignments made me want to elaborate more and explain myself in further detail. The two unit tests that were given out even made me clarify myself in order to prove that I knew what was going on. As Ben Franklin stated, "if you tell me I'll forget it, if you teach me I'll remember, but if you involve me I'll learn." This is exactly what expository writing has done for me. It has helped me to engage with my classmates and peers in ways that are conversational, appropriately address an audience, and have a clear purpose. ■

Questions

❶ How does Brian organize his reflection? Create an outline that details the larger structure of his essay, describing the introduction, body paragraphs, and conclusion.

❷ What kinds of writing moves does Brian make to show how his understanding of literacy and writing has changed?

❸ If Brian was going to post this reflection for a digital portfolio online, how should he write it? What kinds of questions would he need to consider in turning this more traditional essay into a more abbreviated online text that reflects on his time in a writing course?

References, Resources, and Links

References and Resources

Chapter 17

REFERENCES

17:1 Purcell, Kristen, Lee Rainie, Alan Heaps, Judy Buchanan, Linda Friedrich, Amanda Jacklin, Clara Chen, and Kathryn Zickuhr. "How Teens Do Research in the Digital World." *Pew Research Center: Internet, Science & Tech*, 1 Nov. 2012, www.pewinternet.org/2012/11/01/how-teens-do-research-in-the-digital-world/.

17:2 Carr, Nicholas. "Is Google Making Us Stupid? What the Internet is doing to our brains," *The Atlantic,* July/August 2008, www.theatlantic.com/magazine/archive/2008/07/is-google-making-us-stupid/306868/.

17:3 Hargittai, Eszter, Lindsay Fullerton, Ericka Menchen-Trevino, and Kristin Yates Thomas. "Trust Online: Young Adults' Evaluation of Web Content." *International Journal of Communication,* no. 4, 2010.

17:4 Wathen, C. Nadine, and Jacquelyn Burkell. "Believe it or not: Factors influencing credibility on the Web." *Journal of the American Society for Information Science and Technology,* vol. 53, no. 2, 2002, pp. 134–44.

17:5 Sillence, Elizabeth, Pam Briggs, Peter Richard Harris, and Lesley Fishwick. "How do Patients Evaluate and Make Use of Online Health Information?" *Social Science & Medicine,* vol. 64, no. 9, 2007, pp. 1853–1862.

17:6 Walsh, Andrew J. "How Do You Evaluate the Blogs and Websites You Visit?" 13 July 2011, andrewjwalsh.com/blog/how-do-you-evaluate-the-blogs-and-websites-you-visit.

17:7 "Families and Digital Media in Young Children's Learning." *Harvard Family Research Project.* Harvard Graduate School of Education, 19 Feb. 2014, www.hfrp.org/publications-resources/browse-our-publications/research-spotlight-families-and-digital-media-in-young-children-s-learning.

17:8 Head, Alison J. "Learning the Ropes: How Freshmen Conduct Course Research Once They Enter College." Project Information Literacy Research Report, 5 Dec. 2013, papers.ssrn.com/sol3/papers.cfm?abstract_id=2364080.

17:9 Bosker, Bianca. "Wealthier College Students Share, Connect More on Facebook: Study." *The Huffington Post,* 26 June 2013, www.huffingtonpost.com/2013/06/25/college-students-facebook-study_n_3497733.html.

17:10 Parks, Malcolm R., and Kory Floyd. "Making Friends in Cyberspace." *Journal of Communication,* vol. 46, no. 1, 1996, pp. 80-97.

17:11 Savicki, Victor, Dawn Lingenfelter, and Merle Kelley. "Gender Language Style and Group Composition in Internet Discussion Groups." *Journal of Computer-Mediated Communication*, vol. 2, no. 3, 1996.

RESOURCES

"Social Media Research: A Guide to Ethics." Prepared by Dr. Leanne Townsend and Prof. Claire Wallace, with the support from the Economic and Social Research Council of the UK, www.gla.ac.uk/media/media_487729_en.pdf

US National Archives, www.archives.gov/

Library of Congress, www.loc.gov/

University of Massachusetts/Boston's Archives and Special Collections, https://www.umb.edu/library/about/departments/uasc

Chapter 18

REFERENCES

18:1 Head, Alison J. "Learning the Ropes: How Freshmen Conduct Course Research Once They Enter College." Project Information Literacy Research Report, 5 Dec, 2013, papers.ssrn.com/sol3/papers.cfm?abstract_id=2364080.

18:2 Marwick, Alice, and danah boyd. "Networked Privacy: How Teenagers Negotiate Context in Social Media." *New Media & Society,* vol. 16, no. 7, 2014, pp. 1051-1067.

18:3 Marwick, Alice, and danah boyd. "'It's just drama': Teen Perspectives on Conflict and Aggression in a Networked Era." *Journal of Youth Studies,* vol. 17, no. 9, 2014, pp. 1187-1204.

18:4 boyd, danah, and Alice Marwick. "The Conundrum of Visibility." *Journal of Children and Media,* vol. 3, no. 4, 2009, pp. 410-414.

18:5 boyd, danah, and Eszter Hargittai. "Connected and Concerned: Variation in parents' online safety concerns." *Policy & Internet,* vol. 5, no. 3, 2013, pp.,245–269.

18:6 boyd, danah. "Networked Privacy." *Surveillance & Society,* vol. 10, no. 3/4, 2012, pp. 348-350.

18:7 Gibbs, Jennifer, and Heewon Kim. "Invoking the Power of Book Club: An Investigation of Concertive Control in an Online Community." Conference Papers–*International Communication Association*, 2011, pp. 1-30. *Communication and Mass Media Complete.*

18:8 Kutz, EleanorF, Wayne Rhodes, Stephen Sutherland, and Vivian Zamel. "Addressing Plagiarism in a Digital Age." *Human Architecture: Journal of the Sociology of Self-Knowledge IX*, vol. 9, no. 3, 2011, pp. 15-35. scholarworks.umb.edu/cgi/viewcontent.cgi?article=1410&context=humanarchitecture.

18:9 Koosel, Stacey. "Ethnographies of Social Networks: How Artists Negotiate Digital Identity." *interartive.* http://interartive.org/2013/05/ethnographies-social-networks-artist-digital-identity/

RESOURCES

The University of Massachusetts, Boston library guide to beginning research, umb.libguides.com/module1

The University of Massachusetts, Boston academic honestly policy, www.umb.edu/pages/standard_page/19536

Chapter 19
REFERENCES

19:1 boyd, danah. "How Can Qualitative Internet Researchers Define the Boundaries of Their Projects: A Response to Christine Hine." *Internet Inquiry: Conversations About Method,* edited by Annette Markham and Nancy Baym. Sage, 2008, pp. 26-32.

19:2 van Dijck, José. *The Culture of Connectivity: Critical History of Social Media.* Oxford UP, 2013.

19:3 "About." Ethnography Matters. Ethnography Matters, ethnographymatters.net/about.

19:4 Fister, Barbara. "'Reading as a Contact Sport': Online Book Groups and the Social Dimensions of Reading." *Reference and User Services Quarterly*, vol. 44, no. 4, pp. 303-309.

19:5 Koosel, Stacey. "Ethnographies of Social Networks: How Artists Negotiate Digital Identity." *interartive.* http://interartive.org/2013/05/ethnographies-social-networks-artist-digital-identity/

19:6 Hilbert, Martin, and Priscila Lopez. "The World's Technological Capacity to Store, Communicate, and Compute Information." *Science*, no. 332, 2011, pp. 60-65, DOI: 10.1126/science.1200970.

19:7 Sheldon, Jane P. "Gender Stereotypes in Educational Software for Young Children." *Sex Roles*, vol. 51, no. 7/8, 2004, pp. 433-44, deepblue.lib.umich.edu/bitstream/handle/2027.42/45637/11199_2004_article_ny00000326.pdf?sequence=1.

19:8 Mattix, April, and Michelle J. Sobolak. "The Gender Journey in Picturebooks: A Look Back to Move Forward." *Childhood Education*, vol. 90, no. 3, 2014, pp. 229-33, www.tandfonline.com/doi/abs/10.1080/00094056.2014.912061?mobileUi=0&journalCode=uced20.

19:9 Gasser, Urs, Sandra Cortesi, Momin Malik, and Ashley Lee. "Youth and Digital Media: From Credibility to Information Quality." *The Berkman Center for Internet & Society Research Publication Series.* The Berkman Center for Internet & Society, 2012-1, cyber.law.harvard.edu/publications.

19:10 Wilson, Robert E., Samuel D. Gosling, and Lindsay T. Graham. "A Review of Facebook Research in the Social Sciences." *Perspectives on Psychological Science*, vol. 7, no. 3, 2012, pp. 203-20.

RESOURCES

Ethnography Matters ethnographymatters.net/

Wendy Hsu, "On Doing Digital Ethnography" series in *Ethnography Matters*

Part I: ethnographymatters.net/blog/2012/10/27/on-digital-ethnography-part-one-what-do-computers-have-to-do-with-ethnography/

Part II: ethnographymatters.net/blog/2012/12/05/on-digital-ethnography-mapping-as-a-mode-of-data-discovery-part-2-of-4/

Part III: ethnographymatters.net/blog/2013/01/25/on-digital-ethnography-magnifying-the-materiality-of-culture-part-3-of-4/

Part IV: ethnographymatters.net/blog/2013/12/09/ethnography-beyond-text-and-print-how-the-digital-can-transform-ethnographic-expressions/

Mass. Memories Road Show at the University of Massachusetts in Boston, openarchives.umb.edu/cdm/landingpage/collection/p15774coll6

Library of Congress, www.loc.gov

Cowbird.com, cowbird.com/

Fera, Jonathan. "Digital story project captures students' hopes, struggles and resilience." University News. University of Wisconsin, *Whitewater*, 16 Feb. 2015, www.uww.edu/news/archive/2015-02-digital-stories

National Archives, www.archives.gov/

World Digital Library, www.wdl.org/en/

Digital Public Library of America, dp.la/

"Looking for a book?" Old Children's Books, www.oldchildrensbooks.com/looking-for-a-book?page=8

Newbery Medal Winners, ala.org/alsc/awardsgrants/bookmedia/newbery-medal/newberyhonors/newberymedal

Chapter 20
REFERENCES

20:1 Waters, Sue. "Digital Curation: Putting the Pieces Together." *Sue Waters Blog.* Self Published, 13 Oct. 2013, suewaters.com/2013/10/13/digital-curation/.

20:2 Vengoechea, Ximena. "How We Date, Online and Off: Notes From the Field." *The Huffington Post.* TheHuffingtonPost.com, 11 June 2014, www.huffingtonpost.com/ximena-vengoechea/how-we-date-online-and-off_b_5479667.html.

20:3 Kynard, Carmen et al. "E-Portfolio Inspiration from 2013" Digication, johnjay.digication.com/eportfolio_express/Some_E-Portfolio_Inspirations.

20:4 Nunes, Christian. "Digication E-Portfolio: My World In My Words," johnjay.digication.com/my_world_in_my_words/Home.

20:5 Jackson, Laurie J. "Portfolio—Laurie J. Jackson." Self-published, ljjackson4.wix.com/nostalgia.

20:6 Wix.com, www.wix.com.

RESOURCES

Bartlett, Jeff. "Jeff Bartlett Media." *Jeff Bartlett Media.* Self-published, www.jeffbartlettmedia.com.

Portfolio Resources:

www.wix.com

thewritelife.com/freelance-portfolio-sites/

en.wordpress.com/portfolios/

www.elegantthemes.com/blog/tips-tricks/creating-a-killer-online-portfolio-website-using-wordpress

Presentation Resources:

Garr Reynolds Presentation Tips, www.garrreynolds.com/preso-tips/

Garr Reynolds on *Presentation Zen,* www.youtube.com/watch?v=DZ2vtQCESpk and "How To Present Data" https://www.youtube.com/watch?v=h9avFB908k0

Links

Additional Readings

LRIII.1 http://firstmonday.org/ojs/index.php/fm/rt/printerFriendly/3340/2985#33

LRIII.2 https://cyber.harvard.edu/node/95360

LRIII.3 http://scholarworks.umb.edu/humanarchitecture/vol9/iss3/3/

PORTFOLIO RESOURCES

http://www.wix.com

http://thewritelife.com/freelance-portfolio-sites/

https://en.wordpress.com/portfolios/

https://www.elegantthemes.com/blog/tips-tricks/creating-a-killer-online-portfolio-website-using-wordpress

PRESENTATION RESOURCES

Garr Reynolds Presentation Tips http://www.garrreynolds.com/preso-tips/

Garr Reynolds on Presentation Zen https://www.youtube.com/watch?v=DZ-2vtQCESpk and How To Present Data https://www.youtube.com/watch?v=h9avFB908k0 (Short extract from Presentation Zen talk)

Chapter 17

L17:1 http://www.pewinternet.org/2012/11/01/how-teens-do-research-in-the-digital-world

L17:2 http://www.easybib.com/guides/students/research-guide/website-credibility-evaluation/

L17:3 http://www.archives.gov

L17:4 https://www.loc.gov

L17:5 https://www.umb.edu/library/about/departments/uasc

L17:6 http://openarchives.umb.edu/cdm/landingpage/collection/p15774coll6/

Chapter 18

L18:1 http://money.cnn.com/infographic/technology/what-is-the-deep-web/

L18:2 https://www.coastal.edu/library

L18:3 http://umb.libguides.com/c.php?g=351173&p=2368883

L18:4 https://www.umb.edu/pages/standard_page/19536

L18:5 http://scholarworks.umb.edu/humanarchitecture/vol9/iss3/3/

Chapter 19

L19:1 http://ethnographymatters.net/

L19:2 http://ethnographymatters.net/blog/2012/10/27/on-digital-ethnography-part-one-what-do-computers-have-to-do-with-ethnography/

L19:3 http://openarchives.umb.edu/cdm/landingpage/collection/p15774coll6/

L19:4 https://www.loc.gov

L19:5 http://www.archive.org

L19:6 http://www.london.umb.edu

L19:7 http://cowbird.com/story/94106/YesterdayToday/?uiid=widget-1200209079-94106

L19:8 http://cowbird.com/story/27272/Yesterdays_Hard_Copy/

L19:9 http://cowbird.com/story/66164/A_Young_Mans_War_Diary/?uiid=widget-1137227941-66164

L19:10 http://www.uww.edu/news/archive/2015-02-digital-stories

L19:11 https://www.loc.gov/

L19:12 https://www.archives.gov/

L19:13 https://www.wdl.org/en/

L19:14 https://dp.la

L19:15 http://www.oldchildrensbooks.com/looking-for-a-book?page=8

L19:16 http://www.ala.org/alsc/awardsgrants/bookmedia/newberymedal/newberyhonors/newberymedal

Chapter 20

L20:1 http://www.theedublogger.com/

L20:2 http://www.ximenavengoechea.com/

L20:3 http://www.jeffbartlettmedia.com/

L20:4 https://johnjay.digication.com

L20:5 http://ljjackson4.wix.com/nostalgia

L20:6 http://wix.com

A Brief Guide to
Citations

Citations are ever-evolving community practices, ways of citing references and resources that are reshaped as new technologies emerge (as the recent revision of the MLA citation style stresses). As a writer, you need to tend to specific stylistic approaches to show that you are aware of the communities you write to and for as well as their conventions and expectations. While there are many resources (such as Purdue's Online Writing Lab at https://owl.english.purdue.edu/owl/) that provide explanations and examples of how to cite a vast variety of texts, we provide a brief guide here of commonly cited forms using both APA and MLA style.

In this brief guide, we focus on the kinds of citations you will include at the end of a paper, in a "References" or "Works Cited" list (depending on whether you are using APA or MLA style, respectively). You will also include parenthetical in-text citations in your writing that will correspond to these formats. This means that APA in-text citations include authors' names, publication dates, and page numbers—so, they will look something like this, (Brandt, 1996, p. 650)—while MLA in-text citations require only authors' names and page numbers—like this, (Brandt 650). While these differences might seem inconsequential, they speak to the values of the communities that draw upon these styles. Those who use APA—such as fields in the social sciences, like psychology—value timely research, so the date is made more visible using that approach.

Understanding the context that you are writing for involves anticipating your readers' expectations about citation practices. In addition to paying attention to the "how" of these styles (how to format parenthetical in-text citations, how to format a "References" or "Works Cited" list), you should also consider the "why" by questioning what these approaches suggest about the shared ways, values, and expectations of the disciplinary specific communities that use them.

A Note in Regard to MLA Style

The Modern Language Association's eighth edition (MLA 8) relies on a single, standard citation format applicable to every source type. MLA 8 constructs Works Cited entries based on a set of core elements found in most source types, both digital and print. If a given element is not relevant to the type of source you're citing (e.g. page numbers on a web page) it should be omitted from your Works Cited entry. Each element is followed by the punctuation mark shown below, and the last element should be followed by a period.

(1)Author. (2)Title of Source. (3)Title of Container, (4)Other Contributors, (5)Version, (6)Number, (7)Publisher, (8)Publication Date, (9)Location.

The MLA Works Cited entries listed in this section are offered as examples to illustrate the flexibility of MLA 8's core elements.

Article in a Scholarly Journal Found in an Online Database

APA

Author's Last Name, First Initial. (Year). Article title. *Magazine/Journal/Newspaper Title, Volume number*(Issue number), Page numbers. Retrieved from URL of database home page

Brandt, D. (1996). Accumulating literacy: Writing and learning to write in the twentieth century. *College English 57*(6), 649-651. Retrieved from http://www.jstor.org

MLA

Author's Last Name, First Name. "Title of Article." *Name of Periodical*, Volume, Issue, Date, Pages. *Name of Database*, DOI or URL.

Brandt, Deborah. "Accumulating Literacy: Writing and Learning to Write in the Twentieth Century." *College English,* 57, 6, 1996, pp. 649-651. *JSTOR*, DOI: 10.2307/378570.

Website

APA

Author last name, First initial (if available). (Year, Month Day web page was last updated). *Title or description of page.* Retrieved from URL

boyd, d. (n.d.). *danah boyd*. Retrieved from http://www.danah.org/

MLA

Last Name, First Name. *Title of Site.* Publisher (if different from site name), URL.

boyd, danah. *danah boyd*. www.danah.org/.

Article on a Website

APA

Author last name, First initial. (Year, Month Day). Title of article. *Name of website.* Retrieved from URL

boyd, d. (2010, August 23). Learning to hide in plain sight. *Apophenia*. Retrieved from http://www.zephoria.org/thoughts/archives/2010/08/23/social-steganography-learning-to-hide-in-plain-sight.html

MLA

Author's Last Name, First Name. "Title of Work." *Title of Site*, Publisher, Date, URL.

boyd, danah. "Learning to Hide in Plain Sight." *Apophenia*, danah boyd, 23 Aug. 2010, www.zephoria.org/thoughts/archives/2010/08/23/social-steganography-learning-to-hide-in-plain-sight.html.

Blog

APA

Author last name, First initial. (Year, Month Day). Title of blog entry [Description of form]. Retrieved from URL

Baym, N. (2011, September 8). Biting and feeding the hands that feed: Audience-musician interactions online [Web log post]. Retrieved from http://www.onlinefandom.com/

MLA

Author's Last Name, First Name. "Title of Blog Entry." *Title of Blog,* Date, URL.

Baym, Nancy. "Biting And Feeding The Hands That Feed: Audience-Musician Interactions Online." *Online Fandom*, 8 Sept. 2011, www.onlinefandom.com/.

Podcast

APA

Host/narrator/producer/director/writer last name, First initial. (Role of person/persons). (Year, Month Day). *Series* [Audio podcast]. Retrieved from URL

> Montagne, R. & Neary, L. (Hosts). (2010, May 10). Working to stop teens texting behind the wheel. *Morning Edition* [Audio podcast]. Retrieved from http://www.npr.org/templates/story/story.php?storyId=126486142

MLA

Last Name, First Name, role. "Title of Episode." *Title of Program,* season, episode, Sponsor, Date, URL.

> Montagne, Renee, and Lynn Neary, Hosts. "Working to Stop Teens Texting Behind the Wheel." *Morning Edition,* 10 May 2010. www.npr.org/templates/story/story.php?storyId=126486142.

Song

APA

Songwriter last name, First initial. (Year of copyright). Title of song [Recorded by artist if different from song writer]. On *Title of album* [Medium of recording]. Location: Label. (Recording date if different from copyright date).

> West, K. (2016). No more parties in L.A. On *The life of Pablo* [CD]. New York, NY: Def Jam/G.O.O.D. Music.

MLA

Last Name, First Name. "Title of Work." *Title of Album*, Distributor, Date. *Name of Audio Service.*

> West, Kanye. "No More Parties in L.A." *The Life of Pablo,* Def Jam/G.O.O.D. Music, 2016. *Spotify.*

Image

APA

Author Last name, First initial. (Role of Author). (Year image was created). Title of work [Type of work]. Retrieved from URL of website

> Rockwell, N. (Artist). (1943). Rosie the riveter [painting]. Retrieved from http://www.best-normanrock-well-art.com/1943-rosie-the-riveter.html

MLA

Artist's Last Name, First Name. *Title of Art.* Year created. *Name of Site*, URL.

> Rockwell, Norman. *Rosie the Riveter.* 1943. *Best Norman Rockwell Art*, www.best-norman-rockwell-art.com/1943-rosie-the-riveter.html.

Online Video Clip

APA

Producer(s) or author(s). (Year, Month Day). Title [Video type]. Retrieved from URL

> Turkle, S. (2012, April). Connected, but alone? [Video file]. Retrieved from https://www.ted.com/playlists/26/our_digital_lives

MLA

Author's Last Name, First Name. "Title." *Name of Host Site,* Date, URL.

Turkle, Sherry. "Connected, But Alone?" *TED*, Apr. 2012, www.ted.com/playlists/26/our_digital_lives.

Wiki
APA

Title of entry. (Date). In *Name of Collaborative Work.* Retrieved <Month, Day, Year>, from URL

Social media. (n.d.). In *Wikipedia*. Retrieved August 15 2015, from https://en.wikipedia.org/wiki/Social_media

MLA

"Title of Entry." *Title of Wiki*, Publisher, URL.

"Social media." *Wikipedia*, Wikimedia Foundation, en.wikipedia.org/wiki/Social_media.

Book
APA

Author's last name, author's first and middle initials. (Year of publication). *Title of book*. Location: Publisher.

Berthoff, A. (1981). The making of meaning. Claremont, NJ: Boynton/Cook.

MLA

Author's Last Name, First Name. *Title.* Publisher, Year of publication.

Berthoff, Ann. *The Making of Meaning.* Boynton/Cook, 1981.

Anthology or Collection
APA

Editor(s). (Ed(s).). (Year of publication). *Title of anthology/collection*. Location: Publisher.

Wysocki, A. F. (Ed.). (2004). *Writing new media: Theory and applications for expanding the teaching of composition.* Logan, UT: Utah State University Press.

MLA

Last Name, First Name, editor. *Title*. Publisher, Year of publication.

Wysocki, Anne Frances, editor. *Writing New Media: Theory and Applications for Expanding the Teaching of Composition.* Utah State UP, 2004.

A Work in an Anthology
APA

Author(s) of the work. (Year of publication). Title of work. In Editor (Eds.), *Title of edited collection* (pages of work). Location: Publisher.

Knobel, M. & Lankshear, C. (2007). Online memes, affinities, and cultural production. In M. Knobel & C. Lankshear (Eds.) *New literacies sampler* (pp. 199–228). New York, NY: Peter Lang.

MLA

Author's Last Name, First Name. "Title of Work." *Title of Anthology*, edited by First and Last Names, Publisher, Year of publication, Pages.

Knobel, Michele, and Colin Lankshear. "Online Memes, Affinities, and Cultural Production." *New Literacies Sampler,* edited by Michele Knobel and Colin Lankshear, Peter Lang, 2007, pp. 199-228.

Review

APA

Reviewer's name. (Year, Month Day). Title of review. [Review of the work (book, film, etc.) *Title of work*, by A. A. Author (editor, director, etc.)]. *Journal, volume*(issue), pages. Retrieved from URL

Atwood, M. (2013, November 21). When privacy is theft. [Review of *The circle*, by D. Eggers]. *The New York Review of Books*. Retrieved from http://www.nybooks.com/articles/archives/2013/nov/21/eggers-circle-when-privacy-is-theft/

MLA

Reviewer's Last Name, First Name. "Title of Review." Review of *Title*, by Author's First and Last Names. *Name of Periodical*, Date, URL.

Atwood, Margaret. "When Privacy is Theft." Review of *The Circle,* by Dave Eggers. *The New York Review of Books,* 21 Nov. 2013, www.nybooks.com/articles/archives/2013/nov/21/eggers-circle-when-privacy-is-theft/

Part IV:
Digital Toolbox—List of Online Content

Access Part IV: Digital Toolbox online at <u>fountainheadpress.com/writingmoves</u>. The contents of the Digital Toolbox are listed below.

Section 1: Using Digital Tools to Support Reading, Writing, Collaboration, and Creativity

Purpose: Reading in Digital Spaces

THE DESIGN OF READING APPS

Resources for Reading in Digital Spaces
- Adobe Reader
- Notability
- Evernote
- Other Useful Reading Apps

Purpose: Generating Ideas and Planning

Using Mind Maps

THE DESIGN OF MIND-MAPPING TOOLS

Resources and Tools for Mind-Mapping
- Coggle
- MindMup
- Drawing and Sketching Programs/Apps

Using Timeline Creators

THE DESIGN OF TIMELINE CREATORS

Resources for Creating Timelines
- Teachnology Timeline Creator
- Sutori

Using Outlining Tools

THE DESIGN OF OUTLINING TOOLS

Outlining Resources
- MS Word Outline Tool
- Notetaking App Outliners
- Other Outlining Tools: Pages, Google Docs, Outliner
- OWL, the Online Writing Lab at Purdue University

Purpose: Drafting, Collaborating, and Managing Content

Using Multipurpose Document Tools

THE DESIGN OF MULTIPURPOSE DOCUMENT TOOLS

Copyright Acknowledgments

Index